STREET LAW
A COURSE IN PRACTICAL LAW

TENTH EDITION

netw○rks™
There's More Online!

Lee Arbetman, M.Ed., J.D.
Executive Director
Street Law, Inc.

The work of the late Edward L. O'Brien,
Street Law co-founder and co-author
on earlier editions of this text, continues to
focus and strengthen this new edition.

Mc Graw Hill

mheducation.com/prek-12

Copyright © 2021 McGraw-Hill Education

Send all inquiries to:
McGraw-Hill Education
8787 Orion Place
Columbus, OH 43240

ISBN: 978-0-07-681502-9
MHID: 0-07-681502-1

Printed in the United States of America.

2 3 4 5 6 7 LWI 25 24 23 22 21 20

AUTHORS

Lee Arbetman is a graduate of Grinnell College, the University of Massachusetts (M.Ed.) and George Washington University's National Law Center (J.D.). He is the executive director at Street Law, Inc. Arbetman is an active member of the National Council for the Social Studies and a former chair of its citizenship committee. A former winner of the Isidore Starr Award from the American Bar Association, he is co-author of *United States Government: Our Democracy* from McGraw-Hill. Arbetman is also co-author of *Great Trials in American History,* as well as numerous magazine and journal articles. Arbetman developed Street Law's Supreme Court Summer Institute and Legal Diversity Pipeline Programs.

STREET LAW: A Course in Practical Law

The tenth edition of *Street Law: A Course in Practical Law* builds upon the success and popularity of earlier editions. Incorporating their best features, this edition provides new information, practical advice, and inquiry-based, competency-building activities designed to provide students with the ability to analyze, evaluate, and, in some instances, resolve legal disputes. More broadly, Street Law is a powerful civic education vehicle that helps build critical thinking and problem-solving skills as young people prepare for thoughtful, democratic engagement.

This text and the Teacher Manual generally reflect changes in law and legal procedure that have taken place at the national level since the publication of the ninth edition. We have added text and problems dealing with the most current law-related public issues, including intellectual property, marriage equality, immigration, terrorism, and technology.

An entirely new chapter, Environmental Law, has been added to Unit 7, Contemporary Issues in Law. The material in this chapter is of particular interest to young people and of vital importance to all of us. The chapter-based feature "Taking Action: Law and Democracy" challenges students to consider steps they can take to help address some of the nation's most difficult issues. Students are asked to plan inquiries, gather evidence, draw logical conclusions, and articulate reasonable action steps that can be taken to solve problems and strengthen communities.

Another chapter-based feature, "Investigating the Law Where You Live," asks students to find and explain local and state variations in the law. Many aspects of law are not federal and vary significantly from place to place. This feature asks students to explore local laws, procedures and resources where they live and puts greater responsibility on them for the content of the curriculum. Dozens of investigations are included throughout the student text.

Street Law's approach to civic learning (also called democracy education) is to provide practical information and problem-solving opportunities that develop in students the knowledge and skills necessary for meaningful democratic engagement. While the program has been developed and tested extensively with high school students, there is no mistaking the considerable intellectual rigor required to learn about the law—even at this introductory level. The curriculum includes case studies, mock trials, role-plays, small-group exercises, and visual analysis activities. For optimal results, the *Street Law* program strongly encourages the use of community resource people such as lawyers, judges, law students, police officers, consumer advocates, and others. These legal resource people help teachers implement lessons in the classroom.

The program also promotes community experiences such as court tours, observations of legislatures, and police ride-alongs. This approach allows students to be active participants in their own education, and models the civic engagement that is a critical outcome of all high quality social studies programs. Because of the relevance of the topics covered in *Street Law*, and the close connection the curriculum has to the community and to advocacy related to public policy, many teachers also see this course as a platform for launching carefully constructed service learning activities.

Lee Arbetman

Silver Spring, MD

Summer 2019

Advice to Readers: Law varies from state to state and is constantly changing. Therefore, someone confronted with a legal problem should not use this text as a substitute for legal advice from an attorney.

CONTENTS

UNIT ONE

Introduction to Law and the Legal System

CONTENTS

ViewApart/Getty Images

CONTENTS

UNIT FOUR

Consumer Law

Pixtal/age fotostock

ix

UNIT FIVE

Family Law

UNIT SIX

Individual Rights and Liberties

Contemporary Issues in Law

UNIT SEVEN

Appendix

Jill Braaten/McGraw-Hill Education

THE **CASE** OF...

FEATURES

THE **CASE** OF...

FEATURES

FYI For Your Information

Steps to Take

FEATURES

FEATURES

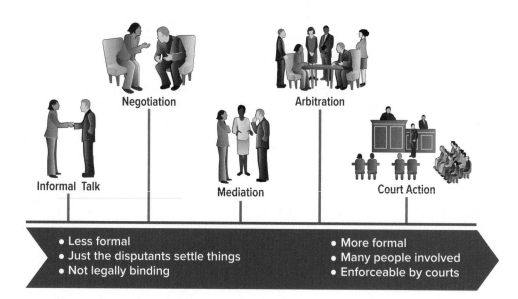

ABOUT STREET LAW, INC.

For more than 45 years, Street Law, Inc. —a nonpartisan, nonprofit organization—has developed practical law curricula, programs, and partnerships that teach people what that law is; how laws are made, implemented, enforced, and changed; and how they can participate in civic life. In the U.S. and abroad, Street Law advances justice through classroom and community education programs that empower people with the legal and civic knowledge, skills, and confidence to bring about positive change for themselves and others.

This tenth edition of the Street Law text reflects the input of many teachers, lawyers, law students, judges and law enforcement officials over four decades. In addition, many of the terrific staff at Street Law, Inc. have made significant contributions to this edition: Cathy Ruffing (lead author on the new teacher manual), Jen Wheeler (lead writer for all of the deliberations), Jose Arevalo, Joy Dingle, Jazmine Donerson, Allison Hawkins, Yolanda Johnson, Ben Perdue, Ben Steele, Erica Wang, and Jennifer Whatley. Several former Street Law staff who have moved on to new career challenges have also left their mark on this edition: Bebs Chorak, Megan Hanson, Lena Morreale Scott, and Judy Zimmer. In the section that follows we gratefully thank the many volunteers who helped with this edition.

As users of previous editions of this program have discovered, young people in Street Law classes experience powerful, interactive learning that is quite distinct from traditional didactic instruction. Classwork is based on dialogue and students have the opportunity to both construct and contest knowledge. Street Law learning is embedded in doing and is part of a social process. Street Law's focus invites students to do real work with content and activities that are authentic.

Street Law, Inc. has also worked globally, delivering its message of law, democracy and human rights education and helping to create a rule of law culture in more than 40 countries.

Special thanks to the committed members of Street Law's Board of Directors and Leadership Circle. These individuals provide support and guidance throughout the year and help us continue to make progress toward our twin goals—Teaching About Law and Advancing Justice for All. The current members of the Board and of the Leadership Circle are listed on the organization's website.

Street Law's staff provide training and technical assistance to school districts, law schools, law firms, law departments, bar associations, juvenile justice programs and community based organizations wishing to implement its programs. Programs and materials are described at www.streetlaw.org.

For additional information and assistance, contact:

Street Law, Inc.
1010 Wayne Avenue
Suite 870
Silver Spring, MD 20910
301-589-1130
learnmore@streetlaw.org

STREET LAW is a registered trademark of Street Law, Inc.

The preparation of the tenth edition involved a particularly rigorous review of all of the content from the ninth edition. To accomplish this, we involved an unusually large number of lawyers and law faculty who brought deep legal expertise. We also received guidance from some Street Law teachers who had extensive experience using earlier editions of the text. The author's daughters, Amy Arbetman and Gwen Arbetman, also provided a careful and helpful review of the new environmental law chapter. This edition would have been impossible without the assistance of the following legal and educational experts: Carrie Anderer, Paul Bock, Erno L. Buky, Ilana Eisenstein, Alene Garcia, Maureen Goble, Amy Hammer, Naomi Cahn, Richard Katskee, Alan Korn, Kelly Koscuiszka Sari Long, Joan Meier, Frances Mendez, Erin Murphy, Kevin Parton, Susan Gross Sholinsky, Claudia Simons, Jacqueline Srour, Katherine Sullivan, Carrie Valiant, and Amanda Wichot. Special recognition is due to Professor Amanda Leiter from American University's law school and her law student research assistant, Jenna Ruddock, for providing a strong draft of the new environmental law chapter. Each of these individuals worked without any form of compensation and under very limited time constraints.

We also wish to thank again the hundreds of individuals who have helped with earlier editions of Street Law.

UNIT 1

Introduction to Law and the Legal System

networks

The first unit of this text sets the stage for your study of law and legal issues. Chapters in this unit answer important questions regarding basic information such as:

- What is law?
- How are laws made?
- What roles can you play in influencing lawmakers?
- How is our legal system organized?
- How can you find and get help from a lawyer?

Knowing the answers to these questions will help you develop skills you will need for the rest of your life.

◀ The phrase "equal justice under law" refers to the goal of the U.S. court system to treat all persons fairly.

▶ Congress passes laws for everyone in the United States to live by.

The question "What is law?" has troubled people for many years. Many definitions of *law* exist. For our purposes, however, law can be defined as the rules and regulations made and enforced by government that regulate the conduct of people within a society.

As a child, you learned about rules first at home and later at school. At home, your parents or guardians made and enforced rules concerning issues such as chores and bedtimes. Later teachers and principals established rules about behavior in school. Rules made and enforced by the government are called laws. The government makes laws that affect almost every aspect of daily life.

One thing is certain: Every society that has ever existed has recognized the need for laws. These laws may have been unwritten, but even preindustrial societies had rules to regulate people's conduct. Without laws, there would be confusion and disorder. This point does not mean that all laws are fair or even good, but imagine how people might take advantage of one another without a set of rules.

A democratic system of government cannot function effectively unless its laws are known and respected by the people the laws are intended to govern. In other words, society must be based on the "rule of law." The rule of law requires that the rules by which we are governed be known in advance and created through democratic processes. Rules should not be made up after the fact by arbitrary actions or decrees. All members of society—average citizens and government officials such as senators, judges, and even the president—are required to support the legal system and obey its laws. Where rule of law exists, no one is above the law.

List 10 of your daily activities (for example, waking up, eating, and going to school). Next to each item, list any laws that affect that activity. What is the purpose of each law that you identified? Would you change any of these laws? Why or why not?

Law and Values

Laws generally reflect and promote a society's values. Our legal system is influenced by our society's traditional ideas of right and wrong. For example, laws against murder reflect the moral belief that killing another person is wrong. However, not everything that is immoral is also illegal. For example, lying to a friend may be immoral but is usually not illegal.

We expect our legal system to achieve many goals. These include:

- protecting basic human rights,
- promoting fairness,
- helping resolve conflicts,
- promoting order and stability,
- promoting desirable social and economic behavior,
- representing the will of the majority, and
- protecting the rights of minorities.

Many of society's most difficult problems involve conflicts among these goals. For example, some laws give preference to minorities. Critics of these laws argue that they promote reverse discrimination and racial conflict. Proponents of such laws, however, argue that they make up for past discrimination and promote fairness by leveling an uneven playing field in society today.

Achieving the goals listed above while trying to minimize conflict is a difficult task for our legal system. Laws must balance rights with responsibilities, the will of the majority with the rights of the minority, and the need for order with the need for basic human rights. Reasonable people sometimes disagree over how the law can protect the rights of some without violating the rights of others. However, everyone must remember that laws are intended to protect people and prevent and resolve conflicts in everyday life.

◄ This sign reflects society's values about right and wrong. *What values are placed in conflict by laws protecting the environment?*

ENTERING
COLLIER - SEMINOLE
STATE PARK
ALL PLANTS AND
ANIMALS PROTECTED
DEPARTMENT OF ENVIRONMENTAL PROTECTION
DIVISION OF RECREATION AND PARKS

THE **CASE** OF...

The Shipwrecked Sailors

Three sailors on an oceangoing freighter were cast adrift in a life raft after their ship sank during a storm in the Atlantic Ocean. The ship went down so suddenly that there was no time to send out an SOS. As far as the three sailors knew, they were the only survivors. They had no food or water in the raft. And they had no fishing gear or other equipment that might be used to get food from the ocean.

After recovering from the shock of the shipwreck, the three sailors began to discuss their situation. Dudley, the ship's navigator, figured that they were at least one thousand miles from land and that the storm had blown them far from where any ships would normally pass. Stephens, the ship's doctor, indicated that without food they could not live longer than 30 days. The only nourishment they could expect was from any rain that might fall from time to time. He noted, however, that if one of the three died before the others, the other two could live a while longer by eating the body of the third.

On the twenty-fifth day, the third sailor, Brooks, who by this time was extremely weak, suggested that they all draw lots and that the loser be killed and eaten by the other two. Both Dudley and Stephens agreed. The next day, lots were drawn

and Brooks lost. At this point, Brooks objected and refused to consent. However, Dudley and Stephens decided that Brooks would die soon anyway, so they might as well get it over with. After thus agreeing, they killed and ate Brooks.

Five days later, Dudley and Stephens were rescued by a passing ship and brought to port. They explained to authorities what had happened to Brooks. After recovering from their ordeal, the two were placed on trial for murder.

The country in which they were tried had the following law: Any person who deliberately takes the life of another is guilty of murder.

PROBLEM 1.2

a. Should Dudley and Stephens be tried for murder? Explain.

b. As an attorney for Dudley and Stephens, what arguments would you make on their behalf? As an attorney for the government, what arguments would you make on the government's behalf?

c. If Dudley and Stephens are convicted, what should their punishment be?

d. What purpose would be served by convicting Dudley and Stephens?

e. What is the relationship between law and morality in this case? Was it morally wrong for Dudley and Stephens to kill Brooks? Explain your answer.

f. Can an act be legal but immoral? Can an act be morally right but unlawful? Explain.

Laws can be based on moral, economic, political, or social values. As values change, so can laws. Moral values deal with fundamental questions of right and wrong. For example, laws against killing promote society's primary moral value—the protection of life. However, even this shared moral value—protection of life—is not absolute or universal because in limited circumstances such as self-defense or war, the law allows intentional killing.

Economic values deal with the accumulation, preservation, use, and distribution of wealth. Many laws promote economic values by encouraging certain economic decisions and discouraging others. For example, the law encourages home ownership by giving tax benefits to people who borrow money from a lender to pay for a home. Laws against shoplifting protect property and discourage stealing by providing a criminal penalty.

Political values reflect the relationship between government and individuals. Laws making it easier to vote promote citizen participation in the political process, a basic American political value.

Social values concern issues that are important to society. For example, it is an American social value that all students are provided with free public education at least through high school. Consequently, all states have laws providing for such education. Like other values, social values can change. In the past, for example, society believed that school sports were not as important for girls as for boys. This value has changed. Laws now reflect the belief that females should be provided with sports opportunities similar to those offered to males.

Many laws combine moral, economic, political, and social values. For example, laws against theft deal with the moral issue of stealing, the economic issue of protection of property, the political issue of how government punishes those who violate criminal statutes, and the social issue of respecting the property of others.

Many Americans tend to think that laws can be passed to solve all of their problems. In 1919, the U.S. Constitution was amended to prohibit the manufacture and sale of alcoholic beverages in this country. The Eighteenth Amendment was passed in response to a significant national problem. However, prohibition of alcohol was extremely difficult to enforce, and 14 years later it was repealed by another constitutional amendment. (The text of the entire U.S. Constitution is available from the National Archives website.)

Some laws designed to protect certain values may interfere with other important values. After the terrorist attacks on September 11, 2001, Congress moved quickly to pass the *USA Patriot Act,* a federal law designed to protect against further attacks. Some people criticized this law, which makes certain searches and electronic eavesdropping easier, as an invasion of the civil liberties Americans cherish. Others believe that, as a country, we may have to sacrifice some liberty for additional security during dangerous times.

▲ Female participation in traditionally male activities is on the rise. *How does this photo reflect society's changing laws and values?*

THE Constitution

After one year from ratification of this article the manufacture, sale, or transportation of intoxicating liquors within, the importation thereof into, or the exportation thereof from the United States and all territory subject to the jurisdiction thereof for beverage purposes is hereby prohibited.

—Eighteenth Amendment

Today, legislators try to deal with the country's devastating drug and gang problems by passing a wide variety of laws. People disagree on what role the law can play in solving these problems. Experience shows that there is a limit to what laws can reasonably be expected to do.

Human Rights

human rights basic privileges a person as a human being

Human rights are the rights all people have simply because they are human beings. To advocate human rights is to demand that the dignity of all people be respected. Both government and private individuals can violate human rights. Human rights apply in people's homes, schools, and workplaces. In fact they apply everywhere. Governments have the duty to respect, protect, and fulfill all individuals' human rights.

The Universal Declaration of Human Rights (UDHR) is a statement of basic human rights and standards for government that has been agreed to by almost every country in the world. (The text of the entire UDHR is available from the United Nations website.) First written and adopted by the United Nations (UN) in 1948 under the leadership of Eleanor Roosevelt, it proclaims that all people have the right to liberty, education, political and religious freedom, and economic well-being. The Declaration also bans torture and says that all people have the right to participate in their government process. Today these rights are generally promoted, recognized, and observed by countries that belong to the UN.

The UDHR is not a binding treaty. However, the UN has established a system of international treaties and other legal mechanisms to enforce human rights. These include the following major treaties:

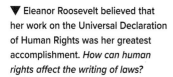

▼ Eleanor Roosevelt believed that her work on the Universal Declaration of Human Rights was her greatest accomplishment. *How can human rights affect the writing of laws?*

- The International Covenant on Civil and Political Rights protects the freedoms of speech, religion, and press and the right to participate in government.
- The International Covenant on Economic, Social and Cultural Rights provides for the right to adequate education, food, housing, health care, protection of property, and employment in safe conditions at an adequate salary.
- The Convention on the Rights of the Child spells out basic human rights to which children everywhere are entitled, including the right to education and to be free from exploitation.

Some believe the right to a clean environment should be added to the Covenants, while others call for a right to economic development for poor countries. The United States has signed and ratified the Covenant on Civil and

Political Rights and has signed but not ratified both the Covenant on Economic, Social and Cultural Rights and the Convention on the Rights of the Child. A treaty must be ratified in order to be binding.

Even when the United States signs a human rights agreement, it often restricts its enforcement within the country. This action is done by announcing that the United States is taking **reservations**, which is a legal way of making a provision less enforceable than it might otherwise be. The government gives reasons for these reservations, including the fact that the treaty would take away the power of individual states to make law under our system of federalism, as well as the belief that other countries should not impose their views on the states. Those who advocate ratification argue that states could still decide how to implement treaties.

reservation a legal way of making a provision less enforceable than it might be otherwise

PROBLEM 1.4

You have been selected to join a group of space pioneers who will establish a colony on a distant planet. In order to create the best possible society, you and your group decide to make a list of the human rights that all space colonists should have.

a. List the three most important human rights that you believe should be guaranteed to all colonists.

b. Compare your list with those of other group members. Explain reasons for your selections.

c. Why do you think some of the rights you listed are more important than others?

d. Do any of the rights you listed conflict with one another? If so, which ones? Why?

e. Compare your list of rights with those listed in the Universal Declaration of Human Rights. Which ones did you include? Which ones did you not include?

f. Are all the human rights you listed also legal rights? When does a human right become a legal right?

Human rights are standards that all countries can use when writing laws. Sometimes human rights become law in a country when the government signs and ratifies an international treaty guaranteeing such rights. Human rights also can become law if they are included in a constitution or if the legislature of a country passes laws protecting or guaranteeing these rights. Even though they may not refer to them as "human rights," there are many provisions that protect human rights in the U.S. Constitution and Bill of Rights and in federal, state, and local laws.

Many of the human rights documents—including the UDHR—mention cultural rights, and it is widely accepted that all people have a right to their own culture. But what does this right to culture mean when culture comes into conflict with other universally accepted human rights? For example, the practice of female infanticide, or the killing of female babies, might be accepted in one culture, but the world community condemns it as a violation of a human right, the right to life. So cultural rights, like many other rights, are not absolute.

Rule of Law

The second president of the United States, John Adams, Jr., said that ours is a "government of laws and not of men." In this phrase he captured the core meaning of the term *rule of law*. Where the rule of law is present, laws are clear, well understood, and fairly enforced. And no one is above the law. The rule of law serves as a safeguard against arbitrary actions by government and also helps protect basic human rights.

A global organization, the World Justice Project, measures adherence to the rule of law in more than 100 countries. They do this through surveys of individual households and expert questionnaires in each country. Through these surveys they have created an annual rule of law index with scores for each country. The index is based on the following eight factors:

- **Constraints on government:** This factor focuses on limits on the power of government and includes checks on executive power by legislatures and courts, as well as checks on governmental power provided by a free media and active civil society.

- **Absence of corruption:** Government officials, including the police, do not use their public office for private gain (for example, by accepting bribes).

- **Open government:** Laws are published, and people have access to this information. They also have mechanisms for complaining about government action.

- **Fundamental rights:** Basic rights to expression, religion, and privacy are protected; government uses fair procedures and people receive equal treatment (no discrimination).

- **Order and security:** Crime is controlled, and people do not resort to violence to resolve problems.

- **Regulatory enforcement:** Government rules and regulations are fair and are enforced without undue influence (no corruption).

- **Civil justice:** The civil justice system is available to people without undue expense or delay, and operates fairly and without corruption.

- **Criminal justice:** The criminal justice system Is fair, free of corruption, operates without undue delay, and deters crime.

Avoiding corruption is obviously one critical factor in assuring strong rule of law. Typically, the Scandinavian countries have the strongest scores in the rule of law index. Countries with massive corruption and where the rulers do not follow the rules have weak rule of law.

Visit the World Justice Project at www.worldjusticeproject.org and look at the most recent rule of law index report to answer the following questions.

a. Identify two countries with stronger rule of law index scores than the United States.

b. Identify two countries with weaker rule of law index scores than the United States.

c. What steps could be taken in the United States to strengthen rule of law?

Balancing Rights With Responsibilities

The emphasis on rights in the United States has led some people to criticize the country for being too concerned with rights, while neglecting responsibilities. Some say that "with every right there comes a responsibility" and urge people to act more responsibly toward one another, their families, and their communities.

While individual rights are important, they must be matched by social responsibilities, these critics say. For example, if people wish to be tried by juries of their peers, they must be willing to serve on such juries. If they want to be governed by elected officials who respond to their values and needs, they not only must vote, but also get involved in other ways: attend election forums, work for candidates, and run for positions on school boards, city councils, and community associations. Many laws also require people to act responsibly. For example, parents must provide their children with adequate food, shelter, and clothing; drivers must obey traffic laws; and all workers must pay taxes.

Critics of the emphasis on rights in the United States point out that "just because you have a legal right to do (or not to do) something does not mean it is the right thing to do." For example, the First Amendment protects freedom of speech and sometimes gives people the right to say hateful and abusive things. However, it does not make such speech morally right.

Others emphasize the pride that Americans take because rights have been extended to women, people of color, and persons with disabilities, all of whom had been previously excluded from full participation in society. Striking the correct balance between rights and responsibilities can be difficult.

◄ Leaders helped minority groups fight for civil rights. *How have laws changed to include women, minorities, and persons with disabilities?*

THE **CASE** OF...

The Apathetic Bystanders

Catherine "Kitty" Genovese was attacked and stabbed to death in 1964 in a highly populated area of Queens, New York. During the half-hour ordeal, 38 people heard Kitty's screams for help and watched from their windows. Twice the killer was scared off by the sound of voices and the realization that he was being watched. However, both times, when it became obvious that nobody was going to call the police, the killer returned to finish off his victim. Rather than give any aid to Kitty, such as calling the police or an ambulance, all 38 bystanders chose to pull their shades, draw their blinds, and ignore Kitty's urgent pleas for help as her life was taken by the deranged attacker.

PROBLEM 1.6

a. Why do you think the bystanders took no action to help Kitty?

b. Did the bystanders commit a crime by not acting? Give your reasons.

c. Did the bystanders do the right thing?

d. Should the law require that citizens help out in cases such as this one?

e. Draft a bystander responsibility law.

---

criminal law the branch of law dealing with crimes and their punishment

felony a serious criminal offense punishable by a prison sentence of more than one year

misdemeanor a criminal offense, less serious than a felony, punishable by a prison sentence of one year or less

civil law all law that does not involve criminal matters, such as tort and contract law. Civil law usually deals with private rights of individuals, groups, or businesses.

civil action a noncriminal lawsuit, brought to enforce a right or redress a wrong

defendant the person against whom a claim is made. In a civil suit, the defendant is the person being sued; in a criminal case, the defendant is the person charged with committing a crime.

plaintiff in a civil case, the injured party who brings the legal action against the alleged wrongdoer

Kinds of Laws

Laws fall into two major groups: criminal and civil. **Criminal laws** regulate public conduct and set out duties owed to society. A criminal case can be brought only by the government against a person charged with committing a crime. Criminal laws have penalties, and convicted offenders are imprisoned, fined, placed under supervision, or punished in some other way. In the U.S. legal system, criminal offenses are divided into **felonies** and **misdemeanors**. Felonies, such as murder or robbery, are more serious crimes. The penalty for a felony is a term of more than one year in prison. For a misdemeanor, the penalty is a prison term of one year or less. Less serious crimes, such as simple assault or minor theft, are called misdemeanors.

Civil laws regulate relations between individuals or groups of individuals. A **civil action** is a lawsuit that can be brought by a person who feels wronged or injured by another person. Courts may award the injured person money for the loss, or they may order the person who committed the wrong to make amends in some other way. An example of a civil action is a lawsuit for recovery of damages suffered in an automobile accident. Civil laws regulate many everyday situations, such as marriage, divorce, contracts, real estate, insurance, consumer protection, and negligence.

Sometimes behavior can violate both civil and criminal laws and can result in two court cases. A criminal case is brought by the government against a **defendant**, the person accused of committing the crime. A civil case is brought by the **plaintiff**—the person or company harmed—against the defendant.

In a famous series of cases, former star football player O.J. Simpson was prosecuted in connection with the deaths of his former wife, Nicole Brown Simpson, and her friend, Ron Goldman. The Los Angeles district attorney was the **prosecutor** in this criminal case. In order to win a conviction, the district attorney had to prove that O.J. Simpson was guilty **beyond a reasonable doubt.** This means that if the jury (or the judge in a case tried without a jury) has any reasonable doubts about the defendant's guilt, then it must vote not to convict. The jury verdict in Simpson's criminal case was *not guilty*.

Several months later, the parents of Ron Goldman brought a civil suit against O.J. Simpson to recover damages resulting from the wrongful death of their son. In a civil case, the plaintiff wins by convincing the jury (or the judge in a case tried without a jury) by a **preponderance of the evidence.** The jury (or judge) needs only to decide if it is more likely than not that the plaintiff's complaint is true. This is a lower requirement for proof than the beyond-a-reasonable-doubt standard used in criminal cases. The reason for the different standards of proof is that a defendant loses money in a civil case but can suffer lengthy imprisonment or even the death penalty as a result of a criminal conviction. The Goldmans won their civil case against O.J. Simpson. Because the public tends not to understand the difference between civil and criminal cases, there was much confusion about how a person could be found not guilty in a criminal case and then responsible in a civil suit for damages for the same act.

prosecutor the state or federal government's attorney in a criminal care

beyond a reasonable doubt the level of proof required to convict a person of a crime. It does not mean "convinced 100 percent," but does mean there are no reasonable doubts as to guilt.

preponderance of the evidence usually the standard of proof used in a civil suit; the burden of proof that a party must meet in order to win the lawsuit. To win, a party must provide evidence that is more convincing than the other side's evidence.

PROBLEM 1.7

Matt and Kenji take Kenji's brother's car without telling him and drive to a local shopping center. Ignoring the sign "Parking for Handicapped Persons Only," they leave the car and enter an electronics shop.

After looking around, they buy a new tablet. Then they buy some sandwiches from a street vendor and walk to a nearby park. While eating, they discover that the tablet does not work. In their hurry to return it, they leave their trash on the park bench.

When Matt and Kenji get back to the shopping center, they notice a large dent in one side of their car. The dent appears to be the result of a driver's carelessness in backing out of the next space. They also notice that the car has been broken into and that a smartphone has been removed.

They call the police to report the accident and theft. When the police arrive, they seize a small, clear bag containing illegal drugs from behind the car's backseat. Matt and Kenji are arrested.

a. List all the things you think Matt and Kenji did wrong.

b. What laws are involved in this story?

c. Which of these are criminal laws? Which are civil laws?

Our Constitutional Framework

The U.S. Constitution is the highest law of the land. Drafted more than two hundred years ago, this remarkable document is the longest-lasting written constitution in the world. It sets forth the basic framework of our government. It also lists the government's powers, the limits on those powers, and the people's freedoms that cannot be taken away by the government.

The principle of **limited government** is a fundamental notion in our Constitution. Before the U.S. Constitution was written and ratified, the individual states were reluctant to give up power to the national government. After all, a revolution had just been fought against the government of the king of England to preserve individual liberty and the freedom to govern independently. As a result, the Constitution created a national government of limited powers, with authority to pass laws only in the areas listed in Article I of the Constitution. Those who criticize the reach of the federal government's power today often cite these historic reasons for limiting its power.

Perhaps nothing is more important in the Constitution than the division of power among the three branches of the federal government: the executive, the legislative, and the judicial. This division is known as the **separation of powers**. The legislative branch, or Congress, writes and passes laws called **statutes**. The executive branch, which includes the president and federal agencies, is primarily responsible for implementing and enforcing the law. To do so, the executive branch makes rules and issues executive orders that have the force of law.

The judicial branch, or the courts, resolves disputes and interprets laws. These rulings may interpret a provision of the Constitution, a statute, or a rule issued by an executive agency.

The three branches of the federal government are independent, but each has the power to restrain the other branches through a system of

limited government a basic principle of our constitutional system. It limits government to powers provided to it by the people.

separation of powers the division of power among the branches of government (executive, legislative, and judicial)

statutes written laws enacted by legislatures

▶ This image depicts the members of the Constitutional Convention formally endorsing their new plan of government. *What is the purpose of the U.S. Constitution?*

Architect of the Capitol

checks and balances. The system was designed to prevent one branch from becoming too powerful and abusing its power. For example, Congress may investigate actions by the president or other executive officials, and members of Congress or the executive branch may be prosecuted in court for violating that law. Another check is the president's power to veto, or refuse to approve, laws passed by Congress. Yet another check is congressional power to impeach the president or federal judges.

One of the most visible and important checks of one branch on another is the courts' power of judicial review. Judicial review enables a court to declare unenforceable any law passed by Congress or a state legislature that conflicts with the country's highest law, the U.S. Constitution. For example, Congress might pass a law prohibiting media criticism of elected officials. If challenged in court, this law would be declared invalid and unconstitutional because it violates the freedom of speech and press guaranteed in the First Amendment to the Constitution. In general, the courts can declare a law unconstitutional either because (1) the government has passed a law that the Constitution does not give it the power to pass or (2) the government has passed a law that violates somebody's rights. Judicial review also gives the courts the power to declare an action of the executive or legislative branch to be unconstitutional. For example, the courts can strike down law enforcement actions that violate a constitutional right.

Just as the Constitution provides checks on the power of each branch, it also reflects the view that the powers of the federal government as a whole should be limited. The federal government can only make laws about certain topics and these topics are listed in the Constitution. States, on the other hand, can legislate on a much wider range of topics. In some areas, the federal and state governments share lawmaking power. This division of power between the states and the federal government is known as federalism. This is why most civil and criminal laws are passed by state legislatures or local governments, and many laws differ from state to state.

The principle of limited government is also manifested in the Bill of Rights, the first 10 amendments to the Constitution. The Bill of Rights defines and guarantees the fundamental rights and liberties of all Americans, including the freedoms of religion, speech, and press; the freedom from unreasonable search and seizure; and other individual rights. The Supreme Court has ruled that most provisions of the Bill of Rights limit the power of state and local governments as well as the federal government.

Every state has a constitution, and most state constitutions include the major principles of the U.S. Constitution. All provide for different branches of government, separation of powers, and a system of checks and balances. Some state constitutions provide greater protection of rights than the U.S. Constitution. The Constitution sets a floor, but not a ceiling, on individual rights. For example, some state constitutions guarantee people greater rights than they have under the U.S. Constitution.

The U.S. Constitution and most state constitutions are difficult to change. The reason is that they were drafted with the belief that they should not be

checks and balances the power of each of the three branches of government (legislative, judicial, executive) to limit the other branches' power, so as to prevent an abuse

veto prohibit; in government, the veto is the power of the chief executive to prevent enactment of a bill (i.e., to prevent the bill from becoming a law)

judicial review the process by which courts decide whether the laws passed by Congress or state legislatures are constitutional

unconstitutional conflicting with some provision of the Constitution

federalism the division of powers between the states and the federal government

Bill of Rights the first ten amendments to the Constitution, which guarantee basic individual rights to all persons in the United States

THE Constitution

Congress shall make no law respecting an establishment of religion, or prohibiting the free exercise thereof; or abridging the freedom of speech, or of the press; or the right of the people peaceably to assemble, and to petition the Government for redress of grievances.

—First Amendment

▶ Federal troops enforced the U.S. Constitution and forcibly integrated this school in Washington D.C. *What is the role of the federal government in protecting individual rights?*

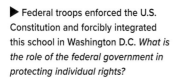

No law, varying the compensation for the services of Senators and Representatives, shall take effect, until an election of Representatives shall have intervened.

—Twenty-Seventh Amendment

changed without careful thought, discussion, and debate. The idea was to make these documents as permanent as possible. However, allowances were made to accommodate necessary changes. The U.S. Constitution may be changed in two ways. An amendment must be proposed either by a two-thirds vote of each house of Congress or at a constitutional convention called by two-thirds of the states. In either case, it must then be ratified, or approved, by legislatures or conventions in three-fourths of the states.

People try to change the Constitution for many reasons. One of the most common reasons for change has been to extend rights that were not originally written into the Constitution. Although ratification is difficult, 27 amendments have been added to the Constitution. These amendments often reflect the changing viewpoints of citizens and their elected representatives. For example, when the original Constitution was ratified in 1789, most states restricted voting to white males who owned property. Since then, various amendments have extended voting rights to people of color, women, and persons aged 18 to 20.

Amendments for a range of issues have been discussed and proposed over the years. Some think there should be a constitutional amendment to provide full congressional representation to the citizens of the District of Columbia. Another proposed amendment would require the federal government to adopt a balanced budget. Other amendments have been proposed to punish flag burning, protect victims of crime, and ban abortions. The Equal Rights Amendment, passed by Congress in 1972, prohibited discrimination on the basis of gender. However, it failed to be ratified by the required 38 states, so it did not become a part of the U.S. Constitution. In 1992, the Twenty-Seventh Amendment became part of the Constitution. This amendment, first proposed by James Madison in 1789, bans midterm congressional pay raises.

PROBLEM 1.8

For each of the following situations determine for whether it involves the principle of separation of powers, checks and balances, judicial review, federalism, or some combination of these principles. Specify the principle or principles involved and explain your answer.

a. A state law requires that a prayer be said each day in public schools. A federal court rules that the law violates a First Amendment clause that prohibits the government from establishing a religion.

b. The U.S. Congress passes a law requiring that Supreme Court sessions be televised.

c. Because a prison is very old and overcrowded, a state court orders the state legislature to spend $100 million on a new prison.

d. A state government passes a law legalizing recreational and medicinal marijuana use despite a federal statute that lists it as an illegal drug. The federal Drug Enforcement Agency seizes drugs from a citizen in this state and prosecutes the person in federal court.

e. The U.S. Supreme Court rules that flag burning is a protected form of free speech under the First Amendment. In response to their constituents' wishes, senators and representatives from several states propose an amendment to the Constitution making it illegal to burn the flag.

f. A federal court serves the president of the United States with a subpoena seeking evidence of a crime. The president refuses to turn over the evidence claiming executive privilege. The U.S. Supreme Court rules that the president's executive privilege power is limited and that he must turn over the evidence.

▶ The U.S. Capitol is home to the legislative branch of the federal government.

The laws that U.S. citizens are expected to obey come from many sources, including federal, state, and local governments. Constitutions set forth laws and establish the structure of government. Legislatures, of course, make laws. In some situations, voters can act directly as lawmakers. Administrative agencies also make many laws. Finally, laws are sometimes made by courts when they decide appeals.

Legislatures

The U.S. Constitution divides the power to make laws between the federal government and the state governments. At both the federal and the state levels, legislatures are the primary lawmaking bodies. The U.S. Congress—the federal legislature—is made up of two houses. The Senate is composed of 100 members, with two from each state, and the House of Representatives has 435 members, with each state represented according to the size of its population. The U.S. Constitution gives Congress the power to pass certain laws that are binding on the people in every state. States have the power to pass laws that apply only within their boundaries.

The lawmaking authority of Congress is exercised through the passage of laws known as federal **statutes**. When Congress passes a federal statute, it affects people in every state. Federal statutes deal with issues of national impact, such as environmental quality, national defense, homeland security, labor relations, veterans affairs, public health, civil rights, economic development, postal services, federal taxes, and social security and other benefits programs.

statutes written laws enacted by legislatures

The states' lawmaking powers are vested in their legislatures, which pass laws called state statutes. Except for Nebraska, every state has a two-house legislature. Most states' legislatures meet on an annual basis; in a few states, the legislatures meet every two years. States pass laws with statewide impact in such areas as education, transportation and traffic, state taxes, marriage and divorce, most criminal laws, and the powers and duties of state government officials. Although tribal governments of Native Americans vary, many place legislative authority, and sometimes executive authority, in a tribal council.

The power of the federal government to pass laws is limited. Congress cannot legislate unless given the power to do so in the Constitution. The states, on the other hand, have broader power to legislate. In general, the states have power to legislate in all those areas over which the national government was not granted power by the Constitution. For example, a state could not enter into a treaty with another country or coin money, as those are among the specific powers assigned to the national government. These powers are set forth in Article I, Section 8, of the Constitution.

In addition to the U.S. Congress and state legislatures, cities, towns, and counties also have lawmaking bodies such as county or city councils, boards of aldermen, and local boards of education. Local governments pass laws known as **ordinances** or regulations. Legislative issues that concern local governments include land use, parking, schools, and regulation of local business. Laws passed by local governments apply only to a county, city, or town. Local lawmaking bodies receive the power to enact ordinances from the state. Many laws important in our daily lives are passed by local governments.

▲ Segregated drinking fountains were common in the American South in the 1960s. *Why was the federal government concerned about this situation?*

ordinance a county or city law

Sometimes federal laws conflict with state and local laws. For example, in the 1960s, federal laws against racial segregation in restaurants and hotels came into conflict with laws in some states that required separate accommodations for African Americans and whites. The courts ruled the state laws invalid based on Article VI of the Constitution, the **supremacy clause**, which states that "the Constitution and the Laws of the United States . . . shall be the supreme law of the land." The Supreme Court has also ruled that Congress has sometimes passed laws about topics that are the proper focus of the states. These laws have been found to be an unconstitutional intrusion on the rights of states. Finally, there are a few topics for which both the federal government and the states have legislative power. For example, while most criminal laws are passed by state legislatures, Congress has also passed a limited number of federal criminal laws.

supremacy clause the provision in Article VI of the Constitution stating that in the event of conflict between state and federal law, the federal law must be applied.

PROBLEM 2.1

Decide whether each of the following is a federal, a state, and/or a local law. Then give one example, not listed here, of a federal, a state, and a local law.

a. No parking on the east side of Main Street between 4:00 P.M. and 6:00 P.M.

b. All persons between the ages of 6 and 16 must attend school.

c. Whoever enters a bank for purposes of taking by force or violence the property or money in custody of such bank shall be fined not more than $50,000 or imprisoned not more than 20 years or both.

d. In order to sell any product on public streets, the seller must first apply for and receive a vendor's permit.

e. No employer of more than 15 persons may discriminate on the basis of race, color, religion, sex, or national origin.

f. All persons traveling on interstate airline carriers are subject to search before entering the airplane departure area.

Investigating the Law Where You Live

Research to learn where on the Internet you can find a list and explanation of your state's statutes.

Legislatures and other lawmaking bodies try to respond to the needs of the citizens they represent by introducing legislation in the form of **bills**. Bills are used to enact new laws or to amend or repeal old laws. Ideas for bills can come from legislators, the executive branch, individual citizens, citizens groups, businesses, or lobbyists representing specific interest groups. A bill passed by the legislature and not vetoed by the executive branch becomes a law.

After a bill becomes a law, the people must obey it. Sometimes, though, the language of a law is open to differing interpretations. It is not always easy to know exactly what a law prohibits or allows. Disputes over what a law means frequently end up in court. A judge who interprets what the legislature means is determining **legislative intent**.

bill a proposed law being considered by a legislature

legislative intent what the lawmakers who passed a law wanted the law to mean. If the language of a statute is unclear, judges will often look at the legislative intent to help them interpret the law.

THE CASE OF...

The Unclear Law

The city of Beautifica has established a lovely park in the city. The city council wishes to preserve some elements of nature, undisturbed by city noise, traffic, pollution, and crowding. The park is a place where citizens can find grass, trees, flowers, and quiet. In addition, there are playgrounds and picnic areas. At one time a road ran through the park. Now the road is closed. The city council has enacted a law requiring that all entrances to the park have the following sign posted: NO VEHICLES IN THE PARK.

▲ Park rules should be clear to everyone.

PROBLEM 2.2

The law seems clear, but some disputes have arisen over its interpretation. Interpret the law in the following cases, keeping in mind what the law says (the letter of the law) as well as the legislative intent. Examine each situation and decide whether or not the vehicle described should be allowed in the park. Write the reasons for your choices. When you finish analyzing all of the situations, rewrite the law to make it clearer.

a. Tony lives on one side of the city and works on the other. He will save ten minutes if he drives through the park.

b. To keep the park clean, trash barrels are located throughout the area. The sanitation department wants to drive a truck into the park to collect the trash from the barrels.

c. Two police cars are chasing a suspected bank robber. If one police car cuts through the park, it can get in front of the suspect's car and trap it between the patrol cars.

d. An ambulance is racing to the hospital with a dying patient. The shortest route is through the park.

e. Elena wants to take her baby to the park in a stroller.

f. A monument is being erected to the city's citizens who died in the Vietnam War. A tank, donated by the government, is to be placed beside the monument.

g. Amul uses an electric wheelchair and wants to visit the park.

h. Roshini wants to fly her toy drone in the park.

Drafting a Bill

No matter where the idea for a bill originates, eventually there must come a time when the bill is drafted—that is, when actual language is written. As you can see from The Case of the Unclear Law, even the simplest language might not be clear enough for people to understand. Legislation is often drafted and redrafted before being introduced and discussed by a legislative body. Despite these efforts, laws are sometimes difficult to read and understand. When misunderstandings occur, one of the basic purposes of law—letting people know what conduct is expected of them or what conduct is prohibited—is lost. When drafting laws, it is useful to ask the following questions to evaluate whether problems are likely to result.

- Is the law written in clear language?
- Is the law understandable?
- When does the law go into effect?
- Does the law contradict any other laws?
- Is the law enforceable? If so, by whom?
- Are the penalties for breaking the law clear and reasonable?

In deciding what a statute means, judges must follow certain rules. One rule is that courts will not enforce laws, particularly criminal laws, that are so vague that it is unclear exactly what conduct is prohibited.

TAKING ACTION: Law and Democracy

Drafting a Law Simulation

The harmful effects of cigarette smoking, both for smokers and for those nearby, continue to make headlines. In your town there is a discussion about prohibiting smoking in certain places. Opinion on this issue is divided. Some restaurant employees want to work in healthier, smoke-free environments. Some restaurant owners are concerned that no-smoking rules will harm their businesses and might result in a loss of jobs. Some citizens believe that smoking should be banned in all public places, including stores, restaurants, workplaces, and even outdoor spaces such as parks.

Still others believe that these restrictions go too far and intrude on the rights of people using a lawful product (cigarettes). They believe that economic forces, rather than government action, will bring the best results. Some restaurants, for example, will choose to be smoke-free in order to attract patrons who care about this issue.

PROBLEM 2.3

You are a member of the citizens advisory group to your town council. Your group has been asked to draft a new ordinance dealing with smoking in public places.

a. List the details that should be included.

b. Create a draft of the ordinance, using the guidelines for drafting laws.

c. Who would support your ordinance? Who would oppose it?

For example, a law that stated "it shall be illegal to gather on a street corner without a good reason" would be considered too vague because the phrase "good reason" is not clear. Another rule says that if there is doubt as to the meaning of a word in a criminal statute, the word must be strictly interpreted against the government. This usually means that words are given their ordinary meaning by the court. These rules are meant to encourage lawmakers to write clear laws and to ensure that people are not punished for failing to obey an unclear law.

Clarity in legal language is important. For that reason, some legislatures now attempt to write in simple, clear English rather than traditional legal language. Those who favor this practice argue that laws have been written in language that is too complex and should instead be written so that a person of ordinary intelligence and education can understand what is expected.

Agencies

Many of the laws that affect you are made by government agencies. Legislative bodies usually deal with problems in only a general way. They authorize administrative agencies to develop rules and regulations to make laws more specific. These regulations influence almost every aspect of our daily lives and have the force of law. For example, Congress passed a law requiring safe working conditions in places of employment. To implement the law, Congress established the Occupational Safety and Health Administration (OSHA). This agency develops specific regulations governing health and safety on the job. These regulations dictate specific requirements, such as the height of guardrails in factories, the number of fire exits, and the type of safety equipment to be worn by employees in various occupations.

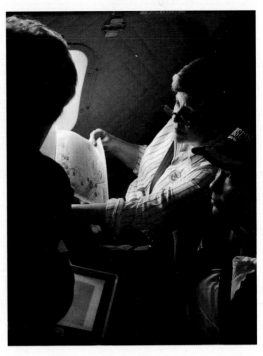

▼ Specific rules and regulations are made by agencies such as the Department of Homeland Security. *Why do you think this agency is needed?*

Another example of a government agency is the Environmental Protection Agency (EPA). It works with other federal agencies, state and local governments, and Native American groups to develop and enforce regulations under existing environmental laws passed by Congress. The EPA sets national standards that help protect human health and safeguard the national environment, with enforcement delegated to state governments. The agency also works with industry and government at various levels on pollution prevention and energy conservation.

In response to the terrorist attacks of September 11, 2001, the federal government created new agencies and reorganized existing ones to increase homeland security. For example, in November 2002 President George W. Bush signed a bill creating a new federal Department of Homeland Security. The department's primary mission is to help prevent, protect against, and respond to acts of terrorism on U.S. soil. An existing agency, the Department of Transportation (DOT), was also reorganized when the Transportation Security Administration (TSA) was created within DOT to protect the nation's transportation systems.

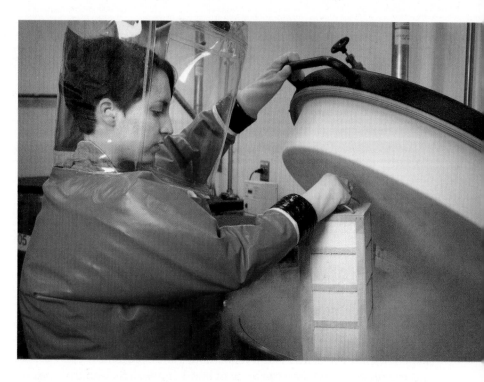

▶ A scientist conducts research to improve diagnostic tests for diseases. *How do administrative agencies work to protect the well-being of individuals?*

CDC/James Gathany

Investigating the Law Where You Live

Visit the official website of your state government. Note that your state has many agencies. Which state agencies are likely to be most important to you at some time in your life?

public hearings proceedings that are open to the public. During these proceedings, evidence is considered and then a decision is reached based on this evidence

The administrative agencies with the greatest impact on your daily life are those at the state and local levels. For example, a zoning commission and other local agencies where you live may have developed a plan that determines what kind of buildings can be located in specific parts of your town. A local agency may hold public hearings to determine whether a new restaurant can serve alcohol or feature live music.

Administrative agencies, then, are really hidden lawmakers, enacting numerous rules and regulations that affect business and industry as well as individuals. For example, regulations govern the amount of pesticides that can be used on produce, the number of animals that can be killed by hunters, the ingredients that can be used in canned food, the costs of phone calls and electricity, the hours of operation for bars and restaurants, the qualifications of people employed in various professions, and hundreds of other issues. In addition to their lawmaking functions, agencies also administer government programs and provide many services.

Regulations issued by these agencies become law without being voted upon. However, agencies usually hold **public hearings** before issuing proposed regulations. These hearings give individuals and businesses an opportunity to express their views on the proposals. In addition, regulations proposed by the federal government must be published in a special newspaper called the *Federal Register*. This allows people to learn about and comment on proposed rules.

Some people criticize rules and regulations created by federal and state agencies. Critics argue that these agencies have created bloated bureaucracies and require wasteful paperwork, interfering with the efficient operation of the marketplace. Others say administrative regulations give meaning to laws passed by legislatures, protect consumers and workers, and are an essential part of modern life.

Complete one of the following exercises as a research project.

a. Find an article in your local newspaper or online about an administrative agency. What is the agency's name? What does it do? Is it part of the federal, state, or local government? What does the article say about the agency?

b. Find evidence of an agency at work in your community. What agency is acting? What action is the agency taking? Is there any way for the public to have an impact on the agency? If so, how? Is the agency part of the federal, state, or local government?

Courts

Law is also made by courts. Think about courtroom scenes you have seen on television. These courts were conducting **trials**. The person who loses a trial can sometimes ask a higher court to review and change the result of the trial. These higher courts are called **appeals** or **appellate courts**. When an appeals court decides a case, it issues a written opinion that sets a **precedent** for similar cases in the future. All lower courts in the jurisdiction where the precedent was issued must follow it. For example, if a state's supreme court ruled that the state's constitution required that school funding be equalized throughout the state—richer and poorer school districts would each have to spend the same amount per student— then all lower courts in that state would have to follow that precedent.

trial a court proceeding

appeals court a court in which appeals from trial court decisions are heard

precedent court decision on a legal question that guides decisions in future cases presenting similar questions

International Lawmaking

International law is usually defined as the law that applies to the conduct of countries. It is most often made when national governments make treaties with each other or with a group of countries. A **treaty** is an agreement or contract between countries. These treaties are sometimes created by the joint action of countries or by actions taken by the United Nations. Various international laws, usually made by treaty, regulate commerce among countries, refugees crossing national borders, ownership of property including copyrights and patents, the environment, and many other areas. The U.S. Constitution provides that treaties are the supreme law of the land if they are signed by the president and then ratified by a two-thirds majority of the U.S. Senate.

treaty a pact between nations; if entered into by the United States through its executive branch, the pact must be approved by "two-thirds of the senators present," under Article II, Section 2 of the Constitution, to become effective

Treaties are also used to determine whether one country has a legal obligation to return someone accused of a crime or terrorist act to another country. The process in which one country asks another country to surrender a suspected or convicted criminal is called **extradition**. According to international law, each country is assumed to have authority over the people within its borders. To overcome this assumption, most countries have signed extradition treaties with other counties. The United States does not have extradition treaties with a number of countries, however, including China and North Korea.

extradition the legal process in which one country or state asks another to surrender a suspected or convicted criminal

▲ The process of European integration has resulted in the creation of the European Parliament, the body that passes the majority of European laws. *Why are so many countries eager to join the EU?*

Important international law has been made by a series of treaties, signed since 1950 by various European countries, which formed the European Union (EU). These treaties established a European Parliament, which has the power to make laws that promote political and economic cooperation among European countries. A very visible example of this has been the EU's agreement to have a common currency called the euro. In 2018, twenty-eight countries belonged to the European Union, and five others were candidates for entry into the EU. Countries that join retain most of their sovereign power to make laws that are binding within their borders. However, in order to benefit all member countries, they do give up power in selected areas by delegating some lawmaking authority to an EU-wide organization.

The United Nations (UN), formed in 1945 and headquartered in New York City, has nearly 200 member countries, as well as many affiliated organizations such as the Commission on Human Rights, United Nations Educational, Scientific, and Cultural Organization (UNESCO), International Monetary Fund (IMF), World Trade Organization (WTO), World Health Organization (WHO), United Nations Children's Fund (UNICEF), International Labour Organization (ILO), and the World Bank. The UN also maintains a system of international courts and has become an important institution in the area of international law. Countries that join the United Nations agree to abide by the provisions of its charter.

The United States was one of the founding members of the UN and has been its biggest financial supporter. Some people in the United States, however, have criticized the UN for being inefficient, bureaucratic, and slow to act, often wasting time and money. Others criticize the United States for not fully supporting UN actions, especially when most UN member countries do not agree with U.S. policy.

◀ The United Nations building in New York City is the center of the organization's activities, which support global cooperation and world peace.

PROBLEM 2.5

The government of a country has been very corrupt for many years and has violated the human rights of many of its citizens by jailing and executing opposition leaders who are all from one ethnic group. The United States and most other countries have been critical of this government for its actions. The opposition groups in the country want to overthrow the government. The government reacts by rounding up and executing hundreds of members of the ethnic group leading the opposition.

The United States and many other governments around the world speak out against this action. The United Nations is considering a resolution authorizing sending UN troops into the country to stop what some are calling genocide, the systematic killing of an ethnic or cultural group. Some member countries believe the UN should not interfere militarily in the internal affairs of another country.

The UN Charter (Article 55) states: "With a view to the creation of conditions of stability and well-being which are necessary for peaceful and friendly relations among nations based on respect for the principle of equal rights and self-determination of peoples, the United Nations shall promote . . . universal respect for, and observance of, human rights and fundamental freedoms for all without distinction as to race, sex, language, or religion."

Article 56 states that all members pledge themselves to take joint and separate action in cooperation with the organization for the achievement of the purposes set forth in Article 55.

a. If you were the president of the United States, would you instruct our UN delegate to support the resolution authorizing the UN to send troops into this country? Explain.

b. Assume the U.S. government does not think sending troops is the best way to solve this problem, but more than two-thirds of the countries in the UN vote in favor of the resolution. Should the United States contribute troops to the UN effort? Explain.

c. After a presidential election and change of administrations in the United States, assume the U.S. government believes that forceful action must be taken against this government, but most other governments come to believe that the UN should not take joint action in this case. Should the United States take action alone?

▶ Community members advocate their cause by publicly expressing their opinions.

One of the most important goals of *Street Law* is promoting positive involvement in public affairs. This chapter discusses advocacy, or how civic engagement can influence the lawmaking process. In our democracy, the people are responsible for making the law, usually through their elected representatives. While voting is, of course, an important obligation of citizenship, an individual's lawmaking role is much broader than voting. Individuals are also responsible for working to change laws that are not helping to solve problems and working for new laws and policies that address problems in their communities, cities, states, or countries.

The Art of Advocacy

Advocacy is the active support of a cause. It also involves the art of persuading others to support the same cause. Advocacy is based on the careful gathering of facts, the development of excellent communication skills, and the creation of an effective plan and time line. In order to advocate effectively, you must determine what level or levels of government are responsible for addressing the problem.

High school students all over the country have become effective advocates on important questions ranging from national issues, such as violence prevention and military activity abroad, to local concerns, such as homelessness and school uniform policies. In some instances students have advocated change with their local schools and town or city councils. In other instances they have communicated with state or congressional representatives. For example, high school students concerned about smoking in student bathrooms lobbied for membership on their school's

Realistic Reflections

TAKING ACTION: **Law and Democracy**

Changing the Law: Research and Role-Play

Work with your classmates in small groups to research one of the proposed laws listed below. Then answer the questions that follow. Each group will share its findings. The proposed laws would:

- require motorcycle riders of all ages to wear an approved safety helmet while riding on public roads.
- legalize the use of marijuana for medical purposes while under the supervision of a doctor.
- require voters to have a state-issued ID in order to vote.
- suspend a person's driver's license for failing to pay court-ordered child support.
- require every worker in the country to carry a national identification card with biometric information, such as a fingerprint, to make sure that all employees have legal status.

PROBLEM 3.1

a. What arguments could be presented for and against the proposed law?

b. What groups, organizations, or businesses are likely to lobby for or against the proposed law? What techniques could they use to influence legislators?

c. How could social media be used to advocate for or against the proposed law?

d. Predict the outcome if your community held a voter referendum on the proposed law. Explain your reasons.

safety committee. When they joined the committee, they worked with the school resource officer, building principal, and assistant principal to convince their county board of education to give them funds to purchase smoke detectors. The students then lobbied their state representative, who was so impressed with their solution that he introduced a bill in the next legislative session to make smoke detectors mandatory in public school bathrooms across the entire state.

Lobbying

Lobbying is a way to influence the lawmaking process by convincing lawmakers to vote as you want them to. The word *lobbying* comes from the seventeenth century, when interested persons would corner legislators in the outer waiting room of the legislature— the lobby. While lobbying often has a negative connotation, it is actually a basic right protected by the U.S. Constitution. Lobbying involves the right of free speech and often other rights, such as assembly, association, and freedom of the press.

A lobbyist is someone who works to convince a lawmaker to vote for or against a particular issue. Anyone can be a lobbyist. As a private individual, you can lobby elected officials on issues that affect your life. You can influence elected officials by expressing your opinions individually or as part of a group, either in person or by letter, petition, phone, or e-mail. Lobbyists also use political contributions, ads, favors, letter-writing campaigns, and other techniques to influence legislation on various issues.

▲ Many individuals and groups lobby for their causes in Washington, D.C.

Steps to Take

Writing a Public Official

- **Write in your own words.** Personal letters are far more effective than form letters or petitions. Explain to the official how the issue will affect you and your friends, family, or job.

- **Keep your letter short and to the point.** Deal with only one issue per letter. If you are writing about some specific proposed bill or legislation, identify it by name (for example, the National Consumer Protection Act) and by number if you know it (for example, H.R. 343).

- **Explain why you are writing.** Ask the official to state his or her own position on the issue. Request a reply and ask the official to take some kind of definite action.

- **Always put your return address on the letter, sign and date it, and keep a copy.** Your letter does not have to be typed, but it should be legible. Perhaps most importantly, it should reach the official before the issue is voted on.

- **Contact public officials by using e-mail or faxing a letter to their office.**

Today, special interest groups and organizations lobby on behalf of every imaginable cause and issue. Businesses and organizations hire professional lobbyists to influence federal, state, and local legislators. For example, the National Rifle Association employs lobbyists to oppose restrictions on gun ownership and use, while Handgun Control, Inc., lobbies for gun control. Literally thousands of professional lobbyists work in Washington, D.C., and in state capitals throughout the country. Those who lobby the federal government must register with Congress and file reports four times a year. In these reports, they must identify their clients and the specific bills on which they are working. They must also indicate how much money they have been paid for their lobbying work. In addition to lobbying for laws, grassroots groups can advocate for candidates.

Professional lobbyists have advantages over **grassroots lobbyists** because they may have more money behind them and they know legislators and their staffs personally. They know where the levers of power are. They know who to talk to and how best to talk to them. Nevertheless, grassroots lobbyists can be very effective, particularly when they join with others. Demonstration of grassroots support by large numbers of people is a very effective lobbying technique because legislators care about what their voters think.

Many critics of the lobbying system in the United States say it enables some people and businesses to "buy legislation." It is true that contributors to political campaigns may have greater access to legislators and greater influence over how they vote on certain issues. However, others argue that lobbying is an integral part of American democracy. They claim that the use of money and influence is a legitimate way for groups to make their views heard. In general, however, issues facing lower-income Americans struggle to gain attention in the political system at least in part because those Americans cannot afford to form associations, contribute money, and hire lobbyists.

lobbying influencing or persuading legislators to take action to introduce a bill or vote a certain way on a proposed law

grassroots lobbyist a person, or group of people, who works to convince a lawmaker to vote for or against a particular issue by participating in rallies, meeting representatives, or letter writing campaigns

PROBLEM 3.2

a. Select a current issue that concerns you. Search the Internet to find sites that deal with this issue. What information is available on each site? Does the information seem reliable? How can you tell? Do any of the sites suggest strategies you could use to lobby for the issue?

b. Select a current issue that concerns you. Write a letter about it to a public official. Use the guidelines listed in the Steps to Take feature on page 31 to help you compose your letter. For example, you may write to your mayor, city council member, state legislator, congressional representative, or senator. E-mail your letter to the elected official and then analyze any reply you receive. Did he or she answer your questions or provide additional information?

c. Do persons with more money have greater influence over legislators than those with less money? If so, is this unavoidable in a society like ours, or should steps be taken to reform the lobbying and campaign finance systems?

Steps to Take

Guidelines for Advocates

Before you begin to advocate, think through these steps for success:

1. **Identify the issue.** Think about your school or community. Is there a problem that needs to be addressed? How do you know it is a problem? Can a new policy or rule address this issue?

2. **Set a goal.** Visualize a better tomorrow by answering the following questions:
   - What solution are you proposing?
   - How will your community be improved if your solution is implemented?
   - What unintentional problems might be caused by your solution?

3. **Become an expert on the issue.** Know the facts. Collect information to support your position. Monitor social media, search the Internet, and interview community members. Learn both sides of the issue.

4. **Recruit allies. Identify roadblocks.** Identify coalitions already working on your issue. Social media features like hashtags, trend feeds, and contact networks can help you recruit allies and identify opponents. Why would opponents be against your proposed policy? What strategies might they use to resist your efforts? Who will be their allies?

5. **Identify your strategies.** To advocate effectively, you will likely use a variety of Take Action Strategies. Consider the following:
   - create a social media group;
   - send out e-mail blasts;
   - conduct a survey;
   - create a petition, either digital or physical;
   - coordinate a public rally, march, or vigil;
   - testify at a public hearing on your issue;
   - lobby in person; or
   - attend a community meeting.

6. **Plan for success.** What needs to be done first, second, etc.? Who will be responsible for what? How will you know you have been successful?

7. **Work with the media.** The media is the best tool to get your solution out to a large audience. Seek to explain your issue and solution in just a few sentences. Incorporate your message into the following strategies:
   - start a social media campaign around the issue;
   - write a blog about the issue;
   - upload a video or participate in a podcast about the issue; and
   - circulate posters, flyers, and brochures.

8. **Create a resource pool.** Money is only one resource that may be useful in your effort. Identify resources that exist within your group. What talents and skills do you and your team have to offer? Do you know a business or organization that may be willing to donate space, food, or other items to advance your cause?

Three Golden Rules for Advocacy

1. **Clarity:** create a single message and stay focused on it.

2. **Quantity:** create as large a network as possible to support your cause.

3. **Frequency:** get your message out to as many people as possible as frequently as possible.

Voting

Voting is a basic constitutional right. Eligible voters may vote for president, vice president, two U.S. senators, and one U.S. representative. They may also vote for governor, state legislators, and numerous other state, county, tribal, and local officials.

Initiative and Referendum

In a representative democracy, laws are usually made by elected legislators acting on the voters' behalf. However, in some situations, the people can vote directly on proposed laws. Initiatives and referenda allow citizens to circulate petitions and put proposed laws on the ballot. An **initiative** is a procedure that enables a specified number of voters to propose a law by petition. The proposed law is then submitted to either the electorate or the legislature for approval. A **referendum** occurs when a legislative act is referred to voters for final approval or rejection. Recent state referenda have been held on issues, such as gun control, gay rights, abortion, environmental protection, and funding for schools, parks, roads, and other government programs. Many states also permit **recall** elections, which allow voters to remove elected officials from office.

Some people argue that allowing voters to express their opinions directly through initiatives or referenda, rather than indirectly through representatives, is a more democratic system of lawmaking. Rather than being a true democracy, the United States is technically a republic because the people elect representatives to vote on laws instead of voting on them directly. Supporters of the initiative and referendum processes point out that they promote direct involvement in lawmaking and reflect the true will of the people. Others argue that allowing direct voting on laws will sometimes result in majority populations voting to take away rights from minorities.

Some form of direct voting exists in 30 states. In 1897 South Dakota became the first state to adopt statewide initiative and popular referendum systems. Most of the states that now have this system adopted it during the first two decades of the twentieth century. Many laws have been proposed through the initiative process, including the right to vote for women, the eight-hour workday for government employees, term

initiative a procedure by which voters can propose a law and submit it to the electorate or the legislature for approval

referendum a procedure in which issues are voted on directly by the citizens rather than by their representatives in government

recall the removal of an elected official from office by a vote of the people

◀ Students get involved in elections by encouraging people to vote.

Ariel Skelley/Getty Images

▲ Women were effective in lobbying. Their defeat of local candidates was especially persuasive in convincing Congress to pass the Nineteenth Amendment. *Why do some people believe that voting is the most important political right?*

limits for elected officials, campaign finance reform, and environmental protection. This system has also been used to pass laws and establish public policy related to affirmative action.

Who Can Vote?

To register to vote, you must be a U.S. citizen by birth or naturalization, at least 18 years old by the date of the election, and a resident of the community in which you register. It is a violation of federal law to falsely claim U.S. citizenship in order to register to vote. You cannot register to vote in more than one place at a time. A few communities have changed their laws to allow those who are 16 and 17 to register and vote in local elections.

Registering to vote is handled by each state. Applicants usually register by completing an application form in person or by mail. The *National Voter Registration Act,* also known as the Motor Voter Act, requires states to make registration forms available not only at motor vehicle departments, but also at numerous state offices, welfare offices, and agencies that serve the disabled. In addition, some organizations and states make voter registration forms available on the Internet. As of 2018, 17 states plus the District of Columbia allowed voters to register on Election Day.

Where states have adopted same-day voter registration, voter participation has increased. In some other states, steps taken to prevent voter fraud have made it more difficult to vote. In 2018 the Supreme Court considered an Ohio law that eliminated people from the voter rolls if they failed to vote in a few elections and then did not respond to a notice from an election official. In a 5-4 decision, the Court found that this law did not violate the Constitution.

A fair election requires that voters have access to information about the candidates, the issues, and the details of the voting process. Many organizations—some partisan and some nonpartisan—provide election information online. The League of Women Voters (www.lwv.org) provides online information about federal, state, and local elections and candidates.

Information about federal elections, including past statistical data, is available from the Federal Election Commission (www.fec.gov). The FEC also provides online access to the National Mail Voter Registration Form, which has been translated into Spanish, Chinese, Filipino, Japanese, Korean, Vietnamese, and Tagalog to encourage registration by language minority groups.

Voting restrictions have been used in the past as a way to prevent certain groups from participating in elections. African Americans did not receive the right to vote until 1870, with the passage of the Fifteenth Amendment. Women gained the right to vote in 1920. Congress did not grant citizenship and therefore the right to vote to all Native Americans until 1924. Until the passage of the *Voting Rights Act* in 1965, some states had barriers such as poll taxes, literacy tests, and character exams that kept millions of people from voting. In 1971 the passage of the Twenty-Sixth Amendment gave 18 year olds the right to vote.

Today there are disagreements in many states about whether it is good policy to require people to have ID cards in order to vote. In 2008 the Supreme Court said in *Crawford v. Marion County Election Board* that requiring voter ID cards did not violate the Constitution. Those in favor of ID cards think that it is now too easy to cast fraudulent votes, while those opposed argue that requiring ID cards is unnecessary and would overly restrict minorities, the elderly, and the poor from being able to vote.

Participating in Elections

According to the U.S. Census Bureau, 70 percent of the voting age population was registered to vote in 2016, and 87 percent of those registered did in fact vote in the presidential election. This means that 61 percent of the voting-age population voted in that election. Typically, turnout in national elections is higher in presidential election years (e.g., 2008, 2012, 2016) and lower in years with only Congressional elections (e.g., 2010, 2014, 2018). Data from recent elections also suggest that lower income people, members of some racial minorities, and persons who have not attended college vote at rates significantly lower than the rate for middle-class whites. Young people typically vote at much lower rates than older people. Many countries—including some of the world's newest democracies—have much higher voter turnout for national elections than the United States.

> ### THE Constitution
>
> *The right of citizens of the United States to vote shall not be denied or abridged by the United States or by any State on account of race, color, or previous condition of servitude.*
>
> —Fifteenth Amendment

> ### Investigating the Law Where You Live
>
> **Learn** more about how to vote in your community. Where and how does one register to vote? Is there a residence requirement? If so, what is it? When and where does one go to vote?

PROBLEM 3.3

a. Make two lists: one of all the reasons for voting and another of all the reasons for not voting.

b. The following proposals have been made to encourage more people to vote. Do you favor or oppose each proposal? Explain your answers.

- Allow people to register and vote on the same day.
- Lower the voting age to 16 so some high school students could vote.
- Keep the polls open for a week instead of one day.
- Automatically register everyone who has a driver's license.
- Allow for voting up to a month early.
- Change election day from a weekday to a weekend day.

DELIBERATION

Should voting be compulsory in the United States?

Free and fair elections are essential to a democracy. They make true representative government possible. Through voting, people express their views about government. They choose leaders who they believe will improve their country and community. But what happens when people choose not to vote? What does that indicate about democracy?

In the United States, voter turnout can vary by state, by election type, and by a number of other factors. Only about 56 percent of eligible voters cast ballots in the 2016 U.S. presidential election. Usually, even fewer voters turn out for state or city elections. A 2016 report from Portland State University revealed that local election turnout in 10 of America's 30 largest cities was less than 15 percent.

Voter turnout varies widely based on age, income level, and race or ethnic group. American voters 65 and older turn out at 30 percentage points higher than 18- to 24-year-olds. Americans earning $100,000–$150,000 per year vote at a rate that is 30–50 percentage points higher than those earning less than $20,000 per year. And in the 2016 election, white American voter turnout was 7 percentage points higher than black Americans, 16 percentage points higher than Asian Americans, and 18 percentage points higher than Hispanic voters.

Some people in the United States are concerned about low voter turnout. They fear that if citizens do not vote, unqualified or bad leaders will be elected or stay in power. They doubt that leaders will be accountable. How can leaders speak for "the people" when so few people actually chose them? They worry that variations in voter participation among different groups mean that the government is not truly representative of everyone.

Not everyone agrees that voter turnout is a problem. Some people want voters to demonstrate their desire to vote, even if that means that turnout numbers remain low. In a 2017 Pew Research Center poll, 39 percent of Americans said that citizens should have to prove they want to vote by registering in advance. There are other concerns that by making voting easier, the government would increase opportunities for voter fraud as well. For some of these reasons, states vary in their registration and voting requirements.

Some people believe that citizens should be required to vote. This is called compulsory voting. In countries where **compulsory voting** exists, voters are not required to vote for any particular candidate, but they must be able to prove they voted. In 22 democratic countries, citizens are required to vote in national elections. In some cases, without a valid excuse, they may face some form of punsihment if they do not vote.

Should voting be compulsory in the United States? Consider the arguments.

YES

Voting should be compulsory in the United States.

Elections with high rates of voter participation are more legitimate because they better represent the will of the people.

Compulsory voting increases voting among people who are poor, are less educated, and were previously disenfranchised. At one point, some U.S. states required voters to pay poll taxes and pass literacy tests. These state requirements aimed to disenfranchise African Americans, but also impacted poor people and illiterate people. The legacy of this practice continues today, as African Americans, poor people, and less educated people turn out to vote at lower rates. Compulsory voting amplifies the voices of people who have previously been disenfranchised, which is good for democracy.

Compulsory voting laws do increase voter turnout. In national elections compulsory voting has increased turnout by 10-15 percentage points and even more in local and regional elections. In Australia, where voting is compulsory, voter turnout averages 95 percent.

Compulsory voting laws reinforce that voting is a vital part of democratic citizenship. Furthermore, compulsory voting can create a feeling of civic duty and responsibility among a nation's people.

NO

Voting should not be compulsory in the United States.

Authoritarian governments often coerce people to vote and to attend political rallies to give the appearance that their leaders are popular. When so many people vote, compulsory voting makes a corrupt election seem legitimate. Voluntary voting makes democracy more transparent.

Compulsory voting may be particularly burdensome to low-income voters who may not have the flexibility to take time off of work to vote. In countries that fine people who don't vote, penalties will also more harshly impact these low-income voters.

There are easier ways to increase voting. Democracies should better educate potential voters about the issues and the candidates' plans. Then people will know what is "at stake" and why they should vote. One strategy is same-day voter registration, which has increased turnout in states with the practice by 3–7 percent.

People who are being forced to vote might not make wise or informed decisions. They may simply vote for someone at random and negate the votes of people who do care. Our democracy does not need more participation by people who do not know or care about the candidates or issues.

GUIDING QUESTIONS

1. What are the two most compelling reasons to support the deliberation question?

2. What are the two most compelling reasons to disagree with the deliberation question?

3. What is one area of this deliberation where the two sides might find common ground?

i Portland State University, "Who Votes for Mayor?," 2016, http://www.whovotesformayor.org/

ii National Conference of State Legislatures, "Same Day Voter Registration," March 27, 2018, http://www.ncsl.org/research/elections-and-campaigns/same-day-registration.aspx.

Campaign Finance Reform

The 200-year tradition of privately financed elections in the United States has been accompanied by 200 years of campaign finance reform. However, efforts to counteract the influence of money on politics have usually been unsuccessful. Politicians have been quick to condemn fundraising scandals but slow to agree on laws to prevent them.

According to the League of Women Voters, those who support campaign finance reform want to improve methods of financing political campaigns for several reasons: to ensure the public's right to know, to combat corruption and undue influence, to enable candidates to compete more equitably for public office, and to promote citizen participation in the political process. Some groups argue for complete public funding of certain elections.

In recent years, federal elections have become extraordinarily expensive. To win, most candidates have to be rich, skillful fundraisers, or both. In fact, the candidate who raises the most money seldom loses the election.

Critics of the current system argue that (1) people of lower or middle income cannot run for office successfully because they cannot raise huge sums of money; (2) special interests receive favors in exchange for substantial campaign contributions; and (3) elected officials spend too much time raising money and not enough time doing their jobs.

Others argue that political contributions are a form of speech protected by the First Amendment to the U.S. Constitution. From their perspective it violates a voter's or a candidate's constitutional rights to limit the amount of money that can be contributed to or spent on a campaign. In addition to their constitutional arguments, those opposed to reform in this area contend that as a practical matter it is difficult, if not impossible, to create enforceable campaign finance reform laws.

▼ Delegates holding signs in support of Barak Obama and Joe Biden in 2008.

In 1976 the Supreme Court ruled in the case of *Buckley* v. *Valeo* that political contributions and expenditures are protected by the First Amendment. In 2010 the Supreme Court extended First Amendment protections to unions and corporations in *Citizens United* v. *Federal Election Commission*. As a result of this case and others, the government cannot restrict independent political expenditures by corporations, unions and other associations of people. And there are First Amendment limits on the government's power to restrict contributions to candidates by individuals.

An independent expenditure is one made by a group that is separate from a candidate and that does not coordinate with the candidate. During the 2018 mid-term elections, more than $1.2 billion was spent on advertisements by such groups.

Jill Braaten/McGraw-Hill Education

Some argue that this spending is good because advertisements inform the people and encourage candidates to take a stand on important issues. Others argue that these expenditures might be not completely independent of campaigns and because of their size could have an undue, corrupting influence on candidates.

A special campaign finance problem arises in states where judges are elected, rather than appointed, to their positions. Some states that initially appoint judges later make them stand before the voters in retention elections. An advantage of electing judges is that this builds a degree of accountability into the system. However, some believe that requiring judges to raise money to finance their campaigns compromises judicial independence. For example, studies of judicial elections have shown that the primary contributors to these campaigns are lawyers and law firms.

PROBLEM 3.4

a. Which of the following proposals is closest to your view of campaign finance reform? Explain your reasons.

- The only way to take money out of politics is to have full federal funding of presidential and congressional elections.

- In a free country with democratic elections, it makes no sense to try to limit how much money voters and candidates can contribute to campaigns. If people have the money and want to spend it on campaigns (either their own campaign or for the candidate of their choice), then they should be able to.

- We have to balance the rights of those who want to contribute money to campaigns against the need to fight corruption and undue influence in politics. The best way to do this is through disclosure laws: let everyone see who is giving money to candidates. If elected officials favor the special interests that funded their campaigns, the voters can vote them out of office in the next election.

b. Which of the following is closest to your view of judicial elections? Explain your reasons.

- Money and judicial elections do not mix. Independent commissions should appoint judges. Politics should be taken out of choosing judges.

- The chief executive—the governor—should nominate judges, and the state legislatures should confirm them. The federal judicial system works this way and should be our model in the states.

- In a democracy we have to trust the people. Judges should be elected just like other officials.

▶ Conflict is part of everyday life.

Effective community advocates work to solve problems in their community by proposing and lobbying for better laws and public policies. In doing so, they often use the legislative process to resolve conflict. Conflict in the public arena—sometimes called controversy—creates an important opportunity to learn about issues that are of public concern in a democracy. The ability to collect the facts about an issue, formulate an opinion, listen to competing ideas, and discuss and debate the best course of action are all valuable civic skills in settling conflict. As you will learn later in this unit, courts can also help resolve conflicts, but most conflict is settled before it ever gets to court.

Because conflict is a natural part of everyday life, it is important to consider how to handle it. We often think of conflict as a problem, but it can also be productive. When conflict is managed responsibly, it can provide a great opportunity to learn. Therefore the most important question is not whether there will be conflict in your life, but how you will respond to it.

There are sometimes disadvantages in going to court to resolve conflict. The court process can be time-consuming and expensive. Going to court can even make some problems worse. For example, in divorces and child custody disputes, going to court often causes extreme anger and bitterness. Some people feel that by going to court, they will lose even if they win!

Methods for Solving Disputes

Among the most common methods for solving disputes out of court are negotiation, arbitration, and mediation. As you will learn, negotiation is the most informal of these methods. Mediation is more formal than negotiation. Arbitration is still more formal, and in some ways it resembles going to court.

Negotiation is the process by which people involved in a dispute discuss their problem and try to reach a solution acceptable to all. It is important to learn to negotiate, because the skills involved in handling conflict responsibly are used every day by people in all aspects of life. You negotiate when you have a disagreement with your parents, your friends, or your teacher and you work out an agreement. The informality of negotiation makes it ideal for many types of problems. Sometimes people hire attorneys to negotiate for them. For example, people involved in auto accidents sometimes hire attorneys to negotiate with the insurance company over payments for injuries or damages to their cars. However, even if you use an attorney to negotiate, you must approve any agreement before it becomes final. Attorneys sometimes file a case in court and then still attempt to work out a **settlement**, or agreement, before the case goes to trial. A large number of civil cases are settled this way, saving both time and money.

It is helpful to think of negotiation in three phases—preparation for negotiation, the negotiation itself, and post-negotiation. Each phase contains steps that encourage a fair negotiation process. Each party in the dispute should follow all of the steps in each phase to make sure the process helps to resolve the problem.

The steps in the first phase help both parties prepare to negotiate. First, all involved should come to the discussion with a sincere interest in settling the problem. Then the issue that is causing the conflict must be identified as clearly as possible. Everyone should think about what is really causing the

negotiation the process of discussing an issue to reach a settlement or agreement

settlement a mutual agreement between two sides in a civil lawsuit, made either before the case goes to trial or before a final judgment is entered, that settles or ends the dispute

---

FIGURE

4.1 Methods of Dispute Resolution

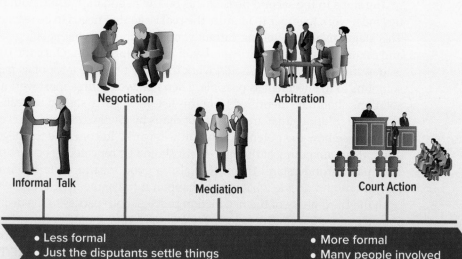

Negotiation

Arbitration

Informal Talk

Mediation

Court Action

- Less formal
- Just the disputants settle things
- Not legally binding

- More formal
- Many people involved
- Enforceable by courts

There are several ways to resolve disputes without violence. **ANALYZE THE DATA** *How is negotiation different from mediation? From arbitration?*

▲ Divorce negotiations often become heated as both parties try to agree upon the best possible solutions to their problems. *Why is it important to separate the demands (positions) from what the parties really want (interests) during the negotiation process?*

arbitration a way of settling a dispute without going to trial. The parties who disagree select one or more impartial persons to settle the argument. If the arbitration is binding, then all parties must accept the decision.

problem and try to separate the demands (positions) from what the parties really want (interests). In the third step, each party should consider the issue from the perspective of the other in order to help them understand the concerns and feelings on the other side of the conflict. Finally, each party should sort out his or her feelings about the problem so each can understand how the interests of the other party differ from their own. After this step, both parties should identify two workable solutions that might resolve the problem.

The steps in the second phase focus on the negotiation itself. Both parties must work together to identify the real issue that needs to be resolved. This stage involves listening carefully, understanding what is being said, and asking questions to clarify and gain more information. Once the issue is identified, both parties should work together to create a list of as many solutions to the problem as possible. Then the two or three most workable solutions should be identified from this list. Each party should be realistic about the solutions that are chosen, perhaps by giving examples so everyone can see how the potential solution will work. To conclude the negotiation, the main points of the agreement should be repeated to be sure that both parties understand them. It is also a good idea to write down the agreement and decide what should happen if the agreement is broken.

In the third phase of the negotiation process, both parties to the dispute should make a few final decisions. For example, they should decide what to tell others about how the problem was handled. Everyone involved should be in agreement on what people outside the negotiation will be told. This step could help deter problems in the future. In addition, both parties should be willing to discuss the problem again if the agreement does not seem to be working.

In **arbitration**, both parties to a dispute agree to have one or more persons listen to their arguments and make a decision for them. The

Steps in a Typical Mediation Session

Step 1. Introduction

The mediator helps the people involved in the dispute feel at ease and explains the ground rules for behavior during the mediation. Such rules can include agreeing to remain seated and agreeing that any party may request a break during the mediation.

Step 2. Telling the Story

Each person tells what happened. The person who brings up the problem usually tells his or her side of the story first. No interruptions are allowed. Then the other person explains his or her side. These people are the disputants.

Step 3. Identifying Positions and Interests

The mediator tries to make certain that each disputant is clearly understood by listening carefully to each side, summarizing each person's view, and asking questions. Sometimes the mediator will encourage the disputants to ask questions and summarize each other's point of view in order to check for understanding.

Step 4. Identifying Alternative Solutions

The disputants think of possible solutions to the problem. The mediator makes a list and then asks each disputant to explain his or her feelings about each possible solution. Sometimes in a difficult situation, the mediator might also meet with each disputant separately to discuss his or her concerns.

Step 5. Revising and Discussing Solutions

Based on the feelings of the disputants involved, the mediator may help the disputants change some of the possible solutions and identify a better solution to which the disputants can agree.

Step 6. Reaching an Agreement

The mediator helps the disputants reach an agreement that both can accept. The agreement is written down. The disputants also discuss what will happen if they find out the agreement is not working for them.

arbitrator is like a judge, but the process is less formal than a trial. Arbitrators, like judges, have the authority to make the final decision, and the parties must follow it (except in nonbinding arbitration). Arbitration is common in contract and labor-management disputes and in some international law cases. Agreements between labor unions and employers include arbitration clauses. This means that the union and the employer agree in advance to submit certain disputes to arbitration and to be bound by the arbitrator's decision.

Mediation takes place when a third person helps the disputing parties talk about their problem and settle their differences. Unlike arbitrators,

mediation the act or process of resolving a dispute between two or more parties

ombudsperson a person who has the power to investigate reported complaints and help achieve fair settlements

mediators cannot impose a decision on the parties. The agreement is the result of the parties' willingness to listen carefully to each other and come up with a reasonable settlement to the problem.

The mediator acts as a neutral third party by listening carefully to both sides. He or she also tries to help the parties understand each other's positions and find ways to resolve the dispute. Mediation is voluntary; the disputants themselves must reach a decision about the problem. Mediation allows the disputants to air their feelings, avoids placing blame, and concentrates on the future relationship between the parties. The key issue is how the disputants will work or live together after the mediation.

Mediation is used to solve a variety of disputes. Community mediation programs help settle disputes between husbands and wives, landlords and tenants, and consumers and businesses. For example, the Better Business Bureau (BBB) may mediate disputes between shoppers and store owners. In other places, neighborhood justice centers help settle disputes between community residents. Government agencies, newspapers, and some universities have **ombudspersons**, people who have the power to investigate complaints and then help the parties reach some agreement. To locate a mediation program in your community, contact your local court, district attorney's office, or social services agency.

The key to the success of both negotiation and mediation is that the ideas for resolving the conflict come from the people who have the conflict. The disputants take responsibility for their actions and work out the problem. Unlike court cases, both of these processes result in an agreement that is focused on the future relationship between the disputing parties. Because the solution comes from the parties, they are more interested in making the solution work.

The parties do not provide the solution in an arbitration. The arbitrator determines the solution. However, parties to a contract often include an agreement to resolve disputes through arbitration because it is faster and less expensive than going to court.

PROBLEM 4.1

Examine the following situations and decide the best method for solving each problem. Consider informal discussion, negotiation, arbitration, mediation, going to court (including small claims court), seeking help from a government agency, and other methods. Explain your answers.

a. Two sisters share a room. However, they disagree over how the room should be arranged and decorated.

b. A new plasma television breaks after two weeks, and the salesperson refuses to fix it.

c. A landlord will not make needed repairs because he believes the tenant caused the damage.

d. A fast food restaurant and an employee disagree over the wages and conditions of employment.

e. The Internal Revenue Service sends you a letter claiming that you owe another $2,000 in taxes. You disagree.

TAKING ACTION: Law and Democracy

Problems at the Mall

Magda, David, and Rashida have been friends since the sixth grade. One of their favorite activities is to go to the mall and look around in the stores. Sometimes they make purchases and sometimes they just window-shop. There are lots of young people who do this, and it is fun to see people and hang out.

Recently, a number of stores at the mall have experienced an increase in shoplifting and vandalism. As a result, the stores have made a policy that no one under 16 years of age can enter without a parent or guardian. The new rules also state that if you are between the ages of 16 and 18 you cannot enter the store in groups larger than two. Other teens have to wait outside until each pair leaves. Store owners have threatened to call the police if the young people give them any trouble about the new policies.

This policy makes Magda, David, and Rashida angry. They believe it is unfair. After all, they are paying customers and spend money in these stores. Why is the rule directed only at young people? They do not want to get into trouble with

the police, but they do not understand why they have to be treated as troublemakers when they have not done anything wrong.

The manager of the shopping mall, along with one of the store owners, has agreed to meet with two of the teens and a mediator to try to find some workable solutions.

PROBLEM 4.2

In preparation for the mediation session, the disputants should consider the following issues:

a. What are your concerns? How would you state the issue in the dispute?

b. What is your starting position (demand)? What are your underlying interests (what do you really want)?

c. What is the best conceivable outcome from your perspective?

d. What do you think the starting position and underlying interests of the other side will be?

e. Identify two workable solutions that would solve the conflict.

Use the list of Steps in a Typical Mediation Session to walk through the process and develop a reasonable solution for the disputants.

▶ The use of juries builds the values of democracy into the court system.

trial courts courts that listen to testimony, consider evidence, and decide the facts in a disputed situation

parties the people directly concerned with or taking part in any legal matter

plaintiff in a civil case, the injured party who brings legal action against the alleged wrongdoer

prosecutor the state or federal government's attorney in a criminal case

defendant the person against whom a claim is made. In a civil suit, the defendant is the person being sued; in a criminal case, the defendant is the person charged with committing the crime.

adversarial system the judicial system used in the United States. It allows opposing parties to present their legal conflicts before an impartial judge and jury.

In the United States, there are many court systems. Each state has its own court system, and the federal court system exists at the national level. Each of these systems has trial and appeals courts. There are also a number of tribal justice systems as well as a system of military justice. The highest court in the land is the Supreme Court of the United States. The Supreme Court hears appeals from the other court systems.

Trial Courts

Trial courts listen to testimony, consider evidence, and decide the facts in disputed situations. Evidence can be anything that might tend to prove or disprove an issue in the case. In a trial there are two **parties**, or sides, to each case. In a civil trial, the party bringing the legal action is called the **plaintiff**. In a criminal trial, the state or federal government initiates the case and serves as the **prosecutor**. In both civil and criminal trials, the party responding to the plaintiff (civil) or prosecution (criminal) is called the **defendant**. Once a trial court has made a decision, the losing party may be able to appeal the decision to an appellate, or appeals, court.

The trial system in the United States is an **adversarial system**. This means it is a contest between opposing sides, or adversaries. The theory is that the trier of fact (the judge or jury) will be able to determine the truth if the opposing parties present their best arguments and show the weaknesses in the other side's case.

The adversarial process is not the only method for handling legal disputes. Many countries have different trial systems. Some European

Judges play a more active role under the inquisitional system (left) than they do in the adversarial system (below). *In what ways are judges more involved in the court proceedings of an inquisitional system?*

countries use the **inquisitional system**, in which the judge is active in questioning witnesses and controlling the court process, including the gathering and presenting of evidence. These judges can order witnesses to appear, conduct searches, present and comment on evidence, and, in general, take the lead role in trying to uncover the truth. This system differs from the adversarial process, in which these matters are left to the competing parties, with a decision being made by the judge or jury based on the arguments and evidence presented.

The adversarial process is sometimes criticized. Critics say that it is not the best method for discovering the truth with respect to the facts of a specific case. They compare the adversarial process to a battle in which lawyers act as enemies, making every effort *not* to present *all* the evidence. According to this view, the goal of trial is "victory, not truth or justice." Despite its drawbacks, the adversarial process is the cornerstone of the American legal system. Most attorneys in the United States believe that approaching the same set of facts from adversarial perspectives will uncover more truth than would other methods.

inquisitional system a European method for handling disputes in which the judge plays an active role in gathering and presenting evidence and questioning witnesses

Judges and juries are essential parts of our legal system. The judge presides over the trial and makes sure that attorneys follow the rules of evidence and trial procedure. In jury trials, the judge instructs the jury as to the law involved in the case and the jury determines the facts, including whether the defendant in a criminal case is guilty or not guilty. Finally, in criminal trials in most states, judges sentence individuals convicted of committing crimes. In nonjury trials, the judge determines the facts of the case and renders a judgment.

The Sixth Amendment to the U.S. Constitution guarantees the right to trial by jury in criminal cases. This right applies in both federal and state courts. The Seventh Amendment guarantees a right to trial by jury in civil cases in federal courts. This right has not been extended to state courts, but many state constitutions provide a right to jury trial in civil cases. However, the fact that a constitution protects the right to trial by jury does not mean that a jury is required in every case. Juries are not used as often as one might think. In civil cases, either the plaintiff or the defendant may request a jury trial. In criminal cases, the defendant decides whether there will be a jury. Most civil cases result in out-of-court settlements or trials by a judge. Most criminal cases are never brought to trial. Instead a **plea bargain**, or pretrial agreement between the prosecutor and the defendant and his or her lawyer, disposes of the case without a trial.

If a jury trial is requested, a jury is selected and charged with the task of determining the facts and applying the law in a particular case. To serve on a jury, you must be a U.S. citizen, at least 18 years old, able to speak and understand English, and a resident of the state. As citizens we have a duty to serve on juries when called upon. At one time, people from certain occupations were exempt from jury service. These included members of the clergy, attorneys, physicians, police officers, firefighters, and persons unable to undertake juror tasks because of mental or physical disability. In some places, these persons are no longer excluded. Convicted felons are usually ineligible for jury service unless their civil rights have been restored. People who are not exempt and are called for jury duty are sometimes excused if they can show "undue hardship or extreme inconvenience."

Jury service is an important civic duty that is necessary to preserve the constitutional right to trial by jury. To determine who is called for jury

plea bargain in a criminal case, the negotiations between the prosecutor, defendant, and defendant's attorney. In exchange for the defendant agreeing to plead guilty, the prosecutor agrees to charge the defendant with a less serious crime, which usually results in a lesser punishment

Steps in a Trial

Step 1. Opening Statement by Plaintiff or Prosecutor

The plaintiff's attorney (in civil cases) or the prosecutor (in criminal cases) explains to the trier of fact (the judge or jury) the evidence to be presented as proof of the allegations (unproven statements) in the written papers filed with the court.

Step 2. Opening Statement by Defense

The defendant's attorney explains evidence to be presented to disprove the allegations made by the plaintiff or prosecutor.

Step 3. Direct Examination by Plaintiff or Prosecutor

Each witness for the plaintiff or prosecution is questioned. Other evidence in favor of the plaintiff or prosecution is presented.

Step 4. Cross-Examination by Defense

The defense has the opportunity to question each witness. Questioning is used to break down the story or to discredit the witness.

Step 5. Motions

If the prosecution's or plaintiff's basic case has not been established from the evidence introduced, the judge can end the case by granting a motion (oral request) made by the defendant's attorney. Also, both before and during a trial, attorneys for either side may ask the judge for legal rulings that affect specific pieces of evidence or even the entire case.

Step 6. Direct Examination by Defense

Each defense witness is questioned.

Step 7. Cross-Examination by Plaintiff or Prosecutor

Each defense witness is cross-examined.

Step 8. Closing Statement by Plaintiff or Prosecutor

The prosecutor or plaintiff's attorney reviews all the evidence presented and asks for a finding of guilty (in criminal cases) or a finding for the plaintiff (in civil cases).

Step 9. Closing Statement by Defense

This is the same as the closing statement by the prosecution or plaintiff. The defense asks for a finding of not guilty (in criminal cases) or for a finding for, or in favor of, the defendant (in civil cases).

Step 10. Rebuttal Argument

The prosecutor or plaintiff may have the right to make additional closing arguments that respond to points made by the defense in its closing statement.

Step 11. Jury Instructions

The judge instructs the jury as to the law that applies in the case.

Step 12. Verdict

In most states, a unanimous decision by the jury is required for a conviction in a criminal case. In civil cases some version of a majority is needed. The exact requirement is determined by state law.

▶ Attorneys for both the defense and the prosecution screen prospective jurors through the process of voir dire examination. *Why might a prospective juror be dismissed?*

voir dire from the French phrase meaning "to speak the truth." It is the screening process in which opposing lawyers question prospective jurors to ensure as favorable or as fair a jury as possible

removal for cause part of the jury selection process. After voir dire, opposing attorneys may request removal of any juror who does not appear capable of rendering a fair and impartial verdict.

peremptory challenges part of the pretrial jury selection. Attorneys on opposing sides may dismiss a certain number of possible jurors without giving any reason. There is one exception: peremptory challenges cannot be used to discriminate based on race.

duty, the clerk of the court uses a list with names of registered voters, licensed drivers, or some combination of the two. Usually a questionnaire is sent to potential jurors to determine whether they are eligible to serve. Employers are required to let their employees take time off for jury service. Most courts pay jurors a small daily stipend, and some courts also provide a transportation fee. Some employers pay their employees during their jury service, but they are not required to do so. To reduce the burden of jury service, many courts have instituted a one-day, one-trial plan. Jurors must show up on the day they are called. A juror selected for a trial on that day must then return for the duration of the trial. If not selected, the juror will not be called again for some period of time, usually at least a year.

After they are selected, jurors are assigned to specific cases after being screened through a process known as **voir dire** examination. In this process, opposing lawyers question each prospective juror to discover any prejudices or preconceived opinions concerning the case. After questioning each juror, the opposing attorneys may request the removal of any juror who appears incapable of rendering a fair and impartial verdict. This is called **removal for cause**. In addition, each attorney is allowed a limited number of **peremptory challenges**. This means the attorneys can have prospective jurors removed without stating a cause.

Juries range in size from 6 to 12 persons, although all federal criminal cases require 12-person juries. In the federal system and most state systems, conviction in a criminal case requires a unanimous verdict. However, about half of the state systems allow for nonunanimous verdicts in civil cases.

a. What reasons can you give for excluding from jury service members of the clergy, attorneys, physicians, police officers, and convicted felons? Should everyone be required to serve on juries? Give your reasons.

b. If you were a defense attorney questioning jurors at the voir dire in a murder trial, what questions would you ask potential jurors?

c. For what reasons might an attorney use a peremptory challenge?

Appeals Courts

In an **appeals court**, one party presents arguments asking the court to review the decision of the trial court. The other party presents arguments supporting the decision of the trial court. There are no juries or witnesses, and no new evidence is presented. Only lawyers appear before the judges to make legal arguments.

Not everyone who loses a trial can appeal. Usually, an appeal is possible only when there is a claim that the trial court has committed an error of law. An **error of law** occurs when the judge makes a mistake as to the law applicable in the case. For example, a judge might give the wrong instructions to the jury or permit evidence that should not be allowed. A judge's error is considered minor as long as it does not affect the outcome of the trial. In cases involving minor errors of law, the trial court decision will not be reversed.

When an appeals court decides a case, it issues a written opinion or ruling. This opinion sets a **precedent** for similar cases in the future. All lower courts in the area where the decision was made must follow the precedent set in the opinion. This is what is meant by courts "making law." However, a higher court has the power to reverse or change the precedent. Courts in other parts of the country are not required to follow the precedent. A court in another jurisdiction or state can disagree with this precedent.

Typically, a panel of judges—or justices, as appellate judges are sometimes called—decides such cases. The panel may consist of three or more judges. Nine justices hear cases argued before the Supreme Court of the United States.

When these judges disagree on a decision, two or more written opinions may be issued in the same case. The majority opinion states the decision of the court. Judges who disagree with the majority opinion may issue a separate document called a **dissenting opinion**, which states the reasons for the disagreement. In some instances, judges who agree with the majority's outcome, but for reasons different from those used to support the majority opinion, may write a **concurring opinion**.

Dissenting opinions are important because their reasoning may become the basis of future majority opinions. As society and the views of judges on appellate courts change, so can legal opinion. An example is the 1896 case of *Plessy* v. *Ferguson*, which upheld racial segregation in

appeals court a court in which appeals from trial-court decisions are heard

error of law a mistake made by a judge in legal procedures or rulings during a trial that may allow the case to be appealed

precedent an appellate court decision on a legal question that guides future cases presenting a similar legal question

dissenting opinion in an appeal, the written opinion of the minority of judges who disagree with the decision of the majority

concurring opinion an additional written court opinion in which a judge or judges agrees with the outcome reached by the court, but for reasons different from those used to support the majority opinion

THE **CASE** OF...

Taking a Car by Mistake

Joe Harper left the key in his 2018 blue sports utility vehicle (SUV) while he ran an errand. When he came back an hour later, he got into someone else's blue SUV by mistake.

This car also had the key in the ignition. Harper, who did not notice it was a different car, started it and drove away. He was arrested for auto theft as a result of his mistake.

At the trial, the judge told the jury it was not necessary for them to consider whether Harper intended to steal the car. Instead, the judge instructed the jury that to find Harper guilty of auto theft, they had to decide only whether he was caught driving a car that was not his. Using these guidelines, the jury found Joe Harper guilty.

This case illustrates an error of law that could be appealed. Auto theft law requires that the accused person must have intended to steal the car. Because Harper did not intend to steal the car, the guilty verdict would be reversed by an appellate court.

Landmark Supreme Court Cases

Visit the Landmark Supreme Court Case website at landmarkcases.org for information and activities about *Plessy* v. *Ferguson* and *Brown* v. *Board of Education*

railroad cars as long as facilities for whites and African Americans were "separate but equal."

U.S. Supreme Court Justice John Marshall Harlan dissented from the majority opinion because it allowed a state to pass regulations based solely on race, which he believed violated the U.S. Constitution. In the 1954 precedent-setting case of *Brown* v. *Board of Education*, some of the reasoning expressed in Justice Harlan's dissent in *Plessy* was accepted by the Supreme Court, and the "separate but equal" doctrine was declared unconstitutional.

State and Federal Court Systems

Figure 5.1 illustrates the two separate court systems in the United States—state and federal. State courts are courts of general jurisdiction. They can hear cases that deal with state law as well as many areas of federal law. The federal courts are courts of limited jurisdiction. Their power is limited to deciding certain types of cases. Federal courts hear criminal and civil cases involving federal law, including the Constitution. They also hear some civil cases involving parties from different states when the amount in dispute is more than $75,000. Federal trial courts are known as U.S. District Courts. If you lose a trial in the U.S. District Court, you may be able to appeal to the U.S. Circuit Court of Appeals in your region. The United States has 94 district courts and 13 circuit courts. The court of final appeal is the Supreme Court of the United States.

State Courts

Most state court systems resemble the federal court system in both structure and procedure. All states have trial courts. These are called superior, county, district, or municipal courts, depending on the state.

State trial courts are often specialized to deal with specific types of legal issues. Examples include family, traffic, criminal, probate, and small claims courts.

Family or domestic relations courts hear actions involving divorce, separation, and child custody. Cases involving juveniles and intrafamily offenses (fights within families) may also be heard. Cases involving juveniles are usually heard in a special juvenile court. Traffic courts hear actions involving violations committed by persons driving motor vehicles. Criminal courts hear cases involving violations of law for which the violators could be punished. Frequently, criminal court is divided between felony and misdemeanor cases. **Probate** courts handle cases involving wills and claims against the estates of persons who die with or without a will. Small claims courts hear cases involving small amounts of money (maximums of up to $10,000, or more, depending on the state). Individuals may bring cases to small claims court without lawyers, though it is sometimes advised that lawyers be present. Filing procedures are easy, and the court fees are low.

Investigating the Law Where You Live

Find out what courts exist in your community. What kinds of cases do they handle? How are the appeals handled in your state? What is the highest court in your state? Where is it located? Search online to find a diagram of your state's court system.

FIGURE

5.1 Federal and State Court Systems

The U.S. judiciary consists of parallel systems of federal and state courts. **ANALYZE THE DATA** How are the systems the same? How are they different?

If you lose your case in the trial court, you may be able to appeal to an intermediate court of appeals or, in some states, directly to the state's highest court. If a state supreme court decision involves only state law, it can be appealed no further. Each state's highest court has the final say on interpretation of state laws and the state constitution. If a state supreme court decision involves federal law or a federal constitutional issue, it may be possible for the losing party to appeal to the U.S. Supreme Court.

Federal Courts

Article III of the U.S. Constitution creates a Supreme Court and gives Congress the power to create lower courts. Congress has divided the United States into 94 federal judicial districts, with a district court known as a federal trial court in each district. The district courts handle a variety of federal criminal and civil cases. Each district court has at least one judge and some have more than 20. There are also federal bankruptcy and tax courts that only handle certain kinds of cases. As the map in Figure 5.2 on the next page shows, some federal judicial districts cover an entire state, while other states have several districts within their boundaries.

Congress placed the 94 districts in 12 regional circuits, each of which has a court of appeals. Court of appeals judges handle appeals of trial court decisions to determine whether district court judges applied the law correctly. Most courts of appeal have between 10 and 15 judges. However the largest court of appeals (for the Ninth Circuit, which includes California) has more than 40 judges. There is also a U.S. Court of Appeals for the Federal Circuit. This court, which meets in Washington, D.C., hears appeals from federal trial courts from all over the country. However, it only hears cases dealing with certain legal topics—primarily international trade, patent law, certain money claims against the federal government, and veterans issues. In creating the U.S. Court of Appeals for the Federal Circuit, Congress believed that its judges would develop special expertise in these complex cases.

Overall, the federal courts handle more than 400,000 cases per year. The federal courts also handle more than 1,000,000 bankruptcy petitions each year. All together, the state court systems handle more than 100 million cases per year. About 1,700 federal judges decide the former matters, and about 30,000 state court judges decide the latter. Federal court judges are appointed by the president and confirmed by the Senate. The U.S. Constitution protects the independence of these judges by providing that they hold office "during good behavior." For the most part, federal judges serve until they resign, retire, or die. Removal of federal judges requires that Congress follow formal impeachment procedures.

Investigating the Law Where You Live

Research to learn more about the federal judicial district in which you live. Which federal court of appeals handles appeals from your local federal trial court? Learn more at **www.uscourts.gov**.

For each case, decide whether it will be tried in a federal or state court. To what court could each case be appealed? Explain. Then give an example, different from those listed, of a case that could be heard in a state court and a case that could be heard in a federal court.

a. A state sues a neighboring state for dumping waste in a river that borders both states.

b. A wife sues her husband for divorce.

c. A person is prosecuted for assaulting a neighbor.

d. Two drivers from the same state crash their cars into each other. One driver sues the other for medical bills and car repairs.

e. A woman who has patented an invention sues another person later claiming to have invented the same item.

FIGURE

5.2 The Federal Judicial Circuits

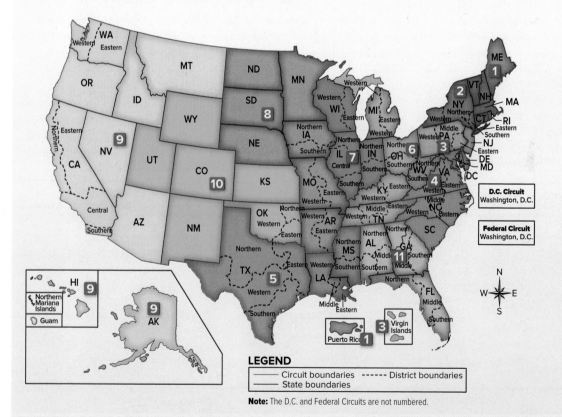

LEGEND

Circuit boundaries ------ District boundaries
State boundaries

Note: The D.C. and Federal Circuits are not numbered.

Congress created district courts to serve as trial courts for federal cases. **ANALYZE THE DATA** *Which federal judicial circuit hears cases from the state where you live?*

Independent Courts

A key element of a democracy is that courts must act impartially and make fair decisions without undue influence by outside forces.

One method of trying to ensure an independent judiciary is to appoint judges for a life term. This is done in the federal system and in a few states. Federal judges are nominated by the president and confirmed by the Senate. Judges who are appointed for a life term can make decisions in cases without being concerned about how it might affect their reelection.

In most state courts, judges are elected. Some believe that the need to raise funds for elections can result in a judge's being biased when deciding a particular case. Others believe that a system of electing judges ensures accountability and is appropriate in a democracy.

Another method of trying to preserve the independence of judges is known as merit selection. Using this approach, a judicial commission made up of lawyers, judges, and sometimes laypeople either decides who will be a judge or sends names of qualified candidates to the governor, who then chooses judges from that list.

In addition to issues of judicial selection and retention, independent courts must have fair procedures, the power of judicial review, and the benefit of an executive branch that will enforce court orders if necessary.

In some countries, judges and courts are not independent. They are influenced or in some cases controlled by the legislature or the president.

Read each of the following situations carefully. For each one, determine whether the actions violate judicial independence. Explain your reasons

a. Marsha Monroe is running for election to be a judge on her state's supreme court. She visits the offices of George Sanchez, the president of a large corporation, and asks for a donation of $1,000 to help in her campaign.

b. Some U.S. senators are unhappy about decisions of some federal judges. When the budget for the federal judiciary comes before Congress, these senators propose a reduction in salary for federal judges.

c. Judge Max Kaufman presides over a case involving a corporation. A distant cousin of his is employed by that corporation and is a witness for the corporation at the trial. Judge Kaufman rules for the corporation.

d. Judge Maureen Kim is running for reelection and knows that crime is a big issue with the voters in her state. In the months just before the election, she hands down some unusually long sentences for drug offenses.

Aaron Roeth Photography

◀ Native American groups govern their own people. *Why do tribal court systems exist?*

Tribal Courts

Many people, especially those who live in states with small Native American populations, do not realize that several hundred Indian tribal groups operate as semi-autonomous nations within the United States. These "domestic dependent nations," as the U.S. government refers to them, retain certain legal authority over their respective reservations.

Sometimes these tribal powers are called inherent powers. These powers include the power to regulate family relationships, tribal membership, and law and order among tribal members on the reservation. Occasionally Congress grants power, such as environmental regulation, to a tribal group. This is called a delegated power. Most Native American groups have justice systems, often called tribal court systems. Tribal courts hear a broad range of both criminal and civil cases involving both Native Americans and non-Native Americans. The jurisdiction of tribal courts varies based on such factors as the location of the offense (on or off the reservation) and the status (Native American or non-Native American) of the defendant and plaintiff.

Military Courts

In many ways, the military acts as another domestic dependent nation of the United States. It has its own set of laws, written by Congress and known as the Uniform Code of Military Justice (UCMJ), and its own system of courts. Of course, the military courts ultimately must abide by the Constitution and by the rulings of the Supreme Court. Military courts are most often called courts-martial and are convened to try U.S. military members who have violated the UCMJ.

Military courts may also be used during wartime to try enemy combatants. The more famous of these tribunals was the Nuremberg trials, held after World War II to prosecute members of Nazi Germany for war crimes. Most recently, military tribunals have been established in Guantanamo Bay, Cuba, to prosecute detainees captured during the War on Terror. These tribunals have been the subject of several Supreme Court cases and

THE **CASE** OF...

Gideon v. Wainwright

In 1963, a case called *Gideon* v. *Wainwright* came before the U.S. Supreme Court. In this case, a Florida man named Clarence Gideon was charged with unlawful breaking into and entering a poolroom. Gideon asked the trial court to provide him with a free lawyer because he was too poor to hire one himself. The state court refused to provide him with an attorney. It said that state law provided free attorneys only to poor defendants charged with capital offenses (those crimes that carry a penalty of death or life imprisonment).

The Fourteenth Amendment to the U.S. Constitution says that no state may deprive a person of life, liberty, or property without **due process** of law. Due process means fair treatment. Gideon argued that to try someone for a felony without providing him or her with a lawyer violated the person's right to due process of law. State courts had been split on the question of whether a free attorney had to be provided to an indigent defendant in a felony case. One powerful argument against Gideon was that the Supreme Court should not be telling the states how to administer their criminal justice systems. However, the Supreme Court agreed with Gideon.

PROBLEM 5.4

a. What precedent did the Supreme Court set with its ruling in *Gideon* v. *Wainwright*? Who has to follow this precedent?

b. Who would have had to follow the precedent if the case had been decided by a judge in a state supreme court?

c. Does the Gideon precedent apply if you are charged with a misdemeanor? Does it apply if you are sued in a civil case?

due process the idea stated in the Fifth and Fourteenth Amendments that every person is entitled to fair treatment by the government. The requirements of due process vary with the situation, but they require at a minimum notice and an opportunity to be heard.

Landmark Supreme Court Cases

Visit the Landmark Supreme Court Cases website at landmarkcases.org for information and activities about *Gideon* v. *Wainwright*.

there is still a great deal of controversy surrounding the tribunals and the due process afforded to the detainees.

The Supreme Court of the United States

The most important legal precedents are established by the U.S. Supreme Court, where nine justices hear each case and a majority rules. All state and federal courts in the United States must follow U.S. Supreme Court precedents. Some of these precedents, such as *Brown* v. *Board of Education*, which ended state-sponsored segregation in public education, are fairly well known by the public. Surveys show, however, that the public has little understanding of how the Court operates.

The Supreme Court does not accept most of the cases it is asked to hear. Each year, the Court is asked to hear more than 7,000 cases. The parties who lost their case in a lower court file a **petition for certiorari**—a request for the lower court to send up its ruling—asking the Court to hear their case. More than 99 percent of these requests are denied. The justices typically hear oral arguments and issue written opinions in fewer than 80 cases each year.

With few exceptions (such as federal voting rights cases), the Court does not have to hear a case it is asked to hear. With so many cases to choose from, it is able to set its own agenda. Most often petitions for certiorari are granted when lower courts have decided the same issue differently because the Court sees its role as making laws uniform across the country. The Court also takes cases that it believes deal with critical national issues. More than half of the petitions each year come from people who cannot afford to pay the $300 filing fee. Usually, these petitioners are incarcerated.

The party who petitions to the Supreme Court is generally the losing party in an appellate case that was argued in a federal circuit court of appeals or a state supreme court. This party's first step is to request in writing that the Court hear the case. The written legal briefs, or legal arguments, initially submitted to the Court emphasize *why* the case should be heard rather than how it should be decided. The party who has won the case in the lower court may submit a brief arguing why the case should not be heard. If the party appealing gets four of the nine justices to agree to hear the case, then the petition for certiorari is granted. This is the one exception to majority rule at the Court.

If the Court decides to hear the case, the parties then write briefs arguing *how* the case should be decided, and an oral argument is scheduled with the Court. During this hour-long argument, which is open to the public, each side usually has 30 minutes to present its case to the justices. The justices, who have already read the briefs and studied the case, ask many questions of the lawyers. After the case has been argued, the justices meet in a private conference to discuss the case, and the process of drafting an opinion begins. While the media tend to emphasize the disagreements among the justices, in a typical term the Court decides more cases 9 to 0 than 5 to 4.

The federal government participates in a significant number of the cases before the Court. Sometimes the U.S. government is a party to the

petition for certiorari *Certiorari* is a Latin word meaning "to be informed of." It is a formal application by a party to have a lower-court decision reviewed by the U.S. Supreme Court, which has discretion to approve or deny any such application.

▼ In 2019, the U.S. Supreme Court included (first row, L-R) Associate Justice Stephen G. Breyer, Associate Justice Clarence Thomas, Chief Justice John G. Roberts, Jr., Associate Justice Ruth Bader Ginsburg, Associate Justice Samuel A. Alito. Back row: Associate Justice Neil M. Gorsuch, Associate Justice Sonia Sotomayor, Associate Justice Elena Kagan, Associate Justice Brett M. Kavanaugh. *How does the Court determine which cases it will hear?*

case. More often, it offers its views to the Court as an *amicus curiae*, or "friend of the Court," with an interest in the case. The Office of the Solicitor General of the United States represents the federal government in the Supreme Court.

When a party files a petition for certiorari and the solicitor general's office also asks the Court to take the case, the Court is much more likely to grant review. In these cases a lawyer from the solicitor general's office may also participate in the oral argument, presenting the federal government's views—and answering the justices' questions—during 10 of the 30 minutes allotted to the party whose side the government supports.

The Court's term begins on the first Monday of each October, and final decisions on cases argued during that term are handed down by the end of June of the following year. In a typical year, about 80 percent of the cases the Court hears come from the federal courts, and 20 percent from state courts. In more than half of the cases argued before the Court, the lower court opinion is reversed.

The nine U.S. Supreme Court justices are nominated by the president and confirmed by the Senate. They have the authority to interpret the meaning of the U.S. Constitution and federal laws. All lower courts must follow these interpretations and other rules of law established by the Supreme Court. The Court's opinions are released electronically the same day they are issued. Later they are published in law books.

In recent years, many of society's most controversial issues have been heard by the Court. These include the death penalty, freedom of speech, gun control, abortion, and civil rights. Because these issues are so significant and because justices are appointed for life, the views of persons nominated to become justices have become very important.

Some individuals criticize the practice of appointing justices on the basis of their personal or political viewpoints. These critics say appointees should be above politics because they sit for life and the Court makes its decisions in private. They say that other criteria should be used to select justices, such as demonstrated experience and expertise as a lawyer or a judge, as well as intelligence, integrity, and good moral character. Others say that the process—presidential nomination and Senate confirmation—is inherently political and that it is impossible to be above politics when it comes to judicial nominations to the Court.

stare decisis the rule stating that precedent must be followed, providing the legal system with predictability and stability

As noted, all lower courts in the United States must follow legal precedent established by the Supreme Court. The rule that precedent must be followed is called **stare decisis**. This Latin phrase literally means "to stand by that which is decided." Following precedent gives the legal system predictability and stability. While the Court usually follows its precedents, it has the power to overturn a rule of law established in a prior case. This action sometimes occurs when society's prevailing views change and the justices want the law to reflect these changes. It may also occur when one or more justices who voted a certain way in an earlier case leaves the Court, and new justices are appointed who disagree with the prior decision. If this happens, the justices may overrule the existing precedent. When the Court decided *Brown* v. *Board of Education* in 1954, it voted to overturn the "separate but equal" rule it had established more than 50 years earlier in *Plessy* v. *Ferguson*.

TAKING ACTION: Law and Democracy

Who Should Be on the Supreme Court?

The president of the United States selects nominees for all federal judgeships, including the U.S. Supreme Court justices, "with the advice and consent of the Senate." The Senate must approve all nominees before they are appointed. Once appointed, justices serve for life unless they resign or are impeached. When the Senate receives a nomination from the president, it sends the nomination to the Senate Judiciary Committee for consideration. The committee schedules a hearing on the nomination. After the hearing, the committee votes. If a majority votes in favor of the nominee, the nomination is sent to the full Senate for consideration. If the majority of the Senate also votes for the nominee, the nominee is confirmed.

▲ U.S. Supreme Court building

PROBLEM 5.5

a. You are legal counsel to the president. One of the Supreme Court justices has just announced his resignation. Many groups and individuals are suggesting names of people they think should be nominated by the president. Write a memo to the president describing the type of person who should be nominated to the U.S. Supreme Court.

b. As legal counsel to the president, look at the following characteristics of potential Supreme Court nominees. Rank them from most important to least important. Be prepared to give your reasons.

- 45 years old
- Asian American (assume there are no Asian Americans on the Court)
- female
- graduated first in class from a top law school
- respected trial court judge
- friend of the president
- believes that affirmative action is unconstitutional
- believes in a woman's right to an abortion
- lives in California (assume there are no current justices from the West Coast)

c. Assume you are a member of the Senate Judiciary Committee. A nominee for the Supreme Court has an excellent reputation as a lawyer and lower court judge but is likely to vote, if confirmed, to overturn the case that established a woman's right to choose an abortion. Voters in your state tend to support the right to choose. How would you vote on the nominee?

International Courts

A number of international courts have been set up by the United Nations (UN) and other international organizations to apply and enforce international law. The International Court of Justice (ICJ), the principal judicial organ of the UN, is located at The Hague in the Netherlands. This court may settle any dispute based on international law that a country submits to it. Both countries involved must agree to have the ICJ settle the dispute.

The International Criminal Court, created by the UN in 1998, began operating in 2003. This court has jurisdiction to try individuals for crimes such as genocide, crimes against humanity, war crimes, and crimes of aggression. Initially, more than 80 UN member countries ratified the treaty setting up the International Criminal Court, but the United States opposed ratification. Opposition in this country is based on the belief that this court might put American citizens, including U.S. military personnel, on trial for political reasons. For example, a member of the U.S. military might be tried because some countries oppose U.S. military policy in some part of the world. Other international courts include the International Court of Justice, the Inter-American Court of Human Rights, the African Court of Human and People's Rights, and the European Court of Human Rights.

▼ The International Court of Justice, also known as the World Court, is located in the Peace Palace in The Hague, the Netherlands. *What kind of disputes does the International Court of Justice settle?*

UygarSirin/Getty Images

► The sixteenth president of the United States, Abraham Lincoln was also a lawyer.

There are more than 1.3 million lawyers, also referred to as attorneys, in the United States. More than 70 percent of them are in private practice. Around 10 percent are government lawyers who work for federal, state, or local agencies. Another 10 percent work for corporations, unions, or trade associations. A small number of lawyers work for public interest or legal aid organizations. An even smaller number are law professors, judges, or elected officials.

Contrary to popular belief, most lawyers rarely go to court. Most law practice involves giving advice, drafting legal opinions, negotiating settlements, or otherwise providing out-of-court legal assistance.

Some lawyers do, however, go to court. They are called trial attorneys or **litigators**. In civil cases, lawyers act as advocates for their clients' positions. Likewise, in a criminal case, the lawyer for the defendant has a duty to do everything possible—without violating a code of professional ethics—to secure the release and acquittal of his or her client.

litigator a trial attorney; a barrister

When Do You Need a Lawyer?

It is important to know when to see a lawyer. Many people think of seeing an attorney only after they get into trouble, but perhaps the best time to consult an attorney is before the problem arises. Preventive advice is an important service that lawyers provide. If you are under 18 and not legally emancipated, you will need a parent or another representative known as a "next friend" to use most of the services that lawyers provide.

David Planchet

You should consider consulting an attorney about a number of common situations. These include:

- buying or selling a home or other real estate,
- organizing a business,
- changing your family status (for example, by divorce or adoption),
- making a will or planning an estate,
- handling accidents involving significant personal injury or property damage,
- signing a large or important contract, and
- defending a criminal charge or bringing a civil suit.

If a question of law is involved, a legal document needs to be drawn up or analyzed, or you are involved in a court case, you will probably need legal help. However, if your problem is minor, you may be able to handle it on your own or with the help of someone other than a lawyer. For example, you can usually sue someone in a small claims court without a lawyer. Likewise, an argument with a spouse may be better handled through a marriage counselor or mediator. Relatives, friends, teachers, members of the clergy, doctors, or accountants may be more appropriate sources of advice in certain situations.

If you are not sure whether you need a lawyer, it may be advisable to see one to help you decide. Many **bar associations**—organizations that license lawyers—and other groups have services to help you decide if you need a lawyer. These are often provided free of charge or for a small fee.

bar associations an organization that licenses lawyers in some states

▼ Involvement in a car accident may require you to seek the advice of a lawyer. *How would a lawyer's services help someone involved in a car accident?*

For each of the following situations, discuss the reasons you may or may not need an attorney.

a. You hit another car in a parking lot. Your insurance agent indicates that the company will pay for bodily injury and property damage.

b. You borrow a friend's car without his knowledge, and he reports it to the police as stolen.

c. You buy a new laptop for $800. One month later, the laptop stops working. You return to the store, and the salesperson tells you he is sorry but these laptops have only a two-week guarantee.

d. You decide to trade in your old car and buy a new one.

e. Two friends are caught robbing the cashier at a local store, and they name you as someone who helped plan the robbery.

f. You are turned down when you apply for a job. You think you were rejected because you are deaf.

g. You do not want your family to inherit the $10,000 you have saved. After being told you will die within a year, you want the money to be used for cancer research.

h. You and your spouse can no longer get along. You want a divorce.

i. You earn $5,000 working in a restaurant during the year. You want to file your federal income tax return.

How Do You Find a Lawyer?

If you need a lawyer, how do you find one who is right for you and your particular problem? Perhaps the best way to find an experienced lawyer is through the recommendation of someone who had a similar legal problem that was resolved to his or her satisfaction. You might also ask your employer, members of the clergy, businesspeople, or other professionals for the name of a lawyer they know and trust.

Probably the best way to find a lawyer is through the recommendation of a friend who used a lawyer for a similar problem and felt well represented. In addition, the *Martindale-Hubbell Law Directory*, available in your public library and online, lists most lawyers in the United States and provides general information about education and professional experience of each lawyer. Lawyers sometimes advertise their services. In many places, advertisements for lawyers appear in newspapers and magazines or on radio and television. In addition, a variety of websites also provide referrals to lawyers.

Lawyers have not always been allowed to advertise. For years, it was considered improper and was forbidden by bar associations and courts. In 1977, the Supreme Court ruled that advertising by lawyers was protected by the First Amendment's freedom of speech clause.

Investigating the Law Where You Live

Find out the contact information for the bar association in your state. Does it provide a lawyer referral service?

▶ Lawyers specializing in certain legal services, such as bankruptcy and personal injury, often advertise on large billboards. *What is the best way to find an experienced lawyer?*

Those in favor of allowing lawyers to advertise think that it helps consumers decide which lawyer to hire. They add that statistics show advertising lowers legal fees through competition. Those against advertising by lawyers think that it encourages lawyers to be salespersons who are likely to make exaggerated claims. They think that lawyers should be hired based on competence and skill, qualities difficult to ascertain through advertising.

Many lawyers now advertise through various means, including on billboards, buses, radio, and television. But the trend is clearly toward online, digitally-driven advertising. Advertising has enabled large, lower-cost law firms, often called legal clinics, to develop, and some have spread nationwide. However, many attorneys and others still consider advertising improper.

In fact, lawyer advertising is a relatively new phenomenon. It began in 1977 when the Supreme Court struck down restrictions on lawyer advertising in Arizona in the case of *Bates* v. *State Bar of Arizona*.

PROBLEM 6.2

Conduct an online search for ads from lawyers and law firms. Enter the phrase "find a family lawyer near me." Analyze three advertisements. What are some advantages of lawyer advertising? What are some disadvantages of lawyer advertising?

Becoming a Lawyer

Some students in high school law classes are interested—or become interested—in becoming a lawyer. The path to becoming a lawyer in the United States usually involves completing a four-year college program, demonstrating strong academic skills, taking the Law School Admission Test (LSAT), completing law school (usually a three-year program) and passing a state-administered bar examination. The rules for eligibility to take the bar exam and to qualify for bar admission are set by each state. However, to receive a license to practice law, one must be a graduate of a law school that meets certain standards, and one must achieve a passing score on the bar examination. In addition, states check the character and fitness of each person who applies for a license to practice law.

In 2018 more than 100,000 students were enrolled in law school. More than 30,000 students graduate from law school each year and, typically, between 60 and 70 percent of those graduates pass a bar exam. Pass rates vary from state to state and even from year to year. In 2016 women outnumbered men for the first time in law school classrooms. The number of students of color enrolled in law schools has increased somewhat over time, but lawyers of color are significantly underrepresented in the legal profession. Many organizations work to increase diversity in the legal profession.

The Law School Admission Test is administered by the Law School Admission Council (LSAC). LSAC provides a great deal of information for students interested in applying to law school (www.lsac.org). LSAC also sponsors dozens of programs and events each year to encourage students from communities that are underrepresented in the legal profession to consider law as a career.

PROBLEM 6.3

a. What job opportunities are available to persons who graduate from law school and pass the bar exam?

b. What are some of the obstacles to becoming a lawyer and how can these obstacles be overcome?

◀ Becoming a lawyer in the United States involves earning a four-year college degree, taking the LSAT, and completing law school.

Solis Images/Shutterstock

UNIT 2
Criminal Law and Juvenile Justice

DO NOT CROSS

networks

Crime is a serious problem in the United States. According to the FBI, a property crime occurred about every 4.1 seconds in 2017, and a violent crime occurred about every 25 seconds. Public opinion polls show that citizens are very concerned about crime and about certain factors, such as illegal drug use and the availability of firearms, that can lead to criminal activity. Most measurements of crime, however, showed overall decreases since 2000.

◄ Crimes committed by both adults and juveniles are a problem in the United States. Most measures of crime have decreased in recent years.

▶ Police duties range from writing speeding tickets to investigating violent crimes.

Crime wears many faces. It may be the thief snatching a woman's purse or the career criminal planning a kidnapping. It may be the person who steals a car for a joyride or the car theft ring that takes it for later sale. It may be the professional criminal who profits from organized gambling, extortion, or narcotics traffic, or the politician who takes a bribe. Crime may be committed by the accountant who cheats on tax returns, the businessperson who secretly agrees to fix prices, the burglar who ransacks homes while the owners are at work, or the cyber terrorist who acts under the claim of a greater cause.

The Nature of Crimes

A **crime** is something one does or fails to do that is in violation of a law. It can also be defined as behavior for which there is a set penalty. Criminal law makes certain conduct "criminal" and other conduct "noncriminal." Decisions as to what constitutes a crime are made by legislatures, which try to protect the public based on what most people believe is right and necessary for the orderly conduct of society.

Certain acts are prohibited or required to protect life and property, preserve individual freedoms, maintain the system of government, and uphold the morality of society. Ideally, the goals of law are to protect human rights for all and to regulate human conduct so that people can live in harmony.

crime an act or failure to act that violates a law and for which a government has set a penalty (usually a fine, jail, or probation)

Many people do not realize that crime victims are also victims of human rights violations. For example, people have a human right to ownership of their own property (Universal Declaration of Human Rights [UDHR], Article 17). Theft crimes violate this right. People also have a human right to protection of their personal security (UDHR, Article 3). Violent crimes such as murder, rape, and assault violate this human right.

PROBLEM 7.1

Assume you are a member of a commission established to evaluate laws. Consider the following acts. In each case decide whether or not the act should be treated as a crime. Then place the letter for each example along a line to create a continuum from left to right. You will rank the examples from "most serious" to "least serious" to "not a crime". Explain your decisions.

a. Robert sells crack cocaine and uses the proceeds to support his mother, who receives public assistance.

b. Marley is a passenger in a car she knows is stolen, although she did not participate in the theft of the car.

c. When Carl's girlfriend tries to leave his apartment after an argument, he takes her car keys and threatens to hurt her.

d. A college student pirates movies that are still showing at local theaters and sells them to her friends.

e. Paulina is caught with a pound of marijuana.

f. Ella leaves a store with change for a $10 bill, knowing that she gave the cashier a $5 bill.

g. Felicia spreads rumors on social media about a boy she doesn't like, causing him emotional harm.

h. Ming refuses to wear a helmet while riding a motorcycle.

i. A company pollutes a river with waste from its factory.

j. Pat gets drunk and hits a child, injuring her severely, while speeding through a school zone.

k. DeShawn observes his best friend shoplifting but does not turn him in.

Crime has long been a major problem in the United States. Governments at all levels—national, state and local—are concerned with preventing crime and with apprehending and prosecuting criminals. The federal government collects data on crime reports and arrests and makes it available online. Much of this data is organized according to what are referred to as seven "index crimes." Figure 7.1 shows recent statistics for such crimes.

7.1 Crimes Reported and Arrests Made, 2017

Type of Crime	Number Reported	Percentage Arrested		Total Number Reported	Percentage Arrested
Larceny/Theft	5,519,107	17.2	Total Property Crime	7,694,086	16.2
Burglary	1,401,840	14.2			
Motor Vehicle Theft	773,139	11.8			
Aggravated Assault	810,825	47.9	Total Violent Crime	1,247,321	41.5
Robbery	319,356	29.4			
Rape	135,755	17.2			
Murder and Non-negligent Manslaughter	17,284	70.6			
			CRIME INDEX TOTAL	8,941,407	19.7

Sources: www.fbi.gov, *Federal Bureau of Investigation, 2017.*

PROBLEM 7.2

Study the crime and arrest data above. Then answer the following questions.

a. According to the information above, what was the most commonly reported index crime in 2017?

b. What percentage of the total reported crimes resulted in an arrest?

c. Of the index crimes reported, for which crimes were people most likely to be arrested? Why do you think this is so?

d. How can citizens act to help police improve arrest rates?

Since the mid-1980s, there has generally been a decrease in the reported number of index crimes. This trend is evident in both violent crimes and property crimes. However, there has been a very large increase during that time in the number of arrests made for violations of drug laws. The policy to aggressively prosecute drug offenses is sometimes called the "war on drugs." This term came into popular use in the 1970s when Richard Nixon was president. During the two terms of Barack Obama's presidency, public opinion polls indicated that Americans thought the country has lost the war on drugs. Polls indicated that treatment programs were preferable to prosecution for many drug users.

Although authorities agree that crime is a major problem, much disagreement exists over the causes of crime and what can be done about it. Among the possible causes of the high crime rate in the United States are poverty, permissive courts, unemployment, lack of education, abuse of alcohol and drugs, inadequate police protection, rising population, lack of parental guidance, a breakdown in morals, an ineffective correctional system, and the influence of the Internet, television, and films. This lack of agreement suggests that the causes of crime are many and complex.

Let's examine some suggested causes of crime in the United States more closely. Some people point to the U.S. economic system, with its wide disparity between higher and lower income, as a factor contributing to the rate of crime. In the 1990s, with a generally strong economy and low unemployment, the crime rate tended to go down. Between 2001 and 2002, the United States experienced a weaker economy and a rise in crime rates. However, between 2006 and 2009 there was a dramatic weakening of the economy but crime rates fell. At other times in U.S. history, a strong economy has not reduced crime, and a weak economy has not caused crime to increase. Most recent research concludes that there is no clear relationship between crime rates and the economy.

Researchers have also looked at data from high-crime urban areas. They have found that poverty by itself is not a good predictor of crime; a more important factor is the stability of the family. For example, many families with few financial resources raise children who are responsible, law-abiding citizens. However, it is also true that poverty and lack of educational and economic opportunities make it more difficult for families to achieve the stability that would help reduce crime.

Would tougher penalties curb crime? Many people think so, but the United States already has some of the harshest criminal laws—as well as the highest **incarceration** rate—of any industrialized nation. According to the Prison Policy Project's 2018 data, the incarceration rate in the United States—698 per 100,000 people—makes the country the "world's prison capital." By comparison, the incarceration rate in Scandinavia is about 60 per 100,000 people, or about one-tenth of the U.S. rate. Tough penalties may deter some people from committing crimes, but compared with the number of crimes committed, only a small number of people ever go to prison. Thus, some experts say that longer prison terms are not the answer. They say the certainty and swiftness of punishment is more important than the length of the sentence.

▲ Many communities organize neighborhood crime watch groups to help monitor suspicious activities. *What approaches has your community taken to prevent crime?*

incarceration imprisonment by the government

McGraw-Hill Education

7.2 U.S. Crime Clock

Crime	2009	2013	2017
PROPERTY CRIME	One every: **3.4 seconds**	One every: **3.7 seconds**	One every: **4.1 seconds**
Larceny/Theft	5 seconds	5.3 seconds	5.9 seconds
Burglary	14.3 seconds	16.4 seconds	22.6 seconds
Motor Vehicle Theft	39.7 seconds	45.1 seconds	40.9 seconds
VIOLENT CRIME	One every: **23.9 seconds**	One every: **27.1 seconds**	One every: **24.6 seconds**
Murder	34.5 minutes	37.0 minutes	30.5 minutes
Forcible Rape	6.0 minutes	6.6 minutes	3.9 minutes
Robbery	1.3 minutes	1.5 minutes	1.7 minutes
Aggravated Assault	39.1 seconds	43.5 seconds	39 seconds

Sources: *U.S. Department of Justice, Crime in the United States, 2009, 2013, and 2017.*

PROBLEM 7.3

Consider the frequency of crimes listed above and answer the questions that follow.

a. Did crimes occur less or more frequently in 2017 than they did in 2009? Do you think these changes are significant in any single category of crime? What pattern is most evident among all the categories? Explain your reasons.

b. What are the possible explanations for these changes? Are there any crimes that people might be reluctant to report? Explain.

c. Do you think the data in the table accurately reflect the crime problem in your community? Explain your answers.

Adequate police protection clearly has something to do with the crime rate, but studies show that simply increasing the number of police officers on the street does not necessarily reduce the crime rate.

Some communities have embraced the idea of **community policing**. This strategy builds closer connections between police and the communities they serve. Police officers who have more direct contact with residents in neighborhoods can more effectively participate in community crime prevention activities, understand the nature and extent of local crime problems, and gather information about criminal activity.

Thinking about crime requires individuals, communities, and governments to go beyond slogans and stereotypes. We should carefully consider each of the suggested causes and the possible solutions to the

community policing a strategy whereby the community works actively with the local police to lower the crime rate in its area

problem. Perhaps the most that can be said is that disagreement exists over the causes of crime and that solutions to the crime problem are not simple.

The National Council on Crime and Delinquency (NCCD) has studied criminal justice in the United States since 1907 and recommends the following strategies for reducing crime:

- Build safer communities with special attention to safe schools, after-school programs, community policing, and prevention of domestic violence and child abuse.

- Reduce the costs and improve the fairness of the criminal justice system.

- Develop cost-effective alternatives to incarceration, reserving prison sentences for those who cannot be safely treated in community-based programs.

- Create effective drug-control policies. Reduce funds spent on catching drug sellers and users; expand funding for drug treatment and job training; and repeal laws requiring mandatory prison sentences for drug possession.

PROBLEM 7.4

a. Not everyone agrees with the NCCD's recommendations. Do you agree or disagree with their recommendations for reducing crime in the United States? Explain your answer.

b. How would you structure an investigation to determine the three most important causes of crime in your community? How could crime be reduced where you live?

c. What steps should the federal government take to reduce crime? What steps should your state government take? What steps should be taken by your local government?

Crime on Campus

While schools are generally safe places, there is ongoing concern about safety issues. The federal government collects data on school safety. According to national data from 2016, about 28 students per 1,000 were crime victims at school. There were more theft and assault crimes in high schools than in middle schools. Bullying was higher in middle schools than in high schools. In 2015 about 6 percent of high school students reported that they had been threatened or injured with a weapon. About 12 percent of public schools reported incidents of cyberbullying among students. In 2015, 25 percent of high school students reported that illegal drugs were made available to them on school property during the previous 12 months.

On February 14, 2019 a gunman opened fire at Marjory Stoneman Douglas High School in Parkland, Florida. The assailant killed 17 students and faculty and wounded 17 others. This was the deadliest shooting at a U.S. high school in history. The shooter, a 19-year-old former student at

► Law enforcement officers work in schools as School Resource Officers (SROs) focusing on law enforcement, student counseling, and law-related education. *How else might a school attempt to reduce crime on campus?*

the school, was captured by police shortly after the massacre. Adding to the tragedy was the fact that officials had received several tips that this person was potentially dangerous.

Student survivors of the shooting organized "Never Again MSD" to demand legislative action on gun violence. They met with their governor, state legislators, and even President Trump. No new federal laws were passed in response to the Parkland shooting, but Florida did raise the age for buying a rifle from 18 to 21. Parkland students continued their civic advocacy in multiple states as part of the November 2018 mid-term elections.

Gangs and Crime

At one time, violent gangs were thought to operate only in the largest cities in the United States. Evidence indicates, however, that gangs are now active in towns and cities of all sizes throughout the country. Most large cities report a dozen or more gangs, while most smaller cities and rural counties report three or fewer gangs. One reason gangs have spread is the lure of profits from the sale of illegal drugs, an activity in which many gangs participate. Many gang members also buy, sell, and steal firearms. The combination of drugs and guns has led to increased gang violence. In 2012 the FBI estimated that there were about 33,000 gangs with more than 1,400,000 members, which indicates the magnitude of the problem.

THE CASE OF...

Weapons on Campus

Sunshine City is a suburb of Metropolis, the largest city in the state. Sunshine Community College (SCC), the only community college in Sunshine City, has 15,000 students. SCC's student population is racially and economically mixed. The college has many student organizations, as well as sports teams. There are mental health counselors on staff.

Sunshine Community College has its share of problems with alcohol and drug abuse. Except for an occasional fistfight, however, until recently it has not had a problem with campus violence. The faculty senate is committed to SCC student safety and recently discussed expanding the campus security force.

Samuel is a 19-year-old student at SCC. He moved to Sunshine City from another state with his family four months ago and started school in the middle of last term. Samuel is a loner, has few friends, and spends most of his time surfing the Internet and playing violent video games. He has not had any disciplinary problems on campus but has been caught shoplifting.

Samuel has had a difficult transition to SCC. His grades are poor, and his general demeanor is gloomy. He is sometimes picked on by other students and sometimes skips classes. Samuel's parents have noticed that lately he has been more withdrawn than usual, and they have been concerned about him. They contacted the mental health center staff, who promised to talk to him. Samuel did not go to the two appointments the counselor scheduled with him.

One Wednesday morning, Samuel left early for his classes, telling his mother good-bye and that he loved her. Although this struck his mother as odd—usually, he was late and did not say anything as he left—she hoped it meant he was feeling better about things.

Before going into the main academic building, Samuel saw Eddie, a quiet classmate who sat next to him in math. Before reaching the front door, Samuel told Eddie that he "had to take care of something" but that he did not want Eddie to be around when "it all went down."

Eddie had the sense that something was wrong and went to find a campus security officer. Officer Lee found Samuel just as he was about to enter the classroom. When the officer questioned Samuel and received a mumbled response, he decided to frisk him for weapons. Under Samuel's jacket was a semiautomatic gun. The actions that Eddie and Officer Lee took helped avoid a major tragedy at SCC.

The police and campus administrators investigated. One student, Trisha, told an administrator that Samuel advised her not to come to school that day. He wanted to keep her safe from danger, as she was always nice to him. The police discovered that Samuel had purchased the gun from someone on the street and also found a disturbing note in Samuel's jacket pocket. In it he outlined his plan to shoot people and remarked, "After today, no one will push me around again!"

PROBLEM 7.5

a. What conditions might have led to Samuel's decision to commit this crime?

b. What, if anything, could have been done to help Samuel? Were there signs on campus or at home that he was at risk?

c. Are there measures in place at your school to prevent acts of violence from occurring? Are additional measures needed? If so, what are they?

▲ Many gangs identify themselves with colors. *How are today's gangs different from those of the nineteenth century?*

What Are Gangs?

In this discussion, *gang* refers to people who form groups that are closed to the general public, for certain common purposes that may or may not include violent criminal activity. While the media have featured gang activity a great deal in recent years, gangs are not new in the United States. In the nineteenth century, gangs existed in many American neighborhoods. They were primarily composed of adults and were usually organized along ethnic lines. Even then gangs had names, rules, emblems, initiation rituals, and distinctive ways of dressing. Early gangs were interested in protecting turf, reputation, and cultural heritage. But not all of these gangs engaged in criminal activity; neither do all gangs today. In fact, some gangs perform community work and operate job-training and other government-funded programs. Generally, however, these are not the gangs that contribute to the crime problem.

Today's gang members range in age from young children to middle-aged adults. While traditional youth gangs are still concerned with issues of status and turf, many gangs now operate with much more sophisticated organizational structures. Many gangs focus on drug trafficking, firearm sales, auto theft, prostitution, and other criminal activities. Others use group-oriented violence or other criminal behavior to defend certain political beliefs that may be racist or sexist.

Gangs often associate themselves with one of several major gang "nations" and choose particular symbols, emblems, colors, phrases, and clothing with which to identify themselves. Gangs often use graffiti to mark, or "tag," particular territory as theirs, to intimidate rival gangs, or to instill fear in citizens of a neighborhood. People who join gangs usually have to endure some initiation ritual or test, such as committing a crime, being beaten, or, for female initiates, having sex with multiple members of the gang. Many gangs, however, are more concerned with prospective members' abilities to sell drugs and make a profit. They may require new recruits to successfully complete a robbery or drug deal or to commit an act of violence. It is not uncommon to have to endure a similar rite to get out of a gang, if getting out is an option at all. Violence, deadly weapons, drugs and alcohol, pride in their group identity, constant danger to themselves and their families, and involvement with the criminal justice system are frequently associated with the lives of most gang members.

Who Joins Gangs and Why?

The majority of gang members are male; about 10 percent are female. However in some high crime areas, 30 percent of gang members may be female. About 12 percent of gang members are Caucasians. In many cases, members' relatives or friends are also involved with gangs. Many gang members live under difficult conditions at home, where their basic

◄ People join gangs for many reasons. *What are the factors that put young people at risk for gang involvement?*

needs are often unmet, and they lack success in school. They are frequently very pessimistic about their job prospects and other opportunities for the future.

While the media and entertainment industry may portray gang membership as appealing only to inner-city minority youth, there is no shortage of gang members in urban, suburban, and rural areas. In addition, the idea that gang members can become financially prosperous as the result of gang membership is just an urban legend. In reality, very few gang members ever find either financial or social success.

Researchers have identified a number of factors that put people at risk for gang involvement: poverty, school failure, substance abuse, family dysfunction, and domestic and community violence. Many gang recruits have low self-esteem and little adult participation in their lives. However, there is no magic formula for predicting whether a person will or will not join a gang. Millions of people face the conditions described above, yet never join gangs.

Some people join gangs to receive attention and to feel a sense of belonging that is missing in other areas of their lives. Other people are the children of gang members and are choosing a similar lifestyle. Still others join because they feel pressure from friends, possibly in the form of threats, or because they believe that once they join they will be protected from police or members of other gangs. To people who see a future without job or financial opportunities, gang membership may appear to be their only alternative. This point may explain why some older members, still lacking opportunities, are not "maturing out" of gangs.

How Can the Gang Problem Be Solved?

Most experts agree that the best way to handle the challenge of gangs is to develop a flexible program that includes prevention, intervention, and suppression (targeting the most violent gang members for prosecution). Communities that are most successful in dealing with gangs take the following actions:

- Operate outreach and intervention programs in which social workers and trained counselors encourage gang members to become involved in positive, nongang activities.

- Provide greater opportunities for young people, including athletics, clubs, tutoring, community service work, and job training.

- Mobilize government agencies, schools, parents, community groups, religious organizations, and other people to increase awareness and develop opportunities for people at risk of joining a gang.

- Organize prevention strategies in which police and probation officers identify gang members (and wannabes) and place them in anti-gang membership programs.

- Prosecute gang members for illegal activity.

- Organize neighborhood watch groups that regularly remove graffiti and make it difficult for gangs to establish a presence or intimidate the community.

PROBLEM 7.6

a. Is there a gang problem in your community? If not, what steps should be taken to prevent such a problem? If there is a problem, how do you know it exists? What steps should be taken to deal with it?

b. Are gangs a serious problem in the United States today? Why do you think people join gangs?

c. Do you think gang membership appeals only to people from disadvantaged socioeconomic groups? Is a group of middle-class or rich youth that hangs out, vandalizes, and sells drugs a gang?

d. Do some television shows, cartoons, online media, movies, and lyrics of popular music encourage violence? What, if anything, should be done about this?

Guns and the Law

Most people own guns for safety and for sport. According to a 2017 Gallup poll, 42 percent of American households reported owning guns. However, guns are frequently used in violent crimes. Efforts by government at various levels to control firearms are very controversial among U.S. citizens, millions of whom believe passionately that their liberty and perhaps their safety will be at risk if gun ownership is restricted. Others believe that the relatively easy availability of certain firearms has aggravated the crime problem. Still others argue that it is not guns, but gun users, who cause violence and that law-abiding citizens have a right to own firearms.

Gun control is a controversial issue. Some groups look to the Second Amendment as protection against government attempts to ban or regulate firearms. Others argue that the language of the Second Amendment should protect a state's right to maintain a militia but should not protect individuals against government efforts to legislate in this area. Many

THE
Constitution

A well regulated Militia, being necessary to the security of a free State, the right of the people to keep and bear Arms, shall not be infringed.

—Second Amendment

◀ Guns can be purchased at licensed stores. *How does the law control gun possession?*

courts have ruled that the Second Amendment gives states a right to maintain a militia. However in a controversial 5-to-4 decision in 2008 *(District of Columbia* v. *Heller)*, the Supreme Court determined that the amendment also protected an individual's right to possess a firearm in one's home for self-defense. The *Heller* decision only applied to the District of Columbia. Two years later, the Supreme Court decided *McDonald* v. *Chicago* which extended *Heller*, protecting Second Amendment rights against violation by state or local governments.

The primary federal gun-control law is the *Gun Control Act of 1968*, passed after the murders of Dr. Martin Luther King, Jr., and Senator Robert Kennedy. It prohibits certain people—such as convicted felons, minors, and undocumented immigrants—from buying or possessing guns.

The act requires serial numbers on all guns and establishes a licensing-fee schedule for firearms manufacturers, importers, and dealers. It prohibits the mail-order sale of all firearms and ammunition, and it also prohibits the interstate sale of handguns. The passage of the *Gun Control Act* set penalties for carrying and using firearms in crimes of violence or drug trafficking, and it set age guidelines for firearms purchased through dealers (handgun purchasers must be at least 21; purchasers of rifles must be at least 18).

The National Instant Criminal Background Check System (NICS) is administered by the FBI. When a person attempts to purchase a gun from a licensed firearm dealer, a check is made to determine if that purchaser is listed in a federal database of persons with criminal histories or certain mental illnesses. The database also contains names of persons who are in the country without legal status. The database is compiled from records provided by state and federal authorities. The federal government has a program to make grants to states to help them strengthen reporting capacity. If the purchaser is listed in the database, the licensed dealer is not allowed to make the sale.

THE CASE OF...

The Gun Control Law

Several District of Columbia residents challenged local firearms laws passed by the Washington, D.C., city council. One of these laws banned handguns in the District of Columbia. Another law required all lawfully owned shotguns or rifles to be kept unloaded and disassembled or else disarmed by a trigger lock.

The residents who challenged the laws want to possess handguns and keep them in their homes for self-defense. One of the residents owns a lawfully registered shotgun but wants to keep it assembled and not bound by a trigger lock. They do not object to the idea of a registration requirement for firearms. Also, they are not seeking to carry any firearms outside their homes. The residents claim that these firearms laws violate their rights under the Second Amendment to the U.S. Constitution.

PROBLEM 7.7

a. Read the language of the Second Amendment on page 78. Do the Washington, D.C., firearms laws violate this Amendment? Explain your reasons.

b. Do the Washington, D.C., residents have a stronger case in challenging the ban on handguns or in challenging the requirement that rifles and shotguns be kept disassembled? Explain your reasons.

c. What is the strongest argument for allowing states to ban or regulate weapons? Explain.

d. What is the strongest argument for prohibiting states from banning or regulating weapons? Explain your answer.

Over the past several decades polling data on gun control has remained relatively consistent, with narrowing majorities supporting greater gun control laws over stronger gun rights laws. By 2017 Americans were almost evenly divided in terms of support for stronger versus weaker gun control laws. In 2018—perhaps as a result of several high-profile mass shootings—57 percent of Americans surveyed said gun laws should be stricter, 31 percent said they were about right, and 11 percent said they should be less strict, according to a national study by the Pew Research Center. On many issues relating to guns, there is a strong partisan divide with Republicans more supportive of protecting the rights of gun owners and Democrats more supportive of stronger gun control laws.

Investigating the Law Where You Live

Find out what gun laws exist in your state. Does your state have a law prohibiting adults from storing or leaving a loaded firearm within easy access of a minor (a "child access prevention," or CAP, law)? Does your state allow citizens who have permits to carry concealed guns?

PROBLEM 7.8

a. Which is a better way to reduce crime—more gun control or less gun control? Give your reasons.

b. What restrictions, if any, should the government place on the manufacture of firearms? The sale of firearms? The possession of firearms? Explain.

c. Should handguns, rifles for hunting, and semi-automatic weapons all have the same legal protections? Explain your reasoning.

d. Research the gun laws in your state. Propose any changes you believe are necessary and give your reasons. How could you get your changes enacted?

7.3 Public Attitudes on Gun Rights versus Gun Restrictions

Issue	% of Respondents Who Strongly or Somewhat Favor
Preventing people with mental illness from purchasing guns	89
Preventing people on federal no-fly or watch lists from purchasing guns	84
Requiring background checks for private sales and at gun shows	85
Creating a federal database to track gun sales	74
Banning high capacity magazines	67
Banning assault style weapons	67
Allowing K-12 teachers and administrators to carry guns at school	43
Expanding conceal carry laws	45
Shortening waiting periods to buy a gun legally	31
Allowing people to carry concealing guns without a permit	18

Source: *Pew Research Center, survey of U.S. adults, September-October 2018.*

Substance Abuse and Crime

The term **substance abuse** has come into general use in recent years. The word *substance* is used to describe all the different kinds of chemicals that people abuse, including alcohol and drugs. This type of abuse has always plagued American society. Substance abuse contributes to many social problems, including the breakup of families, decreased productivity, injuries in the workplace, and automobile crashes. Criminal activity may be caused by substance abuse or the desire for money to purchase alcohol or drugs.

substance abuse the harmful overuse of chemicals, such as drugs or alcohol

Alcohol

Alcohol is the most widely abused substance in the United States today. One reason for this is that drinking alcohol is generally socially acceptable in our society. Alcohol use has been legal for adults 21 years of age and older since the birth of the country—with the exception of a 14-year period from 1920 to 1933 known as Prohibition in which the sale, manufacture, and transportation of alcohol were banned. Not all countries, however, believe alcohol use is acceptable. For example, it is a criminal offense to drink alcohol in many Muslim-majority countries.

Alcohol abuse is detrimental to society. Alcoholism contributes to poor communication and dysfunction in some families. Some people commit spouse abuse, child abuse, and other crimes while under the influence of alcohol.

When considering alcohol and crime, many people focus on the tragic loss of life resulting from drinking and driving accidents. In fact, drunk driving crashes claimed more than 10,000 lives in the United States in 2018. However, many people do not connect alcohol to other forms of violence.

According to the U.S. Department of Justice, alcohol use is a factor in about one-third of all violent crimes committed in the United States. Two-thirds of the victims who suffered violence by a spouse, former spouse, boyfriend, or girlfriend report that alcohol had been a factor.

The term **drunk driving** is used in a general sense to refer to the legal terms **driving while intoxicated** (DWI) and **driving under the influence** (DUI). The legal definition of DWI/DUI refers to a person's blood alcohol concentration (BAC). The BAC indicates the grams per deciliter (g/dl) of alcohol in the blood. A person's BAC can be determined through breath, urine, or blood samples. Alcohol is a mind-altering drug, and tests have shown that thinking and reaction time are affected in varying degrees by the level of alcohol in the bloodstream. Although the legal levels of BAC vary from state to state, an individual generally is considered *impaired* when the BAC is between 0.05g/dl and 0.08g/dl, and *intoxicated* when the BAC is 0.08g/dl or greater.

Every state in the country has a DWI/DUI law. In 2018 almost one million people were arrested for driving under the influence of alcohol. Approximately 29 percent of all highway deaths involved alcohol in 2017, and thousands more are injured each year in alcohol-related car crashes. Use of drugs, either legal or illegal, that impair driving ability is also a violation of DWI/DUI laws. People can receive a variety of different penalties for driving under the influence including:

- monetary fine,
- enrollment in a DWI school,
- community service,
- license suspended (taken away for a period of time),
- license revoked (permanently taken away), and
- jail sentence (some laws require a minimum term).

drunk driving the operation of a motor vehicle while intoxicated (overcome by alcohol to the point of losing control over one's conscious faculties). A drunk person's blood-alcohol concentration is above a predefined level set by state law

driving under the influence/ driving while intoxicated DUI/DWI refers to a person's blood alcohol concentration (BAC). Although the legal levels of BAC vary from state to state, an individual generally is considered impaired when the BAC is between 0.05 g/dl and 0.08 g/dl, and intoxicated when the BAC is 0.08 g/dl or greater.

▶ Devastating accidents can occur when a person drinks alcohol and then drives.

Any combination of the penalties listed above may be imposed on a convicted drunk driver. A repeat offender is likely to receive stiffer penalties, and many states now automatically suspend drivers' licenses for DWI/DUI. In most states, repeat offenders receive a jail sentence. In some states, even a first-time offender must serve a brief jail sentence.

A driver who has been stopped may choose not to take an alcohol test. However, most states have an **implied consent** law under which the driver agrees to submit to a BAC test in exchange for the privilege of driving. In those states, refusal to take the test could result in immediate and automatic suspension of the driver's license for a certain period, even if the driver is not found guilty of DWI.

As drivers or passengers, young people are at a greater risk of being injured or killed in alcohol-related accidents than are people of any other age group. This is because young people are affected by alcohol faster and to a greater extent than adults and because they also tend to be less experienced drivers. For this reason, many states have passed zero-tolerance laws for drivers under the age of 21. These laws make it a crime for drivers under 21 to have *any* alcohol in their blood.

National and local organizations exist to help reduce drunk driving and provide assistance to victims of drunk-driving crashes. Such organizations include Mothers Against Drunk Driving, Students Against Destructive Decisions (formerly Students Against Drunk Driving), and Remove Intoxicated Drivers. These groups have brought greater public awareness of the dangers of drinking and driving.

In addition to laws about underage drinking and driving, many other laws deal with teens and alcohol. As noted earlier, alcohol is frequently present and an aggravating factor when other crimes are committed. Also, there is evidence that alcohol use among teens is a significant health problem, as well as a legal problem. According to the Center for Disease Control (CDC), underage drinking is linked to poor grades, school absences, drug abuse, and physical and sexual assault. Alcohol is relatively easy to obtain and is by far the substance most often abused. In a recent year, the CDC reported more than 4,000 deaths from teen binge drinking.

A number of states have taken measures to hold parents and other adults responsible for either providing alcohol to minors or failing to see that alcohol is being used by minors in their homes. In some circumstances these laws allow parents to be held financially responsible if a minor uses alcohol and is hurt, or hurts someone else. In addition to these civil laws, which allow the adult to be sued for damages, some states have criminal laws, which provide fines and jail time for parents who allow underage persons to possess or consume alcohol or who permit a party in their home in which alcohol is served to minors.

implied consent an unwritten agreement to submit to forms of interrogation or searches in exchange for certain privileges, such as driving or flying

Investigating the Law Where You Live

Conduct research to learn about the laws in your state that deal with penalties for DWI/DUI.

▼ Organizations have focused public awareness on drunk-driving in recent years.

©Henryk Sadura/Alamy

THE CASE OF...

The Graduation Party

Alexis and Neil were the proud parents of Sandra, who was about to graduate from high school. Sandra asked if she could have a graduation party, and her parents agreed. Sandra did not drink, and her parents assumed that her friends did not drink either. They told her she could invite up to 30 people, Alexis and Neil provided soft drinks, sandwiches, and snacks. When guests started to arrive, Sandra's parents went upstairs and did not circulate at the party.

Sandra became nervous that some of the guests had been drinking when she noticed that some of them left the party for brief periods of time and then came back. As planned, the party ended at midnight.

A few days later, Sandra and her parents learned that two of the guests were threatened as they walked home from the party. The sober friend ran and escaped harm. The other friend, who was apparently quite drunk, was sexually assaulted.

PROBLEM 7.9

a. Should the parents of the friend who was assaulted be able to sue Alexis and Neil for monetary damages?

b. Should the police charge Sandra's parents with a crime?

c. How could Sandra and her parents have handled the party differently?

d. Assume you are a teen drinking alcohol with a friend and your friend becomes sick (or that you are using drugs with a friend who overdoses). A few states now have laws so that neither you nor your friend will get in trouble if you call for help. Why do you think these laws were passed? Do you support or oppose these laws? Give your reasons.

Investigating the Law Where You Live

Find out what the state and local laws are concerning drugs where you live.

Drugs

While illegal drug use is not new, it has become increasingly widespread, and its effects have touched nearly everyone in American society. Illegal drug use costs society billions of dollars a year. The flourishing illegal-drug industry has led to a dramatic increase in criminal activity, ranging from murder to high-level government corruption. This has placed an overwhelming burden on the criminal justice system because so many people are arrested for selling or possessing drugs. Between 60 and 85 percent of persons taken into the criminal justice system test positive for one or more drugs at the time of their arrest. The trends in this area are difficult to determine: some cities have outbreaks of crack cocaine, while other cities experience increases in the use of marijuana, heroin, or methamphetamines. Some reports have shown a particularly close relationship between the increased use of crack cocaine and increases in the rate of violent crime in a community.

Possession, distribution, or sale of certain drugs is a crime that may violate federal law, state law, or both. Some drugs, such as heroin, are particularly addictive and can severely harm the personal life of the user. The federal drug law, known as the *Controlled Substances Act*, classifies drugs into five groups, depending on medical use (if any), potential for abuse, and capability to create physical or psychological addiction. The criminal penalties are different for each of the five groups.

Those who sell drugs or possess large amounts of drugs with the intent to sell them often face mandatory jail terms even for their first offense. Under federal law and in some states, those found guilty of being major drug traffickers may face a sentence of "life without parole." Some states treat simple possession of even small amounts of certain types of drugs as felonies. In addition, some states have enacted special drug forfeiture laws, which allow the government to seize property, such as bank accounts, airplanes, automobiles, and even houses, that was used for or acquired through the proceeds of drug crimes.

Since 2009 there has been a trend in some states to direct appropriate defendants into treatment or community-based supervision rather than sending them to prison. And some states have changed mandatory minimum laws to give judges more flexibility in sentencing violators of

FYI For Your Information

The Opioid Crisis

Opioids are powerful medicines legally prescribed by doctors to deal with moderate to severe patient pain. While these drugs are effective for relieving pain, they are also potentially addictive. In addition, when misused they can cause overdose death. Some people who become addicted to opioids turn to less expensive substitutes like heroin or other illegally manufactured substances. Those products can also lead to overdose death. In 2017 there were nearly 50,000 drug overdose deaths from opioids which means that 130 Americans died daily from these overdoses. This number is greater than the number of annual deaths from gun violence and auto accidents combined!

Doctors began prescribing opioids in the 1990s and by the end of that decade overdose deaths began to rise. In 2010 overdose deaths from heroin began rising. In 2013 overdose deaths from synthetic opioids including illegally manufactured drugs such as fentanyl began to spike.

Possibly because opioids were legal and prescribed by medical professionals, the public and government officials were slow to recognize the severity of the crisis. The Centers for Disease Control and Prevention (www.cdc.gov) leads the federal government's effort to combat the opioid epidemic. The CDC works with states to gather data on the extent of the problem, and with medical professionals on safer prescribing practices while also helping educate consumers about opioid misuse and the dangers of overdose. In late 2018 Congress passed, and President Trump signed the *Opioid Crisis Response Act* which increased funding for recovery centers, overdose-reversal treatments, addiction related research, and infrastructure improvements at the southern border (designed to detect illegal drugs coming into the country).

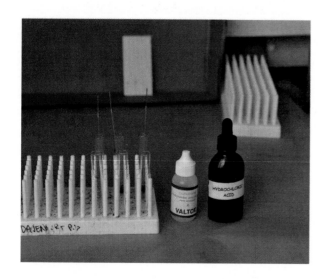

▲ Drug courts require offenders to submit to regular drug testing. *What other conditions set by the drug court must an offender meet?*

Investigating the Law Where You Live

Research drug laws in your state. Are the penalties too harsh, too lenient, or about right? How could you work to improve these laws?

drug laws. By 2018 there were more than 3,100 specialized drug courts implementing a treatment oriented philosophy in place of punishment.

Some people, including a few politicians, have proposed that American society should consider legalizing certain drugs, such as marijuana. These people point to the failure of the "war on drugs" and say that as long as some drugs are illegal, we are creating a market for their illegal sale. Proponents of legalization believe the United States would be better able to control the sale and use of drugs if the laws changed from drug prohibition to drug regulation. They suggest that the United States treat drug abuse as a health problem rather than a crime. It is hypocritical, they claim, to criminalize drug use while allowing the legal sale of alcohol and tobacco, which studies show are very harmful to people's health and cause many more deaths than illegal drugs.

Some people favor legalizing certain drugs either for medical or recreational purposes. As of 2018 ten U.S. states had legalized recreational marijuana use, and another 33 states allowed for medical marijuana use. In 2005 the U.S. Supreme Court determined that federal drug laws could be enforced, even in states that had legalized the use of marijuana. For this reason, criminal penalties remain in place for those prosecuted under federal laws.

Many are opposed to any sort of drug legalization. They believe that legalizing drugs and making them easier to get would lead to greater drug use, cause more deaths, and increase other drug-related problems. These people feel that criminal laws deter drug use and that reducing or eliminating penalties would deliver a message of acceptance. Legalizing drugs, they say, would result in what some people call "the addicting of America" and would endanger our society as a whole.

A middle ground, advocated by some, is decriminalization. Under this approach, police would write tickets (like traffic tickets) for use of certain drugs. This approach does not demonstrate social acceptance of drug use, but users do not go to jail either.

PROBLEM 7.10

a. Are there any controlled substances that should be legalized (still allowing some form of government regulation and even fines)? If so, which controlled substances should be legalized?

b. What are the most convincing arguments in favor of legalizing some controlled substances?

c. What are the most convincing arguments against legalizing any controlled substances?

TAKING ACTION: Law and Democracy

Drugs in the City

The city of Southland has been plagued by a growing drug epidemic. City officials and citizens are especially outraged that adults are using minors to sell drugs for them. This happens because minors often receive lighter sentences than adults do for drug-related offenses. Southland is also facing an influx of drugs and drug dealers from other cities. The mayor has called a special city council meeting to address the problem. Six experts have been asked to testify and present six different approaches to address the problem.

Police Chief Anderson (Law Enforcement Approach): "We cannot be everywhere at once. The department needs 100 more officers. The best way to combat the drug epidemic is to put more officers on the street and arm them with the newest and best weapons. Let's show the drug dealers and their customers that we mean business."

District Attorney Fisher (Restrict Civil Liberties Approach): "I think the city should declare an emergency and clamp down on drug sales on the street. Because of the epidemic, the civil liberties of the citizens of Southland must be temporarily limited. Because minors are selling drugs late at night, we need to institute a 9 p.m. curfew for anyone under the age of 18. I also advocate conducting random searches of students at schools and establishing checkpoints where all cars will be stopped and searched in areas where drug trafficking is high."

Terry Blade (Drug Treatment Approach): "I am an ex-addict who was cured because I was arrested and sent to a good treatment program. I see drug treatment as the best way to cut the demand for drugs, thereby driving the drug dealers out of business. Many addicts are turned away because treatment spaces are limited in this community. I want the city to devote more resources to treating people addicted to drugs."

School Superintendent Lee (Preventive Education Approach): "Education is the real answer to the drug problem. We must address the issue of values as a set of choices every student has: either obey the law or use drugs. I want preventive drug education for every student, starting in the first grade."

Prosecutor Horton (Penalties Approach): "Stiffer penalties are needed. The state legislature should pass tougher mandatory sentences for drug offenders. Anyone aged 15 or older who is convicted of selling drugs should be given a mandatory two-year sentence and be tried as an adult."

Rocio Fuentes (Legalization Approach): "We should legalize drugs. If drugs are made legal, the government can regulate the price and quality of the product, thereby reducing or eliminating the black market for drugs. Drug addicts won't need to commit other crimes in order to obtain money to buy drugs at outrageously high street prices. Finally, our tax dollars won't be wasted chasing drug traffickers and international cartels. The money saved could be used to fund preventive education and treatment programs."

PROBLEM 7.11

a. Use the experts' statements to stage a city council hearing. Then decide which approach will help the city of Southland most. List the six approaches in order of your preference, and give reasons for your rankings.

b. What are the costs and benefits of each approach? What are the problems or risks of each?

c. Could more than one of these approaches be tried at the same time? If so, which ones go together most easily?

d. As a city council member, which approach will you vote for? Explain.

Contact your police or prosecutor's office to learn whether there is a victim's assistance program in your community. If there is one, how does it operate? Is there a victim compensation law? If so, how does it operate?

restitution the act of restoring something to its owner; the act of making good for loss or damage; repaying or refunding illegally obtained money or property

▼ Urban dwellers are more likely to become victims of crime. *What other factors influence a person's likelihood of becoming a victim of crime?*

Victims of Crime

Crime affects us all, but victims suffer most. Victims of crime are found among all segments of society: young, old, rich, lower income, and all racial and ethnic groups. In 2017, just under nine million crimes were committed in the United States. Of these, 1.2 million were violent crimes and 7.7 million were property crimes.

Young people are more likely to be victims of crime than people in any other age group. Persons 12 to 24 years old are typically victims of violent crime at rates higher than any other age group.

Gender, socioeconomic status, race, and location are also factors that influence a person's likelihood of becoming a victim of crime. Except for rape and sexual assault, males are more frequently the victims of violent crime. Persons from lower-income households are more likely to be victims of crime than those with higher incomes. Members of minority groups, urban dwellers, and those who rent their homes are more likely to be victims of crime than persons who are white, non-urbans, and property owners. For example, the homicide victimization rate for African Americans is approximately four times higher than the rate for whites.

In recent years, public interest in aiding victims of crime has grown. Most states now have victim assistance programs. These programs provide victims with counseling, medical care, and other services. Most states also have victim compensation laws. These laws provide financial help for victims, such as paying medical bills, making up lost salary, and, in some cases, paying funeral costs and death benefits to victims' families. Some states allow prosecutors to submit victim impact statements to the court when a person is sentenced for a crime. These statements show the effect of the defendant's crime on the victim's physical and psychological well-being. Some courts also allow victims to testify. In addition, courts sometimes order **restitution**—requiring criminals to pay back or otherwise compensate the victims.

Today, victim advocacy groups are playing a more significant role in the criminal justice system. Their primary functions are to help victims through their trauma and to protect the rights of victims. Most of these groups deal with specific crimes, such as rape, spouse abuse, drunk driving, and child abuse. One highly successful victim advocacy group is Mothers Against Drunk Driving (MADD). MADD has been instrumental in calling attention to the problem of drunk driving and in lobbying for and winning stricter punishment for people caught driving while intoxicated.

Con Tanasiuk/Design Pics

7.4 Prevalence of Violent Crime by Demographic Characteristics

Victim demographic	Number of victims[a]	
	2013	2016
Total	3,041,170	2,900,320
Sex		
Male	1,567,070	1,514,130
Female	1,474,090	1,386,190
Race/Hispanic origin		
White[a]	1,860,870	1,785,680
Black/African American[a]	430,380	377,950
Hispanic/Latino	540,130	488,700
Other	209,800	299,990
Age		
12–17	545,370	313,470
18–24	527,410	461,300
25–34	604,500	689,590
35–49	684,150	700,060
50–64	566,990	541,330
65 or older	112,760	170,640

Note: Detail may not sum to total due to rounding.
[a]Excludes persons of Hispanic or Latino origin.
Source: Bureau of Justice Statistics, National Crime Victimization Survey, 2013 and 2016

PROBLEM 7.12

This table from the federal government shows demographic information about victims of violent crimes.

a. What generalization, if any, can you make from the data in this figure?

b. What additional data would you need to make other generalizations?

Victims' Rights: Megan's Law as Advocacy

Victims' groups can often be successful in helping to pass legislation that provides protection for particularly vulnerable members of society. For example, in the early 1990s, seven-year-old Megan Kanka was abducted, sexually molested, and murdered by a neighbor who, unknown to her parents, was a convicted sex offender. Following this tragedy, through the advocacy of parent groups and communities, voters across the country began enacting local legislation that would help protect children from sex offenders. Within two years of Megan's abduction and murder, all 50 states and the District of Columbia had passed their own versions of Megan's Law, requiring the registration of all convicted sex offenders in the community. There is also a federal law requiring that each state register sex offenders and make this information available to the public. Ex-offenders have challenged these laws in several states, claiming they are being punished twice for the same offense—once by a term in jail and then again by being listed on these registries. In 2003 the U.S. Supreme Court upheld the Alaska and Connecticut versions of these laws, based on the states' interest in maintaining public safety and because the goal of an offender registry is to inform the community, not to judge an offender as currently dangerous to society.

▲ Amber alert sign

Preventing and Reporting Crime

As an effective citizen, you can help fight crime by learning how to protect yourself. This means knowing both how to prevent crime and what to do if you are ever a victim of crime. Reporting a crime alerts police and the community, and thus helps to prevent others from becoming victims. To reduce the risk of crime, take the following steps:

- Report suspicious activity to the police. The police cannot help you if you do not call them.
- Always lock your car and home doors and windows. You can prevent many burglaries by locking up. Also, when at home, do not open the door unless you know who is outside. Cancel newspapers and mail when you are away for an extended period. Do not enter your home if you think someone has broken in. Instead, call police from a neighbor's home.
- Be alert when in high-crime areas such as dark, deserted streets and parking lots.
- Use the "buddy system." Criminals are less likely to target pairs or groups of people.
- Do not flash money in public.
- If you witness a crime or have been the victim of a crime, stay calm and call the police.
- Provide police with as much information as possible. If you can, write down the details, including a description of the suspect.
- You may be asked to file a complaint or to testify in court. Your help will assist the police in preventing future crimes in your community.

Crimes of consumer fraud, identify theft and various forms of cybercrime are also significant and growing problems. Almost all states, for example, have laws against cyberstalking and cyber harassment. Electronic forms of bullying, sometimes called cyber bullying, are also crimes in many states. You will learn more about protecting yourself from these crimes later in *Street Law*.

▶ Survivors of crime can turn to government and private organizations for assistance. *What are two groups that provide help to survivors of crime?*

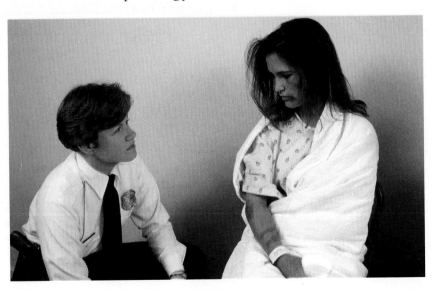

If You Become a Victim

There are two different views on what to do if you believe you are about to become the victim of a crime. The first theory is that you should not fight back. For property crimes, for example, many believe you should give up the property without objection to reduce your risk of injury. The second theory is that you should resist the assailant. Many advocate learning self-defense techniques to protect yourself in the event of a personal crime. Which course should you follow? Every situation is unique, but your safety should always come first.

If you choose to fight back against the assailant, be prepared to risk injury. Know your own limitations. Not everyone has the strength or size to be able to fight back successfully. If the assailant has a weapon, you should assume it is going to be used.

As a general rule, criminals do not want an audience. If you are able to scream, blow a whistle, or make some other type of noise, do so if you know you will be heard. If you cannot run away, sit down so you will not get knocked down. Finally, call the police as soon as you can. Do not wait! The longer you wait to call, the more likely it is that the criminal will get away.

Are witnesses to crimes under any obligation to come to the aid of crime victims? Until recently, the legal answer, as opposed to the moral answer, was no. Most states have had Good Samaritan laws that relieve bystanders from most civil liability when they help people in danger, but they have not required bystanders to help. Now, however, several new state laws require witnesses to offer whatever help they can reasonably provide without endangering themselves. In the case of a violent crime, this simply means reporting the crime to the police. In a number of European countries and some other countries as well, there is a general duty to rescue unless doing so would cause the rescuer harm.

FYI For Your Information

Help for Survivors of Crime

Many federal, state, and local governments, as well as private organizations, have established programs to assist survivors of crimes and their families. These programs include counseling and support groups, advocacy initiatives, and financial assistance to families of victims and survivors of crime. Two such groups are the National Center for Victims of Crime and the Office for Victims of Crime.

The Office for Victims of Crime is a federally administered program that was established by the Victims of Crime Act of 1984. It provides support for policy and legislative initiatives, as well as providing information and services to victims of crime and their families. The Office for Victims of Crime provides information online at **www.ovc.gov**.

CHAPTER **8**
Introduction to Criminal Law

▶ Police officers secure a crime scene to ensure that evidence is not lost.

state of mind what you are thinking; most crimes require that the actor have a guilty state of mind, meaning that he or she purposefully commits the prohibited act

mens rea the Latin term used by lawyers when they discuss the requirements for a guilty state of mind

strict liability the legal responsibility for damage or injury, even if you are not negligent

statutory rape the act of unlawful sexual intercourse by an adult with someone under the age of consent, even if the minor is a willing and voluntary participant in the sexual act

Almost all crimes require an illegal act to be accompanied by a guilty **state of mind**. A guilty state of mind usually means that the prohibited act was done intentionally, knowingly, or willfully. The Latin term used by lawyers when they discuss this requirement for a guilty mind is ***mens rea***. In most cases, mere carelessness is not considered a guilty state of mind. For example, if Meredith accidentally forgot to turn off the stove before leaving for work and the whole apartment building caught fire as a result, she would not be guilty of arson, which is the intentional burning of a person's property. She committed the act but did not have the guilty state of mind.

State of mind is different from motive. State of mind refers to the level of awareness a person has when committing an act, for example intentionally or recklessly. Motive is the person's reason for performing the act. For example, Robin Hood stole from the rich to give to the poor, but his state of mind was intentional, so he would be guilty of a crime.

A few crimes are **strict liability** offenses. These crimes do not require a guilty state of mind. The act itself is criminal, regardless of the knowledge or intent of the person committing it. For example, it is a strict liability crime to sell alcoholic beverages to minors. Selling alcohol to a minor is a crime regardless of whether the seller knew the buyer was underage. Similarly, having sex with an underage partner, or **statutory rape**, is a crime even if the perpetrator believes the person is not a minor. Strict liability often applies to less serious offenses such as parking violations. The state does not have to prove a guilty state of mind, only that a car was parked illegally. Unless a legislature declares in a law that it is a strict liability offense, courts assume that criminal intent is required.

General Considerations

Every crime is defined by certain elements, each of which must be proven at trial in order to convict the offender. Thus, in addition to proving any required guilty mental state, the prosecutor must prove beyond a reasonable doubt that the accused committed all of the elements of the crime. For example, robbery is the unlawful taking and carrying away of goods or money from someone's person by force or intimidation. Thus, the elements of robbery are (1) the taking and carrying away of goods or money, (2) the taking from someone's person, and (3) the use of force or intimidation.

If someone breaks into your house when you are not home and takes your property, the person cannot be convicted of robbery. The person did not take the property from a person (no one was home) and therefore could not force or intimidate anyone. However, the person could be guilty of burglary—breaking and entering into a home with intent to commit a felony—because the elements of that crime do not require the taking from a person or the use of force.

A single act can be both a crime and a civil wrong. For example, if Clay purposely sets fire to Tamika's store, the state may file criminal charges against Clay for arson. Tamika may also bring a separate civil action (lawsuit) against Clay to recover for the damage to her store. To prevail in a civil suit, the plaintiff only needs to prove her case by a preponderance of the evidence (not beyond a reasonable doubt as in a criminal case).

▼ The crime of arson requires a guilty state of mind. *How is state of mind different from motive?*

Anton is a bully. One night while eating at a local diner, he notices Derek eating at a nearby table. Anton does not like the band displayed on Derek's T-shirt, so to show his pals who is in charge, Anton orders Derek to sit at another table. When Derek refuses, Anton punches him in the jaw. As a result of the injury, Derek misses several weeks of work and has to pay both medical and dental bills.

a. Has Anton violated civil laws, criminal laws, or both?

b. Who decides whether Anton should be charged criminally? Who decides whether or not to sue Anton in a civil action?

c. If Anton is charged with a crime and is sued in a civil action, would the civil and criminal cases be tried together? Why or why not?

d. Is going to court the only way to handle this problem? What alternatives are there and which do you think would work best?

State and Federal Crimes

Criminal laws exist at both the state and federal levels. Some acts, such as simple assault, disorderly conduct, drunk driving, and shoplifting, can be prosecuted only in a state court unless they occur on federal property, such as a national park. Other acts, such as failure to pay federal taxes, mail fraud, espionage, and international smuggling, can be prosecuted only in a federal court. Certain crimes, such as illegal possession of drugs and bank robbery, can violate both state and federal law and can be prosecuted in both state and federal courts.

Classes of Crimes

Crimes are classified as either felonies or misdemeanors. A **felony** is any crime for which the potential penalty is imprisonment for more than one year. Felonies are usually more serious crimes. A **misdemeanor** is any crime for which the potential penalty is imprisonment for one year or less. Minor traffic violations are not considered crimes, although they are punishable by law. This chapter deals primarily with felonies and more serious misdemeanors.

felony a serious criminal offense punishable by a prison sentence of more than one year

misdemeanor a criminal offense, less serious than a felony, punishable by a jail sentence of one year or less

Parties to Crimes

The person who commits a crime is called the **principal**. For example, the person who fires the gun in a murder is the principal. An **accomplice** is someone who helps the principal commit a crime. For example, the person who drives the getaway car during a bank robbery is an accomplice. An accomplice may be charged with and convicted of the same crime as the principal. A person who orders a crime or helps the principal commit the crime but who is not present during the crime—for example, someone who loans a bank robber their car—is known as an **accessory before the fact**. This person can usually be charged with the same crime and can receive the

principal the person who commits the crime

accomplice a person who voluntarily helps another person commit a crime; an accomplice is usually present or directly aids in the crime

▶ An accomplice can be charged with the same crime as the person who commits the crime. *Describe the difference between an accessory before the fact and an accessory after the fact.*

accessory a person who helps commit a crime but is usually not present at the crime. An accessory before the fact is one who encourages or helps plan a crime. An accessory after the fact is someone, who knowing a crime has been committed, helps conceal the crime or the criminal

same punishment as the principal. An **accessory after the fact** is a person who, knowing a crime has been committed, helps the principal or an accomplice avoid capture or helps them escape. This person is not charged with the original crime but may be charged with harboring a fugitive, aiding the escape, or obstructing justice. Being an accessory after the fact has been made a separate crime by statute in many jurisdictions. The victim of a crime is not a party to the crime but might be called as a witness at the trial.

PROBLEM 8.2

Harold and Marci decide to burglarize Superior Jewelers. Their friend Carl, an employee at Superior, helps by telling them the location of the store vault. Marci drives a van to the store and acts as the lookout while Harold goes inside and cracks the safe. After Harold and Marci make their getaway, Harold meets a friend, Shawn, who was not involved in the actual burglary. Harold tells Shawn about the burglary, and Shawn helps Harold get a train out of town. David, a former classmate of Harold and Marci, witnesses the crime but does not tell the police, even though he recognizes both Harold and Marci. How will each person be charged? Explain your answer.

Crimes of Omission

Most crimes occur when a person does something or performs some act in violation of a law. In a few cases, however, failing to act—called an omission—may be a crime if the person had a legal duty to act. For example, it is a crime for a taxpayer to fail to file a tax return or for a motorist to fail to stop after being involved in an automobile accident. A person is guilty of a **crime of omission** when he or she fails to perform an act required by a criminal law, if he or she is able to perform the required act.

crime of omission failing to perform an act required by criminal law

THE **CASE** OF...

The Drowning Girl

Abe takes his daughter Jill and her friends Kristi and Chin to the lake. While horsing around on the dock, Kristi deliberately shoves Chin into Jill, causing Jill to fall into the water. Jill lands awkwardly and sinks to the bottom. Hannah, a bystander and an expert swimmer, glares at Kristi but takes no other action. Abe confronts the group, demanding that they do something.

PROBLEM 8.3

a. If Jill drowns, would any of the witnesses be criminally liable?

b. Should any of them be liable? Explain your answer.

Preliminary Crimes

Certain types of behavior take place before or in preparation for committing a crime. These preliminary actions—such as attempt, solicitation, and conspiracy—are crimes in themselves. Sometimes called **inchoate crimes**, they require proof of criminal intent but can be punished even if the harm intended never occurred.

inchoate crimes crimes that are committed before or in preparation for committing another crime

Solicitation

A number of states make it a crime for a person to solicit—or ask, command, urge, or advise—another person to commit a crime. The offense is committed at the time the **solicitation** is made. It does not require that the person solicited, or asked, actually commits the crime. For example, Dennis wishes to kill his wife, Carmella. Lacking the nerve to do the job himself, he asks William to kill her. Even if William refuses, Dennis has committed the crime of solicitation.

solicitation the act of requesting or strongly urging someone to do something. If the request is to do something illegal, solicitation is considered a crime.

Attempt

In most states, an attempt to commit a crime is itself a crime. To be guilty of an attempted crime, the accused must have both intended to commit a crime and taken some "substantial step" toward committing the crime. When someone performs all of the elements of a crime but fails to achieve the criminal result, an **attempt** has occurred. For example, when a person intends to shoot and kill someone but misses or merely wounds the intended victim, the person is guilty of attempted murder. Sometimes the crime is foiled before all the necessary steps are completed, such as when a person purchases a gun and intends to shoot another person but is arrested on the way to the intended victim's house. Courts must then determine whether the actions of the accused constituted a "substantial step" toward the actual commission of the crime or were mere acts of preparation.

attempt an effort to commit a crime that goes beyond mere preparation but does not result in the commission of the crime

Examine the following situations and decide whether any of the individuals involved would be guilty of the crime of attempt.

a. Martin, a bank teller, figures out a foolproof method of stealing money from the bank. It takes him some time to get up the nerve to steal any money. Finally, he makes up his mind and tells his girlfriend, Yuka, that tomorrow he will steal the money. Yuka goes to the police, and Martin is arrested an hour later.

b. Gilbert, an accomplished thief, is caught while trying to pick Lewis's pocket. He pleads not guilty and says he cannot possibly be convicted, because Lewis did not have a penny on him.

c. Rita and Anwar decide to rob a liquor store. They meet at a pub and talk over their plans. Rita leaves to buy a revolver, and Anwar leaves to steal a car for use in their getaway. Rita is arrested as she walks out of the gun shop with her new revolver. Anwar is arrested while trying to hot-wire a car.

d. Amy decides to burn down her store to collect the insurance money. She spreads gasoline around the building. She is arrested while leaving the store to get a book of matches.

Conspiracy

conspiracy an agreement between two or more persons to commit a crime along with a substantial act toward committing the crime

A **conspiracy** is an agreement between two or more persons to commit a crime, coupled with an intent to commit the crime and (in most states) some action or conduct that furthers the agreement. The designation of conspiracy as a crime allows police to arrest conspirators before they complete the crime. It also is meant to prevent other crimes and to strike against criminal activity by groups.

▶ The U.S. government took into custody people, such as Zacarias Moussaoui, believed to have conspired against the United States in the September 11, 2001, terrorist attacks. *Why is the designation of conspiracy as a crime sometimes criticized as a threat to First Amendment freedoms?*

Andrea Booher/FEMA News Photo

For example, the federal government aggressively pursued anyone believed to have conspired with the al-Qaeda network in the terrorist attacks of September 11, 2001. The goal was to punish those involved in the attacks and to prevent any future terrorist activities from being carried out against U.S. interests. However, the designation of conspiracy as a crime is sometimes criticized as a threat to freedom of speech and association. During the Vietnam War, the government charged several people with conspiracy for speaking publicly to young men about how to avoid the draft. Many critics of criminal conspiracy said the accused were being denied a basic right—the freedom of speech.

A criminal conspiracy also occurs when Nick, a drug dealer, persuades Lyle, his associate, to help him kill another rival dealer. If Lyle agrees to Nick's request and then takes steps toward committing the crime, such as buying a gun, both Nick and Lyle are guilty of conspiracy to commit murder, even if the murder is never attempted or accomplished.

In many states and under some federal laws, an **overt** act—an act that is open to view—is required for conviction on a conspiracy charge. The overt act must occur after the agreement but does not have to be illegal. For example, assume several people agree to rob a bank. Then one of them buys a ski mask that is to be worn during the robbery. The requirement for an overt act has been met for all the co-conspirators.

overt open; clear

What happens if one member involved in the conspiracy decides not to go through with the planned crime? In most states, the person who withdraws from the planned crime must also notify law enforcement before the crime takes place in order to avoid criminal liability.

PROBLEM 8.5

Johnson, Hector, and Rajana discuss a plan to commit arson and burn down a fast food restaurant where they work. They purchase kerosene and matches at the local hardware store. The next day, Johnson, Hector, and Rajana load the kerosene and matches into Hector's truck and drive together to the restaurant. They carry the kerosene and matches towards the restaurant, pour kerosene near the restaurant and light a match. A police officer notices them and runs over to arrest them.

a. At what point, if any, are Johnson, Hector, and Rajana guilty of the crime of conspiracy in most states?

b. At what point, if any, are Johnson, Hector, and Rajana guilty of the crime of attempted arson?

c. Assume that Johnson changes his mind and decides not to participate in the arson after he goes to the hardware store with Hector and Rajana to purchase the kerosene and matches. Could he be charged with any crime? If so, what crime?

▶ This reenactment shows a victim of a homicide

Crimes against the person include homicide, kidnapping, assault, battery, robbery, and rape and sexual assault. All of these crimes are serious offenses. A defendant found guilty of any one of them may receive a harsh sentence. The law also protects the defendant from overly harsh penalties by defining various levels of some of these crimes and by considering the circumstances of each offense.

Homicide

homicide the killing of another person. Homicide can be criminal, noncriminal, or negligent.

Homicide—the killing of one human being by another—is the most serious of all acts. Homicides may be either criminal or non-criminal. Criminal homicide is committed with intent, or a plan. It is also considered criminal homicide if a person's reckless actions, without regard for human life, result in the killing of another person. Noncriminal homicide can be classified as either "excusable" or "justifiable" and is not subject to criminal charges.

Criminal Homicide

Murder, the most serious form of criminal homicide, is killing that is done with malice. Malice means having the intent to kill or seriously harm another person or acting in an extremely reckless manner that shows a lack of regard for human life. At one time, there were no degrees of murder. Any homicide done with malice was considered to be murder and was punishable by death. To reduce the punishment for less-grievous homicides, most states now have statutes that classify murder according to the killer's state of mind or the circumstances surrounding the crime.

First-degree murder is usually defined as the act of killing that is premeditated (thought about beforehand), deliberate, and done with malice. It is an action with an intent to kill or cause severe bodily injury or with a depraved indifference to human life. Courts have often found that the premeditation and deliberation can occur very close to the time of the homicide.

Felony murder is any killing that takes place during the commission of certain felonies such as arson, rape, robbery, or burglary. It is not necessary to prove intent; malice is presumed because the homicide occurred during the felony, even if it were accidental. Most states consider felony murder to be first-degree murder regardless of whether malice, premeditation, and deliberation exist.

Second-degree murder is killing that is done with malice, but without premeditation or deliberation. That is, the intent to kill did not exist until the moment of the murder. Second-degree murder includes intentional but spontaneous killings that are unplanned.

Voluntary manslaughter is killing that would otherwise be seen as murder but that occurs after the victim has done something to the killer that would cause a reasonable person to lose self-control or act rashly. A person who kills someone in a violent argument or quarrel without first planning to do so is guilty of voluntary manslaughter. Words alone, no matter how offensive, do not reduce the severity of a murder to voluntary manslaughter. Also, the killing must occur just after the provocation so that the killer does not have an opportunity to "cool down." A typical example of voluntary manslaughter is when a person discovers his or her spouse with someone else and that person kills the spouse's lover in a jealous rage. Voluntary manslaughter is punished somewhat less severely than murder as a concession to the frailty of human character.

Involuntary manslaughter is a killing in which there is no intent to kill at all. It is unintentional killing resulting from conduct so reckless that it causes extreme danger of death or bodily injury. An example of involuntary manslaughter is killing that results from playing with a gun known to be loaded.

Negligent homicide means causing death through criminal negligence. Negligence is the failure to exercise a reasonable or ordinary amount of care in a situation, thereby causing harm to someone.

Investigating the Law Where You Live

Find out what forms of homicide exist under your state's criminal statutes. What is the range of punishments for each level of the crime?

malice ill will; deliberate intent to harm someone

murder the unlawful killing of a person with malice and forethought. Murder in the first degree is planned in advance and done with malice or during the commission of a dangerous felony. Murder in the second degree does not require malice or premeditation but is the result of a desire to inflict bodily harm. It is done without excuse, and is therefore more serious than manslaughter.

premeditated deliberate, or having thought about doing something before actually doing it

felony murder the killing of someone during the commission of certain felonies, regardless of intent to kill

manslaughter the killing of a person without malice or premeditation, but during the commission of an illegal act. Manslaughter can be either voluntary, when intentional but not premeditated, resulting from the heat of passion or the diminished mental capacity of the killer; or involuntary, when unintentional but done during an unlawful act of a lesser nature

negligent homicide causing death through criminally negligent behavior

negligence the failure to exercise a reasonable amount of care in either doing, or not doing something, resulting in harm or injury to another person

Homicide Cases

Read each of the following accounts carefully. For each one, determine who can be charged with the crime of homicide and the degree of homicide for which he or she should be charged. Give reasons for your answers.

a. Walt decidees to shoot his ex-girlfriend Yolanda, whom he blames for all his trouble. As he is driving to her home to carry out the murder, he accidentally hits a jogger who darted out into the road from behind a tree. Stopping immediately, Walt rushes to help the jogger, who is already dead. Assume that Walt was driving at a safe speed and that the collision with the jogger was unavoidable.

b. Belva is cheated when she buys a car from Fast Eddie's Car Mart. She attempts to return the car, but Eddie just laughs and tells her to go away. Every time Belva has to make a repair on the car, she gets angry. Finally, she decides to wreck Eddie's car to get even with him. Following him home from work one evening, Belva tries to ram his car, hoping to bend the axle or frame. Instead of bending the frame, the collision smashes Eddie's gas tank, causes an explosion, and kills him.

▲ The car explosion

c. Alison and Brad need money to pay their bills and decide to rob a bank. Brad drives the getaway car. Alison goes into the bank and pulls out her gun, anouncing, "This is a stickup. Don't move!" The bank guard, Gordon, shoots Alison but misses, killing Dawn, a bank customer.

Some states classify death by gross, or extreme and thus criminal, negligence as involuntary manslaughter. The most common form of negligent homicide is vehicular homicide. This is killing that results from operating a motor vehicle in a reckless and grossly negligent manner. Any death that results from careless driving may lead to a civil suit for damages, but it is usually not considered a criminal offense unless the death results from gross negligence.

Noncriminal Homicide

Some homicides are not considered crimes at all. Noncriminal homicide is killing that is justifiable or excusable, and therefore the killer is deemed faultless. Examples of noncriminal homicide include the killing of an enemy soldier in wartime, the killing of a condemned criminal by an executioner, the killing by a police officer of a person who is committing a serious crime and who poses a threat of death or serious harm, and a killing performed in self-defense or in defense of another person. Also see Chapter 11 on defenses.

Suicide

Suicide, the deliberate taking of one's own life, was once considered a crime. Today courts often treat attempted suicide as a plea for help, requiring the person who attempted it to undergo a psychological examination and receive treatment, often in the form of counseling. Someone who helps another person commit suicide can, however, be found guilty of the crime of murder or manslaughter.

Although many people have suicidal thoughts at some point in their lives, most never attempt suicide. Many people can find help through suicide hotlines, medication, counseling, and other programs for those who may be considering suicide. Despairing individuals may need someone to talk to who can help them see positive alternatives to ending their lives.

Communities have expanded mental health and suicide awareness programs in recent years. Factors that can reduce risk include close personal relationships with friends, family, faculty and staff as well as proper attention to sleep, diet, and physical exercise.

In a typical year there are more suicides than homicides in this country. Teen suicides and attempted suicides are considered very serious public health problems. The elderly have the highest suicide rate, and men have a significantly higher suicide rate than women.

suicide the deliberate taking of one's own life

◀ Safeplaces and other services are available for people who are considering suicide. *How can safeplaces help such individuals?*

©Ilene MacDonald/Alamy

THE **CASE** OF...

The Dying Cancer Patient

Wilfred, age 75, has been suffering from cancer for 10 years. The pain associated with the cancer is severe and has become worse over time. Wilfred's doctors say there is no treatment to either slow down the cancer's growth or substantially reduce the pain. Wilfred asks Martha, his wife of 50 years, to relieve him of the terrible pain. He asks her to bring him a bottle of pills that will help him end his own life. Martha cannot stand watching Wilfred suffer anymore and gives him the pills. He swallows them all, slowly fades off to sleep, and dies.

PROBLEM 9.1

a. Was Wilfred's request related to suicide? Explain your answer.

b. If you were the district attorney in the state where Martha lives, would you file criminal charges against her? Explain.

c. If manslaughter charges were filed and you were on the jury, would you vote to convict Martha? Give your reasons. If Martha were convicted, what sentence should she receive? Why?

d. If the bottle of pills had been given to Wilfred by a physician instead of by his wife, would your answers have been different? Give your reasons.

e. If you were a state legislator, would you be in favor of or against a law allowing assisted suicide? Explain.

There are multiple suicide prevention hotlines in each state. Go to **www.suicide.org** to access your state's hotlines. The national suicide prevention lifeline is 1-800-273-8255. This lifeline provides 24/7 free, confidential support for people in distress. The text telephone number is 1-800-799-4889. The LGBTQ hotline is 1-866-488-7386 (The Trevor Project). A network of trained crisis counselors, **www.imalive.org**, allows for online chat which might be a useful option for someone who doesn't want to make a phone call. You can also use the Internet to find suicide hotlines and prevention programs located in your community.

kidnapping taking away a person against that person's will

unlawful imprisonment confining a person against that person's will and in violation of the law

abduction involves taking away a person against that person's will

Kidnapping

Kidnapping, also called **unlawful imprisonment** or **abduction**, has been recognized as a crime for centuries. Originally this crime referred to stealing children for use as servants or workers, but it now applies to victims of all ages. Kidnapping involves taking away a person against that person's will. When the victim is taken across state lines, this act also violates federal criminal law.

Assault and Battery

Assault is any attempt or threat to carry out a physical attack upon another person. **Battery** is any unlawful physical contact inflicted by one person upon another person without consent. Actual injury is not necessary. The only requirement is that the person must have intended to do bodily harm. Today, there is often not much difference in law or practice between the uses of the words *assault* and *battery*.

Just as there are degrees of murder, there are also different classifications for assault and battery. Many states now have separate statutes for assault with intent to rob and assault with intent to murder. The charge is often defined by the harm inflicted. Thus an assault, even though unarmed, that results in a serious physical injury can be considered an aggravated battery.

Assaults typically result from arguments between people who know each other. In such arguments, rage, often triggered by alcohol or jealousy, may lead to violence. Whether the violence leads to serious injury or death often depends on the presence of a weapon.

Stalking occurs when a person repeatedly follows or harasses another person and makes threats, causing the victim to fear death or bodily injury. Women are the targets of most stalking cases that occur each year. To deal with the growing problem of harassment, most states now have anti-stalking laws. In addition, many states also have laws that criminalize stalking and harassment using electronic communications (sometimes called **cyberstalking**).

Bullying is a version of assault and battery in which peers or acquaintances intimidate, or put others in fear. In 2017 more than 1 in 5 students reported having been bullied during the previous school year. Bullying causes harm to victims, witnesses, and perpetrators and is sometimes seen as a "gateway behavior." When bullying is tolerated, it may teach the perpetrator that threats and aggression are acceptable. Some school-based bullying prevention programs have been effective in reducing bullying.

Sexual assault is a specific kind of assault that can include rape or attempted rape. Sexual assault includes a wide range of victimizations from verbal threats of a sexual nature to unwanted sexual contact between the victim and the offender.

Investigating the Law Where You Live

Research to learn how your state defines *assault*. How does it define *battery*? Are there different classifications of these crimes? Explain them.

assault an intentional threat, show of force, or movement that causes a reasonable fear of, or an actual physical contact with, another person.

battery any intentional, unlawful physical contact inflicted on one person by another without consent. In some states, this ins combined with assault.

stalking the act of following or harassing another person, causing the fear of death or injury

cyberstalking stalking or harassment using electronic communications

bullying a version of assault and battery in which peers or acquaintances intimidate, or put others in fear

sexual assault unwelcome sexual contact against another individual committed through the use of force, threat, or intimidation, or enabled because the victim is incapacitated due to drugs, alcohol, or mental disability

◀ Anti-stalking laws protect people from harassment and threats. *Does your state have anti-stalking laws?*

Crimes Against the Person **105**

▲ Authorities must confirm the rape victim's story in order to proceed with the case. *What are "rape shield" laws?*

rape unlawful sexual intercourse. It is committed when one party forces another party to have sexual intercourse. It implies lack of consent.

statutory rape the act of unlawful sexual intercourse by an adult with someone under the age of consent, even if the minor is a willing and voluntary participant in the sexual act

criminal sexual assault a category of crimes that includes rape, attempted rape, and statutory rape

Like assault and battery, sexual assault can be an attack that is either completed or attempted. Contact without consent might include grabbing or fondling and may, but does not have to, involve force. Contrary to traditional views of male and female roles, both men and women are capable of committing and being victims of sexual assault.

Rape and Sexual Assault

In the past, most laws defined rape only in terms of vaginal intercourse. **Rape** is typically defined today as sexual penetration without consent. Traditionally, the law has recognized the separate crimes of rape and statutory rape. Aggravated rape occurs when the perpetrator uses a weapon or some other form of force to complete the assault. **Statutory rape** is intercourse with someone under the legal age of consent. The legal age of consent varies from state to state.

This area of law is in transition as many states are replacing their rape laws with criminal sexual assault laws, with rape being the most severe form of **criminal sexual assault**. The crime requires a lack of consent on the part of the victim. There is no consent if the victim is unconscious or mentally incompetent or if the victim's judgment is impaired by drugs or alcohol. The perpetrator and the victim can be of either sex. These new laws, therefore, can be used to prosecute women as well as men and can be used to prosecute same sex criminal sexual assault.

Statutory rape differs from rape in a very important way: lack of consent is not an element of the crime. This crime is based on the notion that a minor is incapable of giving legal consent. A male can be prosecuted for statutory rape of a minor even if the victim lied about his or her age. Statutory rape laws are also changing. While these laws were traditionally used to prosecute males for having sex with underage females, the trend now is to recognize that either males or females can commit or be victims of statutory rape. There is also a trend in many states not to charge a person with statutory rape unless the perpetrator is several years older than the victim, although this age-difference requirement is never used to define forcible rape.

States define forcible or statutory rape in a range of ways. States also tend to have specific sentencing laws that require more severe punishments for certain forms of sexual assault. When the victim is under a certain age, over a certain age, disabled, or threatened with a weapon, punishment may be more severe.

fatchoi/iStock/Getty Images

In the past, defendants in rape cases were allowed to present evidence to the jury about the victim's past sexual behavior and reputation in order to show that he or she had probably consented to the act. Most states and the federal system have passed "rape shield" laws, which now prohibit introducing such evidence. To convict a person of rape, some states require other proof that the act took place. This means confirmation of or support for the account provided by the victim, including testimony of a witness, a doctor's report that sexual intercourse took place, or a prompt report to the police.

There is a trend, nonetheless, to be more protective of victims, that is, to make sure the defendant and not the victim is put on trial. Yet it is also true that the sometimes unclear nature of relationships presents challenges for the criminal justice system. While criminal sexual assault is a serious crime, the criminal justice system must also avoid punishing an accused person unless the victim clearly expresses a lack of consent.

In recent years, the term **acquaintance rape** (also known as **date rape**) has been used to describe a sexual assault by someone known to the victim. Many victims of acquaintance rape do not report the assault, perhaps because they do not realize an attack that occurs on a date or social encounter can in fact constitute a rape.

Investigating the Law Where You Live

Learn how *criminal sexual assault* is defined in your state. How is this crime punished where you live? What is the legal age of consent in your state's statutory rape law?

acquaintance rape sexual assault by someone known to the victim, such as a date or neighbor)

PROBLEM 9.2

For each case below, assume that the two people have sexual intercourse. Assume that the police find out about the sexual activity in each instance. How should each situation be handled?

a. At midnight, a man breaks into the home of a woman he does not know. He goes to her bedroom, awakens her, pulls out a knife, and threatens to stab her unless she has sex with him. She tells him that she does not want to have sex. But then she says, "If you are going to do this, you'd better use a condom." He agrees.

b. A famous boxer serves as a judge at a beauty contest. After the contest, he invites an 18-year-old contestant to his hotel room. She meets him there. Later, she says he forced her to have sex.

c. A male college student, age 19, and a female high school student, age 15, go out on a date. After attending a party, they agree to have intercourse in his car. The legal age of consent in this state is 16. The next day, he brags about this on campus, and she goes to the police. There is some evidence that he is part of an informal organization of male students who are involved in a competition to have sex with as many young women as possible.

d. Leo and Nina are college juniors who have had three dates. On these dates, they have never engaged in any sexual activity beyond a brief good-night kiss. On their fourth date, he invites her to an all-night drinking party at his fraternity house. She drinks too much, goes up to his room alone around 1:00 a.m., and falls asleep. In the morning, she wakes up to discover that she and Leo had intercourse during the night.

CHAPTER **10**
Crimes Against Property

▶ Crimes against property include arson, the deliberate burning of property.

This chapter focuses on crimes in which property is destroyed, such as arson and vandalism, and crimes in which property is taken against the will of the owner, such as larceny. Cybercrimes, which can occur against both property, such as identity theft, and a person, such as cyberstalking, are also discussed in this chapter.

In recent years the number of traditional property crimes committed has fallen, in part because Americans have developed better crime prevention behaviors. These behaviors include security lighting, home and automobile alarm systems, steering wheel locks, greater attention to locking doors and windows, and a tendency to carry less cash due to the increased use of credit cards.

Arson

arson the deliberate and malicious burning of another person's property

Arson is the willful and malicious burning of a person's property. In most states, it is a crime to burn any building or structure, even if the person who burns the structure owns it. Moreover, burning property with the intent to defraud an insurance company is usually a separate crime, regardless of the type of property burned or who owns the property.

At various times arson has also been a form of racial violence. To help federal prosecutors deal with a rash of racially motivated church arsons, Congress passed the *Church Arson Prevention Act of 1996*. This act helps oversee the investigation and prosecution of arson at places of worship across the United States. The act also increases the penalties for those who commit such crimes.

Aaron Roeth Photography

Vandalism

Vandalism, also known as malicious mischief, is willful destruction of, or damage to, the property of another. Vandalism is responsible for millions of dollars in damage each year. It includes such things as breaking windows, ripping down fences, writing graffiti, and breaking off car hood ornaments. Depending on the extent of the damage, vandalism can be either a felony or a misdemeanor.

vandalism the deliberate destruction or defacement of another person's property; also known as malicious mischief

---

PROBLEM 10.1

a. Why do people sometimes commit acts of vandalism?

b. What, if anything, can be done to reduce vandalism?

c. If you saw two college students throwing rocks through the windows of their high school at night, would you report the students to the police? Why or why not? Suppose you saw two friends throwing rocks through the windows of a neighbor's home. Would you report your friends to the police? Why or why not? Did you answer both questions the same way? If not, explain why.

Larceny

Larceny is the unlawful taking and carrying away of the property of another person against his or her will with intent to permanently deprive the owner of it. In most states, larceny is divided into two classes—grand and petty—depending on the value of the stolen item. Grand larceny involves the theft of anything above a certain value, sometimes $100 or more, and is a felony. Petty larceny is the theft of anything of less value, for example less than $100, and is a misdemeanor.

The crime of larceny also includes keeping lost property when a reasonable method exists for finding the owner. For example, if you find a wallet that contains the identification of its owner but nevertheless decide to keep it, you have committed larceny. Likewise, you may be guilty of larceny if you keep property delivered to you by mistake.

Shoplifting is a form of larceny. It is the crime of taking items from a store without paying or intending to pay for them. Some states have a separate crime called **concealment,** which is the crime of attempted shoplifting. Commission of this crime is particularly common among young people.

Shoplifting results in business losses of billions of dollars each year. The costs are usually passed on to consumers in the form of higher prices. Consequently, everyone ends up paying for shoplifting.

larceny the unlawful taking of another's property with the intent to steal it. Grand larceny, a felony, is the theft of anything above a certain value (sometimes $100 or more). Petty larceny, a misdemeanor, is the theft of anything below a certain value (for example, $100).

shoplifting a form of larceny in which a person takes items from a store without paying or intending to pay

concealment the crime of attempted shoplifting that is recognized in some states

a. Why do you think people shoplift? List the reasons.

b. What could be done to address each of the reasons for shoplifting you listed? Which would be most effective? Why?

c. If you saw a stranger shoplifting in a store, what would you do? Would your answer be different if you knew the person?

d. A movie star is caught shoplifting thousands of dollars worth of merchandise. It is her first offense. What penalty should she receive? Would the penalty you recommend be different if she were not famous?

▼ There are several ways store owners can reduce shoplifting. *How do sensor tags on clothing reduce shoplifting?*

Embezzlement

Embezzlement is the unlawful taking of property by someone to whom it was entrusted. For example, the bank teller who takes money from the cash drawer or the stockbroker who takes money that should have been invested are both guilty of embezzlement. In recent years, a number of states have merged the crimes of embezzlement, larceny, and obtaining property by false pretenses (intentional misstatements of fact) into the statutory crime of theft.

Robbery

Robbery is the unlawful taking of property from a person's immediate possession by force or intimidation. It is both a crime against a person and a crime against property. Unlike other theft offenses, it involves two harms: theft of property and actual or potential physical harm to the victim. In most states, the difference between robbery and larceny is the use of force. Hence, a pickpocket who takes your wallet unnoticed is guilty of the crime of larceny. A mugger who knocks you down and takes your wallet by force is guilty of the crime of robbery. Robbery is almost always a felony, but many states impose stricter penalties for armed robberies—thefts committed with a gun or other weapon.

Extortion

Extortion, popularly called blackmail, is the use of threats to obtain the property of another. Extortion statutes generally cover threats to do future physical harm, destroy property, or injure someone's character or reputation. For example, a person who threatens to injure you or your property unless you give him your car is guilty of the crime of extortion.

Burglary

Burglary was originally defined as breaking and entering the dwelling of another person during the night with intent to commit a felony therein. Modern laws have broadened the definition to include the unauthorized entry into any structure with the intent to commit a crime, regardless of the time of day. Many states have stiffer penalties for burglaries committed at night, burglaries of inhabited dwellings, and burglaries committed with weapons.

▲ After being charged with illegal business practices, Enron corporation laid off many employees in 2002. *How are larceny and embezzlement different? How are they similar?*

embezzlement the taking of money or property by a person to whom it has been entrusted; for example, a bank teller or a company accountant

robbery the unlawful taking of property from a person's immediate possession by force or intimidation

extortion taking property illegally through threats of harm

burglary breaking and entering a building with the intention of committing a crime

Steps to Take

Identity Theft

Despite the great benefits society has gained from technological advances, technology has also spawned the development of a new kind of crook: the identity thief. There are millions of victims of identity theft each year. This thief steals a piece of personal information such as your Social Security number, your bank account number, or a credit card number and uses it to commit a fraud or further theft. Everyday actions such as throwing out your garbage, sending a rent check to your land-lord, or ordering a book online put you at risk for identity theft. If someone steals and uses your personal information, it can cost you hundreds or thousands of dollars. Identity theft can also cost you your credit rating and good name, not to mention the significant time and emotional expense of trying to clean up the mess. While it might not be possible to prevent identity theft altogether, you can take steps to minimize your exposure to this crime. An excellent resource to learn more about identity theft is www.consumer.gov.

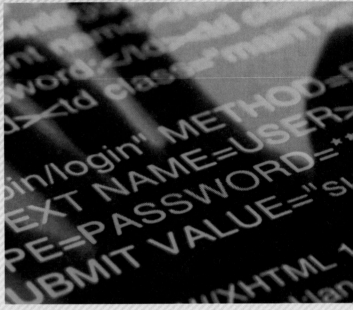

▲ A secure website

- **Check your credit report.** Order your credit report from each of the three main credit bureaus (www.equifax.com, www.transunion.com, www.experian.com), and check each for accuracy.

- **Be wary of any unsolicited or unfamiliar e-mails requesting personal information.**

- **Protect your personal information in your own home.** This point is especially important if you have roommates or other people who have access to your home.

- **Create passwords that are not easy to guess for your Internet, bank, credit card, and phone accounts.**

- **If you work, ask about security proce-dures in place to protect your personal records and hiring information.** Do not leave your purse or wallet unattended.

- **Do not give out personal information unless you know who you are dealing with and are satisfied that your informa-tion will be handled in a secure manner.** This applies to transactions over the phone, through the mail, or on the Internet.

- **Guard your mail and trash from theft.** Ask a friend to pick up your mail while you are away from home. Tear up or shred mail and other items containing your personal or financial information.

- **Do not carry your Social Security card with you, and avoid giving out your Social Security number when possible.** Instead, ask that a unique identification number be assigned to you.

- **Pay attention to your bank, credit card, and charge card statements as well as your billing cycles. Report any inconsis-tencies you discover.**

- **Recovering from identify theft.** If you are a victim, visit www.identifytheft.gov to report the crime and create a recovery plan.

Forgery

Forgery is a crime in which a person falsely makes or alters a writing or document with intent to defraud. This usually involves someone signing the name of another person to a check or some other document without his or her permission. It can also mean changing or erasing part of a previously signed document, such as the amount on a check. **Uttering,** which is a separate crime in many states, is offering to someone a document as genuine although it is known to be a fake.

Receiving Stolen Property

If you receive or buy property that you know or have reason to believe is stolen, you have committed the crime of **receiving stolen property.** Knowledge that the property is stolen may be implied by the circumstances, for example, buying goods out of the trunk of an automobile or for a price that is unreasonably low. In most states, the severity of punishment for the crime is related to the value of the goods received.

▲ Forgery is a serious crime. *Why is it dangerous to give someone a signed check without filling out the rest of the check?*

forgery the act of making a fake document or altering a real one with the intent to commit fraud

uttering offering to someone as genuine a document known to be a fake

receiving stolen property receiving or buying property that is known or reasonably believed to be stolen

PROBLEM 10.3

Ivan met with his friend Anthony, who was driving a flashy new red convertible. Ivan knew that neither Anthony nor his family owned this car, but it looked good, so he got in and let Anthony take him for a ride. Ivan also knew that Anthony used drugs and sometimes took other people's things and sold them to get money to buy cocaine. Anthony offered to sell Ivan a smart phone he had in the back seat of the car for $40. Ivan agreed to pay him the money.

a. Have any crimes been committed? If so, which crimes and by whom?

b. Why does society make receiving stolen property a crime? Should it be?

c. Would you ever buy something for an extremely low price from a friend? How would you know for sure it was not stolen?

Unauthorized Use of a Vehicle

Several crimes may occur when a person unlawfully takes a motor vehicle without the owner's consent. The crime, which is called **unauthorized use of a vehicle** (UUV), is committed if the person only intends to take the vehicle temporarily. This crime includes joyriding.

unauthorized use of a vehicle unlawful taking of a car by someone who intends only to use it temporarily

Ingram Publishing/age fotostock

carjacking a crime in which the perpetrator uses force or intimidation to steal a car from a driver

cybercrime describes a wide range of actions that involves computers and computer networks in criminal activities

However, if the person intends to take the car permanently, then the crime may be larceny or auto theft. These crimes usually have stiffer penalties than UUV. The crime of **carjacking** occurs if a person uses force or intimidation to steal a car from a driver. Carjacking is a federal crime and is punishable by a sentence of up to life in prison.

Cybercrime

Cybercrime, also called computer crime, describes a wide range of actions that involve computers and computer networks in criminal activities. Computers are often used in both crimes against property and crimes against the person. Some of these activities are based on traditional crimes, such as theft or stalking, in which computers or networks are used to accomplish the crime. Other crimes uniquely involve technology and did not exist before the development of computers and the Internet. Examples of these crimes include spamming, denial-of-service attacks and "phishing" (attempts to illegally acquire personal information). Although some people believe that antispam laws violate free speech rights, spammers have been prosecuted, fined, and given stiff prison terms for using spam to transmit malicious software or to defraud victims through social engineering.

Illegal downloading, or the duplication and distribution of media such as TV shows, music, software, and movies, is often called "piracy" and can take many forms. Media companies contend that piracy reduces legitimate sales and harms the economic interests of the underlying artists and performers. Steep civil fines, as well as possible jail terms, await those who are convicted of stealing this kind of copyrighted content.

▶ Computer viruses can delete information and damage your computer. *How has the U.S. government attempted to deal with computer crime?*

Mark Dierker/McGraw-Hill Education

Federal law protects copyright owners from unauthorized reproduction, adaptation, or distribution of their recordings. Generally it is acceptable practice to use legally purchased media across all personal devices. There are also numerous legal online services that permit the streaming of music, movies, and television shows for a monthly fee.

As people have turned to Internet-based solutions both as a means of socializing and for storing confidential data, cyber harassment, identity theft, and cyber blackmailing have become increasingly large problems. They have also raised complicated legal issues.

In 2015 the U.S. Supreme Court had to decide one of these issues in *Elonis* v. *United States*. In that case the defendant was convicted of using social media to post vengeful rants, sometimes in the form of rap lyrics. The defendant was arrested and convicted under a federal law that "prohibits the use of interstate communication of threats to harm individuals." The defendant appealed his conviction, claiming that his expression was protected by the First Amendment. He argued that his rants were art not threats. Some of the threats were directed against his wife. She testified that she was "terrified" after reading the postings. The Court had to decide whether the intent of the speaker or the reasonable reaction of the person receiving the message should govern its interpretation of the statute. The justices ruled that the intent of the speaker is what matters in a case like this.

▲ Filtering software is used to protect children from adult content available on the Internet. *What is the Children's Internet Protection Act and how does it work?*

Another common Internet crime is the transmission of obscene images, movies, and sounds. Concerned that children may be harmed by such material on the Internet made available on public school and library computers, Congress passed the *Children's Internet Protection Act in 2000*. This act requires that all public schools and libraries purchase and install filtering software on all of their student-accessible computers and establish certain Internet safety policies or risk losing federal funding for technology. However this law seems outdated in some ways because most students now have their own smartphones.

State and federal authorities have created special units that deal with Computer Hacking and Intellectual Property (CHIP) crimes. These units have specially trained personnel who prosecute computer intrusions, copyright and trademark violations, and other Internet crime, including Internet fraud and Internet child pornography. They also work with consumers and the high-tech community to encourage reporting of computer crime. The FBI provides the Internet Crime Complaint Center at **www.ic3.gov** for this purpose. Because the Internet has a global reach, the U.S. Department of Justice works with judges, prosecutors, and investigators in countries around the world to prevent and prosecute cybercrime. State and federal law enforcement officers in the United States also collaborate to prevent computer- and cyber-based terrorist attacks.

Congress passed the *Computer Fraud and Abuse Act of 1986* to provide the government with a specific law to prosecute hackers. The law made it a crime to modify, destroy, or disclose information gained from unauthorized entry into a computer. The law also makes it illegal to intentionally give or receive passwords that would permit unauthorized access to systems. The law is jointly enforced by the U.S. Secret Service and the FBI. By 2003, all 50 states had also enacted laws specifically dealing with computer crime.

Another type of computer crime occurs when someone illegally copies software he or she has purchased. Data indicate that

▼ Copyright laws apply to music downloading. *How can copyright laws be broken by users of digital music?*

John Flournoy/McGraw-Hill Education

software companies lose billions of dollars each year to illegal copying. A person who opens a software package is agreeing to use the software on one computer only. This person is allowed to make copies of the software only to use as a backup. Placing software on more than one computer without the publisher's permission is illegal and violates federal copyright laws. The violator is subject to a possible jail term and a fine of up to $250,000. Violators can include individuals, businesses, and schools.

Software piracy is a serious global problem. Companies in the United States lose money and employees lose jobs as a result of piracy. Computers have become a way of life for almost everyone in today's society. Courts, Congress, state legislatures, and law enforcement officials will continue to deal with new criminal law problems as computer technology evolves.

PROBLEM 10.4

In each case below, decide whether or not the act should be treated as a crime. Then for those that should be a crime, rank the acts from most serious to least serious. Explain your reasons.

a. Evan goes to the website where he usually buys music and realizes there is a glitch in the code which allows him to download three songs without paying for them.

b. Perrisha supervises Bill at work. She suspects that he is visiting pornographic websites instead of working. She looks at his history of websites visited, which confirms her suspicions. She fires him.

c. Dominique and Harold launch a computer virus designed to slow down the U.S. air traffic control system in hopes that they can cause airplanes to crash.

d. David, 31, poses as a teenage boy at an online social networking site that is popular with high school students and arranges to meet a high school junior for a date.

e. Someone pretending to be with the Public Bank sends you an e-mail message saying there is a problem with your account and requesting that you send information, including your social security number, so that the problem can be corrected.

f. Nelly downloads her top 20 favorite songs from various sources and saves them to her personal music folder. The next day, Nelly uploads the songs to a peer-to-peer network so that her friends can download the songs to their personal music folders.

g. The night before a 10-page paper is due, Annelisa copies and pastes several pages of information from an online public encyclopedia, then writes a few pages herself. She does not cite her source and tries to pass off the entire paper as her original work.

▶ A number of possible defenses are available to defendents.

For a conviction to occur in a criminal case, the prosecutor must establish beyond a reasonable doubt that the defendant committed the act in question with the required intent. The defendant is not required to present a defense but can instead simply force the government to prove its case. However, a number of possible defenses are available to defendants in criminal cases.

No Crime Has Been Committed

The defendant may present evidence to show that (1) no criminal act was committed or (2) there was no criminal intent. In the first case, a defendant might attempt to show that she was carrying a gun but had a valid license, or a defendant might attempt to show that he did not commit rape because the woman had consented. In the second case, the defendant might attempt to show that he mistakenly took another person's coat when leaving a restaurant. In this situation, the defendant is innocent of a charge of larceny if it was an honest and reasonable mistake.

Defendant Did Not Commit the Crime

Often no doubt exists that a criminal act has been committed. In such cases, the question is: who committed it? In this situation, the defendant might present evidence of a mistake in identity or offer an **alibi**—evidence that the defendant was somewhere else at the time the crime was committed.

alibi a Latin word meaning "elsewhere;" an excuse or plea that a person was somewhere else at the time a crime was committed

©Ocean/Corbis

Developments in science and technology have made it possible to use biological evidence, called **DNA evidence,** to connect an offender conclusively to a crime. An offender who does not leave fingerprints at a crime scene might leave biological evidence—a single hair, for example—at the scene without knowing it. It is possible to then conduct a DNA test to determine whether that hair or other piece of evidence belongs to the defendant. Although the state can use DNA evidence to prove that the defendant was at the scene or committed the crime, a defendant can also use DNA evidence to prove that he or she *did not* commit the crime. All states give defendants at least a limited right to access DNA evidence, but as of 2018, the Supreme Court had not ruled on whether there is a constitutional right to obtain DNA evidence.

Defendant Committed the Act, but it Was Excusable or Justifiable

Sometimes an otherwise criminal act may be considered excusable or justifiable. Defenses in this category include self-defense, defense of property, and defense of others.

The law recognizes the right of a person who is unlawfully attacked to use reasonable force in self-defense. It also recognizes the right of one person to use reasonable force to defend another person from an attack that is about to occur. There are, however, a number of limitations to these defenses.

A person who reasonably believes there is imminent danger of bodily harm can use a reasonable amount of force in self-defense. However, a person cannot use more force than appears to be necessary.

If, after stopping an attacker, the defender continues to use force, the roles reverse, and the defender can no longer claim self-defense. Deadly force can usually be used only by a person who reasonably believes that there is imminent danger of death or serious bodily harm. In most states a person is also allowed to use deadly or nondeadly force to defend a third person if the person defended could claim self-defense.

Reasonable nondeadly force may be used to protect property. However, some states have passed Stand Your Ground laws that give people the right to use deadly force to defend their property against unwarranted intrusion. In general, police can only use deadly force in self defense when they have reasonable cause to believe a suspect poses a significant threat of death or bodily harm to the officer and others.

▲ Scientific developments allow the use of DNA evidence to connect an offender to a crime. *How else may DNA evidence be used?*

DNA evidence biological evidence, derived from testing samples of human tissues and fluids, that genetically links an offender to a crime

TEK IMAGE/Getty Images

a. Ms. Urbanski kept a pistol in her home as protection against intruders. One evening, she heard a noise in the den and went to investigate. Upon entering the room, she saw a man stealing her television. The burglar, seeing the gun, ran for the window, but Ms. Urbanski fired and killed him before he could escape. In a trial for manslaughter, Ms. Urbanski pleaded self-defense. Would you find her guilty? Why or why not? Would it matter if the state had a Stand Your Ground Law?

b. A police officer responds to a call about a young person with a gun sitting on a park bench. Upon arriving at the park in his cruiser, the officer tells him three times to "show your hands." The person did not show his hands and may have reached toward his belt. Within two seconds of arriving, he was shot and killed by the police officer. The young person turns out to be 12 years old and the gun turns out to be a toy. Is this a justifiable use of force by the officer? Explain.

Defendant Committed the Act but Is Not Criminally Responsible

Some defenses in a criminal case rest on the defendant's lack of criminal responsibility. Although it is acknowledged that he or she committed the criminal act, he or she may be considered not criminally responsible. In this category are the defenses of infancy, intoxication, insanity, entrapment, duress, and necessity.

Infancy

Traditionally, children of a young age, usually under age 7, were considered legally incapable of committing a crime. Children between the ages of 7 and 14 were generally presumed incapable of committing a crime, but this presumption could be shown to be wrong. Under modern laws, many states follow some version of this common-law approach. Other states simply provide that children under a specified age shall not be tried for their crimes but shall be turned over to the juvenile court. Children under the specified age have the defense of **infancy.**

infancy the legal defense of a person considered not yet legally responsible for his or her actions; the time before which a person becomes entitled to the legal rights and responsibilities normally held by citizens

Some states either do not have a defense of infancy or allow prosecutors to decide whether to try a child as an adult, giving them more discretion to deal with juvenile delinquency on a case-by-case basis. These policies sometimes lead to the controversial result of trying a child for a heinous crime as an adult and allowing a long prison sentence. However as of 2016, mandatory life sentences without the possibility of parole for juveniles has been ruled to be unconstitutional. The Supreme Court has also banned the use of the death penalty for defendants who were juveniles at the time they committed their crime.

Intoxication

Defendants sometimes claim **intoxication** as a defense—that is, they claim that at the time of a crime, they were so drunk on alcohol or high on drugs that they did not know what they were doing. As a general rule, voluntary intoxication is not a valid defense for a crime. However, it may sometimes be a valid defense if the crime requires proof of a specific mental state. For example, Grady is charged with assault with intent to kill. He claims he was drunk. If he can prove that he was so drunk that he could not have formed the intent to kill, his intoxication may be a valid defense. Grady can still be convicted of the crime of assault because specific intent is not required to prove that crime. However, if Grady had decided to kill the victim before he got drunk, or if he got drunk to get up enough nerve to commit the crime, then intoxication would not be a defense. This is because the required mental state—the intent to kill—existed before Grady's drunkenness occurred.

Insanity

Over the centuries, the **insanity defense** has evolved as an important legal concept. Ancient Greeks and Romans believed that insane people were not responsible for their actions and should not be punished like ordinary criminals. Since the fourteenth century, English courts have excused offenders who were mentally unable to control their conduct. The modern standard grew out of an 1843 case involving the attempted murder of the British prime minister.

The basic idea is that people who have a mental disease or disorder should not be convicted if they do not know what they are doing or if they do not know the difference between right and wrong. In the United States about half of the states and the federal government use this standard. The other states hold that accused persons must be acquitted if they lack the *substantial capacity* to appreciate the nature of the act or to conform their conduct to the requirements of the law.

During criminal proceedings, the mental state of the accused can be an issue in determining whether (1) the defendant is competent to stand trial, (2) the defendant was sane at the time of the criminal act, and (3) the defendant is sane after the trial. The insanity defense applies only if the accused were insane at the time of the crime. Insanity at the time of the trial may delay the proceedings until the accused is competent to stand trial or can understand what is taking place. However, insanity during the trial does not affect the defendant's criminal liability.

▲ The defense of infancy rests on the defendant's lack of criminal responsibility. *How does this defense vary among states?*

intoxication a state of drunkenness or similar condition created by the use of drugs or alcohol

insanity defense defense raised by a criminal defendant stating that because of mental disease or defect, the defendant should not be held responsible for the crime committed

Investigating the Law Where You Live

Find out how law enforcement deals with very young defendants where you live.

Stockbyte/Getty Images

▲ Some prisoners claim that they are insane and therefore should not be found guilty of a crime. *How should a person who successfully pleads insanity be punished?*

In most states, there are three possible verdicts: guilty, innocent, or not guilty by reason of insanity. In some states, the last verdict results in automatic commitment to a mental institution. In others, the judge or jury exercises discretion, sometimes in a separate hearing, to determine commitment of the accused. Some of the states have the verdict guilty but mentally ill. Defendants found guilty but mentally ill can be sent to a hospital and later transferred to a prison once they are judged sane.

To prove insanity, the defense must produce evidence of a mental disease or disorder. Psychiatrists usually give testimony in these cases. Both the defense and the prosecution may have psychiatrists examine the defendant, and the testimonies are often in conflict. The decision as to whether insanity is a valid defense rests with whoever—judge or jury—decides the facts of the case.

There is a great deal of controversy about the insanity defense. A few states have abolished it entirely in their state courts. According to polling information, Americans believe that this defense has been successfully used by many heinous criminals. In reality, however, this defense is seldom used. Virtually all studies conclude that it is used in only about one percent of criminal cases. When it is used, it is seldom successful.

Investigating the Law Where You Live

Find out how your state's criminal code defines insanity. Then write a brief definition based on your findings.

entrapment an act by law enforcement officials to persuade a person to commit a crime that the person would not otherwise have committed. If proven, entrapment is a valid defense to a criminal charge.

PROBLEM 11.2

a. What is the insanity defense? How does it work?

b. Should the insanity defense be kept as it is, changed in some way, or abolished? Explain your answer.

Entrapment

The **entrapment** defense applies when the defendant admits to committing a criminal act but claims that he or she was induced, or persuaded, by a law enforcement officer to commit the crime.

There is no entrapment when a police officer merely provides the defendant with an opportunity to commit a crime; rather, it must be shown that the defendant would not have committed the crime if not for the inducement of the police officer. Entrapment is difficult to prove and cannot be claimed as a defense to crimes involving serious physical injury, such as rape or murder.

◄ Entrapment is difficult to prove.

PROBLEM 11.3

Can entrapment be claimed as a valid defense in any of the following cases? Explain your answer.

a. Mary, an undercover police officer masquerading as a prostitute, approaches Edward and tells him that she'll have sex with him in exchange for $50. Edward hands over the money and is arrested.

b. Jan, a drug dealer, offers to sell drugs to Emilio, an undercover officer posing as a drug addict. Emilio buys the drugs, and Jan is arrested.

c. Rashid, an undercover FBI agent, repeatedly offers Sammy a chance to get in on an illegal gambling ring, with the promise that he will win big. After refusing several offers, Sammy, who has no history of gambling and who just lost his job, finally gives Rashid $200 as a bet. Rashid immediately arrests Sammy.

Duress

A person acts under **duress** when he or she does something as a result of coercion or a threat of immediate danger to life or personal safety. Under duress, an individual lacks the ability to exercise free will. For example, suppose someone points a gun at your head and demands that you steal money or be killed. You steal the money. Duress would be a good defense in this case if you were prosecuted for theft. It may also be used as a defense if the threat is made to a third party such as a family member. Duress is not a defense to homicide.

duress unlawful pressure on a person to do something that he or she would not otherwise do. Duress may be a defense to a criminal charge.

Necessity

An individual acts under **necessity** when he or she is compelled to react to a situation that is unavoidable in order to protect life. Suppose, for example, that a group of people is left adrift in a lifeboat so heavy with cargo that it is in danger of sinking. The group throws the cargo overboard to make the lifeboat lighter and more manageable. In this case, necessity would be a good defense to a charge of destruction of property. Necessity is not a defense to homicide.

neccessity a defense to a criminal charge that shows a just and lawful reason for the defendant's conduct

CHAPTER **12**
Criminal Justice Process:
The Investigative Phase

► Arrests must be based on probable cause.

The criminal justice process includes everything that happens to a person from arrest through prosecution and conviction to release from the control of the state. The vast majority of crimes that occur are investigated and prosecuted under state laws. There are, however, many federal crimes that are handled in the federal criminal justice system. The federal and state systems are similar in many ways, but each state has certain features that make it unique.

Typically the process moves through certain stages, and the person arrested might gain his or her freedom at any stage. Some are freed almost immediately at the police station, and some regain their freedom only after serving time in a correctional institution. At various points in the investigation, trial, and sentencing process, the prosecutor may drop the case for lack of evidence, or the judge may declare a mistrial if the jury is unable to reach a verdict.

Jason Pack/FEMA

This chapter deals with the investigation phase of the process, including how the U.S. Constitution limits what police can do. The next three chapters cover proceedings before trial, the trial itself, and sentencing and corrections. The juvenile justice process is discussed in Chapter 16.

Arrest

An **arrest** takes place when a person suspected of a crime is taken into custody. An arrest is considered a seizure under the Fourth Amendment, which requires that seizures be reasonable. A person can be taken into custody by a police officer in one of two ways: with an arrest warrant issued by a judge or without a warrant if there is probable cause.

An **arrest warrant** is a court order commanding that the person named in it be taken into custody. A warrant is obtained by filing a complaint before a judge or magistrate. The person filing the complaint is generally a police officer but may be a victim or a witness. The person making the complaint must also describe and swear to the facts and circumstances of the alleged crime. If, on the basis of the information provided, the judge finds probable cause to believe that an offense has been committed and that the accused committed it, a warrant will be issued. On many occasions, police do not have time to get a warrant. In certain felony cases and in misdemeanor cases, they may make a warrantless arrest in public based on probable cause.

Probable cause to arrest means having a reasonable belief that a specific person has committed a crime. This reasonable belief may be based on much less evidence than is necessary to prove a person guilty at trial. For example, suppose the police receive a radio report of a bank robbery. An officer sees a man matching the description of the bank robber waving a gun and running away from the bank. The officer would have probable cause to stop and arrest the man, but that evidence alone might not be enough to convict him of the crime.

There is no exact formula for determining probable cause. When arresting without a warrant, police must use their own judgment as to what is reasonable under the circumstances of each case. In all cases, probable cause requires more than mere suspicion or a hunch. Some facts must be present that indicate that the person arrested has committed a crime.

Courts have allowed law enforcement officials to use what is known as a **drug courier profile** to help establish probable cause for arrest. Drug courier profiles are often based on commonly held notions concerning the typical age, race, personal appearance, behavior, and mannerisms of drug couriers. Police may use a profile to provide a basis to stop and question a person. However to make an arrest, police need individualized suspicion. Simply fitting a profile is not enough to support an arrest. When courts review an investigatory stop or the seizure (arrest) of a person, they consider whether "the totality of the circumstances" justify the action of the police.

Police may also establish probable cause based on information provided by citizens in the community. Information and statements from victims or witnesses can be used to obtain an arrest warrant. Police also

arrest to take a person suspected of a crime into custody

arrest warrant a court-ordered document authorizing the police to arrest an individual on a specific charge

probable cause a reasonable belief, known personally or through reliable sources, that a specific person has committed a crime

drug courier profile using commonly notions of what typical drug couriers look and act like in order to be able to question a person without establishing individualized suspicion

use tips from informants to establish probable cause if they can convince a judge that the information they have obtained is reliable.

In determining the reliability of an informant's tip, a judge will consider a number of circumstances. These include whether the informant has provided accurate statements in the past, how the informant obtained the information, and whether the police can **corroborate,** or confirm, the informant's tip with information from other sources.

corroborate to confirm information

12.1 Sequence of Events in the Criminal Justice Process

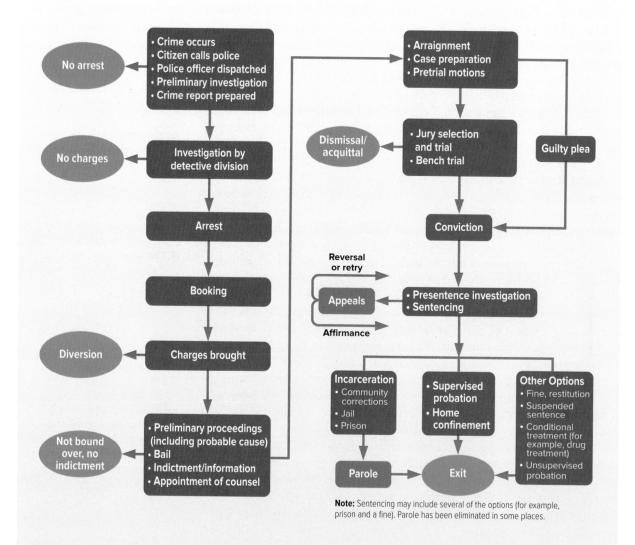

Note: Sentencing may include several of the options (for example, prison and a fine). Parole has been eliminated in some places.

The criminal justice process includes everything that happens from the arrest through prosecution, conviction, and eventual release from control by the state. Additional information is provided in Chapters 13–15. **ANALYZE THE DATA** *What happens after charges are brought against the individual?*

The police receive a tip that a drug pusher named Richie will be flying from New York City to Washington, D.C., sometime on the morning of September 8. The informant describes Richie as a tall man with reddish hair and a beard. He also tells police that Richie has a habit of walking fast and that he will be carrying illegal drugs in a brown leather bag. The police have received reliable information from this informant in the past. On the morning of September 8, the police watch all passengers arriving from New York City. When they see a man who fits the description—carrying a brown leather bag and walking fast—they arrest him. A search of the bag reveals a large quantity of cocaine.

a. Do you think the police had probable cause to arrest Richie? Explain.

b. Should the police have obtained a warrant before arresting Richie? Why or why not?

c. Assume the police have not received a specific tip but they know that crack cocaine is being brought regularly on trains from one specific city to their city by teenagers hired by older drug dealers. They see a 16-year-old African American male arriving in their city by train from a city that has been the source of crack cocaine dealings. He is alone and is carrying a small canvas bag. Should the police be able to stop and question him? Under what circumstances should they be able to search or arrest him?

reasonable suspicion evidence that justifies an officer in stopping and questioning an individual believed to be involved in criminal activity; based on less evidence than probable cause but more than a mere hunch

stop and frisk to "pat down" or search the outer clothing of someone whom the police believe is acting suspiciously

▼ An officer pats down a suspect's outer clothing. *When can an officer stop and frisk a person?*

A police officer does not need probable cause to stop and question an individual on the street, but the officer must have **reasonable suspicion** to believe that the individual is involved in criminal activity. Reasonable suspicion is based on even less evidence than probable cause, but it must be more than a mere hunch. If the officer has reasonable suspicion that the person is armed and dangerous, he or she may do a limited pat-down of the person's outer clothing—called a **stop and frisk**—to remove any weapons the person may be carrying. This is called a "Terry stop" because stop and frisk was first approved by the Supreme Court in the case *Terry* v. *Ohio*.

Even if a police officer does not have probable cause or reasonable suspicion, the officer may go up to any individual and ask to speak to him or her. The person may decline and continue his or her activity, and the officer is not legally permitted to take the person's silence or departure into account in determining probable cause or reasonable suspicion. In all states, however, if the person runs from the police upon being asked for identification, that flight may

Aaron Roeth Photography

give the officer reasonable suspicion to stop the person again, at which point the person is not free to walk away. This occurence is especially true with stops in high crime areas.

The most common kind of police-citizen interaction occurs when a person is stopped for violating traffic laws. The detention in this common situation is usually brief, lasting only as long as it takes the officer to check identification and registration, and typically ends when a citation (a ticket)—or if the driver is lucky, a warning—is issued. The U.S. Supreme Court has ruled that police can order all passengers out of a car when making a lawful traffic stop.

THE **CASE** OF...

The Unlucky Couple

After an evening at the movies, Lonnie Howard and his girlfriend, Melissa, decide to park in the empty lot behind Briarwood Elementary School. They begin talking and start drinking the beer they brought with them. After several beers, the couple is startled by the sound of breaking glass and voices from the rear of the school.

Unnoticed in their darkened car, Lonnie and Melissa observe two men loading office furniture and electronics equipment from the school into the back of a van. Quickly concluding that the men must be burglars, Lonnie decides he should leave the parking lot. He revs up his engine and roars out of the parking lot onto Main Street.

Meanwhile, unknown to Lonnie and Melissa, a silent security alarm has also alerted the local police to the break-in at the school. Responding to the alarm, Officer Vicki Ramos heads for the school. She turns onto Main Street just in time to see one vehicle—Lonnie's car—speeding away from the school.

PROBLEM 12.2

a. If you were Officer Ramos, what would you do in this situation? If you were Lonnie, what would you do?

b. If Officer Ramos chases Lonnie, will she have probable cause to stop and arrest him?

c. How do you think Officer Ramos would act after stopping Lonnie? How do you think Lonnie and Melissa would act?

d. Role-play this situation. As Officer Ramos, decide what you would say and how you would act toward the occupants of the car. As Lonnie and Melissa, decide what you would say and how you would act toward the police officer.

e. What could Lonnie and Melissa do if they were mistakenly arrested for the burglary? What could they do if they were abused or mistreated by Officer Ramos?

f. Assume Lonnie takes a baseball bat from the back of the car and begins to wave it after being stopped by Officer Ramos. Would it be legal for Officer Ramos to use deadly force?

Steps to Take

What To Do If You Are Arrested

- **Do not struggle with the police.** Be polite. Avoid fighting or swearing, even if you think the police have made a mistake. Resisting arrest and assaulting a police officer are usually separate crimes that you can be charged with even if you have done nothing else wrong. If you believe you have been assaulted by the police, be sure to write down the officer's name and badge number. If possible, also write down the names and phone numbers of any witnesses.

  Give your name, address, and phone number to the police. You have a right to remain silent and not answer questions about the alleged crime. If you tell police you do not want to speak with them, they should stop questioning you about the crime. Anything you do say, however, can be used against you in court.

  You may be searched, photographed, and fingerprinted. Notice carefully what is done but do not resist. If any personal property is taken from you, ask for a written receipt.

  As soon as possible after you get to the police station, call a trusted relative or friend. Tell this person where you are, what you have been charged with, and what your bail or bond is. (See Chapter 13 for information about bail.)

  Please note that this information applies to adults who are arrested. When juveniles are taken into custody, a parent or guardian must be notified and there is no right to bail. There may also be other differences between juvenile and adult arrest procedures and the steps you should take. (See Chapter 16 for information about the juvenile justice system.)

- **When you are arrested for a minor offense, you may, in some places, be released without having to put up any**

money. This is called an unsecured bond or citation release. If you do not qualify for a citation release, you may have to put up some money before release. This is called posting a cash bond or collateral. Ask for a receipt for the money.

- **When you are arrested for a serious misdemeanor or felony, you will not be released immediately.** Ask the friend or relative you have called to get a lawyer for you. If you cannot afford a lawyer, one will be appointed by the judge at no cost to you when you are first brought to court.

  Before you leave the police station, be sure to find out when you are due in court. *Never be late or miss a court appearance.* If you do not show up in court at the assigned time, a warrant may be issued for your rearrest.

- **Do not talk about your case with anyone except your lawyer.** Be honest with your lawyer, or he or she will have trouble helping you. Ask that your lawyer be present at all lineups and interrogation sessions. Most criminal defense lawyers recommend that you not talk to police about the crime until you speak with a lawyer.

Television crime shows suggest that much of a police officer's work involves deadly force. In fact only a small percentage of interaction between the police and the public involves the use of force. When force is used, it usually does not involve police use of a weapon or other type of deadly force. A police officer may use as much force as is reasonably necessary to make an arrest. However, most police departments limit the use of deadly force to incidents involving dangerous or threatening suspects. The U.S. Supreme Court has ruled that deadly force "may not be used unless it is necessary to prevent escape, and the officer has probable cause to believe the suspect poses a significant threat of death or serious physical harm to the officer or others."

If a police officer uses too much force or makes an unlawful arrest, the accused may bring a civil action seeking monetary damages for a violation of the federal *Civil Rights Act*. The government could also file a criminal action against the police. In addition, many local governments have processes for handling citizen complaints about police misconduct. Note, however, that a police officer is never liable for false arrest simply because the person arrested did not commit the crime. Rather, it must be shown that the officer acted maliciously or had no reasonable grounds for suspicion of guilt. Also, if an arrest is later ruled unlawful, the evidence obtained as a result of the arrest may not be used against the accused.

THE **CASE** OF...

The Dangerous Car Chase

In March 2001, Victor Harris, who was 19 years old, was speeding at 73 miles per hour on a stretch of road where the speed limit was 55 miles per hour. A police officer activated his blue flashing lights to signal Harris to pull over, but Harris sped away. The officer chased Harris and radioed his dispatch for assistance.

Deputy Timothy Scott joined the pursuit along with other officers, and most of the chase occurred on a two-lane highway. At one point, Harris pulled into a shopping-center parking lot, where he collided with one of the patrol cars and then continued fleeing down the highway. Deputy Scott, now the lead pursuit vehicle, decided to stop Harris by ramming him from behind. He sought and received permission from his supervisor, who said "go ahead and take him out."

Scott pushed his bumper into the rear of Harris's vehicle, which ran off the road, overturned, and crashed. Harris was badly injured in the crash, which left him a quadriplegic. He sued Scott for violating his Fourth Amendment rights, saying that Scott used excessive force to seize him.

PROBLEM 12.3

a. What arguments can Harris make that his rights were violated?

b. What arguments can Officer Scott make that his use of force did not violate Harris' rights?

c. How should this case be decided? Explain.

d. Draft a policy that the police could use to determine when a chase is justified.

The use of deadly force by police was thrust into the spotlight late in 2014 following a series of heavily publicized cases in which police officers shot unarmed African American males. This spurred protests across the country and launched a national dialogue about the strained relationship between law enforcement and some minority communities. Shortly after these killings, two New York City police officers were shot and killed while in their cruiser by a gunman who then committed suicide. A note left by the gunman suggested that these were "revenge killings." These events—all of which occurred in a five month period—highlighted the problem of violence both by and against law enforcement.

Search and Seizure

Americans have always valued their privacy. They expect to be left alone, to be free from unwarranted snooping or spying, and to be secure in their homes. While there is no explicit right to privacy in the U.S. Constitution, the Fourth Amendment sets out the right to be free from "unreasonable searches and seizures" and establishes conditions under which search warrants may be issued. Like others in the Bill of Rights, this right limits the power of government, not the actions of private citizens. If an individual violates your privacy, however, you may be able to sue the person in civil court.

Balanced against the individual's reasonable expectation of privacy is the government's need to gather information. In the case of the police, there is the need to collect evidence against criminals and to protect society against crime.

The Fourth Amendment does not give citizens an absolute right to privacy, and it does not prohibit all searches—only those that are unreasonable. In reviewing whether the police acted reasonably in conducting a search, courts carefully consider the facts and circumstances of each case, sometimes called the "totality of the circumstances." Traditionally, courts have found searches and seizures of private homes to be reasonable only when authorized by a valid warrant. In practice today, warrantless searches are very common (except for searches of homes) as long as they are reasonable. The courts have recognized certain situations in which warrantless searches are considered to be reasonable and allowed.

The U.S. Supreme Court has sometimes used the concept of "reasonable expectation of privacy" to help determine whether a search was reasonable or unreasonable. Courts ask: did the person in a particular situation have an expectation of privacy, and does society consider that expectation in this instance to be reasonable? In one such case, the Supreme Court found that a person did not have a reasonable expectation of privacy in garbage left in a plastic bag for pickup on the curb in front of his house. The police were allowed to search this person's garbage without first obtaining a warrant.

Although the language of the Fourth Amendment is relatively simple, search and seizure law is complex. There are many exceptions to the basic rules. Once an individual is arrested, it may be up to the courts to decide whether any evidence found in a search was legally obtained. If a court finds that the search was unreasonable, then evidence found in the search cannot be used at the trial against the defendant. This principle—the **exclusionary rule**—does not mean that the defendant cannot be tried or convicted, but it does mean that evidence seized in an unlawful search cannot be used at trial.

exclusionary rule a legal rule that generally prohibits the use of illegally obtained evidence against the defendant at trial; generally applies to violations of a defendant's Fourth, Fifth, or Sixth Amendment rights

▶ Police officers search a house to collect evidence against criminals. *What is the exclusionary rule?*

PROBLEM 12.4

Examine the following situations. Decide whether the search violates the Fourth Amendment. Explain your decisions.

a. The police see Dell standing at a bus stop in an area known for drug dealing. They stop and search him, finding drugs in his pocket.

b. After Brandon checks out of a hotel, the police ask the hotel manager to turn over the contents of the wastebasket, where they find notes planning a murder.

c. Jill's ex-boyfriend breaks into her apartment and looks through her desk for love letters. Instead he finds drugs, which he gives to the police.

d. Pam is seen shoplifting in a store. Police chase Pam into her apartment building and arrest her outside the closed door of her apartment. A search of the apartment reveals a large quantity of stolen goods.

e. Sandi is suspected of receiving stolen goods. The police go to her house and ask Claire, her roommate, if they can search the house. Claire gives them permission, and they find stolen items in Sandi's dresser.

TAKING ACTION: Law and Democracy

Policing the Police

Ever since the development of the modern police force in London by Sir Robert Peel in 1829, determining the best way to police the police—to investigate and hold them accountable for following laws as they enforce them—has been an ongoing challenge. In most municipalities, city government is headed by an elected mayor or a city manager hired by an elected city council. In either case, the mayor or city manager has the power to hire and fire the police chief. If voters are dissatisfied with the work of the police force, the mayor or the city manager will have a strong incentive to either improve the work of the force or hire a new chief who will do a better job.

Police departments handle complaints from citizens through an internal affairs unit. In small departments, one officer handles citizen complaints in addition to other duties. In larger departments, citizen complaints are handled by a specialized unit, often staffed by supervisors.

A number of jurisdictions have taken additional steps that involve persons independent of the police department in the review of police conduct. Among the most common structures are the following:

Civilian Complaint Review Board Model: The civilian complaint review board is usually made up of citizen volunteers who review findings that the police department's internal affairs unit proposes in response to complaints from citizens. In some jurisdictions, the complaint review board relies on the police investigation to make a determination. In others, the review board has staff members who investigate the complaints. This process is more open to the public and can help build trust in the community, but the volunteers on the board may know little about police work.

Police Commission Model: The police commission has independent authority over the operation of the police department. Commission members are usually appointed by elected officials such as the mayor and/or city council. In some cases the commission employs a staff of investigators to review complaints. The commission can recommend disciplinary action to the chief of police, when appropriate, or independently impose discipline when necessary.

Office of Professional Accountability Model: An outside expert is brought in as the head of the police department office of internal affairs. This expert is appointed by the mayor and confirmed by the city council. This model blends inside expertise with outside accountability.

Special Prosecutor Model: It is possible to prosecute a police officer for excessive use of force. For example, an officer who kills a suspect in a situation where lethal force cannot be justified can be prosecuted for homicide. As a practical matter, prosecutors have to work very closely with police officers and are generally very reluctant to seek grand jury indictments against them. Some people suggest the use of a special prosecutor, totally independent from law enforcement, to handle such cases.

PROBLEM 12.5

a. Critics of investigations by a police department's internal affairs unit talk about a "blue wall of silence" blocking a thorough investigation. What do you think this phrase means?

b. What are the strengths and weaknesses of each model described above? Which approach would you recommend for your community? Explain your reasons.

Searches With a Warrant

search warrant a court order issued by a judge or magistrate, giving police the power to search a person or to enter a building to search for and seize items related to a crime

bona fide a Latin term, meaning "in good faith"; characterized by good faith and lack of fraud or deceit

affidavit a written statement of facts sworn to or made under oath before someone authorized to administer an oath

A **search warrant** is a court order. It is obtained from a judge who is convinced that there is a **bona fide** (genuine) need to search a person or place. Before a judge issues a warrant, someone, usually a police officer, must file an **affidavit**—a sworn statement of facts and circumstances—that provides the probable cause to believe that a search is justified. If a judge issues a search warrant, the warrant must specifically describe the person or place to be searched and the particular things to be seized.

Once the search warrant is issued by the judge, the search must be conducted within a certain number of days specified in the warrant. Also, in many states the search must be conducted only in the daytime, unless the warrant expressly states otherwise. Finally, a search warrant does not usually authorize a general search of everything in the specified place. For example, if the police have a warrant to search a house for stolen 32-inch televisions, it would be unreasonable for the police to look in desk drawers, envelopes, or other small places where such televisions could not possibly be hidden. However, the police can seize evidence related to the case and any other illegal items that are in plain view when they are properly searching the house for the televisions.

When the police have a warrant to search a house, the Fourth Amendment's reasonableness requirement usually means that they must knock, announce their purpose and authority (that is, that they are police officers), and request admission. The police generally cannot enter a house forcibly—even with a search warrant—unless they have met the "knock and announce" test described above.

▼ Search warrants must state the specific place to be searched and the particular items to be seized. *What other requirements must police follow with a search warrant?*

Aaron Roeth Photography

However, the U.S. Supreme Court has allowed for "no-knock" entries when circumstances present a threat to the officers or where evidence would likely be destroyed if advance notice were given (such as in drug cases). In 2006 the Supreme Court allowed the use at trial of evidence obtained after police entered a house without following "knock and announce" rules.

Searches Without a Warrant

By law, searches of private homes usually require a warrant. However, the courts have recognized some situations in which searches are reasonable and may be legally conducted without a warrant.

- **Search incident to a lawful arrest.** A search that is part of, or incident to, a lawful arrest is considered reasonable. This allows the police to search a lawfully arrested person and the area immediately around that person for hidden weapons or for evidence that might be destroyed. This is called a "wing span" search. If the arrest occurs next to or in the accused's car, police may also search the passenger compartment of the car, but usually not the trunk. The Supreme Court has also allowed a "protective sweep" through an arrested person's home in search of other potentially armed persons.

- **Stop and frisk.** A police officer who reasonably thinks a person is behaving suspiciously and is likely to be armed may stop and frisk the suspect for weapons. This protects the safety of officers and bystanders who might be injured by a person carrying a concealed weapon. The Supreme Court has also said that seizing an illegal substance (such as drugs) during a valid frisk is reasonable if the officer's sense of touch makes it immediately clear that the object felt is an illegal one. This is known as the "plain feel" exception.

- **Consent.** When a person voluntarily agrees, the police may conduct a search without a warrant and without probable cause. Normally, a person may grant permission to search only his or her own belongings or property. In some situations, however, one person may legally allow the police to conduct a search of another person's property. For example, a parent may usually allow officers to search a child's property. While one spouse cannot give consent for a warrantless search of his or her home when the other spouse is present and objects to the search, in 2014 the Court held that a co-resident could give consent to search if the objecting resident had been removed from the property for a reasonable purpose (in that case, being lawfully arrested).

▼ Transportation Security Administration agents are authorized to search people boarding a plane without a warrant. *Is it reasonable to allow a search dog to sniff around a person or their luggage even when there is no probable cause?*

THE **CASE** OF...

Fingers McGee

While on duty, Officer Yomoto and Officer Jones receive a radio report of a robbery at the Dixie Liquor Store. The report indicates only that the suspect is male, about six feet tall, and wearing old clothes. Meanwhile, Fingers McGee is finishing up some shopping at a nearby store and has just seen the owner of the Dixie Liquor Store chasing a man. The man was carrying a paper sack and what appeared to be a knife as he ran down the street. McGee thinks the man looks like Mark Johnson, a drug addict, and he thinks the man was running toward Johnson's house located at 22 Elm Street. Officers Yomoto and Jones encounter Fingers McGee on a street corner and begin to ask him questions.

> ### PROBLEM 12.6
>
> **a.** Role-play this encounter. As the officers, decide what questions to ask McGee. As McGee, decide what to tell the officers.
>
> **b.** Assume McGee tells the police what he knows. What should the police do then?
>
> **c.** Should the police get a search warrant before going to Johnson's house? If they go without a warrant, do they have probable cause to arrest him? Why or why not?
>
> **d.** If the police decide to enter Johnson's house, should they knock and announce themselves or break in unannounced?
>
> **e.** If the police enter the house, can they arrest Johnson? Where can they search, and what, if anything, can be seized? Role-play the scene at the house.

- **Border and airport searches.** Customs agents are authorized to search without warrants and without probable cause. They may examine the baggage, vehicles, purses, wallets, and similar belongings of people entering the country. Body searches or searches conducted away from the border by customs agents are allowed only where there is reasonable suspicion of criminal activity. In view of the danger of terrorist activities, security personnel and airlines are permitted to search all carry-on luggage and to search all passengers by means of fixed and hand-held metal detectors. Since the September 11, 2001, terrorist attacks in New York, Washington, D.C., and Pennsylvania, these searches can take place several times from the moment a passenger enters the airport until he or she boards the flight. Part of the rationale for border and airport searches is that people have a reduced expectation of privacy in these two settings and accept a certain amount of intrusion by government into their privacy.

- **Vehicle searches.** A police officer who has probable cause to believe that a vehicle contains contraband may conduct a search of the entire vehicle, as well as any containers in the vehicle that might contain the contraband, without a warrant. This point does not mean that the police have a right to stop and search any vehicle on the street. The right to stop and search must be based on probable cause.

- **Plain view.** If an object connected with a crime is in plain view and can be seen from a place where an officer has a right to be, it can be seized without a warrant. For example, if an officer legally stops a car for a traffic violation and sees a gun lying on the car seat next to the driver, he or she may seize it without a warrant. Likewise, if an officer has gained legal entrance into a suspect's house and sees drug paraphernalia on a coffee table, the officer does not need a warrant to seize the **contraband**, or illegal items.

- **Hot pursuit.** Police officers in hot pursuit of a suspect are not required to obtain a search warrant before entering a building that they have seen the suspect enter. It is also lawful for the police to seize evidence found in plain view during hot pursuit of a suspected felon.

- **Emergency situations.** In certain types of emergency situations, the police are not required to get a search warrant. These situations include searching a building after a telephoned bomb threat, entering a house after smelling smoke or hearing screams, and other situations in which the police do not have time to obtain a warrant from a judge. The U.S. Supreme Court has also allowed warrantless entries of a person's home where the police have probable cause to believe that failure to enter immediately without a warrant will result in destruction of evidence, escape of the suspect, or harm to the police or another individual inside or outside the building. This exception has been limited by the Supreme Court to serious crimes.

contraband any items that are illegal to possess

▼ Although the Fourth Amendment protects students at school, the Supreme Court has given school administrators broader power than the police to search students and their possessions. *How has the Supreme Court helped schools address the issue of drugs?*

Public School Searches

As you have learned, the Fourth Amendment does not protect citizens against all government searches and seizures, only unreasonable ones. In its consideration of the extent to which students at public schools enjoy Fourth Amendment rights while they are at school, the U.S. Supreme Court has granted school authorities broad discretion to search students who are minors.

The touchstone of the Supreme Court's analysis under the Fourth Amendment in criminal searches is the reasonableness, considering all the circumstances, of the particular government invasion of an individual's personal security. In public school cases, however, the main concern is whether a search is reasonable in the context of the school's legitimate interests.

Hemera/age fotostock

THE **CASE** OF...

Student Drug Testing

Tecumseh High School offers a variety of extra-curricular activities for its students. These activities include choir, band, color guard, Future Farmers of America (FFA), Future Homemakers of America (FHA), and the academic team, as well as athletics and the cheerleading squad. The majority of the school's 500 students participate in one or more of these activities.

At the start of the 1998 school year, the school district adopted the Student Activities Drug Testing Policy. While the school acknowledged only a minimal problem with drugs, they adopted this policy to prevent a bigger problem from developing. The policy required drug testing of all students who participated in any school-sanctioned extracurricular activity. Specifically, in order to participate in an activity, each student had to sign a written consent agreeing to be tested for drug use on several occasions: prior to participating in the activity, randomly during the year while participating in the activity, and at any time while participating in the activity upon reasonable suspicion.

According to the policy, students to be tested at random are called out of class in groups of two or three. The students are directed to a restroom, where a faculty member serves as a monitor. The monitor waits outside the closed restroom stall for the student to produce the urine sample. The monitor pours the contents of the vial into two bottles. Together the faculty monitor and the student seal the bottles. The student signs a form, which the monitor places with the filled bottles into a mailing pouch in the presence of the student. The bottles are then sent to be tested at a designated laboratory. Random drug testing was conducted in this manner on approximately eight occasions during the 1998 and 1999 school years.

There are no academic penalties for refusing to take the test or for a negative result, and results of the tests are not shared with law enforcement authorities. Students who refuse to submit to the policy simply cannot participate in the extracurricular activity. In two school years, a total of 484 students were tested as part of this policy. Four students tested positive.

Two students, neither of them athletes, challenged this policy in federal court as a violation of their right to privacy. The trial court sided with the school, but the federal court of appeals reversed the decision. The school board has appealed to the U.S. Supreme Court, which has agreed to hear the case.

Several years earlier, the U.S. Supreme Court upheld the policy of an Oregon high school to conduct random, suspicionless searches of student athletes at a high school with a serious drug problem. In that case, school officials had determined that the student athletes were among the leaders of the "drug culture" at the school.

PROBLEM 12.7

a. How is the Tecumseh case like the Oregon case? How is it different? How is this case similar to and different from the *New Jersey* v. *TLO* case?

b. What are the most convincing arguments challenging the policy for the students?

c. What are the most convincing arguments in justifying the policy for the school?

d. How should this case be decided? Explain.

e. Assume that the case is decided in favor of the school. Will this mean that schools can test all students? Faculty and staff? Should schools be able to test everyone for drugs? Explain your reasons.

In the 1985 case of *New Jersey* v. *TLO*, an assistant principal suspected a student of violating the public high school's rule against smoking. The principal searched the student's purse and found evidence of marijuana use. Although the U.S. Supreme Court recognized that a student does have a reasonable expectation of privacy while at school, it nevertheless upheld the search by the principal. Instead of requiring that the school have probable cause to suspect a student of criminal activity, as in a traditional criminal search, the school authority only needs to have reasonable suspicion that a search will turn up evidence that the student is violating either school rules or the law.

Because drug use is a serious issue in some schools, courts have given elementary and secondary schools great discretion in devising ways to combat the problem. For example, the courts allow schools to search student lockers on the theory that lockers belong to the school and that students do not have a reasonable expectation of privacy in property owned by the school. However, in 2009 the Supreme Court found a strip search of a middle school student suspected of hiding ibuprofen in her underwear to be unreasonable. The Court said that the school officials overreacted to vague accusations that the student was violating a school rule.

Landmark Supreme Court Cases

Visit the Landmark Supreme Court Cases website at landmarkcases.org for information and activities about *New Jersey* v. *TLO*.

Suspicionless Searches

Searches and seizures are usually considered unreasonable if there is no *individualized* suspicion of wrongdoing. For example, the police could not search all the people gathered at a street corner if they suspected that only one of them possessed evidence of a crime. They could search only the person upon whom their individual suspicion is focused so that the privacy rights of the others on the corner are protected.

The U.S. Supreme Court has recognized some limited circumstances in which this requirement of individualized suspicion need not be met. For example, the Court has upheld suspicionless searches conducted in the context of a program designed to meet special needs beyond the goals of routine law enforcement. These special circumstances include fixed-point searches at or near borders to detect illegal immigrants, highway sobriety checkpoints, and mandatory drug and alcohol tests for railroad employees who have been involved in accidents. The Court found these searches to be reasonable and in support of a special need beyond ordinary law enforcement. These searches continue to be controversial because they seem to depart from the Fourth Amendment's traditional requirement that searches be based on probable cause. In the 1990 case of *Michigan Dept. of State Police v. Sitz*, the Supreme Court determined that properly conducted sobriety checkpoints are constitutional. However, some states have determined that such checkpoints that have been allowed by the Court in fact violate their state constitutions and have banned them.

Police Searches and Technology

Each of the cases below deals with how the police perform searches involving technology. Analyze the fact patterns carefully. Balance the individual's interest in privacy against the government's justification for these investigatory techniques. Then decide whether or not the Supreme Court should allow the high tech search.

a. Police officers suspected Antoine Jones of trafficking drugs. In order to track his movements, they put a GPS device on Jones's car. They got a warrant before attaching the device but the warrant was for a limited time. The police tracked the movements of his car around the clock for four weeks, exceeding the scope of the warrant. Using information gathered from the GPS, police established the location of Jones's operations and were able to arrest him.

Jones argued that placing the GPS device on his car violated his right to be protected from unreasonable searches by gathering personal data about him that a reasonable person would feel was private. The police said that placing the GPS wasn't a search, but was instead just like having an officer follow Jones's car around on public streets, which is a normal part of police investigations.

b. David Riley was arrested in 2009 after the police found loaded firearms in his car during a lawful traffic stop. After the arrest, police officers took Riley's phone and looked through the messages, contacts, videos, and photos that Riley had stored on it. Officers found evidence in Riley's phone that linked him to a shooting, and he was charged with that crime. Riley argued that the police looking through his phone was an unreasonable search under the Fourth Amendment. The police said that looking through the things that people are carrying—a search incident to a lawful arrest—is an established part of arrest procedure.

Racial Profiling in Police Investigations

Racial profiling involves the use of race as a factor in identifying people who may break or have broken the law. Profiling can take the form of inappropriate police action based on ethnicity, national origin, or religion as well as race. Profiling occurs when, for example, an airport security guard selects a person from a racial or ethnic group to be searched solely because of his or her appearance. Critics of racial profiling, including civil rights advocates and some police professional organizations, say that it violates the people's constitutional right to equal protection before the law as well as the presumption of innocence. They also say it is an ineffective law enforcement tactic, it reinforces racial stereotypes in society, and it creates negative relations between police and citizens.

The general rule is that it is inappropriate for an officer to stop a person *solely* because of his or her race, ethnicity, national origin, or religion. However, in some situations officers may appropriately consider these factors among others in deciding whom to stop. For example, if an eyewitness to a robbery describes the robber as an African American man, a police officer may use race as a factor in deciding to stop an African American man that she sees running from the immediate vicinity of the crime.

▲ Racial profiling is a controversial issue. *When is it appropriate for a police officer to use race in deciding whom to stop?*

racial profiling the use of race as a factor in identifying people who may break or who may have broken the law

TAKING ACTION: Law and Democracy

Should Anything Be Done About Racial Profiling?

A committee of state legislators is meeting to discuss solutions to the issue of racial profiling. A study by the state government shows that African American drivers are 35 percent more likely to be stopped and searched by police than are drivers of other races. A survey of people who have been pulled over by law enforcement in the state shows that a majority of people felt that they were stopped for legitimate reasons. However, one in three African Americans and one in four Latinos felt they had been unfairly stopped. Many complained of abusive treatment by police.

Assume that you are a state legislator on the committee trying to solve these problems. Read the following excerpts from proposals offered by committee members.

Gomez: The problem is that police are not used to dealing with people from other cultures and have stereotypes of people of other races. All police should receive training on diversity and how to be culturally sensitive.

Wu: This practice has gone on for so long because people are not aware of their rights. When people are stopped, they should immediately be told why and be given a card that lists their rights along with a business card listing the name and contact information of the officer.

Letaliano: Police officers are not being disciplined for their inappropriate behavior because the police chiefs are unaware of what is going on. We need to collect data regularly to make police officers more aware of why they are really stopping people and to keep them accountable to the public. Each time a driver is stopped, the officer should be required to fill out a form detailing the time and date, driver's age, probable race, gender, and the reason for stopping the person.

Reynolds: The U.S. Constitution and state laws already prohibit searches not based on probable cause. The police department already has internal complaint procedures that people can follow if they feel they were stopped because of their race. This is enough to protect citizens. To do more could make the police reluctant to stop people who might be criminals.

Al-Aziz: It's too hard for citizens to prove that they were stopped illegally. All stops by police should be videotaped so we can see how the police treat the suspect and then take disciplinary action against officers who act improperly.

Debouche: We can't rely only on laws or the police department to solve the problem. The answer is to have a board made up of ordinary citizens that hears complaints and has the power to take disciplinary action against officers who act inappropriately.

PROBLEM 12.8

a. Which of these proposals seems most likely to help address the issue as you see it? Give your reasons.

b. Invite members of your community to participate in this activity. Be sure that representatives from both law enforcement and a group concerned about racial profiling are invited. Is there evidence that racial profiling is a problem in your community? If so, what is the evidence? What can be done to deal with the problem? If it is not a problem where you live, what measures can be taken to keep it from becoming a problem?

Determine whether profiling was used in making each of the following decisions. Give your reasons.

a. Two African American men are driving over the speed limit on a highway where police know drugs are being transported to a part of the city with a large African American population. A police officer stops them for speeding and then conducts a complete search of their car, including their trunk, to look for drugs. They do not find any drugs.

b. After a terrorist attack, the government decides to use more telephone wiretaps to gather information in communities that have mosques.

c. A man reports overhearing two Spanish-speaking men in a coffee shop planning to rob a specific jewelry store the next day. The witness could not see the men's faces and does not know their names. The next day the police go to the store and question two "Latino-looking" men who are sitting in a car outside.

d. A woman entering the United States holds a passport from a country with which the United States was recently at war. A customs agent detains her for questioning.

> ### THE Constitution
>
> *No person . . . shall be compelled in any criminal case to be a witness against himself, nor be deprived of life, liberty, or property, without due process of law.*
>
> —Fifth Amendment
>
> *In all criminal prosecutions, the accused shall . . . have the Assistance of Counsel for his defence.*
>
> — Sixth Amendment

Interrogations and Confessions

After an arrest is made, standard police practice is to question, or **interrogate**, the accused. These interrogations often result in confessions or admissions of guilt. The accused's confessions or admissions may later be used as evidence at trial.

interrogate to question a witness or suspected criminal

Balanced against the police's need to question suspects are the constitutional rights of people accused of a crime. The Fifth Amendment to the U.S. Constitution provides citizens with a protection against **self-incrimination**. This means that a suspect has a right to remain silent and cannot be forced to testify against himself or herself at trial. This protection rests on a basic legal principle: the government bears the burden of proof. Suspects are not obliged to help the government prove they committed a crime or to testify at their own trial. Under the Sixth Amendment, a person accused of a crime has the right to the assistance of an attorney.

self-incrimination giving evidence and answering questions that would tend to subject one to criminal prosecution

The U.S. Supreme Court has held that a confession is not admissible as evidence if it is not voluntary and trustworthy. Using physical force, torture, threats, or other techniques that could force an innocent person to confess is prohibited. In the 1964 case of *Escobedo* v. *Illinois*, the Supreme Court said that even a voluntary confession is inadmissible as evidence if it is obtained after the defendant's request to talk with an attorney has been denied. The Court reasoned that the presence of Escobedo's attorney could have helped him avoid self-incrimination.

► *Miranda* warnings are read to suspects in custody if the police want to interrogate them. *How has the Miranda rule changed in recent years?*

MIRANDA WARNING

1. YOU HAVE THE RIGHT TO REMAIN SILENT.
2. ANYTHING YOU SAY CAN AND WILL BE USED AGAINST YOU IN A COURT OF LAW.
3. YOU HAVE THE RIGHT TO TALK TO A LAWYER AND TO HAVE HIM PRESENT WITH YOU WHILE YOU ARE BEING QUESTIONED.
4. IF YOU CANNOT AFFORD TO HIRE A LAWYER, ONE WILL BE APPOINTED TO REPRESENT YOU BEFORE ANY QUESTIONING IF YOU WISH.
5. YOU CAN DECIDE AT ANY TIME TO EXERCISE THESE RIGHTS AND NOT ANSWER ANY QUESTIONS OR MAKE ANY STATEMENTS.

WAIVER

DO YOU UNDERSTAND EACH OF THESE RIGHTS I HAVE EXPLAINED TO YOU? HAVING THESE RIGHTS IN MIND, DO YOU WISH TO TALK TO US NOW?

Landmark Supreme Court Cases

Visit the Landmark Supreme Court Cases website at landmarkcases.org for information and activities about *Miranda* v. *Arizona*.

Miranda warnings rights that a person taken into custody must be informed of by police or other officials before questioning begins. These include the right to remain silent, to contact a lawyer, and to have a free lawyers provided if the person arrested cannot afford one.

Although some defendants might ask for an attorney, others might not be aware of or understand their right to remain silent or their right to have a lawyer present during questioning. In 1966, the Supreme Court was presented with such a situation in the case of *Miranda* v. *Arizona*. In its decision, the Court ruled that Ernesto Miranda's confession could not be used at trial because officers had obtained it without informing Miranda of his right to a lawyer and his right to remain silent. As a result of this case, police are now required to inform people taken into custody of the so-called Miranda rights before questioning begins.

Suspects sometimes complain that they were not read their Miranda rights and that the entire case should therefore be dropped and charges dismissed. Failure to give **Miranda warnings**, however, does not affect the validity of an arrest. The police have to give Miranda warnings only if they want to use statements from the accused at the trial. In fact, in his second trial, even though the court could not use his confession as evidence against him, Miranda was convicted based on other evidence.

The controversial *Miranda* case illustrates the delicate balance between the protection guaranteed to the accused and the protection from crime provided to society. This balance is constantly changing, and the effect of *Miranda* has been altered by more recent cases.

THE **CASE** OF...

The Juvenile and the Miranda Warnings

In 1995, teenagers Michael Alvarado and Paul Soto attempted to steal a truck in a shopping mall parking lot in Santa Fe Springs, California. Alvarado approached the passenger side door of the truck, and Soto, holding a .357 Magnum pistol, approached the driver. The driver refused to give Soto the keys, so Soto shot and killed him. Alvarado then helped Soto hide the gun.

Both Alvarado and Soto were convicted of second-degree murder and robbery. Alvarado was convicted in large part because of incriminating statements he made about his involvement in the shooting during a two-hour interview with a police detective about a month after the murder.

At the time of the interview, Alvarado was a 17-year-old high school student. The detective contacted Alvarado's mother, who agreed to bring him to the police station for questioning. When Alvarado arrived with his parents, the detective denied the parents' request to remain with their son during the interview. While they waited in the lobby, Alvarado was questioned alone. During the two-hour session, the detective twice asked Alvarado if he wanted to take a break. Alvarado admitted to his role in the killing. At the end of the interview he went home. Alvarado was never advised that he had a right to remain silent, to consult a lawyer prior to answering questions, or to leave the police station.

PROBLEM 12.10

a. What are the strongest arguments that Alvarado should have been given Miranda warnings at the beginning of the questioning by the detective?

b. What are the strongest arguments that there was no need to give Alvarado Miranda warnings in these circumstances?

c. If you were a judge on an appeals court hearing this case, how would you analyze the issue of whether Alvarado was in custody and being interrogated? Should his age and experience be a factor? Explain.

d. Should Alvarado have done anything differently? Should the detective have done anything differently?

In one case, the Supreme Court created a public safety exception to the *Miranda* rule. In this case, a police officer was arresting a rape suspect thought to be carrying a weapon in a grocery store. The officer asked the suspect where his gun was before advising him of his rights. The suspect then pointed to a nearby grocery counter, where the gun was found. The Court held that police may ask questions related to public safety before advising suspects of their rights. The Court has also limited the Miranda rule to require the warnings only if the support is subject to custodial interrogation. **Custodial interrogation** means that the person is in custody (not free to leave) and is being interrogated (questioned) by the police. Remember that defense counsel will ask the judge before trial to exclude the results of an illegal search. Similarly, defense counsel will ask the judge at a pretrial hearing to exclude any statement given by the defendant in violation of the Miranda rule.

custodial interrogation
questioning by law enforcement officers after a person has been taken into custody or otherwise deprived of his or her freedom of movement

Aaron Roeth Photography

► Police use fingerprints to investigate the crime.

booking the formal process of making a police record of an arrest

Before a criminal case is scheduled for trial, several pretrial actions must take place. Most of these proceedings are standard for every case. Depending on the circumstances and the result of preliminary proceedings, the case will be set for trial unless the charges are dropped or the accused pleads guilty.

Booking and Initial Appearance

After an arrest, the accused is taken to a police station for **booking**, the formal process of making a police record of the arrest. At this time, the accused is asked to provide information, including name, address, date of birth, place of employment, and details about any previous arrests.

Then the accused is usually fingerprinted and photographed. In certain circumstances, the police are allowed to take fingernail clippings, hand-writing specimens, or blood samples for possible DNA analysis. Urine tests to ascertain drug use have also become a common booking requirement.

Within a limited period following arrest and booking, the accused must appear before a judicial officer, usually a judge or magistrate. At this initial appearance, the judge explains the defendant's rights and explains the exact nature of the charges. The defendant has an attorney appointed or is given the opportunity to obtain one. The judge may also set bail.

In *Gideon* v. *Wainwright*, the U.S. Supreme Court guaranteed the right to free counsel at trial for low-income persons charged with a felony. In a later case, the Court ruled that a low-income defendant cannot be subjected to imprisonment unless provided with counsel. This case extended *Gideon* from only felony cases to misdemeanors that carried a punishment of jail time. However, some states do not provide counsel at the initial appearance. Studies have shown that indigent defendants without counsel at the initial appearance get higher money bail and spend more time in jail before trial than defendants represented by counsel at the initial appearance.

In a misdemeanor case, the defendant is asked at the initial appearance to enter a plea of guilty or not guilty. In a felony case, the procedure is somewhat different. The defendant is informed of the charges and advised of his or her rights, as in a misdemeanor case, but does not enter a plea until a later stage in the criminal process, known as the felony **arraignment.** In some jurisdictions, the defendant may be entitled to a preliminary hearing to determine if there is probable cause to believe that a crime was committed and that the defendant committed it. The arraignment and the preliminary hearing are discussed later in this chapter. The most important part of the initial appearance is deciding whether the defendant will be released from custody and, if so, under what conditions.

arraignment a court session at which a defendant is charged and enters a plea. For a misdemeanor this is also the defendant's initial appearance, at which the judge informs him or her of the charges and sets the bail

Bail and Pretrial Release

In determining how to deal with an arrested person at the pretrial stage, the judge will consider whether the person is likely to show up for trial as well as whether the person is a danger to the community. In general, the judge will have four options: (1) releasing the person with no conditions (called release on personal recognizance); (2) releasing with non-monetary conditions (various forms of monitoring in the community); (3) setting a cash bail amount which must be paid to the court in

THE Constitution

"Excessive bail shall not be required, nor excessive fines imposed, nor cruel and unusual punishments inflicted."

— Eighth Amendment

◀ Bail bond companies have gone out of business in some places. *Why might this be?*

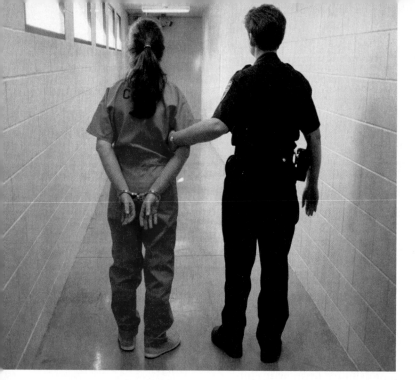

▲ To be eligible for pretrial release, a defendant must be considered a low risk of failing to show up for trial. *What factors should a judge consider when determining whether a defendant will return for trial?*

personal recognizance a release from legal custody based on a defendant's promise to show up for trial. An alternative to cash bail, this practice is used if the judge decides that the defendant is likely to return.

order for the person to be released; or (4) ordering the person detained without bail. Pretrial release systems vary from state to state, and the federal system is also different than most state systems.

Bail may be paid directly to the court. The entire amount may be required, or in some places, the defendant may be released after paying just a portion of the total amount (for example, 10 percent). If a person released on bail fails to return, the court will keep the money. If the defendant does not have the money, a bond company may put up a bail bond in exchange for a fee. For example, a defendant with bail set at $2,000 might be released after paying a $200 premium to the bond company. If a bond is posted, the bond company will be required to pay the amount of the bond to the court if the defendant does not report for trial. The bail bond company might also require that another person sign to guarantee the bond. When the defendant shows up for trial, the amount of the bond is returned to the company, but the company keeps the premium.

The Eighth Amendment to the U.S. Constitution states that "excessive bail shall not be required." However this does not specify how much is excessive, and a poor person unable to raise any money could be detained in jail before trial or conviction. Some people consider this unfair, and some courts and legislatures have developed programs to release defendants without requiring any money.

In order to be eligible for release on **personal recognizance,** or personal bond, the defendant must promise to return and must be considered a low risk of failing to show up for trial. In determining the likelihood of the defendant's return, judges consider factors such as the nature and circumstances of the offense and the accused's family and community ties, financial resources, employment background, and prior criminal record.

In addition to personal recognizance programs, courts may set other nonmonetary conditions designed to ensure the return of the defendant. These conditions include placing the defendant in the custody of a third party or requiring the defendant to maintain or get a job, to reside at a certain address, or to report his or her whereabouts regularly.

Despite the advantages of these programs, there can be problems in releasing defendants, even though they have not yet been found guilty of the crime with which they have been charged. Statistics indicate that some defendants commit crimes while out on bail.

Supporters of pretrial release say that it prevents punishment prior to conviction and gives defendants the freedom to help prepare their cases. Supporters also claim that the U.S. justice system rests on the presumption that defendants are innocent until proven guilty and that setting high bail or holding a person in jail before trial goes against that presumption.

a. What is the purpose of the constitutional right to protection from excessive bail? Should it apply to all people?

b. Are there any circumstances in which a person should be released without any bail requirements? Are there any circumstances under which a person should not be released on bail of any kind? Explain.

c. Do you think the bail system needs to be reformed? If so, how?

Information

In most states, a defendant will proceed to trial for a misdemeanor based on a prosecutor's **information,** which details the nature and circumstances of the charge. The information is a formal criminal charge filed with the court by the prosecutor without the aid of a preliminary hearing or a grand jury. It is based on the evidence a prosecutor collects during his or her preliminary investigation that suggests that the defendant in custody committed the crime in question. A defendant charged with a misdemeanor is not entitled to a preliminary hearing or a subsequent grand jury review. A few states use the information system in felony prosecutions as well.

information a prosecuting attorney's formal accusation of the defendant, detailing the nature and circumstances of the charge

▼ Prosecutors conduct preliminary investigations to determine whether the defendant committed the crime. *What is included in the prosecutor's information?*

Dave and Les Jacobs/Getty Images

Bail Hearing

The following people have been arrested and charged with a variety of crimes. For each case, decide whether the person should be released and, if so, under what conditions: (1) bail (release after a certain amount of money is paid; set an amount), (2) personal recognizance (release with no money), (3) conditional release (release under certain conditions; set the conditions), or (4) pretrial detention (no release).

Case 1

Name: Marta Garcia   Age: 26
Charge: Possession of crack cocaine
Residence: 619 30th Street; lives alone; no family or references.
Employment: Unemployed
Education: 11th grade
Criminal record: As a juvenile, five arrests, mostly misdemeanors. As an adult, two arrests for petty larceny and a conviction for possession of dangerous drugs. Probation was successfully completed.
Comment: Arrested while leaving a train station with a large quantity of crack cocaine. Urine test indicates use of narcotics.

Case 2

Name: Gloria Hardy   Age: 23
Charge: Prostitution
Residence: 130 Riverside Drive, Apt. 10; lives with female roommates.
Employment: Call girl; earns $2,500 per week.
Education: Completed high school.
Criminal record: Five arrests for prostitution, two convictions. Currently on probation.
Comment: Allegedly involved in prostitution catering to wealthy clients.

Case 3

Name: Stanley A. Wexler   Age: 42
Charge: Possession and sale of crack cocaine
Residence: 3814 Sunset Drive; lives with wife and two children.
Employment: Self-employed owner of a drugstore chain; annual salary $400,000
Education: Completed college; holds degrees in pharmacy and business administration.
Criminal record: None
Comment: Arrested at his store by undercover police after attempting to sell a large quantity of crack cocaine. Alleged to be a big-time dealer. No indication of drug usage.

Case 4

Name: Michael D. McKenna   Age: 19
Charge: Assault
Residence: 412 Pine Street; lives alone; parents are in prison.
Employment: Waiter; earns $400 per week
Education: 10th grade
Criminal record: Six juvenile arrests (possession of marijuana, illegal possession of firearms, and four burglaries); convicted of firearms charge and two burglaries; spent two years in juvenile facility.
Comment: Arrested after being identified as assailant in a street fight. Alleged leader of a street gang. Police consider him dangerous. No indication of drug usage.

Case 5

Name: Chow Yang   Age: 34
Charge: Possession of stolen mail and forgery
Residence: 5361 Texas Street; lives with his wife and two children by a prior marriage.
Employment: Works 30 hours per week at a service station; earns minimum wage.
Education: 8th grade
Criminal record: Nine arrests, mostly vagrancy and drunk and disorderly conduct. Two convictions: (1) driving while intoxicated (fined and lost license) and (2) forgery (completed two years' probation).
Comment: Arrested attempting to cash a stolen Social Security check. Has a drinking problem.

Preliminary Hearing

A **preliminary hearing** is a screening process used in about half of the states. It is used in felony cases to determine whether there is enough evidence to require the defendant to stand trial. At a preliminary hearing, the prosecutor is required to establish before a judge that a crime probably has been committed and that the defendant probably did it.

In most of these states, the defendant has the right to be represented by an attorney, to cross-examine prosecution witnesses, and to call favorable witnesses. If enough evidence supports the prosecutor's case, the defendant will proceed to trial. If the judge finds no probable cause to believe that a crime was committed or that the defendant committed it, the case may be dismissed. However, dismissal of a case at the preliminary hearing does not always mean that the case is over. The prosecution may still submit the case to a grand jury for further review of the charges.

preliminary hearing pretrial proceeding at which the prosecutor must prove that a crime was committed and establish the probable guilt of the defendant. If the evidence presented does not show probable guilt, the judge may dismiss the case.

Grand Jury

A **grand jury** is a group of 16–23 people charged with determining whether there is sufficient cause to believe that a person has committed a crime and should stand trial. The Fifth Amendment to the U.S. Constitution requires that before anyone can be tried for a serious crime in federal court, there must be a grand jury **indictment,** or formal charge of criminal action. About half of the states regularly use grand juries instead of a preliminary hearing for serious crimes to determine the probability that a particular defendant committed the alleged crime. Some states utilize both procedures.

To secure an indictment, a prosecutor presents evidence to convince members of the grand jury that a crime has been committed and that there is probable cause to believe that the defendant committed it. Neither the defendant nor his or her attorney has a right to appear before a grand jury. A judge is not present and rules of evidence do not apply. The prosecutor is not required to present all the evidence or call all the witnesses as long as the grand jury is satisfied that the evidence presented amounts to probable cause. The proceeding is secret, not public.

Historically, the grand jury—standing between the accuser and the accused—was seen as a guardian of the rights of the innocent. If a majority of the grand jurors do not believe that sufficient evidence has been presented, no indictment will be issued, and the complaint against the defendant will be dismissed. In some instances, the grand jury system has protected citizens from being harassed by the government. Grand juries at both the state and federal level are also used to investigate organized crime and public corruption cases. In some states, grand juries also investigate civil matters such as the condition of prisons and the monitoring of elections.

grand jury a group of 16 to 23 people who hear preliminary evidence to decide whether there is sufficient reason to formally charge a person with a crime

indictment a grand jury's formal charge or accusation of criminal action

THE Constitution

"No person shall be held to answer for a capital or otherwise infamous crime, unless on presentment or indictment of a Grand Jury...."

— Fifth Amendment

Think about the pros and cons of the grand jury system. Should the grand jury system be kept as is, changed, or discarded? Explain your answer.

Felony Arraignment and Pleas

After an indictment or information is issued, the defendant is required to appear in court to enter a plea. If the defendant pleads guilty, the judge will set a date for sentencing. If the defendant pleads not guilty, the judge will set a date for trial and ask whether the defendant wants a jury trial or a trial before a judge alone, called a "bench trial."

nolo contendere Latin phrase meaning "no contest"; a defendant's plea to criminal charges that does not admit guilt but also does not contest the charges. It is the equivalent to a guilty plea, but cannot be used as evidence in a later civil trial for damages based on the same facts.

pretrial motion a document by which a party asks the judge to make a decision or take some action before the trial begins

Nolo contendere is a plea in which the defendant does not admit guilt but also does not contest the charges. It is equivalent to pleading guilty. The only advantage of this plea to the defendant is that it cannot be used as evidence in a later civil trial for damages based on the same set of facts. After such a plea, there is no trial. Instead, the defendant proceeds directly to the sentencing phase.

Pretrial Motions

An important preliminary proceeding is the **pretrial motion.** A motion is a formal request that a court make a ruling or take some other action. Prior to trial, a defendant may file motions seeking to have the case dismissed, to examine certain evidence in possession of the state, to postpone the trial to a later date, to change the location (venue) of the trial, or to suppress certain evidence.

▶ One common pretrial motion is a request to change the location of the trial. _How might media attention influence a trial and its outcome?_

Exactstock/Superstock

The Exclusionary Rule

The Fourth Amendment protects citizens against "unreasonable searches and seizures" by the government. But it does not say what happens if the police violate the amendment. To give force to the amendment, the Supreme Court has interpreted it as requiring an **exclusionary rule.** This rule states that any evidence illegally seized by law enforcement officials cannot be used to convict the accused at trial. It also applies to evidence obtained from illegal questioning of the accused.

The exclusionary rule is used by criminal defense lawyers when they file a motion to suppress evidence. This motion asks the court to exclude any evidence that was illegally obtained. If the judge agrees that the evidence was obtained in violation of the accused's constitutional rights, it will be suppressed. However, this does not mean the evidence is returned to the defendant. For example, if the police illegally seize contraband, such as marijuana, it cannot be used at trial, but the marijuana will not be given back to the defendant. In fact, illegally obtained evidence or confessions may be used at other stages of the process, such as a probable cause or sentencing hearing.

The exclusionary rule has been used in federal courts since 1914. However, the rule was not extended to state courts until the 1961 Supreme Court case *Mapp* v. *Ohio*. This famous case applied the exclusionary rule to the states. Over the years since the Mapp decision, courts have modified and reevaluated the exclusionary rule, but the basic premise remains.

The exclusionary rule does not prevent the arrest or trial of a suspect. However, in some cases, it does mean that people who committed a crime might go free. This could happen because when an important piece of evidence is excluded from the trial, the prosecutor may not have enough other evidence to obtain a conviction. As a result, the case might be dropped or the defendant might be acquitted.

The exclusionary rule is very controversial. Many people claim that it is a legal loophole that allows dangerous criminals to go free. They also point out that many other countries have no such rule; instead, those countries punish the police for violating citizens' rights. Others say the rule is necessary to safeguard our rights and to prevent police misconduct. The two major arguments in support of the rule are judicial integrity and deterrence. **Judicial integrity** is the idea that courts should not be parties to lawbreaking by the police. **Deterrence** means that police will be less likely to violate a citizen's rights if they know that illegally seized evidence will be thrown out of court.

As a practical matter, police are sometimes more concerned with arrests than with convictions. They might make arrests primarily to seize contraband, to gather information, or to disrupt criminal activity, regardless of whether the evidence can legitimately be used to convict the suspect of a crime.

In recent years, the U.S. Supreme Court has decided several cases that have established a "good faith" exception to the exclusionary rule. This means that if police act in good faith—even if there is a minor flaw in following correct procedure—the

exclusionary rule a legal rule that generally prohibits the use of illegally obtained evidence against the defendant at trial; generally applies to violations of a defendant's Fourth, Fifth, and Sixth Amendment rights

judicial integrity as used in discussing search and seizure, this is an argument for the use of the exclusionary rule, which emphasizes that courts should not permit lawbreaking by the police

deterrence measures taken to discourage illegal actions

▼ The police must be sure that evidence is acquired legally. *Why is the exclusionary rule controversial?*

Landmark Supreme Court Cases

Visit the Landmark Supreme Court Cases website at **landmark-cases.org** for information and activities about *Mapp v. Ohio*.

evidence will be admissible. In one of these cases, police officers were handed an improper warrant by a magistrate and they used it to search. In another case, an officer believed he could stop a car for having one tail light out, even though the actual state law required both lights to be out. In both cases, the Supreme Court said that reasonable mistakes of either fact or law should not bar the use of evidence obtained by police. The key, according to the Court, was that the officers acted reasonably.

PROBLEM 13.3

a. What is the exclusionary rule? How does it work?

b. Why do you think the Supreme Court adopted the exclusionary rule? What are some arguments in favor of the rule? Against the rule? Do you favor or oppose the rule? Explain your answer.

c. What is the good faith exception to the exclusionary rule? What are some arguments in favor of the good faith exception? Against it?

Plea Bargaining

Contrary to popular belief, most criminal cases—more than 90 percent—never go to trial. Rather, most defendants who are charged with a crime plead guilty before trial. In minor cases, such as traffic violations, the procedure for pleading guilty is simple. The defendant signs a form waiving the right to appear in court and mails the court a check for the amount of the fine. In major cases, guilty pleas result from a process of negotiation among the person accused of the crime, the defense attorney, and the prosecutor.

This process is known as **plea bargaining.** It involves granting certain concessions to the defendant in exchange for a plea of guilty. Typically, the prosecution will allow the defendant to plead guilty to a less serious charge or recommend a lighter sentence on the original charge in exchange for a guilty plea. Because prosecutors are often burdened with heavy caseloads, they have an incentive to offer a plea bargain to a defendant in order to save the time, cost, and uncertainty involved in a trial.

plea bargaining in a criminal case, the negotiations between the prosecutor, defendant, and defendant's attorney. In exchange for the defendant agreeing to plead guilty, the prosecutor agrees to charge the defendant with a less serious crime, which usually results in a reduced punishment

Defense attorneys are important in any negotiation of a guilty plea. They must consult with their clients and agree only to what the clients want. Low-income defendants who have public defenders or court-appointed attorneys may be at a disadvantage, as these attorneys may not have the same amount of time to work on their cases as do private attorneys.

When accepting a guilty plea, the judge must decide whether the plea was made freely, voluntarily, and with knowledge of all the facts. A judge has the power to reject a plea. Thus, once a defendant pleads guilty, withdrawing the guilty plea and appealing the subsequent conviction are very difficult.

Plea bargaining is controversial. Critics charge that plea bargaining allows dangerous criminals to get off with light sentences. People more concerned with the plight of the defendant argue that the government should be forced to prove guilt beyond a reasonable doubt at trial.

They say that a prosecutor with a weak case can use the plea bargaining system to unfairly influence a defendant to accept a lesser charge in lieu of risking a longer sentence if he or she is convicted at trial. Finally, victims of crime argue that their rights are completely overlooked in the plea bargaining process that occurs between the prosecutor and the defendant.

Some jurisdictions have abolished or limited plea bargaining. Supporters of plea bargaining argue that without it, the criminal justice system will be overwhelmed by the number of cases coming to trial. Others say that eliminating plea bargaining will provide greater justice because the government will drop (not prosecute) weak cases, and defendants will still plead guilty when the government's case is very strong.

A plea bargain is really a contract between the prosecutor and the defendant. If the defendant fails to live up to the terms of this contract—for example, by not testifying against a co-defendant—the prosecutor can withdraw the plea bargain offer. Similarly, if the prosecutor fails to live up to the terms of the agreement, the defendant can ask the judge to reinstate the plea bargain.

Investigating the Law Where You Live

Research to find out whether plea bargaining is used where you live.

PROBLEM 13.4

a. Should plea bargaining be allowed? Do you think plea bargaining offers greater advantages to the prosecutor or to the defendant? Explain the reasons for your answer.

b. Do you think anyone accused of a crime would plead guilty if he or she were really innocent? Explain your answer.

▼ Many cases conclude with a plea bargain and never go to trial. *How does the process of plea bargaining work?*

Comstock/Getty Images

▶ Persons accused of a crime have a right to a trial.

due process the idea stated in the Fifth and Fourteenth Amendments that every person involved in a legal dispute is entitled to a fair hearing or trial. The requirements of due process vary with the situation, but they require at a minimum notice and an opportunity to be heard.

The idea of **due process** of law, or fair procedures, means little to the average citizen unless and until he or she is arrested and charged with a crime. The reason is that many of the basic rights set out in the U.S. Constitution apply to people accused of crimes. Accused people are entitled to have a jury trial in public and, without undue delay, to be informed of their rights and of the charges against them, to confront and cross-examine witnesses, to compel witnesses to testify on their behalf, to refuse to testify against themselves, and to be represented by an attorney. These rights are the essence of due process of law. Taken together, they make up the overall right to a fair trial.

Right to Trial by Jury

The right to a jury trial in criminal cases is guaranteed by the Sixth Amendment to the U.S. Constitution. It is applicable in all federal and state courts. However, a jury is not required in every case. In fact, juries are not used very often.

moodboard/Getty Images

Most criminal cases are resolved by guilty pleas before ever reaching trial. Jury trials are also not required for certain minor offenses—generally, those punishable by less than six months in prison. Furthermore, defendants can **waive**, or give up, their right to a jury trial and instead have their cases heard by a judge in a bench trial. In some states, waivers occur in the majority of cases that are tried.

Jury panels are selected from voter registration or tax lists and are supposed to be generally representative of the local community. In some communities potential jurors are selected from drivers' license rolls. In federal courts, juries consist of 12 persons. While many states also use 12-person juries, they are not required to do this by the U.S. Constitution. The U.S. Supreme Court requires only that trials in state court have at least six jurors. Juries in federal courts must reach a unanimous verdict before finding a person guilty. Similarly, most states require unanimous verdicts in criminal cases, but the Court, in interpreting the Constitution, has not required unanimous verdicts in criminal cases that are tried in state courts.

Once the potential jurors for a case are assembled, the prosecutor and defense lawyer select the members of the jury through a process called **voir dire**. This is the process by which lawyers select jurors to hear a case. They do this by asking prospective jurors questions to determine possible bias. Either lawyer can request that a potential juror be eliminated for some specific reason by using a **for-cause challenge**. A for-cause challenge could be used, for example, if a juror knew the defendant or the victim. Each side also has a limited number of **peremptory challenges**, which do not have to be based on a specific reason. In some cases each party hires consultants to help them make judgments about which prospective jurors are most likely to be favorable to their side.

The Supreme Court has ruled in a number of cases that attorneys may not exclude prospective jurors from serving on a jury solely because of their race, gender, or national origin. Preventing discrimination in the selection of jurors has been a challenge for the justice system. Supreme Court decisions indicate that criminal trials with juries selected in a discriminatory manner harm the defendant, injure the persons removed from the jury for discriminatory reasons, and damage society in general. The Sixth Amendment right to trial by jury is considered a basic constitutional right in the United States. Citizen involvement in the criminal justicce system is a value of our democracy. Most countries around the world, however, do not have jury trials.

waive to give up some right, privilege, or benefit voluntarily

voir dire from the French phrase meaning "to speak the truth." It is the screening process in which opposing lawyers question prospective jurors to ensure as favorable or as fair a jury as possible

for-cause challenge a lawyer's request that a potential juror be eliminated for some specific reason, for example, if a juror knew the defendant or the victim in the case

peremptory challenge part of the pretrial jury selection. Attorneys on opposing sides may dismiss a limited number of possible jurors without giving any reason. There is one exception: peremptory challenges cannot be used to discriminate based on race.

PROBLEM 14.1

a. Why is the right to a jury trial guaranteed by the Bill of Rights? Why might someone choose not to have a jury trial?

b. Do you think jury verdicts should be unanimous? Why or why not?

c. Do you think juries should deliberate and come to a conclusion in private, or should this proceeding be televised and made public? Explain.

"In all criminal prosecutions, the accused shall enjoy the right to a speedy and public trial, by an impartial jury of the State and district wherein the crime shall have been committed..."

—Sixth Amendment

Right to a Speedy and Public Trial

The Sixth Amendment to the U.S. Constitution provides a right to a *speedy* trial in all criminal cases. The Constitution does not define speedy, and courts have had trouble deciding what this means. To remedy this problem, the federal government and some states have set specific time limits within which a case must be brought to trial. Without the right to a speedy trial as an element of due process, an innocent person could await trial—in jail—for years.

If a person does not receive a speedy trial, the case may be dismissed. However, defendants often waive their right to a speedy trial because of the unavailability of an important witness or because they need more time to prepare their cases. In addition, pretrial motions made by the defendant can delay the start of the trial—sometimes for years. Before dismissing a case, courts will consider the cause and reasons for the delay and whether the defendant was free on bail or in jail during the pretrial period.

PROBLEM 14.2

a. Why is the right to a speedy trial important?

b. How soon after arrest should a person be brought to trial? What are some reasons for and against bringing a defendant to trial quickly?

c. Do you think that televising criminal trials is a good idea? Explain.

FYI For Your Information

Jury Nullification

Jurors and juries have a great deal of power in the U.S. legal system. Some see the jury box, like the ballot box, as an essential element of democracy and as a check on the government.

Juries determine the facts provided at trial and apply the law based on instructions from the judge. However, there is a long history in the United States of juries sometimes disregarding the law and the judges' instructions when they believe they must do so in the interest of justice. This disregard is called jury nullification. For example, during the nineteenth century, some juries refused to convict people who hid runaway slaves, even though it was illegal to do so at that time. Today, juries sometimes refuse to convict when they believe a law is unfair or is being unfairly enforced.

While legal scholars acknowledge the history of jury nullification in the United States, some experts believe that expanded use of this extraordinary power could lead to an undermining of the rule of law. Others argue that it is an effective way for citizens in a democracy to check government abuse of power.

Right to Compulsory Process and to Confront Witnesses

Defendants in criminal cases have a right to compulsory process for obtaining witnesses. This means that the defendant can get a **subpoena**—a court order—requiring a witness to appear in court to testify. Without this basic right, defendants would have great difficulty establishing a defense.

The Sixth Amendment provides people accused of crimes with the right to confront (be face to face with) the witnesses against them and to ask them questions by way of cross-examination. Although a defendant has the right to be present in the courtroom during all stages of the trial, the U.S. Supreme Court has said that this right may be restricted if the defendant becomes disorderly or disruptive. In such instances, a judge has the power to remove the defendant from the courtroom, to cite him or her for **contempt of court**, or, in extreme circumstances, to have the defendant bound and gagged.

The right to confrontation is sometimes modified for child witnesses, especially in abuse cases. Many courts in these cases install closed-circuit television cameras. This practice enables the child to testify on camera in a room separate from the one in which the defendant is located and reduces the potential for additional harm to the child.

THE Constitution

"In all criminal prosecutions, the accused shall enjoy the right...to be confronted with the witnesses against him; to have compulsory process for obtaining witnesses in his favor, and to have the Assistance of Counsel for his defence."

—Sixth Amendment

subpoena a court order to appear in court or turn over documents on a specified date and time

contempt of court any act to embarrass, hinder, or obstruct the court in the administration of justice

THE **CASE** OF...

The Tape-Recorded Witness Statement

Crawford and his wife went to a man's apartment, where a fight broke out between Crawford and the man. The man was stabbed during the fight, after which he called the police. Crawford was arrested later that night. The police interrogated him and his wife separately. Crawford claimed that the man had attempted to rape his wife and that he acted in self-defense. His wife's story, which the police tape-recorded, did not match his. Crawford was eventually tried and convicted of attempted murder. State law where he lived did not allow one spouse to testify in a criminal case against the other spouse without that spouse's consent. Crawford did not agree to have his wife testify at his trial. However, the prosecutor played a tape-recording of what she told police. On appeal, Crawford argued that use of this tape recording violated his Sixth Amendment right to confront a witness against him because there was no way to cross-examine the recording.

PROBLEM 14.3

a. What are the strongest arguments for Crawford?

b. What are the strongest arguments for the state?

c. How should this case be decided?

Freedom From Self-Incrimination

Freedom from self-incrimination means that you cannot be forced to testify against yourself in a criminal trial. This right comes from the Fifth Amendment and can be exercised in all criminal cases. Defense attorneys may counsel their clients not to take the stand for their own protection. In addition, the prosecutor is forbidden to make any statement drawing the jury's attention to the defendant's refusal to testify. While defendants in a criminal case have a right not to testify, they also have a right to take the stand and testify if they wish. (In some other countries, defendants in criminal cases are required to testify.) A defendant does not have to answer an inappropriate question if her attorney objects to it and the judge sustains, or agrees with, that objection. If the defendant takes the stand, the prosecutor will be able to cross examine the witness, point out inconsistent statements, and generally try to impeach the defendant's credibility.

Related to the constitutional right against self-incrimination is the concept of **immunity**. Being granted immunity means that a witness cannot be prosecuted based on information provided in a testimony. A person with immunity must answer all questions—even those that are incriminating. Prosecutors often use immunity laws to force people to testify against codefendants or others involved in the crime.

immunity freedom from; protection from some action, such as being sued or prosecuted

indigent term used to describe a defendant who does not have the financial means to hire an attorney

---

PROBLEM 14.4

a. Suppose you are a defense attorney. What are the advantages and disadvantages of having a criminal defendant testify at trial?

b. If you were a member of the jury in a criminal trial, what would you think if the defendant refused to testify? Would you be affected by the judge's instruction not to draw any conclusion from this?

c. If a defendant is forced to stand in a lineup, give a handwriting sample, or take an alcohol breath or urine test, does this violate the privilege against self-incrimination?

d. Do you think that U.S. law should be changed so that defendants are required to testify in criminal cases? Explain.

Landmark Supreme Court Cases

Visit the Landmark Supreme Court Case website at landmarkcases.org for information and activities about *Gideon* v. *Wainwright.*

Right to an Attorney

The Sixth Amendment provides that "In all criminal prosecutions, the accused shall enjoy the right to . . . have the Assistance of Counsel for his defence." At one time, this meant that, except in capital cases—those involving the death penalty or life imprisonment—a defendant had the right to an attorney only if he or she could afford one. However, in 1938, the U.S. Supreme Court decided a case that required the federal courts to appoint attorneys for **indigent** defendants—those without financial means—in all federal felony cases.

Twenty-five years later, in the case of *Gideon* v. *Wainwright* (1963), the Court extended the right to counsel to all felony defendants, whether in state or federal court. In 1972, the Court further extended this ruling by requiring that no imprisonment may occur, even in misdemeanor cases, unless the accused is given an opportunity to be represented by an attorney.

The right to the assistance of counsel is basic to the idea of a fair trial. In a criminal trial, the state (the people) is represented by a prosecutor who is a lawyer. In addition, the prosecutor's office has other resources, including investigators, to help prepare the case against the accused. At a minimum, the defendant needs a skillful lawyer to ensure a fair trial.

As a result of these Supreme Court decisions, criminal defendants who cannot afford an attorney have one appointed to them free of charge by the government. These attorneys may be either public defenders or private attorneys. The public defender's office is supported by the government. The job of the public defender's office is to represent poor people in criminal cases. Private lawyers appointed by the court to handle criminal cases for indigent defendants are typically paid less than private lawyers hired directly by a defendant. Many public defenders are highly skilled and have a great deal of experience handling criminal defense cases. Some people criticize the overall quality of representation that poor criminal defendants receive in this country. These critics say that criminal defendants with money to hire their own lawyers have a much better chance of being found not guilty than do economically disadvantaged defendants.

▲ It is important for a criminal defendant to have a skillful defense attorney. *In what ways can an attorney help a defendant prepare for trial?*

Investigating the Law Where You Live

Find out if there is a public defender where you live. If not, how does the state provide legal representation for indigent defendants? How well does this system work in terms of ensuring justice?

PROBLEM 14.5

a. Assume a defendant wants to handle his or her own defense. Should this be allowed? Do you think this is a good idea?

b. Assume a lawyer knows that his or her client is guilty. Is it right for the lawyer to try to convince the jury the person is not guilty? Explain.

Criminal Appeals

If the jury returns with a "not guilty" verdict, this is normally the end of the case. The state—or prosecution—cannot appeal after the defendant has been acquitted of the offenses for which he or she was tried. The Fifth Amendment's **double jeopardy** language means that a defendant cannot be prosecuted a second time for the same offense after either an acquittal or a conviction. If the verdict is "guilty," then the sentencing will follow. While a defendant cannot be prosecuted twice for the same crime by one state, it is possible for the federal government—a separate sovereign—to prosecute a defendant charged with a state crime in the same facts in federal court if those facts also constituted a federal crime.

double jeopardy a defendant cannot be prosecuted a second time for the same crime. This limit on government power is based on the Fifth Amendment.

ThinkStock/SuperStock

"The privilege of the writ of habeas corpus shall not be suspended, unless when in cases of rebellion or invasion the public safety may require it."

—Article I, Section 9, Clause 2

mistrial the termination of a trial before its normal conclusion because of procedural error, statements by a witness, judge, or attorney which prejudice a jury, a deadlock by a jury without reaching a verdict after lengthy deliberation (a "hung jury"), or the failure to complete a trial within the time set by the court. A new trial must be ordered and the case starts over from the beginning.

petitioner one who signs and/or files a petition. The party initiating or appealing a case to the Supreme Court is referred to as the petitioner.

appellant one who signs or files an appeal of a trial decision

respondent the party that wins the case and has to respond to the appeal to the higher court by the petitioner

writ a judge's order, or authorization, for something to be done

habeas corpus Latin for "you have the body"; a writ (court order) which directs the law enforcement officials who have custody of a prisoner to appear in court with the prisoner to help the judge determine whether the prisoner is being held lawfully

Once the trial judge has entered the final judgment in the case, defendants who think they have been wrongly convicted have several options. The defendant can ask the judge to overturn the jury's verdict and enter a verdict of not guilty, or he or she can ask the judge to set aside the jury's verdict, declare a **mistrial**, and ask for a new trial. These strategies are seldom successful. The defendant can also appeal to a higher court. An appeal requests that a higher court review and change the decision of the trial court. In the appeal, the defendant can challenge either the conviction or the sentencing decision.

Sometimes the defendant will want to hire a different lawyer for the appeal. This happens because lawyers who do trial work may not specialize in appellate work. It might also happen because the defendant's appeal may be based on an alleged violation of the Sixth Amendment, which guarantees the right to effective assistance of counsel. Depending on the resources available, the public defender's office may or may not be available to provide assistance to indigent defendants who wish to appeal.

Trial courts determine questions of fact, such as guilty or not guilty in a criminal case, and appellate courts determine questions of law. In order to win an appeal, the side that lost at the trial—now called the **petitioner** or **appellant**—must convince the appeals court that there were serious errors of law made at the original trial. On appeal, the side that won at trial is called the **respondent** or appellant. Appeals courts tend to defer to trial judges and are not usually eager to overturn the result of the trial. If there are legal errors of a minor nature, the outcome of the trial will not be changed. Sometimes an appeals court will say that the constitutional right of the defendant is to a fair trial, not to a perfect, or error-free, trial.

In addition to appeals, the defendant may apply to a court for help by seeking a **writ**, which is an order from a higher court to either a lower court or to a government official, such as the warden of a jail or prison. The writ of **habeas corpus**—which literally means "to produce the body"—claims that a defendant is being held illegally and requests release. The writ can sometimes be used when an appeal could not be. For example, a defendant might use a writ to argue for his innocence based on DNA testing that occurred after the trial, a point that could not be made using an appeal.

The writ of habeas corpus can be filed with a state court for alleged state law violations or with a federal court for alleged violations of federal law. The writ of habeas corpus gives criminal defendants the right to ask for relief from confinement, but of course filing this writ does not necessarily mean that the court will grant the relief. Post-conviction procedures can vary from state to state.

► Imprisonment is just one of several sentencing options.

The final phase of the criminal justice process begins with sentencing. When found guilty, the defendant will be sentenced by the judge or, in a few states, by the jury. The sentence is perhaps the most critical decision in the criminal justice process. It can determine a defendant's fate for years or, in some cases, for life.

Sentencing Options

Most criminal statutes set out a basic sentencing structure, but judges generally have considerable freedom in determining the actual type, length, and conditions of the sentence. Depending on the state, judges may choose from one or a combination of the following options:

- A **suspended sentence** is given but does not have to be served at the time it is imposed. The defendant may have to serve the sentence later if he or she is rearrested on another charge or violates a condition of probation.

- The defendant can be released on **probation** under the supervision of a probation officer after agreeing to meet certain conditions, such as getting a job, staying drug-free, or not traveling outside the area during the probation period.

suspended sentence a sentence issued by the court but not actually served. The individual is usually released by the court with no conditions attached.

probation a system of supervised freedom, usually by a probation officer, for persons convicted of a criminal offense. Typically, the probationer must agree to certain conditions such as getting a job, avoiding drugs, and not traveling outside a limited area.

home confinement the type of sentence in which the defendant must serve the term at home and usually can leave only for essential purposes, such as work or school

fine a monetary penalty imposed upon someone

restitution the act of restoring something to its owner; the act of making good for loss or damage; repaying or refunding illegally obtained money or property

work release the type of sentence in which a defendant is allowed to work in the community but is required to return to prison at night or on weekends

death penalty a sentence to death for commission of a serious crime, such as murder

- Under **home confinement**, the defendant is sentenced to serve the term at home. Normally, the only time this defendant can leave the home is for essential purposes such as work, school, or a doctor's appointment. The defendant is sometimes required to wear an electronic monitoring device so that his or her activities can be observed by the probation officer.

- The defendant might be required to pay the government a **fine**, or an amount of money set by the court.

- A defendant who is required to pay **restitution** must make up for whatever loss or injury was caused to the victim of the crime.

- Under **work release**, the defendant is allowed to work in the community but must return to prison at night or on weekends.

- A defendant who is imprisoned must serve a term in jail or prison. Some states require that a definite sentence be given, in which case the judge specifies the exact amount of time to be served, for example, two years. Some states provide for an indeterminate term, in which case the sentence is stated as a minimum and maximum term, for example, not less than three years nor more than ten years. Some judges allow defendants in misdemeanor cases to serve short jail sentences on weekends.

- If the defendant is sentenced to die for his or her crime, it is called a death penalty. In some states and in the federal court system, judges have the option of handing down the **death penalty** for the most serious offenses. This controversial issue is discussed later in this chapter.

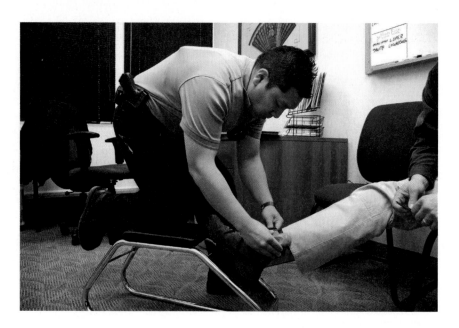

▶ Electronic monitoring devices are often used for home confinement. *What are the advantages and disadvantages of such a sentence?*

THE **CASE** OF...

The Three Strikes Law

California lawmakers passed the "Three Strikes" Law in March 1994, following the high-profile kidnapping and murder of 12-year-old Polly Klaas. Her abductor was a violent offender out on parole, living in the Klaas family's community. Outraged by this awful crime and eager for the legislature to get tougher on crime, California voters overwhelmingly approved Proposition 184. This law was designed to deter offenders from committing new crimes by requiring longer prison terms for criminals who had been convicted of felonies in the past. By the late 1990s, about 40 states had some form of recidivist statute, a law designed specifically to punish serious repeat offenders.

Under California's Three Strikes Law, a "strike" is a conviction for a serious or violent felony. When a defendant has one strike, conviction for the second strike results in doubling the usual sentence for that crime. If a defendant is convicted of a third felony, the law requires that he or she receive a sentence of at least 25 years to life, with no possibility of parole before 25 years.

While strikes one and two must be for serious or violent felonies, *any felony conviction* will qualify as the third strike, whether or not the felony was serious or violent. In addition, certain offenses (called "wobblers") can be prosecuted as either misdemeanors or felonies, at the discretion of the prosecutor or the judge. Finally, the Three Strikes Law is retroactive and is not limited to crimes committed in California. Therefore, convictions from before the law was passed (1994) or in other states can count as strikes.

In November 1995, Leandro Andrade attempted to steal five G-rated videotapes but was arrested upon leaving the store. Two weeks later, Andrade was arrested outside another store for attempting to steal more videotapes. The total value of all the tapes was approximately $150. Andrade, a longtime heroin addict, had a 15-year criminal history with five felonies and two misdemeanors on his record. None of the previous convictions were for violent offenses. Prosecutors determined that he already had two strikes under the California law when the prosecution for the most recent thefts commenced. Under California law, petty theft with a prior conviction is one of the so-called wobblers, misdemeanors that can be prosecuted as felonies. Andrade, then 37, was convicted and sentenced to 25 years to life for *each* of the two petty theft counts (strikes three and four). According to the Three Strikes Law, those sentences must be served consecutively, not concurrently, so Andrade will not become eligible for parole for 50 years.

A federal appeals court found his sentence "grossly disproportionate" to the crime and a violation of the Eighth Amendment's prohibition against cruel and unusual punishment. Prosecutors for the state of California appealed to the U.S. Supreme Court.

PROBLEM 15.1

a. Why did California pass the Three Strikes Law? Why do you think these laws have become so popular in the United States?

b. What are the most convincing arguments for upholding Andrade's sentence?

c. What are the most convincing arguments for reversing the sentence?

d. How should the Supreme Court decide the Andrade case? What arguments might the dissenting justices make?

e. As a matter of public policy, do you support or oppose laws like the Three Strikes Law? What information would you need to come to a decision on this matter?

Investigating the Law Where You Live

Research to find out if your state has a special sentencing law for repeat offenders. If so, how does it work?

presentence report a probation officer's written report that gives the sentencing judge information about the defendant's background and prospects for rehabilitation

retribution punishment given as a kind of revenge for wrongdoing

deterrence measure taken to discourage criminal actions; usually some form of punishment. It is the belief that punishment will discourage the offender from committing future crimes and will serve as an example to keep others from committing crimes.

Many considerations must be made in the sentencing process. These include the judge's theory regarding corrections and what he or she believes is in the best interest of society and the individual. In addition, most states authorize a **presentence report**. This report, prepared by the probation department, contains a description of the offense and sets out the circumstances surrounding it. The report also describes the defendant's past criminal record; provides data on the defendant's social, medical, educational, and employment background; and includes a recommended sentence.

The presentence report may also describe the harm to the victim. In many states, victims are given the opportunity to provide the judge with a statement—orally, in writing, or in some instances via videotape—about the impact of the crime. If the victim has been killed, family members are allowed to provide victim impact statements. After receiving the presentence report, victim impact statements, and recommendations from the prosecuting and defense attorneys, the judge will impose the sentence.

Some people criticize the system of sentencing as giving too much discretion to the judge. Two people who commit the same crime may receive very different sentences, which some view as an injustice. To combat the problem of inconsistency in sentencing, the U.S. Congress passed a federal sentencing guideline law in 1988 that listed the sentences that judges were to impose for specific federal crimes. States have since passed similar laws to limit the discretion of judges in sentencing. These guidelines typically determine sentences based on the conduct and the criminal history of the defendant in question, though some guidelines have been challenged as racially based because of differences in punishments for crimes more often committed by white people than those committed by people of color. In reviewing these sentencing laws, the U.S. Supreme Court has said that the guidelines do not create mandatory standards but are only advisory. This means that judges must consider the guidelines in determining sentences, but they retain discretion.

In general, the Supreme Court defers to the legislative branch when reviewing sentencing laws. However, in 2012, the Supreme Court reviewed an Alabama statute and found that mandatory life sentences without the possibility of parole were unconstitutional for juvenile offenders.

Purposes of Punishment

Over the years, the criminal sentence has served a number of different purposes, including retribution, deterrence, rehabilitation, and incapacitation. At one time, the primary reason for punishing a criminal was **retribution**. This is the idea behind the saying "an eye for an eye and a tooth for a tooth." Instead of individuals seeking revenge, society, through the criminal justice system, takes on the role of punishing those who violate its laws.

Another reason for punishing criminals is **deterrence**. Many people believe that punishment discourages the offender from committing

◀ Rehabilitation programs help inmates change their behavior so they can lead productive lives after release. *What kind of education and training should an inmate receive?*

another crime in the future. In addition, the punishment is meant to serve as an example to deter other people from committing similar crimes.

A third goal of punishment is **rehabilitation**, or helping convicted persons change their behavior so that they can lead useful and productive lives after their release. Rehabilitation is based on the idea that criminals can overcome the social, educational, or psychological problems that caused them to commit a crime and that they can be helped to become responsible members of society. Educational, vocational, and counseling programs in prisons and jails are designed to rehabilitate inmates.

A fourth reason for punishment is **incapacitation**. This means that the criminal is physically separated from the community and the community is protected as a result of this incapacitation. While confined in prison, the offender does not pose a threat to the safety of the community.

rehabilitation the process through which a convicted person is changed or reformed, in order to lead a productive life rather than commit another crime

incapacitation a reason for criminal punishment that stresses keeping a convicted person confined to protect society

Parole

In most states, the actual length of time a person serves in prison depends on whether **parole** is granted. Parole is the release of a convicted person from prison before his or her entire sentence has been served. Depending on the state, a person might become eligible for parole after serving a minimum sentence specified by the judge or law. In other states, people automatically become eligible for parole after serving a portion of the total sentence.

Eligibility for parole is not a right but, rather, a privilege. Inmates may go before a parole board that makes the decision. Some inmates are never paroled and serve their full sentences in prison. The federal prison system and some states do not allow for parole.

parole release from prison before the full sentence has been served, granted at the discretion of a parole board

Investigating the Law Where You Live

Has your state abolished parole? Should they do this?

Aaron Roeth Photography

Critics of parole say this is better because it gives certainty to the sentence and improves deterrence. Others believe that inmates should be evaluated periodically and released early if there is evidence that they have been rehabilitated.

pardon order that releases a person from legal punishment

A defendant who receives a **pardon** from the president (for a federal crime) or from a governor (for a state crime) is able to leave confinement. A pardon means, in effect, that the crime did not happen. A sentence can also end when the president or governor **commutes** a sentence which typically means reducing the sentence to time already served.

commute to change sentence to another less severe

As of 2018 there were 2.3 million people in the nation's 3,100 jails and 2,000 prisons. Another 4.5 million people were being supervised in the community on parole or probation. This total represents slightly more than 2 percent of all U.S. residents.

PROBLEM 15.2

With only **5 percent** of the world's population, the United States has approximately **25 percent** of the world's prison population. What are the advantages and disadvantages of policies that lead to such a high rate of incarceration?

Capital Punishment

capital punishment the death penalty; putting a convicted person to death as punishment for a crime

Capital punishment, also known as the death penalty, is the most controversial sentence given to defendants. It has a long history in America. The first person executed for murder among settlers in America was hanged in 1630. In colonial years, the death penalty was imposed for a number of different crimes. Gradually, capital punishment was restricted to the most serious crimes—usually murder and rape. In 1977, however, the U.S. Supreme Court held that the death penalty was an unconstitutional punishment for the crime of rape of an adult. In 2008, the Court found that a state law providing the death penalty for the rape of a *child* was a disproportionate punishment (it did not fit the crime) and a violation of the Eighth Amendment.

The issue of capital punishment has been debated for years. Public protest against the death penalty gradually reduced the number of executions from a peak of 199 in 1935 to only 1 in 1967. For the 10 years after that, executions were halted while the courts studied the legality of capital punishment.

In the 1972 case of *Furman* v. *Georgia*, the U.S. Supreme Court held that the death penalty as then applied was unconstitutional because juries were given too much discretion in assigning this sentence. States then rewrote their capital punishment laws. In 1976, the Court ruled that the new laws were constitutional as long as aggravating and mitigating circumstances were considered. Executions soon resumed.

At the end of 2018, state and federal prisons held about 2,700 inmates on death row. The number of inmates executed has gone down over time. In 2018, 25 people were executed, 23 of them by lethal injection. As of 2018, 31 states and the federal government had the death penalty as a punishment option. Since 1978 when the death penalty was reinstated,

1,481 defendants have been executed (as of August, 2018). In 2018, juries imposed the death penalty in only 39 cases.

In 2007 all executions were temporarily stopped when the Supreme Court agreed to hear a case that challenged lethal injection procedures as cruel and unusual punishment in violation of the Eighth Amendment. Lethal injections resumed in 2008, but cases continue to challenge this method of execution as unreasonably cruel and in violation of the Eighth Amendment.

Most capital punishment laws call for a two-part trial. In part one, the jury decides guilt or innocence. The defendant usually knows whether he or she may face the death penalty if convicted. If the defendant is found guilty, the jury decides in part two of the trial whether the defendant should receive the death penalty or a lesser punishment. Judges and juries are required to consider both aggravating and mitigating circumstances. **Aggravating circumstances** are factors that suggest the defendant deserves a more severe punishment. Examples include a gruesome murder, crimes involving children, or previous convictions of the accused. **Mitigating circumstances** are factors that suggest the defendant deserves a less severe punishment. Examples include the defendant's age, lack of a criminal record, or a history showing that the victim had previously abused the defendant.

Opponents of capital punishment claim that no one who values life can approve of the death penalty. They claim that religious and moral objections to killing also apply to the government's policy of executing criminals. They further argue that the death penalty does not deter murder, citing statistics showing that murder rates are the same or higher in states with the death penalty as in those without it. Opponents also argue that the death penalty is applied in an unfair manner, that members of minority groups are more likely to receive it, and that it violates the Eighth Amendment's ban against "cruel and unusual punishment."

Some arguments against capital punishment point to the fact that there have at times been wrongful convictions, that is, a person who did not commit the crime was convicted and sentenced to death. Much of the proof of wrongful convictions has been based on advances in modern technology, such as the use of DNA evidence.

▲ Capital punishment often occurs in the same facility where the prisoner is incarcerated.

aggravating circumstances factors that tend to increase the seriousness of an offense. The presence of such circumstances must be considered in the sentence.

mitigating circumstances factors that tend to lessen the seriousness of an offense. This presence of these factors must be considered in the sentence.

Investigating the Law Where You Live

Find out if your state has capital punishment. If your state does not have capital punishment, how does it punish those convicted of the most severe crimes?

David R. Frazier Photolibrary, Inc.

In some cases, evidence of innocence was discovered after an execution. In recent years, policy makers have considered how to deal with this problem in light of the possibility—even if remote—that someone might be waiting to be executed for a crime that he or she did not commit.

One approach to dealing with a wrongful conviction is the use of a sentence of life in prison without parole. This sentence protects communities from repeat offenders while preserving the option of freeing a person later found to have been unjustly convicted.

The death penalty existed at the time the Bill of Rights was drafted and ratified. While wanting to prohibit cruel and unusual punishment, it is clear that the Framers did not intend to prohibit capital punishment. Advocates of the death penalty say that it is a just punishment for those who commit the most serious crimes. Advocates also argue that the threat of death does deter crime because people fear death more than any other punishment. In states where capital punishment is not favored by the voters, legislatures can (and have) abolished it. But, proponents argue, the Court should leave it up to the states and not undermine democratic practice by banning the death penalty nationwide.

A national Gallup opinion poll released at the end of 2017 showed an eight point drop in support for the death penalty from one year earlier, with 58 percent in favor for murder convictions. As recently as 1994, 80 percent of Americans supported the death penalty. While overall support for the death penalty has declined, nearly 40 percent of those surveyed have consistently favored greater use of the death penalty. A reliable source of information on the death penalty can be found at the Death Penalty Information Center, www.deathpenaltyinfo.org.

FYI For Your Information

The Innocence Project

National programs such as The Innocence Project (www.innocenceproject.org) focus on exonerating inmates using DNA evidence. These programs also use recanted confessions, new witnesses, DNA analysis, and other new technology to obtain exonerations. Under the supervision of law professors, law students conduct crime scene investigations, gather evidence, interview witnesses, and write briefs and motions that are filed in court. Hundreds of innocent inmates have been released as a result of this work.

The projects have also been involved in reforming the criminal justice system so that fewer innocent people are convicted.

THE CASE OF...

The Death Penalty for Defendants with Intellectual Disabilities and Juvenile Defendants

The following cases present situations in which the death penalty is called into question.

Case 1

Daryl Atkins and an accomplice abducted Eric Nesbitt, robbed him, and drove him to an ATM, where security cameras recorded them forcing him to withdraw more cash. They then took Nesbitt to an isolated location and shot him eight times. Atkins had a history of felony convictions. Both he and his accomplice were convicted of the killing in a Virginia state court.

During the penalty phase of the trial, Atkins's lawyer presented evidence from a psychologist showing that Atkins had a mild intellectual disability. The jury imposed the death penalty and the Virginia Supreme Court upheld the sentence. The case was then appealed to the U.S. Supreme Court. At issue was whether it is a violation of the Eighth Amendment's cruel and unusual punishment clause to impose the death penalty on a person with a mild intellectual disability.

Case 2

In September 1993, Christopher Simmons broke into the suburban St. Louis, Missouri, home of Shirley Crook with the intention to rob and possibly kill her. Simmons and a friend bound the victim's hands and feet with duct tape and drove her to a nearby state park. At the park, Simmons pushed Crook off a bridge and into the Meramec River, where she drowned. Simmons was 17 years old at the time of the murder. Before the crime, he had told several friends about his plan to burglarize a home and kill the occupants, noting that they could do it and "get away with it"—or not be charged with and punished for it—because they were juveniles.

Simmons and his friend were arrested the following day, and Simmons confessed on videotape at the police station. He was found guilty, and his initial appeal to the Missouri Supreme Court resulted in his conviction being affirmed. Several years later, the state supreme court reconsidered the case, concluding that a national consensus opposed execution of juvenile offenders. As a result, the state supreme court reversed Simmons' sentence of death. The state then appealed the case to the U.S. Supreme Court.

PROBLEM 15.3

a. What happened in each of these cases to call the death penalty into question? Why were Daryl Atkins and Christopher Simmons given the death penalty?

b. What are the strongest arguments for upholding the state supreme court decision in each of these cases? What are the strongest arguments for reversing it?

c. Assume there has been a trend in the states not to impose the death penalty in cases involving defendants or juvenile defendants with intellectual disabilities. Should that have any impact on the U.S. Supreme Court's decision? Explain your answer.

d. Assume there has been a trend in other countries not to impose the death penalty in cases involving defendants or juvenile defendants with intellectual disabilities. Should that have any impact on the U.S. Supreme Court's decision? Explain your answer.

e. How should each of these cases be decided by the U.S. Supreme Court? Give reasons for your answer.

▶ Inmates' lives are controlled by many rules. *Should inmates lose all rights when they are sent to prison? If not, which rights should they keep?*

Corrections

Once a person is convicted of a crime, the state or federal government places the offender in the corrections system. Several treatment and punishment options are available, including community corrections, halfway houses, jails, and prisons.

What is the difference between jails and prisons? Jails are run by cities and counties. They are used by local law enforcement officers to detain people awaiting trial and to hold mental patients, drug addicts, alcoholics, juvenile offenders, and felons on a temporary basis as they await transfer to other facilities. Jails also hold people convicted of minor crimes for which the sentence is one year or less. Prisons are operated by federal or state governments. They are used to incarcerate people convicted of more serious crimes, usually felonies, for which the sentence is more than one year.

Life Behind Bars

A prison or jail inmate's life is controlled by rules. Inmates are told when to get up and when to go to sleep. Mail and phone calls are screened. Access to radio, television, the Internet, and books is controlled. Visitation is limited, and inmates are subject to constant surveillance and searches. Some inmates work at prison jobs, which usually pay very little. Others spend almost all day locked in their cells.

Until the 1960s, courts had a hands-off policy toward prisons. Inmates had few, if any, rights. Prison officials could make almost any rules they wanted. As a result, harsh treatment, solitary confinement, and beatings were all fairly common.

Over the years, courts have established and enforced some prisoners' rights, yet the U.S. Supreme Court has often said that people who enter prison must give up certain rights. Still, inmates do retain limited versions of some rights after entering prison. These include the right to be free from cruel and unusual punishment, the right to freedom of religion, the right to due process, the right to medical treatment, and the right to meaningful access to the court.

While inmates still have some access to the courts, the Supreme Court has ruled that they must use all established channels of complaint within the institution before they can ask a court to resolve their issues. The courts are generally reluctant to second-guess administrators in the day-to-day operation of jails and prisons. When a prison rule or practice is challenged by an inmate, judges will usually uphold the prison practice if it is reasonably related to "legitimate penological interests."

Prison Policy

During the 1990s and into the twenty-first century, the number of people incarcerated in the United States increased significantly. The rate of incarceration is six to ten times higher than that of most developed countries. This increase was caused by a get-tough-on-crime policy that resulted in more criminal defendants going to prison for longer periods. An increasing use of mandatory sentences and a lengthening of some prison terms added to prison populations.

With more prisoners entering the correctional system, jail and prison capacity has increased. The cost of expanding existing prisons and building new ones, along with the cost of maintaining the larger number of inmates in prison—estimated to average more than $30,000 per inmate per year—has placed an enormous strain on state and federal budgets. To cut costs, many prison officials have reduced or eliminated inmate education, counseling, recreation, and vocational training programs.

While some voters have cheered the "lock 'em up" philosophy that has led to the increased inmate population, fewer have been as enthusiastic

FIGURE

15.1 Changes in the Criminal Justice System Population*

YEAR	Probation	Jail	Prison	Parole	Total
1990	2,670,234	405,320	743,382	531,407	4,350,300
2001	3,392,751	631,240	1,330,980	731,147	6,592,800
2016**	3,700,000	750,000	1,500,000	840,000	6,790,000

* Federal and state figures are combined.
** 2016 figures are estimates.

Source: U.S. Department of Justice, Bureau of Justice Statistics.

The number of offenders in the criminal justice system has increased over the last 20 years. ANALYZE THE DATA *Can you identify a trend in these numbers?*

about paying the increased costs. Some maintain that the federal and state governments have locked up too many offenders. These critics argue that some of the money spent on prisons would be better spent on prevention and treatment programs, and that some inmates—those convicted of minor drug offenses, for example—should be returned to their communities with supervision and support. Others argue that vigorous prosecution and longer prison terms are the right approach because they have brought a significant reduction in crime, which has led to safer communities. Since 2016, there has been a decline in the number of people in jail or prison and on parole or probation.

PROBLEM 15.4

a. Should prisoners have rights? If so, what rights should they have? Make a list of these rights.

b. If you were a prison warden, what rules would you make to control the prisoners? List these rules.

c. Should the criminal justice system be more selective about who is locked up?

d. Do you support tough-on-crime sentencing or a greater emphasis on community-based treatment and prevention programs? Give your reasons.

Reentering Society

More than 600,000 adult offenders leave prison every year and return to their communities. According to the National Institute of Justice, within three years, more than half of those released from prison become repeat offenders.

The U.S. Department of Justice, working with other federal agencies, started a program called **reentry** designed to reduce serious crime committed by ex-offenders. This initiative targets both adult and juvenile offenders. It has three distinct phases. Phase one programs begin in correctional institutions and focus on providing education, mental health services, substance abuse treatment, job training, and mentoring for convicts to psychologically prepare them to reenter society. Phase two programs focus on the actual transition back into the community, including decisions about where to live, how to find a job, and ways to reestablish ties with members of the community. This phase also provides mental health and substance abuse treatment. The final phase helps link individuals who have left the supervision of the justice system with a network of social services agencies and community-based organizations. These groups can provide long-term support and mentoring relationships between convicts and counselors to help complete the transition back into society.

Planning for successful reentry begins when the defendant enters the correctional system. Reentry programs are important because the overwhelming majority of inmates will at some point return to their communities. Adequate preparation of inmates—and of the community—for reentry can reduce recidivism.

Investigating the Law Where You Live

Is the prison population growing, shrinking, or staying the same in your state? Explain the change if any.

reentry a program created by the U.S. Department of Justice designed to reduce serious crime committed by ex-offenders

▲ Reentry programs provide counseling and long-term support. *What challenges do ex-offenders face in reentering society?*

PROBLEM 15.5

In almost all states, felons lose their right to vote while in prison. In some states that right is automatically restored after a sentence is completed. In other states, the ex-felon must apply for a restoration of voting rights, sometimes after a waiting period of several years after the completion of a sentence. In still other states, felons permanently lose their right to vote.

a. What are the strongest arguments for and against restoring the voting rights of felons after they complete their sentences?

b. A number of democracies around the world allow their prisoners to vote in elections on the theory that this helps with their rehabilitation. Do you support or oppose this policy? Give your reasons.

Investigating the Law Where You Live

Do ex-felons in your state have their voting rights restored? Should they?

Access to Medical Care for Inmates

An estimated 80 percent of inmates are poor, and many are incarcerated with chronic medical problems, mental health problems, or both. According to the World Health Organization, "everyone should have access to health care services they need, when and where they need them, and without suffering financial hardship." (Human Rights Day, 2017) In a 1976 case the U.S. Supreme Court ruled that not providing adequate medical care to prisoners is a violation of the Eighth Amendment's protection against cruel and unusual punishment. But how much care is required for "adequate care"?

Governments pay most of the cost of medical care for inmates, but more than half of the states also allow prisons to charge co-pays for medicine and medical services. Inmates who typically have very little money—and come from families with very limited resources—may have to choose between making a co-payment and purchasing toothpaste.

One reason for the co-pays is to raise revenue in light of the rising cost of health care services. The other reason is to discourage inmates from seeking medical care when it is not really needed. However, co-pays might have the effect of reducing preventive care and, in the context of a confining prison, leading to the spread of disease with ultimately higher costs for the prison.

PROBLEM 15.6

What level of health and mental health services should be provided to inmates? For example should inmates receive an annual physical and as well as regular dental and eyesight screenings?

a. Do you agree or disagree with charging inmates co-pays for health services? Give your reasons.

b. How does access to health care relate to other issues in this chapter (e.g., the decision to incarcerate, re-entry, etc.)?

▶ For serious offenses, youth can be committed to a juvenile institution.

In the United States, juveniles in trouble with the law are treated differently from adults. However, this has not always been the case. In earlier times, children were put into jails along with adults. Long prison terms and corporal punishment, involving striking the juvenile's body, were common. Some children were even sentenced to death for crimes that seem relatively minor by today's standards.

History and Overview of Juvenile Courts

In the mid-nineteenth century, reformers began to argue that the failure of the family was the cause of delinquent behavior. In other words, parents had failed to teach their children proper values and respect for authority. The solution that evolved was for a separate juvenile court to assume the responsibility that had been the parents' job. Instead of punishing young people through the adult system, a separate juvenile court would seek to rehabilitate them by taking a moralistic approach and trying to help them learn community values.

▲ Truancy, or skipping school, is a status offense. *What other acts are considered status offenses?*

parens patriae Latin for "parent of the country"; the doctrine that allows the government to take care of minors and others who cannot legally take care of themselves

delinquent offender a minor who has committed an act that, if committed by an adult, would be a crime under federal, state, or local law. Such offenders are usually processed through the juvenile justice system.

status offender a minor who has committed an act that would not be a crime if committed by an adult, such as truancy from school, running away from home, or being habitually disobedient.

Under this philosophy, the first juvenile court was set up in Cook County, Illinois, in 1899. Juvenile courts were designed to be informal, allowing the court to act as a parent or guardian for the child. The right of the state to intervene in the life of a child is based on the concept of **parens patriae,** a Latin term meaning "parent of the country." Using this concept, the court assumed the role of a parent and was permitted to do whatever it thought was necessary to help the child. Hearings were closed to the public so the youth's identity and personal information would remain private. In addition, the juvenile court used terms different from those used in the adult court. (See the FYI feature "Juvenile and Adult Law Terms.")

Today, juvenile courts generally handle three groups of juveniles: delinquent offenders, status offenders, and neglected or abused children. **Delinquent offenders** are youths who have committed acts that would be crimes if committed by adults under federal, state, or local law. Most of this chapter targets how youth charged as delinquents are treated in the juvenile justice system.

Status offenders are youths who have committed acts that would not be crimes if committed by adults. Status offenses include running away from home, skipping school, violating curfew, refusing to obey parents, or engaging in certain behaviors such as underage consumption of alcohol. Status offenders are considered to be unruly or beyond the control of their parents or legal guardians; they are persons, minors, or children in need of supervision (PINS, MINS, or CHINS).

Neglected or **abused children** need the court's protection from a parent or guardian. A neglect case occurs when a parent or guardian is charged with failing to provide adequate food, clothing, shelter, education, or medical care for the child. An abuse case occurs when a child has been sexually, physically, or emotionally abused. In either case, a judge must decide whether the child needs the protection of the court. The next step is to determine whether the child should remain with the family while under court protection. The judge has several options to choose from and works closely with social service agencies. Such agencies can provide a range of services, including counseling and treatment. The judge usually sets certain conditions for the child to remain with his or her family, such as participation by the parents in a counseling program or a later hearing to monitor the progress of the case. The judge may also decide to place a child with relatives or in foster care.

In most states, juvenile court jurisdiction extends through age 17. A juvenile who reaches the age of majority can be prosecuted only in adult court. However, as discussed later in this chapter, all states have processes in place that allow some juveniles to be tried in adult court under exceptional circumstances mostly related to the severity of the crime.

Since 1899, the juvenile justice system has continued to be defined in part by the tension between a "humanitarian" philosophy that emphasizes rehabilitating the offender and a "control" philosophy that emphasizes punishing the offender. This tension has played a major role in determining the current system's practices. It is important to remember that this system continues to evolve as courts, legislatures, and voters try to resolve the tension between society's sometimes conflicting needs for rehabilitation and punishment of juvenile offenders. While this chapter provides a general overview of juvenile justice, this system varies significantly from state to state.

neglect the failure of a parent or guardian to properly feed, clothe, shelter, educate, or tend to the medical needs of a child

abused children minors who have been sexually, physically, or emotionally mistreated

Investigating the Law Where You Live

Find out the age that juvenile court jurisdiction ends in your state.

PROBLEM 16.1

a. Why did reformers want to change the way children were treated? What steps did reformers take to make changes? When did these changes begin to take place?

b. What is *parens patriae*? Do you agree with this idea? Explain.

c. What is the difference between a delinquent offender and a status offender?

d. Which philosophy—humanitarian or control—is more appropriate for juveniles who have been found delinquent? Should there be a balance between the two? Explain.

e. According to the juvenile justice system, what is considered to be a case of child neglect? What is considered to be child abuse? How are such cases handled?

Juvenile Justice and Delinquency Prevention

The Office of Juvenile Justice and Delinquency Prevention (OJJDP), a part of the U.S. Department of Justice, is a federal agency responsible for addressing the public safety issues of juvenile crime and youth victimization in the United States. It is guided by the *Juvenile Justice and Delinquency Prevention Act*, which was designed to promote greater accountability in the juvenile justice system. Federal funds are available to state and local governments to combat juvenile crime through prevention and intervention programs as well as improvements to the juvenile justice system.

The OJJDP has determined that an effective juvenile justice system should work to do three main things. First, it must ensure the safety of the community at large. Second, it must hold the juvenile offender accountable for his or her delinquent acts. Third, it must enable the juvenile to become a capable, productive, and responsible citizen. Learn more at **www.ojjdp.gov.**

Status Offenses

Status offenders are youth who commit acts that would not be crimes if committed by adults. Special problems arise when the juvenile justice system is confronted with a status offender. Juveniles who fall into this category face charges such as being "beyond control," "habitually disobedient," or truant from school.

Status offenders may be emotionally troubled youth who need medical help, emotional help, or both. Many status offenders are runaways or young people with alcohol or drug problems. Some are trying to escape abusive or other difficult home situations. Many runaway and homeless youth leave home because of conflict with a parent or guardian. Although most runaways return home of their own accord, some are located by a parent, guardian, or friend and persuaded to return home, while others are picked up by the police and referred to the juvenile justice system.

A number of programs have been set up to help runaways. The primary resource for runaway and homeless youth is a national network of shelters. The nationwide toll-free phone number that runaways can call for assistance is 800-RUNAWAY. Those in need may also visit **www.1800RUNAWAY.org.** In addition to shelter, these programs provide other services related to the issues that often cause the youth to run away.

Status offenses make up about 20 percent of all juvenile arrests. Federal law requires that juvenile status offenders be represented in court hearings, but the nature and quality of this representation varies from state to state and presents a major challenge to the juvenile justice system. A number of reform movements attempt to improve legal representation of young people charged with status offenses and to make certain that they are allowed to attend and participate in hearings that affect them.

Investigating the Law Where You Live

Learn more about what programs and resources are available for runaways in your area.

As a general rule, a single act of unruly behavior is not enough to support a finding that a juvenile is in need of court supervision. Rather, most states require proof that the young person is habitually disobedient or has repeatedly run away, skipped school, or been out of control. Some status offenders also commit delinquent acts, and juvenile courts have to struggle to determine how best to treat these youth who cross over into delinquent behavior.

Due to problems at home, parents sometimes ask the court to file a PINS (person in need of supervision) petition against their child. Children charged with status offenses may defend their conduct by showing that it was justified or that the parents were unreasonable and at fault. In such cases, the PINS petition might be withdrawn by the court and replaced by a neglect petition against the parents. The court might also order or refer the families for services.

▲ Many status offenders are runaways. *Where can runaways find help on the streets?*

PROBLEM 16.2

a. Do you think courts should intervene in disputes between parents and children? If not, why not? If so, why and under what circumstances?

b. Should attendance at school be mandatory? Why or why not? What should be done about students who are chronically absent from school?

Ingram Publishing

TAKING ACTION: Law and Democracy

Hearing on a Curfew for Teens

As communities have become concerned about violence by and against young people, teen curfew laws have become more common. Some people welcome the idea of such curfews. Others feel they violate the rights of teens and are unevenly enforced.

PROBLEM 16.3

Read the proposed curfew law:

IT WILL BE AN OFFENSE FOR PERSONS UNDER THE AGE OF 18 TO BE OUT OF THEIR HOMES FROM 10:00 P.M. TO 6:00 A.M. SUNDAY THROUGH THURSDAY NIGHTS. ON FRIDAY AND SATURDAY NIGHTS THE CURFEW SHALL BEGIN AT MIDNIGHT. VIOLATORS WILL BE FINED $100. EXCEPTIONS ARE YOUNG PEOPLE CHAPERONED BY ADULTS, ATTENDING A PLANNED COMMUNITY ACTIVITY, OR TRAVELING TO OR FROM WORK.

▲ A curfew reminder

After reading the law, identify who in the community is likely to oppose the law. Who is likely to support the law? Then divide into six groups:

- **Group one is the city council.** You will conduct a hearing and decide whether to enact the law, change it, or not act on it, based on the testimony you hear from the community.
- **Group two is the police department.** Your group opposes the law and will testify against it. You believe the curfew will require too much time and energy to enforce and that existing laws are sufficient to combat drug abuse, violence, and other problems.
- **Group three is "Families Against Violence."** Your group supports the law and will testify in favor of it. Parents and students in your group believe the curfew will reduce drug sales and use, help parents with out-of-control children, and promote family communication about following rules.
- **Group four is the local merchants association.** Your group opposes the law and will testify against it. Teens are important customers—and employees—at local stores, restaurants, and movie theaters, and the merchants believe the curfew will harm business.
- **Group five is the school board.** Your group supports the law and will testify in favor of it. The board members believe that students should be home doing their homework and preparing for the next school day.
- **Group six is comprised of teenagers.** Your group will testify against the proposed law and argue that it is not fair to treat teens as either criminals or irresponsible members of the community.

Group one should meet to decide how to run the hearing and to discuss what questions it will ask the other groups. The other groups should meet to further develop their testimony. Additional groups can be invited to the hearing. After the hearing, the city council should deliberate and decide whether to pass, not to pass, or to amend this law.

Karl Polverino/Getty Images

Juvenile Justice Today

In the 1960s, many people argued that the juvenile court system was providing harsher treatment than the adult system without the procedural safeguards and constitutional rights that defendants would have in adult courts. Beginning in 1966, this movement found support in the U.S. Supreme Court with the *Gault* case. In addition, several later decisions began to change the theory and operation of the juvenile justice system.

The *Gault* decision gave young people many of the same rights as adults, but it also left some unanswered questions. The Court decided in *In re Winship* (1970) that a juvenile charged with a criminal act must be found "delinquent by proof beyond a reasonable doubt," the same standard required in adult criminal court. However, in *McKeiver* v. *Pennsylvania* (1971), the Court decided that jury trials were not required in juvenile cases. It expressed concern that jury trials could hurt juveniles by destroying the privacy of juvenile hearings.

THE **CASE** OF...

Gerald Gault

Gerald Gault, 15, was taken into custody and accused of making an obscene phone call to a neighbor. At the time he was taken into custody, his parents were at work and the police did not notify them of what had happened to their son. Gault was placed in a detention center. When his parents finally learned that he was in custody, they were told that there would be a hearing the next day, but they were not told the nature of the complaint against him.

Mrs. Cook, the woman who had complained about the phone call, did not show up at the hearing. Instead, a police officer testified to what he had been told by Mrs. Cook. Gault blamed the call on a friend and denied making the obscene remarks. No lawyers were present, and no record was made of what was said at the hearing.

Because juries were not allowed in juvenile court, the hearing was held before a judge, who found by a preponderance of the evidence that Gault was delinquent and ordered him sent to a state reform school until age 21. An adult found guilty of the same crime could have been sent to a county jail for no longer than 60 days.

In the *Gault* case, the U.S. Supreme Court held that juveniles should receive many of the same due process rights as adults. Specifically, the Court ruled that juveniles charged with delinquent acts were entitled to four rights: (1) the right to notification of the charges against them, (2) the right to an attorney, (3) the right to confront and cross-examine witnesses, and (4) the right to remain silent.

PROBLEM 16.4

a. Make lists of the fair and unfair things that happened to Gerald Gault. Explain.

b. How would you change the unfair things on your list to make the proceedings fairer for Gerald Gault? Why is it important to change these things?

c. What adult rights were not granted to juveniles in the *Gault* case? Should adults and minors have the same legal rights?

d. Do you agree with the *Gault* decision? Why or why not?

More recently, a series of court decisions and legislative actions have changed the informality of juvenile court proceedings. Some courts even grant spectators and newspaper reporters access to juvenile court proceedings. Although juveniles now possess many of the same rights as adults, the U.S. Supreme Court has made it clear that not all of the procedures used in an adult criminal court apply in a juvenile court proceeding.

The federal government has also played a major role in guiding the juvenile courts. The *Juvenile Justice and Delinquency Prevention Act of 1974*, reauthorized in 2018, requires that the Department of Justice's Office of Juvenile Justice and Delinquency Prevention (OJJDP) oversee changes ordered by Congress. OJJDP works as a partner with state and local units of government to improve the juvenile justice system. The federal act required the juvenile court system to change the way it treated both status offenders and delinquent offenders. For example, status offenders were removed from institutions, or "deinstitutionalized." Juvenile offenders remaining in institutions were separated from incarcerated adults. In addition, each state took responsibility for developing community alternatives to incarceration and for improving the juvenile justice system. OJJDP also asks states to address the serious problem of the disproportionate confinement of minority youth of color. Studies have shown that minority youth are more often placed in government-run institutions while white youth are placed in private facilities to meet their special needs.

OJJPD and state juvenile justice agencies have supported innovative programs to keep minor offenders out of the justice system. These programs, sometimes called diversion or informal adjustment, operate to keep juveniles from being prosecuted.

Prosecuting Juveniles in Adult Court

The trend toward prosecuting juveniles in adult court began in the later 1980s and early 1990s during a time of heightened concern about violent juvenile crime. Some people believed that the juvenile justice system was not equipped to deal with more serious juvenile offenders. By 2000 each state and the District of Columbia had at least one mechanism for trying juveniles in adult court. The issues of prosecuting juveniles as adults is the most controverisal issue in juvenile justice today.

juvenile waiver allows juvenile court judges to send juveniles to adult court (depending on the charge and after a hearing) for prosecution

The most common approach was called **juvenile waiver,** which allowed juvenile court judges to waive juveniles to adult court (depending on the charge and after a hearing) for prosecution. In some states the juvenile court orders a juvenile case manager to conduct a waiver investigation and to recommend to the court whether the youth should be waived into adult court or remain in juvenile court. The investigation consists of background on the youth's family, education status, psychosocial ability, and physical stature.

statutory exclusion requires certain offenses committed by juveniles to be prosecuted in adult court

The second most common approach was passing a state law that *required* certain offenses committed by juveniles to be prosecuted in adult court. This approach is called **statutory exclusion,** or automatic transfer. The third approach, called **direct file,** gave prosecutors discretion to file charges against juveniles in adult criminal court. Many states use two or even all three mechanisms. Studies have shown that youth transferred to adult court re-offend at higher rates than those treated in juvenile court. Even with judicial and legislative changes that allow for the prosecution of juveniles in adult court, the majority of juveniles are still treated in the juvenile justice system.

Critics of prosecuting juveniles in adult criminal court cite high repeat offending rates as well as new research on youth brain development that shows that the brains of young people continue to develop into their 20s. This development is in the portion of the brain that affects impulse control, the capacity for independent thought, and the ability to resist peer pressure. While young offenders are still responsible for their behavior, this research suggests that policy makers should focus on sentencing laws that address punishment and treatment within the juvenile justice system, rather than dealing with these juveniles in the adult system.

> **direct file** gives prosecutors discretion to file charges against juveniles in adult criminal court

YOU BE the JUDGE

Determining Juvenile Status

Describe the factors you would consider in determining whether each person should be tried as a juvenile or as an adult. If you need additional information in order to make a recommendation, what information would you need?

a. Marshall, 15, is accused of robbing a woman at gunpoint. He has a long juvenile record, including acts of burglary, and has bragged about the robbery to friends.

b. Leigh, 17, is accused of killing a pedestrian while driving a stolen car. She has never been in trouble before, is remorseful about the killing, and claims that she planned to return the car after a short joyride.

c. Carter, 14, is accused of selling drugs for his older brother. According to the police, one day a customer stole the money Carter had collected. The police claim that Carter then stabbed the customer with a knife. He has been arrested twice before for selling drugs, but the charges were dropped.

d. Angela, 15, is taken into custody for carrying a handgun without a license. This is the second time she has been taken into custody for a weapons violation. Her brother was killed in a drug deal one year earlier. Angela says she carries a gun because she does not feel safe.

DELIBERATION

Should violent juvenile offenders be treated as adults?

How should young, violent offenders be treated? At the heart of this question is another: How responsible are juveniles for their actions? For most crimes, a person can only be convicted if she does something illegal intentionally, knowingly, and willfully. Basically, to be guilty, a person must know something is wrong and still commit the act on purpose. So, a two-year-old who started a fire would not be treated in the same way as an adult who committed arson to collect insurance money. Nor would a person who is proven insane be punished the same as a sane person who committed the same crime.

For many years, the criminal justice system treated all offenders the same way. Adults and children accused and convicted of crimes had the same rights and faced the same punishments. That changed around 1900. Reformers convinced lawmakers that they should create a separate justice system for juveniles. The idea was that sometimes parents cannot (or will not) take care of or control their children, so the government must step in and take over. Juvenile "correctional facilities" would help young offenders to "correct" their behaviors so they could lead productive lives.

Juvenile justice systems vary from state to state. One difference is in how the state determines who is a juvenile and, therefore, who is entitled to special treatment in the juvenile justice system. In nearly all states, an 18-year-old accused of a crime is automatically sent to the adult criminal system. In some cases, depending on the crime, an accused juvenile may be transferred into the adult criminal system. In some states, the prosecutor or a neutral juvenile court judge makes the decision about whether a juvenile should be tried as an adult.

It matters whether a young person is processed through the criminal system or the juvenile system. Young offenders convicted in the adult criminal system almost always face harsher sentences. They are in jail with adult criminals. Though some adult jails and prisons offer rehabilitation programs, it is much less likely when compared to juvenile facilities. Once the offenders leave prison, their criminal records become permanent and public, whereas juvenile records are usually sealed from public view.

Some state governments are reconsidering their policies about whether juvenile offenders should be treated as adults. They want to make punishments more severe. A 2018 riot at a juvenile justice center had some community members calling for reform of their policies. Some advocates argued that violent juvenile offenders were better suited for the adult criminal system. Other advocates, however, argued that the detention center needed to offer more effective rehabilitation programs, instead.

Other state governments are considering very different changes. They want to make it possible for more juveniles to stay in the juvenile system. Since 2007, seven states that once automatically placed youth in adult courts have raised the age at which a young person can be tried as adult.

How should we strike the balance between punishment and rehabilitation? Should violent juvenile offenders be treated as adults?

Should violent juvenile offenders be treated as adults? Consider the options.

YES

Yes, treat violent juvenile offenders as adults.

Punishment could discourage future crime. "[They think] 'Nothing's going to happen to me. I'm a juvenile,'" says a Florida attorney of frequent juvenile offenders. Youth who know they could be sent to adult prison might be discouraged from committing serious crimes.

One purpose of punishment is to keep our community safe. If criminals are in jail, they cannot hurt the rest of society. In the juvenile system, young violent criminals get back on the streets when they become "adults" in the eyes of the law, regardless of how much time they served. If rehabilitation did not work, they are then free to commit more crimes.

Prosecuting and punishing someone in the adult system is less expensive than going through the juvenile justice system. For example, it costs the Virginia government more than $100,000 a year to keep a juvenile offender in a juvenile correctional center. It costs just $25,000 to imprison an adult. Charging juveniles as adults could allow state governments to use that money for other purposes.

Teens know right from wrong. They also know the consequences of their actions. They should be punished accordingly.

NO

No, do not treat violent juvenile offenders as adults.

Most adult prisons are not geared toward rehabilitation. The experience of a tough adult prison, combined with a juvenile's still developing brain, can lead to becoming a worse criminal while in prison.

Through rehabilitation, young people can re-enter society and lead productive lives. Some juvenile facilities are not providing necessary rehabilitation services, which leads people to believe that rehabilitation doesn't work. Rather than pushing juvenile offenders toward an adult system, the government should ensure that rehabilitation programs are using researched best practices.

Researchers found bias in the criminal justice system. African-American and Hispanic youth are much more likely to be tried as adults and sentenced to adult prisons than white minors accused of the same crimes. A study of the New Jersey criminal justice system revealed that over a five-year period, prosecutors asked to try 1,251 minors as adults. Nearly 90 percent were black or Hispanic.

In the past 10 years, scientists have discovered that brains do not fully mature until the age of about 25. The parts of the brain that control anger and allow people to anticipate consequences are particularly slow to develop.

GUIDING QUESTIONS

1. What are the two most compelling reasons to support the deliberation question?

2. What are the two most compelling reasons to disagree with the deliberation question?

3. What is one area of this deliberation where the two sides might find common ground?

Procedures in Juvenile Court

Suppose a young person is accused of a delinquent act. What happens to this person from the time he or she is taken into custody until release from the juvenile justice system? The exact procedures vary from state to state, but the general process is similar throughout the country.

Taking into Custody On the whole, young people may be taken into custody for the same reasons the police might arrest an adult. However, juveniles also can be taken into custody for status offenses. These offenses include running away from home, truancy, underage use of tobacco or alcohol, and other actions suggesting the need for court supervision.

After taking a juvenile into custody, the police have broad authority to release or detain the juvenile. If the offense is minor, the police may give the juvenile a warning, release the juvenile to his or her parents, or refer the case to a social service agency. If the offense is more serious or if the young person has a prior record, the police may detain the youth and refer him or her to juvenile court.

Intake is the informal process by which court officials or juvenile intake case managers decide if a complaint against a juvenile should be referred to juvenile court. This decision is usually made after interviewing the youth and considering the seriousness of the offense, the youth's past record, his or her family situation, and other factors.

It is estimated that as many as one-third of all complaints in the juvenile system are disposed of during the intake process by dismissal, diversion, or transfer. Most of the cases disposed of are dismissed. Some youths are diverted, which means that they receive educational and treatment services without going through juvenile court. In addition, in some states a prosecutor may decide to charge a juvenile as an adult and request a waiver hearing.

intake the informal process in which court officials or social workers decide if a complaint against a juvenile should be referred to juvenile court

▶ Juveniles taken into custody can be detained and referred to juvenile court. *Describe the instances in which a juvenile offender may be released.*

Colleen Cahill/Design Pics

16.1 The Juvenile Justice Process

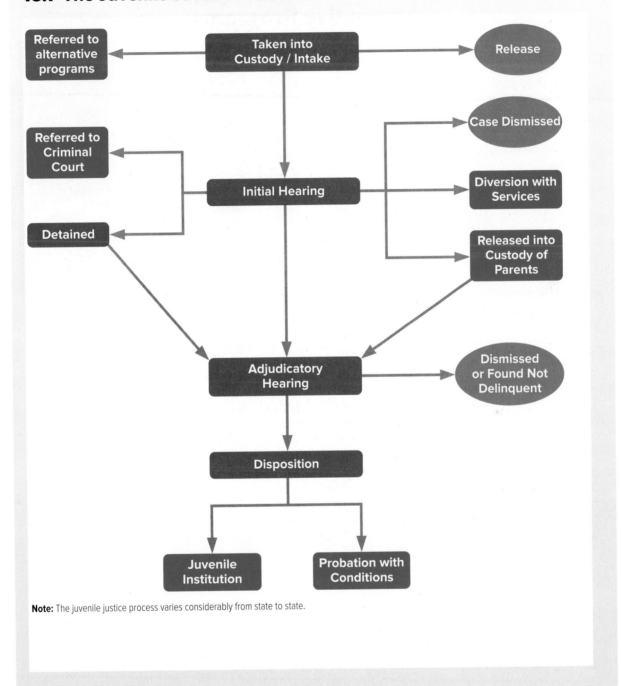

Note: The juvenile justice process varies considerably from state to state.

There are several different outcomes for an offender in the juvenile justice process.
ANALYZE THE DATA *What may happen to a juvenile after he or she is taken into custody?*

Alternative Programs

Alternative programs that focus on accountability, youth development, and community involvement, rather than punishment, have developed within the juvenile justice system. Some divert young people out of the juvenile justice system and into services that deal with problem behaviors or difficult challenges. Some programs provide counseling, while others focus on education or job training.

The fastest-growing alternative program is called **youth court.** There are more than 1,500 youth courts in the United States, and the concept has spread to other countries. About half of the youth courts operate in the juvenile justice system, while others are situated in school or community-based settings. Although there are several different program models, the basic idea behind all youth courts is that young people sentence their peers.

In most youth court programs, the person charged with an offense must admit to having committed the offense before being accepted into youth court. Typical offenses dealt with by youth courts include theft, assault, vandalism, disorderly conduct, and alcohol and marijuana use. The sentences imposed by the peer juries include community service, essays, written and oral apologies to victims, and workshops. Also, most youth courts require offenders to serve on juries to sentence other youth offenders.

▲ A youth court in progress

Youth courts are based on a philosophy called **restorative justice.** The idea behind restorative justice is that criminal acts are not just random acts against the state—they harm victims, offenders themselves, and whole communities. Sentences that reflect restorative justice principles include ways for offenders to repair the harm done to victims, to understand the impact of their actions, and to learn new skills while connecting to their communities in positive ways.

PROBLEM 16.5

a. Evaluations of youth court programs show that the rate of re-offending is very low. Why do you think youth court programs are so successful?

b. What benefits do youth courts offer to juvenile offenders, their families, and the community? Are there any disadvantages?

c. What do you think about the idea of restorative justice? Is this the best approach in dealing with all juvenile offenders? Explain your reasons.

d. Do crimes such as vandalism and shoplifting (sometimes called "gateway crimes") lead to more criminal activity if they go unpunished? If so, what sorts of consequences should vandals and shoplifters face? Explain your reasons.

e. If a judge, a prosecutor, or a police officer in your area does not want to refer an offender to juvenile court, what alternative programs are available for youth in your community?

Initial or Detention Hearing Young people who are taken into custody and formally referred to juvenile court are entitled to an **initial hearing** on the validity of their arrest and detention. At this initial hearing, the state must generally prove two things: that an offense was committed and that there is reasonable cause to believe that the accused committed it. If the state wants to further detain the juvenile, it must prove that the juvenile is a danger to himself or herself or others, is likely to run away if released, or has a past record that warrants detention. If the juvenile does not have an attorney, the court will usually assign one at this time and set a date for a hearing on the facts.

The U.S. Supreme Court has not ruled that juveniles have a constitutional right to bail. Therefore, no money bond is set, and the juvenile court may decide either to release juveniles to their parents or other adults or to detain them until trial. In the 1983 case of *Schall* v. *Martin*, the Supreme Court justified what is referred to as **preventive detention** of juveniles on the grounds that it serves the legitimate purpose of protecting the community and the juveniles themselves from the consequences of future crime. Preventive detention is based on a judge's decision that a juvenile is better off in detention than in his or her own home. Federal law requires juveniles who are detained to be held separately from adults who have been accused of crimes.

> ## PROBLEM 16.6
>
> **a.** Should juveniles have the same right to bail as adults? Why or why not? When should they be detained?
>
> **b.** Should juveniles be detained separately from adults in all cases? What should happen if a small town has only one jail or the juvenile detention center is full?

Adjudicatory Hearing A juvenile charged with a delinquent act is given a hearing. Generally known as an **adjudicatory hearing,** or a fact-finding hearing, its purpose is the same as that of an adult trial—to determine the facts of the case. Unlike an adult trial, however, a juvenile hearing is generally closed to the public, and the names of the accused and the details of the offense are withheld from the press. Although juveniles do not have a constitutional right to a jury trial, a few states do provide for juries in juvenile cases.

At the adjudicatory hearing, the juvenile will be represented by an attorney. A parent or guardian will also be present. The attorney can examine and cross-examine witnesses in an effort to force the prosecution to prove its case beyond a reasonable doubt. If the judge finds the juvenile nondelinquent (not guilty), he or she is free to go. If the judge decides that the facts as set out in the petition are true, the court will enter a finding of delinquent. This is similar to a conviction in adult court proceedings.

youth court a proceeding for sentencing minors who have taken responsibility for their actions. The system aims to involve the community directly and to teach the young offenders the impact of their acts.

restorative justice a concept in criminal justice that emphasizes reparation to the victim or the affected members of the community by the offender, as by cash payment or by community service

initial hearing a preliminary examination of the validity of a youth's arrest, during which the state must prove that an offense was committed and that there is reasonable cause to believe the accused youth committed it. Decisions are made about further detention and legal representation, and a date is set for a hearing on the facts.

preventive detention detaining a person if the individual is a danger to himself/herself or the community

adjudicatory hearing the procedure used to determine the facts in a juvenile case; similar to an adult trial, but generally closed to the public

▲ Juveniles on probation must follow a set of conditions, including regular meetings with a probation officer. *What are other examples of conditions of probation?*

disposition the final sentence or result of a case

Dispositional Hearing The dispositional hearing is perhaps the most important stage in the system for juveniles who are found delinquent. At this hearing, the judge decides what sentence, or **disposition**, the offender should receive. The judge's sentence is usually based primarily on the predisposition report prepared by the probation department. This report is the result of an investigation of the juvenile's social, psychological, family, and school background.

In making their dispositions, courts are supposed to provide for individualized treatment geared toward rehabilitating the offender. In practice, however, courts balance the needs of the offender against the obligation to protect the community. Sentencing options include probation, community service, fines, restitution, placement in a community treatment program, or commitment to a state institution.

Probation is the most common disposition. The judge can impose a number of conditions on a juvenile placed on probation. For example, the juvenile might be ordered to attend school regularly, hold a steady job, attend counseling sessions at a treatment center, take weekly drug tests, be home by 8:00 P.M., or stay away from certain people. A juvenile on probation usually has to meet with a probation officer on a regular basis. If the conditions of probation are not met, the youth can be sent back to court for another hearing. At that time, the judge can decide to send the juvenile to a group home or a residential facility.

For serious offenses, the youth can be committed to a juvenile residential facility. Most courts have the power to place a youth in such a facility for an indeterminate length of time. This means that no matter what the offense, the offender can be detained for up to the maximum period allowed by state law. This varies based on state law as well as the youth's needs.

In certain cases, it lasts until the young person reaches the age of majority, and it can continue in some states until age 21. Most juveniles, however, do not serve the maximum sentence. The exact time of release is usually determined by the agency that operates the institution.

Postdisposition Most states give young people the right to appeal decisions of a juvenile court. However, because the U.S. Supreme Court has never ruled on this issue, the provisions for appeal vary greatly from state to state.

When released from an institution, a juvenile may be placed in **aftercare**. This is the equivalent of parole in the adult system. Aftercare usually involves supervision by a parole officer who counsels the juvenile on education, jobs, vocational training, or other issues.

aftercare the equivalent of parole in the juvenile justice system. A juvenile is supervised and assisted by a parole officer or social worker.

Reentry programs are also needed for juveniles and exist on a limited basis. The transition back to school is a particularly difficult juvenile reentry problem. Some juvenile offenders had academic problems before being placed in a state institution and continued to fall behind academically while in the institution. Where effective juvenile reentry programs are not in place, the likelihood of re-offending is increased.

Having a Record A juvenile who is found delinquent does not have a criminal record, as would someone who is tried as an adult. If asked, a juvenile may legally say that he or she has not been convicted of a *crime*—a legal term that refers only to the adult system. In general, juveniles who are adjudicated do not lose any civil rights and can still register to vote upon reaching adulthood. However, juvenile records can cause problems later. In many states, some or all information on juvenile cases becomes public record. Therefore individuals and agencies, including employers, may be able to access it. A juvenile record often is also considered in sentencing adults, so that defendants with no adult criminal record may still receive a harsher sentence if they have a juvenile record.

▼ Some employers have access to juvenile records, which may cause problems for an adult seeking a job. *What do most states require in order to expunge a person's juvenile record?*

In a few states, juvenile records are automatically sealed or **expunged** (destroyed) when the juvenile reaches the age of 18 or 21, giving the individual a "clean slate." In most states, however, the record continues to exist unless the person, now an adult, officially requests that his or her record be expunged. To be eligible for such a request, most states require that several years have passed since the offense and that the person not have committed any further offenses during that time. If the person with the juvenile record meets these conditions, he or she can go before a judge to request that the record be expunged. If the judge approves the request, there will no longer be a public record of the person's involvement in the juvenile justice system.

PROBLEM 16.7

Should employers who conduct background checks on job applicants be able to access juvenile court records? Give reasons for your opinion.

FYI For Your Information

Juvenile and Adult Law Terms

Juvenile Law Term	Adult Law Term
Offense	Crime
Take into Custody	Arrest
Petition	File Charges
Denial	Not Guilty Plea
Admission	Guilty Plea
Adjudicatory Hearing	Trial
Found Delinquent	Found Guilty
Disposition	Sentencing
Detention	Jail
Aftercare	Parole

Challenges Facing the Juvenile Justice System

Since 1997 the number of youths detained or placed in residential facilities has steadily declined. However, the United States still detains more young people than any other industrialized country, and the majority of youth detained are not being held for a violent offense. African American youth are taken into custody at five times the rate of white youth, and Latino youth are also overrepresented in the juvenile justice system. Reformers urge state and local authorities to examine their policies and procedures that have led to disproportionate minority contact with the juvenile justice system.

Critics of the juvenile justice system claim that current practice is not as effective as it could be either in helping troubled youth or in keeping communities safe. The Annie E. Casey Foundation, one of the organizations most active in juvenile justice reform efforts, states that "youth should remain at home and be supervised in the community rather than being separated from their families and placed into residential facilities when they do not pose a significant risk to public safety." The Foundation also finds evidence of mistreatment of juveniles in some residential facilities. For LGBTQ youth, the rates of mistreatment are particularly high. Educational opportunities in residential facilities are typically limited which makes re-integration into school upon release more difficult. For youth who should be confined, reformers urge replacing large juvenile institutions with smaller, treatment-orientated facilities.

The justice system's approach to serving young people has improved dramatically since earlier periods in our history when juveniles could be executed for relatively minor offenses. But the promise of safe and humane care for all juveniles remains a challenge.

PROBLEM 16.8

Research the juvenile justice system in your state. What improvements have been made in recent years? What challenges remain? How would you go about meeting these challenges?

UNIT 3
Torts

When people think about the law, they often think about the police and about criminal law. Most law, however, is not criminal law but civil law. Tort law—the largest area of civil law—deals with some of society's most controversial issues. For example, should cigarette manufacturers who place a warning on cigarette packages be required to pay damages to a smoker who develops lung cancer as a result of smoking? Tort law encourages people to act responsibly by awarding money or damages to victims who are harmed by wrongdoers. While tort law cases can be resolved by lawsuits, far more are settled without going to court. Mediation, negotiation, and arbitration are frequently used to settle tort cases.

◀ The primary goal of civil law is to protect people by helping them avoid problems and resolve disputes.

CHAPTERS IN BRIEF

CHAPTER **17**
Torts: A Civil Wrong

Chapter 17 defines *tort law* and identifies parties in a civil lawsuit. It also helps you apply basic concepts such as liability, settlement, and damages.

CHAPTER **18**
Intentional Torts

Chapter 18 defines the two general types of intentional torts: actions taken to deliberately harm another person and actions taken to harm property. The chapter also discusses how the judicial system treats intentional torts. Finally, defenses to intentional torts are described.

CHAPTER **19**
Negligence

Chapter 19 explains the concept of negligence. The chapter then explores the legal elements of negligence: duty, breach of duty, causation, and damages. The defenses a person charged with negligence might use are also outlined.

CHAPTER **20**
Strict Liability

Chapter 20 describes torts in which defendants are held to strict liability standards because they engaged in extremely hazardous activities. The chapter explains how this area of law may serve as an incentive for careful and safe practices at work and at home.

CHAPTER **21**
Torts and Public Policy

Chapter 21 reviews the function of the tort law system as it relates to public policy. Then the chapter challenges you to evaluate the importance and fairness of the tort system as you assess current tort reform efforts.

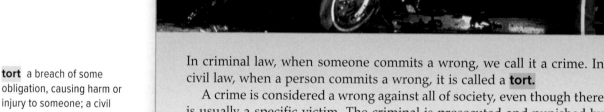

▶ Automobile crashes may result in civil lawsuits.

tort a breach of some obligation, causing harm or injury to someone; a civil wrong, such as negligence or libel

plaintiff in a civil case, the injured party who brings legal action against the alleged wrongdoer

judgment a court's decision in a civil case

defendant the person against whom a claim is made. In a civil suit, the defendant is the person being sued; in a criminal case, the defendant is the person charged with committing a crime

damages money asked for or paid by court order to a plaintiff for injuries or losses suffered

In criminal law, when someone commits a wrong, we call it a crime. In civil law, when a person commits a wrong, it is called a **tort.**

A crime is considered a wrong against all of society, even though there is usually a specific victim. The criminal is prosecuted and punished by the state. By contrast, civil law deals with wrongs against individuals. A harmed individual becomes the **plaintiff** in a civil lawsuit. The plaintiff seeks to win a **judgment** against the **defendant,** or accused wrongdoer. A defendant who loses the judgment in a civil case will not be punished with jail or other penalties associated with criminal law. Instead he or she will be ordered to compensate the plaintiff for harm done, usually by paying monetary **damages.** In certain instances a court might also order the defendant to stop the troubling behavior.

Although a tort and a crime are two different legal categories, the same illegal activity can be both a crime and a tort. For example, a person who breaks into a house has committed a crime and can be prosecuted by the state. The offender has also committed a tort, and the victim may sue to recover monetary damages.

The Idea of Liability

The rules that govern civil wrongs are called tort law. Tort law deals with basic questions such as (1) who should be **liable,** or responsible, for harm caused by human activities, and (2) how much should the responsible person have to pay. Almost any activity—driving a car, operating a

CDC/James Gathany

business, speaking, writing, or using property—can be a source of harm and therefore of tort liability. Knowledge of torts can help people resolve their conflicts, often without going to court.

Tort law also establishes standards of care that society expects from people. Simply put, the law requires us to act with reasonable care toward people and their property. Failure to exercise reasonable care that causes harm may result in legal liability. The person harmed may sue the person who acted unreasonably for damages. Requiring payment of damages compensates the victim for losses and encourages more reasonable behavior.

Whenever a person is injured, someone must bear the cost of the harm. Broken bones create medical bills that must be paid. A hospitalized person will miss work and lose earnings. Damaged property costs money to repair. Less tangible costs, such as emotional suffering, may also be a cost of an injury.

Tort law is concerned with determining who must pay. When a person either purposely or through carelessness causes injury to another, society usually thinks that the wrongdoer, rather than the victim, should bear the cost of the harm. However, sometimes an injury is partially or entirely the fault of the victim, or nobody is at fault, as in the case of true accidents. In such cases, tort law provides no **remedy,** or something to make up for the harm done. As a result, the victim will usually have to bear the costs of the injury.

Liability—legal responsibility for harm—is not the same as moral responsibility. A person may be morally at fault for harming someone but not civilly liable for the injuries. For example, assume you lie to a friend about the correct time, causing her to miss a job interview. As a result, she does not get the job. The lie would be morally wrong and would cause harm but would not usually result in civil liability. In contrast, someone may be civilly liable for injuries to another without being morally at fault. For example, in strict liability cases the law makes certain parties bear the cost of injuries even though there is no proof of fault. However, moral fault is one of the many considerations that courts often look at in developing the law of torts and drawing up the rules of who will pay for injuries people suffer.

▲ The question of liability is not always clear when athletes are injured during participation in a sports event. *Why does tort law provide no remedy for this type of situation?*

liable legally responsible

remedy what is done to compensate for an injury or to enforce some right

liability legal responsibility; the obligations to do or not do something. The defendant in a tort case incurs liability for failing to use reasonable care, resulting in harm to the plaintiff

Read the descriptions of each of the following cases. Each involves an injury. Assume that a civil suit is brought by the injured person. For each case, (1) identify the plaintiff and the defendant or defendants, and (2) determine whether the defendant should pay for the plaintiff's damages. Explain your answers.

a. Nineteen-year-old Carrie is babysitting for her four-year-old niece Jill. Carrie leaves Jill alone in the living room and goes into the kitchen for some privacy to call her boyfriend. From the kitchen she can hear but not see Jill. While Carrie is out of the living room, Jill falls off a chair and is hurt.

b. Ben, a defensive tackle on the school football team, tackles a teammate in a full-contact practice. When the teammate hits the ground, his shoulder is dislocated.

c. Mr. Ghosh owns a large apartment building. When his janitors wax the lobby floor, they place a 12-inch-square sign near the front door that reads: "Caution. Wet Floors." Mrs. Gonzalez is hurrying home from shopping with two large bags of groceries. She does not see the sign and slips and falls on the freshly waxed floor, injuring her knee and arm.

d. Corina leaves a sharp knife on the kitchen table after making a sandwich. A three-year-old neighbor who has been invited over to play with Corina's daughter climbs up onto a chair, grabs the knife, and seriously cuts his finger.

e. Jamal, a school bus driver, has a heart attack one morning while driving the bus carrying students to school. As Jamal loses consciousness, the bus slams into a wall, injuring several of the students. One month earlier during a routine check up, Jamal's doctor had warned him of his heart condition.

f. Matt and Emily are sitting in the upper deck of the stadium behind first base at a major league baseball game. A foul ball hit by their team's star player bounces off a nearby railing, smacking Matt in the head and giving him a concussion.

g. Jess, an expert auto mechanic, continues to drive her car, even though she knows that the brake linings are badly worn. Driving below the speed limit on a rain-slick road at night, she slams on the breaks and skids into a bicyclist who is riding one foot away from the right curb.

▼ Liability for injuries sustained at sporting events, at school, and at home can be difficult to determine. *What factors are considered when determining liability?*

U.S. Air Force photo by Staff Sgt Alan Garrison

Tort law provides a legal process for injured persons to recover monetary damages from wrongdoers who cause them harm. The two parties can simply meet and discuss how to compensate the injured person. The agreement they reach is called a **settlement.** If, however, they cannot agree on compensation, or if the wrongdoer insists that he or she was acting reasonably when the injury occurred, then the injured party may decide to sue. In such instances, a trial may be conducted to decide the rights and liabilities of both parties.

Settlements are much more common than trials. Approximately 95 percent of tort cases filed in court are settled without a trial. For cases that do go to trial, there can be delays of a year or more between the time the case is filed in court and the trial.

The following example illustrates the tort law process. Evan claims that Martha shoved him, causing him to fall down a flight of stairs and break his leg. Evan wants $5,000 from Martha to compensate for his injury. This dispute can be resolved in at least three different ways.

First, Martha could acknowledge that she acted unreasonably and agree to pay a settlement of $5,000. However, a settlement does not have to be for the full amount demanded, and usually the amount is a result of a compromise between the two parties. Besides negotiating a settlement, other forms of dispute resolution could allow Martha and Evan to avoid a civil trial.

Second, Martha could argue that she did not act unreasonably—that Evan ran past her, bumped into her, and then tripped down the stairs—and refuse to pay any monetary damages. If Evan wanted to recover the money, he would have to sue Martha in court.

In a third scenario, Martha might admit nudging Evan a bit but claim that she should have to pay only $4,000, because the $5,000 Evan wants includes money for a new video game console and three games that Evan bought when he was home in bed for two weeks. Here, the dispute is not about liability but about the amount of damages. In this situation, Evan might accept Martha's $4,000 offer, or he might sue Martha for $5,000. However, there is risk in not accepting the $4,000. If a court decides that Martha did not act unreasonably, then Evan might not recover any damages at all!

▲ Injured persons can be compensated by negotiating a settlement with the wrongdoer. *What other methods could help the parties involved avoid a civil trial?*

settlement a mutual agreement between two sides in a civil lawsuit, made either before the case goes to trial or before a final judgment is entered, that settles or ends the dispute

The Idea of Torts: Yesterday, Today, and Tomorrow

The concept of a tort is not new. Judges in England were deciding tort cases as far back as the fifteenth century. Tort law has always tried to weigh the usefulness of certain conduct against the harm that conduct might cause.

Tort law is generally based on **common law.** This is law made by judges through court decisions, generally in state appellate courts. These decisions are written down, and appellate decisions become **precedents** used to decide future cases. Tort law may also be based on **statutes,** or written laws. For example, in some states, laws specifically provide that a person who is injured as a result of someone furnishing alcohol to a minor may be awarded damages in civil court. The damages are paid by the person who served the alcohol to the minor. In other states, this same law exists as a result of an appellate court decision (a precedent), rather than the passage of a statute.

There are a number of specific torts, which are described later in this chapter. There is also a saying that "for every interference with a recognized legal right, the law will provide a remedy." If you can convince a judge that you deserve compensation for some injury, you may occasionally be able to recover damages without fitting your case into an existing category of tort protection.

Tort law seeks to balance usefulness and harm. For example, how safe must a drug be before the manufacturer is not considered legally responsible in the event that the drug harms somebody? If a drug is discovered that saves the lives of many cancer patients but causes the deaths of a few, should the drug manufacturer be liable for the deaths?

common law a system in which court decisions establish legal principles and rules of law

precedent appellate court decision on a legal question that guides future cases representing similar questions

statutes written laws enacted by legislatures

▶ Tort law balances usefulness and individual choice with harm. *Should cigarette companies and drug manufacturers be held liable for side effects or illness incurred by people who use their products?*

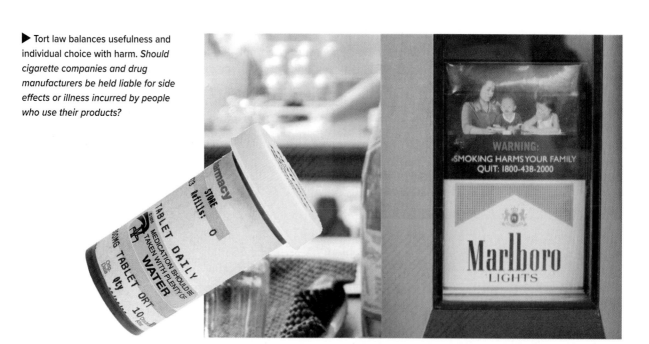

THE **CASE** OF...

The Lung Cancer Death

Mrs. Garrett dies of lung cancer at the age of 42. Her family brings a civil suit against ABC Tobacco Company, the manufacturer of the cigarettes she had smoked daily for the previous 20 years. Her doctors say that cigarette smoking was the major factor in her death.

PROBLEM 17.2

a. If you were the Garrett family's attorney, what arguments would you make at the trial? What evidence would you want to introduce during the trial?

b. If you were the attorney for the ABC Tobacco Company, what arguments would you make for the company at the trial? What evidence would you want to introduce to support your arguments? How would such evidence help your case?

c. If you were the Garrett family's attorney, would you want a jury to decide this case? Would it be better to try this case before a judge? Why?

d. Assume that each package of ABC cigarettes has carried the following warning to consumers for the past 20 years: "Caution: Cigarette smoking can be harmful to your health." How should this case be decided? Explain the reasons for your decision.

Tort law also tries to preserve individual choice. Since the mandatory government warning about the dangers of smoking is prominently displayed on the package, adults are permitted to purchase cigarettes. Many people believe that this product may be more harmful than useful. However, some people argue that letting adults purchase cigarettes preserves their individual choice and that the warning allows the individual to make an informed choice. Others criticize this government decision and argue that the sale of cigarettes should be further restricted or banned.

Tort law is often at the forefront of public controversy in the United States. It is closely related to economic and political policy decisions. As you will see throughout this unit, tort cases often involve a clash of values and interests. As a result, arriving at fair solutions is rarely easy.

Types of Torts

Tort liability exists for three major categories of conduct: intentional wrongs, acts of negligence, and activities for which strict liability is imposed. An **intentional wrong** is an action done with the intent of having a physical or mental effect on another person, his or her property, or both. For example, Ali is mad at Tom, so he intentionally smashes a window of Tom's car. Tom may sue Ali to recover the cost of the damage to his window.

intentional wrong also called an intentional tort; an action taken deliberately to harm another person and/or his or her property

In another example, Lucy writes a letter telling her friends that Andrew is a drug addict, even though she knows this is not true. Andrew may recover damages from Lucy for harm to his reputation caused by her intentional lie.

Intentional torts may also be crimes. In these cases, the defendant can be prosecuted by the state as well as sued by the plaintiff. However, punishing a criminal does not make up for the harm to the victim. A separate civil tort action is used to recover monetary damages.

negligence the failure to exercise a reasonable amount of care in either doing or not doing something, resulting in harm or injury to another person

The most common tort is negligence. **Negligence** is an unintentional tort. It occurs when a person's failure to use reasonable care causes harm. If a drunk driver accidentally hits a pedestrian, the driver is negligent. Although the driver might not have intended to hurt the pedestrian, he or she acted unreasonably in driving drunk and will be liable for the harm caused to the pedestrian.

strict liability the legal responsibility for damage, or injury even if you are not negligent

Strict liability differs from both negligence and intentional wrongs. It applies when the defendant is engaged in an activity so dangerous that there is a serious risk of harm even if he or she acts with utmost care. In order to recover damages in a strict liability case, a plaintiff is not required to prove that the defendant was negligent or intended to cause harm. For example, you are hit by a brick falling from a building being demolished. In this case, you do not have to prove that the contractor was careless or intended to hurt you. Demolishing buildings is so dangerous that contractors are automatically responsible if a passerby is injured. For the most part, three groups of people face strict liability: (1) owners of dangerous animals, (2) people who engage in highly dangerous activities, and (3) manufacturers and sellers of defective consumer products.

Not all injuries to you or your property will lead to a recovery under tort law. In some instances, harmful behavior may not be a tort. In other cases, the person causing the harm may have a legal defense to a tort action. In still other cases, the defendant may be liable but may simply be unable to pay for the harm caused to the plaintiff.

PROBLEM 17.3

Determine whether a tort has been committed in each situation below. If there is a tort, is it an intentional wrong, an act of negligence, or an activity for which strict liability should be imposed? Explain.

a. José trips over his untied shoelace while running to catch a bus, breaking his ankle.

b. Mr. Slifko buys a strong painkiller at the drugstore and takes the capsules according to the directions on the package. He has an extremely bad reaction to the drug and has to be taken to the hospital.

c. Chen drinks too much alcohol at the office holiday party. His supervisor, Ruth, advises him to take a taxi home, but he thinks he will be okay if he drives slowly. Not noticing a stop sign, he strikes and kills a pedestrian crossing the street.

Taking Your Case to Court

Tort law is **civil law**. Civil law deals with disputes between individuals or groups of individuals. In a civil case, the injured party may sue the party who caused the damage. This differs from criminal law, in which the state brings charges against the accused. Criminal law deals with actions that are defined as crimes against the general public, even if there is an individual victim.

In some situations, an act can be both a tort and a crime. This may lead to two separate actions—civil and criminal—against the defendant. For example, Chen (Problem 17.3) may be sued for driving while intoxicated and killing a pedestrian. Chen may also be charged with the crime of negligent homicide or manslaughter for his actions.

The criminal case will be brought by the state, which must prove beyond a reasonable doubt that Chen was guilty. A **standard of proof** must be met. It is the amount of evidence the prosecutor must present in order to win the case.

The victim's family may also sue Chen in civil court. In the civil case, the victim's family will attempt to recover damages for the wrongful death. The civil court will use **preponderance of the evidence** as the standard of proof. This standard requires that to win, more than 50 percent of the weight of the evidence must be in the plaintiff's favor. The civil standard is easier to meet than the criminal standard. This is appropriate, because the penalties for those found liable in a civil action are less severe than the penalties for those found guilty of a crime. A person does not go to jail for committing a tort but instead pays damages to those injured.

Who Can Be Sued?

Almost anyone can be sued, including individuals, groups of individuals, organizations, businesses, and even units of government. Plaintiffs sometimes sue several different defendants at once. Typically, plaintiffs try to sue a defendant who has enough money to pay for the damages. This is called looking for a defendant with **deep pockets.** For example, suppose you slip on a wet rag that the janitor left on the floor of a local restaurant. You break your leg as a result of the fall. You will probably sue the restaurant owner rather than the janitor because the owner will usually have deeper pockets—more money—from which to pay monetary damages.

People can sue employers for torts committed by employees in the course of their employment. The reason for this rule is that the employer is usually in a better position than the employee to handle the cost of the suit. The employer, for example, may purchase liability insurance or raise prices to cover the costs associated with a lawsuit. In addition, imposing financial responsibility on the employer encourages employers to be very careful when hiring, training, assigning, and supervising employees.

Children who commit torts may also be sued for damages. To recover damages from a **minor,** you must prove that the child acted unreasonably for a person of that age and experience. Because most children do not have deep pockets, plaintiffs often sue the child's parents.

civil law all law that does not involve criminal matters, such as tort and contract law. Civil law usually deals with private rights of individuals, groups, or businesses.

standard of proof the level of certainty and the degree of evidence necessary to establish proof in a criminal or civil proceeding. The standard of proof in a criminal trial is generally beyond a reasonable doubt, whereas a civil case generally requires the lesser standard of preponderance of the evidence

preponderance of the evidence usually the standard of proof used in a civil suit; the burden of proof that a party must meet in order to win the lawsuit. To win, a party must provide evidence that is more convincing than the other side's evidence.

deep pockets a description of the person or organization, among many possible defendants, best able to pay damages and therefore most likely to be sued in a tort case

minor a child; a person under the legal age of adulthood, usually 18 or 21

THE **CASE** OF...

The Spilled Peanut Butter

Mr. Grant is in Foodland Supermarket doing the weekly grocery shopping. His four-year-old daughter Jenny is seated in the shopping cart. As they pass a large peanut butter display, Jenny reaches out and pulls a jar off the shelf. The display collapses, and a dozen jars come tumbling down. Some of the jars break, spreading peanut butter and glass all over the floor. Mr. Grant scolds Jenny severely as he wheels her down the aisle.

Ten minutes later, Mrs. Hightower slips and falls on the peanut butter. She breaks her hip in the fall and suffers several deep cuts from the broken glass. Because she is elderly, the hip injury develops complications and may never heal properly.

PROBLEM 17.4

a. Whom should Mrs. Hightower sue for damages? Why?

b. Which possible defendant is likely to have the deepest pockets?

c. Who, if anyone, was at fault in this case? Give your reasons.

d. What methods other than a civil trial could the plaintiff use to deal with this situation? How would these methods work?

▼ Children who commit torts may be sued for damages. *How are parents often involved when their child commits a tort?*

For example, suppose a child leaves toys on the front step, injuring a visitor who trips on them. The visitor may sue the parents and try to prove that they were negligent in either failing to supervise their child or in allowing a hazard to exist on their property.

Certain defendants are **immune,** or protected, from some kinds of tort suits. In some situations, social traditions dictate that for public policy reasons certain groups of people should not be sued, even though their conduct may have been improper. These immunities include suits against governments and certain government officials. Generally, courts do not allow children to sue their parents or vice versa. Historically, courts have also refused to allow spouses to sue each other in tort actions. This restriction was due to the traditional idea that the spouses were one legal entity! Times change and so do tort laws. Today many states allow spouses to sue each other for certain torts. Even where these intrafamily immunities remain, brothers and sisters may be able to sue each other in civil actions.

apply pictures/Alamy

The federal and state governments are also immune from tort liability unless they **waive,** or give up, this immunity. The notion of government immunity comes from England, where there was a tradition that "the king can do no wrong." Today the federal government, through the *Federal Tort Claims Act,* has agreed to be held liable in civil actions for negligent acts or omissions by government employees. While the *Federal Tort Claims Act* does not allow citizens to sue the federal government for most intentional torts, other laws may allow citizens to recover damages from the federal government for intentional violations of their rights. Similar laws exist at the state level.

The president, federal judges, and members of Congress are completely immune from tort liability for acts carried out within the scope of their duties. However, in the 1997 case of *Clinton* v. *Jones*, the U.S. Supreme Court found that the president was not immune from being sued while in office for a tort he allegedly committed before he was president. Other high-ranking officials, including presidential aides and members of the cabinet, have qualified immunity, meaning that they can be sued only if they knew or should have known that their acts were violating the legal rights of another person.

Sometimes there can be more than one plaintiff or injured party in a situation. In some cases, hundreds of people may be injured by one action. When this happens, the injured parties may form a "class" and bring their lawsuit together. This is called a **class action.** For example, if an entire town gets its drinking water from the same source and an industrial plant pollutes the water, the townspeople may file a class action suit against the company. The settlement or damage award will be divided among the people who bring the suit.

People wishing to file a tort action should hire an attorney to file the legal papers, to negotiate with the other side, and, if necessary, to represent them at trial. Some lawyers will work for a **contingency fee,** which means the lawyer does not charge the client an hourly fee. Rather, the lawyer receives a portion of the recovery—typically between 30 and 40 percent—if the plaintiff wins. If the plaintiff loses, the attorney does not receive a fee. However, the plaintiff might have to pay certain reasonable expenses such as the cost of filing the lawsuit. This arrangement allows a person who might otherwise be unable to afford an attorney to be represented in a tort action. The contingency fee is, of course, something of a gamble for the attorney. Lawyers rarely agree to this type of arrangement unless the plaintiff has a strong case and a good chance of recovering money damages.

The contingency fee may not always be a good arrangement for the plaintiff. For example, a lawyer may be able to negotiate a large settlement with an insurance company without even filing a case in court. In such a case, it may be better for the plaintiff to hire a lawyer on an hourly basis or for an agreed-upon, overall fixed fee. Otherwise, the plaintiff could end up paying the attorney much more money through a contingency fee arrangement.

immune exempt from penalties, payments, or legal requirements; free from prosecution

waive to give up some right, privilege, or benefit voluntarily

class action a lawsuit brought by one or more persons on behalf of a larger group

contingency fee the fee paid to an attorney based on a percentage of the sum the client is awarded or settles for in a lawsuit

THE **CASE** OF...

The Steering Wheel Failure

Sarah buys a new car at Town and Country Motors. Just before her first scheduled maintenance visit (at 3,000 miles), she hears a strange noise in her steering wheel. She tells the service manager about the sound, and he notes it on the work order. After picking up the car the next day, she has a serious accident when the steering suddenly fails. The car is totaled, and her medical bills from the accident are more than $30,000.

PROBLEM 17.5

a. Could Sarah bring a civil action? Who are the potential defendants in this case?

b. Who do you think would win? Why?

c. Should Sarah hire a lawyer on a contingency-fee, hourly, or fixed-fee basis? Explain your reasoning.

d. What methods other than a civil trial could the plaintiff use to deal with this situation? How would these methods work?

THE **CASE** OF...

The Airline Explosion

On December 21, 1988, a bomb was smuggled onto an international flight from Frankfurt, Germany, to New York City. The flight carried 259 passengers, many of them students returning to the United States from a European trip, along with a crew of 11. The bomb exploded over Lockerbie, Scotland, killing everyone on board. The bombers were later identified as being from Libya.

▲ Airplane wreckage

PROBLEM 17.6

a. Could the families of those who died in the explosion bring a class action? Explain your answer.

b. Who are the possible defendants in this case? Explain your answer.

c. Which defendant, if any, should be held liable for the deaths?

d. How much should a family receive in damages for the wrongful death of a loved one? Explain your answer.

Insurance

Americans buy billions of dollars of liability insurance every year so that when an accident occurs, the injured party can recover money from the wrongdoer's insurance company, not from the wrongdoer. While insured persons must sometimes go to court, most tort cases between insurance companies and injured persons are settled without resorting to a trial.

Liability insurance is a contract, or agreement. The insured person agrees to make payments—known as premiums—to the insurance company, and the company agrees to pay for damages caused by the insured persons for the length of the contract. Insurance companies set a limit on how much they will pay. Usually the contract requires the insurance company to provide an attorney to defend the insured person in court.

Most doctors, lawyers, and other professionals carry liability insurance to protect themselves against malpractice suits. These are lawsuits brought by clients or patients who claim that a professional person provided services in a negligent manner. Plaintiffs in malpractice cases sometimes win verdicts or settle for large sums of money—sometimes millions of dollars. Without liability insurance, doctors and lawyers would be personally liable for these verdicts.

liability insurance the type of coverage or insurance that pays for injuries to other people or damage to property if the individual insured is responsible for an accident during the term of the contract

contract a legally enforceable agreement between two or more people to exchange something of value

premiums payments made for insurance coverage

malpractice failure to meet acceptable standards of practice in any professional or official position; often the basis for lawsuits by clients or patients against their attorney or physician

THE **CASE** OF...

The Expensive Insurance Premium

Dr. Sam Akiba, a surgeon, complains that he must pay $100,000 each year in premiums for adequate malpractice insurance. This insurance protects him against having to pay claims made by a patient or a patient's family in the event that the patient suffers injury or death due to a medical error during surgery.

PROBLEM 17.7

a. What might happen to Dr. Akiba if he did not carry malpractice insurance?

b. Why do you think Dr. Akiba's insurance premium is so high?

c. Who pays the cost of Dr. Akiba's insurance?

d. What actions can be taken to lower these insurance premiums?

▲ A doctor at work

Purestock/SuperStock

Manufacturers often carry liability insurance to protect against lawsuits brought by customers who are injured when using the manufacturers' products. For manufacturers and professionals alike, the cost of insurance is usually added into the price of their products or services. This method allows them to spread the costs of insurance among all of their customers or clients.

Homeowners and renters may also carry liability insurance. These policies cover the loss of or damage to the insured person's property. For example, if your personal property is taken during a burglary, you can ask the insurance company for money to replace the stolen items. This process is more practical than suing the burglar.

While many different types of liability insurance exist, very few insurance policies cover intentional harm caused by the insured person. Therefore, a home owner's insurance policy will not pay damages if the home owner assaults a guest.

Insuring a Car

Auto insurance is the most important liability insurance for young people. In 2017, more than seven million automobile accidents were reported to police in the United States. These accidents resulted in nearly 40,000 deaths and more than 2.9 million injuries. So it is not surprising that most states require drivers to carry insurance and that many drivers purchase more insurance than their state requires.

Auto insurance protects you by promising to pay for certain possible losses. Insurance can pay for the cost of repairing your car, medical bills, lost wages, and pain and suffering arising from injury. When you buy auto insurance, you can choose various coverage combinations. Coverage depends on the kind of protection you want and how much you can afford to pay. Common kinds of coverage include liability, medical, collision, comprehensive, uninsured motorist, and personal injury protection (PIP)—sometimes called "no fault."

Your auto liability insurance pays for injuries to other people and property if you are responsible for the accident. This type of insurance may include representation in court by the insurance company's attorneys or payment of your legal fees. Liability coverage pays for damages up to, but not more than, the limits listed in your policy. If injuries and property damage are greater than the policy limits, you will have to pay the difference.

Liability policies generally have three limits on how much a person can collect: (1) a limit on injuries per person, (2) a limit on total injuries to all persons involved in the accident, and (3) a limit on property damage per accident. For example, a "100/300/50" policy would pay up to $100,000 per person for personal injury, $300,000 per accident for all personal injuries, and $50,000 per accident for property damage. Sometimes an injured person brings a lawsuit against the driver or car owner who is responsible for the injuries sustained in an accident.

Because the damages in these cases can be very high, you should carefully consider how much insurance you carry on your car. For example, a $50,000 limit on injuries per person might be far less than the damage incurred in a serious accident. If you were negligent and caused an accident, you would be liable for the amount in excess of your insurance policy limit.

Your **medical coverage** pays for your own medical expenses resulting from accidents involving your car or the car you are driving. It also pays for the medical expenses of any passengers in your car, no matter who is at fault. The amount of medical benefits and the kind of medical costs covered, such as hospital bills and office visits, are limited in the policy. For example, medical coverage may be limited to $100,000 per person injured. This amount is usually in addition to the coverage you receive through your health insurance.

Your **collision coverage** pays for damage to your own car, even if the accident was your fault. Collision coverage usually pays up to the actual value of the car but not for its replacement with a new car. You can lower the cost of collision insurance by including a **deductible**, which is an amount that you agree to pay toward repairs before the insurance company pays anything. For example, a $100 deductible means that if your car has $250 in damages, you will pay $100 and the insurance company will pay the remaining $150. The higher the amount of the deductible, the less expensive the collision insurance.

medical coverage insurance which covers an individual's own medical expenses resulting from accidents

collision coverage insurance that pays for damage to the insured's own car caused by an automobile collision

deductible the amount an insured person agrees to pay toward repairs before the insurance company pays anything

PROBLEM 17.8

You have an eight-year-old car with a market value of only **$4,000**. The annual cost of collision insurance is **$500**. If your state does not require collision insurance, should you continue to purchase it? Give your reasons. Should you carry liability insurance? Explain.

THE **CASE** OF...

The Nonstop Car

Pulling into the left lane to pass a slow-moving truck, Terrell saw the traffic light ahead turn yellow. "If I step on it, I'll make this light," he thought. He accelerated, exceeding the speed limit slightly. Just then an oncoming car made a left turn in front of him. Terrell hit the brakes, but it was too late, and they crashed. A few seconds later, pinned against the steering wheel, he saw the other driver, Candace, stagger out of the car, bleeding and holding her shoulder in pain.

PROBLEM 17.9

a. Who should be responsible for the medical bills and car repair bills resulting from this accident?

b. In most cases, who pays for repairs resulting from auto accidents?

comprehensive coverage the portion of an insurance policy that protects an individual against automobile damage or loss from other than collisions. It includes damages and losses due to fire, vandalism, or theft.

uninsured and underinsured motorist coverage insurance that protects drivers from those with no insurance or inadequate insurance. It compensates the injured for the personal injuries or damage the uninsured driver caused.

Your **comprehensive coverage** protects you against damage or loss to your car from causes other than collisions. For example, comprehensive coverage includes damages due to vandalism, fire, or theft. Read your policy carefully to determine whether valuables in your car, such as a an audio system, are covered in case of theft. Insurance policies sometimes include—usually at an extra charge—coverage for towing or car rental costs.

Your **uninsured and underinsured motorist coverage (UM/UIM)** protects you from other drivers who do not have insurance or do not have enough insurance. The policy pays you for the personal injuries or damage they cause. Be sure to find out whether your policy pays for damages caused by uninsured or underinsured motorists and whether it pays only for personal injuries or also includes damages to your car. Uninsured and underinsured motorist coverage is usually an inexpensive and worthwhile addition to your policy.

Some states require personal injury protection (PIP) coverage. PIP is sometimes called no-fault insurance. If you have PIP coverage your own insurance company will pay up to a certain amount for personal injury damages you sustain in an accident, regardless of who is at fault. With this type of coverage, you may be prohibited from suing the other party for those damages. Notice the difference between PIP and liability insurance. With liability insurance, the other driver's company would pay you if that driver was at fault. If you were at fault, your company would pay the other driver. It sometimes requires a court case to determine who was at fault. With PIP insurance, your own company pays for your personal injury damages (such as medical bills and lost wages). You do not make a claim against the other driver. Some people criticize PIP or no fault insurance because the benefits are limited to a certain amount of money and usually cover only certain personal injury damages (like medical bills or lost wages), but not pain and suffering or damage to your car. In many states, however, the injured person may still be able to sue the other party when damages are higher than the PIP limits, or if the injury is considered serious.

PROBLEM 17.10

Reread The Case of the Nonstop Car. Assume that the accident happened in a state without no-fault insurance and that both Terrell and Candace had insurance coverage. Each had a policy covering all types of losses that included a $250 deductible for collision insurance. Also assume that Terrell was at fault.

a. Whose insurance company would pay for Candace's hospital and car repair bills?

b. Whose insurance company would pay for Terrell's hospital and car repair bills?

c. What do you think would happen if the damages to Candace and her car were greater than the limits of Terrell's policy?

d. If the damages were less than the policy's limits, would Terrell have to pay any money to get his car fixed?

▼ Workers' compensation systems can restrict the recovery of damages if the accident is the result of an employee's refusal to follow safety rules. *Should workers' compensation pay for the injury if the worker without the hard hat is injured?*

Workers' Compensation

Every state has a workers' compensation system that operates to automatically compensate, or pay, employees who are injured on the job. Employers make regular contributions to a state fund or buy insurance for this purpose. Workers are compensated for injuries that occur in the course of their employment. However, they do not have to go to court to prove that their employer was at fault. Workers also receive a portion of their salary while they are recovering and unable to work. Many states provide employees with two-thirds of their regular salary. In exchange, the injured employee usually gives up the right to sue his or her employer. Accidents that occur while the employee is commuting to or from work are rarely covered.

Unlike the plaintiffs in typical tort cases, workers can usually recover monetary damages for their injuries even if they were negligent. However, workers' compensation statutes generally deny recovery when the accident was caused by the employee's intoxication. In addition, nearly half of the states either reduce or prohibit recovery when a worker's refusal to follow safety rules caused the accident. For example, a welder who is blinded on the job after ignoring repeated warnings to wear safety goggles would not be able to recover money under workers' compensation statutes in some states.

Glow Images

The amount of money awarded for a specific injury is limited according to a schedule the state determines. The schedule sets the amount a worker can recover based on the seriousness of the injury, the amount of time the worker is expected to be out of work, and the worker's average weekly wage. Workers cannot usually recover additional damages from the employer through a civil tort action. Workers' compensation is the **exclusive remedy,** or the only compensation, for on-the-job injuries.

exclusive remedy the only solution, or compensation, available to a plaintiff in a particular legal situation

A worker who is injured on the job must notify the employer. Often the employer will ask a doctor to certify the injury. Then either the employer or the injured employee will file a claim. After the claim is filed, the injured employee will regularly receive a workers' compensation payment, just like a paycheck. The payments will continue until the employee can return to work or recovers from the injury.

Many states have a workers' compensation commission that hears claims and decides how much money will be given to injured workers. If the commission decides that little or no money should be given, the injured person may appeal to a court.

THE **CASE** OF...

The School Slip and Fall

Mrs. Braun is the art instructor at the local high school. Dale is a student. One day the maintenance staff forgot to display a warning that the floors had been mopped and were wet. The stairway to the art studio was so slippery that Dale fell down the stairs, breaking his arm. Mrs. Braun was teaching class at the time. When she heard the noise of his fall, she ran out to see what was wrong. She, too, slipped and broke her ankle.

PROBLEM 17.11

a. Who is responsible for Dale's injury? For Mrs. Braun's injury?

b. From whom can Dale recover damages? Is there a limit to the amount he can recover?

c. From whom can Mrs. Braun recover damages? How will she recover these dam-

ages? Is there a limit to the amount she can recover?

d. Why does the law treat these two injured people differently? Is this fair? Explain.

Echo/Getty Images

▶ Intentional torts are deliberate acts that cause harm.

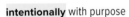

intentionally with purpose

Small children have a natural understanding of what it means to act **intentionally**. When a parent scolds a child for breaking something, the child may plead, "But it was an accident. I didn't do it on purpose!"

A person who plans to perform a certain act, and then does so, is said to have acted with intent. For example, a child who knocks a glass off the table on purpose does it intentionally, even if the child genuinely hoped the glass would land softly on the rug unharmed, rather than shattering.

Intentional torts an action taken deliberately to harm another person and/or his or her property

Actions taken deliberately that harm another person or their property are called **intentional torts**. There are two general types of intentional torts: those causing injury to persons and those causing harm to property. In the law of torts, the required intent is to do the forbidden act—knocking the glass off the table—not a bad motive or a desire to cause harm.

Types of Damages

compensatory damages in a civil case, money the court requires a defendant to pay a winning plaintiff to make up for harm caused. This harm can be financial (for example, lost wages, medical expenses, etc.), physical (for example, past, present, and future pain and suffering), and, in some jurisdictions, emotional (fright and shock, anxiety, etc.).

A person who proves that someone else committed an intentional tort against him or her can recover damages to make up for the harm caused. These are called **compensatory damages** because the award compensates for harm caused by the defendant. For example, when Gus is punched by Seth, Gus may be able to receive damages of $6,000 to cover his medical bills.

Compensatory damages can also include lost wages, as well as "pain and suffering." To receive these types of damages, the plaintiff has to prove existing and future losses—such as medical bills, reduced or lost wages, and pain and suffering—with reasonable certainty. Juries decide how much money will fully compensate the injured person for any pain and suffering.

nominal damages a token amount of money awarded by a court to a plaintiff to show that the claim was justified, even if the plaintiff is unable to prove economic harm

In some cases, the plaintiff recovers only **nominal damages**, or a token amount of money awarded by the court to show that the claim was justified. These are symbolic awards of money that are paid even if the plaintiff is unable to prove economic harm. Nominal damages are awarded to recognize that the defendant acted wrongfully, even though he or she did not cause substantial injury or loss. For example, suppose Juan slapped Matthew in a heated argument. In court, it is shown that even though Juan wrongfully slapped Matthew, Matthew suffered no serious injury. The court might award $1 in nominal damages to Matthew.

punitive damages awards in excess of the proven economic loss. In a tort action, they are awarded to the plaintiff to punish the defendant and to warn others not to engage in such conduct.

Punitive damages are the amounts of money the court awards to the plaintiff to punish the defendant for malicious, willful, or outrageous acts. Punitive damages also serve as a warning to others not to engage in such conduct.

It is possible for both nominal and punitive damages to be awarded even where there is little or no actual harm that would justify compensatory damages. Suppose that Kate shoots a gun at Mark and misses him. This action is an intentional tort. The court could award nominal damages (because there was no actual harm inflicted) and punitive damages (because Kate's act was so outrageous).

Sometimes people sued for intentional torts do not have to pay any damages at all, even though they did exactly what the plaintiff claims. In these instances, the defendant may have a legal defense.

THE **CASE** OF...

The Mischievous Child

Jeremy, Eric's five-year-old child, was playing in the backyard when his neighbor, an elderly woman named Helen, went outside to sit down. Jeremy pulled the lawn chair away just before Helen sat down. Helen was unable to catch herself and fell to the ground. As a result, she fractured her hip.

Jeremy did not intend to hurt Helen and did not believe she would be hurt. The child was aware, however, that if he pulled away the chair as Helen was sitting down, she would almost certainly land on the ground.

PROBLEM 18.1

a. Did Jeremy act intentionally? Is a five-year-old too young to act intentionally? To understand the significance of his actions?

b. Did Jeremy cause Helen's fall? Explain the reasons for your answer.

c. Can Helen sue Jeremy and force him to pay for her injuries? Can she sue Eric?

d. Should it matter that Jeremy did not mean to hurt the woman?

e. Would the legal outcome be different if the child had been running in the yard and tripped over the chair just as Helen was sitting down, resulting in the same injury to her? Explain your answer.

Torts That Injure Persons

Several acts are classified as intentional torts causing injury to a person or persons. The following sections explain the five most common types of intentional torts.

Battery

A **battery** occurs when a person intentionally causes a harmful or offensive contact with another person. The perpetrator is liable for all resulting damages, regardless of whether he or she wanted or expected the contact to cause injury. For example, Elaine became angry at Ravi and shoved him toward an open window. Although the shove was not hard, he fell backward through the window and suffered serious injuries. While Elaine did not want him to suffer such serious injury, she will be liable for damages if Ravi sues her for battery.

What constitutes a harmful or offensive contact? Certainly a punch in the nose or a gunshot through the chest is a harmful and offensive contact. But what about an unwanted kiss on the cheek? The law considers "offensive" to be whatever would offend an average person in society. For example, most people would not be offended by a light tap on the shoulder accompanied by a pleasant "Excuse me, sir, do you have the time?" Such a touch would not be considered a battery, even if it somehow led to an injury.

Assault

The tort of **assault** occurs when a person goes beyond mere words and intentionally makes someone fear an immediate, harmful or offensive contact. An assault can be an intentional threat, show of force, or movement that causes a reasonable fear. For example, if Jeb throws a rotten tomato at Colin's head, Jeb has committed the tort of assault, even if Colin ducks at the last instant and does not get hit. If Colin fails to duck and the tomato hits him, there has been both an assault and a battery. While battery requires a harmful or offensive contact, assault merely requires fear that a harmful or offensive contact is about to occur.

For assault to occur, the fear of harmful or offensive contact must be reasonable or well founded. For example, assume Simon is sitting at a traffic light and Monica is crossing the street in the intersection in front of Simon's car. Monica suddenly becomes overwhelmed by a terrible feeling that Simon is going to step on the gas and run her over. As a result

▲ Battery is one of the most common intentional torts. *In what ways does the definition of battery help protect a victim's dignity from being violated?*

battery any intentional, unlawful physical contact inflicted on one person by another without consent. In some states, this is combined with assault. A battery can also be a crime.

assault an intentional threat, show of force, or movement that causes a reasonable fear of, or an actual physical contact with, another person. It can be a crime or a tort.

of this fear, she has a heart attack. There is no assault in this case because Monica's fear was not reasonable. Also, Simon did not intend to make her fear an immediate, harmful or offensive contact.

As the result of an assault, the plaintiff may be able to recover compensation for mental suffering, such as fright or embarrassment, along with any physical injury that directly results from the assault.

PROBLEM 18.2

a. Lenny is a successful—and very rich—bank robber. He is also careful not to harm bank tellers. In fact, he always uses weapons without bullets. Unfortunately for Lenny, he holds up one bank too many, and the police catch him. The day before he is caught, he sticks an unloaded gun into the face of Cynthia, the teller at the Last National Bank. Cynthia wants to bring a civil suit against Lenny for assault. Will she be successful?

b. The tort of battery can be committed against someone who is asleep or unconscious, but the tort of assault cannot. Explain.

Infliction of Emotional Distress

intentional infliction of emotional distress a tort in which a defendant purposely engages in an action that causes extreme emotional harm to the plaintiff

Intentional infliction of emotional distress, a relatively new tort, has been recognized by the courts only since about 1940. A person commits this tort by intentionally using words or actions that are meant to cause someone extreme anxiety or emotional distress. Actual physical injury is not required for the plaintiff to recover damages for infliction of emotional distress. However, courts do require that the defendant's conduct be quite outrageous and that the plaintiff prove extreme distress. Mere insults are not enough to form the basis of a lawsuit for infliction of emotional distress.

When the actions of bill collectors, insurance adjusters, and landlords have been truly outrageous and excessive, courts have sometimes allowed plaintiffs to recover damages. For example, in one case, a young man owed a store money. The store tried to collect the debt from the youth's father by falsely claiming that he guaranteed the son's debt, making late-night calls to the father, and sending letters telling the father that his credit had been revoked. In this case, the court found that the store had intentionally caused the father severe emotional distress.

Extremely outrageous conduct by restaurants, hotels, or transportation companies can also sometimes form the basis for the tort of intentional infliction of emotional distress. These businesses and certain others have a special obligation to deal with the public in a courteous manner.

Recovery for this tort is sharply limited in order to keep the legal system from being flooded with lawsuits brought by persons suffering from unkind and inconsiderate acts. In addition, there is some value for a free society in letting angry people express their anger without fear of being sued. Among the legal defenses sometimes used are that the defendant's conduct was not outrageous or was in a category of protected expression, that the plaintiff is overly sensitive, and that a reasonable person would not suffer extreme distress as a result of the defendant's conduct.

THE **CASE** OF...

The Case of the Funeral Protest

Members of a small church in Kansas, the Westboro Baptist Church, believe that God hates America because it tolerates homosexuality, particularly in the military services. They work to spread this message by staging protests, frequently at military funerals. The church members have stated that they often stage demonstrations at military funerals for the publicity it generates for them.

In 2006, members of the church traveled more than 1,000 miles to picket at the funeral in Maryland of Matthew Snyder, a Marine. They carried signs that read, "Thank God For Dead Soldiers" and "You're Going to Hell," as well as signs that criticized the Catholic Church and the military. Though Matthew Snyder was not gay, the church members displayed the signs as a form of protest against the fact that the U.S. military allowed homosexuals to serve.

At the funeral, the protestors stood more than 1,000 feet away from the church, on a designated public right-of-way, where their signs were not visible to funeral-goers entering the church. The protestors did not yell, act violently, or engage in civil disobedience. Though Matthew Snyder's father, Albert, knew the church would be picketing his son's funeral, he only learned of the language on the protesters' signs by watching news coverage of the funeral and protest. Mr. Snyder became physically ill when he saw the signs on television and felt they were directed at his son.

Mr. Snyder sued the church and its minister, Rev. Phelps, for the tort of intentional infliction of emotional distress.

According to Mr. Snyder, the demonstration targeted him and caused him harm during a time of bereavement. He pointed out that his son was not

a public figure, nor was the funeral a public event. The church members intended to upset him. He also argued that the church members' speech is not protected by the First Amendment because speech by private individuals directed at private individuals is not protected.

Rev. Phelps and the church members believed that their speech was protected under the First Amendment's freedom of speech clause. Their signs were statements of public concern and did not refer directly to Matthew. They were in a public place, did not have a direct confrontation with the funeral attendees, and Mr. Snyder did not even see their messages in person.

PROBLEM 18.3

a. What is the strongest argument in support of allowing Mr. Snyder to recover damages?

b. What is the strongest argument for the church?

c. Based on the information provided, if you were the trial judge how would you decide this case?

Give a specific example of a situation in which you believe someone should be able to recover damages for intentional infliction of emotional distress. Write the dialogue, showing exactly what each party said and did. Determine the amount of damages that should be awarded.

False Imprisonment

false imprisonment the intentional or wrongful confinement of another person against his or her will

Being able to sue for **false imprisonment** protects a person's right to be free from unreasonable restraint. False imprisonment occurs when someone intentionally and wrongfully confines another person against his or her will. For example, assume that a restaurant manager tells an employee to get out of the walk-in refrigerator so she can lock up and go home. When the employee takes too long, the manager shuts the refrigerator door with the employee still inside and leaves for the night. The restaurant manager has committed the tort of false imprisonment.

Suspected shoplifters sometimes sue shopkeepers who detain them as they attempt to leave the store. In balancing an individual's right to be free from confinement and a shopkeeper's right to protect his or her property

THE **CASE** OF...

The Captured Shoplifter

Kathleen is looking around in a clothing store. As she passes a rack of skirts, she takes one and slips it under her jacket. Thinking that no one has noticed, she turns to leave the store. The store manager, however, has been watching her on the surveillance camera. As she passes the cash register, he stops her before she leaves the store.

PROBLEM 18.5

a. The store manager has several ways he can proceed. Rank the following options in order of most reasonable to least reasonable:

1. The manager calls the police and keeps Kathleen in his office until they come.

2. The manager tells an assistant manager to keep Kathleen in the back room until the police arrive. The assistant manager is called away on another task, and he ties Kathleen's hands and feet together so she cannot run away before the police can get there.

3. The manager locks Kathleen in the storage room for about seven hours, until he is ready to close the store for the day. Then he takes her to the local police station.

4. The store manager tells his armed security guard to arrest Kathleen. The guard pulls his gun, takes Kathleen to the back of the store, and then calls the police.

5. The store manager stops her, takes the skirt back, yells at her in front of other customers, and then he lets her go home.

b. Would any of these options qualify as false imprisonment? If so, which ones and why? What should a shopkeeper do if he or she catches a shoplifter?

from theft, the law recognizes a shopkeeper's privilege to temporarily detain a person suspected of shoplifting. However, shopkeepers must act reasonably, using no more restraint than is necessary to protect their property.

Torts Related to Defamation

A person's reputation is protected by laws prohibiting **defamation**. Defamation includes acts that harm a person's reputation and can be classified as oral or written. Oral statements that harm reputation are called **slander**; written defamation is called **libel**. Traditionally damages were more difficult to prove for slander than for libel. However, social media has made it easier to prove some spoken statements.

Defamation occurs when someone makes a false statement about another person that is communicated to a third party, causing harm to the person's reputation. If a patient yells, "You're a drunken butcher!" to his surgeon, it is not slander if no one else hears the statement. However, if the patient yells this false statement in the hospital hallway where others can hear it and the doctor's reputation is harmed, a tort has been committed.

Proving that the offensive statement is *true* is a complete defense in a defamation lawsuit. For example, Sid brings his car to a garage and yells at the mechanic, "You ruined my transmission!" in front of other customers. This statement might be harmful to the mechanic and his business. But if Sid can prove that the mechanic did ruin his transmission, he has a good defense to slander claims.

defamation written or spoken expression about a person communicated to a third party that is false and damages that person's reputation

slander spoken expression about a person that is false and damages that person's reputation

libel a written expression about a person that is false and damages that person's reputation

THE **CASE** OF...

The Very Unpopular Photographer

A newspaper article reported that a certain photographer, famous for his candid but unauthorized photos of celebrities, was "the most hated photographer" in town. The same article reported that this photographer had installed listening devices outside the homes of celebrities. The photographer sued the newspaper for defamation. At the trial, the newspaper called as witnesses several of the celebrities who testified about the listening devices (bugs) they had discovered.

▲ Paparazzi at work

PROBLEM 18.6

a. What should the photographer have to prove to win his defamation case?

b. In what way do you think the photographer was harmed by the article?

c. What defense, if any, might be available to the newspaper?

d. How should this case be decided? Give your reasons.

Paul Bradbury/Getty Images

The law also protects opinion. Assume a movie critic watches a new movie and, in her review, is particularly critical of one actor's performance. The review may harm the actor's reputation and economic interests, but such statements are usually protected as opinion.

In the United States, freedom of speech and freedom of the press are very important. Therefore, courts balance a person's right to protect his or her reputation against the public's interest in receiving a wide range of information. For this reason, the U.S. Supreme Court has established rules making it difficult for public figures to win damage awards against the media. To win a defamation suit against the media, a public figure must prove not only that a statement was false and caused harm, but also that the statement was made with actual malice: the statement was made with knowledge of its falsity or with a reckless disregard for whether or not the statement was true. These rules make it difficult for celebrities and other famous people to sue the media and win. In a sense, famous people sacrifice some protection of their reputations.

Torts That Harm Property

Tort law protects a person's property in two ways: (1) it protects against interference with the owner's exclusive use of the property, and (2) it protects against the property being taken or damaged. Two kinds of property are protected: **real property** (land and the items attached to it, such as houses, crops, and fences), and **personal property** (property that can be moved, such as cars, computers, and clothing). The legal system in the United States is very protective of private property rights.

Real Property

Everyone has seen signs that read "Private Property—Keep Out" or "No Trespassing." The tort of **trespass** occurs when a person enters another person's property without permission. The owner can recover damages from the trespasser even if there is no harm to the property because the law protects the owner's exclusive right to the property.

In a technical sense, a trespass occurs every time you cut across a neighbor's lawn on the way to the grocery store. Obviously, landowners rarely sue people who merely walk across their property. But what would you do if someone committed a continuing trespass by going onto your property without permission and erecting a sign advertising a nearby restaurant?

In some cases, tort law protects against harm caused by someone who never physically enters your property. A **nuisance** occurs when there is an unreasonable interference with your ability to use and

real property land and all items attached to it, such as houses, crops, and fences

personal property property or belongings that can be moved, such as cars, clothing, furniture, and appliances

trespass the unauthorized intrusion on, or improper use of, property belonging to another person. This can be the basis of an intentional tort case or a criminal prosecution.

nuisance an unreasonable interference with the use and enjoyment of one's property, usually repeated or continued for prolonged periods of time

▼ Posting "No Trespassing" signs can help protect property. *In what other ways does tort law protect property?*

amygdala_imagery/Getty Images

Real Property and Reasonable Interference

Read each case carefully. Is there an unreasonable interference with property? If a nuisance does exist, decide on a fair remedy. Explain the reasons for your answers.

a. Mr. Iwamoto works the 11 p.m. to 7 a.m. shift at the plastics factory and then comes home to sleep. On his way to school every weekday at about 8 a.m., Darrell drives by Mr. Iwamoto's house with his sound system blaring loud music. The music frequently awakens Mr. Iwamoto.

b. A passenger on a commuter train uses his cell phone to make and receive business and personal calls each day during his one-hour ride to work.

c. Morgan owns a restaurant next to High Penn's oil refinery. The refinery occasionally emits gases and odors that make people feel sick. Morgan, believing that this hurts her restaurant business, brings a suit against the oil refinery. High Penn argues that (1) the refinery was properly constructed, (2) there is no way to operate the refinery without emitting these occasional gases and odors, and (3) the refinery was in operation before Morgan opened her restaurant.

d. Commercial advertisements constantly appear in the inbox of your personal e-mail account. The ads are for products that do not interest you. You did not request information about these products.

e. In order to earn the extra money they need to send their two children to college, Larry and Meg operate a small auto repair and body shop in their garage. After returning from their day jobs, they work on cars until about 10 p.m. The noise produced when they rev car engines disturbs their neighbors.

f. Adriana Stein is a successful musician who travels extensively to give concerts. To enjoy some peace and relaxation when she is not traveling, she buys a house in the countryside only five miles from the nearest airport. As the surrounding metropolitan area grows, air traffic at the airport increases. Eventually, the airport needs to build another runway to accommodate the increased traffic. Experts report that the runway can be built in only one location at the airport. Airplanes using this runway would descend directly over Adriana's house, creating loud noise and disrupting the quiet of the countryside. In response to the airport's plan to build the runway, Adriana organizes her neighbors into a citizen action group called RAMP (Residents Against More Planes). The group sues the airport, seeking an injunction to stop the planning and construction of the new runway.

▲ A jet approaches the airport.

enjoy your property. Courts will balance the usefulness of the activity complained of against the harm caused.

You do not have a right to be free from all interference with your property, only unreasonable interference. For example, Ari and Brenda are neighbors. One Sunday, Ari has 20 guests for a barbecue in his backyard, and Brenda is unable to watch the baseball game on her computer while lying outside on her hammock. This one-time event is not a nuisance. If Ari were to cut his lawn at six o'clock every Sunday morning, however, that would probably be a nuisance.

You can recover damages if you win a nuisance suit. In some cases, you may also be able to get a court order requiring the defendant to stop the activity. This court order is called an **injunction**. An injunction requires that a person do, or not do, a specific act.

injunction a court order requiring a person to do, or refrain from doing, a particular act

Personal Property

Tort law provides compensation to someone whose personal property is taken, damaged, or interfered with. Suppose a burglar breaks into Laura's house and steals her computer. If the person is arrested, there will be a criminal prosecution for burglary. Laura could also sue the thief in civil court for a tort called **conversion**. Conversion occurs when someone unlawfully exercises control over the personal property of another person. Of course, it might be difficult for Laura to collect money damages from this defendant.

conversion in tort law, the taking or controlling of another's property without consent. If the property is not returned to the rightful owner, the court can force the defendant to give the plaintiff the monetary value of the property.

A series of privileges has developed for protecting property. You can always use nonviolent means to protect real property or to recover personal property. However, use careful judgment in these cases. Telling your friend that she has taken your book bag may work well; yelling at a fleeing thief to drop your wallet is likely to fail!

Defenses to Intentional Torts

Even if a plaintiff proves that the defendant has committed a tort, the defendant can still escape liability if he or she has a valid defense. **Consent** is the most common defense to many intentional torts. This defense means that the plaintiff consented, or agreed, to the harmful conduct and thus gave up the right to sue later. In the sport of boxing, punches are thrown that in almost any other situation would be serious batteries. However, boxers sign a contract consenting to be punched during a match. Of course, if one boxer tries to stab another with a knife, this would be an assault, as the consent did not involve weapons and was limited to punches.

consent written, spoken, or assumed agreement to something

Consent can be written, spoken, or simply assumed based on the situation. For example, children may knock each other down while playing, but this conduct does not constitute a battery. It is assumed that children may accidently bump into each other while running and playing. In another example, suppose you were seriously injured in an auto accident and taken to the hospital for emergency surgery. Ordinarily, you would sign a consent form giving the doctor permission to perform the operation, but in an emergency, when your physical or medical condition makes it impossible to sign a form, the law assumes that you consent to lifesaving surgery.

Privilege is another defense to intentional torts. Privilege justifies conduct that would otherwise be a tort, because the defendant's interests (or those of the public) require it. Privilege also often justifies conduct that would otherwise be a tort because public policy is best served by permitting such behavior.

Legal authority is one such privilege that can be applied to many different situations. For example, a police officer has legal authority to restrain a person's liberty while carrying out an arrest, and therefore an officer has a valid defense to a false imprisonment suit. Parents have legal authority to use reasonable force to discipline their children. Owners have legal authority over their property and may use reasonable force to recover their property from a thief, even though they would otherwise be committing the acts of false imprisonment, battery, or assault.

privilege (1) an advantage, right to preferential treatment, or excuse from a duty others must perform; (2) a right that cannot be taken away; (3) the right to speak or write personally damaging words because the law specifically allows it; (4) the right and the duty to withhold information from others because of some special status or relationship of confidentiality. These privileges include spousal, doctor-patient, and attorney-client.

PROBLEM 18.7

The Kings own a store in a crime-ridden section of town. As victims of break-ins in the past, they buy a guard dog to protect their store. The dog is trained to attack on command. It stays in the store from 11 p.m. to 7 a.m. while the store is closed. One night, a man breaks into the store and is attacked by the dog. The man is caught and convicted of burglary. After the judge gives him a suspended sentence, the burglar sues the Kings for the injuries caused by the dog. How would you decide this case?

◀ Consent can be implied based on the situation. *Can a child be charged with battery if he knocks down another child during play?*

©Westend61/SuperStock

self-defense the right to defend oneself with whatever force is reasonably necessary against an actual or reasonably perceived threat of personal harm

Perhaps the best-known privilege is **self-defense**. If Julie attacks Amanda, then Amanda can use reasonable force to protect or defend herself. If Julie later sues Amanda for battery, Amanda will be able to use self-defense to justify her actions, as long as the force she used was not excessive. Deadly force—force that may cause life-threatening harm—would be considered excessive unless Amanda's life was in danger.

Defenders who take control of a situation and become aggressors commit battery and have no self-defense claim. For example, while self-defense allows Amanda to defend herself against Julie, it does not allow her to teach Julie a lesson or to seek revenge. Self-defense also allows someone to come to the rescue of another person and to use the same amount of force the victim could have used to repel the attacker.

defense of property the use of reasonable force, which would otherwise be illegal, to defend your home or other property

Defense of property is another privilege that allows people to use reasonable force to defend their homes or property. Deadly force is generally not considered reasonable when defending property. However, in some states there is a "stand your ground" law—sometimes called the Castle Doctrine—that enables homeowners to defend their property using deadly force.

YOU BE the JUDGE

Intentional Torts and Legal Defenses

Read each of the following accounts carefully. For each one, identify the plaintiff and the defendant. Does the defendant have a legal defense? Give reasons for your answers.

a. During the last inning of a baseball game, the star pitcher loses control of an inside pitch. As a result, the ball hits the batter, shattering two bones in his arm.

b. Josh has an appointment to have an oral surgeon remove a tooth that has been causing him discomfort for some time. While Josh is under anesthesia, the surgeon notices that two other teeth are emerging in a crooked position. She believes the crooked teeth are likely to cause Josh pain in the future, so she removes them as well.

c. While horsing around, Sandy throws a snowball at a friend on a crowded city street corner. The snowball misses the friend but hits an elderly man, who falls to the ground and is injured.

d. Maya, a prison guard, is physically attacked by an angry inmate. The inmate knocks Maya down and kicks her in the head and ribs. Maya responds to the inmate in a similar fashion.

e. Wendy breaks into the first floor of Amy's house and begins to steal valuable property. Hearing the intruder, Amy comes downstairs wielding a baseball bat. Seeing this, Wendy drops the property and runs toward the front door of the house. Amy runs after her and hits her on the head with the bat, knocking her unconscious.

▶ Public works projects can create risks of harm through negligence.

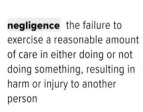

negligence the failure to exercise a reasonable amount of care in either doing or not doing something, resulting in harm or injury to another person

Tort law establishes standards of care that society expects from people. **Negligence** is conduct that falls below the standard established by law for protecting others against unreasonable risks of harm. But what does this mean? The word *negligence* comes from the root word *neglect*. This may lead us to think of negligence as forgetfulness, inattentiveness, or lack of care about others. But tort law requires us to analyze negligence as it relates to a person's conduct. Even a person who cares a great deal about the welfare of others may be negligent if his or her conduct creates an unreasonable risk of harm. On the other hand, a person who is totally unconcerned about the safety of others may not be negligent if his or her conduct does not subject another person to an unreasonable risk of harm.

These are some examples of negligent conduct:

- Dr. D'Angelo, a surgeon, forgets to remove a clamp from a patient's body while operating and stitches up the patient.

- Monica leaves a loaded rifle on the floor where her younger brothers and sisters usually play. A child is shot.

- A city employee working in a manhole forgets to replace the cover when he goes to lunch, and a pedestrian falls in and is injured.

- A drug company markets a birth control device for women without conducting adequate medical testing. A woman develops a serious illness from using the device.

Ingram Publishing

Elements of Negligence

Unlike intentional torts, many of which have specific names, negligence is a very broad category that deals with many kinds of wrongful conduct. While the different types of wrongful conduct may not have separate names, they do have something in common. For a plaintiff to win a negligence action against the defendant, each of the following four **elements** must be proven by a preponderance (majority) of the evidence:

1. **Duty:** The defendant, or accused wrongdoer, owed a duty of care to the plaintiff, or injured person.
2. **Breach of duty:** The defendant's conduct breached or violated that duty.
3. **Causation:** The defendant's conduct caused the plaintiff's harm.
4. **Damages:** The plaintiff suffered actual injuries or losses.

All these elements must be proven or the plaintiff will not prevail. For example, in the case of the drug company described on the previous page, the woman bringing the lawsuit would have to prove each of the elements of negligence by a preponderance of the evidence against the company. Specifically, she would have to prove that the company had a duty of care to its customers to adequately test any new birth control product before selling it, that the company breached this duty through its failure to adequately test the device, and that this breach resulted in a defective product that caused actual damage (ill health, hospital bills, and so on) to her.

As in intentional torts, defendants in negligence cases sometimes have legal defenses. These defenses, which are explained below, are different from those used in intentional torts.

Duty and Breach

Everyone has a general **duty,** or legal obligation, to exercise reasonable care toward other persons and their property. Negligence law is primarily concerned with compensating victims who are harmed by a wrongdoer's action or inaction that **breaches,** or violates, this standard of reasonable care. If a mechanic fixes the brakes on your car without using reasonable care and skill, and this faulty repair causes you to have an accident, you can recover damages from the mechanic as the result of his or her negligence.

What if someone is harmed by another person's inaction? For example, Brian is drowning in a lake and Jennifer, an expert swimmer, passes by in a boat. Does she have a legal duty to rescue Brian? While she may have a moral obligation to help, she generally does not have a legal duty to act unless there is some special relationship between them. For example, if Jennifer is a lifeguard and Brian is drowning in an area she is supervising, then Jennifer has an obligation to respond.

elements the conditions that make an act unlawful

duty a legal obligation

breach the violation of a law, duty, or other form of obligation, including obligations formed through contracts or warranties, either by engaging in an action or failing to act

The Spilled Coffee

In 1994, 79-year-old Stella Liebeck bought a cup of coffee from the drive-through window at a fast-food restaurant. While the car in which she was a passenger was stopped to allow her to put cream and sugar in her coffee, she balanced the cup between her knees and attempted to remove the lid. The coffee spilled, causing third-degree burns to over six percent of Liebeck's body and causing her to spend eight days in the hospital and undergo skin graft operations. Liebeck sued the restaurant for damages.

The restaurant was part of a large national chain that served its coffee at approximately 180°F (82°C), despite the fact that coffee at such a high temperature is too hot to drink. At the trial, the chain's quality control manager testified that the sale of any food over 140°F (60°C) would create a burn hazard.

The restaurant argued that, according to its surveys, many of its customers take coffee back home or to work with them and consume it there, so the higher temperature is necessary to assure that it will still be hot when consumed. They also claimed that many customers choose this particular chain specifically because they do serve their coffee so hot. However, the chain was also aware that, between 1982 and 1992, approximately 700 claims had been filed by people burned by their coffee.

The jury awarded Liebeck $160,000 in compensatory damages (finding her 20 percent at fault for her own negligence) and $2.7 million in punitive damages (the equivalent of two days of the chain's coffee sales). The trial judge reduced the amount of punitive damages to $480,000, and the parties eventually came to a confidential (secret) settlement agreement for an undisclosed amount.

The case launched a public debate about the appropriateness of lawsuits with high damage awards in situations such as this one.

PROBLEM 19.1

a. Who is the plaintiff in this case? Who is the defendant in this case?

b. What, if anything, did the defendant do wrong? What, if anything, did the plaintiff do wrong?

c. Did the defendant cause the plaintiff harm on purpose? Did the defendant's conduct in some way cause the harm suffered by the plaintiff?

d. What duty of care, if any, did the defendant have toward its customers? Did the defendant uphold or breach that duty? Explain your answers.

e. Do you agree or disagree with the outcome of this trial? Give the reasons for your answers.

f. What are the arguments for and against the award of punitive damages in a case like this one?

The Reasonable Person Standard

Everyone has a duty toward everyone else in society: the duty to act reasonably. If you act unreasonably, then you have breached this duty. If the breach causes damage, then you may be liable for damages.

To help judge whether certain conduct is negligent, the law has developed an imaginary person—"the reasonable person of ordinary prudence or carefulness." The reasonably prudent person does not represent the typical, average individual. Rather, this is an idealized version of such a person. This person acts the way a community expects its members to act, not exactly as they do in fact act.

How does the reasonable person behave? The reasonable person considers how likely a certain harm is to occur, how serious the harm would be if it did occur, and the burden involved in avoiding the harm. The likelihood and seriousness of the harm are balanced against the burden of avoiding the harm.

For example, assume a pedestrian is about to cross a road where there is very little traffic. The harm to be avoided, of course, is being hit by a car. How likely is it that such an accident will occur? Not likely. How serious would the harm be if it did occur? Very serious. How difficult would it be to avoid this harm? Not difficult at all; simply look both ways before crossing. Our reasonably prudent person looks both ways before crossing such a street.

In a second example, the walkway to a secluded home in the woods has a crack in it. The crack is large enough to cause a person to trip and fall. This is the harm the homeowner needs to avoid. In this instance, the likelihood of the harm is small, the harm would probably not be serious, and the cost of avoiding it (fixing the walkway) may be substantial. Even our reasonably prudent person may decide not to fix this crack in the walk. However, it may be reasonable to post a sign warning of the danger, because the burden (cost) of the sign would be less than the burden of making the repair.

Tort law also requires that you use reasonable care to protect other persons from harm when they are on your property. In general, though, you are not liable if a trespasser is injured on your property. For example, if a trespasser walks across your lawn, trips on a sprinkler, and sprains her ankle, she will not be able to recover damages from you.

An exception to the general rule occurs when the trespasser is a child too young to appreciate a dangerous condition on your property. The law requires landowners to use reasonable care to eliminate a dangerous condition on their land or to otherwise protect children when the condition presents an unreasonable risk of serious injury where children are likely to trespass. Because of this law, sometimes called the **attractive nuisance** doctrine, construction companies generally fence in excavation sites.

Most people who enter your property are probably not trespassers. Generally they are either guests in your home or businesspeople and customers visiting your workplace. In most states, you have a legal duty to warn guests of any known danger on your property. For example, if your front porch is being repaired, you have a duty to warn your guests to avoid this dangerous situation.

attractive nuisance doctrine that says if a person keeps something on his or her premises that is likely to attract children, that person must take reasonable steps to protect children against dangers the condition might cause

If you own a store or other business establishment and the public enters your property for a business purpose, the law imposes an even higher duty. Business owners have a duty to use reasonable care to inspect their property to make it safe for business visitors. For this reason, a restaurant owner is not merely required to warn customers of a slippery sidewalk on a snowy day but is obligated to use reasonable care to make the sidewalk safe. This may be done by shoveling the snow or spreading salt or sand.

The law assumes that reasonable people do not break the law. Therefore, if someone violates a law, he or she is automatically considered to have breached the duty to act reasonably. If the breach causes injury, then the wrongdoer is negligent. For example, most states have laws prohibiting leaving an unattended vehicle running. Such laws were established because of the risk that such cars can easily be stolen. What would happen if you borrowed your friend's car to run an errand, left it running while you ran into a store, and it was stolen? Have you breached your duty to act responsibly? Can your friend sue you for the value of the car if it can be recovered?

Certain professionals, such as doctors, plumbers, and pilots, are considered to have the abilities of reasonably skilled persons qualified to be members of their professions. For this reason, a plumber who repairs a kitchen sink that later leaks and damages the floor cannot defend against

▲ Business owners have a duty to make their establishments safe for customers. *What responsibility do homeowners have to guests in their home?*

THE **CASE** OF...

The Unfenced Swimming Pool

The Garcia family built a large swimming pool in their backyard. The pool was two feet deep in the shallow end and nine feet deep near the diving board. They placed lights around the pool that turned on automatically at dusk. They also placed four large "Danger—Deep Water" signs around all sides of the pool.

One day, a four-year-old who lived a block away wandered onto their property, entered the pool, and drowned. The child's parents sued the Garcia family for not fencing in the pool.

PROBLEM 19.2

a. How should this case be decided?

b. Suppose the Garcias had fenced in the pool and the child had climbed the fence and drowned. Should the child's parents be able to recover damages in that situation?

Dennis MacDonald/Alamy

THE **CASE** OF...

Liability for Serving Alcohol

Lance is a 16-year-old high school junior. He gathers the alcohol left over from his parents' New Year's party and decides to throw a party at his house on a Saturday night when his parents are out of town. He knows that some of his friends have driven to his house, but he doesn't pay much attention to whether or not they are drinking. He sees his friend Abby finish a beer, grab her car keys, and walk out the door to go home. Stefan, another friend, leaves with Abby to get a ride home. Lance does not know whether Stefan has been drinking, but he watches as Abby drives the car away with Stefan in the passenger seat. As Abby pulls her car onto the highway, she swerves and hits another car head-on. Stefan and the driver of the other car are seriously injured.

▲ A head-on collision

PROBLEM 19.3

a. Who can sue whom in this situation?

b. What duty did Lance have in this situation? Did he violate that duty?

c. What duty, if any, do Lance's parents have in this situation? Did they violate that duty? Would it make a difference if his parents had been at home?

d. Now assume that Lance is a 25-year-old bartender who serves Abby and Stefan, who are both over 21, although he knows that they are intoxicated. The rest of the facts remain the same. Answer questions **a.** and **b.** using this scenario.

e. Is it fair to hold Lance responsible in either situation? Give your reasons.

f. Some bars have "designated driver" programs. Why have they done this? Should people who hold private parties in their homes do anything special to protect their guests from drinking and driving? What, if anything, could be done?

a tort action by claiming that he completed the job as skillfully as the ordinarily prudent person. The work must be at the level of the ordinarily prudent plumber.

Minors are liable for torts they commit. However, the standard used in negligence cases involving minors is not the same as the standard used for adults. Instead, the law compares the minor's conduct with reasonable conduct for others of the same age, intelligence, and experience. When a minor reaches the age of majority, the adult standard of care applies. There is one important exception to this rule: when minors engage in what is ordinarily considered an adult activity, such as driving a car, they are held to the adult standard of care.

THE **CASE** OF...

AIDS Liability

Tyler is infected with HIV, the virus that causes AIDS. He is new in town and wants to meet people and make friends. However, he does not want anyone to know about his HIV status. He eventually meets and becomes romantically involved with Audrey. He has unprotected sex with her, but he still does not disclose his HIV status to her. Audrey contracts the virus as a result of her relationship with Tyler.

PROBLEM 19.4

a. Did Tyler have a duty to tell Audrey about his condition? Explain.

b. Would it make a difference if AIDS were an easily curable disease?

c. What, if anything, should Audrey be able to recover in damages from Tyler? Explain.

Causation

If a plaintiff proves that the defendant owed him or her a duty and that this duty was violated, there still must be proof that the defendant's acts *caused* harm to the plaintiff. While it seems like common sense to require a causal connection between the act complained of and the plaintiff's injury, the concept is sometimes troublesome to apply. See The Case of the Great Chicago Fire for an example of such difficulty.

When you think about the element of **causation,** you must consider two separate issues: **cause in fact** and **proximate cause.** Cause in fact is easy to understand. If the harm would not have occurred without the wrongful act, the act is the cause in fact. If Mrs. O'Leary had not placed the lantern too close to the cow, it would not have been kicked over, and the Great Chicago Fire would not have occurred. Her act was the cause in fact of the fire.

It is often hard to draw the line in proximate cause situations. The basic idea behind proximate cause is that there must be a close connection between the wrongful act and the harm caused. In other words, the harm caused must have been a foreseeable result of the act or acts. Negligence law does not hold people responsible for harm that was completely unforeseeable.

The difficult part of causation is establishing proximate cause. Would it have been fair to make Mrs. O'Leary pay for all of the damage caused in the Chicago fire? A certain amount of damage from her wrongful act was foreseeable (reasonably predictable). At some point, however, the damage to the city of Chicago was greater than what could have been foreseen, or anticipated, when Mrs. O'Leary negligently placed the lantern too close to the cow's rear leg in the shed.

causation the reason an event occurs; that which produces an effect. It is one of the four elements that must be proven in a negligence case. Causation is subdivided into cause in fact and proximate cause.

cause in fact one of the elements a plaintiff must prove in order to establish causation in a negligence suit. It means that if the harm would not have occurred without the wrongful act, the act is the cause in fact of the harm.

proximate cause in negligence law, this concept limits damages the defendant must pay to only those harms that are reasonably predictable consequences of the defendant's wrongful acts.

THE **CASE** OF...

The Great Chicago Fire

In 1871, a major fire destroyed much of the city of Chicago. After a thorough investigation, the cause of the fire was determined. It began in Mrs. O'Leary's shed when a cow she had been milking kicked over a kerosene lantern she had placed too close to the cow's rear leg.

▲ The Great Chicago Fire

> ### PROBLEM 19.5
>
> **a.** Was Mrs. O'Leary negligent in placing the lantern so close to the cow's leg?
>
> **b.** Should she have had to pay for all the damage caused by the fire? Explain.

Assume, for example, that your car wrongfully crosses the double yellow line and collides with a truck. It turns out that the truck is carrying dynamite, which explodes and kills a person two blocks away. Your negligent crossing of the yellow line is the cause in fact of the harm to the person two blocks away. However, most courts would say that your negligence was not the proximate cause of this death. Crossing a double yellow line does not usually result in harm two blocks away. That harm was not reasonably foreseeable. This case would be decided differently, though, if the person who died was a pedestrian on the sidewalk close to the collision.

Sometimes the negligence of more than one person harms someone. For example, suppose two cars, each negligently driven, collide with each other and, as a result, injure a pedestrian on a nearby sidewalk. Each driver is responsible for the pedestrian's injuries. If one driver is unable to pay, the other driver may have to pay the entire amount of the damages.

Damages

A plaintiff who proves that a duty existed, that it was breached, and that both forms of causation occurred still must prove that there were actual **damages** to recover in a negligence action. The basic idea behind damages is that the plaintiff should be restored to his or her pre-injury condition, to the extent that this can be achieved with money.

Courts allow plaintiffs to recover money for hospital bills, lost wages, damage to property, reduced future earnings, and other economic harm. Plaintiffs may also recover monetary compensation for noneconomic harm such as pain and suffering, emotional distress, and permanent physical losses (for example, loss of a limb or blindness). However, in some states, a plaintiff must first prove economic harm—even if only one dollar—before an award for noneconomic harm such as pain and suffering can be made.

damages the injuries or losses suffered by one person due to the fault of another

As a freshman college prank, Carolyn decides to remove a stop sign from an intersection and put it in her dormitory room. To avoid being noticed, she chooses a stop sign at the intersection of a little-used country road and a two-lane state highway several miles out of town. The night after her prank, a motorist from out of state drives through this intersection and is struck by a car traveling at 50 miles per hour along the state highway. Both motorists are seriously injured, and their cars are totally demolished. They recover from their injuries after several months. The police suspect a college prank and, after some investigating, are able to find out who removed the sign. The injured motorists bring a civil action against Carolyn, claiming extensive damages.

a. Can the injured motorists prove that Carolyn's act caused their harm? Explain your answer.
b. Assume that the plaintiffs can prove duty, breach, and causation. List all the types of damages each plaintiff might have suffered. Could they recover all of these damages? Explain your answer.

Defenses to Negligence Suits

People can recover damages for injuries when they are able to prove each of the elements of negligence by a preponderance of the evidence. However, even when all the elements can be proven, the defendant may be able to raise a valid legal defense. One group of legal defenses in negligence cases is based on the plaintiff's conduct.

One traditional legal defense is **contributory negligence.** This means that as a plaintiff, you cannot recover damages from the defendant if your own negligence contributed in any way to the harm you suffered. For example, suppose a train station attendant warns a passenger not to walk in an area where ice has formed on the platform. The passenger walks there anyway, falls, and is hurt. The passenger might sue the railroad for allowing ice to remain on the platform. However, by ignoring the warning and stepping on the ice, the passenger failed to act reasonably. If the passenger sues for damages, the railroad will be able to use the defense of contributory negligence, a defense based on the plaintiff's conduct.

When both parties are equally at fault, the contributory negligence rule perhaps provides a fair result: neither party can recover damages from the other. However, the contributory negligence defense also allows for a very slight amount of negligence on the part of the plaintiff to give the defendant a complete legal defense. This is true even when the damage to the plaintiff is great and the defendant has been very negligent. Many people think this produces an unfair result. Therefore, this defense has been eliminated in most states.

contributory negligence a legal defense in which it is determined that the plaintiff and defendant share the fault for a negligence tort. If proven, the plaintiff cannot recover damages.

Cigarettes and the Law

Prior to the mid-1990s, tobacco companies were usually able to defend against lawsuits brought by smokers who were harmed by smoking cigarettes. They did so by claiming that the smokers had assumed the risks related to smoking, based on the warning printed on cigarette packages. In 1994, despite testimony earlier that year before Congress that smoking was not addictive, documents surfaced showing that tobacco company executives actually had a great deal of information about the addictiveness of nicotine and the harm caused by smoking. Not surprisingly, in the next few years, many class action lawsuits were filed in state courts to recover damages from cigarette companies.

In 1998, the leading cigarette manufacturers settled these lawsuits. Not only did they promise to pay an estimated $246 billion to the states over 25 years, but they also agreed to restrict the way they market cigarettes to the public. The cigarette companies also agreed to pay special attention to restricting young people's access to cigarettes. Some of these restrictions include not advertising on billboards or within public transportation systems, not using cartoon characters to sell tobacco products, and not sponsoring concerts or other events at which young people will be present. In addition, the cigarette companies agreed to dedicate $300 million toward public education efforts to reduce underage tobacco use and to educate consumers about causes and prevention of diseases associated with the use of tobacco products.

A wide variety of local ordinances and state laws restrict smoking in the United States. One common approach is to prohibit smoking in workplaces and public facilities.

Today, vaping—the act of inhaling and exhaling vapor from an electronic cigarette or similar device—is increasingly replacing traditional cigarette smoking. Vaping is now the most popular tobacco product among teens and young adults. This has led to renewed concerns about how tobacco-related products are marketed to youth. For example, in 2018, the federal government issued warning letters to companies that sell e-cigarette liquids in "kid-friendly" packaging that resemble juice boxes, candies, and cookies. The federal government has been particularly focused on these issues because evidence shows that when youth are exposed to nicotine, it affects the developing brain and may cause them to be more likely to be addicted to nicotine in the future.

DYING FOR A MENTHOL?
undo the death toll call 1-800-NO-BUTTS

VIACOM

Signs are often posted to give notice of a certain danger. *If someone is injured or drowns at this beach, can the property owner be held liable?*

Most states now allow a defense called **comparative negligence.** This means dividing the loss according to the degree to which each person is at fault. For example, Paul and Javier are in a car crash and Paul sues Javier for the $20,000 in damages that he suffers. If the jury finds that Paul was somewhat negligent himself—for example, by not wearing his seat belt—the damages will be reduced. If Paul was 10 percent at fault and Javier was 90 percent at fault, Paul will receive $18,000. If Paul was 30 percent at fault, he will receive only $14,000. But if he was more than 50 percent at fault, he will receive no damages in many states, and Javier might be able to sue Paul for some damages. Javier's action against Paul is called a **counterclaim.**

Sometimes two or more people commit a negligent act against a third person. If Paul and Javier had each negligently collided and injured Charles, who was in a third car and was not at fault, Charles could recover damages from both drivers. They might be able to divide their liability to Charles between themselves, according to each one's degree of fault. However, if one of the defendants was unable to pay, the other defendant might have to pay all of the damages.

Another legal defense in negligence cases is **assumption of risk.** It is used when a person voluntarily encounters a known danger and decides to accept the risk of that danger. For example, a hockey fan knows that a puck can be deflected off a player's stick, over the glass that surrounds the rink, and into the seats. A fan who buys a seat knows the risk and agrees to accept the danger. If a fan is hit by the puck, assumption of risk will be a complete defense for the team or the players involved should the injured fan try to sue.

This defense is also used when a warning is posted that gives notice of a certain danger. For example, many hotels operate swimming pools without hiring lifeguards. The hotels post large "Swim at Your Own Risk" signs near the pools.

Even without a warning notice, everyone knows that knives are sharp and may cause injury. When someone accidentally slices off a finger while cutting cucumbers, the knife manufacturer will not be held liable. The injured party assumed the risk by using the knife.

comparative negligence in a tort suit, a finding that the plaintiff was partly at fault and, therefore, does not deserve full compensation for his or her injuries. For example, if an accident was 40 percent the plaintiff's fault, the plaintiff's damages are reduced by 40 percent.

counterclaim a claim made by a defendant against the plaintiff in a civil lawsuit

assumption of risk a legal defense to a negligence tort, whereby the plaintiff is considered to have voluntarily accepted a known risk of danger

DELIBERATION

Should a sports league be held liable for brain damage in its former players?

Football, soccer, ice hockey, and wrestling are all popular sports in the United States, each with youth, college, and professional leagues. Though millions of Americans enjoy participating in these sports, their athletes are prone to head injuries. In 2017, around 2.5 million high school students reported having a concussion related to sports or physical activity.

Concussions are mild traumatic brain injuries. In sports, a concussion often occurs because of a hard hit to the head or a quick and unexpected rotation of the head. Symptoms include headaches, drowsiness, loss of consciousness, memory loss, and irritability. Research reveals that repeated head injuries—concussions, but also milder head injuries—can cause long-term damage, leading to chronic traumatic encephalopathy (CTE). CTE can only be diagnosed after death. Family members of those diagnosed with CTE report having noticed changes in thinking, feeling, and behavior, including cases of depression, anxiety, unpredictable mood changes, and suicidality.

A small 2017 study found CTE in 99 percent of deceased former professional football players, 91 percent of deceased former college football players, and 21 percent of deceased former high school football players whose brains were donated to the study. As the study noted, the results were likely impacted by so-called "selection bias"—that is, participants in the study were those more likely to have exhibited signs of CTE and brain trauma while they were alive. Still, the rate of CTE in former professional and college football players were higher than researchers had expected.

Some family members of deceased former athletes diagnosed with CTE believe that sports leagues should be held civilly liable for brain damage caused when their family members played in the league. This would mean that sports leagues pay for the damages suffered by these players. It may mean paying for medical expenses and it may also mean paying for wages that were lost as a result of the players' injuries.

Holding a league liable for these injuries could have devastating effects. There are about 460,000 college athletes, 1 million high school football participants annually, and more than 2.3 million youth soccer participants. Holding a league liable could mean ending the league because the cost is too high. As a result, players might lose their college scholarships, schools might lose income, and millions of athletes might lose the opportunity to play the game they love.

Since a 2005 report on CTE, thousands of concussion-related lawsuits have been filed in the United States, including lawsuits against youth, college, and professional sports leagues. Many of these lawsuits contended that the league failed to protect its players from the risks associated with head injuries. Some lawsuits even claimed that the leagues knew about the risks associated with head injuries but did little or nothing to prevent them.

Sports leagues argue that they are not liable for brain injuries and the effects suffered by their former players. Many sports, they say, involve some inherent danger, which is a risk an athlete takes in deciding to play. In fact, many leagues ask players to sign waivers acknowledging the risks with the sport and signing away the league's liability should injuries occur.

Should a sports league be held liable for brain damage in its former players? Consider the options.

YES

A sports league should be held liable.

Head injuries sustained in sports are brought on by factors that are under the league's control, including weak rules that do not protect athletes from head injuries, or a lack of trained medical staff.

Many athletes in sports leagues sustain some head injury as a result of playing in the league. Many head injuries go unreported, including subconcussive hits, which are not as immediately impactful as concussive hits, but still have the same long-term effects.

Many sports leagues were aware of the links between head injuries and serious brain diseases like CTE before they actually took measures to decrease head injuries in their leagues. As early as 1994, some American professional sports leagues became aware of the critical dangers of repeated head injuries.

Players filed lawsuits filed against several sports leagues in the wake of published research about CTE. As a result, many leagues changed their policies and practices around head injuries. Leagues created new rules, trained staff, purchased safer equipment, and developed head injury protocols. Because these players could hold their leagues liable, these systemic changes took place.

NO

A sports league should not be held liable.

Anyone who watches these sports knows they can be dangerous and may involve hits and jolts to the head. Athletes knowingly take risks when they step onto the field. Leagues should not be held liable for the risks that athletes knowingly take.

Holding leagues liable could make the leagues too expensive to continue. This would have massive ripple effects, including ending athletic scholarships and ending high school and youth sports leagues.

It is difficult to determine whether the long-term effects of head injuries are a result of an athlete playing in a particular league. Brain injuries take a long time to be recognized and many people sustain head injuries outside of sports leagues entirely. It would be impossible to conclude that a particular league was at fault.

Most leagues have done their best to keep up with safety practices. Leagues regulate safety equipment and train officials to uphold safety standards. Some leagues have player safety commissions that examine safety issues and update rules. It is not fair to hold sports leagues liable for player injuries despite the best efforts of the leagues to prevent them.

GUIDING QUESTIONS

1. What are the two most compelling reasons to support the deliberation question?

2. What are the two most compelling reasons to disagree with the deliberation question?

3. What is one area of this deliberation where the two sides might find common ground?

YOU BE the JUDGE

Determining a Defense to Negligence

Analyze each case below. Identify the plaintiff and the defendant and decide whether the defendant has a legal defense. Assume the state has a comparative negligence law.

a. Olivia and her friends go to an amusement park, and she decides to ride the scariest roller coaster. After each rider is seated, the attendant secures that rider with a safety bar. Olivia tells her friends that she does not need the safety bar. After the first large hill, she detaches it. Later in the ride, Olivia is thrown from the roller coaster and is severely injured.

b. A large sign posted at the foot of the lifeguard station warns of a very dangerous undertow beyond the first sandbar. There are buoys floating around the sandbar. Howard swims out beyond the sandbar and drowns before the lifeguard is able to reach him.

c. At the beginning of the semester, the chemistry teacher distributed instructions explaining how to use the Bunsen burner safely—including which liquids are flammable and a reminder to keep them away from the burners. She does not, however, discuss these instructions with the students. During a lab experiment in the middle of the semester, one student spills a flammable liquid on a lit burner and is badly burned.

d. Shayna takes her four-year-old son Damien to a local public playground. The playground has clearly posted a sign that reads "WARNING: CHILDREN AGES 5 AND UP. ADULT SUPERVISION RECOMMENDED." As Damien is making his way across the monkey bars, one of the bars comes loose. Damien falls and suffers a substantial head injury.

e. It is a snowy, icy day. Eric is walking home from school when he spots some friends walking the next block over. Eric begins to run towards them, taking a shortcut through the courtyard of an office building. He suddenly slips and falls hard on the ice-covered courtyard, breaking his shoulder.

f. Amy just got her driver's license and is on her way to meet some friends at the mall. She forgets to use her left turn signal before switching from the right lane to the left lane. At the same time, a drunk driver on the opposite side of the road swerves into Amy's lane. Fortunately, Amy and the drunk driver suffer only minor injuries, but both cars are completely totaled.

g. While shopping with his mother in a local sports equipment store, Jake, age 9, steps onto a treadmill that is on display. He touches the on/off switch, unaware that it is plugged in. Jake is immediately thrown from the treadmill, sustaining injuries.

▲ Safety bars prevent injury.

▶ The company in charge of this demolition is liable without fault if a bystander is injured.

strict liability the legal responsibility for damage or injury even if you are not negligent

In tort law, one exception to the requirement of fault is **strict liability**, also known as liability without fault. Strict liability means that the defendant is liable to the plaintiff regardless of fault or negligence. In some situations, even if the defendant acted in a reasonable and prudent manner and took all the precautions necessary, liability is imposed without proof of fault. Strict liability is applied to ultrahazardous activities such as storing or transporting dangerous substances or using explosives. It is also applied to harm caused by dangerous animals and to harm caused by the manufacture and sale of defective products to consumers.

Proving negligence involves establishing four elements: duty, breach, causation, and damages. To prove strict liability, however, you must prove only causation and damages. However, you must also convince the court that the activity that caused the harm is the type of unreasonably dangerous activity to which strict liability should be applied. Public policy and common sense require people who conduct dangerous activities to accept responsibility for any harm they caused, even if they were not negligent.

Dangerous Activities

Strict liability applies to activities that are seen as unreasonably dangerous. Activities are considered unreasonably dangerous when they involve a risk of harm that cannot be eliminated even by reasonable care. These activities may be socially useful or necessary; but because of their potential for harm, those who engage in them are held to the strict liability standard. For example, assume that a demolition company has been hired to dynamite an old downtown building. While demolition may be necessary, it is inherently dangerous to use dynamite in a populated area. No amount of care by the demolition team can totally eliminate the risk. Therefore, the law imposes strict liability. This means that the demolition company must assume the risk of any foreseeable harm, even if the company is careful and not negligent.

Companies conducting dangerous activities know that they are strictly liable for any harm they cause. Therefore, they include this potential cost in the price they charge for the work. In the example above, the company using the dynamite has a financial incentive to be as careful as possible because of strict liability.

▲ The concept of toxic torts was developed in response to companies guilty of industrial pollution. *What must the injured parties do before they can recover damages from an industrial polluter?*

PROBLEM 20.1

In which of the following situations should the plaintiffs be able to recover damages based on strict liability? Explain your reasons.

a. Anytown's waste treatment plant develops a leak, and harmful bacteria are released into the water supply. Hundreds of families become sick.

b. Anita takes her car to a mechanic for repairs. As she enters the garage, she slips on spilled motor oil and breaks her ankle.

c. Donna drives by a construction site in a downtown shopping district. Following a sudden blast from the site, a piece of cement crashes through her windshield and injures her.

d. Kyung Lee is eating lunch at a cafeteria. A waiter races by and spills a pot of coffee on Kyung Lee's arm, badly burning him.

toxic torts a lawsuit against a manufacturer of a toxic substance for harm caused by the manufacture or disposal of that substance

In recent years, a concept called **toxic torts** has been introduced in court to address harm resulting from the use of toxic chemicals and other hazardous materials. Historically, some industrial manufacturers disposed of their wastes by dumping them into the nearest river or other convenient location. It was not until the 1960s that the public began to understand that prolonged exposure to toxic chemicals could cause illness and even death.

The toxic torts concept was developed to allow injured parties who are harmed by the manufacture or disposal of hazardous materials to recover damages from industrial polluters if the injured parties can establish causation. For example, when a Massachusetts mother found that her son and a dozen other neighborhood children had leukemia, she successfully sued a chemical company that had contaminated local drinking water by dumping its waste products into a nearby stream.

PROBLEM 20.2

Ms. Mattingly, a well-to-do farmer, has a legal right to apply pesticides to her fruit trees. One year, she decided to hire a crop-dusting airplane to spread a pesticide on her orchard. An unexpected gust of wind blew the chemical onto a neighbor's beehives, killing all the bees. The neighbor sued Mattingly for the value of the 60 beehives. Mattingly argued that a good fruit farmer has to apply pesticides and that the crop duster had exercised extreme caution in applying the chemicals.

a. Was Ms. Mattingly negligent? Should strict liability apply to this case? Give your reasons.

b. How should Ms. Mattingly defend this case?

c. How would you decide this case? Explain your answer.

Animals

The law has traditionally held owners strictly liable for any harm caused by their untamed animals. Even the owner of a tamed wild animal such as a lion may be held strictly liable for any harm it causes because of the nature of the animal itself. The situation differs, however, for household pets. Typically states have one of two types of dog bite laws. Some states have a "one bite" rule, meaning that the dog owner cannot be sued successfully the first time his or her dog bites someone. Other states have strict liability which means the owner can be sued for the first bite as long as the plaintiff did not provoke the dog.

An owner who is negligent can also be sued for harm caused by a dog bite. For example, some states and localities have leash laws requiring that pets be kept under the owner's control and on a leash in public places. If you violate the duty to keep your pet under control, you can be sued by a plaintiff who is harmed based on your negligence. In extreme situations, a pet owner might even be held criminally responsible for the harm caused by a pet if the owner knows that the pet is dangerous or cannot be controlled.

▼ Leash laws require pet owners to keep their pets restrained and under control. *Would a dog owner be liable if his or her dog attacked and injured someone in a public place?*

THE **CASE** OF...

The Dangerous Dog

Five-year-old Matthew opens a gate and walks into his neighbors' yard to play with their dog, a pit bull terrier. The dog—which had never attacked anyone before—attacks Matthew, badly mauling his hand. Matthew's parents sue the dog's owners for not keeping the animal inside or in a pen in the yard. The owners defend themselves by saying that even though there have been reports of attacks by other pit bull terriers, their dog had been affectionate with family members and had never shown any dangerous or destructive tendencies.

> **PROBLEM** 20.3
>
> **a.** What arguments can you make for Matthew's parents?
>
> **b.** What arguments can you make for the dog's owners?
>
> **c.** How should this case be decided? Explain the reasons for your answer.
>
> **d.** Would you have decided this case differently if Matthew had been 15? What if he had been 35? What arguments could you make for each situation? How would they differ?

Defective Products

Harm caused by defective products is a significant social problem. **Product liability**—the legal responsibility of manufacturers or sellers for injuries caused by defective products—is an important legal issue. In fact, some lawyers specialize in product liability law. Millions of people seek medical treatment from injury related to a product. In many cases, the manufacturer is held strictly liable for harm caused by the defective product. In some instances, injured consumers bring cases together as a class action against a manufacturer.

The U.S. Consumer Product Safety Commission (CPSC) was created in 1972 to deal with this problem. It protects the public by issuing and enforcing mandatory product standards or, in some cases, banning consumer products. The commission has the power to force many dangerous products off the market and advises consumers on product safety. The CPSC also maintains a website (**www.cpsc.gov**) describing recent product recalls and allowing consumers to report injury-causing incidents experienced with products.

As a matter of public policy, manufacturers and sellers are frequently held strictly liable for harm caused by their products. Strict liability is meant to create a strong incentive for companies to design safe products, to test products thoroughly, and to include clear directions and warnings on products. Strict liability causes companies to spend more money on research and development, safety features, and insurance. This increase in spending usually results in higher prices for consumers. Some people criticize these higher prices, while others say that safer products are worth the extra cost.

An unsafe product that causes many injuries and subsequent lawsuits may become too expensive to compete successfully with safer products in the marketplace. For example, in the 1990s, more than

Product liability the legal responsibility of manufacturers and sellers for injuries caused by defective products they produce or sell

THE CASE OF...

The First Responders

Gabriella, a doctor, is a member of the first-responders team her city established in case of a bioterrorist attack. As part of her preparation for such an event, Gabriella and her colleagues are each required to be vaccinated for smallpox, a highly infectious and deadly disease that kills 30 percent of those who contract it. The government believes that the smallpox virus could be used in a terrorist attack. Even though Gabriella does not want to receive the vaccination because she knows there is a minor risk (1 in 1,000,000) that she could contract smallpox, she is forced to do so in order to keep her job.

PROBLEM 20.4

a. If Gabriella becomes sick after having the vaccination, should the drug company that manufactures the vaccine be held strictly liable for Gabriella's injury?

b. Is the risk of getting sick from the vaccine unreasonable? Do the benefits outweigh the dangers?

c. What arguments can the drug company make to defend itself? Identify the public policy issues that the company might use in its defense.

d. Should Gabriella be able to sue the government for forcing her to take a drug she doesn't want to take? Why or why not?

5.8 million Americans began taking weight-loss drugs, including a product called fen-phen. About 20 percent of those taking fen-phen developed serious heart problems, and some of them lost normal heart function. In a successful class action, plaintiffs recovered damages from the pharmaceutical company that made fen-phen. As a result of the law suit and actions taken by the federal Food and Drug Administration (FDA), fen-phen is no longer on the market in the United States.

The fear of expensive lawsuits may also discourage the production of new and useful—but unavoidably dangerous—products such as vaccines. Some people argue that this is a reasonable restraint on research and development. Other people argue that the government should provide some type of insurance or immunity from lawsuits as an incentive for companies to develop new products in the spirit of progress.

Courts have been reluctant to apply strict liability to unavoidably unsafe products whose benefits clearly outweigh the dangers. Certain vaccines are unavoidably risky to use. For example, even when the rabies vaccine is properly tested, prepared, and labeled, some people who receive it have become sick. However, if untreated, rabies leads to death. Because the benefits of the vaccine have proven to outweigh the danger, strict liability does not apply. This point does not mean that the rabies vaccine drug manufacturers are automatically protected from any liability. If a drug that causes harm has not been properly tested, prepared, or labeled, the plaintiff may be able to recover damages based on negligence rather than on strict liability.

Defenses to Strict Liability

There are very few defenses in strict liability cases. The defendant's best strategy may be to argue that the plaintiff should have to prove negligence in a particular case and that sound public policy does not require the use of a strict liability standard. It is almost always more difficult for the plaintiff to win a negligence suit, because there must be proof of the defendant's fault, or breach of duty.

While you do not have to prove fault in a strict liability case, you do have to prove both causation and damages. Therefore, a defendant could try to show that there is no causation or that there are no damages. For example, suppose that a person has a heart attack and dies instantly while driving a car with faulty brakes. That person's family might argue that the car manufacturer is strictly liable. However, if the defect (the faulty brakes) did not cause the damage (the death), the manufacturer would not be liable.

In product liability cases, manufacturers or sellers may have a defense if the consumer misuses a product or ignores clear safety warnings. Many courts, however, require manufacturers to anticipate some misuse and to make products safe against any foreseeable misuse. For example, a manufacturer should assume that a stool intended as seating at a kitchen counter might also be used as a stepladder. The stool should be built to hold a person whether seated or standing.

THE **CASE** OF...

The Exploding Tire

Myra purchased a new set of tires and had them mounted and balanced at the store. Several months later, Myra was killed in an accident on a two-lane highway. She was driving at or near the speed limit in dry weather when a front tire exploded, causing her to lose control and crash into a ditch.

Investigators found that one of the tires that had not exploded was overinflated by 15 pounds. Myra's wife filed a lawsuit against the tire store and the tire manufacturer.

PROBLEM 20.5

a. What are the strongest arguments available to the plaintiff in this case?

b. What are the strongest arguments available to the defendants in this case?

c. Should the plaintiff be able to use strict liability in this case or should the plaintiff be required to prove that the defendant was negligent? Explain your answers.

d. How should this case be decided? Give the reasons for your answers.

▶ Tort reform is one of several important issues for many people.

As a matter of public policy, the tort law system should serve to (1) compensate harmed persons in a prompt and efficient way, (2) fairly allocate benefits to victims and costs to wrongdoers, and (3) deter conduct that is unreasonably risky or dangerous. However, some argue that our tort law system does not always meet these goals. Critics generally claim that:

- The amount of money awarded to plaintiffs is sometimes unreasonably high.
- Going to court has become too expensive, with lawyers getting too much of the money awarded.
- Civil courts take too long to resolve disputes.
- Tort law is so complicated that it can be difficult to determine who is at fault.
- The injured party should sometimes receive compensation for a loss, regardless of whether the other party was at fault.

Tort Reform

tort reform the movement that focuses on changing the process of settling tort claims. It emphasizes methods other than going to court or establishes limitations on how much money the winning party may receive.

As a result of the concerns listed earlier in this chapter, a movement called **tort reform** has developed. Some efforts at reform target the process of settling tort claims. These efforts could require participants to try to settle a tort case before beginning a trial. In some civil courts, for example, the judge is required to ask the parties whether they have tried to settle the case outside of court before a trial starts. For some cases, a judge will send the parties to a mediation service in an attempt to settle the case without a trial. Some states have laws, such as no-fault auto insurance, that eliminate the need for civil suits in certain types of auto accident cases.

Another strategy for changing the process of settling tort claims is to reduce the amount of time a plaintiff has to file a lawsuit for damages after an injury. Every state has laws setting deadlines for filing lawsuits. In most states this law, known as the **statute of limitations**, requires that a tort claim be filed within either two or three years from when the injury is suffered. However, there is significant variation from state to state, with limits as short as one year and as long as six years, depending on state law.

statute of limitations a deadline for filing a lawsuit that requires a tort claim to be filed within a certain period after the injury was suffered. In most states, the statute of limitations for filing a tort lawsuit is either two or three years.

Other tort reform efforts target the outcome of tort cases. These efforts most often focus on limiting damage awards. In particular, tort reformers contend that punitive damage awards, as well as damage awards for pain and suffering, should be limited—or "capped." They argue that the tort system would still provide a remedy for injured plaintiffs based on damages proven at trial but that caps would limit large, emotionally driven jury awards.

frivolous lawsuits cases without merit, sometimes filed in an effort to force the defendant to offer a cash settlement rather than going to the expense of defending the lawsuit

Some critics also argue that plaintiffs and their lawyers sometimes bring **frivolous lawsuits**, or cases without merit, in an effort to force businesses to offer a cash settlement rather than going to the expense of defending themselves at a trial. Some reformers see the system used in England as the remedy for frivolous lawsuits. The English rule requires the losing party to pay the other side's legal expenses. Reformers argue that this rule would not be a hardship on plaintiffs with strong claims because, if they won, the defendant would pay both the damages and the plaintiff's legal expenses. However a plaintiff with a questionable case would be reluctant to sue, because losing would result in a court order to pay legal fees for both sides.

Those who support the current system in the United States contend that tort reformers are trying to fix a system that is not broken. They cite data showing that only a small number of cases on the civil docket are tort cases. In fact, more than 95 percent of tort cases are resolved without going to trial. Supporters of the current system also point out that the media frenzy caused by the coverage of a few cases with large damage awards misleads the public on this issue.

In addition, existing legal practice protects defendants against frivolous lawsuits, as judges can easily dismiss these cases or order the plaintiff to pay the defendant's legal fees in the event of a truly frivolous suit. Those who favor the current system also argue that the English system would be unfair. Tort cases can be complex, and liability is not always clear. A plaintiff with a reasonably good case might be reluctant to sue a company for fear of losing and having to pay the defendant's legal fees, potentially leading to personal bankruptcy.

One of the strongest arguments in favor of the current system is that tort law provides a strong incentive to produce safe products and deliver safe services. Knowing that harmful products or practices will be costly encourages careful product development and testing as well as proper training and supervision of service providers.

Legislators have the challenge of passing laws that represent a sensible balancing of interests. Laws need to provide people with reasonable access to the justice system. Laws should encourage safety. At the same time, the tort system must not impose unreasonably high costs on product and service providers or encourage people to bring frivolous lawsuits. Unreasonably high costs can lead to higher prices for consumers, loss of jobs, failure to develop needed products, and loss of services.

Investigating the Law Where You Live

Are there any limits on damage awards in your state? Should there be? Are there current efforts to reform tort laws where you live?

THE **CASE** OF...

The New Car That Was Used

The issue of whether the Constitution provides a limit on punitive damages has been presented to the Supreme Court a number of times. In a case decided by the Court in 1996, an Alabama doctor purchased what he thought was a new BMW, later finding out that the car had been repainted before he purchased it. He sued BMW. BMW said its policy had been to sell damaged cars as new if the damage could be fixed for less than 3 percent of the cost of the car. A jury awarded the doctor $4,000 (the lost value of the car) in actual damages as well as $4 million in punitive damages. The state supreme court reduced the punitive damage award to $2 million. BMW appealed the punitive damage verdict to the U.S. Supreme Court, arguing that such an excessive award was basically unfair and violated the due process clause of the Fourteenth Amendment.

PROBLEM 21.1

a. What happened in this case?

b. What issue was presented to the Court?

c. What are the strongest arguments on each side of the issue?

d. Do you agree with the Court's decision? Give your reasons.

e. One way to look at this case is that punitive damages do not present a constitutional issue, and the Supreme Court should let state courts and legislatures decide these matters. What do you think about this position?

In a 5-4 decision, the Court agreed with BMW. The Court found that punitive damages could be allowed and were constitutional, but that they could not be "grossly excessive."

UNIT 4
Consumer Law

networks

For many years, the legal expression caveat emptor, a Latin phrase meaning "let the buyer beware," summed up consumer law. Consumers, or people who buy goods and services from a seller, had to look out for unfair and misleading sales practices before buying, or be prepared to suffer the consequences. Today the law is more balanced. Consumer law establishes a variety of rights and responsibilities to make the marketplace fair for both buyers and sellers.

◀ The Federal Reserve is the nation's largest financial institution.

CHAPTER **22**
Contracts

▶ A contract is a legally binding agreement.

contract a legally enforceable agreement between two or more people to exchange something of value

breach the violation of a law, duty, or other form of obligation, including obligations formed through contracts or warranties

offer a specific proposal by one person to another to make a deal or contract

acceptance the act of agreeing to an offer and becoming bound to the terms of a contract

A **contract** is an agreement between two or more persons to exchange something of value. A contract legally binds parties to do what they promise. A party who fails to live up to such a promise has **breached** the contract. When you agree to buy something, you usually form a legal contract. If you pay to ride a bus, then you form a legally binding contract because you promise to pay money in exchange for the bus ride.

The law of contracts reaches into many aspects of our daily lives. For example, even when you buy lunch at a restaurant and tickets to see your favorite movie, you are entering into contracts. To protect yourself as a consumer, you need to understand how contracts are formed and how they affect your rights and responsibilities.

Elements of a Contract

To be legally binding, a contract must have certain elements. There must be an **offer** by one party and an **acceptance** by another. An offer must be directed to a specific person. For example, the menu at a fast-food restaurant listing the prices is not an offer, because it is not directed at anyone in particular. When you place your order, however, you make an offer. When they begin cooking your food, the restaurant has accepted your offer, and a contract has been formed. The law infers acceptance from certain actions, such as signing a contract or beginning to carry out the terms of an agreement.

Jupiterimages/Getty Images

For a contract to be valid, there must also be an exchange of **consideration**. This means something of value is given for something else of value. For example, when you buy a new shirt at a store, your consideration is the money you pay, and the merchant's consideration is the item you are buying. The items being exchanged do not have to be of the same value. The law allows consumers and merchants to make both good deals and bad deals.

People entering into a contract must be legally **competent** to make contracts. For example, they cannot be mentally ill or intoxicated. Also, agreements to do something illegal or against public policy are not enforceable.

If Lorenzo says to Christine, "I will sell you my phone for $50," this is an offer. If Christine says, "OK," or if she pays the $50 to Lorenzo, or if she signs an agreement to pay $50, then there is an acceptance. The exchange of the phone for the money is the exchange of consideration. Both parties are competent, and the agreement is not to do something illegal or against public policy. Therefore, a contract has been made.

You should not be too quick to enter into a contract. Always make sure that you understand and agree with all the terms of the contract before you accept them. Otherwise, it may be too late to back out of the deal.

consideration something of value offered or received that must be present in every valid contract voluntarily

competent a person's having the capacity and function to make legal decisions on their own behalf

PROBLEM 22.1

Read each of the following situations and decide whether a contract has been made. Give your reasons.

a. An auctioneer says, "Do I hear a bid for this antique sofa?" Someone in the crowd says, "$300."

b. Yukiko says to Basil, "I'm going to sell my car for $500." Basil replies, "All right, here is the money. I'll take it."

c. The citizens of a small town collect $1,000 and offer it as a reward for the capture of a suspected criminal. The sheriff captures the suspect and seeks the reward.

d. Megan's father promises to pay her $1,000 when she turns 18. On her eighteenth birthday, she seeks the money.

e. Standing at one end of a long bridge, Shelly says to Lynn, "I'll give you $5 if you walk across the bridge." Lynn says nothing but starts walking across the bridge.

f. Liz offers Sharon $100 to steal four hubcaps for her new sports car. Sharon steals the hubcaps from a car dealership, brings them to Liz, and asks for the money.

Minors and Contracts

A minor is a person under the age of legal majority, which is 18 in most states. Minors may make contracts. However, as a general rule, they cannot be forced to carry out their promises and may cancel or refuse to honor their contracts. Minors who cancel contracts usually must return any goods or consideration still in their possession. This rule is designed to protect minors from being taken advantage of because of their age and lack of experience. As a result of this rule, minors may have a tough time getting credit. Many stores require minors to have a parent or other adult **cosign** any major contract. The adult cosigner is responsible for making payments if the minor does not honor the deal.

Minors may, however, be held to contracts that involve necessities, such as food, clothing, shelter, or medical aid. Minors can be required to pay for the reasonable value of such goods and services. In most states, a minor who continues making payments on a contract after reaching the age of majority is considered to have **ratified** (formally approved) the contract. After the contract has been ratified, it can no longer be canceled without some type of penalty.

cosign to sign a legal document, guaranteeing to pay off the debt or contract if the original signer defaults or if the contract is unenforceable against the original signer

ratify to confirm a previous act even though it was not approved beforehand

PROBLEM 22.2

Kara, 17, wants a computer of her own. She goes to a local electronics store to purchase a new laptop. The laptop costs $950. She offers to put down $150 and make monthly payments on the remaining amount. Because Kara is only 17, the manager of the store refuses to sell her the laptop.

a. Is this fair? Is this legal?

b. What concerns might the store manager have about selling a computer to a minor?

▶ Minors often want to buy big-ticket items, such as laptops. *Can minors be held responsible for any contracts they enter into?*

Written and Oral Contracts

Most contracts may be either written or oral (spoken). However, certain kinds of contracts must be in writing to be enforceable. These include contracts for the sale of land or real estate, contracts for the sale of goods priced at $500 or more, agreements to pay another person's debt, and agreements for services that will not be performed within one year from the date of the agreement.

The law favors written contracts. For your protection, it is always better to have a written contract if possible. Otherwise, it can be difficult to prove that a party promised to do something. If there is a written contract, a court will not consider evidence of promises made before the signing of the contract, except when the written contract is unclear or one party was tricked into entering the contract.

▲ Illegal contracts, such as an agreement to commit a crime, are not enforceable in court. *Describe some other situations in which the court would not enforce a contract.*

PROBLEM 22.3

Ruth made an oral agreement to sell her used racing bicycle to Mike for $400. A few days later, she got an offer of $600 from Paul and orally accepted this higher offer. Prior to delivering the bicycle, Ruth decided she did not want to sell it anymore. Both Mike and Paul sued her for breach of contract.

a. What will the court do?

b. Is this decision fair? Explain your answer.

c. How would the case be different if the agreement with Paul were in writing?

Illegal Contracts

Some contracts are unenforceable in court because they are illegal or against public policy. For example, an agreement between two persons for the sale of illegal drugs could never be enforced in court.

Courts sometimes find that a contract is so unfair, harsh, and oppressive that it should not be enforced. Such a contract is considered to be **unconscionable**. The law usually allows freedom of contract, and consumers are allowed to make bad deals as well as good ones.

unconscionable (1) unfair, harsh, oppressive; (2) a sales practice or term in a contract that is so unfair that a judge will not permit enforcement of it

THE **CASE** OF...

The Unfair Contract

A furniture store required an unemployed woman on public assistance to sign its standard contract for credit every time she made a purchase at the store. One of the terms of the contract stated that the store would own every item the woman purchased until all the items were fully paid for. The woman made several purchases at the store, signing this same standard contract each time.

After several years of making all her payments, she purchased a couch and missed two payments. The store believed it had the right, under the contract, to take back all the items the woman had ever purchased there.

A court of appeals found a portion of the contract to be unconscionable and did not enforce this unfair term in the agreement. The woman had to return the couch, but she was able to keep all the items she had already paid for.

▲ Reading a contract carefully.

PROBLEM 22.4

a. Why did the court refuse to enforce the entire agreement in this case?

b. Was the court's decision fair to the owner of the furniture store? Explain.

c. What should the contract have said to make it fair to both parties?

For example, courts will usually enforce a contract that requires someone to pay a very high price for something. On rare occasions, though, a court may not enforce an extremely unfair contract (or an unfair clause in a contract).

A court is more likely to find an extremely unfair contract unconscionable when (1) the consumer is presented with a contract on a take-it-or-leave-it basis, and (2) there is very uneven bargaining power between the parties (as when an experienced seller is dealing with an inexperienced consumer). For example, imagine trying to bargain with the utility company over your electric bill. Despite the uneven bargaining power and take-it-or-leave-it basis, the utility company can usually require you to pay your bill.

Fraud and misrepresentation are also grounds for invalidating a contract. **Fraud** is a false statement about an important fact that is made to induce, or persuade, a person to agree to a contract. For example, if a sports memorabilia salesperson fakes a famous baseball player's signature on a baseball card and sells it, the unsuspecting buyer can cancel the contract and may win damages in court after uncovering the fraud. Although salespersons may not lie about a product's features, they are usually not required to volunteer information about the negative aspects

fraud any deception, lie, or dishonest statement made to cheat someone or induce him or her to agree to a contract

of a product unless they are asked. Only in rare instances, when a special relationship of trust exists between buyer and seller, will courts require the disclosure of negative information. Therefore, it is important for consumers to examine products carefully and to ask a lot of questions before making a purchase.

Breach of Contract

When a contract is formed but one party fails to carry out its end of the bargain, then there has been a breach of the contract. In civil court, you can ask for a number of different remedies for breach of consumer contracts. First, you can sue for expectation damages. **Expectation damages** are the difference between the value that would be expected if the breaching party had fulfilled its promise and the value of what the injured party actually received. For example, assume you order four video games through an online merchant and pay $120, but the company sends you only two games. Assume that the market value of the two games is $60. The expectation damages would be $60—the difference between the full value of what you were promised ($120) and the value of what you actually received ($60) in the mail. You would not have to return the games you received.

Another remedy is **rescission** and **restitution**. When you ask the court for this remedy, you ask it to cancel, or rescind, the contract (rescission) and order the person you are suing to give back, or refund, any money you have already paid (restitution). This releases you from any further obligations under the contract, but you will have to return any benefit already received under the contract. Assume, for example, that you sign a contract to purchase a set of cookware and a pan melts the first time it is exposed to a direct flame. In such a case, you might seek rescission and restitution. You would get your money back and would have no further obligations under the contract, but you would have to return the cookware set.

expectation damages money the breaching party in a contract dispute must pay to make the other party as well off as if the contract had not been breached

rescission the act of canceling a contract and treating it as if it never existed

restitution the act of restoring something to its owner; the act of making good for loss or damage; repaying or refunding illegally obtained money or property

▼ Remedies for breach of contract in online transactions can be sought in civil court. *Describe the three types of civil remedies.*

A third type of civil remedy is **specific performance**. With this remedy, the buyer asks the court to order the seller to carry out the specific terms of the agreement. For example, if you ordered goods that were never delivered, the court could order the company to deliver the goods to you. In the case of specific performance, you would still have to pay for the goods.

A suit for breach of contract in which you sue for expectation damages or for specific performance is designed to place you in approximately the same position you would have been in had the contract been successfully completed. A suit for rescission and restitution is designed to return both the buyer and the seller to the positions they were in before the contract began.

The amount of damages awarded for breach of contract is often affected by the **duty to mitigate** damages. *Mitigate* means "to make less severe." The law usually requires an injured party to take reasonable steps to mitigate damages. For example, suppose Martin received several offers of $100 for the used mp3 player he was selling. Gina agreed to buy the item for $150, but she later refused to follow through on the purchase. Martin would be required to mitigate his damages. In other words, if he could still sell the used mp3 player for $100, his damages for a breach of contract claim against Gina would be only $50.

PROBLEM 22.5

Read each of the following situations in which a consumer has a problem with the seller. If the consumer has to go to court, what is the best remedy? Why? Could either of these situations result in a criminal prosecution? Explain your answers.

a. Jeanine takes a formal, floor-length dress that originally belonged to her mother to the local dry cleaner. When she picks up the dress, she finds several holes in it. The attendant at the dry cleaner claims the holes were there when the garment was brought in. Jeanine is certain that they are the result of the cleaning.

b. The Zhou family hires the Weed Out Chemical Company to spray their lawn twice a month during the spring and summer months of May, June, July, and August. Weed Out sends a monthly bill to the Zhous. By June 10, Weed Out has not yet sprayed, although it sent a bill in May, which the Zhou family paid. Weed Out is behind schedule with its spraying with many of its customers because there is great demand for its product, which contains a successful new formula that is not yet available from other local companies.

▶ Smart consumers comparison shop for warranty protection.

warranty a guarantee or promise made by a seller or manufacturer concerning the quality or performance of goods offered for sale

A **warranty** is a promise or guarantee made by a seller that goods offered for sale are not defective and will perform properly. A warranty may also contain a statement of what the seller will do to remedy the problem if the goods do not perform as promised. If the seller does not live up to the promises made in the warranty, the sales contract has been breached.

Warranties give consumers some very important rights. You should always be aware of the warranties that exist when you make a purchase. However, not all warranties are the same, so it is worthwhile to compare warranties when shopping. When you look at a warranty, consider the duration (how long does it last?), the scope (what parts or problems are covered or excluded?), and the remedy (what do you get under the warranty if the product fails, and what must you do to get the remedy?). You should also check your own state's warranty laws. They may describe other rights that are not in the warranty.

Express Warranties

express warranty a statement of fact or a demonstration concerning the quality or performance of goods offered for sale

An **express warranty** is a statement—written, oral, or by demonstration—concerning the quality or performance of goods offered for sale that becomes a part of the bargain between the parties. For example, if a salesperson tells you, "This TV will not need any repairs for five years," the salesperson has created an express warranty. Similarly, an express warranty is created if you purchase a vacuum cleaner from an appliance store after seeing a demonstration of the vacuum picking up small particles from a deep-pile rug. Because oral warranties and warranties by demonstration are difficult to prove, it is always best to get a written warranty.

E. Audras/PhotoAlto

259

Express warranties are created by statements of fact. Not everything a seller says creates a warranty. If the seller's statement is merely an opinion or an obvious exaggeration, it is considered **puffing,** or sales talk, and cannot be relied on. For example, a used-car dealer advertising "Fantastic Used Cars" is engaged in puffing. Therefore, no warranty is created. No customer should rely on such statements of opinion or obvious exaggeration.

What happens if your TV quits working or your watch will not keep time? The first thing to do is check to see if the warranty is still in effect. One TV may be guaranteed for 90 days, while another may be covered for a full year. Your warranty may provide a remedy when certain things go wrong. So check to see if the failure is covered by the warranty. You may be able to return the item for a refund, exchange it for a replacement, or have it repaired.

Sellers do not have to give written warranties. However, if they do, the *Magnuson-Moss Warranty Act* requires that the written warranties (1) disclose all the essential terms and conditions in a single document, (2) be stated in simple and easy-to-read language, and (3) be made available to the consumer before a sale. Written warranties must also tell you exactly what product parts or problems are covered, what is not covered, and what the seller will do to correct problems that occur while the warranty is in effect. For example, the warranty must explain what repairs are covered and who will make them. The act does not apply to products that cost $15 or less.

Under the *Magnuson-Moss Warranty Act,* warranties are labeled as either full or limited. Under a full warranty:

- A defective product will be fixed or replaced at no cost, including removal and reinstallation, if necessary.
- The consumer will not have to do anything unreasonable (such as shipping a piano to a factory) to get the warranty service.
- The product will be fixed within a reasonable time after the consumer complains.
- If the product cannot be fixed after a reasonable number of attempts, the consumer can get either a refund or a replacement for the product.
- The warranty applies to anyone who owns the product during the specified warranty period (not just the first purchaser of the product).

Any protection less than this is called a limited warranty. Such a warranty usually covers some defects or problems of a product but not others. For example, the limited warranty on a television might cover the cost of new parts but not the labor involved in installing the new parts. Or it might cover only certain parts. To learn what is covered, read the entire warranty carefully.

For an additional price, sellers sometimes offer an extended warranty. This gives the buyer protection over a longer period of time. Buyers should consider whether the additional price is justified in terms of savings from repairs that might be incurred over the longer period of time.

23.1 One-Year Limited Warranty

Your Excellent Digital Camera Warranty

Excellent Digital Cameras fully guarantees this entire product against defects in material or workmanship for one year from purchase date.

Defective product may be brought or mailed, postage prepaid, to purchase place, authorized service center, or Service Department, Excellent Digital Cameras, Inc., 3rd & Maple Streets, Arlington, PA 15616, for free repair or replacement at our option.

Warranty does not include cost of inconvenience, damage due to product failure, transportation damages, misuse, abuse, accident, or commercial use.

For information, write the Consumer Claims Manager at the previously listed Arlington address. Send the owner's name, address, name of store or service center involved, model, serial number, purchase date, and a description of the problem.

This warranty provides specific legal rights. You may have other rights that vary from state to state.

This warranty becomes effective upon purchase. Mailing the enclosed registration card is one way of establishing the purchase date, but it is not required for warranty coverage.

PROBLEM 23.1

Read and evaluate the one-year warranty provided above for a digital camera and then answer the following questions.

a. Who is making the warranty? Who will be responsible for making any repairs—dealer, service center, manufacturer, or independent repairer?

b. How long is the warranty in effect? Does the buyer have to do anything to make the warranty effective?

c. What is covered—the entire product or only certain parts? What is promised—repair, replacement, labor, postage? Is this a full or a limited warranty? Why?

Implied Warranties

Many consumers believe they have no protection if a new product without an express warranty does not work. In many cases, however, consumers are protected—even though they may not realize it—by an implied warranty. An **implied warranty** is an unwritten promise, created by law, that a product will do what it is supposed to do, even if no express promise is made. Implied warranties apply only to products sold by dealers of that product. They do not apply to goods sold by casual sellers. For example, if a friend sells you her bicycle, no implied warranties are involved. But if you buy a bicycle from a cycling store, there will be an implied warranty that the bicycle will perform reasonably well as a bicycle should. The three types of implied warranties are (1) warranty of merchantability, (2) warranty of fitness for a particular purpose, and (3) warranty of title.

implied warranty the unwritten minimum standard of quality the law requires of products offered for sale

warranty of merchantability an implied promise that the item sold is of at least average quality for that type of item

A **warranty of merchantability** is an unwritten promise that the item sold is fit to be sold and will perform in at least an average way for that type of item. For example, a computer game must play, a saw must cut, and a freezer must keep food frozen. A buyer always gets an implied warranty of merchantability from a selling dealer unless the seller expressly disclaims it. Be especially wary of goods marked with disclaimers such as "as is" or "final sale." Using a disclaimer, a seller can legally avoid responsibility for the quality of the product. If the product comes with a written warranty, the *Magnuson-Moss Warranty Act* prohibits disclaiming an implied warranty, and several states also prohibit "as is" sales.

warranty of fitness for a particular purpose a seller's promise, implied by law, that the item sold will meet the buyer's stated purpose

A **warranty of fitness for a particular purpose** exists when a consumer tells a seller before buying an item that it is needed for a specific purpose or will be used in a certain way. A salesperson who sells an item with this knowledge makes an implied promise that the item will fulfill the stated purpose. For example, suppose you tell a salesperson you want a waterproof watch and the salesperson recommends a watch, which you then buy. An implied warranty of fitness has been created. If you go swimming and water leaks into the watch, the warranty has been breached.

warranty of title the seller's promise that he or she owns and may transmit title to the item being offered for sale

A **warranty of title** is a seller's promise that he or she owns the item being offered for sale. Sellers must own the goods in order to transfer title or ownership to the buyer. If a person sells stolen goods, the warranty of title has been broken.

▶ Car dealers often advertise "certified used cars" to show that they have been inspected and approved by a mechanic. *What warranty protection is typically available when you purchase a used car?*

Consumers who are harmed by products may be able to sue for damages because the manufacturer or seller has breached the warranty. Consumers may also be able to recover damages based either on the negligence of the manufacturer or seller or on a legal theory known as **strict liability.**

You should remember that if you fully examine goods—or have the opportunity to do so—before making a purchase, the implied warranty may not apply to those defects you should have discovered during the inspection. Therefore, *carefully inspect any goods you buy for defects.* Be especially careful with used cars. It is wise to have a mechanic you trust examine the car before you purchase it.

Be sure to carefully read all instructions that come with a product. If you fail to use the product properly, or if you use it for an improper purpose, you may invalidate the warranty.

strict liability the legal responsibility for damage or injury even if you are not negligent

---

PROBLEM 23.2

Is a warranty created in any of the following situations? If so, what type of warranty is it? Has the warranty been breached?

a. Juan sells Terri his used car. As Terri drives home, the car breaks down. The cost of fixing the car is greater than the sale price.

b. Deidre buys a dress after telling the sales clerk that she plans to wash it in a washing machine. The clerk replies, "That's fine. This material is washable." Deidre washes the dress in her washing machine and the dress shrinks.

c. A salesperson tells Neva, "This is the finest digital camera on the market. It will last for years." Eight months later, the button that advances the photos stops working.

d. Scott steals a diamond ring from a jewelry store and sells it to Maria after telling her his mother gave it to him.

e. Trina orders a book from a bookstore's website. The website says "Hardcover Edition, $12.95," and includes a picture of the book's cover. Five days later, Trina receives the paperback edition of the book.

f. Ned buys a new sofa from a furniture store. One of the legs falls off two weeks after delivery.

THE **CASE** OF...

The Guitar That Quit

Shari wants to buy a new guitar. She shops around to compare prices at a few different music stores. City Music offers the best price at $300, so Shari buys the guitar there. On the sales receipt is a clause that reads: "This constitutes the exclusive statement of the terms of agreement between the parties. Seller makes no warranties either express or implied with respect to this product." The third time Shari plays the guitar, the neck breaks.

PROBLEM 23.3

a. What should Shari do about the broken guitar? What should the store do to address Shari's problem?

b. Is it possible that a guitar with a higher price and a warranty would have been a better deal?

c. Assume that there is a large sign by the cash register that reads: **All Guitars Sold "AS IS."** How would you react to such a sign? Explain the reasons for your answer.

Disclaimers

disclaimer a clause or statement in a contract or agreement that limits responsibility for anything not expressly promised

A **disclaimer** is an attempt to limit the seller's responsibilities should anything go wrong with a product. The clause quoted in The Case of the Guitar That Quit (above) is a disclaimer. It is an attempt by the store to avoid responsibility for anything that goes wrong with the guitar. The quoted clause makes it clear that an express warranty is not being offered. But does the clause disclaim the implied warranty?

Sellers can usually disclaim the implied warranty of merchantability by using such expressions as "with all faults" or "as is." Unless these or other easily understood words are used, the seller must actually use the word *merchantability* in disclaiming the implied warranty of merchantability. In addition, to be effective, the disclaimer must be written and placed so as to be easily seen by the consumer. Because the sales receipt for the guitar did not say "as is," "with all faults," or "merchantability," it is probably not effective as a disclaimer of the implied warranty of merchantability. However, a large (as is) sign by the cash register would be an effective disclaimer. When consumers buy from a dealer, the customer will always receive the basic protection of the implied warranty of merchantability unless there is an effective disclaimer.

Sellers sometimes use disclaimers to limit the consumer's remedy. For example, a contract may read, "It is expressly understood and agreed that the buyer's only remedy shall be repair or replacement of defective parts. The seller is not liable in damages for injury to persons or property." Suppose the warranty limits the remedy to "repair or replacement of defective parts" and this remedy is not sufficient. That is, after repeated attempts at repair, the product still does not work. In such cases, the buyer can usually seek other remedies, for example, getting a refund. However, courts will usually require that the buyer give the seller a reasonable opportunity to repair the product.

CHAPTER **24**
Credit and Other Financial Services

▶ Credit cards offer consumers a convenient alternative to cash.

credit (1) a deduction from what is owed; (2) purchasing goods with delayed payment, as with a credit card; (3) money that is loaned

Claudia Dewald/Getty Images

Consumers have three main sources from which to pay for goods and services in the marketplace: cash, bank accounts (including checking and savings), and **credit**. Everyone knows what cash is, and virtually all sellers accept it. Yet it is not always convenient to use cash as a method of payment in today's global marketplace. Bank accounts and credit offer consumers convenient alternatives to paying cash for goods and services.

The largely electronic nature of bank accounts and credit sometimes presents more complex problems for consumers. When using a bank account or credit—unlike using cash—there is no physical reminder of how many dollars and cents you have in your pocket to spend. There are also special risks associated with these financial arrangements. This chapter will focus on the use of bank accounts and the payment devices associated with them as well as the use of credit to pay for goods and services.

The Basics About Bank Accounts

Checking and savings accounts are the most common types of bank accounts that people use to manage their money. Banks offer checking accounts to consumers as convenient places to deposit cash and checks for safekeeping. From a checking account, the consumer can easily withdraw money to pay bills and to make purchases. To withdraw money, an account holder can write checks to vendors and creditors, withdraw cash directly from an automatic teller machine (ATM), or make purchases using debit cards. Many smart consumers also open savings accounts into which they deposit a certain amount of money each month. Although an account holder can link an ATM or debit card to a savings account, many believe it is better to limit access to savings accounts so that money will be available in case of an emergency. Smart consumers also use savings accounts as a way to save for a special purchase or vacation.

The key to maintaining a checking account is to record all deposits and withdrawals so that you do not spend more than what is in the account. You can record deposits and withdrawals in the check register that came with your checks or you can use your bank's on-line service. You may also be able to purchase a home finance software product.

Many banks offer overdraft protection, which can assure the account holder that checks written on and debits made from the account will be honored up to the limit of the overdraft protection. This service is like a line of credit and is typically offered only to customers with a good credit history and for a certain amount—up to $1,000, for example. Interest is charged, usually on a daily basis, until the line of credit is repaid.

Banks are required by law to provide account holders with periodic information regarding their accounts. For a checking account, this information often includes copies of the checks you have written that have been paid, and a monthly statement. The statement details the status and activity on your account during that period, including all deposits and withdrawals. It is important that you review these statements to ensure that there has been no unauthorized activity on your account. Nearly all banks also allow online banking, and you may be able to review your monthly transactions on the bank's secure website.

If you encounter a problem with an electronic funds transfer (EFT) or debit card transaction on your monthly statement, the *Electronic Fund Transfer Act* provides you with protection, but only if the errors are of a computational nature, such as withdrawals of the wrong amount or unauthorized withdrawals. You must file a written complaint within 60 days of the date the statement was mailed. The bank must investigate the error within 10 business days, but if the bank credits the amount in dispute to your account during the investigation, it can take up to 45 days. If no error is found at the end of the investigation, the

▼ Smart consumers should review monthly bank statements and accounts for all checks written. *What is overdraft protection? How does it work?*

©Terry Vine/Blend Images LLC

bank can take back the money it credited to you, provided that it sends you a written explanation. If you do not file a complaint within 60 days, you could lose the total amount of money in question.

Banking Fees

Banks usually charge fees for maintaining a checking account, so it is important for consumers to shop around for the best deal. Some accounts are free, some carry a monthly service charge, and some may pay interest on the funds in your account. Standard charges often include fees for ordering checks, for writing more checks than the maximum decided upon at the time you open the account, for failing to keep a minimum balance in the checking account throughout the month, and for "bouncing" checks because there was not enough money in the account. You may also be charged a small fee by your bank to use ATMs, usually for those it does not operate, as well as a "guest" fee by the bank that does. At some banks if you are able to keep a certain amount of money in your account, most fees are waived. If you are having a problem with a bank or other financial institution, go to **www.consumerfinance.gov**, the website of the Consumer Financial Protection Bureau (CFPB). This government agency makes sure banks, lenders, and other financial companies treat consumers fairly.

ATM and Debit Cards

As mentioned above, banks also offer their customers electronic funds transfer cards—more commonly known as ATM cards—as an alternative to writing checks or having to go into a bank to withdraw money from an account. These embossed plastic cards look like a credit card but are connected to a bank account belonging to the card holder. They allow you to withdraw money from your bank account at an automatic teller machine using your personal identification number (PIN).

Banks also regularly issue debit cards, sometimes called "check cards," to their customers as a convenient way to make purchases without the added costs associated with credit cards. Debit cards look like credit cards, complete with your name, the credit card company symbol, a unique 16-digit account number, and an expiration date. However, debit cards are not credit cards and do not have the same legal protections as credit cards. Debit cards may be used anywhere that major credit cards

▲ Transactions with an ATM card are deducted from your checking account. *What are the advantages to using an ATM card?*

are accepted and are used to make purchases in the same way as a credit card. Instead of borrowing the money and paying interest on a balance, as you would on a line of credit, the amount of the purchase is deducted directly from your bank account, and the total amount you can spend is limited to your account balance. In some types of debit card transactions, you will be required to sign a receipt when making a purchase. In other types of debit card transactions, you may be asked to enter a special code or PIN. And in other instances, you may only have to swipe the card through a card reader. The amount of the purchase will be deducted from your bank account, usually fairly quickly.

Lost and Stolen Checkbooks and Bank Cards

Carrying a checkbook is safer than carrying cash because only the authorized signers on the account are allowed to use checks to withdraw funds from the account. If you lose a checkbook or it is stolen, you must notify your bank and ask them to cancel all of the checks in the book. This action is called **stop payment**. By law, the bank may charge you a small fee to stop payment on a check, but it cannot charge you to stop payment on each of the checks in your checkbook if it is lost or stolen.

Although carrying bank cards is typically safer than carrying cash, there are significant risks to consumers if an ATM or debit card is stolen or lost. Because ATM cards often require the use of a PIN to access cash from an account, it is more difficult for someone to make unauthorized withdrawals using your card if you keep your PIN secret.

On the other hand, a debit card can be used like a credit card and does not always require the use of a special code. Thus, anyone can use your debit card as they would a credit card and make purchases that drain money out of your bank account.

With lost or stolen credit cards, your liability is limited to $50 regardless of when you discover the loss. By contrast, your liability for lost or stolen ATM or debit cards depends on how quickly you notify your bank. If you notify the bank within two business days of discovering that your ATM or debit card is lost or stolen, you cannot be charged more than $50. If you discover unauthorized use of your card and notify your bank within 60 calendar days of the date your statement was mailed, your liability is limited to $500. If, however, you fail to notify your bank within this 60-day period, your potential loss from a lost or stolen ATM or debit card is not limited.

Although banks are prohibited from imposing greater liability on a consumer than what is provided for under the law, a bank may voluntarily provide greater protection by reducing a consumer's potential loss in the event of a stolen ATM or debit card. Make certain you understand your bank's rules regarding your potential liability for your ATM and debit cards. You should also read your monthly bank statement carefully to monitor your account for unauthorized activity. Many people also monitor their account activity through online banking. In some cases, a bank or credit card company will call you if they suspect unauthorized activity on your account.

stop payment a depositor's order to a bank to refuse to honor a specified check drawn by him or her

Onoky/SuperStock

For protection, any person with credit cards should keep a list of the following information for each card: (1) the name of the company issuing the card, (2) the account number on the card, and (3) the number to call if the card is lost or stolen. Some people recommend photocopying both sides of all credit cards and keeping these records in a safe place.

FYI For Your Information

p2p Payments

A number of private companies have developed apps that allow for person to person (p2p) payments. Users link to their bank account and are able to exchange funds with others who use the same app. Fees are typically low and transactions among people who trust each other are generally safe. These apps should not be used for financial transactions or sales with persons you do not know. Be sure to learn how these types of apps work and what transactions might not be protected before use.

THE **CASE** OF...

The Lost Wallet

Bridget went to the beach on a sunny Saturday afternoon, but didn't notice that her wallet had fallen out of her beach bag. On Monday morning, she realized that her wallet was gone when she reached into her bag for bus fare. Worried that someone might be using her debit and credit cards, she looked up her checking account balance online, but no unauthorized purchases had been made using her debit card.

Unfortunately, when she called her credit card company, she discovered that $500 had already been charged to her account. Bridget was so upset about the unauthorized purchases on her credit card that she forgot to call her bank to notify them of the lost debit card.

PROBLEM 24.1

a. For what amount, if any, is Bridget liable on her credit card?

b. Suppose Bridget goes to make an ATM withdrawal from her bank account the following Thursday and finds that all of the money in her account—$755—is gone. What if she immediately notifies the bank about the problem? Would she have been better off if she had notified the bank on Monday when she discovered that her debit card was gone? Explain your answers.

c. Do you think a consumer's liability should be different for lost credit cards than for lost debit cards? Why or why not?

d. Why might a bank agree to provide better protection to its customers than what is required by law?

▲ Some consumers use credit cards for everyday things such as food and gasoline, while others use credit cards for big-ticket items only. *What is an annual percentage rate?*

creditor a person who provides credit, loans, money, or delivers goods or services before payment is made

debtor a person who owes money or buys on credit

finance charge additional money owed to a creditor in exchange for the privilege of borrowing money

interest money paid for the use of someone else's money; the cost of borrowing money. Money put in a savings account earns interest, while borrowing money incurs an interest charge.

unsecured credit credit based only on a promise to repay in the future

secured credit credit for which the consumer must put up some kind of property as protection in the event a debt is not repaid

collateral money or property given as security in case a person is unable to repay a debt

default failure to fulfill a legal obligation, such as making a loan payment or appearing in court on a specified date and time

An Introduction to Credit

Using credit means borrowing money or buying goods or services now in exchange for a promise to pay in the future. People who lend money or provide credit to others are called **creditors**. People who borrow money or buy on credit and delay paying for the goods or services are called **debtors**. Debtors usually pay creditors additional money over the amount borrowed for the privilege of using the credit. This additional money owed to the creditor is the **finance charge**. It is based on the **interest** charged plus other fees.

The two general types of credit are unsecured and secured. **Unsecured credit** is credit extended in exchange for a promise to repay in the future. The consumer is not required to pledge property in order to obtain the credit. Most credit cards and store charge accounts are examples of unsecured credit.

Secured credit is credit for which the consumer must put up some property of value—called **collateral**—as protection in the event the debt is not repaid. A borrower who does not make the required payments is said to **default** on the loan. If a borrower defaults on a secured loan, the lender can take the collateral.

For example, a person who buys an automobile may be required by the lender (often a bank) to post the car as collateral until the debt is paid off. If the buyer defaults on the loan and fails to pay it off, the lender can repossess and sell the car, using the proceeds of this sale to pay off the debt.

How Credit Works

Today, many stores and companies (including banks) issue credit cards and allow their customers to maintain charge accounts. Consumers can use credit cards to buy gasoline, go out to dinner, buy clothing, pay bills, and many other things. Some cards can also be used to obtain cash advances from banks and ATMs.

Credit cards are embossed with the account holder's name and identification number. They entitle the holder to buy goods or services on credit. Some companies provide these cards free of charge, while others charge a yearly fee. Lenders charge interest on unpaid balances. Consumers are usually given a credit limit and can make purchases costing up to that limit. If you exceed that limit, the creditor may or may not permit the charge to go through; even if they do, they may impose an over-limit fee. You should be aware of your credit limit and stay within that amount. Exceeding your limit could lead to a negative credit report or termination of your account.

Companies issuing credit cards send or email monthly statements indicating how much you owe. Most credit card companies allow you to pay the balance over time by making a minimum monthly payment. You then are charged interest on the unpaid portion of the bill. The interest rate can be as high as 30 percent or more on unpaid balances. If you pay the entire amount on or before the due date indicated on the bill, however, there is no extra charge.

To more easily compare the rates charged by different companies, you can ask what **annual percentage rate (APR)** is charged. This rate is calculated the same way by all lenders. The APR is the percentage cost of credit on a yearly basis. Federal law requires creditors to give the APR when consumers ask about the cost of credit.

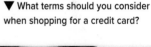

annual percentage rate (APR) the interest rate paid per year on borrowed money

Using a credit card can provide important consumer protections that are not available using other types of payment. However, fees can accrue when balances are not paid in full each month. Therefore, it is unwise to use a credit card to make a purchase that cannot be paid for on the same month's credit card statement. If you purchase an item using a credit card and pay for it over a period of months, the interest payment and other charges will make the item much more expensive than you expected.

Choosing a Credit Card Wisely

When deciding which credit cards or charge accounts to maintain, you should find out the annual fee, if any; the percentage rate charged on money owed; and whether interest is charged from the date of the transaction or only on balances unpaid at the end of the billing period. Providers of credit compete with each other to get new customers. Some offer credit without a fee or at very low interest for a certain period of time. Be sure to find out what the interest rate and annual fee will be after the introductory period. Some have agreements with airlines by which frequent-flyer miles can be earned and redeemed for airline tickets or other merchandise. Others provide cash rebates, insurance benefits, or the status of a particular card color

▼ What terms should you consider when shopping for a credit card?

(such as silver, gold, or platinum) which may carry additional benefits. Annual interest rates may vary by 10 percentage points or more, so it pays to shop very carefully for credit.

Credit cards are in such wide use today that certain goods and services may be difficult to obtain without one. For example, some car rental companies will not rent to people without a major credit card. While credit cards are an important convenience for many consumers, others use their cards repeatedly to obtain "instant loans." If they regularly make purchases with credit cards, they might then be unable to pay the balance on time. The interest rate on unpaid credit card balances is almost always higher than the interest on a bank loan, so using credit cards for this purpose is usually not a good idea.

Purestock/SuperStock

Billing Errors

Billing errors can be a real problem. It takes time and energy to sort them out, and they can cost you money if you do not discover them right away. To avoid problems, check all sales slips, save receipts and canceled checks, and go over each monthly statement carefully.

If you do encounter a billing error, the *Fair Credit Billing Act* provides you with a measure of protection. Billing errors include items not delivered, unauthorized charges, failure to properly list return credits or charges, and errors in computing the amount owed. Problems with the quality of a purchased item are not billing errors. This law requires that if you complain *in writing* about your billing error within 60 days of the date your monthly statement that first showed the error was mailed, creditors must acknowledge and respond to your complaint within 90 days. Phone calls do not protect your rights under this act. The written complaint must include your name, address, account number, and the nature and amount of the error. You may withhold payment of the disputed amount pending the investigation; however, undisputed amounts must be paid as normally required. Until your complaint is settled, the law forbids the creditor from reporting the matter to a credit bureau.

If it is determined that the bill is correct, you may have to pay a finance charge on the unpaid amount in dispute. However, a creditor who does not follow the requirements of the law may not collect the first $50 of the disputed amount, even if the bill turns out to be accurate. A consumer can sue such a creditor for damages and can also recover attorney's fees.

When Should You Use Credit?

To make an informed decision about a credit purchase, you must first answer this question: Is it worth having a car, television, vacation, or other item before you have saved enough money to pay the entire purchase price, even though you will pay more for it in the long run?

Most American families answer "yes" to this question. In fact, many households are seldom debt free. In 2018, the average credit card debt per indebted household was nearly $7,000. This is the average figure for credit card debt carried from month to month.

Extensive use of credit is here to stay, but consumers should know that credit purchases usually cost more than cash purchases. In addition, studies show that consumers who use credit spend more and buy more often. This is the reason many merchants offer "easy credit."

As a general rule, consumers who spend more than 20 percent of their take-home salary to pay off debts (excluding mortgages) are using too much credit. Consumers who skip payments to cover living expenses or who take out new loans to cover old loans are also using too much credit.

▼ Many families use credit to buy big-ticket items. *How does a consumer know if he or she is using too much credit?*

24.1 A Billing Statement

PAYMENTS SHOULD BE ADDRESSED TO
UNITED VIRGINIA BANK CARD CENTER
7818 PARHAM RD. P.O. BOX 27182
RICHMOND, VIRGINIA 23270

UNITED VIRGINIA BANK CARD
STATEMENT

ACCOUNT NUMBER
4366–040–878–000

STATEMENT CLOSING DATE
02/12/19

CREDIT LIMIT	CREDIT AVAILABLE
2,500	1,831.28

CUSTOMER REPRESENTATIVE TELEPHONE NUMBER
(804) 270–8474

JOHN Q. CONSUMER
1000 MAIN STREET
ANYWHERE, USA

INQUIRIES SHOULD BE ADDRESSED TO
UNITED VIRGINIA BANK CARD CENTER
7818 PARHAM RD. P.O. BOX 27172
RICHMOND, VIRGINIA 23270

POSTING DATE	REFERENCE NUMBER	TRANSACTION DATE	TRANSACTION DESCRIPTION			AMOUNT
01/18	*76145324	01/07	DODGE STATE PARK	FT WAYNE	IN	30.03
01/25	*81983773	01/03	ECONOMY HOTEL, INC.	ASHEVILLE	NC	69.71
02/08	21575724	01/27	THRIFTY MOTEL	SOUTH HILL	VA	56.51
02/09	22161982	02/05	SNAP SHOT CAMERA	WASHINGTON	DC	125.67
02/09	56672234	02/04	THE PASTA HOUSE	CHERRY HILL	NJ	46.92
			FINANCE CHARGE – LATE PAYMENT FEE			10.00

Your account is past due.
Please pay the minimum amount due to avoid further finance charges and possible harm to your credit record. If your payment has already been mailed, please accept our thanks.

VISA   **VISA**

TYPE OF CREDIT	PREVIOUS BALANCE	CREDITS	PAYMENTS	NEW TRANSACTIONS	PERIODIC RATES	CORRESPONDING ANNUAL PERCENTAGE RATES	BALANCE ON WHICH COMPUTED	FINANCE CHARGE	NEW BALANCE
ADVANCES	.00	.00	.00	.00	1.66%	19.99%	.00	.00	.00
OTHER EXTENSIONS OF CREDIT	425.00	.00	100.00	338.84	1.50%	18.0%	325.00	4.88	668.72
TOTALS	425.00	.00	100.00	338.84	ANNUAL PERCENTAGE RATE	18.0%	325.00	4.88	668.72

171870

PAST DUE	20	00
CURRENT DUE	20	00
MINIMUM PAYMENT DUE	40	00

TO PAY IN INSTALLMENTS PAY THIS AMOUNT BY THE PAYMENT ◄— DUE DATE

DUE DATE
03/12/19

To avoid additional FINANCE CHARGES on other extensions of credit, pay this amount by the payment due date.

NOTICE: SEE REVERSE SIDE FOR IMPORTANT INFORMATION

PROBLEM 24.2

Examine the billing statement above and answer the following questions.

a. Who is the creditor? Who is the debtor?

b. What is the new balance? How did the creditor arrive at the new balance?

c. How much credit is available on this account? How did the creditor determine the available credit?

d. Assume the debtor had a store receipt from Snap Shot Camera for $77.67. Draft a letter to the creditor about this billing error.

The Cost of Credit

As mentioned earlier, you should shop for credit just as you would shop for other products and services—by comparing costs and the terms of the agreement. The cost of credit includes interest and other finance charges. Because there are different methods for calculating interest rates, always ask for the APR. This number is calculated the same way by all lenders, so you can use it to compare rates from various lenders.

Interest Rates

usury the unlawful act of charging interest for various types of credit at rates higher than than the state's legal limit

Each state sets limits on the amount of interest that can be charged for various types of credit. Charging any amount above the legal limit is called **usury**. Lenders who charge interest rates above the legal maximum may be liable for both civil and criminal penalties. There is no federal usury law.

Interest rate ceilings, or limits, vary from state to state. Generally, however, loans from banks or finance companies carry interest rates from 10 to 30 percent per year. Department stores often charge about 1.5 percent per month, or about 18 percent per year, but these rates can vary widely depending on the lender and the economic conditions at the time. Most store charge cards are now issued by banks. Interest rates on installment contracts for consumer goods, such as new cars or furniture, also vary widely.

variable interest rate interest charged for credit at a rate that changes slightly from time to time, going up or down within certain limits, depending on changes in the economy

Some credit card companies now offer **variable interest rates** to consumers. With a variable rate, the amount of interest the card holder is charged changes slightly from time to time. The rate is computed based on conditions in the economy and can go up or down with the changing economy.

Typical variable interest rates for new credit card holders range widely, often from 10 to 30 percent or more. Although some cards may offer 0 percent or another very low rate, these are usually introductory terms. Find out when these introductory rates expire and what the interest rate will be after that. Credit card companies may lower these rates over time if your credit is good, but the rates can also increase if the issuer thinks you are a credit risk.

Borrowers should carefully review the information provided by the lender to determine how often the interest rate can change and how much it can change at each adjustment, as well as over the entire term of the loan. When the rate changes, your minimum required payments may also change. While your payments may start out low, they could increase over time if the interest rate also increases.

PROBLEM 24.3

Think of an item you would like to have now but could purchase only by using credit and paying later.

a. Name at least two institutions where you could shop for the credit you need to buy the item you want.

b. What interest and other fees might each creditor charge?

c. How would you determine which lender to use?

Other Charges

In addition to the interest paid on a credit purchase, other charges may be added to the basic price. Some of these additional services are offered as options by credit card companies, while others are unavoidable costs of having credit. These costs include:

- **Credit property insurance**—Insures the purchased item against theft or damage.

- **Credit life/disability insurance**—Guarantees payment of some or all of the balance due if the buyer should die or become disabled during the term of the contract.

- **Service charge**—Covers the seller's cost of bookkeeping, billing, and so on.

- **Penalty charge**—May include court costs, repossession expenses, and attorney's fees. In addition, many credit card companies charge a late payment penalty fee and increase your interest rate if you fail to make timely payments.

FYI For Your Information

Credit Cards on Campus

Many young adults obtain their first credit card when they attend college. Historically credit card companies and banks have marketed credit cards aggressively to college students. In many instances college students who obtained credit cards could not afford to incur debt or were not financially responsible. As a result, in 2009 Congress passed a law designed to stop abusive credit card marketing practices.

The Credit Card Accountability, Responsibility and Disclosure Act—the Card Act—forbids banks and credit card companies from handing out free gifts to students in order to entice them into filling out credit card application forms. Young adults under the age of 21 who apply for credit must now demonstrate the ability to pay or have a cosigner in order to be approved.

Costly Credit Arrangements

Consumers may fall prey to **loan sharking**. Loan sharks are people who lend money at high, often usurious (illegal) rates of interest. They promise "easy credit" and appeal to people who have problems obtaining and keeping good credit. Usurious loans are illegal under state laws. There are, however, a variety of legal but costly credit arrangements that consumers should also avoid.

loan sharking lending money at high, often illegal, interest rates

balloon payment a financing agreement in which the last payment of a loan is much higher than the regular monthly payments

acceleration clause a provision in a contract that makes the entire debt due immediately if a payment is not made on time or if some other condition is not met

bill consolidation a form of credit in which the lender combines all of a person's debts into a single monthly payment. In effect, this is a refinancing of a person's existing debts, often with an additional, higher interest charge

Some credit agreements call for **balloon payments**. In such agreements, the last payment is much larger than the monthly payments. Consumers may find it difficult to make the final payment, so carefully consider any agreement that calls for a large final payment. If you cannot make this payment, you may have to return the item to the seller even though you have made all the other required payments.

An **acceleration clause** permits the creditor to accelerate the loan, making all future payments due immediately in the event a consumer misses a single payment. Some auto sales finance agreements have acceleration clauses. If you miss a payment, you may suddenly owe the creditor the entire amount of the loan. Cars can be repossessed for this reason.

You should also beware of **bill consolidation**, or combining all your debts into a single one. Lenders sometimes claim you can wipe out all your bills by making one "easy" monthly payment to them, which they will distribute to your creditors. However, the consolidation loan may require payments over a longer period of time and at a higher rate of interest. Some lenders also charge a substantial fee for these loans. They may subtract the fee from your monthly payment to them before paying off your creditors, so you wind up falling deeper in debt.

Credit unions may offer the best terms to borrowers who want to consolidate debts, as they may lend you an amount sufficient to pay off all your bills. Then the credit union becomes your only creditor. Depending on your creditworthiness, they may also offer you a better interest rate than other lenders.

Truth in Lending

To prevent credit abuses, Congress passed the *Truth in Lending Act* in 1968. This law requires creditors to give you certain basic information about the cost of buying on credit. The creditor must tell you—*in writing and before you sign a contract*—the finance charge and the APR. The finance charge is the total amount you pay to use the credit, including interest charges and any other fees. The APR is the percentage cost of credit on a yearly basis. The law also requires creditors to give you information about variable-rate loans (for which your payments may increase over time).

Additionally, the law requires that consumers be given a copy of the disclosure form containing the credit information and be told the rules and charges for any late payments. Violators can be subject to both civil and criminal penalties, and consumers who sue creditors under this act may recover damages, court costs, and attorney's fees.

THE **CASE** OF...

The 50/50 Credit Plan

Linda wants to buy a new washing machine. The sales clerk at The Washer Mart tells Linda, "This washing machine is a good buy—only $500. But don't worry if you don't have the cash. I can arrange easy credit for you; only $50 down and $50 a month for 12 months. Just sign here." Linda signs the paperwork and pays $50. The washing machine is delivered to Linda's house the next day.

PROBLEM 24.4

a. What is the total price Linda will pay for this washing machine under the contract? How much of this is interest? What is the annual interest rate? Is this a fair price? Explain.

b. What might happen if Linda misses a payment to The Washer Mart?

c. Would it be better for Linda to buy the washing machine on her credit card, which charges monthly interest of 1.5 percent (18 percent annually)?

What Lenders Want to Know

Any store, bank, or credit card company that lends money or extends credit wants to know that the money will be repaid. Before making a loan, the lender will want to know several things:

- Is the consumer a reliable person? For example, a person who moves or changes jobs frequently might not be considered reliable.
- Does the consumer have a long-term steady income?
- Does the consumer have a high enough income to pay for the items to be purchased?
- Does the consumer have a good record in paying off other loans?

Lenders are in business to make money; thus, it is understandable that they would ask questions such as these. However, lenders have sometimes unfairly denied credit and loans for reasons such as the applicant's race, gender, or source of income. A federal law, the *Equal Credit Opportunity Act,* protects consumers against credit discrimination based on sex, marital status, race, color, religion, national origin, age, or source of income.

The Federal Trade Commission (FTC) handles credit discrimination complaints against finance companies, retail stores, oil companies, and travel and entertainment credit card companies. The Consumer Financial Protection Bureau (CFPB) and bank regulatory agencies, such as the Federal Reserve Board, the Comptroller of the Currency, and others handle complaints against banks and bank credit cards. If you think you have been discriminated against, you can complain to one of these agencies or sue the creditor in court.

Many states also have their own laws that forbid credit discrimination. Complaints should be directed to the state or local consumer affairs office or human rights commission.

Investigating the Law Where You Live

Is there a consumer affairs agency in your state? If so, what services does it provide?

▲ Payday loans are usually made to borrowers with bad credit who would not qualify for a bank loan. Interest rates can be very high. Critics of payday loans say they are made to people who will need to borrow again before their next pay day to make payments on their existing loan, creating a long term cycle of debt. The lenders contend that they are providing an important community service by making these small loans to people to help them cover general expenses. Some states have banned these loans. *Is there a payday law in your state?*

What If You Are Denied Credit?

When you apply for credit, the lender or creditor evaluates your application according to certain standards. They may investigate you personally or pay a credit bureau to check your credit record. Many do both. Credit bureaus operate nationwide and often share information about consumers. The Internet has increased the amount of information about consumers that is available to lenders and creditors. Information in a credit bureau's files can be a key factor in determining whether you can get loans, credit cards, or other forms of credit in the future.

If a credit report indicates that you are a high credit risk, the creditor will probably deny credit or offer credit on less favorable terms. Also, if you are trying to get credit for the first time and have no credit record at all, the lender may deny credit. Sometimes lenders deny credit or a loan based solely on information in the application, without taking the time to order a credit report.

The *Equal Credit Opportunity Act* requires that creditors and lenders tell consumers why they were turned down. The reasons given must be specific. For example, "applicant does not meet our standards" is not specific enough. On the other hand, "insufficient income" is a specific reason. It tells you how your circumstances must change to qualify for credit.

Another federal law protects you from inaccurate credit bureau reporting. The *Fair Credit Reporting Act* requires creditors who deny credit based on information received from a credit bureau to tell you that fact. The creditor must also give you the name and address of the credit bureau that supplied the consumer report.

You are a loan officer at a local bank. Each of the following people is seeking a loan. Based on the information provided, evaluate each applicant and make a decision regarding each loan request. Explain your reasons.

a. Erika is the mother of four children. Her only income consists of public assistance payments of $1,020 per month and $100 per month from the pension of her deceased husband. She wishes to buy a new oven and refrigerator that cost a total of $1,100. She lives in a public housing development where her rent and other household expenses average about $950 a month.

b. Jerry is a carpenter seeking work wherever he can find it. Depending on the weather and other factors, he is subject to seasonal unemployment. He currently brings home about $1,200 per month but has no money in the bank. His monthly expenses include car and insurance payments of $350, minimum credit card payments of $50, and rent of $500. He would like to borrow $7,500 to buy a motorcycle.

c. Tamike, 20, is in her second year of college. She has excellent grades and plans to attend medical school after graduation. Until recently, her parents paid her bills, but she is now on her own. She is seeking $4,000 for her college tuition and expenses. She has never borrowed money before, but she plans to repay all loans after finishing medical school.

Under a law passed by Congress in 2003—the *Fair and Accurate Credit Transactions (FACT) Act*—*every* consumer is entitled to a free annual credit report from each of the three national credit bureaus. The reports can be obtained online at **www.annualcreditreport.com** or by calling 1-877-322-8228. For a small fee, consumers can also obtain their credit scores.

If you discover false, misleading, incomplete, or out-of-date information in your file, you should request *in writing* that the credit bureau recheck its information and correct the errors. The credit bureau is required by law to make such corrections. If the credit bureau does not cooperate in correcting your credit file, you may complain to the FTC , the Consumer Financial Protection Bureau (CFPB), or your state attorney general, or you can sue the credit bureau in court. If after reinvestigating the information the bureau still believes that it is correct, you have the right to have your version of the dispute inserted in the file. If the information being reported about you is accurate, the credit bureau can report it for seven years. After this period of time, the information is removed from the file.

Default and Collection Practices

Consumers who use credit sometimes have difficulty making all their payments. Problems can arise because the consumer is too deeply in debt or because of unexpected unemployment, family illness, or a variety of other reasons. A consumer who does not pay a debt is said to be in **default**.

What a Consumer Can Do in Case of Default

If you have problems paying your bills, consider the following options:

• Reassess your financial lifestyle to determine how the problem arose. If you are not already on a budget, consider starting one.

• Notify each creditor of the problem and ask to have the term of debt extended (resulting in smaller monthly payments) or to have the amount of the debt reduced or refinanced. Keep in mind that refinancing over a longer period usually results in increased finance charges.

• Contact a consumer credit counseling service or a family service agency that offers free or low-cost financial counseling to those in need.

• Seek financial assistance from friends or relatives to reduce the debt to a manageable level.

Bankruptcy If taking the steps listed above does not resolve your problem, you may have to declare **bankruptcy**. This is a procedure through which a person places assets under the control of a federal court in order to be relieved of debt. Many people are surprised to learn that the majority of civil cases filed in federal courts are bankruptcies. For the twelve-month period ending December 31, 2018, almost 750,000 consumers filed for bankruptcy in the United States.

Under Chapter 13 of the federal bankruptcy law, a wage earner can make an arrangement, supervised by a federal court, to pay off some or all of what is owed to creditors over an extended period of time. A more severe form of bankruptcy is called a Chapter 7 bankruptcy. Under Chapter 7, the federal court takes control of most of the debtor's assets

▲ Bankruptcy is just one of the options people have when they cannot pay their bills. *How does bankruptcy work?*

default failure to fulfill a legal obligation, such as making a loan payment or appearing in court on a specified date and time

bankruptcy the procedure under the Federal Bankruptcy Act by which a person is relieved of all debts once he or she has placed all property and money in the court's care

Investigating the Law Where You Live

Research to learn what agencies and organizations in your community provide financial counseling services. Do they charge a fee for their services?

(some states allow the debtor to keep certain items), sells them, and pays off as much debt as possible. Generally, the money received from the sale of the assets is not enough to fully pay all creditors.

A declaration of bankruptcy has serious long-term consequences for the debtor. Records of personal bankruptcy remain in credit reports for 10 years. Even after that time, it may be very difficult to obtain credit or borrow money. In addition, some debts are not wiped out through bankruptcy. Taxes, alimony, child support, and student loans must still be repaid.

Creditor Collection Practices

Creditors have many ways of collecting money from consumers who are unwilling or unable to pay their debts. It is understandable that creditors take action to recover money or property owed them. However, some bill collectors have engaged in unsavory practices. As a result, some debtors suffered family problems, lost their jobs, and had their privacy invaded.

These practices prompted Congress to pass the *Fair Debt Collection Practices Act* in 1978. This act protects consumers from abusive and unfair collection practices by third-party debt collectors but does not apply to creditors collecting their own bills. Under the act, the debt collector's communications are limited to reasonable times and places. False or misleading statements, as well as acts of harassment or abuse, are strictly prohibited.

repossess to take back a debtor's property because the debtor failed to repay a debt

▼ When unpaid bills pile up the creditor can repossess the object that the borrower used the money to buy.

Calls and Letters If you receive unfair, deceptive, or harassing phone calls or letters from a debt collector, you should report the collection practice to the FTC, the CFPB, or to your local consumer protection agency. You can stop a debt collector from contacting you by writing a letter telling him or her to stop. After receiving your letter, the debt collector must not contact you again except to say that there will be no further contact or to tell you that the debt collector or creditor intends to take some specific action. Remember that sending this letter does not make the debt go away. You could still be sued by the debt collector or the original creditor.

Repossession Consumers sometimes post collateral when they take out a loan or sign credit sales contracts. The creditor can usually **repossess**, or take back, the collateral if the borrower defaults on the loan or obligation. Most states do not permit creditors to repossess collateral if doing so would involve violence or disturbing the peace. Usually the creditor will hire a repossession company to take back the collateral. This may happen late at night to reduce the chance of violence.

After repossessing the collateral, the creditor can sell it and then apply the proceeds of the sale to the amount owed. Debtors are also charged for any costs incurred in the repossession and sale. After the sale, the debtor is entitled to get back any amount received by the seller that is in excess of the amount owed (plus expenses). However, if the sale brings in less than the amount owed (plus expenses), the creditor can still demand that the debtor pay the difference.

Court Action Creditors may sue debtors in court for the exact amount owed on the debt. At times, the trouble and expense of suing in court make creditors avoid this method. However, creditors often sue debtors in small claims court. You will learn more about small claims court later in this unit.

THE **CASE** OF...

The Missed Payment

Orlando buys a used car from Top Value Cars for $5,000 and signs a contract agreeing to make monthly payments for three years. After paying $3,000, he misses two payments because of unexpected medical bills. Top Value needs to determine which debt collection method to use. Read each option and consider whether the action is legal and fair to Orlando. What arguments could creditors make in support of each option? What arguments could debtors make against them? Is there an option not listed below that would be better?

PROBLEM 24.6

a. Top Value could hire someone to repossess the car. If Top Value takes this route, incurring expenses of $300, and is able to sell the car for $2,000, will Orlando get any money back? Will he still owe money to Top Value even though he no longer has the car?

b. Top Value has previously contracted with a collection agency that has an impressive record of getting consumers to pay their debts. The collector sends a letter every day to both the consumer's home and place of business demanding payment and threatens to contact the consumer's employer about the debt. The collector also calls the debtor at home and at work, leaving messages every hour, beginning at 6 a.m. until 11 p.m. Is this contact reasonable, or does it amount to harassment? Would it be any different if one of Top Value's employees conducted the debt collection activities? Is it proper for a debt collector or a creditor to threaten to contact a debtor's employer?

c. Top Value could file a suit in small claims court against Orlando to sue him for the unpaid amount on the contract. Is this a reasonable first step in the collection process? Is there something else the creditor could do before resorting to a court action?

Just because you are sued does not mean the creditor is entitled to collect the disputed amount. Consumers may have legitimate defenses, such as the fact that the goods were defective. For this reason, *if you ever receive a summons to go to court, don't ignore it*. If you cannot appear in court on the date set in the summons, contact the court clerk to arrange for a postponement of the trial. In addition, contact a lawyer immediately. If you are unable to afford one, you may call the local legal services or legal aid office.

The main thing to avoid when being sued is a **default judgment**. This is a judgment entered for the plaintiff (creditor) against the defendant (debtor). Most default judgments occur simply because the defendant fails to show up in court. If the debtor fails to show up, a default judgment could be entered for the creditor even if the debtor had a good reason for failing to make a required payment.

Garnishment and Attachment A creditor who wins a judgment against a consumer may still have trouble collecting if the consumer does not pay voluntarily. It was once common practice to put people in prison for not paying their debts. This action is no longer allowed, except in some cases of failure to pay court-ordered child support.

One solution creditors use is to get a court order that forces the debtor's employer to withhold part of the debtor's wages and pay it directly to the creditor. This is called **garnishment**. The federal *Wage Garnishment Act* limits the amount that can be garnished to 25 percent of the debtor's take-home pay (pay after taxes and Social Security deductions). The act also prohibits employers from firing employees who have their wages garnished for a single debt. State laws may further limit and sometimes completely prohibit garnishment.

Creditors can also get possession of a debtor's money or property by **attachment**. This is a court order that forces a bank to pay the creditor out of a consumer's bank account or that allows the court to seize the consumer's property and sell it to satisfy the debt.

default judgment a ruling against a party to a lawsuit who fails to take a required action (for example, failing to file a paper on time)

garnishment the legally authorized process of taking a person's money, generally by taking part of the person's wages in order to pay creditors

attachment the act of taking a debtor's property or money to satisfy a debt, by court approval

▶ Many companies use telemarketing to reach consumers.

Although most sellers are honest, some are not. Dishonest sellers may use deceptive or unfair sales techniques. In order to protect themselves, consumers should learn to recognize and avoid deceptive sales practices. This chapter introduces you to such sales practices, tells how sellers use them to deceive buyers, and teaches you how to recognize these deceptive techniques.

Telemarketing Sales

telemarketing the practice of selling or marketing goods and services by phone

Telemarketing, the practice of selling or marketing goods and services by phone, is a popular sales technique. There are two kinds of telemarketing sales. The first occurs when the consumer receives an unsolicited call from the telemarketer. The other type happens when the consumer makes a call, usually to a toll-free number, in response to a print, radio, or other type of ad.

As with any marketing technique, consumers should take steps to ensure that they are dealing with a legitimate seller. Consumers should listen carefully to be sure that they understand the terms of the sale. In particular, consumers should ask how much they will have to pay, when the payments will have to be made, and what steps they can take to cancel the order, if necessary. Consumers should be very skeptical of any telemarketer who tells them they have just "won" something or who asks for payment by money order or cash.

The Federal Trade Commission (FTC) and the Federal Communications Commission (FCC) have many regulations to help protect consumers from telemarketers. Some of these regulations restrict when and how a telemarketer can contact you:

Darren Greenwood/Design Pics

- Telemarketers are restricted to calling you between the hours of 8 A.M. and 9 P.M.
- After you ask a telemarketer not to call you, it is illegal for them to call you again.

Other rules regulate the information a telemarketer must provide:
- They must tell you who is calling and that it is a sales call.
- Telemarketers must tell you the total cost of products or services offered and any restrictions—such as all sales being final and nonrefundable—before you pay.
- For prize promotions, they must tell you the odds of winning, that no purchase or payment is necessary to win, and any conditions for receiving the prize.
- It is illegal for telemarketers to lie or misrepresent any information.

In 2003, the FTC established the National Do Not Call Registry, which allows consumers to place their phone numbers on a list to reduce the number of unsolicited calls from telemarketers. You can register all your phone numbers for free at **www.donotcall.gov** or by calling 1-888-382-1222. After your phone numbers are registered, you may file consumer complaints in the same way that you registered. Some telemarketers may still call you, even if your numbers are registered. However, you can ask the telemarketer not to call you. The Do Not Call Registry does *not* limit calls from political organizations, charities, or companies with which you already have a relationship. Calls from these sources are not considered to be telemarketing calls. If you answer the phone and hear a recorded message, it is a robocall. Most sales-related robocalls are illegal. Do not press any number to speak to a "live operator." Just hang up. You might also be able to use your smartphone to block the number of the robocall.

FYI For Your Information

Telemarketing Scams

According to the Federal Trade Commission (FTC), telemarketing fraud robs people in the United States of billions of dollars each year. The FTC lists the following "offers" as the most common telemarketing scams:
- prize sweepstakes or lottery winnings in which you must buy something, give a credit or debit card number, wire money as a shipping or processing fee, or pay a tax on your winnings to collect something
- "free" travel packages
- credit card or loan scams
- investments, business opportunities, and other "get-rich-quick" schemes
- fake charities
- If a caller you do not know asks for personal information—your social security number, credit card number or bank account number—you should hang up.

Door-to-Door Sales

Door-to-door sales are no longer common in many places. Where such sales practices do occur, most sellers offer products and services consumers need or want. Some, however, use high-pressure tactics and smooth talk to get you to buy things that you otherwise would not buy. Once in the door, this type of salesperson will not take no for an answer and will do almost anything to make the sale.

Some state laws and a FTC rule give consumers a "cooling-off" period of three business days after they have signed any contract for more than $25 with a door-to-door salesperson. During this period, consumers can notify door-to-door sellers in writing that they wish to cancel the contract. It is best to send this letter by registered mail and to keep a copy. The FTC rule also requires door-to-door salespeople to tell their customers about the right to cancel and to put this notice in writing. If the seller does not do this, the consumer may be able to cancel the contract at any time by sending a letter to the seller. The "cooling off" rule applies to sales at the buyer's home, workplace, or dormitory, or at facilities rented by the seller on a temporary basis. The rule also applies if the buyer invites the seller to make a presentation at the buyer's home.

Advertising and the Consumer

Advertising is everywhere—on radio, television, and Internet sites; in newspapers and magazines; on billboards, bus shelters, and park benches; before movies and at sports arenas. Sellers use advertising to inform potential customers about their products. Ads help consumers by telling them about new goods and services and by letting them know when certain products or services are being sold at a reduced price. Some ads are even entertaining. While ads can be helpful, they can also mislead and deceive. Federal and state laws prohibit false or deceptive advertising.

A basic rule about advertising is that each advertising claim must be **substantiated** by the seller or advertiser before the ad runs. This means that a seller or advertiser must have a reasonable basis for any objective claims that it makes in its ads. For example, if a toothpaste manufacturer claims that its product reduces cavities, whitens teeth, and freshens breath, it must have some evidence or proof that backs up this claim. If the advertiser does not have a reasonable basis for a claim, then the advertisement is unfair and deceptive and in violation of the *Federal Trade Commission Act*.

In many states, a seller distributing a deceptive ad can be ordered by the FTC to stop that or similar advertising. The FTC can also order advertisers to correct deceptive ads by providing more information, such as disclosures or warnings, or requiring that information be stated more clearly on a product or in an advertisement. The FTC can also order **corrective advertising**. This means that the advertiser must distribute future ads that correct the deceptive impression left by the false or misleading ad. For example, a well-known mouthwash company once advertised that its product cured sore throats and colds. When an

substantiated provided with a reasonable basis for objective claims that are made by a seller or advertiser in its ads

corrective advertising a remedy imposed by the Federal Trade Commission requiring that any false claim in an advertisement be admitted and corrected in all future ads for specified period of time

investigation proved this claim false, the FTC ordered that all new ads state that the product did not cure sore throats or colds.

Although false or misleading ads are illegal, one type of ad is usually an exception to this rule. Ads based on the seller's opinion, personal taste, or obvious exaggeration are called **puffing**. While perhaps not literally true, ads that puff are not illegal. For example, a used-car dealer that advertises the "World's Best Used Cars" is engaged in puffing. A reasonable person should know better than to rely on the truthfulness of such a statement. Similarly, in announcing a sale at a furniture store, an ad reads: "2,750 items of furniture have to go *tonight!*" This ad is not literally true, but again, a reasonable consumer should understand that this is just "seller's talk."

In contrast, consider an advertisement that reads: "Important New Invention—Improves Auto Fuel Efficiency by 20%!" If the advertised product is not a new invention or does not improve automobile fuel efficiency by the amount claimed, this ad is deceptive and therefore illegal. The ad is not puffing, because it is not based on the seller's opinion, personal taste, or an obvious exaggeration. Rather, if untrue, it misleads consumers about important facts concerning the product.

The difference between illegal advertising and puffing may be slight, so consumers should be on guard. If an ad misleads consumers about an important fact concerning the product, it is probably illegal. If the ad is merely an exaggeration or a nonspecific opinion, it is probably puffing and therefore legal.

▲ Consumers encounter ads hundreds of times each day. *In what unusual places have you seen advertising?*

puffing an exaggerated statement or advertisement as to the desirability or reliability of a product or service

Bring to class three examples of puffing. For each, explain why the ad is not illegal, even though it may not be literally true. Find these ads in the newspaper, on a storefront sign, on the radio or television, or on the Internet.

One of the most controversial types of advertising involves tobacco. Tobacco advertising is controversial because smoking is the nation's leading preventable cause of death. More people in the United States die from illnesses related to smoking each year than from AIDS, car accidents, fires, homicides, suicides, and drunk driving combined. As a result, there have been efforts to eliminate or restrict tobacco advertising. For example, the U.S. Congress has enacted laws requiring health warnings on all packages and in all ads for cigarettes and smokeless tobacco products. Congress has also banned cigarette and smokeless tobacco advertising on radio and television. In addition, advertisements for tobacco products, like those for other products, must be truthful and accurate.

Even if the government does not bring about changes in the private sector through regulation, sometimes such restrictions can be agreed upon by the industry itself. For example, in 1998, the tobacco industry settled massive lawsuits brought against it by many states on behalf of their citizens to recover health care costs associated with tobacco-related illnesses. A primary concern in the lawsuits was the impact that tobacco

▼ Tobacco advertising is controversial. The government has set laws requiring health warnings on all tobacco products.

ads had on children. As part of that settlement, the tobacco companies agreed to restrict the way that they advertise, including banning ads on billboards and in transit systems. The tobacco companies also agreed not to use cartoon characters to sell their products or to distribute free samples of cigarettes or smokeless tobacco products at events to which minors are admitted.

PROBLEM 25.2

Some states are raising or considering raising the legal age for the purchase of tobacco products from 18 to 21. Some of these laws also target e-cigarettes in response to an increase in youth vaping.

a. How are tobacco and e-cigarette sales regulated in your state? Are changes in the law needed?

b. If you wanted to advocate for increasing the age for the sale of tobacco and e-cigarettes from 18 to 21, what other groups might support this change? What groups might oppose this change?

THE **CASE** OF...

Easy Money

Mr. and Mrs. Johnson were struggling to make ends meet and to feed their family of five. They decided that they needed to borrow money to pay their expenses for the month. They considered going to a bank for a loan, but they knew they each had poor credit histories, and they did not want to be paying off interest over a long period of time.

They were very interested when they read the following ad in the newspaper:

EASY MONEY: Having trouble paying bills? Need a short-term loan just to get you through a rough time? We offer quick loans to anyone regardless of credit background. No interest payments. Just a nominal processing fee. Call today!! 1-555-EZ-MONEY.

The offer sounded too good to be true. The Johnsons were skeptical, but they called anyway. The operator said she would be happy to offer them a no-interest loan of $2,000, repayable in six easy monthly installments. All the Johnsons had to do was pay a one-time fee of $200 to process the paperwork.

The Johnsons did not have to meet anybody from the loan company, and nobody bothered them at their home. They scraped together the $200 and sent Easy Money, Inc., a money order.

When they had not received their money in three weeks, they began to worry. They again called the number listed in the paper, but the line had been disconnected. Finally, after two more weeks, they realized they were not going to get their loan and would never see the "processing fee" again.

PROBLEM 25.3

a. Did any unfair or deceptive practices take place in the Johnsons' story? Explain.

b. What could the Johnsons have done to prevent their loss?

c. What can they do now? Can any state or federal agencies help them?

Bait and Switch

The bait-and-switch sales technique involves an insincere offer to sell a product on terms that sound almost too good to be true. The seller does not really want to sell the product, or "bait," being offered. The bait is simply used to get the buyer into the store. Once the consumer is in the store, he or she finds that the product is much less appealing than expected. Furthermore, on some occasions, the store may have a very limited quantity of the "bait," or the product may not be available at all. The seller then tries to "switch" the consumer to a more expensive item.

Salespersons who use the bait-and-switch technique are told to "talk down," or disparage, the advertised product and then encourage the consumer to buy a higher-priced item. As an incentive, salespeople may receive a higher commission if they sell the higher-priced item. The Federal Trade Commission has rules against use of the bait-and-switch selling technique and will take appropriate action when it receives complaints from consumers. Many state and local agencies also handle such complaints. If state law prohibits bait and switch, a consumer may be able to cancel a contract with a seller who has used this technique.

Sellers can legally advertise specials at very low prices to get customers into their stores without violating the bait-and-switch law. The items offered in these specials are sometimes referred to as "loss leaders," because the seller may lose money or make very little money on them. It is legal to advertise a loss leader, so long as the seller has an adequate supply of the item in stock and does not disparage the item in order to switch the buyer to a more expensive product.

PROBLEM 25.4

Kara and her brother Aaron are shopping for a new motorcycle. They see an ad in the Friday newspaper that says, "Come to Big Wheel for the Best Deals on the Slickest Wheels in Town! This weekend only, a 250 cc street bike, only $1,395!"

When they arrive at Big Wheel, the salesperson tells them that the street bike is not very powerful, tends to vibrate above 40 miles per hour, and is uncomfortable for long trips. He suggests that they test-ride a 500 cc, four-cylinder motorcycle on sale this weekend for $2,795.

a. What is the best way for a customer to handle an aggressive seller?

b. Has the salesperson used the bait-and-switch technique, or was the advertised product a loss leader for Big Wheel? Would it matter if Kara and Aaron arrived at the store on Saturday at noon and were told that all the 250 cc cycles had already been sold? Do they have a right to buy one at the advertised price? Give reasons for your answer.

c. Assume that Kara and Aaron purchase the larger bike for $2,795 but later find out that another store across town is selling the same bike for $2,400. What, if anything, can they do?

Internet Commerce

Online commercial activity, or e-commerce, offers consumers tremendous shopping opportunities ranging from books and clothing to financial services and groceries. Online search tools can provide extensive information about a wide variety of products. E-commerce also offers the ability to engage in comparison shopping for the best price and value with minimal effort. While e-commerce offers important advantages, many offline frauds operate just as readily online, including phony contests, fraudulent business opportunities, and health-related products promising instant weight loss or cancer cures.

Federal laws prohibiting fraud and deceptive practices also apply to e-commerce. Marketers are increasingly using e-mail messages or other online advertising to sell their products and services. Some consumers find unsolicited commercial e-mail—also known as "spam"—annoying and intrusive. More importantly, some consumers have lost money by responding to bogus offers that arrived in their e-mail inbox or have had their computers infected by harmful software attached to spam or pop-up ads. This software can take over your computer, causing, among other things, disclosure of personal financial information.

One particular type of online fraud called "phishing" has been especially effective with unwary consumers. Phishing occurs when Internet fraudsters send spam or pop-up messages that look like and claim to be from a business or organization you may have dealt with, such as an Internet service provider (ISP), bank, online payment service, or even a government

▼ Many people purchase daily necessities such as groceries over the Internet. *How can consumers protect themselves when making purchases online?*

Caia Images/Glow Images

agency. The message may ask you to "update," "validate," or "confirm" your account information or face serious consequences. The crook is trying to trick you into divulging your personal financial information in order to take money from your accounts or run up bills in your name.

Internet auctions are popular with consumers. Here, they can buy and sell goods in a massive marketplace. Auction sites give buyers a virtual international flea market through which to browse for nearly everything, and they give sellers a storefront from which to display anything they want to sell. While Internet auctions provide a great service for consumers and those looking to make money, buyers should take precautions to protect themselves. Buyers should:

- Research any product before you bid on it so you know what is a fair price.
- Understand the rules of the auction site, including the terms and conditions of the sale and who pays shipping costs.
- Identify the seller and read any feedback from other customers.
- Evaluate the methods of payment available to you and decide on one that is most secure, such as using a credit card or a third-party **escrow** service that will hold your money until you receive and approve the merchandise.
- You may also want to inquire whether the product you are buying is still covered under the manufacturer's warranty. Otherwise, products sold in an Internet auction do not generally come with a warranty, unless the seller is an authorized dealer of that product.

escrow money or property that a neutral party, such as a bank, holds for someone until that person fulfills some obligation or requirement

The basic steps to take when shopping online are similar to those that are important if you shop in a store or by telephone:

- know whom you are dealing with,
- know what you are buying and how much it will cost,
- pay by credit card to ensure maximum protection,
- make sure you understand the terms of the deal, and
- print and save records of your online transactions.

In addition, the federal Mail Order Rule provides additional rights with respect to the timing of your purchases. Sellers must comply with the promises in their ads, such as "Will be rushed to you within a week." If no shipping date is stated, the merchandise must be shipped within 30 days of the seller's receipt of your order. If the seller does not ship within 30 days, you have the right to cancel the order.

To protect yourself online, it is also critical to use antivirus and anti-spy software, as well as a firewall, and to update them all regularly. Further, use and protect your passwords.

PROBLEM 25.5

Visit an Internet auction site. How does the site work? What are the advantages and disadvantages of using this site?

Repairs and Estimates

Even the highest-quality products sometimes require repair. It is always a good idea to find out ahead of time how much the repairs will cost. Sometimes service mechanics will give an oral estimate of the cost of the repair but then have you sign a repair agreement that says that you authorize all repairs deemed necessary. You should always get a written estimate and insist that any repairs not listed on the repair agreement be made only after you give your specific approval.

Some communities have laws that require repair shops to give written estimates. Frequently, these laws limit the percentage difference allowed between the estimate and the final bill. You should also watch out for "free estimates." Sometimes the estimate is free only if you agree to have the shop make the repairs.

Being careful ahead of time is particularly important, because if you refuse to pay for repairs after they have been made, the repair shop or garage may be able to place a **lien** on the repaired item. This means the repair shop can keep the item until you pay the bill.

lien the right to take possession of or hold a debtor's property until the debt for the property is paid in full

To protect yourself and your property when having repairs done, remember the following steps:

- Become familiar with how cars and major appliances operate.
- Get estimates from several repair shops. Find out if there is a charge for each estimate.
- Ask for and keep an itemized written estimate.
- Insist that any repairs not listed on the estimate be made only after you give your approval.
- Consider requesting that replaced parts be returned to you.
- Search online for companies that compile consumer ratings of local service providers.

THE **CASE** OF...

The Costly Estimate

Nicole's car is running rough, so she takes it to City Repair Shop. The mechanic there tells her the car needs a tune-up and estimates the cost at $175. Nicole tells the mechanic to go ahead with the tune-up, but when she returns later to pick up the car, the total bill is $325.

PROBLEM 25.6

Did Nicole do something wrong? Did the repair shop do something wrong? What can happen if she refuses to pay the bill? Explain your answers.

▲ Getting an estimate

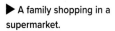
▶ A family shopping in a supermarket.

Becoming a smart consumer involves learning about several issues related to buying and selling. The first part of this chapter will help you think more critically about advertising and other factors that influence your purchases. Next, you will look at how laws at the federal, state, and local levels protect consumers. Finally, you will study practical steps that you can take before and after making a purchase to either avoid or remedy consumer problems. These steps include comparison shopping, gathering information about products and services, negotiating with sellers, writing effective complaint letters, working with government agencies and organizations, and using the court system (especially small claims court).

Influences on Consumers

While smart consumers understand contracts, warranties, deceptive sales practices, credit arrangements, and collection practices, they also understand the factors that influence their shopping habits.

They think about whether they need a product, whether they can afford it, and how they can purchase it carefully. Smart consumers also know the difference between *wanting* and *needing* a product. Of course, all consumers sometimes splurge and buy things they really do not need. But smart shoppers don't spend so much on things they want that they cannot afford what they really need.

Consumers often buy things in response to advertising. Television, radio, print, and Internet advertising is geared toward specific groups of people. For example, sellers know that young adults are an extremely important market for certain goods and services, so they develop specific ads for this audience. The ads, often purchased for television shows, movies, or publications that particularly appeal to young adults, are designed to increase sales of the products advertised. Many ads provide useful information about products or announce a sale. Other ads attempt to influence you to purchase a product that you do not need or want and cannot afford.

Ads That Appeal to Our Emotions

Advertisers try to connect with consumers on a personal level by creating ads that appeal to our emotions. There are several techniques, examples of which can be found in television, radio, newspaper, and online ads. Smart consumers learn to identify these techniques so they can separate the product from the characters and images in the ads.

Some ads *associate* products with popular ideas or symbols, such as family, motherhood, wealth, or sex appeal. These ads try to convince you that purchasing the products will associate you with the same ideas or symbols. Nearly all perfume ads in magazines, for example, include photos of beautiful women. The message to consumers is: if you use this perfume, you will be as beautiful as the woman in our ad.

The *bandwagon approach* is a technique that promotes the idea that everyone is using the product. Automotive manufacturers sometimes claim, for example, that their car, truck, or minivan is "best selling in its class in America . . . three years running." The message to consumers is: because others have bought our product, you should too.

Related to the bandwagon approach is *celebrity appeal*. This technique uses athletes or movie stars to advertise the product. One example of a celebrity ad shows a professional athlete promoting sports equipment. Some products even bear the name and endorsement of a celebrity spokesperson. These people bring glamour and style to ads, but these endorsements did not necessarily mean the products are worth a higher price or are of high quality.

► Smart consumers learn to separate the product from the characters and images in its ads. *Why do some companies use celebrities to advertise their products?*

Still other ads try to convince consumers by resorting to the *claims of authorities*, such as doctors, or by citing test results or studies that appear to be scientific. Ads for certain medicines include the phrase "recommended by doctors." Of course, smart consumers would want to know which doctors had recommended it and for what symptoms.

PROBLEM 26.2

Identify an advertisement for a product you would consider buying. If the ad appeared in a newspaper or magazine, cut it out and bring it to class. If it appeared online, print it out. If it was aired on the radio or television, either record the ad or write a description of it and bring it to class. Answer the following questions about your ad:

a. What product or service does the ad promote?

b. Who is the intended target audience for this product or service?

c. If the ad appeared on radio or television, at what time and during what program did it appear? If it appeared in print or online, in what publication or website did it appear? Why do you think the advertiser chose to run the ad at this time and place, and in this context?

d. What information do you need in order to make a wise choice about this product or service? How much of this information does the ad provide? What information does the ad not provide? Where could you get this information?

e. How does the ad try to persuade you to buy the item? What makes the ad effective?

f. Create an ad that would encourage your friends to buy one of the following products: jeans, a portable music system, perfume, new basketball shoes, a meal at a fast-food restaurant, or a high definition (HD) television. What ideas did you use to appeal to your audience as you designed your ad? Do professional advertising people use these ideas?

Consumer Protection

The federal, state, and local governments all pass and enforce laws to protect the consumer. As you read the following pages, and whenever you think about consumer protection problems, ask yourself: What are my rights under federal law? What are my rights under state law? What are my rights under local law?

Federal Consumer Protection

The U.S. Congress has passed many laws that protect consumers in several ways. First, these laws prohibit unfair or misleading trade practices, such as false advertising, unfair pricing, and mislabeling.

Second, federal laws set standards for the quality, safety, and reliability of many goods and services. Failure to meet these standards can result in legal action against the seller. For example, the *Consumer Product Safety Act* allows the government to ban, seize, or prevent the sale of harmful products. This law also allows the federal government to create standards requiring that dangerous products be made safer for the consumer.

Third, many federal agencies enforce consumer laws and regulate what products reach consumers. For example, the Federal Trade Commission (FTC) has the power to prohibit unfair or deceptive trade practices—such as false advertising—and can take legal action to stop such practices. The Consumer Product Safety Commission (CPSC) helps protect the public from unreasonable risk of injury associated with consumer products. The CPSC also provides safety information about products that consumers might want to buy.

▼ Federal law requires that most food labels contain the list of ingredients and nutritional information. *How does this help consumers?*

Fourth, Congress passes laws and agencies issue rules to improve the operation of the marketplace. In many instances, these laws and rules are designed to give consumers better information about products. For example, in 1992, Congress passed the *Nutrition Labeling and Education Act*. In 2006, the federal government began requiring most food manufacturers to list the amount of transfats on nutrition labels. These laws require that most food product labels list ingredients and nutritional information in a form that most people will be able to understand. This allows consumers to make smarter dietary choices. In 2014, the Food and Drug Administration (FDA) began requiring that calorie information be listed on menus and menu boards in chain restaurants.

DELIBERATION

Should we further regulate unhealthy foods and drinks?

A gallon of sugary soda: 1,500 calories. A one-pound chocolate, caramel, and peanut candy bar: 2,216 calories. A large bacon cheeseburger and fries: 1,580 calories. Each item is a quick, easy, inexpensive purchase at the store.

According to the Department of Health and Human Services, American diets regularly exceed the recommended caloric intake of 1,600 to 2,400 calories per day for adult women and 2,000 to 3,000 calories per day for adult men. Nearly half of all Americans' calories come from two categories: flours and grains, and fats and oils. Three-fourths of the population does not eat enough fruits and vegetables on a regular basis.

The Center for Disease Control has generally defined obesity as a weight that is higher than what is considered healthy for a given height. In the United States, heart disease, stroke, and type 2 diabetes are all considered obesity-related conditions and are all preventable. In 2008, the estimated annual medical cost of obesity in the United States was $147 billion.

Many health care professionals have labeled American obesity a crisis. One proposed solution to this crisis has been to increase government regulation of unhealthy foods and drinks. Additional regulation of unhealthy foods and drinks could come in many forms, from limiting portion sizes, to banning unhealthy additives, to regulating food advertising, and more.

A variety of government regulations already exist. In 1990, the *Nutritional Labeling and Education Act* required that all packaged foods and drinks include a label with nutritional information. In 2008, more than 50 percent of Americans said that they used nutrition labels to make food decisions. Similarly, the 2010 *Affordable Care Act* required that restaurant chains with 20 or more stores post calories on their menus and menu boards.

These regulations exist thanks in part to more than 100 years of jurisprudence. The 1911 Supreme Court case *Hipolite Egg Co*. v. *United States* cited the interstate commerce clause of the Constitution in upholding the federal government's power to regulate food and drugs. In similar cases that followed, the Supreme Court often upheld laws meant to protect the American public's health.

Critics believe that calls for additional regulations of unhealthy foods and drinks go too far. Americans who choose to eat unhealthy foods are making a choice and the government should not interfere with that choice. And, the federal government's power to regulate food is not without limits. In the early 1900s, the federal government attempted to eliminate the Coca-Cola Company's use of caffeine in its beverages. The case, *United States v. Forty Barrels and Twenty Kegs of Coca-Cola* (1916), resulted in a middle ground decision, with the company agreeing to reduce but not eliminate caffeine content in its beverages.

Should we further regulate unhealthy foods and drinks? Consider the options.

The government should further regulate unhealthy foods and drinks.

The government already regulates alcohol and tobacco, which can cause great harm to consumers. Unhealthy foods and drinks can harm consumers as well, so they, too, should be further regulated.

Unhealthy foods and drinks—both type of food and portion size—have contributed to obesity in four in ten Americans. High obesity levels increase healthcare costs, which impact all Americans, not just the obese. Further regulating food and drinks would decrease obesity in the United States and decrease health care costs.

Regulating the marketing of unhealthy food and drinks could be one solution to the problem. "We are hard-wired to notice food...there is so much food marketing and advertising trying to convince us to eat—especially junk food and other high-calorie food." Deborah Cohen, physician and researcher at the Rand Corporation said.

The human body sends internal signals for food, but also responds to external signals like images and smells. Eating is also linked to mood boosts and easing boredom and stress. Additional regulations on food and drink may help combat these internal and external signals to eat.

The government should not further regulate unhealthy foods and drinks.

The government's health education regulations are working. Obesity rates among young kids fell from 13.9 percent to 8 percent from 2003 to 2012. American teenagers in 2009-2010 exercised more, ate more fruits and vegetables, and drank fewer sugary drinks than kids the same age in 2001-2002 did.

Other government regulations have led to a decrease in caloric intake. Adults consumed about 118 fewer calories a day in 2009-2010 than four years earlier. Some have attributed this decline to consumers reading nutrition labels, which are a government regulation.

Regulating unhealthy foods and drinks deprives Americans of the freedom to make their own choices. "...it treats us all as children who can neither be trusted to make our own choices or be held responsible for those choices," says Michael D. Tanner at the Cato Institute.

New regulations will drive up costs. When the government adds regulations, businesses need to spend money to comply with those regulations. That cost is passed along to consumers, who will pay more for goods. This will most impact low-income households, who spend comparatively more on food than high-income households.

GUIDING QUESTIONS

1. What are the two most compelling reasons to support the deliberation question?
2. What are the two most compelling reasons to disagree with the deliberation question?
3. What is one area of this deliberation where the two sides might find common ground?

class action a lawsuit brought by one or more persons on behalf of a larger group

remedy what is done to compensate for an injury or to enforce some right

cease and desist order an order given by an administrative agency or a judge to stop some illegal or deceptive activity

consent decree a voluntary agreement to stop a practice that is claimed to be illegal

restitution the act of restoring something to its owner; the act of making good for loss or damage; repaying or refunding illegally obtained money or property

State and Local Consumer Protection

States also have their own consumer protection laws and agencies. Many of these laws prohibit unfair and deceptive trade practices. State laws allow consumers to file complaints in state court and with state agencies. They also enable agencies, such as the state attorney general's office or the state office of consumer affairs, to sue on behalf of consumers in order to halt illegal practices. In some cases, consumers can join together to bring **class action** lawsuits, which allow one or more persons to seek redress on behalf of an entire group.

Like federal consumer protection laws, state laws give the government power not only to stop unfair and deceptive practices, but also to provide consumers with a variety of remedies. A **remedy** makes up for harm that has been done. Remedies include **cease and desist orders,** a process by which an agency can require a business to stop a forbidden practice; **consent decrees,** which are voluntary agreements to end a practice that is claimed to be illegal; and **restitution,** in which a business refunds or repays any money illegally obtained.

Cities and counties may also have consumer protection laws. These laws are usually passed to deal with specific consumer issues that arise at a local level. For example, some cities have "truth-in-menus" laws. Under these laws, if the menu reads "fresh salmon," the restaurant cannot serve salmon that has been frozen. Some cities have also banned the use of transfats in restaurant cooking oil.

Protecting Your Rights as a Consumer

Consumers can encounter a wide variety of problems. This section will help you avoid some of these problems and will explain how to deal with any difficulties that may arise.

PROBLEM 26.4

You and a friend are planning a summer bicycle trip across your state. You own a very old bicycle and have decided to shop for a new road bike to use on this trip. List at least five ways you would gather information before making this purchase.

What to Do Before Buying

Generally, making large purchases on impulse is not wise. When shopping for products or services, learn as much as possible about them before buying. Careful consumers always compare prices and products before purchasing "big-ticket" items. This activity is called *comparison shopping.* They purchase the product only after considering other products that could also meet their needs.

For major purchases, careful shoppers use the library or the Internet to research consumer reports about competing brands. You could also ask your friends for product recommendations.

After you have determined what product you need, you may discover that it is available from more than one seller in your community. It makes good sense to buy from a seller with a good reputation, especially for important purchases. Contact your local Better Business Bureau (BBB) and conduct online research to determine whether there have been complaints about a particular seller.

Policies regarding products and services may differ among sellers. For some products, there may be additional charges for delivery, installation, and service. A price that seems lower from one seller may really be higher when extra charges are added in. Also check the seller's return policy. A very low price where all sales are final may not turn out to be such a good deal if you decide that you are unhappy with the product after you have purchased it. Sometimes a shopper may even spend a little more money to purchase an item from a seller with an outstanding reputation for service or the ability to deliver the item quickly and install it free of charge.

Before making a purchase, consumers should read the warranty carefully. Different manufacturers and sellers may provide different warranty coverage on very similar products. When studying the warranty, be sure to find out what you must do and what the seller or manufacturer must do if you have a problem with the product. A warranty that requires you to ship a broken product to a faraway place for repair at your expense may not be of much value to you.

▼ Many people buy big-ticket items with their own money. *What should a smart consumer do before buying an expensive item?*

If you are required to sign a contract as part of the purchase, be sure that you read and understand the entire contract and that all blanks have been filled in before you sign. If you have trouble understanding the contract, ask the store for permission to take the contract to someone who can help you understand it before you sign it. You may not want to deal with a store that will not let you do this.

Finally, do not believe everything you hear from the seller. Just because a seller says, "This is a real bargain!" does not make it true. You have to determine for yourself through careful shopping whether it is a bargain.

Steps to Take

Things to Consider Before Making a Purchase

- **Determine exactly what product or service fits your needs.**

- **Compare brands.** Read about various brands in consumer magazines and on the Internet. Ask friends for recommendations.

- **Compare sellers.** Check out a seller's reputation. Find out if there are extra charges. Learn about the seller's policy regarding exchanges or refunds.

- **Read and compare all warranties.**

- **Read and understand the contract (or get someone else to help you do this).**

- **Determine the total purchase price (including interest).**

What to Do After Buying

Sometimes even careful shoppers have problems. When this happens, it is important to remain calm and be persistent. Often, smart consumers can solve their own problems. When they cannot, it is very likely that an agency or organization in their community will be able to provide the needed help.

The first thing to do after buying a product is to inspect it. If you do not receive the exact product you purchased or if it has a defect, take it back to the seller and ask for a replacement or refund.

You should always read and follow the instructions provided and use the product only as recommended by the manufacturer. If the instructions are unclear or seem incomplete, contact the seller. Misuse of a product may be dangerous and may also cause you to forfeit your legal rights! Be sure to report any problem with a product as soon as possible. Trying to fix the product yourself could make the warranty void. If you believe the product is dangerous, or if you have been injured by the product, consider reporting the information to a government agency such as the Consumer Product Safety Commission.

If you experience a problem with a product, you should always try to contact the seller first. Reputable businesspeople are interested in a customer's future business, and most problems and misunderstandings can be cleared up with a face-to-face discussion or a telephone call. If you are not successful, then all future contacts should be in writing or documented in a log or journal.

Many companies have consumer affairs departments, but you may get faster action by writing directly to the company president. Review the following list of suggestions for writing a consumer letter of complaint:

- Include your name, address, phone number(s), e-mail address, and account number, if appropriate.
- Be brief, polite, and to the point. Do not be sarcastic or angry.
- Include all important facts, such as date and place of purchase, and information identifying the product, such as model and serial number.
- Explain the problem, what you have done about it, and what you want to have done.
- Include copies of documents relating to your problem. Do not send originals.
- Type the letter if possible. If this is not possible, print it neatly.
- Keep a copy of whatever you send, and any response you received.
- Before you mail the letter from your post office, ask for a return receipt, which will cost extra. This receipt will be signed by the company when it receives your letter and then returned to you. If you wind up in court with your problem, the receipt is your proof that the company was notified of the problem.

THE **CASE** OF...

The Cheap Vacation Home

David and Michele Cole were watching television after dinner one night when the phone rang. A pleasant-sounding person on the line told them that people in their community had a chance to purchase brand-new vacation homes for only $40,000. The homes were located in a beautiful, wooded setting just two hours by car from where the Cole family lived. In order to take advantage of this low price, the seller said that the Coles had to make a 20 percent down payment immediately. The rest of the money could be paid over the next 10 years with no interest.

The Coles had been thinking about buying a little place away from the city for weekend escapes, and this deal seemed too good to be true. They gave the seller their credit card number for the down payment of $8,000. The seller promised to send literature about the dream home.

Unfortunately, the literature never arrived. When the Coles complained to their state's office of consumer affairs, they found that others in their community had also been tricked. Fortunately, a thorough investigation enabled authorities to locate the persons responsible for this fraudulent sales scheme.

PROBLEM 26.5

a. What steps could the Cole family have taken initially to avoid this problem?

b. What remedies could the office of consumer affairs ask for?

c. Draft a law that would reduce the chances that this situation would happen again.

▲ Although they have been careful, some shoppers still experience problems. *What information should a consumer present when returning an item?*

If the seller still refuses to help you, consider contacting the product's manufacturer. If you do not know the name of the manufacturer, ask your librarian or look online for the *Thomas Registry of American Manufacturers*, which lists thousands of products and their manufacturers. If the seller is part of a chain store, consider writing to the corporate headquarters of the store. If you do not know the address of the manufacturer or the corporate headquarters, go to your local library and look it up in *Standard and Poor's Register of Corporations*, or look it up on the Internet.

Consider sending copies of your letter to local and state consumer protection organizations and to your local Better Business Bureau. If you still are not satisfied, it may be time to seek outside help. Many agencies and organizations exist for this purpose and may be able to help you. For example, you could take your complaint to a consumer protection agency, a media "action line," or a small claims court. You may also wish to contact an attorney at this point.

Jeff and Kristin Burt saw a newspaper ad for a brand-name flat screen TV set on sale at Tally's Electronics Shop. They rushed down to Tally's, where they bought a new 42-inch model for $1,000. Several weeks later, the TV completely lost its picture. A TV service mechanic who came to their home told them that the power supply had malfunctioned and that repairs would cost $600. The next morning, Jeff and Kristin returned to the store and asked to speak to Mr. Foxx, the salesperson who had sold them the TV.

a. Role-play the meeting between the Burts and Mr. Foxx. What should the Burts say, and what should Mr. Foxx say?

b. If Mr. Foxx refuses to help, what should the Burts do? If they decide to write a letter of complaint, to whom should they send it? What information should be included in the letter? Write a letter of complaint for the Burts.

c. What should the Burts do if they do not get a response to their letter within a reasonable amount of time?

Consumer Protection Agencies and Organizations

Use the Internet to search for consumer protection agencies and organizations. In many instances, complaints can be made online. Also check the beginning of the white pages of your telephone directory for information about local community resources. Many directories also have a section that provides a comprehensive listing of government agencies. Look in that section under "Consumer and Regulatory Agencies" to find the phone numbers of organizations that can help you with a consumer problem.

Some communities have arbitration programs to help with consumer complaints. These programs arbitrate disputes between buyers and sellers who have not been able to settle a problem. If you choose to use such a service, be sure to ask for and read a copy of the rules before you file your case. In some instances, the decision of the arbitrators is binding on both the business and the consumer; in others, only on the business; and in still others, on neither party. The party bound by the decision usually agrees not to pursue any other remedy, such as going to court.

Consumer Groups Many private organizations help consumers. National organizations such as the Consumer Federation of America, the Consumers Union, and Safe Kids Worldwide educate consumers and lobby for passage of consumer protection legislation.

The Consumer Federation of America (**www.consumerfed.org**) is primarily an advocacy organization that works to promote policies that help protect consumers on the federal and the state level. It also works to educate the public about consumer issues and developments in consumer law.

▶ Many consumers rely on product reports in magazines. *Have you ever used product reports to help you make a decision about a purchase?*

The Consumers Union (**www.consumersunion.org**) is a nonprofit, independent testing organization that provides unbiased reports to consumers about products and services, personal finance, health and nutrition, and other consumer concerns. CU publishes the well-known *Consumer Reports,* which many people refer to when making decisions to purchase goods and services in the marketplace.

Safe Kids Worldwide (**www.safekids.org**) is the only international non-profit organization that is dedicated solely to the prevention of unintentional injury to children. This advocacy group works for the production of safer products and lobbies for laws and regulations aimed at protecting the safety of children. Safe Kids also educates the public about harmful goods and services.

Private state and local consumer groups may give advice, investigate complaints, contact sellers, try to arrange settlements, and make legal referrals. To find similar organizations in your community, or search online, contact a local university, your state attorney general's office, or a member of your city council.

Business and Trade Associations One of the best-known consumer help organizations is the Better Business Bureau (BBB). Better Business Bureaus are supported by private businesses; they are not government agencies. While BBBs have no law-enforcement power, they do monitor business activity and try to promote high standards of business ethics. In many places, the BBB investigates consumer complaints, contacts the company involved, and tries to mediate a settlement. Reasonable complaints can often be settled with the BBB's help, but BBBs usually act only as mediators and cannot force a business to settle. In communities that do not have a BBB, you can contact the local chamber of commerce.

Media Many local newspapers as well as radio and television stations have special "action line" or "consumer affairs" services that help consumers. Publicity is a powerful weapon, and many consumers find that they can settle problems simply by contacting, or even threatening to contact, the media. To use these services, contact your local newspaper or radio and television stations using their websites.

Professional Associations Many business and professional people belong to associations that act on behalf of the entire profession or occupation. While such an association may have no legal enforcement powers over its members, a consumer complaint may result in pressure on, or dismissal of, the offending member. For example, if you have a complaint against an attorney, you can contact the bar association for your state.

State and Local Government All states, as well as many local governments, have consumer protection groups. These groups deal with everything from regulating public utilities to making sure you get a fair deal when you have your car repaired. Consumer protection groups are often located within the state attorney general's office, consumer affairs bureau, consumer protection agency, public advocate's office, or public utilities commission. To learn more about what the attorneys general in all of the states are doing to address local and national consumer protection issues, visit the National Association of Attorneys General at **www.naag.org**.

There are also more than 1,500 state boards that license or register members of more than 550 professions and service industries. Commonly regulated under these boards are accountants, architects, attorneys, barbers, bill collectors, doctors, electricians, engineers, funeral directors, teachers, nurses, plumbers, and real estate agents. Professional and occupational licensing was started by state legislatures to protect the public. These state boards set rules and standards for the occupation, prepare and give exams, issue or deny licenses, and handle consumer complaints. State boards have the power to **revoke** (take away) or suspend licenses for violations of established standards.

Finally, many places have mediation centers to help consumers solve problems without going to court. Some of these centers are operated by local governments, while others are sponsored by Better Business Bureaus or other private organizations.

revoke to take back or cancel

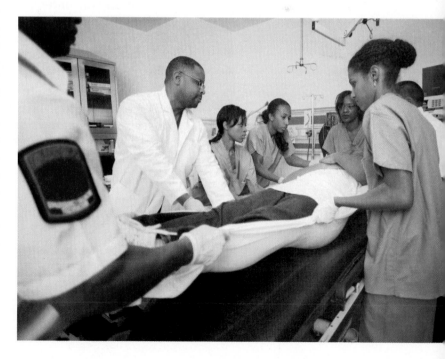

▼ State licensing boards, such as those for nurses and doctors, help protect consumers. *What kind of issues do state boards address?*

Choose a service that you have used, such as medical care, legal aid, auto repair, public transportation, or a hair salon.

a. Is there a professional association, licensing board, or other agency that could assist you if you had a problem with this service? Conduct research using your local phone book and/or the Internet to identify sources of help for consumers.

b. What steps must a consumer take to register a complaint with this agency or association?

c. What power does this agency have?

Federal Government It is usually best to try to solve your consumer problem on a local level. For certain problems, though, the federal government may provide you with the only remedy. Even if a federal agency cannot help, it may suggest a way to solve your problem. Some of the major federal consumer protection agencies and their contact information are described below:

- **Federal Trade Commission (FTC)** As the federal government's main consumer protection agency, the FTC seeks to prevent unfair or deceptive trade practices as well as problems with bills, credit, and warranties. Consumers can file a complaint at **www.ftc.gov** or by calling 1-877-FTC-HELP.

- **Food and Drug Administration (FDA)** The FDA regulates the safety of food, drugs, cosmetics, and medical devices through a testing program, and can order unsafe products off the market. Consumers can file complaints regarding FDA-regulated products either directly with the FDA or with regional consumer complaint coordinators in each state. Contact information can be found at **www.fda.gov** or by calling 1-888-INFO-FDA.

- **Consumer Product Safety Commission (CPSC)** The CPSC makes and enforces safety standards for many consumer products. It can ban, seize, or require warnings for unsafe products. You can file a complaint regarding an unsafe product at **www.cpsc.gov** or by calling 1-800-638-2772.

- **U.S. Postal Service (USPS)** The USPS investigates mail fraud and other mail problems. Consumers can contact the USPS regarding services or problems with their mail at **www.usps.com** or by calling 1-800-ASK-USPS.

- **Federal Communications Commission (FCC)** The FCC regulates consumer practices and interactions that take place over communications devices such as the radio, television, and telephone. The FCC receives consumer complaints at **www.consumercomplaints. fcc.gov** or by phone at 1-888-CALL-FCC.

- **Consumer Financial Protection Bureau (CFPB)**—The CFPB was created by an Act of Congress in 2010. Its mission is to watch out for American consumers in the market for financial products and services. CFPB receives complaints online at **www.consumerfinance.gov/complaint/** or by phone at 1-855-411-2372.

- **Department of Transportation (DOT)**—Various consumer protection offices within the department set standards for safe air, rail, bus, and automobile travel as well as handling complaints from passengers. Passenger and consumer complaints must be filed with the agency governing the type of travel in which you are engaged:

  - For defects related to automobile performance and products, contact the National Highway Traffic Safety Administration at **http://www.nhtsa.gov/** or by calling 1-888-327-4236.

  - For mass transit-related issues (buses and subways), visit the Federal Transit Administration Safety and Security online at **www.transit-safety.volpe.dot.gov**.

  - To report air travel safety issues, visit the Federal Aviation Administration at **www.faa.gov** or call 1-866-TELL-FAA.

▼ The United States Postal Service is just one of the many federal consumer protection agencies. *How does the USPS help consumers?*

PROBLEM 26.8

What federal agency discussed earlier in this chapter could help with each of the problems described below? Explain. Could a local or state agency also be helpful with any of the problems? If so, which agency?

a. Your parents are considering buying an exercise bike for home use and are concerned that your younger brother may be injured if he plays with or uses it incorrectly.

b. You buy an airline ticket for a job interview in another city. When you arrive at the airport, you find that the plane is already full. You cannot board the flight and therefore will miss your scheduled interview.

c. A friend has lost an arm in a serious accident. Her doctor is planning surgery that will result in the use of a new type of artificial limb. You want to learn more about the safety of this product before your friend's surgery.

d. A vocational school in your community runs an advertisement that promises job placement for every graduate. You are suspicious about this claim.

Direct Action by Consumers

Sometimes consumers who have concerns with an organization's business practices take **direct action** to make their voices heard. Direct action refers to actions that consumers take to make an impact on a business's or other organization's operations or profits. These steps can include letter-writing campaigns, boycotts of certain goods, press conferences, and picketing or other types of demonstrations. In recent years, for example, some students have organized direct-action campaigns to protest the treatment of the workers in developing countries who make clothing sold to students.

Taking Your Case to Court

Suppose you cannot settle your complaint and a consumer agency has been unable to help. Sometimes your complaint may form the basis for a criminal action against the seller. Whether or not a crime is involved, you can take your case to civil court. Anyone can go to court.

▲ Sweatshops are often the target of direct action by consumers. *Why might consumers be concerned about this issue?*

direct action an action that consumers take to make an impact on a business's or other organization's operations or profits

fraud an intentional deception, lie, or dishonest statement made to cheat someone that results in harm

Criminal Court

In some cases, a seller's action may be a crime. Such acts can be prosecuted as criminal **fraud**. Criminal fraud occurs when a salesperson knowingly misstates or misrepresents some important fact with the intent to defraud you, resulting in harm.

For example, suppose you sign a contract with a builder to construct a deck on your home. You pay the builder several thousand dollars to purchase the necessary materials. However, the builder does not intend to build the deck. He simply uses the scheme to take your money. In such a case, you are the victim of a crime. You should contact the police or your local prosecutor. Cases like this one can be prosecuted by the government in criminal court. State laws not only provide a fine or jail term (or both) for a convicted defendant, but also may require that the defendant pay back the defrauded consumer.

Civil Court

If a civil dispute involves a large amount of money, the case will be brought in the local civil trial court. Taking a case to court can be costly and time consuming. In some places, free or low-cost legal services may be available to consumers who cannot afford to hire an attorney.

Small Claims Court

In the early twentieth century, court reformers recognized that the typical civil court was too slow, expensive, and complicated for many minor cases. These reformers proposed a "people's court" designed to give citizens their day in court for small claims. Today, every state has a small claims court system. There is often a small claims court in each region of every state, where you can sue for small amounts of money. Each state or local jurisdiction has a different monetary upper limit on the cases that qualify for small claims actions, ranging from a few hundred to several thousand dollars.

The small claims court system offers citizens many advantages over the traditional court system. Filing a suit in small claims court is very inexpensive, as attorneys are not required (in some states they are not allowed), and there are few time-consuming delays. There are no juries in small claims court; a judge decides all cases. The judge will typically make a decision about your case immediately. To find out how small claims courts operate in your state, contact the clerk of the court before filing a claim.

▼ Criminal activities such as real estate fraud often result in houses standing empty. People involved may face charges in a criminal court. *What is criminal fraud?*

©Natalia Bratslavsky/age fotostock

Taking Your Complaint to Small Claims Court

Filing a suit in small claims court involves three general steps:

1. **File the Claim.**

    a. **Eligibility.** Discuss your case with the court clerk by calling or visiting the local courthouse. The clerk will be able to determine whether the court can handle your claim. You may also be able to get this information by visiting the Web site for your local court system.

    b. **Paperwork.** If you have a claim that is appropriate for small claims court, you will be required to fill out some forms and pay a filing fee. This fee varies among jurisdictions, but it usually ranges from $30 to $100 depending on the amount of the claim. To fill out the forms, known as a "Complaint" or "Statement of Claim," you will be asked for the name and address of the party you are suing, the reason for your complaint, and the amount you are asking for. The amount of the claim should be based on the loss you have incurred.

2. **Prepare for Your Day in Court.**

    a. **Notification.** In most states, the court will notify you and the defendant of the date and place of the hearing. You should confirm that your jurisdiction takes responsibility for notifying the defendant, because your case cannot proceed unless the other party receives notice of the lawsuit.

    b. **Evidence.** You should gather all the evidence necessary to present your case. This includes receipts, letters, canceled checks, sales slips, and estimates of repair. If a defective product is involved, be sure to bring it along,

▲ Small claims court

if possible. Contact all witnesses to be sure they come to court. Uncooperative witnesses can be subpoenaed. This means they can be ordered to appear in court. If you have time, visit the court before your hearing so you will know what to expect. Also, practice presenting your case to a friend beforehand.

3. **Go to Court on Time AND with Confidence.**

    a. **Punctuality.** Be on time for court on the date scheduled for the hearing. If for any reason you cannot make it, call the court clerk to ask for a postponement, called a continuance.

    b. **Confidence.** When your hearing begins, the judge will ask you to tell your story. Do this by presenting your facts, witnesses, and any evidence you may have. Do not get emotional. Be prepared for questions from the judge. After both sides have presented their stories, the judge will make a decision.

David R. Frazier Photolibrary, Inc.

TAKING ACTION: Law and Democracy

Mock Trial: *James Phillips* v. *The Sound Shop*

FACTS

James Phillips purchased wireless earbuds from The Sound Shop and later tried to exchange them because they did not work. The date of the sale was November 14, and the return was 10 days later. The sales slip says: "Fully guaranteed for five days from the date of purchase. If defective, return it in the original box for store credit." The store refused to make the exchange, and James brought this action in small claims court.

EVIDENCE

James has (1) the sales slip for $124.95 plus tax and (2) the broken earbuds. He claims to have thrown away the original packaging.

WITNESSES

For the plaintiff:

1. James Phillips
2. Pam Phillips, James's sister

For the defendant:

1. Al Jackson, the salesperson
2. Hattie Babcock, the store manager

COURT

The judge should allow James to make his case and should give the store representatives a chance to tell the court why the money should not be returned. At the end, the judge should make a ruling and provide reasons for the decision.

WITNESS STATEMENT: James Phillips

"I went into The Sound Shop to buy wireless earbuds. I paid the $124.95 price, and he gave me the earbuds in their original box. When I got home, they didn't work. I went back to the store to get my money back, but the salesperson wouldn't return it. He said I should have brought the earbuds back right away. I explained to him that my mother had been sick and that I had been busy taking care of her. Here are the broken earbuds and the receipt as proof."

WITNESS STATEMENT: Pam Phillips

"When James got home that day, he was excited and wanted to show me something. He called me into his room to show me his new earbuds. I put them in my ears, but when he played the music, nothing happened."

WITNESS STATEMENT: Al Jackson

"I sold him the wireless earbuds, but as far as I know, it worked. All the display models worked well enough, so why shouldn't the boxed ones straight from the factory? He probably dropped them on his way home. Or maybe he broke it because he didn't know how to use them correctly."

WITNESS STATEMENT: Hattie Babcock

"As Mr. Jackson said, all the other wireless earbuds have worked fine. We've never had a single complaint. Our store policy is not to make refunds unless the merchandise is returned within five days in the original box. The guarantee even says this. That's why Mr. Jackson didn't give him his money back. Otherwise, we'd have been more than happy to give him credit toward a new purchase. Personally, I agree with Mr. Jackson. James probably didn't bring back the box because it was all messed up after he dropped it."

PROBLEM 26.10

a. Role-play a small claims court hearing. Participants should be divided into groups of five, each with a judge and four witnesses. Witnesses should testify and answer questions from the judge. When all testimony is complete, each judge should announce his or her ruling. Was the decision the same for each hearing?

b. Is this an effective way to resolve this type of problem? Explain.

▶ Consumers should be aware of the legal issues related to buying a car.

In this chapter you will learn about four of the most important purchases you are likely to make: buying a car, renting a place to live, paying for college, and obtaining health insurance. Concepts you have already studied in this unit–contracts, warranties, comparison shopping, credit, and others–apply here as well.

Buying a Car

When you shop for a car, you should consider: (1) safety, (2) price, (3) quality, (4) warranty, and (5) fuel economy. Unfortunately, many consumers fail to compare safety features and other factors when shopping for a car.

Safety features are important because, in an average year, there are more than six million automobile accidents. Federal law requires car dealers to provide a pamphlet that outlines the safety features of all new cars. This pamphlet includes information on acceleration and passing ability, stopping distance, and tire load. In addition, a prospective buyer should always check visibility from the driver's seat. Check for blind spots, windshield glare in strong sunlight, and positioning of inside and outside mirrors. You should also check whether you can reach all the controls while sitting in the driver's seat with the seat belts fastened, and consider what protection is afforded by bumpers, safety belts, and air bags. If you have child safety seats, be sure they fit the car. Also consider fuel efficiency. Cars that are fuel efficient can save money and help protect the environment.

Niko Guido/Getty Images

In considering price, remember that virtually no one pays the sticker price for a new or used car. Discounts are common. The size of the discount depends on the time of year, your negotiating ability, special sales, manufacturer's bonuses, rebates, and other factors.

You should compare quality, fuel economy, warranties, and the dealer's capability to make repairs the same way you compare safety features and price. Many new cars have "bumper-to-bumper" warranties covering most parts, except batteries and tires, against defects for 36,000 miles or 36 months, whichever comes first. Some manufacturers warrant the engine and drivetrain for a longer period. Other manufacturers offer a warranty as part of the purchase price but also make available an extended warranty (a service contract) for an additional cost. Warranties vary, so be certain that you read and fully understand exactly what protections the warranty provides.

In some instances, used cars come with warranties—often for a short period of time. The Federal Trade Commission requires used-car dealers to place a large sticker—a "Buyer's Guide"—in the window of every vehicle offered for sale. The sticker must indicate whether the vehicle comes with an express warranty. If it does, the sticker must detail what the warranty includes. If the sticker says the car comes "as is," this means no warranty is provided. In some places, however, state law prohibits a car from being sold "as is." Finally, the sticker will advise you to get all promises in writing and to have the car inspected by a mechanic before you buy it.

Although car warranties are now easier to read and protections have been expanded, there are still time or mileage limits (or both) on warranties. Also, a warranty may become void if you fail to perform scheduled maintenance or if you misuse the car. Always be sure the warranty and any additional promises are in writing. Keep these papers in a safe place.

▼ Examine both the inside and outside of a car before you buy. *What information is available to consumers on the window sticker of a car for sale?*

Clerkenwell/Getty Images

Internet Resources for Car Buyers

Car shoppers can get price information for used cars, pricing for new cars, quality reviews, and information on available financing at the Kelley Blue Book website (**www.kbb.com**). Begun in 1926, the Kelley Blue Book is the industry standard for evaluating cars. Much of the information is also available in Spanish.

Safety information is available from the U.S. Department of Transportation's National Highway Transportation Safety Administration (**www.nhtsa.dot. gov**), which has a special online feature that allows you to compare crash and rollover tests for various cars, light trucks, vans, and SUVs. Tire information is also available at this site.

When buying a car—particularly your first car—remember that each state requires motor vehicle owners and drivers to have liability insurance. Statistically, younger drivers are involved in more accidents than more experienced drivers, so insurance costs can be quite high. Shop carefully for auto insurance and be sure that you understand what your policy covers. Sometimes discounts are available for students with good grades.

PROBLEM 27.1

In addition to the purchase price, what other costs should you consider when you are deciding to purchase a car? Where can you find information about each of these costs?

Financing a Car

Most new-car buyers and many used-car buyers make their purchases on credit. Buyers may select the length of the repayment period, which may be as long as five years. The longer the repayment period, the lower the monthly payments will be. However, longer repayment periods also result in a larger amount paid in interest. Figure 27.1 shows the total interest charges on a $6,000 loan for a used car at a 5 percent interest rate over various repayment periods. Actual interest rates for car loans will vary depending upon a variety of factors, including whether the car you are purchasing is new or used. Interest rates also vary based on your lender, your creditworthiness, and general economic conditions.

Automobile financing is usually available from car dealers, banks, credit unions, and finance companies. When you are comparing finance charges among lenders, make certain that you are comparing the same down payment and repayment periods for each loan. In comparing terms, you will mostly be concerned with the annual percentage rate (APR). The *Truth in Lending Act* requires that creditors give you written disclosure of important terms of the credit agreement before you sign it, including APR, total finance charges, total amount financed, and charges for late payments. However, you should also read all the terms carefully so that you can answer the following questions:

- Will finance charges be refunded if the loan is repaid early?
- Will there be fair warning in the event of a repossession?
- Is there a penalty for late payments? If so, how much?
- Will all payments immediately become due if a payment is missed?

In general, the better your credit score and the shorter your loan repayment schedule, the lower the interest rate will be. Interest rates for new car loans are typically slightly lower than interest rates for used car loans. If you need an auto loan, comparison shop for the best deal and read the contract carefully. Get help if you don't understand the contract.

THE **CASE** OF...

The Used-Car Purchase

Having saved $1,000 from her part-time job, Sasha responded to an ad for "Like New! One-Owner Used Cars." A salesperson for A-1 Used Cars watched Sasha wander around the lot until she was attracted to a bright-red compact car. Sasha told the salesperson that this car looked just right for her. He replied, "You've made a good choice. This is an excellent car. It will give you many years of good service."

Although the sticker price was $6,550, the salesperson thought that he might be able to get Sasha a $50 discount because she was "a nice young kid getting her first car." After conferring with the sales manager, he explained to Sasha that she could have the car for $6,500 and that the dealer could arrange to finance the car and sell her all the necessary auto insurance.

Sasha knew that she would need a loan and that auto insurance was required by law. Her excitement increased as it appeared that all her needs could be met in one stop.

Sasha saw a sticker on the car's window indicating that this car came with a warranty.

The salesperson told her that A-1 Used Cars would make any repairs to the engine for damage not caused by her misuse for 30 days or 10,000 miles, whichever came first. Now she felt confident about using all of her savings as a down payment. After all, what repair bills could she have with such a nice car accompanied by a terrific warranty?

PROBLEM 27.2

a. Make a list of things Sasha should have done or thought about before going to A-1 Used Cars.

b. Make a list of things Sasha should have done at A-1 before agreeing to buy the car.

c. What promises, if any, did the seller make to her? Did he say anything that could be considered puffing? If so, what?

d. What are the advantages and disadvantages to Sasha of obtaining financing and insurance from the dealer?

e. Does the warranty provided make this a better deal or a worse deal? Explain.

27.1 Interest on a $6,000 Loan

Amount Borrowed	APR (Annual Percentage Rate)	Term of Loan (in months)	Monthly Payment	Total Finance Charge
$6,000	5%	24	$263.23	$317.52
$6,000	5%	36	$179.83	$473.88
$6,000	5%	48	$138.18	$632.64

PROBLEM 27.3

Nathan is buying a used car for $7,000. He can make a down payment of $1,000 and needs to borrow the remaining $6,000. Assume that credit is available only from the source listed above.

a. What is the total cost of the car if the term of the loan is 24 months? 36 months? 48 months?

b. If Nathan borrows the money, which credit arrangement would be least expensive in the long run? Most desirable?

Leasing a Car

Rather than buying, many consumers opt to lease cars. Under a lease agreement, the consumer does not own the car but pays a monthly fee to drive the car for a certain time period. At the end of the term, the consumer can pay an agreed-upon amount—which may equal the rest of the car's value—to purchase the car. More often, he or she returns the car, pays any required end-of-lease charges, and "walks away," owning nothing. The lease agreement usually restricts mileage and wear and tear, imposing additional fees for exceeding the limits on those terms. The agreement also includes provisions for an initial down payment, security deposit, and other fees. The customer should make sure that the warranty covers the entire lease term as well as the number of miles he or she is likely to drive.

Typically, monthly lease payments are lower than monthly loan payments. However, you do not own the car at the end of the lease as you do after paying off a loan. Under the federal *Consumer Leasing Act*, consumers have a right to information about the costs and terms of a vehicle lease.

Rather than buying or leasing a car, some people take advantage of car sharing. In many urban areas, car sharing companies make cars available for rent by the hour. Consumers rent the car by phone or online, pick it up from a reserved parking spot, use it, and then return it to the same parking spot. Rental fees usually include fuel and insurance. Drivers may need to be 21 or older. Many people who car share make more use of other transportation options such as walking, biking, and public transit. Car sharing also reduces traffic congestion and fuel consumption.

Investigating the Law Where You Live

Find out what procedures you must follow to register a car and obtain license plates in your community.

What to Do in the Event of an Auto Accident

- **Check for injuries.** Get medical help if it is needed.

- **Route traffic around the accident.** Set up road flares or another emergency signaling device to alert other drivers of the accident. Another motorist or bystander can also stand at a safe distance at the side of the road and caution motorists to slow down and drive around the accident. This action keeps everyone safe.

- **Call the police, even if the accident is minor.** Some insurance companies may require the police report of the accident.

- **Exchange information with the other driver(s).** Include names, addresses, and phone numbers; license and registration numbers; makes, models, and years of cars; and names, addresses, and phone numbers of insurance agents.

- **Look for witnesses to the accident.** Get the names, addresses, phone numbers, and e-mail addresses of any witnesses. This includes passengers in all vehicles involved in the accident. Doing so can prevent disagreement concerning how the accident actually happened.

- **Do not tell the other driver(s) the extent of your insurance.** Do not confess guilt, do not indicate that your insurance company will take care of everything, and do not sign any paper indicating you were not injured.

- **Note the name and badge number of the police officer who comes to the scene of the accident.** Your state law may require that you file an accident report with the police.

- **Make careful notes about the accident while the information is fresh in your mind.** Be sure to describe the specific damages to all vehicles involved. Also note details such as the location of the accident, weather conditions, road conditions, and visibility.

- **Contact your insurance agent as soon as possible after the accident to file a claim.** Give your agent as much information as possible about the accident. Follow his or her instructions carefully to avoid problems later.

Renting a Place to Live

When young people complete their education, many rent a place of their own to live. Some families own their homes. To finance a home purchase, most people obtain a loan called a **mortgage** from a lender—a bank or other financial institution. With a mortgage, the lender pays the seller of the home the purchase price, and the buyer makes regular payments to the lender over a long period of time, usually 15 or 30 years. The buyer pays interest to the lender in return for the ability to repay the loan over many years. Depending on interest rates and the **term**, or length, of the loan, a buyer might make payments of more than $200,000 in order to pay off a $100,000 mortgage.

Most mortgages are **fixed-rate mortgages** in which the interest rate remains the same throughout the term of the loan. Some mortgages, however, are **adjustable-rate mortgages** in which the interest rate can change over time. Some begin with very low interest rates, which may initially make the loan more affordable.

However, some purchasers have found that these interest rates adjust upward faster than their ability to make higher monthly mortgage payments. This problem can lead to missed payments and eventually to **foreclosure**. When there is a foreclosure, the bank or other lender gets a court order that lets it take back the property and resell it. The money

mortgage a loan in which land or buildings are put up as security

term a length or duration of time

fixed-rate mortgages a home loan in which the interest rate remains the same throughout the term of the loan

adjustable-rate mortgages a home loan in which the interest rate can change over time

foreclosure a bank's taking possession of a property to resell it, due to the owner's failure to make mortgage payments

▼ Choosing a place to live is very important to consumers.

Juice Images/Glow Images

that comes in from that sale is used to satisfy the debt still owed by the borrower. Some lenders have been criticized for offering adjustable rate mortgages to borrowers who did not have the financial resources to make the monthly payments when the interest adjusted upward.

Many people eventually own a home, but initially almost all young people are renters. A renter, or **tenant**, pays the owner, or **landlord**, a certain amount of money in return for the right to live for a period of time in property owned by the landlord.

Leases: A Special Kind of Contract

The landlord-tenant relationship is created by a type of contract called a **lease**, or rental agreement. A lease specifies the amount of rent that must be paid and the length of time for which the dwelling may be rented. It also states the rights and duties of both landlord and tenant.

Before you rent an apartment or a house, you should do at least two things to protect your interests. First, completely inspect the dwelling to ensure that it meets your needs and is in good condition. Second, because most leases are written to the advantage of the landlord, carefully read the lease. If you do not understand or cannot read the lease, get help from someone else before signing it. The following list includes issues you should consider before renting:

- In what kind of area or neighborhood do you wish to live?
- What are the costs, including rent, utilities, and security deposit?
- What is the condition of the apartment or house? Will any repairs be made by the landlord before you move in?
- How long will the lease last, and how can it be ended? Can you sublet this apartment or add other tenants to the lease?
- Will the landlord make or pay for repairs after you move in?
- What services will the tenant receive?
- Are there any special rules (for example, no pets or no guests)?
- Do you understand all the **clauses** in the lease? Are any of them unacceptable to you?

tenant a person who rents a property

landlord the property owner who leases or rents space

lease a rental contract between a landlord and a tenant for the use of property for a specified length of time at a specified cost

clause a paragraph, sentence, or phrase in a legal document, such as a contract, lease, or will

---

PROBLEM 27.4

Assume that you are looking for a new apartment. You are married and have a two-year-old child and a small dog.

a. What should you look for when inspecting an apartment? Make a list.

b. What questions would you ask the landlord?

THE **CASE** OF...

The Summer Rental

A college student moves to a resort town to work for the summer. After searching the classi-fied ads in the local newspaper, she finds an apart-ment for rent. She phones the landlord and after seeing the apartment tells him she will rent it for three months. After a month, she moves to a cheaper apartment down the street. The landlord demands rent for the two remaining months, but the young woman claims she does not owe any money because the lease was not in writing.

PROBLEM 27.5

a. Is the student obligated to pay the additional two months' rent?

b. Would it make a difference if the landlord rented the apartment immediately after the student moved out?

c. What should the woman have done when she found the cheaper apartment?

d. Role-play a phone call between the woman and the landlord after she finds the cheaper apartment and wishes to get the landlord's permission to move.

After you have inspected a rental house or apartment, you will probably be asked to fill out a **lease application**. The landlord uses this form to determine whether you qualify for the rental property. You will be asked for information such as your name, age, address, place of employment, source of income, and a list of previous residences. You will also be asked for credit references, including from previous land-lords. Landlords use this information to determine your ability to pay the rent. If the landlord approves your lease application, you will then be asked to sign a lease.

A lease is a legal contract in which both the landlord and the tenant agree to certain obligations. A lease usually includes the date the tenant may move in, the amount of the rent, the dates on which the rent is to be paid, and the term or length of the lease. It also includes the amount of any security deposit, the conditions under which the rent may be raised, and information about whether the tenant can sublet the rental property to someone else. The lease also states the rules governing repairs, maintenance, and other conditions in the apartment or house.

Depending upon your particular situation, one type of lease may be better than another. For example, if you are planning to rent for only a short period of time, or if your job often requires you to move on short notice, you might prefer a **month-to-month lease**. While this type of lease usually enables you to leave after giving 30 days' notice, it has the disadvantage of allowing the landlord to raise the rent or evict you with just 30 days' notice as well. You should also keep in mind that renting an apartment on a month-to-month basis will usually be more expensive than entering into a long-term lease.

lease application a form the landlord uses to determine whether someone qualifies for a rental property

month-to-month lease a lease enabling the tenant to leave with 30 days' notice and the landlord to raise the rent or evict the tenant with 30 days' notice

Another type of lease allows a tenant to move in with the understanding that the lease is for an indefinite period. This arrangement is called a tenancy at will. Tenants who remain in an apartment after their lease has expired are usually considered to be tenants at will. There is very little protection for either the landlord or the tenant in a **tenancy at will**, because the tenant may leave—or be asked to leave—at any time. Often, however, such a lease will have a provision requiring that the party who wants to end the lease give the other party fair notice, such as 30 days.

A lease for a fixed period of time is called a **tenancy for years**. This type of lease generally prevents the landlord from raising the rent or evicting the tenant during the term of the lease. If you are planning to rent for a long period of time, this may be the best type of lease for you.

Written leases can sometimes be difficult to read and understand. To protect yourself, be sure to read all clauses in your lease carefully before signing it. Never sign a lease unless all blank spaces are filled in or crossed out. If you are unsure of anything in the lease, ask to take it home and consult with a representative of a tenant organization, legal aid office, private law firm, or others experienced with leases. Also make sure that any promises made by the landlord are written into the lease. For example, if the landlord promises to paint the apartment before you move in, get the promise in writing.

Leases with a term of one year or longer must be in writing to be enforceable in court. However, leases for less than one year may not have to be written to be legally effective, and an oral agreement may be binding. To avoid problems, you should always get a written lease that is signed and dated by both you and the landlord. If there is only an oral agreement and problems arise, one of you may remember the terms of the agreement differently than the other.

Landlord-Tenant Negotiations

In many places, housing is in great demand and short supply. In this kind of market, landlords generally have the upper hand and can often tell tenants to "take it or leave it." Negotiating with a landlord about rent and other lease terms can be difficult, but it may be worth a try.

▲ Tenants should understand all parts of their lease agreement before they sign the paperwork. *Why might a tenant want to negotiate with the landlord before signing the lease?*

tenancy at will an arrangement in which a tenant remains on rented property beyond the end of the lease with the understanding that the tenant may leave, or be asked to leave, at any time.

tenancy for years any lease for a fixed period of time. This type of lease specifies that the tenant may live on the property for a single, definite period of time, during which the landlord may not raise the rent or evict the tenant.

Negotiating works best if you know your rights and know what you want. If you do negotiate with a landlord, it is best to be assertive, yet tactful and polite. Landlords want to know you will be a good tenant. But tenants expect something in return—namely, fair treatment and a clean, well-maintained place to live.

It may be possible to change parts of the lease. To strike a section from a lease, both the tenant and the landlord or rental agent should cross out the particular clause and put their initials and the date next to the change. If anything is added to the lease, be sure the addition is written on all copies of the lease and is initialed and dated by both the landlord and the tenant.

Some landlords ask that you sign a standard form lease because it is usually written to the landlord's advantage. It may even contain clauses that are unenforceable in court. The lease reprinted in Figure 27.2 contains many provisions found in standard form leases. Since landlord-tenant laws differ from state to state, a few of the clauses in this lease could be illegal in some states. You should learn about the landlord-tenant laws in your particular state.

PROBLEM 27.6

a. What are the key provisions of the lease in Figure 27.2? Who is the landlord? Who pays the utilities? Is the tenant allowed to have a pet?

b. As a tenant, would you object to any of the provisions in this lease? If so, which ones?

c. As a landlord, would you add any clauses to the lease? If so, draft them.

The following pages provide information on several of the clauses in the lease in Figure 27.2. This material is designed to help you read and understand a lease and avoid problems. After a person signs a lease and moves into a rental home, both the landlord and the tenant take on certain rights and duties. Most of these are spelled out in the lease, but others exist regardless of whether or not they are expressly stated in the lease.

If the tenant violates a provision of the lease—for example, does not pay the rent—the landlord can go to court and attempt to have the tenant evicted. The tenant may be able to defend against the landlord in court and prevent the eviction.

27.2 A Rental Agreement

RANDALL REAL ESTATE CO.
PROPERTY MANAGEMENT, INVESTMENT PROPERTY, SALES, INSURANCE

THIS AGREEMENT, Made and executed this _____ day of _____A.D. 20___, by and between RANDALL REAL ESTATE COMPANY, hereinafter called the Landlord, and _____,
hereinafter called the Tenant.

WITNESSETH, That Landlord does hereby let unto Tenant the premises known as Apartment No. 301, at 12 Marshall Street, Johnstown, Virginia, for the term commencing on the _____day of _____, 20___, and fully ending at midnight on the _____ day of _____, 20___, at and for the total rental of _____ Dollars, the first installment payable on the execution of this agreement and the remaining installments payable in advance on the _____ day of each ensuing month, to and at the office of RANDALL REAL ESTATE COMPANY, 1000 Columbia Road, Johnstown, Virginia.

On the _____ day of _____, 20___, a sum of _____ shall become due and payable. This sum shall cover the period up to the _____ day of _____, 20___; thereafter, a sum of _____ shall be due and payable on the _____ day of each month.

AND TENANT does hereby agree as follows:
1. Tenant will pay the rent at the time specified.
2. Tenant will pay all utility bills as they become due.
3. Tenant will use the premises for a dwelling and for no other purpose.
4. Tenant will not use said premises for any unlawful purpose, or in any noisy or rowdy manner, or in a way offensive to any other occupant of the building.
5. Tenant will not transfer or sublet the premises without the written consent of the Landlord.
6. Landlord shall have access to the premises at any time for the purpose of inspection, to make repairs the Landlord considers necessary, or to show the apartment to tenant applicants.
7. Tenant will give Landlord prompt notice of any defects or breakage in the structure, equipment, or fixtures of said premises.
8. Tenant will not make any alterations or additions to the structure, equipment, or fixtures of said premises without the written consent of the Landlord.
9. Tenant will pay a security deposit in the amount of $_____, which will be held by Landlord until expiration of this lease and refunded on the condition that said premises are returned in good condition, normal wear and tear excepted.
10. Tenant will not keep any pets, live animals, or birds of any description in said premises.
11. Landlord shall be under no liability to Tenant for any discontinuance of heat, hot water, or elevator service, and shall not be liable for damage to property of Tenant caused by rodents, rain, snow, defective plumbing or any other source.
12. Should Tenant continue in possession after the end of the term herein with permission of Landlord, it is agreed that the tenancy thus created can be terminated by either party giving to the other party not less than Thirty (30) days' Written Notice.
13. Tenant shall be required to give the Landlord at least thirty (30) days' notice, in writing, of his or her intention to vacate the premises at the expiration of this tenancy. If Tenant vacates the premises without first furnishing said notice, Tenant shall be liable to the Landlord for one month's rent.
14. Both Landlord and Tenant waive trial by jury in connection with any agreement contained in the rental agreement or any claim for damages arising out of the agreement or connected with this tenancy.
15. Landlord shall not be held liable for any injuries or damages to the Tenant or his or her guests, regardless of cause.
16. In the event of increases in real estate taxes, fuel charges, or sewer and water fees, Tenant agrees during the term of the lease to pay a proportionate share of such charges, fees, or increases.
17. Tenant confesses judgment and waives any and all rights to file a counterclaim, or a defense to any action filed by the Landlord against the Tenant and further agrees to pay attorney's fees and all other costs incurred by the Landlord in an action against the Tenant.
18. Tenant agrees to observe all such rules and regulations which the Landlord or his agents will make concerning the apartment building.

IN TESTIMONY WHEREOF, Landlord and Tenant have signed this Agreement the day and year first herein- before written.

Signed in the presence of

_____   _____
_____   _____
_____   _____

Paying the Rent
Tenant will pay the rent at the time specified. (Clause 1)

A tenant's most important duty is paying the rent on time. Leases generally state the amount of rent to be paid and the dates on which it is due. Most leases require payment on the first day of each month. If you and the landlord agree to a different day, be sure that it is written into the lease and that both parties have initialed the change.

Courts and legislatures in many states have decided that in situations in which a house or apartment is made unlivable by fire, landlord neglect, or other causes, the tenant cannot be forced to pay the rent. Keep in mind, however, that tenants have a duty to pay the rent and that landlords generally have a right to evict tenants who do not pay it. It is best not to assume that you are excused from paying rent.

Raising the Rent
In the event of increases in real estate taxes, fuel charges, or sewer and water fees, Tenant agrees during the term of the lease to pay a proportionate share of such charges, fees, or increases. (Clause 16)

rent-control a law that limits how much existing rents can be raised. Large cities often have such laws.

Generally, landlords cannot raise the rent during the term of a lease. When the term is over, the rent can normally be raised as much as the landlord wants. Some leases, however, include provisions (like Clause 16 in the sample lease) that allow for automatic increases during the term of the lease. Many landlords include such clauses to cover the rising costs of fuel and building maintenance. A lease with an escalation clause is usually not favorable to a tenant.

Another factor that can affect whether the landlord may raise the rent is **rent control**. Large cities may have such rent-control laws, which put a limit on how much existing rents can be raised. Cities with rent-control laws use various standards to control the rise in rents. Some places limit rent increases to a certain percentage each year. In other places, rent increases are tied to the cost of living or improvements in the building or are allowed only when a new tenant moves in. Rent-control laws slow down the rising cost of housing. However, there are many arguments for and against rent control. Wherever the system has been tried, it has been controversial.

▼ Landlords should keep the dwelling in a condition fit for living. *Is the landlord or the tenant responsible for making these repairs?*

Upkeep and Repairs
Landlord shall be under no liability to Tenant for any discontinuance of heat, hot water, or elevator service, and shall not be liable for damage to property of Tenant caused by rodents, rain, snow, defective plumbing, or any other source. (Clause 11)

In the past, landlords did not have a duty to maintain the premises or to make repairs to a rented house or apartment. In the few places where this is still true, tenants have to make all repairs that are needed to keep the property in its original condition. Clause 11 from the sample lease implies that the tenant must continue to pay the rent.

This is the case whether or not the landlord provides a dwelling fit to live in. In some states, this provision is unenforceable. Today, most states require landlords to keep houses or apartments in a condition fit to live in. The landlord is also responsible for maintaining common areas such as hallways and lobbies.

Many state courts and legislatures say that a **warranty of habitability** is implied in every lease. This means that the landlord promises to provide a place fit for human habitation. The warranty of habitability exists whether or not it is written into the lease. Thus, if major repairs are needed, the landlord has a duty to fix the problems.

warranty of habitability the implied, or unwritten, obligation of a landlord to provide a unit fit for human habitation

PROBLEM 27.7

a. If you were a landlord, what repairs and maintenance would you expect the tenant to perform? Make a list and explain each item.

b. If you were a tenant, what repairs and maintenance would you expect the landlord to perform? Make a list and explain each item.

c. Would it make a difference to your list if your state had a warranty of habitability? Explain.

In addition to the implied warranty of habitability, many communities also have housing codes. These codes set minimum standards for repairs and living conditions within rental houses or apartments. Landlords are required by law to meet the standards of the housing code, and they may lose their licenses to rent if the standards are not maintained. Housing codes differ from area to area, but in most places, tenants have the right to call a government housing inspector to examine their apartments for code violations.

Although most places hold landlords responsible for major repairs, remember that the landlord's duty to make repairs differs from place to place and from lease to lease. It is always best to make sure the responsibility for repairs is spelled out in the lease. Also, remember that tenants have a duty to notify the landlord when repairs are needed. If someone is injured as a result of an unsafe or defective condition, the landlord cannot be held liable unless he or she knew or should have known that the condition existed.

Use of the Property *Tenant will use the premises for a dwelling and for no other purpose.* (Clause 3)

Tenants pay for the right to use a landlord's property. As a general rule, tenants may use the property only for the purposes stated in the lease. For example, if you rented a house to be used as a residence, you would not be allowed to use it as a restaurant or, in some places, as a daycare facility.

TAKING ACTION: Law and Democracy

Lease Negotiation

Read the following information, then work in groups of four. In each group, two classmates should role-play the landlords (the Randalls), and two others should role-play the tenants (the Monicos). The Monicos should inspect the apartment and ask all the questions a tenant should ask before signing a lease. The Randalls should find out everything a landlord needs to know before renting to a tenant. The landlords should give a copy of the lease to the tenants. The tenants should discuss the lease and reach a decision on whether to sign it. Use Figure 27.2 for this activity.

The Randalls own an apartment building in the city of Johnstown. They have a two-bedroom apartment for rent. They require all their tenants to sign a two-year lease and to pay a security deposit equal to two-months' rent. The rent is $900 per month plus utilities, which average about $75 a month. In addition, no pets are allowed in the building. The Randalls are eager to rent the apartment right away because it has been empty for two weeks and they are losing money.

The Monicos have just moved to Johnstown, where they have new jobs. Mrs. Monico's job may last only one year, and they may then have to move back to Williamsport, a city 100 miles away. They have a three-year-old son and a dog. Based on their salaries, the Monicos wish to pay only $750 a month in rent and utilities. They want a nice neighborhood and are a little worried about crime in Johnstown.

The Monicos need an apartment right away because Ms. Monico starts work in three days. The couple sees an ad for the Randalls' apartment. They do not know much about the neighborhood but decide to go and look at the apartment anyway.

The apartment has two bedrooms, a living room, a dining area, and one bathroom with a bathtub but no shower. It is on the second floor and has a small balcony overlooking a parking lot. The paint is peeling in the larger bedroom, and a small window is broken in the bathroom. The kitchen has a new refrigerator and sink, but the stove is old and worn and has a missing handle. The front door and the door to the balcony have locks that could easily be opened by an intruder.

PROBLEM 27.8

After the role play, answer these questions:

a. Did the Monicos ask any questions about the neighborhood or about the building as a whole? Should they have?

b. What was decided regarding the amount of rent and other costs of the apartment? In reality, can tenants ever convince landlords to take less than they are asking? Give the reasons for your answer.

c. In discussing the condition of the apartment, did the tenants get the landlords to agree to any repairs?

d. Did the Monicos ask about such facilities as laundry, parking, and playgrounds? Should they have?

e. Are there any special rules in the lease that the Monicos did not like? Did they ask the landlords to discuss these rules? If so, what was decided? Could the Monicos have done a better job of negotiating these rules? Explain.

f. Is it worthwhile for tenants to try to negotiate with landlords? Can tenants be hurt by doing this? Explain.

g. The Monicos also make jewelry in their spare time and are interested in selling it online to supplement their incomes. Do they need to ask about internet access before signing a lease? Can they conduct this activity under the lease they have been offered? What should they do?

Sample Housing Code

The following are examples of provisions included in a typical housing code.

Maintenance and Repair

- Floors and walls shall be free of holes, cracks, splinters, or peeling paint.
- Windows and doors shall be weatherproof, easily operable, free of broken glass, and equipped with workable locks.
- Stairs and walkways shall be in good repair, clean, and free of safety hazards.
- Roof shall be free of leaks.

Cleanliness and Sanitation

- Each unit shall be generally free of rodents and insects.
- Common areas shall be free of dirt, litter, trash, water, or other unsanitary matter.

Use and Occupancy

- Each unit shall have a minimum of 120 square feet of livable floor space per occupant.

- Each bedroom shall have a minimum of 50 square feet of floor space per occupant.
- Each unit shall have a private bathroom.
- Each common area shall be accessible without going through another apartment.

Facilities and Utilities

- Sinks, lavatories, and bathing facilities shall be in working order.
- Every room shall have a minimum of two electrical outlets and will have no exposed wiring.
- Water, electricity, gas, heating, and sewer services shall be in good operating condition.
- Halls, stairways, and common areas shall be adequately lighted.
- The building shall be free of fire hazards and secure from intruders.

Most leases contain clauses that permit **eviction** if the landlord reasonably believes that the tenants have committed crimes or allowed the commission of crimes on the rented premises. Even if the lease does not contain a clause banning criminal activity, the landlord may still be able to have the tenants evicted. Judges frequently enforce such requests from landlords.

A lease may specify the names, ages, and number of people who will live on the premises. Although having occasional guests will not violate such a lease, there can be problems if the number of people permanently occupying the premises changes, as happens after the birth or adoption of a child or after getting married.

Although tenants have a right to use the rental property, they also have a duty to take care of the property and return it to the landlord in the same general condition in which it was rented. Tenants generally are responsible for the upkeep of the premises, including routine cleaning and minor repairs. Major repairs and upkeep of common areas, such as apartment hallways, are normally the responsibility of the landlord. However, the landlord and tenant may make different arrangements if they mutually agree to do so.

eviction the action by a landlord of removing a tenant from a rental unit

THE **CASE** OF...

The Unsavory Visitors

The Larkins were excited about the birth of their first child. On the day they returned home with the new baby, the Larkins' friends gathered at their apartment to greet them. The Larkins did not notice that two of their friends had some marijuana, which they took into the back bedroom and smoked. However, their landlord, who was also present for the occasion, did notice. A week later, the Larkins received a notice that they were being evicted for allowing drug use in their apartment.

▲ Moving out after being evicted

PROBLEM 27.9

a. Does the law allow the Larkins to be evicted for what their friends did in their apartment? Should the law allow this?

b. Does the Larkins' ignorance of their friends' possession and use of marijuana affect your answer to question **a**?

c. After the Larkins receive the landlord's notice of eviction, are there any steps they can take to prevent her from evicting them?

d. Should the government assist private landlords in identifying possible drug users and sellers and in evicting them? What are the arguments for and against doing this?

Tenants are not responsible for damages that result from normal wear and tear or ordinary use of the property. For example, tenants are not liable for worn spots in the carpet caused by everyday foot traffic. In contrast, damages caused by a tenant's misuse or neglect are known as **waste**. For example, a tenant whose dog has severely scratched the landlord's hardwood floors would be responsible for this damage. The landlord can force the tenant to pay for such repairs. Moreover, tenants have a duty to let the landlord know when major repairs are needed and to take reasonable steps to prevent unnecessary waste or damage.

Security Deposits *Tenant will pay a security deposit in the amount of $_____, which will be held by Landlord until expiration of this lease and refunded on the condition that said premises is returned in good condition, normal wear and tear excepted.* (Clause 9)

In most places, landlords have the right to ask for a security deposit. This deposit is an amount of money—usually one month's rent, but

waste damages caused by a tenant's misuse or neglect of property. The landlord can force the tenant to make repairs or can sue for damages.

Investigating the Law Where You Live

Find out what the law is in your area regarding security deposits.

Purestock/Getty Images

Security Deposits

- Before signing the lease, inspect the apartment, and make a list of all existing defects or damages. You can take pictures of any damage and keep these in the event of a dispute.

- Give a copy of the list to the landlord, and keep a copy for yourself.

- Always get a receipt for the amount of the security deposit.

- Ask to be paid interest on your money. In many places, you are entitled to this.

- Before moving out, inspect the apartment and make a list of all damages.

- Clean the apartment. Repair any damage for which you are responsible, and remove trash so you will not be charged for cleaning or repairs.

- Have a friend go through the apartment with you in case you later need a witness.

sometimes more—that is held by the landlord to ensure that the tenant takes care of the apartment or house and abides by the terms of the lease. If the tenant damages the landlord's property, the landlord may keep the security deposit (or a part of it) to pay for the damage. Also, if the tenant does not pay all the rent, the landlord may be able to keep the security deposit to cover the portion of the rent still owed.

Some states put a limit on the amount of the security deposit. Some also require landlords to pay tenants interest on the money and to return it within a specified time after the end of the lease. When a landlord requires a security deposit, the tenant should always get a receipt and should keep it until the deposit is returned. The tenant may also ask that the money be placed in an interest-paying bank account (whether or not this is required by state law).

Security deposits are sometimes the subject of disputes between landlords and tenants. Whether the deposit is returned to you depends on whether damages to the property result from normal wear and tear or from tenant misuse or neglect. To protect yourself, make a list of all defects and damages that exist at the time you move in. Keep a copy of the list for your records, and give another copy to the landlord.

When moving out, you should inspect the apartment or house again and make a list of any damages. Sometimes an inspection with both the landlord and the tenant present can help avoid any disagreements. If there are no damages, the landlord should return your money within a reasonable period of time. When a lease expires, most states require the landlord to either return the full amount of the security deposit to the tenant or provide an itemized list of deductions. In some states, you can

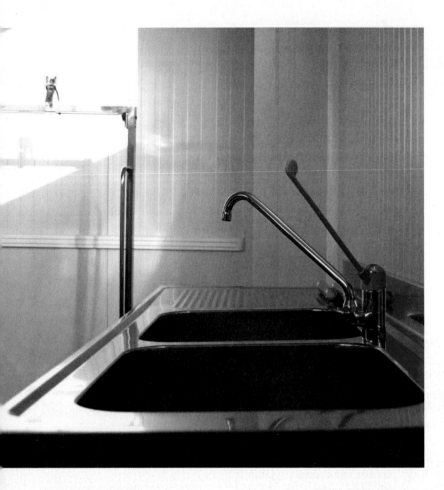

sue for punitive damages if the landlord fails to return the security deposit or give you the list of deductions. In every state, you have the right to sue the landlord in small claims court if you disagree with the reasons for not returning the security deposit.

Finally, tenants generally have no right to make any changes in the structure or character of the property without the permission of the landlord. Even if the landlord agrees to changes or improvements, the improvement becomes the property of the landlord if it cannot be removed without serious damage to the premises. For example, if you build new cabinets in the kitchen, they become a **fixture** of the property and cannot be removed when you move out at the end of the lease. Fixtures are items attached to the property in such a way that their removal would damage the property. As noted, fixtures belong to the owner of the property.

▲ Inspect the apartment and make a list of all the damages before signing the lease. *Why is it important to inspect the apartment both before you move in and after you move out?*

fixture (1) anything attached to land or a building; (2) those things, that once attached, may not be removed by a tenant

PROBLEM 27.10

In each of the following situations, the tenant is moving out and the landlord wants to keep part of the tenant's security deposit. Decide who should pay for the damages.

a. The tenant moves without cleaning the apartment. The landlord is forced to remove trash, clean the walls and floors, wash the windows, and clean out the oven and refrigerator.

b. The toilet overflows in the apartment above that of the tenant moving out. The water leaks through the floor, ruining the ceiling and carpet in the tenant's apartment below.

c. The tenant's pet stains the carpet. The tenant was trying to paper train a puppy. The lease allowed one small pet.

d. The walls are faded and need repainting.

e. The roof leaks, ruining the hardwood floors. The tenant has never told the landlord about the leak.

Responsibility for Injuries in the Building *Landlord shall not be held liable for any injuries or damages to the Tenant or his or her guests, regardless of cause.* (Clause 15)

Many standard form leases contain clauses stating that the tenant cannot hold the landlord responsible for damages or personal injuries that result from the landlord's negligence. For example, the lease may say that the tenant cannot sue the landlord if the tenant is injured because of a broken guardrail that the landlord should have repaired.

This type of clause is known as a **waiver of tort liability**. Under this provision, the tenant agrees to **waive**, or give up, the usual right to hold the landlord responsible for personal injuries. Most courts will not uphold such a clause. Therefore, if you or your guest is injured as a result of a landlord's negligence, you can usually recover damages no matter what the signed lease says. However, you are always better off getting a lease without this type of clause so that you can avoid going to court if at all possible. A few courts still enforce waivers of tort liability.

Landlord Access and Inspection *Landlord shall have access to the premises at any time for the purpose of inspection, to make repairs the Landlord considers necessary, or to show the apartment to tenant applicants.* (Clause 6)

Most leases give landlords and their agents the right to enter the premises to make repairs, collect the rent, or enforce other provisions of the lease. This provision is called a **right of entry or access** clause. Taken literally, this provision would allow the landlord to enter your apartment at any time, day or night, without your permission.

The law in almost every state, however, requires that visits by the landlord be at a reasonable time and that reasonable notice of the visit be given to the tenant. Moreover, landlords do not usually have the right to enter your apartment or house without your permission simply to snoop around or to check on your housekeeping.

Rules and Regulations *Tenant agrees to observe all such rules and regulations which the Landlord or his agents will make concerning the apartment building.* (Clause 18)

Some leases require tenants to obey all present and future rules that landlords make concerning their property. In most cases these rules are reasonable, but not always. Typical examples include rules against having pets; rules against keeping bicycles or other items in the halls; and rules concerning visitors, cooking, storage, children, building security, and hanging pictures on the walls.

It is important to read and understand all the rules and regulations before you move into a building. Otherwise, you may lose your security deposit or be evicted for violating the apartment rules.

waiver of tort liability a lease clause in which the tenant agrees to give up the usual right to hold the landlord responsible for personal injuries

waive to give up some right, privilege, or benefit voluntarily

right of entry or access the provision of a lease that allows a landlord and his or her agents to enter a tenant's premises to make repairs, collect rent, or enforce other provisions of the lease

▼ Most courts will not uphold a waiver of tort liability included in a lease. *Why should landlords always be sure their property is in good repair?*

THE **CASE** OF...

The Dormitory Rape

One Saturday night, Audrey was asleep in her college dormitory room. Her roommate was away for the weekend. There was a guard at the front door to the dormitory, and all the students were supposed to use that door to enter and leave the building after dark. Earlier in the evening, someone had gone out a side door and failed to shut it securely, but no guard ever checked it that night. Audrey was awakened after midnight by a strange man in her room, who then sexually assaulted her. Although she later notified the police, they never found the man.

PROBLEM 27.11

a. Should the college have a responsibility to provide security for dormitory residents? If so, did the college provide adequate security in this instance?

b. What other measures might the college have taken to ensure the security of the dormitory residents?

If you are going to sign a lease that requires you to obey all rules—even those made in the future—it is best to have the lease state, "The tenant agrees to follow all *reasonable* rules and regulations."

PROBLEM 27.12

a. Suppose you own a three-bedroom house that you wish to rent. Make a list of all the rules and regulations you would want tenants to obey while living in your house.

b. Suppose you are a tenant seeking to rent the house in question **a.** Which rules would you consider reasonable, and which would you consider unreasonable?

c. If tenants do not like some of the landlord's rules and regulations, what should they do?

Sublease of a House or Apartment *Tenant will not transfer or sublet the premises without the written consent of the Landlord.* (Clause 5)

Clause 5 is a **sublease clause**. It requires you to obtain the landlord's permission before subleasing the apartment or house. A sublease takes place when the tenant allows someone else to live on the premises and pay all or part of the rent.

For example, suppose you sign a one-year lease on a small house. After six months, you find a larger house and want to move. If the landlord agrees, a sublease clause would allow you to rent the small house to someone else for the remainder of the lease. In a sublease situation, the original lease remains in effect. This means that if the new tenant fails to pay the rent, you are still responsible for paying.

To avoid continued responsibility under the lease, a tenant can seek a **release**. If the landlord gives a release, the tenant is excused from all duties related to the apartment or house and the lease.

sublease clause the provision of most standard leases that requires the tenant to obtain the landlord's permission before allowing someone else to live on the premises and pay all or part of the rent

release (1) giving up of a claim or right by a person; (2) a landlord's act of excusing a tenant from all duties related to the apartment or house and the lease

◀ Some leases include a list of rules and regulations about such things as pets, visitors, and hanging pictures on the walls. *Why is it important to read and understand the rules and regulations before you move in?*

Landlords do not have to agree to the tenants' requests to sublease. Therefore, you are better off with a lease that says, "The landlord agrees not to withhold consent unreasonably." Under such a lease, you would be able to sublease except when the landlord could give a good reason for refusing. Remember, even if your lease lets you sublease, you are still responsible for paying the rent if the person to whom you sublet does not pay.

PROBLEM 27.13

a. Why do most leases require the tenant to get the landlord's permission before subleasing an apartment?

b. Assume the lease requires the tenant to get the landlord's permission before subletting. Bimal, the tenant, leaves town and lets his friend Daniel take over the lease. The landlord allows the sublease, but Daniel never pays the rent. Does Bimal still owe the landlord the rent?

Quiet Enjoyment One of a tenant's most basic rights is the **right to quiet enjoyment** of the property. This simply means that a tenant has a right to use and enjoy the property without being disturbed by the landlord or other tenants. Of course, there is always some noise involved in living in a building with other people. Nevertheless, each tenant should be able to live in relative peace.

Tenants have a right to quiet enjoyment even if it is not stated in the lease, and landlords have a duty to ensure that no tenant unreasonably disturbs the other people in the building. A tenant who is annoyed by noisy or otherwise bothersome neighbors should send a written complaint to the landlord and keep a copy of it.

right to quiet enjoyment a tenant's basic right to use and enjoy a rented or leased property without unnecessary disturbance by the landlord or other tenants

PROBLEM 27.14

Luis and Angelina Allende sign a one-year lease, and they are pleased when they move into a beautiful old apartment building in their favorite part of town. Soon after moving, however, they discover that the building is incredibly noisy and disorderly. During the first week, their next-door neighbor throws several wild parties, keeping the Allendes up all night. They also discover that when their neighbor isn't having parties, he is receiving visitors at all hours of the day. These visits are almost always accompanied by loud music, shouting, and constant coming and going. The partying often spills into the halls, and the Allendes are frequently hassled by visitors.

The Allendes complain to the landlord on a dozen occasions, but the late-night parties and noisy visitors continue. Finally, the Allendes decide they have had enough, and they move out. The landlord then sues the Allendes, claiming that they owe her eleven months' rent. Will the Allendes have to pay?

▲ Although it may not be stated in the lease, all tenants have a right to quiet enjoyment of the property. *Can a tenant play a musical instrument without violating the rights of other tenants?*

Paying for College

The cost of attending a four-year college in 2018 had more than doubled since 1988. In fact, the cost of attending a public college—while still less expensive than a private college—had more than tripled since 1988. To help control these costs, some students now attend a community college for two years and then transfer to a four-year institution, saving tens of thousands of dollars in tuition and fees!

Many students and their families must borrow money to pay for college. By the time they graduate, almost 70 percent of students at four-year institutions will have some student loan debt. In 2018, the average student loan debt among graduating seniors was over $35,000.

Student loans are often a young person's first exposure to the world of credit and debt. Private or government-sponsored student loan programs can provide the only means for some students to attend college. Student loans, however, create debt that must be managed and paid back, just like a credit card bill or a car loan. Borrowers sometimes default on student loans just as they do on other commercial loans. In deciding whether and how much to borrow for school, you should carefully consider the following:

▲ The responsibility of paying for college provides some young people with their first experience of credit and debt. What are important issues to consider when borrowing money for school?

- What is the total cost for tuition, fees, and books?
- How much additional will living expenses cost? Will you be living at home, on campus, or in an apartment? Alone or with roommates? How will you pay for your meals?
- Are there other sources of income that will help pay your expenses? Can your parents contribute part of the cost? Will you have a job during the school year? Do you have any money in savings? How much can you save from working over the summer?
- Are full or partial scholarships available?
- When will your loans become due after you finish school?

Some student loan programs are quite borrower-friendly. Various loan programs exist, including those where either a parent or the student is the borrower. Others allow the student to be the primary borrower but require a co-borrower as added assurance that the loan will be paid back. A co-borrower is someone who promises to pay the debt in the event the student defaults on the loan. Many banks and universities

offer private loans for education expenses. Students should carefully pursue all government-supported loan options before considering private loans because government-supported loan programs typically have lower interest rates. In addition, government-supported loans may have other desirable options. For example, repayment of student loans can be deferred while you are in school, and many lenders offer grace periods, forbearance periods (if you encounter a difficult financial situation during the repayment period), consolidation programs, and graduated payment programs that allow your payments to start out low and increase as your income increases.

You can get more information about student loan programs from any college or university, as well as online from private lenders, loan servicing companies, and the federal government. The following websites are a good starting place to learn about student loan programs:

- Visit FAFSA (Free Application for Federal Student Aid) online at **www.fafsa.ed.gov**.

- The Smart Student Guide to Financial Aid at **www.finaid.org**.

- The Consumer Financial Protection Bureau at **www.consumerfinance.gov/ paying-for-college/**.

▲ Student loan programs are available from private lenders as well as the federal government. *What are the advantages of federal student loans?*

Investigating the Law Where You Live

As of 2018, 17 states offered programs to make two years of community college tuition free for some high school graduates. Does your state have such a program?

PROBLEM 27.15

What are the advantages of taking out student loans rather than using credit cards to pay for college expenses?

How might a person determine whether it is worth incurring debt in order to attend college?

Health Care

Just as people need to insure their cars and homes in order to protect against financial harm from unanticipated accidents or damage, people also need to insure their health to protect against financial harm from illness or injury. It is estimated that the majority of bankruptcies filed in the United States are due to health care bills.

At one time, unless you were employed and participating in your employer's health plan, or qualified for Medicare or Medicaid, it was difficult and expensive to get insurance on your own. Rates were high and

©Andersen Ross/Blend Images LLC

there were no subsidies available from the government to defray the costs. Available insurance frequently had limited coverage or required very high out-of-pocket expenses. People who were sick could be denied coverage altogether due to a "preexisting condition." As a result, many people in the United States were either uninsured or underinsured.

In 2010, Congress passed the *Patient Protection and Affordable Care Act* ("ACA"), frequently called "Obamacare" after the U.S. president who was the driving force behind the legislation. Under this law, since 2014, people have been able to buy health insurance from a health insurance exchange or marketplace run by the states or the federal government. The ACA, as originally enacted, required all Americans to have health insurance or pay a penalty, a concept known as the **individual mandate**. The individual mandate was considered important because, in order for health insurance to work, the pool of insured people needs to include both sick and healthy people. This way, the risk of loss is spread among all the members of the insured pool. Without the individual mandate, many people would only buy health insurance when they were sick, and the insurance pool would soon be out of money from paying too many insurance claims from doctors and hospitals. Congress eliminated the penalty in a 2017 law.

People can satisfy the individual mandate either by buying insurance from the marketplace or through their employers or if they qualify for coverage under Medicare or Medicaid. Most people still obtain their health insurance coverage through their employers. Employers usually subsidize a part of their employees' coverage. If you have a job that provides this benefit obtaining your coverage through your employer is usually a good deal. As a result of the ACA, some states have expanded Medicaid coverage to cover all individuals who earn less than 133 percent of the poverty limit. In 2018, the federal poverty limit was about $25,000 for a family of four.

If you do not have employer sponsored health insurance, there are different levels of plans available from the marketplaces—designated "gold", "silver" and "bronze"—and they generally vary based on the amount of copays and deductibles you will have to pay. Depending on your income, you may also be eligible to have part of the cost of your insurance paid by the government. This is known as a **subsidy**. Subsidies are available only when you buy a silver level plan. Visit **www.healthcare.gov** to see the options available for purchasing health insurance.

When you buy insurance from the marketplace or through your employer, you will be given an opportunity once a year to sign up for coverage. This is known as open enrollment and it generally occurs in the fall of each year. You may also get a special enrollment opportunity to sign up for coverage when you start a new job, or when you experience significant life changes, such as marriage, divorce or having a baby.

When you buy insurance, you pay a monthly **premium** for your insurance policy. Your policy will also have an annual **deductible**, or amount that you must pay out of your own pocket before your insurance company will pay anything. There are also likely to be fees associated with each visit to the doctor or being treated in the hospital. These are known as **co-payments** or coinsurance amounts. Generally, the higher your premium payment, the lower your annual deductible and copay amounts.

individual mandate a requirement by law that most Americans purchase or otherwise obtain health care or pay a tax penalty

subsidy money that is paid, usually by a government, to keep the price of a product or service low or to help a business or organization to continue to function

premium a payment made for insurance coverage

deductible the amount an insured person agrees to pay toward repairs before the insurance company pays anything

copayment an amount of money that a person with health insurance is required to pay at the time of each visit to a doctor or when purchasing medicine

Higher copays may be associated with certain types of care. This is because health plans want to encourage you to get your care from cost effective providers. For example, the copay may be several hundred dollars to get care in a hospital emergency room, where care is very expensive, and only $25 to be treated at an urgent care center.

When choosing coverage, it is important to see if the doctors, hospitals and drugs that you ordinarily use participate in the health plan's provider network. Health plans typically contract with a network of providers and establish what is known as a **formulary**, or list, of covered drugs. If you go to a provider who is out of network or your doctor prescribes a drug that is not on formulary (or not a preferred drug) you may pay more or the services may not be covered. Also, depending on your health plan, you may need a referral from your primary care physician before visiting a specialist, getting tested, or being admitted to a hospital for non-emergency treatment.

While the ACA has expanded the availability of health care coverage, there are still people who are uninsured. For instance, undocumented immigrants are not covered by the ACA. Additionally, since not all states have expanded Medicaid, the extent to which you have health care coverage may still depend upon the state in which you reside. Even with the ACA and other programs, nearly 9 percent of Americans (almost 30 million people) did not have health insurance in 2018.

If you do not have health insurance, there are still avenues for obtaining emergency health care treatment. For instance, the *Emergency Medical Treatment and Active Labor Act* ("EMTALA") requires hospitals to provide all patients with a medical screening to determine whether you have an emergency medical condition, and stabilizing treatment if you do. This law does not prevent the hospital from billing you for their services, but hospitals (especially nonprofit hospitals) may have charitable care policies and extended payment plans available.

formulary an official list giving details of medicines that may be prescribed

PROBLEM 27.16

For each of the following, has a good health care choice been made? Why or why not?

a. John is young and very healthy so he does not think he needs health insurance and does not want to pay the monthly premiums of $700. He lets the open enrollment period pass without signing up. Six months later, he tears a muscle in his arm playing basketball and needs surgery. The cost of the surgery is $20,000.

b. Miguel, who is insured, visits his doctor every year for his annual exam and pays the $25 copay. During one visit, the doctor determines that Miguel has high cholesterol, which can be easily remedied with diet and exercise.

c. Teresa, who is insured, has been feeling tired for weeks but she is too busy to visit her doctor and does not want to pay the $50 copay. Later, she faints at work and has to be taken to the emergency room in an ambulance. The doctors determine she is anemic and should have been taking a simple iron supplement. The copay at the hospital is $250.

TAKING ACTION: **Law and Democracy**

The Health Care Controversy

The ACA has been extremely controversial since its enactment. Under the ACA 30 million Americans began to have health insurance, insurance companies were prohibited from denying coverage based on preexisting conditions, and children could remain on their parents' policy until age 26. These features were popular with the American public. Supporters of the ACA claimed it would reduce health care costs. According to factcheck.org, the ACA did not initially reduce health care costs, but it might have contributed to a slower rate of increase in health care costs.

There are both conservative and liberal critics of the ACA. Conservatives say the law imposes too many costs on businesses and taxes on individuals and infringes on people's freedom to purchase less comprehensive insurance at a lower cost, or no insurance at all. Some conservatives favor a "repeal and replace" approach in which a different national health care plan is adopted. Other conservatives favor eliminating the law completely, leaving health insurance to the private insurance market.

On the other hand, many liberals believe the ACA does not go far enough because so many people remain without insurance. They believe that health care is a fundamental right and that Medicare for All is a better approach. (Medicare is the federal program that provides health care coverage for those who are over 65 years old or disabled.) While Medicare for All would insure everyone, taxes would be raised to pay for the expanded coverage. They also state that the United States is the only highly developed country in the world that does not have some form of universal health care system.

There have been a number of legal challenges to the ACA. A group of plaintiffs challenged the constitutionality of the ACA when it was first passed by Congress. In a 2012 Supreme Court case, a narrowly divided Court upheld the individual mandate as a lawful exercise of the federal government's taxing power. While this decision left most of the ACA intact, political and legal challenges continued.

PROBLEM 27.17

Conduct research on the health care controversy. What changes, if any, should be made in our national health care policy? Give your reasons.

UNIT 5
Family Law

netw⊕rks

The family is a basic unit of society. It is the most intimate and important of all social groups. A strong family can help its members when they have problems in their lives. In fact, families are the strongest influence on what kind of person you turn out to be. Law and government also have an effect on individuals and families throughout their lives. As you study this unit, you will learn about law as it affects families.

◄ Although family life is private, it is influenced by laws and government.

► The law affects every stage of an individual's life.

The law is involved every time a birth, death, marriage, or divorce takes place. In fact, the law affects families in many different ways throughout the course of a person's life. For the most part, family law is determined by each state and there are important differences in family law from state to state.

Law From Birth to Death

The law affects children beginning at birth. When a child is born in the United States, a birth certificate is issued by the state, and the parent can apply for a Social Security number for the child. When children reach a certain age, parents are required by law to send their children to school or to provide proof of homeschooling. Each state has a law requiring vaccinations for children entering public school. State laws may exempt parents from this requirement for medical, philosophical, or religious reasons.

Francisco Cruz/Purestock/SuperStock

As young people reach a certain age, they often take a test, given by the state, to get a driver's license. The age at which a person can drink alcoholic beverages is also regulated by law. Males are required by law to register for Selective Service when they turn 18. State laws set requirements that must be met before anyone can be married.

The law also creates the basic rights and responsibilities of parents. For example, parents are entitled to tax deductions for each dependent child. The *Family and Medical Leave Act* allows employees unpaid time off from work to care for newborns, newly adopted children, or sick relatives. Parents are required to provide basic necessities such as food, clothing, shelter, and medical care for their children. A non-custodial parent (of either gender) can be required to provide support for his or her child until age 18 or in some states until age 21.

States also have laws that affect relationships among family members. Chapter 30, "Parents and Children," examines the line between permissible parental discipline and child abuse. Other laws govern areas such as marriage, adoption, foster care, child abuse and neglect, alimony, custody, divorce, and support.

There are even laws that apply after a family member dies. A **will** is a legal document that explains how a person wants his or her property distributed after death. Courts typically enforce a person's wishes expressed in a will. Writing a will that covers money, property, and digital assets could minimize the problems your family might have after you die.

If you die without a will, state law determines who receives your property. State law usually requires that a portion of the property go to your spouse if you are married. The remainder of your property may go to your children, parents, grandchildren, brothers, or sisters, depending on the state law where you live. Having a will ensures that your property goes to whomever you wish in the amounts you choose.

In most states, persons can legally make wills when they reach the age of majority, usually 18 or 21. However, some states allow persons as young as age 14 to make wills if they are married, **emancipated,** near death, or in other special circumstances. If a minor dies, their property, such as money and clothes, goes to their parents or legal guardians, who decide what to do with it.

▲ Laws govern how a person's property is divided after he or she dies. *Why is it important to write a will?*

will a legal document that states what a person wants done with his or her belongings after death

emancipated the condition of having reached legal adulthood; usually at age 16, 18, or 21

Marmaduke St. John/Alamy

In addition to the areas mentioned on the previous page, what other issues in the family are regulated by law? Does the law regulate too much or too little of family life? Explain your answers.

What Is a Family?

If asked to identify a family, most of us would say we know one when we see one. We are surrounded by families wherever we go, and most of us live in family settings. However, families come in all shapes and sizes, and defining the term *family* can be difficult.

Legally, the word *family* is used to describe many relationships: parents and children; people related by blood, marriage, or adoption; or a group of unrelated people living together in a single household, sharing living space and housekeeping responsibilities. Because the word *family* does not have a precise definition, many laws define the term when they use it. For example, zoning laws that set aside certain areas for single-family homes define a family in a certain way. Laws involving insurance, Social Security, or inheritance may define a family in other ways.

▼ Family structure has changed over time. *Give specific examples that show how families have changed.*

©Bananastock/Alamy

PROBLEM 28.2

Examine the group of photos shown here. For each photo, answer the following questions:

a. Is this a family? Why or why not?

b. Is this living arrangement common where you live?

c. How does the law affect this living arrangement?

d. What are the characteristics of a family? How would you define the term *family?*

e. Are divorced spouses still a family? Would you answer differently depending on whether they have children? If a parent remarries?

28.1 Changes in American Families, 1990–2017

Year	1990	2000	2010	2017
Marriages performed	2,243,000	2,384,000	2,096,000	2,236,496
Divorces granted	1,182,000	1,163,000	872,000	787,251
Married couples	53,317,000	54,493,232	58,410,000	63,739,000
Married couples with children	24,961,000	24,835,505	24,575,000	24,555,000
Average size of household	2.63	2.59	2.59	2.53
Families with both partners working	22,053,000	22,674,000	27,894,000	31,013,000
Unmarried couples living together	2,856,000	4,736,000	7,744,711	8,500,000
Unmarried couples with children	891,000	1,675,000	1,765,000	3,028,000

Sources: U.S. Bureau of the Census; U.S. Department of Health and Human Services; CDC

PROBLEM 28.3

a. Study the data above. What do you think are the most significant changes in American families since 1990? In your opinion, why have these changes occurred?

b. Identify any ways in which these patterns are reflected in your own family.

c. What do you think families will be like in the future?

The American family has changed dramatically over the past 100 years. One change has been a reduction in size. In 1900, average family size was 5.7 persons. Figure 28.1 shows that by 2017, the average family had shrunk by more than 50 percent. Today, some couples have fewer children or, in some cases, no children at all.

Families have also changed because women's and men's roles have changed. During the early part of the twentieth century, most married women did not work outside their homes. Today, however, the majority of married women hold jobs outside their homes, and many fathers have become more involved in parenting. Other changes include men and women marrying at a later age—or not at all.

Changes in marriage practices have changed the face of the U.S. family. Single-parent families and unmarried couples raising children have both become more common. Blended families with stepparents and stepchildren are common. In some families, grandparents are raising the children.

Laws that fit old ways of understanding the family have been challenged. New laws have been written, and judges have decided cases that help resolve conflicts and challenges that today's families face.

▶ Marriage is a legal relationship, as well as, for most couples, an economic, social, and emotional relationship.

Marriage can be a personal, social, economic, legal, and, for some, a religious relationship. While only about 50 percent of adult Americans are currently married, more than 70 percent of all Americans will be married at some time during their lives. This chapter examines the legal aspects of marriage. It describes the steps that one must follow to get married, the requirements for a legal marriage, the debate about marriage equality, the difference between formal and common-law marriage, and what to do about partner abuse.

Getting Married

To legally marry, most states require that a couple follow certain steps:

- **Marriage license.** All states require a marriage license. When they apply for a marriage license, the couple will be asked to provide certain information, such as proof of age and identity. They then must swear to the truth of the information they provided and pay a small fee.

- **Administrative requirements.** A few states require the couple to have blood tests which would make them aware of certain diseases that might affect their health and their partners. A few states also have a short waiting period between the time the license is issued and the time the ceremony can be performed.

- **Wedding ceremony.** A wedding ceremony can be either religious or civil. Typically weddings are conducted by members of the clergy or by public officials such as judges or justices of the peace. The law does not require any set format. After the ceremony, the couple will receive a marriage certificate. Some states recognize common-law marriage, which does not require a ceremony.

No state requires premarital counseling as a prerequisite to obtaining a marriage license, although some states encourage it. However, many people believe that premarital counseling encourages couples to enter marriage more thoughtfully and helps to reduce divorce rates.

PROBLEM 29.1

a. Marriage involves many considerations. Rank the following considerations in order of importance: money, desire for children, sexual relations, religious beliefs, similar racial or ethnic backgrounds, common interests, relationships with in-laws, faithfulness, and age differences. Are there any other factors that you consider important to a successful marriage? Explain your answer.

b. Make a list of all the questions you would ask yourself before deciding to get married. Make a separate list of questions you would ask your partner. Are any of the questions the same? Do any of these questions involve the law?

c. What social, religious, and legal arrangements would you have to make in order to get married?

▼ Applying for a marriage license is one of the most important steps in getting married. *Why do states require couples to obtain a marriage license?*

THE **CASE** OF...

Loving v. Virginia

In 1958, Richard Loving, a white man, and Mildred Jeter, an African American woman, decided to get married. Legal residents of Virginia, they went to Washington, D.C., to get around a Virginia law forbidding marriage between caucasians and people of color. After their marriage ceremony, they returned to Virginia, where they were arrested and charged with violating the ban on interracial marriage. The Lovings pleaded guilty and were each sentenced to one year in jail. The judge agreed to suspend the sentence if the Lovings would leave Virginia for 25 years. The Lovings moved to Washington, D.C., but appealed their case to the U.S. Supreme Court. They asked that the state law against interracial marriages be declared unconstitutional.

PROBLEM 29.2

a. What arguments do you think the state made in favor of the law? What arguments do you think the Lovings made against the law?

b. How would you decide this case? Explain.

c. Some marriage regulations are appropriate, and others are not. Should states regulate marriage based on age? Mental capacity? Physical disability? Health? Sexual orientation? Religious, ethnic, or racial differences? Explain.

Legal Aspects of Marriage

Marriage is a legally recognized status for two persons who agree to live together as partners. It creates legal rights and duties for each party. To be married, a couple must meet certain legal requirements.

In the United States, marriage laws are set by the individual states. State laws vary, but most states have the following requirements:

- **Age.** A couple wishing to marry must meet certain age requirements. Usually, both women and men must be 18 years old. Some states allow younger couples to get married if their parents consent and/or if a judge agrees. Some states also allow a couple under the minimum age to marry if the woman is pregnant.

- **Relationship.** Every state forbids marriage between close relatives. It is illegal for a person to marry his or her parent, child, grandparent, grandchild, brother, sister, uncle, aunt, niece, or nephew. Many states also prohibit marriages between first cousins. Most of these laws are based on bloodlines. Marrying or having sexual relations with a close relative is a crime known as **incest.** Any resulting marriage is void, meaning that it never existed legally.

- **Number of Persons.** Marriage is legally limited to two persons. Marrying someone who is already married is illegal. Having more than one spouse is a crime known as **bigamy.**

Investigating the Law Where You Live

Find out the law in your state regarding who may legally marry.

incest sexual relations between people who are closely related to each other

bigamy the crime of being married to more than one person at a time

- **Gender.** Marriages between persons of the same sex used to be considered legally invalid. However, public attitudes and the law in this area have changed. States began to recognize same-sex marriages in 2004, and in 2015 the U.S. Supreme Court decided a case that required all states to permit same-sex marriages.

- **Consent.** Both persons must agree to the marriage. No one can be forced to marry someone against his or her will. For example, no one can be forced to marry at gunpoint.

As a general rule, if a marriage is legal in one state, it will be recognized as legal in all other states. However, if a couple goes through a wedding ceremony without meeting the requirements for a legal marriage, the marriage may be annulled. **Annulment** is a court order declaring that a marriage never existed. It is different from a **divorce,** which is a court order that ends a valid marriage. In other words, a divorce means that two people are no longer married. An annulment means that two people were never legally married.

The grounds for annulment vary from state to state, but common reasons for annulment include the following:

- **Age.** One or both spouses were too young to be married.
- **Bigamy.** One spouse was already married.
- **Fraud.** One spouse lied to the other about an important matter, such as the desire to have children.
- **Lack of consent.** One spouse was forced to marry against his or her will, was too drunk or incapacitated to understand that a wedding was taking place, or was insane.

Laws place many restrictions on marriage. They prescribe who can marry, some of the obligations created by marriage, and how marriage can be ended. However, states cannot prohibit marriage between consenting adults without a good reason.

Many U.S. marriages take place in a church, mosque, or synagogue. Customs and religious traditions play an important role in married life in the United States. These customs and traditions, however, may not be used as justification for ignoring established civil laws governing marriage.

In 1878, George Reynolds, a Mormon living in Utah, was arrested and charged with the crime of bigamy. At the time, many Mormons regarded plural marriages as a religious obligation. Some believed that refusal to practice **polygamy** when circumstances permitted would lead to "damnation in the life to come." Reynolds argued that the anti-bigamy law violated his constitutional right to freedom of religion. After his conviction, he appealed his case to the U.S. Supreme Court.

▲ Some couples have civil wedding ceremonies, while other couples choose to have religious wedding ceremonies. *What legal requirements are common to marriage, regardless of ceremony?*

annulment a court or religious order that declares a marriage never legally existed

divorce the ending of a marriage by court order

polygamy the practice of having more than one spouse at the same time. Polygamy is illegal in the United States.

In the case of *Reynolds* v. *United States,* the Supreme Court upheld the anti-bigamy law. It ruled that a religious belief cannot justify an *illegal act.* Reynolds could believe anything he wanted, but he could not put into practice a belief that society condemned. Today, the Mormon Church condemns polygamy and excommunicates members who practice it.

Common-Law Marriage

Common-law marriage is a marriage without a license, a wedding ceremony, or a certificate. It is created when two people agree to be married, hold themselves out to the public as spouses, and live together as if married. As of 2018, about a dozen states either recognized common-law marriages or recognized these marriages if created before a certain date.

Some of these states require a couple to have lived together for a certain number of years before they are considered legally married. In others, there is no minimum waiting period if a couple agrees that they are married, lives together, and represents themselves as spouses. If a couple separates after entering into a common-law marriage, they must divorce legally before either may remarry, or they can be charged with the crime of bigamy.

States that do not allow common-law marriages do, however, recognize such a marriage if it originated in a state that recognizes common-law marriage. If a marriage is legal in the state where it begins, other states usually recognize that marriage as legal.

common-law marriage a marriage created without the legal ceremony by a couple living together and publicly presenting themselves as married. Such a marriage can be formed only in certain states.

Investigating the Law Where You Live

Does your state recognize common-law marriage? Should it recognize common-law marriage?

THE **CASE** OF...

The Common-Law Marriage

Rick Schwartz and his girlfriend, Sarah Brown, live together in Montana, a state that recognizes common-law marriage. They talk about having a wedding but never do. They are in love and think it is simpler to tell people that they are married. They buy a house together, open a joint bank account, and are known everywhere as Mr. and Mrs. Schwartz. One day Sarah gets bored and leaves Rick. She soon finds a new boyfriend, Dylan. Coming from a traditional background, Dylan insists that they get married before living together.

PROBLEM 29.3

a. What are the requirements of a common-law marriage?

b. Do Rick and Sarah have a valid common-law marriage? Why or why not?

c. Can Sarah marry Dylan? Will she have to divorce Rick first? Why or why not?

d. Should all states allow common-law marriage? Explain your reasons.

▲ Both spouses are often held financially responsible for family items or services that either one of them purchases. *How is this different from the traditional view of financial responsibility in a marriage?*

Financial Responsibilities

In the past, the law considered the husband to be the head of the household. He had a duty to support his wife and children. In return for this support, he was entitled to his wife's household services and companionship. The law reflected this traditional view by giving husbands the legal right to make decisions such as where the family would live and how money would be spent. Over the past half century, however, this view of marriage has been challenged by economic and social changes in our society. In many ways, the law has also changed to reflect the idea that marriage is a partnership between equals. Spouses are now required to support one another in accordance with their respective needs and abilities. Many states hold both spouses financially responsible for necessary family items or services that either of them purchases.

Property Ownership

Who owns property acquired during a marriage? At one time for opposite-sex marriages, the law considered a husband and wife as one person. This meant that the husband owned the property and the wife had no property rights. Any money or property a woman owned before marriage or acquired during marriage became the property of her husband. In 1887, states began to pass married women's property rights acts that changed the law. These acts gave married women the right to own and control their own property.

Today, for the most part, property (both assets and debts) owned by either spouse before the marriage remains the property of that person throughout the marriage. This is true in both opposite- and same-sex marriages. This is called **separate property.** Although each spouse may still collect separate property by gift or inheritance, generally, property acquired by either spouse individually or by the couple during a marriage is called **marital property** upon divorce.

separate property a system under which property owned by either spouse before the marriage remains that person's property throughout the marriage, and any property acquired during the marriage belongs to the person who acquired it

marital property property acquired during a marriage, including joint bank accounts, real estate, automobiles, etc. Such property is considered to be owned equally by both spouses.

During marriage, couples may decide together whether to combine all of their property and earnings or keep them separate. The longer the marriage lasts, however, the more difficult it may be to track each spouse's separate property.

Decisions in a Marriage

Married life involves many decisions and responsibilities. Couples need to cooperate, share, and make decisions about their lives together. For instance, how will housework be divided? Who will handle the money? Will they have children? How will any children they have be brought up? What if the parents come from different religious traditions? Today, some couples use prenuptial agreements to put some of these decisions in writing. A **prenuptial agreement** is a written document made before marriage that sets forth certain rights and responsibilities of the spouses (for example, whether any alimony will be paid in the event of a divorce).

In most matters, spouses are free to make their own decisions and to work out their own problems. Except in rare cases, the law does not interfere in everyday family life. There are, however, some issues to be aware of:

- **Name change.** Many spouses have traditionally taken the others' last names as a matter of social custom. However, neither spouse is legally required to do so. Legally, a spouse can keep their maiden name, take their spouse's name in combination with their own (for example, Smith-Larkin), or use the spouse's name. Some people have a professional name they use at work and a family name they use in their personal lives.

- **Support.** In most states, spouses have equal responsibility to support each other and to support their children. Spouses share equally the duty to pay for necessary family items bought by either of them.

- **Privileged communications.** The law considers certain relationships private and confidential. Attorney-client, doctor-patient, and spousal relationships are all considered privileged. Neither person can be

▲ Property ownership can become an issue if a marriage ends. *What is separate property? Marital property?*

prenuptial agreement a contractual agreement between a couple prior to marriage. It often includes provisions for the disposal of property in the event of separation, divorce, or death.

▲ The issue of having and raising children is an important decision in a marriage. *What are some basic decisions a couple must make when they decide to have children?*

forced to disclose information received as part of the relationship. The only information that is covered by this privilege is confidential communications between spouses that occur during the marriage.

Historically, a spouse who was a witness at a trial could not testify against his or her spouse unless the spouse consented, or agreed. However, the U.S. Supreme Court has decided that one spouse may testify against the other in federal criminal prosecutions without the spouse's consent. Usually spouses cannot testify against each other in a civil case. A person can testify against a spouse under certain circumstances, such as when one spouse is accused of abusing the other. Communications between parents and children are not considered privileged.

- **Inheritance.** If one spouse dies, the other is usually entitled to a share of the deceased's estate. This amount varies from one-third to one-half, depending on state law. One spouse may leave the other a different amount of money in a will—either more or less than the statutory share. However, the surviving spouse usually has the option to give up the amount in the will and to take the statutory share instead. Even if a spouse is left out of a will, state laws usually give the survivor the right to receive a portion of the estate.

a. Raul is in an auto accident with a delivery truck. At the hospital, he tells his wife, Serena, that the accident was all his fault. Later, in a lawsuit for damages resulting from the accident, the delivery company subpoenas Serena to testify about Raul's statements at the hospital. Does Serena have to testify against her husband? What if Raul had made the statements to his daughter? Could she be forced to testify about those statements?

b. Brent has argued with his wife, Liza, for years. In a fit of anger, he rewrites his will, leaving his entire fortune to charity. If Brent dies, will Liza be left with nothing? Explain your answer.

c. James and his husband, Edward, both work for local companies. The company James works for is experiencing financial difficulties. He is offered a better position with a company 400 miles away. Edward is doing very well in his job and would rather not move. How do they decide what to do? Who has the legal right to make the final decision? Who should have that right?

Intimate Partner Violence

Intimate partner violence can occur across the entire spectrum of relationships. While this section addresses the issue primarily in the context of marriage, it is important to remember that similar problems and legal issues apply in other intimate relationships, regardless of age, race, sexual orientation, gender identity, income, sex or disability.

Intimate partner violence occurs among families of all economic backgrounds and in all settings—urban, suburban, and rural. Experts believe this is an underreported crime. Victims suffer injuries ranging from psychological and financial abuse to severe battering and murder. In fact, spousal assaults are more likely to result in serious injuries than assaults committed by strangers. More than 10 percent of all murders in the United States involve people who are related, and many of these are spousal killings. Both women and men can be abusers, but women suffer more than 80 percent of the injuries inflicted by spouses. In homes where a spouse is abused, there is also a higher risk for child abuse.

Abuse is a psychological phenomenon, not just violence. It is also rarely a one-time incident. Perpetrators typically repeat the behavior, often with increasing severity. Intimate partner violence, however, often remains behind closed doors and may go undetected or ignored by friends and neighbors.

Historically, the police and the courts were reluctant to get involved in domestic disputes. In fact, until the late 1800s, it was legal in most states for a husband to beat his wife. Even after spousal battering was outlawed, police often refused to respond to requests for assistance from battered women or to arrest abusive husbands. Police officers hesitated to become involved in domestic disputes, in part because they believed this was not

Investigating the Law Where You Live

Find out how police and prosecutors handle domestic violence in your community.

a crime but rather a relationship problem. In the past, most police officers were taught to either "counsel" the abuser and the victim or to make the abuser leave the home for several hours or more to "cool down."

These practices have changed. Most modern police departments now encourage officers to arrest spouses or domestic partners who are suspected of assault. Some states have enacted statutes that require arrest if there is probable cause to believe an assault or other crime has been committed, even if the injured spouse or partner refuses to sign a complaint against the abuser. Advocates of mandatory arrest point to studies that show that arrest is the most effective way to prevent repeated abuse. Opponents of mandatory arrest argue that victims should have some control over the process and cite studies showing that mandatory arrest and prosecution sometimes lead to increased violence.

Even when there is an arrest, prosecutors sometimes do not bring charges against abusive spouses and partners and may be more willing to reduce the charges than in cases of assault between two strangers. Some judges may merely dismiss those abuse cases or give warnings or probation to those who are found guilty. They cite the need to protect family privacy or to promote domestic harmony as the reason for their inaction. However, other judges recognize that there may be little family harmony to protect when one family member is abusing another.

The federal *Violence Against Women Act* of 1994 created an Office on Violence Against Women in the U.S. Department of Justice. This law addresses domestic violence, sexual assault, rape, and stalking. It also creates protections against teen dating violence, establishes nationwide enforcement of protection orders, and expands stalking laws to include cyberstalking. This office also has a special program to reduce dating violence, assault, and stalking on campus. Go to **www.ovw.usdoj.gov** for more information.

Despite advances in the law and in society's recognition of the problem, partner abuse continues to be difficult to combat because of the complexity of abusive relationships and the lack of resources to help partners and children who leave abusers. Several factors contribute to this cycle of violence, often including a victim's belief that the abuse is

▼ The federal *Violence Against Women Act* approved spending for counseling and legal assistance programs. *Why is it important for adults and children to learn about the cycle of abuse that can occur in families?*

Women face economic, cultural, and personal barriers to leaving an abusive relationship. *How do these barriers make it difficult to leave?*

somehow his or her fault and that he or she can make the situation better. An abuser often apologizes, promises to change, and begs the partner not to leave. Abusers sometimes threaten their victims and even other members of the victim's families.

Additionally, some women face particularly daunting barriers to leaving an abusive relationship.

- Women fear retaliation from their abusers if they try to leave, go to the police, or press charges.
- Often, the woman is not the family's primary wage earner, and she faces economic hardship and no place to live if she leaves or if her husband goes to jail, especially if she has children.
- A woman may face pressures to stay, including community mistrust, cultural norms, language barriers, and immigrant status.
- A woman may feel that to leave would hurt the family by breaking up the marriage and taking the children away from their father.

While many victims of abuse can receive help through counseling, spouse abusers usually need sanctions as well as treatment to help them learn to change their pattern of behavior. Spousal abusers may frequently be addicted to alcohol or drugs and must deal with their addiction as well as their abusive behavior. Some independent men's organizations, in addition to services started by battered women's programs and courts, offer men counseling, treatment, and support. Social service agencies and faith-based organizations often can refer men to nearby programs. Some of the best programs are affiliated with local trial courts.

At one time, husbands could not be criminally prosecuted for raping their wives. All 50 states and the District of Columbia now recognize marital rape as a crime. In addition, a battered spouse who has been raped can file a civil lawsuit for damages against their spouse.

a. Why do you think that in the past courts did not prosecute husbands for raping their wives?

b. Assume you are a prosecutor. A woman files a complaint against her husband, stating that he forced her at knifepoint to have sexual intercourse with him. She tells you that she and her husband have been arguing violently for years. Would you file a rape charge against the husband? Explain your answer.

c. Assume that the facts are the same as in question b, except that the husband and wife are legally separated. Should it make any difference in proving rape that the couple is separated rather than living together?

THE **CASE** OF...

Partner Abuse

Late one night, you hear screams and the sounds of crashing furniture coming from the apartment next door. You look out in the hall and see your neighbor, Ms. Darwin, being slapped and punched by her husband. Before she can get away, Mr. Darwin pulls her back in and slams the door. You hear breaking glass and more screams. You know that Mr. Darwin has a drinking problem. You also know that this is not the first time he has beaten his wife.

PROBLEM 29.6

a. If you were the Darwins' neighbor, what would you do? Would you call the police? If so, what would you tell them? If you would not call the police, explain why not.

b. If you were a police officer, what would you do in this situation? Would you question the couple? Would you arrest the husband? Would you remove the wife or the husband from the house?

c. If you were the husband, how would you react to the police in this situation? If you were the wife, how would you react? Would you press charges against your husband? Would you stay in the home? Would you do something else?

d. Suppose you are a judge confronted with the Darwin case. Would you send Mr. Darwin to jail? Would you take some other action? What other information would you want?

e. Besides calling the police, what are some other things Mrs. Darwin could do about the problem?

Steps to Take

What to Do If Partner Abuse Occurs

Both victims and abusers need to seek help to end the cycle of abuse. The first incident of domestic violence is rarely the last. Victims of abuse can take the following steps:

- **Call the police.** Assaulting anyone is a crime, and many consider arrest to be the most effective means of halting spouse abuse. Even if the police do not make an arrest, a police report can support later legal action. For instance, victims can later (1) testify against their spouses, (2) request protective orders, or (3) file for divorce.

- **Consult a domestic violence advocate.** Various organizations can provide victims of intimate partner violence help in sorting through their situation and thinking through options. They might also be able to assist with economic support and safe housing as well as identifying opportunities to participate in a support group or receive individual counseling.

- **Obtain a protective order.** Courts can order an abuser to (1) stop the abuse, (2) cease all contact with his or her spouse or partner, (3) leave the home, (4) get counseling, or (5) do something else. Violating a court order is considered contempt of court, and a person found guilty of contempt can be jailed, fined, or both.

- **Move out/Kick out.** Despite the significant barriers they face, it is possible for the victim to leave the home, and help may be available. Many communities have protective shelters where a woman and her children can live temporarily. Either the police or crisis hotline personnel can help a victim locate a shelter. The National Domestic Violence Hotline is 800-799-

▲ Talking to police

SAFE (7233), or online at www.thehotline.org. However, in some cases it is better to stay in the home and get a "kick out" order against the abuser.

- **Obtain a legal separation or divorce.** If a couple is legally separated, one spouse usually has no right to enter the other's home without permission. Local bar associations, legal aid offices, family courts, and women's organizations can give victims information about divorce.

- **Get Help at School.** An increasing number of schools have policies in place that enable them to make sure abusers and victims do not attend the same classes. *Title IX of the Education Act Amendments of 1972* requires schools to consider disciplinary action when notified of interpersonal abuse that impairs a student's equal access to education (i.e., makes the victim not want to go to school).

DELIBERATION

Should the government require health-care providers to report domestic abuse?

Imagine you are in a relationship. In a rage, your partner hits you. These blows injure your face. You want to go to the hospital for treatment, but you know that doctors are required by law to report this violent incident to the police. You wonder: Will a report prevent more abuse by holding your partner accountable? Or will a police report lead to retaliation from your partner?

Now, imagine yourself as an emergency room doctor. You are treating a woman with injuries to her face. You suspect that her partner caused the injuries. The partner is sitting nearby. You wonder: If you ask about the abuse, will the partner retaliate against the woman? Will she not come back for treatment in the future because she fears you will report her partner to the police?

Domestic violence is the abuse of an intimate partner. The abuse can be physical, psychological, or sexual. Women and men around the world are subjected to domestic violence, in opposite-sex and same-sex relationships.

About 32 percent of women and 28 percent of men will be victims of physical violence, and 16 percent of women and 7 percent of men will be victims of unwanted sexual contact by an intimate partner in their lifetime. Crime rates, however, tell a different story about reporting domestic violence. In 2015, 0.5 percent of women and 0.05 percent of men reported being the victim of intimate partner violence. Because intimate partner violence is so personal, it influences the victim's decision to report the crime. Intimate partner violence crimes are highly underreported.

Preventing domestic abuse is complicated and involves many groups working together. Some states have tried to reduce domestic abuse by creating laws that require health-care providers to report it. These are called "mandatory reporting" laws. There are three categories of mandatory reporting laws: (1) laws requiring reporting injuries caused by weapons; (2) laws mandating reporting for injuries caused as a result of violence; and (3) laws that specifically address reporting in domestic violence cases. Colorado, for example, requires that health-care providers report injuries that they believe to be intentional to local police, including injuries resulting from domestic violence. Tennessee requires health-care providers who know, or have reasonable cause to suspect, that a patient's injuries are the result of domestic violence to report that information to the state's department of health statistics.

Not all states include domestic violence in their mandatory reporting laws and some states do not have any mandatory reporting laws at all. Hawaii's mandatory reporting law requires that health-care providers treating serious knife or firearm injuries report the cases to police, but there is no mention of domestic violence. Wyoming does not have any mandatory reporting laws at all. A 2017 report found that 31 states do not include domestic violence in their mandatory reporting laws, if they have mandatory reporting laws at all. Three states include domestic violence in their mandatory reporting laws but allow exemptions if the victims are adults.

With such a disparity in the state laws, should the federal government require health care providers to report domestic abuse?

Should the government require health-care providers to report domestic abuse? Consider the options.

YES

They should be required to report domestic abuse.

Many domestic abuse survivors do not call the police, which means that the government has difficulty assessing the scope of the problem. A federal mandatory reporting law would improve the government's collection of data about the prevalence of domestic abuse and allow it to dedicate additional resources and support to help survivors and create effective prevention programs.

Mandatory reporting improves survivor safety by treating domestic violence as a criminal matter rather than a "family matter." This policy would send an important message that domestic violence is a serious crime—abusers would be arrested and face criminal charges.

Mandatory reporting allows authorities to find abusers. Since domestic violence is underreported, governments cannot protect survivors adequately. When health-care providers report suspected domestic violence, the criminal justice system can protect the survivor. Evidence of abuse that health-care providers record can also be used against abusers in court.

Police and health-care providers should work together to solve the problem of domestic violence. By involving health-care providers in nationwide reporting, doctors around the country will receive training on domestic violence and have increased awareness of the issue.

NO

They should not be required to report domestic abuse.

Mandatory reporting weakens doctors' ability to offer effective interventions for domestic violence. If survivors hide their situation from health-care providers to avoid mandatory reporting, doctors cannot refer them to appropriate resources like counseling, shelter, and legal services. Instead of mandatory reporting laws, states should instead support training for health-care providers so that they can better identify and support victims of domestic violence.

Mandatory reporting violates provider-patient confidentiality. Some patients do not want abuse reported. Many health-care providers want to honor that decision.

Survivor safety should be the most important goal in responding to domestic violence. Mandatory reporting may work against this goal. Some survivors of domestic violence report that they are discriminated against when they report their abuse, which may lead survivors to avoid the police and other mandatory reporters. If health-care providers become mandatory reporters, survivors may avoid medical treatment when they need it most.

Mandatory reporting denies survivors the right to make their own life decisions. Not allowing survivors to decide if they want to report abuse continues the harmful stereotypes of domestic abuse survivors as weak and helpless.

GUIDING QUESTIONS

1. What are the two most compelling reasons to support the deliberation question?
2. What are the two most compelling reasons to disagree with the deliberation question?
3. What is one area of this deliberation where the two sides might find common ground?

Legal Issues for Single People in Serious Relationships

In recent years, there have been increases in the number of unmarried couples living together and in the number of unmarried couples with children. In the past, if a couple lived together, shared household duties and expenses, and then split up, they could usually go their separate ways without legal obligation. On the other hand, if the couple had been married, numerous laws would have set out their legal rights and duties concerning divorce, division of marital property, spousal support, and other issues.

The situation is changing for single people in serious relationships. Unmarried adults should know that legal issues can arise when single people live together. Certain legal rights and duties may exist between the partners.

Some unmarried couples develop a **cohabitation agreement**—a written or oral contract that outlines how they want to deal with their money, property, or responsibilities during and after their relationship. At one time, courts would not enforce agreements between unmarried couples with respect to support or property ownership. Courts did not require that one member of the couple make payments, sometimes called **palimony,** to the other after the breakup. If an unmarried couple separated, any property went to the person who had legal title to it. In relationships in which the man was the wage earner and the woman was the homemaker, the man often got all the property. In these situations, the wage earner owned any property acquired with his wages.

The rules began to change in the mid 1970s. Since then, some state courts have enforced cohabitation agreements between unmarried couples, including same-sex couples. In *Marvin* v. *Marvin,* the California Supreme Court ruled in 1976 that unmarried adults who voluntarily live together can make contracts regarding their earnings and property rights. A few states recognize such property rights without the existence of a contract, and some states do not do so even if there is a contract.

Marriage Equality

The U.S. government provides many rights and protections to heterosexual married couples. These include Social Security benefits, veteran's benefits, health benefits, hospitalization visitation, certain tax benefits, pensions, and family leave. Until 2000, these benefits were only available to opposite-sex married couples.

As America entered a new century, the legal landscape began to change. On July 1, 2000, Vermont became the first state to recognize **civil unions**. Civil unions extended certain traditional marriage rights to same-sex

▲ Legal issues can arise between people who live together, whether or not they are married to one another. *What do you think some of these legal issues might be?*

cohabitation agreement a written or oral contract outlining how unmarried couples want to deal with their money, property, or responsibilities during and after their relationship

palimony the support payment that one partner may make or be ordered by a court to make to the other when an unmarried couple, romantically involved and living together, breaks up and no longer cohabitates

civil union a legal status that allows two persons to establish a relationship that protects many of the same spousal benefits that would apply to partners in a traditional marriage

couples, including many spousal benefits. Civil unions also provided the same protections with respect to children as those provided to a married couple. One important difference between civil unions and marriage was that only marriage conferred federal benefits and protections.

A few states and localities also provided limited spousal rights for same-sex couples, irrespective of state marriage laws, through **domestic partnership** laws. These laws required employers who offered their employees fringe benefits such as medical and dental insurance, life insurance and disability insurance to offer the benefits to domestic partners in the same way the benefits were already available to spouses.

In 2004, Massachusetts became the first state to recognize legal marriages between people of the same sex. Several states also began to recognize same-sex marriage. At the same time, some states passed laws as well as constitutional amendments prohibiting same-sex marriage and refusing to recognize same-sex marriages entered into in other states. While this cultural and legal issue was extremely divisive, there was also movement in public opinion polls toward national acceptance of same-sex marriage.

Outside the United States, Denmark created a civil union law in 1989, and in 2001, the Netherlands became the first country to legalize same-sex marriage. Most of the countries in Europe then followed with either civil union or same-sex marriage laws. In 2005, Canada granted same-sex couples the right to marry. By 2018, 26 countries recognized same-sex marriage.

In the United States many states followed Massachusetts in recognizing same-sex marriages. By 2015, 37 states permitted same-sex marriages as a result of state court rulings, state laws, or federal court appeals decisions.

▲ As a result of a 2015 Supreme Court decision, same sex marriage is now legal in all states. *What are the benefits of legal marriage over civil unions and domestic partnerships?*

domestic partnership allows an employee's heterosexual or homosexual live-in partner to receive the same employment and health benefits a spouse would receive

The Marriage Equality Cases

In 1996 Congress passed and President Bill Clinton signed into law the *Defense of Marriage Act* (*DOMA*). This law created a federal definition of marriage as the union of a man and a woman. *DOMA* neither required nor prohibited states from recognizing same-sex marriages. It allowed each state to decide whether it would recognize a same-sex marriage created in another state. After *DOMA* was passed, a number of states banned same sex-marriages.

In 2012 the Supreme Court of the United States ruled in a 5-to-4 decision that *DOMA* violated the Constitution because it discriminated against same-sex couples. In response to this Supreme Court decision, many federal courts of appeal struck down state same-sex marriage bans. The U.S. Court of Appeals for the Sixth Circuit did not strike down the laws and constitutional amendments that banned same-sex marriage in

Michigan, Ohio, Kentucky, and Tennessee. Several same-sex couples from these states filed lawsuits in federal court against the bans.

James Obergefell and his husband, John Arthur, were married in Maryland, but lived in Ohio—a state that did not recognize same-sex marriage. Arthur was terminally ill. After John Arthur died, Obergefell sued Richard Hodges, director of Ohio's Department of Health, when the department refused to list Obergefell as the surviving spouse on Arthur's death certificate. Obergefell won his case in federal trial court, but the U.S. Court of Appeals for the Sixth Circuit reversed the trial court's decision, upholding the Ohio law banning same-sex marriage. In 2015, the U.S. Supreme Court agreed to hear Obergefell's case.

Obergefell v. Hodges presented two questions to the Supreme Court: (1) does the Fourteenth Amendment require a state to license same-sex marriages, and (2) does the Fourteenth Amendment require a state to recognize a same-sex marriage that was lawfully created out of state? In a 5-to-4 decision, the Supreme Court decided that the answer to both questions was "yes."

The majority found that the right to marry is a fundamental right protected by the Fourteenth Amendment's due process and equal protection clauses for both same-sex couples and opposite-sex couples. The Court's decision stated that marriage protects children and families and is a critical part of the nation's social order. Excluding same-sex couples from the right to marry causes them harm and is inconsistent with the nation's commitment to equality. Because all states had to recognize same-sex marriages (the answer to question 1), states could not refuse to recognize a same-sex marriage created out of state (the answer to question 2).

The dissenting justices found that states should be free to establish their own definition of marriage, and that the definition should be determined by the votes of the people who live there. They argued that taking the power to make this decision away from the states undermines democracy. At least some of the dissenting justices were not against same-sex marriage; they were, however, against finding a national right to same-sex marriage in the Constitution.

PROBLEM 29.7

a. Think about the argument put forth by the four dissenting justices in this case. Can you construct a counter argument to their argument? How would you counter the dissent?

b. After the Court's ruling in *Obergefell* v. *Hodges*, assume that a same-sex couple seeks a marriage license from a state official whose religious conviction prohibits the recognition of same-sex marriage. Must the official provide the license? How could this conflict be resolved?

c. When the Fourteenth Amendment was ratified in 1868, it seems unlikely that either the drafters or the ratifiers of the Amendment thought that the Constitution would require all states to recognize same-sex marriage. Whether or not you support same-sex marriage, what is your view about whether the Fourteenth Amendment requires states to recognize same-sex marriage?

▶ Parents are responsible for their children's education.

The relationship between parents and children is a special one. Being a parent involves many rewards and also many responsibilities. Parents have a legal obligation to care for, support, and discipline their children. When parents are unable or unwilling to fulfill their responsibilities, the legal system may intervene. This chapter explores the legal rights and responsibilities of parents and children.

Responsibilities Between Parents and Children

Parents are legally responsible for their children in many ways. Most importantly, they must provide the necessities of life. They must also provide for their children's social and moral development, and they must set limits on and supervise their children's behavior.

Paternity

No one can be forced to marry someone against his or her will; such a marriage would be invalid and could be annulled. When children are involved, however, the law requires parents to support their children whether or not the parents are married, dating, living together or apart, and regardless of where the child lives.

For example, if a man denies being a child's father, the mother may bring a **paternity suit,** or action in court to establish his fatherhood, and force him to pay for prenatal care and child support. If the mother is a

paternity suit a lawsuit brought by a woman against a man she claims is the father of her child. If paternity is proven, the man is legally responsible for contributing to the support of the child.

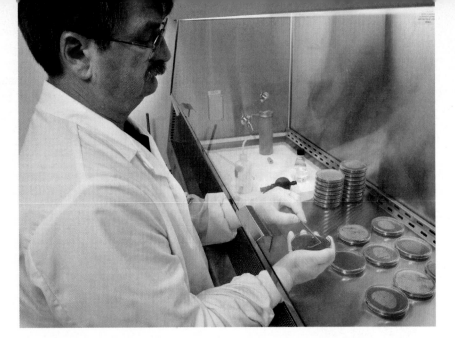

▲ DNA testing is used to determine paternity. *What does the* Family Support Act of 1988 *require of all states?*

minor, some states allow her parents to bring the suit. The *Family Support Act of 1988* requires all states to assist mothers and children in obtaining paternity testing and to allow paternity suits until the child is 18 years old. Government lawyers can assist in finding missing parents and help mothers and fathers prove paternity.

Blood samples can be used to prove that a particular man is not a particular child's father. For example, if both the mother and the alleged father have blood type A and the child has blood type B, the man cannot be the child's father. A child cannot have type B blood unless either the father or the mother has that type.

Blood type alone, however, cannot prove that a man is a child's father. Courts typically use DNA tests to prove paternity. This method tests blood or tissue for genes that link a specific parent and child. Test results are extremely accurate and greatly reduce the uncertainties that once plagued paternity suits.

PROBLEM 30.1

Martha becomes pregnant. She claims that Michael is the father, but Michael denies it and refuses to marry her or support the child. Does the law require Michael to marry Martha? Does the law require unmarried people to provide support for their children?

Support

The most basic responsibility of parents is to support their minor children. Parents must provide the basic necessities of life, including food, clothing, shelter, education, and medical care. These are things minor children cannot provide for themselves.

All parents—regardless of income, marital status, or age—are required to support their minor children. The amount of support a family can give, of course, depends on what it can afford. Parents with lower incomes, for example, would not be in a position to provide expensive clothes, lavish housing, or fancy meals.

Generally, the law makes parents equally responsible for child support. This does not mean that each parent pays the same amount of money but that each parent provides according to his or her ability. Support is a legal requirement whether the parents are unmarried, married, separated, or divorced. In the event of divorce, a court order will usually indicate the amount each parent must provide.

Investigating the Law Where You Live

Find out what agency handles child support enforcement in your state.

THE **CASE** OF...

The Child with an Intellectual Disability

When Diem and Kim divorce, the court orders Diem to pay $250 per month in child support for their six-year-old daughter, Meena. Meena has an intellectual disability and is not expected to ever function at a level higher than that of a second grader. She lives with her mother and will probably never be capable of living independently. When Meena reaches the age of 18, Diem files a motion seeking to end his child support payments.

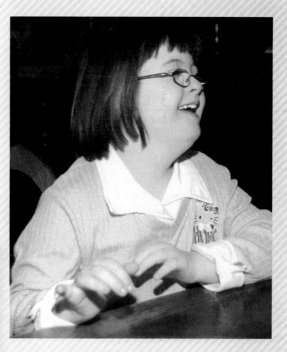

▲ A child with an intellectual disability

PROBLEM 30.2

a. How should the court rule in this case?

b. What is the general rule for how long parents must financially support their children? Should that rule be different if the child is mentally or physically disabled?

c. What other conditions might make it reasonable to require that a parent support a child who is no longer a minor?

Traditionally, the parents' duty to support their children ended when each child reached the age of majority (18 in most states). However, because of the importance of education today, some states have rules that parents must provide reasonable post-secondary school support. In addition, most states have adopted a rule that requires parents to support their adult disabled children.

Emancipation

Parents are usually not required to give financial support to an adult child. Parents' legal responsibility ends when their children become emancipated. Emancipation means that children are free from the legal custody and control of their parents. **Emancipation** normally takes place automatically when the child reaches adulthood—age 18 in most states. It also can occur when a child gets married, joins the armed forces, or becomes financially self-supporting. Some states also provide for emancipation at an age younger than 18 if a minor successfully petitions the court for this legal status.

To convince a court to grant emancipation in those states that recognize it, a minor would have to show proof of a steady source of income

Investigating the Law Where You Live

Find out Does your state require parents to provide reasonable post-secondary school support? If not, should it?

emancipation the freeing of a child from the control of parents and allowing the child to live on his or her own or under the control of others. It usually applies to adolescents who leave the parents' household by agreement or demand. Emancipation may also end the responsibility of a divorced parent to pay child support.

Realistic Reflections

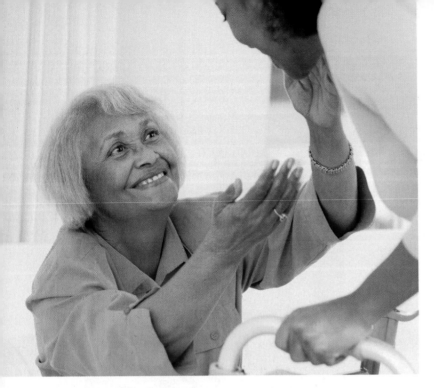

and a permanent place to live. Parents and other adults can attend the emancipation court hearing and testify either for or against granting emancipation. Emancipation is rarely granted, and when it is, the minor must still wait until the legal age of majority to vote or drink alcohol.

Family Responsibility Laws

A long tradition of law and social custom has called upon adult children to support their parents when the parents are in need. In some states, children are not legally required to support their elderly or disabled parents. Most states, however, have passed **family (filial) responsibility laws** that require adult children to care for their elderly parents. Other states have abolished these laws, and almost all states limit the support obligation to an amount the relative can reasonably afford.

▲ Many adult children support their elderly or disabled parents. *What are family responsibility laws?*

family (filial) responsibility laws laws that require adult children to care for their elderly parents

PROBLEM 30.3

Rose, 42, owns a successful business. Her mother Irma, 65, will retire from her job at the end of the year. However, Irma's meager savings and Social Security payments are not enough for her to continue paying rent where she lives. Irma can move to a publicly supported home for the elderly but would prefer to stay in her own apartment. Does Rose have a legal obligation to support her mother? Should the law require adult children to support their parents when they are in need? Do people have a moral obligation to support their needy parents?

Education

All children in the United States have a right to a free public school education through the twelfth grade. Each state sets standards for its public school system, but parents have a right to choose the kind of school to which to send their children—public, private, parochial, or homeschool. School attendance is generally required for children ages 6 to 16, although state laws vary. A child who misses school without justification is considered a **truant.** Because states generally hold parents responsible for their children's welfare and education, parents who fail to send their children to school may be fined or arrested.

Some parents decide that the traditional public or private school system is not adequate to meet the needs of their children and that they would rather educate their children at home. Prior to the 1980s, many states did not permit children to be homeschooled. All 50 states and the District of

truant a child who stays away from school without permission

Columbia now allow a child's formal education to take place at home under certain circumstances, such as having dedicated space in which instruction takes place, meeting state curricular requirements, and participating in mandated achievement testing. In 2016 about 1.7 million school-aged children were being homeschooled. This number is just over 3.0 percent of the school-age population in the United States. The number of home schooled children fluctuates somewhat with economic conditions. When the economy is weak, for example, some parents who would place their children in private schools home school instead.

A federal law, the *Individuals with Disabilities Education Act (IDEA),* provides for a public school education for children with disabilities. Under the law, children with physical, mental, and emotional disabilities who need special services in order to learn are entitled to an evaluation and an appropriate individualized education plan. Children who need services must be granted specialized instruction, as well as any related services necessary for the child to benefit from the program. Such services may include transportation, speech and language therapy, and psychological or psychiatric counseling. These services are all provided at no cost to the child or family.

Parents are not usually legally required to pay for college tuition. However, if they are financially able to, many parents do. Some divorce decrees require parental financial support through college for the parent's children.

Investigating the Law Where You Live

Research to learn more about what parents in your state must do in order to homeschool their children.

THE **CASE** OF...

The School at Home

Michelle and Larry Novitzki have four children. Two are of school age. Larry is a high school graduate, and Michelle has a college degree. They began educating their children at home because they disapproved of the public school's sex education classes, were concerned about violence in schools, and believed that the children would learn more in a less structured environment. They designed lessons that related to activities around their home and community.

The Novitzkis use books and materials approved by the state board of education and have set aside one room to serve as a classroom. The children receive instruction six hours a day, year-round. Both children score above average on standardized tests and appear to psychologists to be healthy and normal. An educational official claims that the Novitzkis' program does not satisfy the state's compulsory education law.

PROBLEM 30.4

a. Should the Novitzkis be allowed to instruct their children at home? Are their reasons for wanting to do so valid?

b. What are the advantages and disadvantages of homeschooling?

c. What qualifications, if any, should a parent have in order to teach his or her children at home?

d. Should homeschooled students be able to participate on school sports teams or play in the school band? Explain.

e. Draft a rule that will guide education officials in determining whether a home schooling family is in compliance with the state's compulsory education law.

TAKING ACTION: Law and Democracy

Should Higher Education in Public Institutions be Tuition Free?

Some argue that providing a free public education through high school is not sufficient to ensure that the United States has a globally competitive workforce. Some people believe that a two-year community college education should be available tuition free to all. Still others believe that a public four-year college or university education should be tuition free to either all or to those who can show economic need.

One aspect of the argument for tuition-free higher education focuses on the development of a globally competitive workforce. Another element is that such programs would promote equal educational opportunity for those who desire higher education but cannot afford the cost of education beyond high school. Free or dramatically reduced tuition would also ease the burden of student debt for many students.

The cost of tuition-free programs would be supported by higher taxes. Many believe that tuition-free higher education is not politically realistic or practical and that our current system of higher education is the envy of the world and should be maintained as is.

PROBLEM 30.5

a. Should Congress pass a law providing for free tuition at two-year public colleges? At four-year public colleges and universities? If so, should tuition be free for all or should there be a sliding scale for cost based on economic need?

b. Instead of a federal law, would you prefer that each state make its own decisions about tuition-free access? What are the benefits of a national decision? Of a state-by-state approach?

c. What are the strongest arguments for tuition-free higher education? Against tuition-free higher education?

Medical Care

Parents have a legal duty to protect and supervise their children's health. They must provide proper medical and dental care. For example, children must be up to date on vaccinations—with some exceptions for medical, philosophical, or religious reasons—before entering school.

Children usually need their parents' permission to obtain medical treatment. For example, suppose a 14-year-old boy wants cosmetic surgery. Without his parents' permission, a doctor could not perform such surgery. Parents have a right to supervise medical care, but they can also be charged with neglect if they ignore their children's health problems. In very serious cases, a court may permit a doctor to treat a child without parental consent. Doctors may also act in life-threatening emergencies without permission from either a parent or a court.

Care and Supervision

Parents may decide what is best for their children as long as they do not abuse or neglect them. There are no minimum requirements for the number of hours parents must spend with their children. Both parents may work, and their children may be left home alone. However, state laws govern the age at which a child may be left alone in the home, so parents must be sure that someone responsible is caring for their young children at all times. These laws concerning child care and supervision vary from state to state.

Discipline

Parents have a right and a duty to supervise their children. Likewise, children have a legal obligation to obey their parents and to follow reasonable rules. Parents can ask children to do chores around the house. Parents may also decide where their children live, what school they attend, what religion they practice, and other aspects of their lives. However, parental authority is not absolute. Children do not have to obey parents who order them to do something dangerous or illegal. Parents who resort to unreasonable actions to discipline their children can be charged with child abuse or child neglect.

Children who continually disobey their parents or run away from home may be charged as status offenders. Status offenses are acts that are not illegal if committed by adults. Status offenses include running away from home, skipping school, refusing to obey parents, or engaging in immoral or dangerous behavior. A status offender may be placed under court supervision. When this happens, the child is known as a PINS, CHINS, or MINS—a person, child, or minor in need of supervision. Under these circumstances, courts may order counseling or special schooling or, in serious cases, may place the child in a foster home or other alternative facility until the family can be reunified.

PROBLEM 30.6

Consider the following situations. In each case, decide whether the parents have the legal authority to make the decision involved. What arguments can you make in support of the parents? In support of the child?

a. Mr. McBride disapproves of the lifestyle of his 19-year-old son, Larry, who regularly smokes marijuana. When Larry refuses to stop using the drug, Mr. McBride cuts off financial support to Larry, including college tuition.

b. Hiroshi, a high school senior, does not want to move to a new city with his parents. He wants to finish high school with his friends. His parents insist that he live with them.

c. Mr. and Mrs. Parham think that their 16-year-old daughter is mentally ill and needs psychiatric treatment. The daughter objects, but her parents decide to commit her to a mental institution.

Parental Responsibility for Children's Acts

Parents who fail to exercise proper supervision and control over their children may be held legally responsible for their children's acts. This point is especially true if they aid or encourage improper conduct. For example, a parent who allows an underage child to drink and drive may be held liable if the child causes an accident.

Almost all states hold parents civilly liable for certain acts of their minor children, such as property damage, theft, or vandalism. The action of contributing to the delinquency of a minor is recognized as a crime by some states. A parent who encourages a child to sell drugs, for example, could be charged with this crime. Some states pass and try to enforce laws that make parents criminally responsible for certain delinquent acts, such as vandalism, committed by their children. Other states see such laws as unworkable and believe they shift responsibility away from the children, who should be held accountable for their own actions.

Historically, parents were not held responsible for injuries caused by their children. This applied whether the injuries were accidental or intentional, unless the parents were somehow to blame. For example, if a parent gave a child a gun to play with, or failed to adequately supervise a child, the parent could be liable for injuries caused by the actions of the child.

Today, some states make parents legally responsible, up to a certain dollar amount, for harm caused by their children. This amount varies from approximately $1,000 to $60,000 or more, depending on state law. A rule known as the **family car doctrine** makes parents responsible for damages caused by any driver in the family. If a teen driver causes an accident while driving the family car, the parents may have to pay for any damage.

family car doctrine a legal rule stating that the owner of a car will be liable for damage done by any family member driving the car

---

PROBLEM 30.7

Vanessa, 14, stays out late at night and often misses school. She seems to have a lot of cash and nice clothes. When her parents ask where she gets the money, she says she earns it from babysitting. Her parents suspect that she's involved in selling drugs. One night Vanessa and her boyfriend break into a neighbor's house, steal a television, and sell it to get money for drugs. A neighbor sees them buying drugs, calls the police, and Vanessa and her boyfriend are arrested.

a. Have Vanessa's parents adequately supervised their daughter? If not, what should they have done differently? Can parents' actions affect the actions of their children?

b. Should Vanessa's parents have to pay for the neighbor's television? Why or why not?

c. Should parents be held criminally responsible for the actions of their children? If so, under what circumstances?

Earnings and Employment

In many families, children who work are allowed to keep and spend their own money. Nevertheless, parents have the legal right to take the earnings of their minor children. Children may keep only the wages that their parents allow them to keep. However, parents have no right to use money from other sources that legally belongs to their children. If a minor receives an inheritance or recovers damages in a lawsuit, for example, this money is the child's to set aside in a bank account until he or she reaches adulthood.

Child Abuse and Neglect

Child abuse takes many forms. It occurs whenever any adult or older child inflicts or threatens to inflict intentional physical, emotional, or sexual harm on a child. **Child neglect** occurs more frequently than child abuse and involves the failure to properly feed, clothe, shelter, educate, supervise, or tend to the medical needs of a child. Abuse and neglect are among the leading causes of death of children in the United States.

Abuse and neglect of children have effects that go far beyond the obvious immediate dangers. Being abused or neglected as a child increases the likelihood of arrest as a juvenile. Truancy and attempted suicide often result from emotional abuse. Moreover, abused children frequently grow up to be abusive adults.

child abuse neglect or mistreatment of a child

child neglect the failure of a parent to properly feed, clothe, provide shelter for, educate, supervise, or provide for the medical needs of a child

---

FIGURE

30.1 Child Abuse Reported, 1962–2017

Year	Cases
1962 (prior to reporting laws)	662
1976 (first year reported)	1.1 million
1980	1.1 million
1990	2.6 million
2000	2.8 million
2010	3.3 million
2017	4.1 million

Source: National Committee to Prevent Child Abuse and Children's Bureau, HMS

Reporting laws have resulted in an increased number of reported cases of child abuse. ANALYZE THE DATA *By how much did the number of reported cases change in the more than 40 years between 1976 and 2017?*

Not surprisingly, most youths who run away from home have suffered physical or emotional abuse and neglect. Nearly three-fourths of all female runaways have been sexually abused, and so have many male runaways. Older teenage runaways are sometimes termed "throw-aways." These are children whose parents refuse to care for them.

Abused children often are not in a position to do anything about their abuse. Accordingly, every state has laws requiring doctors, nurses, teachers, social workers, and other adults to report suspected cases of abuse or neglect. Accusing someone of child abuse without reasons to suspect the person of abuse might provide the basis for a civil lawsuit. You will not be held legally liable, however, for a mistaken report made in good faith. In fact, if you are obligated under state law to do so, failure to report suspected abuse can lead to criminal or civil penalties, or both.

Sexual Abuse

pedophile a person who engages in the sexual abuse of a minor

Reported cases of child sexual abuse have increased dramatically in recent years. Sexual fondling, using a child in pornography, and making a child view pornography all constitute sexual abuse, along with other forms of sexual contact. The sexual offender, often called a **pedophile,** may be a person the child knows and trusts, such as a family member, a family friend, a child-care worker, a school employee, or even a clergy member. The abuser can be an older child, an adult, or even a parent. Child sexual abuse can cause physical injury to the child as well as serious emotional and psychological harm.

Despite the benefits we enjoy from the Internet, growing use of the Internet by children and adults has provided child abusers with another way of preying on juveniles through online forums. Child sexual abusers prey on a child's obedience, trust, and embarrassment. In the online context, they often lie to a child about who they are, their age, and the basis of their interest in the child. In all contexts, abusers often use threats to prevent a child from reporting the abuse.

PROBLEM 30.8

For each situation, decide whether or not the action of the parent or parents should be considered child abuse or neglect. Explain your answer. If you find abuse or neglect, what should be done to protect the child?

a. Sixteen-year-old Theresa returns home late one evening. As punishment, her parents ground her for a week.

b. Eighteen-year-old Shawn and his two-year-old son, Jeffrey, live with his mother. Shawn has to be at work at 9 p.m., but his mother does not get home until 10 p.m. Shawn feeds Jeffrey, puts him to bed, and leaves him asleep and alone for the hour or so until his mother returns home.

Increasingly, parents are bringing civil suits against child abusers and their employers who work with their children. The suits typically charge an employer with negligence for not properly overseeing employees or screening job applicants for a history of child abuse. As a result, it is now common for organizations that employ adults who work with children to require a job applicant to submit to fingerprinting as part of a criminal background check.

Some people say that children may imagine episodes of sexual abuse. However, most psychologists stress that young children lack the sexual experience to make up stories of sexual abuse by themselves. Moreover, while it is possible for an older child to invent such a story, such instances are considered unusual. Therefore, any time a minor reports sexual abuse, his or her story should be taken seriously and thoroughly investigated.

If a child does report sexual abuse, the police should be notified immediately. An investigation will determine whether the child is in immediate, ongoing danger and whether the case should go to trial. If the alleged abuser is a parent or someone who lives with the child, the child may be removed from the home. Most states currently allow child victims to testify in court through closed-circuit television or by means of videotaped questioning to save them from the trauma of having to face their abusers.

THE **CASE** OF...

A Parent, Drug Use, and Neglect

Jenna is the mother of six-year-old Kimberly. The police recently searched their apartment for drugs and found it to be a "shooting gallery" for heroin. Syringes were found, and Jenna and others present were arrested. Kimberly witnessed the raid.

There is no definite evidence that Jenna is using drugs, although she has a history of drug use and is currently in a drug rehabilitation program. She claims that her boyfriend comes into her apartment with his friends and that they use drugs without her permission. Jenna has a full-time job as a secretary, and Kimberly is doing well in school. She loves her mother and does not want to be taken from her home.

The state law regarding child neglect reads: "Neglect means the negligent treatment or the maltreatment of a child by a person responsible for the child's welfare under circumstances indicating harm or threatened harm to the child's health or welfare. The term includes both acts and omissions on the part of the responsible person."

PROBLEM 30.9

a. The state brings a neglect petition against Jenna. What are the arguments for and against finding Kimberly to be a neglected child?

b. If you were the judge, would you find neglect in this case? Why or why not?

c. If Kimberly is found to be neglected, would you terminate parental rights and remove her from the home? What other orders might you issue?

d. Do you think a parent who uses drugs is committing neglect? Does it make a difference if the child is aware of the drug use? What other factors should be considered before neglect is found to exist?

Steps to Take

How to Report Child Abuse or Neglect

- **To whom do I make a report?** To make a child abuse or neglect report, call the National Child Abuse Hotline, 1-800-4-A-CHILD, or visit online at www.childhelp.org. The hotline will tell you how to contact your local child protective services (CPS) agency. You also may want to talk to a teacher, counselor, medical professional, or other trusted adult. If you believe the child is in immediate danger, contact the police.

- **Who must report suspected cases of child abuse?** Usually, medical practitioners, teachers, child-care professionals, school officials, and social workers must report suspected cases of abuse to the authorities.

- **Who may report?** Suspected cases of child abuse can be reported by anyone suspecting that a child is being mistreated. This includes the child who believes he or she is being abused.

- **What conditions should I report?** You should report any situation that indicates abuse or neglect of a child. This may include unexplained bruises or burn marks; constant hunger or repeated inappropriate dress for the weather; major weight gain or loss; or chronic uncleanliness, exhaustion, or school absences. You may also want to talk to the child's teachers or another trusted adult. If a child is in immediate danger or if you witness a child being physically harmed, call the police for immediate response.

- **What happens if I report someone?** After you make the report, a CPS worker will ask for all the information you have. Then the CPS worker will visit the family to determine whether the child in question

▲ Receiving help from a CPS worker

is in immediate danger and whether it is necessary to call in the police or a doctor. Under extreme circumstances, the child may be removed from the home immediately. In such cases, the child is placed in foster care or with another family member who does not live in the same household. Otherwise, the CPS worker will interview the parents, observe the physical and emotional conditions of the household, and decide whether there is a need for counseling or family support services.

- **Must I give my name when I make a report?** Giving your name is not required. However, it might assist the CPS worker in gaining more information and enable the authorities to take legal action against the abuser. Also, you might be required to testify in court.

▶ One goal shared by foster care and adoption is to place children in safe and healthy homes.

Children do not always live with their biological families. Neglected or abused children may be removed from the family home, placed in foster care, and sometimes placed for adoption. For a variety of reasons, some parents decide to give up their children for adoption, often at birth.

Foster Care

In extreme cases of child abuse, neglect, or deaths in the family, courts may decide that parents are unable to care for their children. The state becomes the child's **temporary legal guardian,** making most decisions about that child's life while the child's parents retain limited legal rights. Judges and social workers then decide where and with whom the child will live. In 2017, over 450,000 children spent time in foster care in the United States. **Family foster care** is a system of licensed families in each state who act as temporary parents for children who cannot live with their families.

temporary legal guardian the state's role in making most decisions for children whose parents are temporarily unable to care for them. The parents usually retain limited rights.

family foster care a system of licensed families in each state who act as temporary parents for children who cannot live with their families

Ian Boddy/Science Photo Library/Alamy

▲ Some children are placed in the care of relatives rather than in the foster care system. *What are the advantages to kinship care?*

group home a residence in which several children in foster care live together under the supervision and care of licensed individuals

kinship care placement of a vulnerable youth in the continuous care and supervision of relatives who are not his or her parents as directed by a social services or other child welfare agency. Such an arrangement also often occurs informally.

family reunification the process a family goes through to make the necessary changes to provide a safe home for a foster child to return to

terminate parental rights a court decision ending the rights of an unfit parent, leaving the child available for adoption by the foster family, relatives, or others

adoption the legal process of taking a child of other biological parents and accepting that child as your own, with all the legal rights and responsibilities there would be if the child were yours by birth

Foster parents have temporary physical custody of children and care for them day to day. They do not have legal custody of the child. Children may also live in **group homes,** where several children in foster care live together. **Kinship care** is the placement of children with relatives who are not their parents. If the state places children with relatives, the law requires that these relatives be licensed like any other foster family.

Foster care is meant to be only a temporary solution. Judges regularly review the case and are required to do everything they can to provide children with permanent homes. Courts first try to help the families make the necessary changes to provide safe homes so that children can return. This solution—**family reunification**—is the most common outcome for children in foster care. If the court finds that there is no way for the child to safely return home, then the judge may **terminate parental rights**. When this happens, children may be adopted by their foster families, relatives, or others.

Each year, more than 20,000 young people reach the age of majority (18 in most places) and "age out" of the foster care system. After that happens, no one has custody of these young people. In many cases, they leave the system without the life skills or the support systems that are common for most people their age. The *Foster Care Independence Act of 1999* was passed by Congress to provide funding so that states could provide independent living services for these youth until age 21. Other federal programs help with college and vocational school tuition for youth who age out of the foster care system. Studies have shown that youth aging out of the foster care system are at high risk of poverty, homelessness, substance abuse, and domestic violence. Many become involved in the criminal justice system.

Some people are critical of the operation of the foster care system, believing that governments are too quick to take children away from their birth parents and that most youngsters would do better even in a difficult home environment than in the foster care system. Others believe that the government is too slow to identify a permanent plan for children after they have been taken from the parents.

Adoption

Adoption is the legal process by which an adult or adults become the legal parent(s) of another person. Though adults usually adopt children, most states also permit adults to adopt another adult. The law places few restrictions on who can legally adopt whom. Therefore, most adults—regardless of marital status, race, religion, or age—are eligible to adopt anyone else. In practice, however, adoption agencies and courts try to make a child's new family as much like their family of origin as possible.

Removing Children From the Family

- **Preliminary protective hearings** are held either immediately before or immediately after a social services agency removes a child from the family and places the child in protective custody. If there is immediate danger to the child, social services may remove the child until an emergency hearing can be held, usually within two or three days. A judge identifies the child's immediate needs and decides whether there is a good reason for the child to stay in the care of the state until a full hearing can be held.

- **Jurisdictional hearings** are held to hear testimony from the social service agency, the parents, and the court-appointed guardian for the child (a *guardian ad litem* or Court-Appointed Special Advocate [CASA] worker). If the court finds clear evidence of abuse or neglect, the child is placed in the care of the state. If not, the child is returned to the home.

- **Disposition hearings** determine where, and with whom, the child should live. This is sometimes combined with the jurisdictional hearing. Dispositional decisions must be reviewed regularly by the judge, with the goal of returning the child to the family from which he or she was removed.

- **Permanency hearings** are held to find a permanent, stable home for the child. All youth in foster care have a voice in where they want their permanent home to be. For most, the goal is reunification with their family. For others, adoption, guardianship, or emancipation may be the best outcome.

- **Termination of parental rights hearings** are held when the court feels a parent cannot and will not be able to provide a safe home for a child. When the parents' rights are terminated, the child may be adopted.

Adoption agencies therefore are sometimes reluctant to place children with a single parent or with parents of a different race or religion.

Most adoptions are arranged through public or private adoption agencies. When they apply to an agency, people wishing to adopt are investigated and evaluated to determine whether they would be suitable parents. While public agencies usually charge little or no fee for this service, private agencies often charge substantial fees for their services. Some people work through agencies to adopt children living in other countries. Other people turn to "go-betweens," who arrange for pregnant women to turn over their babies to adoptive parents without going through an adoption agency. Some states allow this practice and license the go-betweens. Other states refer to the practice as "black-market adoption" and make it illegal.

Learn more about whether your state law allows adopted children to find out the identity of their birth parents. What does the law provide?

surrogate mother a woman, other than the wife, who agrees to be artificially inseminated to carry the resulting child to term, and to release legal custody to the individual or couple immediately following birth

People who wish to adopt must also apply to a court to have the adoption legally approved. An attorney often takes the legal steps to make the adoption final. An adoption agency will submit its report on the adopting parents and will seek written consent from the birth parents. In most states, consent is required, but in some cases, even if the birth parents refuse or cannot be found, courts may still grant adoptions that they decide are in the best interest of the child. Children over a certain age—often 12 or 14—must also consent to the adoption.

In most states, when the court approves an adoption, it issues a temporary order. The agency or birth parents remain the legal guardians for a specified waiting period, such as six months or a year. After this waiting period, a new birth certificate is issued showing the adopting parents as the parents of the child. The child and the adoptive parents then assume the same rights and responsibilities as biological children and their birth parents.

Some couples who cannot conceive their own biological children may rely on a surrogate parent. Some individuals without a spouse or partner may also use this arrangement. A **surrogate mother** is someone who agrees to carry a child to term for the individual or couple through artificial insemination or in vitro fertilization. The surrogate and the couple typically sign a contract before the child is born in which the surrogate consents to the child's adoption and releases all parental rights. State laws vary widely on the legality of surrogacy contracts and the terms that may be included in them. Some states permit them and others do not.

Do you think adopted children should have a right to know who their birth parents are? Traditionally, adoption records were sealed, and adopted children were not allowed to find out the names or whereabouts of their birth parents. However, adoptive children are often interested in learning about and meeting their birth parents. All states now allow adoptees at least some access to their own adoption records. In most states, a court order is needed to access this information.

▶ Sealing adoption records is a controversial issue. *Should adopted children be able to find out the names of their birth parents?*

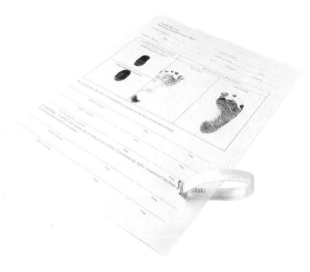

©Comstock/Alamy

TAKING ACTION: Law and Democracy

Interracial Adoptions

The U.S. Supreme Court first addressed the roles of race, ethnicity, and religion in court cases involving child custody and adoption in 1984. The Court ruled that a judge should not consider the race or races of a child's parents when deciding whether to take a child from a home. In 1994, Congress passed a law allowing the race of adoptive parents and the child to be used as a factor in deciding whether to allow adoptions.

However, this law was reversed in 1996 when Congress passed a law specifying that no adoption could be delayed or denied on the basis of race. This legislation, however, applies only to adoption agencies receiving federal funds. In many instances, race is one of the factors considered by social workers, courts, and private-sector adoption agencies in determining the homes where children should be placed. Read the proposed law and the arguments below.

Proposed State Law: In making decisions regarding the adoption of a child, the race of the child and the adoptive parents shall not be considered as a factor.

Arguments in Favor of the Law: At any given time, there are typically more white families than families of color wishing to adopt children. There are several reasons for this disparity. Whites in the United States tend to be wealthier overall than other racial groups. If adoptions are limited to same-race parents, children of color will most likely wait longer periods than white children to be adopted. All children's needs for safe and healthy homes should be given more weight than the adoptive parents' race. In addition, allowing racial preference in adoption is a form of discrimination. The law should promote equality.

Arguments Against the Law: Many races and ethnicities in U.S. society have a history of being oppressed. It is important to place children of historically oppressed races and ethnicities in homes that will practice and preserve the traditions of their cultural heritage, promote knowledge and pride in their cultural history, and equip children with the coping skills necessary to live in a society in which discrimination still exists. Even if they strive to promote cultural knowledge and self-respect, white parents who adopt children of color will find it difficult to foster such an environment. White parents tend to associate socially with other white people, practice traditions from a Western European background, and often lack knowledge of other cultures. Children of color who are raised by white parents risk being confused about their identities, unaware of the accomplishments and history of people of their own race and culture, and unprepared to function well in either culture.

PROBLEM 31.1

a. Debate the proposed law. Should it be adopted? Explain the reasons for your answer.

b. Should the religion of the adoptive parents and the child be considered in making adoption decisions? Explain your answer.

c. Should a single parent be able to adopt a child? Explain your answer.

d. Should same-sex couples be able to adopt children? Explain your answer.

Scarpetta v. *The Adoption Agency*

Olga Scarpetta, 32, comes from a wealthy, religious California family. During an affair with a married man, she becomes pregnant. Olga thinks her pregnancy will embarrass her family, so she goes to New York to have the baby. The child is born May 18 and placed with an adoption agency four days later. On June 1, Olga signs a document giving the agency full authority to find new parents for the child.

The agency places the infant with the DeMartino family on June 18. Dr. DeMartino and his wife have previously adopted a four-year-old boy from the same agency.

Within two months after the birth, Olga changes her mind and asks for her baby. The agency refuses and will not tell her who has adopted the child. After several weeks of arguing with the agency, Olga goes to court. She tells the judge that she was physically and emotionally distraught following childbirth. She is now sure that she wants to keep the child. Her family has learned of the birth and also wants Olga to get her baby back.

PROBLEM 31.2

Read the following opinions and decide which one you agree with most. Give reasons for your choice. Note that the adoption agency is the defendant in this case, because the DeMartinos have not yet received final legal custody of the child. The court must decide whether to return the child to the birth parent or to leave the child with the adoptive parents.

Opinion A

For many reasons, this court believes it is in the child's best interest to leave the child with the adoptive parents, the DeMartinos.

First, Ms. Scarpetta waited six weeks after giving up the child for adoption before requesting the child's return. During this period, the DeMartinos formed a strong attachment to the child and made many sacrifices because they had every reason to believe the child would be their own.

Second, the DeMartinos' situation is much more secure than Ms. Scarpetta's. She is unmarried and, from the evidence before us, appears to be emotionally unstable. As for the DeMartinos, the agency selected them because they had already adopted a four-year-old boy and proved themselves to be able to provide for the child's moral and physical well-being. They can give the attention of two parents to the child. To take away the baby at this point would cause them a great deal of suffering.

Finally, Ms. Scarpetta freely gave up the child, and the agency acted in a proper manner in obtaining her consent.

Opinion B

There is a legal presumption that unless proven to be unfit, the birth mother is best suited to provide support and care for her child. This court believes that Olga Scarpetta is a fit birth parent.

First, Ms. Scarpetta was under great pressure when she placed the child for adoption. She had just gone through an unplanned pregnancy, labor, and delivery. She was worried about the reaction of her devoutly religious family. Her decision could not have been freely made under these circumstances.

Second, she now clearly wants the child and is able to provide for the child's welfare. Her wealthy family also supports her in this decision and will no doubt help her if she needs financial assistance.

Finally, there is no evidence that she will be an unfit parent. Even though the DeMartinos may be good or even better parents, they should not be given rights ahead of those of the birth mother.

▶ Separation and divorce can be painful experiences for children, as can living with unhappily married parents.

When problems arise in a marriage, they can sometimes be resolved with help from friends, family members, or counselors. Sometimes, however, spouses may consider ending their marriage. When this occurs, it involves serious and often difficult changes for the entire family. This chapter covers procedures for ending a valid marriage through separation or divorce, as well as the many legal issues raised by divorce, including child custody, alimony, child support, and property division. If parents remarry or find a new life partner, new relationships are created for stepparents and children. All these changes involve the law.

Marriage Problems

Some of the difficulties a couple may experience in a marriage are conflicts with in-laws or relatives, job and career pressures, adultery, conflicts about children, sexual problems, and a breakdown in communication. Alcohol or drug abuse, money problems, and loss of shared goals or interests may also affect a couple's relationship.

S. Olsson/PhotoAlto

▶ A breakdown in communication is one of the most common problems in a marriage. *How are separation and divorce similar? How are they different?*

marriage counselor a person who is trained to help couples settle their marital problems

Minor disagreements are usually settled by the couple themselves or with the help of family members and friends. Major differences may require the couple to seek the help of a marriage counselor, psychologist, or social worker. A **marriage counselor,** for example, can help them explore the reasons for their problems and, ideally, work out a solution. The American Association for Marriage and Family Therapy can help couples find a local qualified marriage counselor. Couples can also ask for help from their friends, family, or members of the clergy.

Separation and Divorce

If a married couple decides that their marriage has broken down and cannot be repaired, the partners usually have several legal options:

- **Separation.** The couple may decide to live apart. This may be for a short cooling-off period, or it may be permanent. In either case, the couple is still legally married and may reunite at any time.

- **Divorce.** A divorce is a court order that legally ends a valid marriage. After a divorce is final, each partner may legally remarry.

Separation

Just as the process for beginning a marriage is governed by state law, so is the process of ending a marriage. Some of the states require a couple to live apart for some period prior to obtaining a final divorce. This period can range from a few months to more than a year. During this time, both spouses can consider the consequences of ending the marriage and can get their affairs in order so that they can go on with their separate lives.

separation agreement a written document that lists the continuing legal rights and duties of each spouse when a couple separates, including alimony, child custody, support, and division of property

If a married couple chooses to separate, they still have legal and financial responsibilities to each other and to their children. They remain spouses, and neither can legally remarry. For these reasons, a **separation agreement** is a good idea. This is typically a written document that sets out the couple's agreed-upon terms for child custody and visitation, child and spousal support, division of property, and other issues. It is often the result of a negotiation between the spouses or, in some cases, a judge's order.

After the couple signs a separation agreement, it becomes a legally enforceable contract. For example, if one spouse refuses to pay promised support money or will not leave the home as agreed, he or she can be taken to court by the other.

A separation agreement can say almost anything the couple wants it to say. Separation agreements do not have to be approved by a court. After the parties have agreed to the terms of the contract, each side must abide by it. However, in certain cases, the partners may choose to go to court to have a judge approve the agreement. In this case, after it is signed, the agreement cannot be changed unless the court changes it or both spouses agree to the change. If a couple later decides to seek a divorce, the terms of the separation agreement usually form the basis for the final divorce **decree,** which is issued by the court. For this reason, it is useful for each party to get legal advice before signing a separation agreement.

decree an official decision of a court, setting out the facts found in a case and the legal results. It orders that the court's decision (for example, a divorce decree) be carried out.

Divorce

Divorce rates rose very rapidly from 1960–1980 but have been generally declining since then. The rate of divorce is lower for couples with college degrees than for those without them. **Divorce** is the process by which a couple legally ends their marriage and divides their property. This does not mean, though, that the couple's legal relationship is ended. There may be continuing financial obligations and, if there are children, continuing rights and responsibilities that the parents must share.

divorce the ending of a marriage by court order

Ending a marriage can be expensive. Legal fees, alimony, child support payments, and the cost of maintaining two households are likely to pose a financial challenge. Divorce can also be emotionally difficult for all those involved—the spouses, children, friends, and extended family. This is why it is important that couples carefully consider this step, which will have long-term effects on their lives and the lives of their children.

▼ Blended families are formed when parents with children from previous relationships get married. *Describe the challenges a divorcing couple might face.*

Second or third marriages can bring additional challenges. There may be existing alimony, child support payments, or debts to resolve. Children and parents from previous marriages often form a "blended family." Children gain stepparents, and spouses gain stepchildren.

Jack Hollingsworth/Corbis/age fotostock

▲ Resources are available for children who are affected by divorce.

For all these reasons, a couple should be aware that divorce is a serious step that will affect them and their children for the rest of their lives. A couple should not decide to seek a divorce in the heat of anger or without at least trying to work out their problems. This is why states recommend—and some require—a period of separation before they will grant a divorce.

When they have decided to seek a divorce, couples can proceed in several ways. Some divorcing couples hire lawyers to prepare their cases. However, it is not always necessary to have attorneys involved in every aspect of a divorce. **Pro se** (or do-it-yourself) divorce kits and classes are available in many places. To learn more about this alternative, check with your local court, library, bookstore, or legal aid office. If the divorce involves disagreements over children, large sums of money, property, or anything else substantial, then each spouse should have an attorney or consult a family mediation service.

A family mediator can work with a couple to guide them through a series of negotiations designed to reach an agreement which satisfies both parties. Unless the divorce is pro se, the agreement is usually reviewed by each person's lawyer before being filed in court. Mediators sometimes can help divorcing couples reach a settlement without the time, expense, or hard feelings of the traditional adversary process. Working with a mediator can also be beneficial because the partners involved know the most about their own situation and are in the best position to devise solutions that will work. However, mediation will not always be a good option (e.g., in domestic violence cases).

PROBLEM 32.1

Bill and Rachel married when both were 19 years old. One year later, they had a baby. After two years of marriage, they fight constantly and are miserable. They are unsure about a divorce, but both think it might be better to live apart for a while. Bill works as an auto mechanic, making $2,200 a month. Rachel works as a teller in a local bank, making $1,750 a month. They rent an apartment for $850 a month and spend $600 a month on child care. They also have $2,000 of joint credit-card debt and own the following assets: $750 in a savings account; a used, but paid for, car worth $6,000; furniture and appliances.

a. Do Bill and Rachel have any choices besides divorce? Explain.

b. Do Bill and Rachel need a lawyer? Do they each need their own lawyer? Who else could help them?

c. List the things that Bill and Rachel must decide before agreeing to a separation.

A new approach to divorce, called **collaborative divorce,** is similar to family mediation. Collaborative divorce uses informal discussions and conferences attended by both parties and their lawyers to settle all issues. Lawyers agree to withdraw from the case if their clients decide to contest the divorce in court. This provides an incentive for the parties to collaborate and not litigate. Other specialists, such as child development and financial experts, sometimes have a role in the process. Lawyers who do this work have special training.

At one time, most states allowed divorce only if one spouse could show that the other spouse had done something wrong or was at fault. Typical faults, or grounds for divorce, under this system included:

▲ Typical grounds for divorce include mental and physical cruelty. *Why have many states changed their laws to include no-fault divorce?*

- **adultery,** or sexual intercourse between a married person and someone other than his or her spouse;
- abandoning one's spouse or **desertion,** with no intention of returning or of reassuming the duties of marriage;
- acts of emotional or psychological abuse that are considered to be **mental cruelty** against one's spouse;
- acts of violence or physical abuse that constitute **physical cruelty** against one's spouse; and
- some form of mental illness or **insanity.**

Proving that one spouse was at fault was often difficult, and divorce tended to cause great embarrassment. In many cases, a finding that one spouse was at fault would preclude him or her from receiving any support after the marriage ended.

The laws have changed and most states now also maintain a **no-fault divorce** system. To obtain a no-fault divorce, one spouse does not have to prove that the other spouse did something wrong. Instead, a spouse has to show only that there are disagreements that cannot be resolved, or **irreconcilable differences.** The marriage has completely broken down and is beyond repair. Many states also allow divorce when a couple can show that they voluntarily lived apart for a certain period of time—several months to more than a year, depending on state law—whether or not it was a formal period of separation.

Many states still have laws allowing divorce based on the fault grounds listed above. Most couples who choose to get a divorce do not use these fault grounds; instead they obtain no-fault divorces.

However, some argue that divorce has been made too easy and that divorce rates would go down if states required proof of fault before

collaborative divorce a form of divorce that involves informal discussions and conferences attended by both parties and their lawyers to settle all issues

adultery voluntary sexual intercourse between a married person and someone other than his or her spouse

Investigating the Law Where You Live

Find out the grounds for divorce in your state. Does your state allow no-fault divorce? How long does it take to obtain a divorce in your state?

Ingram Publishing/SuperStock

desertion the act of abandoning one's spouse with no intention of returning or of reassuming the duties of marriage. Desertion is usually grounds for divorce.

mental cruelty acts of emotional or psychological abuse against one's spouse

physical cruelty acts of violence or physical abuse against one's spouse

insanity a defense used in criminal law cases. The insanity defense varies from state to state and is based on the idea that the defendant could not tell right from wrong.

no-fault divorce a divorce in which neither party is charged with any wrongdoing. The marriage is ended on the grounds that there are irreconcilable differences (i.e., basic disagreements) that caused the marriage to break down.

irreconcilable differences disagreement between a couple that is grounds for a no-fault divorce

covenant marriage a special type of marriage in which the couple surrenders, in advance, their right to a no-fault divorce

custody the care and keeping of something or someone, such as a child

granting a divorce. Partially in response to this argument, some states have lengthened the time it takes to get a no-fault divorce. On the other hand, forcing a couple to stay married until fault can be proven can perpetuate domestic violence.

Several states have passed a law enabling couples who are planning to marry to choose a **covenant marriage** instead of obtaining a regular license to marry. Couples choosing a covenant marriage agree in advance—in writing—to make no-fault divorce more difficult to obtain. For example, a state covenant marriage law might require a longer period of separation—up to several years—before a no-fault divorce could be granted. Covenant marriages aim to reduce the divorce rate by limiting access to relatively easy divorces and encourage lifelong commitments by both partners. In some states couples who are already married also have the option to convert their existing marriage to a covenant marriage.

PROBLEM 32.2

a. The divorce rate is lower now than it was 30 years ago. Develop a hypothesis to explain why.

b. Explain the difference between a fault divorce and a no-fault divorce.

c. Do you think that couples should be allowed to obtain no-fault divorces? What are the arguments in favor of allowing no-fault divorce? Should couples wanting to divorce be required to demonstrate fault by one party? What are the reasons to require demonstration of fault?

d. Do you think states should make it harder or easier to get a divorce? Why?

Child Custody

If a couple with children separate or divorce, important questions arise: Who will take care of the children? With whom will the children live? In legal terms, the question is: who will have **custody** of the children?

Custody decisions are important because the parent with custody decides most aspects of the child's life, such as where the child will live and go to school. Custody may be temporary, or it may be permanently awarded to one parent. After it is awarded, unless circumstances change significantly, it is rarely changed. For example, if the custodial parent became a drug addict, the court could order a change of custody.

The noncustodial parent is usually given visitation rights. He or she can visit with the child on certain days and at certain times of the year. Both parents are required to contribute to the support of a child. The parent who has custody makes these contributions in the day-to-day life of the child. The noncustodial parent makes these contributions in the form of a regular monetary payment to the parent who has primary custody of the child.

Sometimes courts award custody to both parents. With **joint custody,** both parents have full responsibility for the child's supervision, and both have an equal say in important issues such as schooling and religion. The child may live part-time with each parent but need not spend the same amount of time with each parent. For example, a child who attends school near one parent might spend school nights with that parent and weekends with the other parent.

Joint custody has become more common. Some state laws specify that joint custody is presumed to be the best option unless one parent proves unfit to raise the child. On the other hand, joint custody is successful only when both parents want responsibility for the child or children.

joint custody a custody arrangement in which divorced or separated parents have equal rights in making important decisions concerning their children; also called joint legal custody. Joint physical custody means shared parenting in which the child spends a significant amount of time with each parent. It is possible to have joint legal custody along with sole physical custody.

PROBLEM 32.3

Wilma and Robert are getting divorced. They have a four-year-old child. Both are employed full-time, and they plan to live about 10 miles apart after the divorce.

a. What are the advantages and disadvantages of a joint custody arrangement for Wilma and Robert?

b. What are the advantages and disadvantages of sole custody with visitation awarded to the noncustodial parent?

c. What other information would you want to know before deciding the best custody arrangement?

d. If they choose joint custody, will both Wilma and Robert have to agree to the arrangement? What will happen if they cannot agree?

▼ Noncustodial parents are usually allowed scheduled visits with their children. *Why do you think decisions regarding custody issues are among the most difficult a judge must make?*

tender years doctrine the presumption (now rejected by most states) that a young child is always better off living with his or her mother

best interest of the child a doctrine used to determine custody by examining factors that will best benefit a child

kinship care placement of a vulnerable youth in the continuous care and supervision of relatives who are not his or her parents as directed by a social services or other child welfare agency. Such an arrangement also often occurs informally.

▼ Many grandparents and other close relatives raise children whose parents cannot do so because of substance abuse, divorce, or other problems. *What is kinship care?*

If parents cannot agree on custody or the court does not approve their agreement, the decision is made by the court. Traditionally, the law presumed that young children were better off with their mothers. This presumption was called the **tender years doctrine.** Today, most states have laws that require courts to treat men and women equally in custody disputes.

In determining custody, courts apply a standard of what is believed to be in the **best interests of the child.** This is often difficult to determine. Courts consider factors such as the emotional and economic stability of the parents; which parent has stronger bonds with the child; and which parent has been the primary care provider. Courts often consider the children's desires, especially if they are old enough to understand the ramifications of their wishes or are over a certain age (in many states, age 12). To help with this decision, judges often assign a social worker to study the parents and children. The results of this study are used as the basis for a custody recommendation.

Increases in substance abuse, incarceration, divorce, and other family and community problems have resulted in many grandparents and other close relatives raising children whose parents cannot do so. This caregiving relationship is called **kinship care.** Several million children are being raised by a relative, more than half of the time a grandparent.

Many states have passed laws that allow grandparents to petition for visitation rights if the child's parents will not voluntarily grant visitation to them. However, challenges to these laws brought by parents have been upheld in many states. In a 2000 case, the U.S. Supreme Court struck down a state law that allowed visitation by any person who could show that such visitation would be in the best interests of the child. The Supreme Court was concerned that such a broad granting of visitation rights—even to family members, including grandparents—would undermine a parent's fundamental interest in the care, custody, and control of his or her children.

Some custody disputes become so bitter that one parent takes the children from the other parent and hides them. This action may involve moving permanently to another state or country, or the parent and children may move repeatedly to avoid being found. Thousands of parents have resorted to this illegal means of opposing a court's custody decision. Such abductions may account for the majority of children reported missing each year. The *Federal Parental Kidnapping Prevention Act* prevents parents who abduct their children from getting new custody orders in a different state. It also provides resources to help custodial parents locate their missing children.

▲ Some missing children may be the victims of parental abduction. *What laws have been passed to help address the issue of parental abduction?*

Each state also has a law stating that a valid custody decree entered in one state is valid in all states. Therefore, a parent without custody cannot usually remove his or her children from their home state and attempt to obtain a different custody order in another state. In addition, most states have statutes that make parental kidnapping or custodial interference—taking or hiding a child from a parent who has custody—a crime. To report a suspected child abduction, contact the National Center for Missing and Exploited Children at **www.missingkids.com**.

Alimony, Property Division, and Child Support

Since the development of no-fault divorce, most divorce disputes center on two issues: children and money. The major financial issues are alimony, child support, and property division. These issues are frequently negotiated between the parties on their own, through their attorneys, or in mediation. The parties then make a brief courtroom appearance to finalize the divorce.

U.S. Census Bureau statistics show that most women suffer financial hardship as a result of divorce, but most men experience financial improvement. This is not surprising, given the number of women who stay in the home to care for children, especially when the children are young. Upon divorcing, many women face financial hardship because they have been out of the workforce for a period of time, because a majority of children of divorced parents live primarily with their mothers, and because women sometimes face wage disparities in the workplace. In addition, some non-custodial parents are behind or not making child support payments. With increased government enforcement of support awards, the percentage of custodial parents receiving full support payments from non-custodial parents was at about 40 percent in 2017.

Alimony

alimony a court-ordered allowance a husband or wife (or an ex-husband/ex-wife) pays to his or her spouse after a legal separation, after a divorce, or while the case is being decided

Alimony, also called spousal support or maintenance, is money paid by one spouse to help support the other spouse after a divorce. It can cover household and personal expenses, work-related costs, educational expenses, and recreation costs. Alimony was traditionally paid by men to support their ex-wives, but the U.S. Supreme Court ruled in 1979 that state laws restricting alimony awards to women only were unconstitutional.

Alimony is based primarily on need, although the duration of the marriage is often a factor. As a result, alimony awards vary greatly from case to case. When awarding alimony, courts consider the couple's standard of living as well as the financial status and wage-earning capacity of each spouse. Sometimes **rehabilitative alimony** is awarded temporarily to help one spouse regain or develop job skills needed for future employment. Alimony is not awarded in all cases. The decision whether or not to award alimony and for how long is left to the discretion of the court, based on the circumstances of the case.

rehabilitative alimony after a divorce, money awarded to a spouse for the purpose of regaining or developing job skills

An important consideration in awarding alimony is how long the payments should continue. Many people advocate that alimony should continue until the spouse no longer has the financial need for it, which could mean that payments continue indefinitely. Other people, however, feel that such an arrangement undermines the goal of ending the relationship for good. They say that the purpose of alimony is not to equalize incomes forever but rather to give the disadvantaged spouse an opportunity to reestablish his or her life as an independent person after the divorce. Under this theory, support payments should be made for a limited period of time, thereby encouraging both parties to move on with their lives.

Alimony typically ends when the recipient marries a new partner.

▼ Property division is an important issue for couples getting divorced. *How are property division and alimony different?*

Note that alimony and property division are separate concepts that are related to the process of divorce. Property includes all physical possessions, income, and debt that have been acquired by the family during the marriage. Alimony consists of future payments of support money after the end of the marriage.

Property Division

Dividing property owned by the couple is another important issue during a divorce. It involves deciding who gets the house, the car, the furniture, the bank account and so on, as well as responsibility for debts. In general, property division is determined according to what the court considers to be fair and equitable for both spouses. The judge may consider the length of the marriage and the economic circumstances of each spouse, including employment history and future income-earning prospects.

The laws of the state in which the couple live will determine what happens to that property if the marriage ends. Nine states—Arizona, California, Idaho, Louisiana, Nevada, New Mexico, Texas, Washington, and Wisconsin—as well as Puerto Rico have old **community property** systems. These systems, generally derived from French and Spanish law, usually provide that all property acquired during the marriage belongs equally to both spouses, no matter who earns or purchases it. Regardless of the duration of the marriage, if the couple breaks up, either by death or divorce, each spouse is entitled to any separate property brought into the marriage, as well as one-half of the community property acquired during the marriage.

Most states follow a system of **equitable distribution** when dividing assets and debts at the end of a marriage. In these states, each spouse is entitled to his or her separate property acquired during the marriage. The marital property, however, is divided based on a variety of factors, including need, financial and nonfinancial contributions of each party to the acquisition of property, and length of marriage. The goals of equitable distribution are to balance ownership rights and claims by both spouses and to consider obligations each spouse has to third parties, such as children or lenders.

community property property acquired during a marriage that is owned by both husband and wife, regardless of who earned it or paid for it

equitable distribution a system for dividing property at the end of a marriage in which each spouse is entitled to his or her separate property brought into or acquired during the marriage. Marital property is divided according to factors such as need and length of the marriage.

PROBLEM 32.4

a. Lloyd and Veronica were married four months ago. Before they were married, Veronica inherited a large tract of land from her grandfather. Now that they are married, to whom does the land belong?

b. Frances and Leon are married and have two children. Frances is an architect making $75,000 a year. Leon is an artist who earns very little money. Frances uses some of her income to buy a vacation home. If Frances and Leon divorce, who owns the vacation home in a community property state? In an equitable distribution state?

c. Which is fairer: an equitable distribution or a community property system? Why?

THE CASE OF...

The Medical School Degree

Roberto and Marta Flores sought a divorce to end their 11-year marriage. At first, the case seemed simple. The couple had no children, little property to divide, and, with California's no-fault divorce law, seemingly little to argue about. However, at the time of the divorce, Roberto argued that he deserved part of his ex-wife's income as a physician because he had worked to support the family—and pay some of her tuition—while she went to school to earn her medical degree.

Roberto claimed that he was entitled to a share of Marta's total projected lifetime income as a doctor. He estimated that Marta was likely to earn over $3 million in twenty years of medical practice. She countered that while he might be entitled to reimbursement for part of the cost of her education, he is not entitled to share in the *potential future value* of her degree. She argued that there is no way to reasonably predict what she will earn in her career. She might decide to provide medical services in another country or to work in a community medical clinic where she would earn very little. In either case, her income could be far less than what Roberto predicts.

PROBLEM 32.5

a. What happened in this case? What is Roberto asking for?

b. What is fair reimbursement: the cost of Marta's education or the value in terms of her potential increased earnings? Explain your answer.

Child Support

Both parents still have a legal duty to support their children after divorce. Therefore, divorcing couples with children need an agreement or court order regarding child support. Usually, only one parent actually makes child support payments. The other parent—often the parent with primary physical custody—supports the child by taking care of daily needs such as food, clothing, and shelter. The level of support is based on the noncustodial parent's ability to pay and the amount necessary to cover the child's needs. Child support is usually paid until the child becomes an adult or is emancipated, unless the parties agree to a longer period of support, such as through college.

When one parent fails to provide the agreed-upon financial support, the other may seek a court order requiring payment. The *Family Support Act of 1988 (FSA)* was passed by Congress to help in enforcing support orders. Child support guidelines are set by each state and also by Native American groups. This law requires states to expand their child support enforcement procedures and parent-locating services. The guidelines consider many factors, including both spouses' incomes and the number and ages of their children. Some deviation from these guidelines is allowed, but a court must provide clear reasons for such a variation. The FSA allows child support payments to be deducted from a parent's salary and permits states to track parents by means of their Social Security numbers and other data.

Each of the following situations involves a divorce. Should either spouse pay alimony, child support, or both? If so, which spouse should pay what? How much should be paid, and for how long?

a. Miguel, a successful plumbing contractor, earns $75,000 per year. His wife, Carmen, stays at home and takes care of their four children. When Miguel and Carmen divorce, the two older children—a junior in high school and a freshman in college—wish to stay with Miguel. The two younger children prefer to stay with Carmen.

b. Angela, a government social worker, divorces her husband, Leroy, an occasionally employed freelance writer. He has been staying home, taking care of their two-year-old son. Angela's yearly salary is $33,000; Leroy has earned $6,000 in the past 12 months. The child will live with his mother.

Stepparents

After divorce, many people remarry and create new blended families. More and more families in the United States include stepparents who can play important roles in the lives of children, especially when married to custodial parents. The relationship that develops is different in every family. In many cases, a stepparent takes on a role that is different from a birth parent but something like an additional parent.

State laws vary about the rights and responsibilities of stepparents. In a few places, stepparents are required to support their stepchildren as long as they are living with them. In some places, if the stepparent has acted **in loco parentis,** or in place of the parent, this responsibility may continue after the stepchild has moved out. If the marriage ends in divorce, stepparents usually cannot claim custody of the stepchild, though they may be able to seek visitation rights.

Stepparents are not considered full legal parents unless they adopt their stepchildren. Adoption is usually only possible if the child's noncustodial parent consents, dies, or if a court has terminated the non-custodial parent's rights.

For example, assume that Jay and Marla marry and have a son, Brian. When Jay and Marla divorce, Brian lives primarily with Marla, and she marries Larry. Only if Jay consents to the adoption will Larry be able to adopt Brian because the adoption would end Jay's legal rights as Brian's parent.

in loco parentis Latin for "in place of a parent"; person or institution (such as a school) that is entrusted with a minor's care and has intentionally assumed some or all of the rights of a parent over the minor

▼ Many stepparents play an important role in the lives of their spouses' children. *What can stepparents do to become full parents?*

Kali Nine LLC/Getty Images

CHAPTER **33**
Government Support for Families and Individuals

▶ Many types of government support exist for families in need.

Since the Great Depression of the 1930s, Congress has passed laws creating social programs that provide economic, educational, and health benefits to millions of Americans. Government social programs are a continuing source of controversy in the United States, a society that prizes individualism, self-reliance, and free enterprise. The New Deal programs that were created to relieve suffering brought on by the Great Depression were met with gratitude by some and with outraged cries of "creeping Socialism" by others. Federal, state, and local governments spend tens of billions of dollars on social service programs each year. Even with these expenditures, millions of Americans live in poverty, unable to secure adequate housing, nutrition, and health care. As governments struggle with mounting deficits, support for social programs has become an increasingly contested issue.

Approximately 12 percent of Americans were living in poverty in 2017. According to the Census Bureau, nearly 40 million Americans lived below the poverty threshold in 2017. The federal government set this poverty threshold in 2019 at $25,094 for a family of four. The poverty rate is highest for persons under 18 and lowest for persons over 65.

Many Americans assume that government programs exist only to help the poor. However, some government programs offer benefits to families at all income levels. Programs that are directed toward lower income Americans include Temporary Assistance to Needy Families (TANF), Supplemental Nutrition Assistance Program (SNAP), Medicaid, and public housing. Programs that benefit Americans of all income levels include

Ingram Publishing

Social Security, Medicare, veterans' benefits, and unemployment compensation. In addition, some American families who are in the middle and upper income levels receive mortgage interest deductions—tax breaks for owning a home—on their income taxes each year.

PROBLEM 33.1

a. List five major causes of poverty in the United States. Which of these problems can government programs help solve? How? Which of these problems can government not solve? Explain the reasons for your answers.

b. Should people receiving money under social programs receive the same amount no matter what state they live in? Why or why not?

Economic Benefits for Individuals and Families

People of all income levels and in all living situations need, and often rely upon, economic benefits provided through government programs. For example, some people count on their Social Security benefits to help support them in their retirement. Others depend on welfare, SNAP, and Medicaid to provide for basic necessities for their children.

Social Security

When you apply for a job, your employer will ask for your Social Security number. While this may seem unimportant now, your Social Security number will be a valuable benefit when you retire. Social Security works like an insurance policy. When you work, social security taxes are automatically deducted from your wages by your employer, who pays a matching amount to the federal government. After you reach retirement age, you are entitled to benefits based on the amount of money you and your employers paid into the Social Security fund. To be eligible for Social Security benefits, a person must have worked at least 40 quarters (about 10 years) at jobs with Social Security contributions.

Most Americans—men, women, and children—have Social Security protection either as workers or as dependents of workers. However, not all Americans are eligible to receive such benefits, including public sector employees who participate in a state government pension plan that provides benefits in replacement of social security. The following list summarizes some of the major provisions of the Social Security law.

- **Retirement benefits.** In order to receive full social security benefits, a person must wait until their full retirement age. Full retirement age depends on when a person was born; as of 2017 it was age 66 and two months. The full retirement age will increase by two months each year until it reaches age 67 for people born in or after 1960. The age at which a person retires makes a difference. Retiring later will increase the monthly benefit one receives.

- **Disability benefits.** Workers who are blind, injured, or too ill to work can receive monthly checks if the disability is expected to last at least 12 months or to result in death. Spouses and children of such workers are also eligible to receive benefits.
- **Survivor's benefits.** When a worker dies, their family becomes eligible to receive payments. This is like a government life insurance policy.

To illustrate how Social Security works, consider the case of Melody, a single parent with two children. Melody worked in a bakery for five years. She then became seriously ill and had to stop working. After a required waiting period, Social Security will send Melody and her children a monthly check until Melody is able to return to work. If Melody dies, Social Security will continue to provide benefit checks to each of her children until they reach age 18, or until they reach age 22 if they are full-time students.

Supplemental Security Income

The federal Supplemental Security Income (SSI) program provides money for elderly, blind, and disabled people who are in need. This program provides monthly benefits at a standard rate across the country. States may also provide benefits in addition to these federal benefits. To receive SSI benefits, a person must be age 65 or older, be legally blind, or have a major disability that prevents them from working for a year or more. Applications for SSI are handled by local Social Security offices.

Temporary Assistance to Needy Families

Until 1996, Aid to Families with Dependent Children (AFDC)—often referred to as "welfare"—was the joint federal-state program that provided aid to needy families with dependent children.

AFDC was controversial. Critics argued that welfare discouraged people from working because welfare payments were reduced when income from employment increased. Others argued that it broke up families, because many states would not pay AFDC benefits if the father lived in the home. Still others contended that the programs cost too much.

In response to some of the controversy surrounding AFDC, Congress passed the *Personal Responsibility and Work Opportunity Reconciliation Act of 1996*, which replaced AFDC with Temporary Assistance to Needy Families (TANF). This law changed welfare dramatically. TANF has considerably changed the way welfare benefits are granted and administered.

▼ Workers who are blind can receive Social Security benefits. *What other types of benefits are available through Social Security?*

Realistic Reflections

TANF has a much stricter work requirement than AFDC had. In order to receive benefits under TANF, most recipients must work, volunteer, or attend a vocational program for at least 20 hours a week or risk losing benefits, depending on the state's program. Recipients also receive at least one year of health care benefits while they are making the transition from welfare to work.

There are other restrictions on receiving TANF benefits. For example, many families with an adult who has received federal assistance for a total of five years may not receive cash aid under TANF. Many immigrants to the United States, regardless of whether they are documented or undocumented, are barred from receiving TANF benefits. Parents who are still minors themselves are required to live in an adult-supervised home and to continue their education or receive vocational training in order to qualify for benefits.

TANF also requires states to set up and maintain child-support payment enforcement programs. The law provides rules and procedures that make it easier to monitor and track parents who are delinquent on child-support payments. The law also makes it easier to establish paternity for child-support purposes.

▲ Many welfare offices have been renamed "empowerment centers." *How does this change reflect changes in federal welfare law?*

Supplemental Nutrition Assistance Program (SNAP)

Nearly 15 million households were "food insecure" in 2018, meaning that they lacked reliable access to a sufficient amount of affordable, nutritious food. SNAP (formerly food stamps) provides a safety net by helping low-income people buy food. As of 2017, benefits average about $1.40 per person per meal. SNAP benefits can only be used to purchase food and are available to low-income households that purchase and prepare their meals together. The program targets people most in need, such as households with children or an elderly or disabled person. Even full-time workers can be eligible for SNAP benefits if their gross income is below 130 percent of the poverty line. Legal immigrants who have lived in the United States for at least five years and legal immigrants who are children or disabled can apply for SNAP benefits. Undocumented immigrants are not eligible.

The SNAP program is funded primarily by the U.S. Department of Agriculture. While there are national standards, states may implement certain restrictions, such as disqualifying a person who owns a car valued over a certain amount from receiving SNAP benefits. SNAP benefits are given each month on a plastic card called an Electronic Benefit Transfer (EBT) card that works like a debit card and can be used in retail stores. This system reduces loss, theft, and fraud, and it reduces the stigma for customers who no longer have to redeem paper food stamps. Those who receive SNAP benefits are also required to engage in work and training activities similar to those required under TANF.

Unemployment Compensation and Veterans Benefits

Unemployment insurance is a joint state-federal program that provides temporary income for eligible workers who lose their jobs through no fault of their own. Each state sets its own requirements for eligibility, benefit amounts, and length of time benefits can be paid.

The United States Department of Veterans Affairs (VA) is an agency of the federal government that offers a wide variety of benefits and services to veterans, including health care. Eligibility for most VA benefits is based upon honorable discharge from the active military.

Investigating the Law Where You Live

Find out what public housing options if any exist in your community. What services do they provide?

▼ Homeowners receive tax deductions on the interest paid as part of their mortgage loans. *Why was this benefit created? Does it help all homeowners?*

PROBLEM 33.2

Governments in Canada and many countries in Europe provide their citizens with far more benefits than the U.S. government provides to its citizens. However, citizens in nations with more benefits pay higher taxes to finance these "safety net" programs that provide support for those in need. This difference reveals contrasting views about the role government should play in protecting citizens from hunger, homelessness, and illness.

a. What is your view of government safety net programs?

b. What costs would U.S. taxpayers face if the government were to expand our safety net programs?

c. What costs might we face if we decide to reduce safety net programs?

Housing Assistance and Mortgage Interest Deductions

Federal, state, and local governments offer programs designed to provide low-income people with housing assistance. These programs include government-operated housing projects, direct payments of portions of rent, and low-interest loans and insurance to help people buy their own homes.

The mortgage interest deduction is a provision under the federal tax code that allows homeowners to reduce their taxable income by the amount of interest paid on their home loan. This benefit was designed to encourage home ownership and make homes more affordable, so these deductions are enjoyed by those who are able to buy their own homes. Although there are a number of first-time

Housing Assistance

On any day in the United States in 2017, more than 500,000 people—one-fourth of them children—could be homeless. Many of the homeless are employed but cannot afford existing housing. Experts estimate that more than half of the families eligible for federal housing assistance do not receive it. Information about renting and federal rental assistance programs is available from the U.S. Department of Housing and Urban Development at **www.hud.gov/rental_assistance.**

home buyer programs to help lower-income families buy homes, the majority of people that benefit from this deduction are from middle and higher income brackets.

Health Benefits

Access to affordable health care is a problem of great and growing importance in the United States. As of 2019 more than 30 million Americans had no health insurance and millions more were underinsured.

In 2010, Congress passed *The Patient Protection and Affordable Care Act*. This law requires many employers to provide access to health insurance to their employees and expands Medicaid coverage for needy families. In addition, the law requires most Americans (unless they have a religious objection) to purchase health insurance. This section of the law is often referred to as the "individual mandate" requirement. The individual mandate proved most controversial. In 2012, the law was challenged in the U.S. Supreme Court. The federal government argued that it had the ability to pass this legislation under the government's powers to regulate interstate commerce set forth in Article I, Section 8, Clause 3 of the U.S. Constitution. Opponents of the legislation disagreed and contended that it was unconstitutional for the federal government to require a person to purchase health insurance. The Supreme Court upheld the law but not because of the federal government's interstate commerce power. Instead the Court viewed the penalty for not complying with the individual mandate as a federal tax supported under the Sixteenth Amendment's taxing power. In December 2017 Congress passed a tax bill that eliminated the tax penalty for individuals without health insurance.

Medicare

Medicare is a federal health insurance program for people age 65 or older. It also aids people of any age with permanent kidney failure requiring dialysis or a transplant, as well as certain disabled people. Those

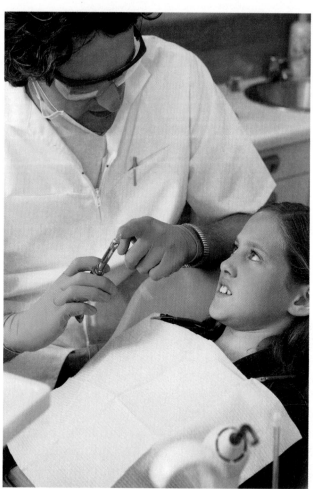

receiving Medicare can usually obtain medical care through physicians of their own choosing. Medicare has two parts: hospital insurance and medical insurance. Hospital insurance helps pay for major hospital expenses and certain follow-up care, such as hospice care and some health care. Medical insurance helps pay for physicians' office fees, physical and occupational therapists, and other medical expenses, including prescription drug coverage. Local Social Security Administration offices receive applications for Medicare, assist people in filing claims, and provide information about the program.

Medicaid

Medicaid is a government program that provides private medical care to low income and disabled people. The program is jointly funded by the federal and state governments and administered by the states. It covers most common medical services, including hospital and outpatient care, nursing-home services, hearing aids, eyeglasses, prescription drugs, dental care, physicians' office fees, medical supplies, and transportation to and from hospitals or doctors' offices.

Recipients of Temporary Assistance to Needy Families may also be eligible for Medicaid benefits, with a few exceptions. Depending on the state in which they live, recipients of Supplemental Security Income may automatically receive Medicaid.

For example, a single adult who fails to meet the work requirement may not be eligible for Medicaid. Most Medicaid expenditures go to persons over age 65 or to those who are blind or totally disabled. Elderly and disabled persons are eligible for Medicaid if they are U.S. citizens or legal immigrants, live in the state where they apply, and have an income below a set amount.

▲ In addition to hospital care, Medicaid also provides dental care. *What other services are covered by Medicaid?*

Investigating the Law Where You Live

Learn more about where in your community a person can apply for Medicare and Social Security benefits.

PROBLEM 33.3

a. Do you think having some form of health insurance is a necessity? Should access to affordable health care be thought of as a right? Explain your answers.

b. Should the government be able to force Americans to purchase health insurance or face financial penalties? Why or why not?

Fancy Photography/SuperStock

Family and Medical Leave Act

In 1993, Congress passed the *Family and Medical Leave Act (FMLA)* to help parents who want to stay at home with their babies, as well as workers who need time off to care for ailing relatives. The legislation guarantees working adults up to 12 weeks of unpaid leave during any 12-month period for any of the following reasons: (1) for the birth and care of the employee's child, (2) for the placement of a child for adoption or foster care with the employee, (3) to care for a spouse, child, or parent who is suffering from a serious health condition, (4) to take medical leave when the employee is unable to work because of a serious health condition, or (5) for qualifying emergencies that arise when the employee's spouse, child, or parent is on covered active military duty or has been notified of an upcoming order to active duty. In addition, the *FMLA* provides eligible employees up to 26 weeks of unpaid leave to care for a covered service member with a serious illness or injury.

The *FMLA* does not apply to everyone. For example, only employers with 50 or more employees are covered by federal law.

Employees who are eligible for *FMLA* leave are usually restored to their former job or an equivalent position after their leave is over. However, there is an exception for "key employees" who are the most highly paid employees in the company or region. In their cases an employer may be able to deny their reinstatement after taking *FMLA* leave if the reinstatement would cause serious economic injury to the employer's operation.

In addition to the *FMLA*, several states have passed their own family and/or medical leave laws. These laws usually mirror the federal law but also provide some additional protections.

Educational Benefits

Government support for educational benefits ranges from primary and secondary public education to child development programs for younger children. Some states also provide financial assistance for obtaining a higher education. In addition, grants and loans are available through the federal government.

Elementary and Secondary Public Schools

The government is involved in education at all levels. Both state and local governments are responsible for providing public elementary and secondary education for all students. In fact, state and local governments decide most education policy. Typically, approximately 12 percent of the funding for elementary and secondary schools comes from the federal government. State and local governments fund their public schools primarily through a combination of state income taxes and real property taxes. All 50 state constitutions provide for the right to a public education. Children between certain ages—typically 6 through 16—are required to attend school. Federal law requires schools to provide special educational services to students with physical and mental disabilities.

PROBLEM 33.4

The U.S. Constitution does not provide a legal right to education, and the responsibility for public education in this country has historically been left to the individual states. Although each state constitution provides children in that state with the right to a public education, they do not necessarily provide children with the resources for any particular quality of education. Because public schools are funded largely from property tax revenue, wealthy communities are able to generate more revenue to spend on educating their children than are lower income communities. As a result, students in the wealthier districts are, on average, better prepared for college or for jobs. Some argue that this resource disparity violates the principle of "equal opportunity for all" and urge states to provide funds to equalize spending across the state regardless of local property tax revenues.

a. What are two arguments that would support such a policy?

b. What are two arguments that could be used to oppose such a policy?

c. What is your view? Explain.

Investigating the Law Where You Live

What early childhood education programs exist in your community?

Head Start and Early Head Start

Head Start and Early Head Start are programs run by the U.S. Department of Health and Human Services. These comprehensive child development programs serve children from birth to age five, pregnant women, and their families. These programs are administered through the coordination of local, state, and federal governments in an effort to increase school readiness of young children in from low-income families. Head Start and Early Head Start provide a range of services in education and early childhood development; medical, dental, and mental health; nutrition; and parental involvement. The programs are designed to respond to each child's and family's individualized developmental, ethnic, cultural, and linguistic needs.

Colleges and Universities

States also provide funds for higher education. Many four year colleges and universities as well as almost all community colleges are operated by the state. Tuition at these institutions is generally less expensive than at private colleges and universities and may be further reduced for students who are residents of the state.

States generally provide some funding, such as scholarships, grants and loans, for college students to finance their college education. However, the vast majority of college students who seek financial aid to pay for college receive that aid through the federal government and private loan and grant programs.

Grants Federal Pell Grants are available from the U.S. Department of Education to financially eligible students to obtain an undergraduate or professional degree. These are grants that do not have to be repaid, unlike loans which require repayment. Federal Opportunity Grants are available to undergraduate students with exceptional financial need. The most comprehensive government website for grants for education is www.ed.gov. At this site you can search and apply for grants and signup for e-mail alerts about federal funding.

Federal Work Study The Federal Work Study (FWS) Program supplies colleges and universities with funds to provide jobs, usually on-campus, for financially needy undergraduate and graduate students. In addition to on-campus jobs, students may work at a federal, state, or local public agency, a private nonprofit organization, or a private for-profit organization as part of their involvement in the FWS program. This program enables students to earn at least federal minimum wage to help them pay for their educational expenses while attending school. In addition, the Federal Work Study Program can help students gain valuable work experience in their chosen field of study before they leave school.

Loans Loan programs are available from the U.S. Department of Education (www.studentaid.ed.gov) to help students finance their college degrees. A variety of federal education loans exist. Some loans go to the students directly, while others go to the students' parents. All loans, regardless of the program or the source, must be repaid. A range of financial assistance is available directly from colleges and universities, including loans, scholarships, tuition waivers, grants, fellowships and employment opportunities.

Various branches of the military offer special college loan repayment programs as enlistment incentives. The student makes a commitment to serve in the military, and in return the military pays a set percentage of the student's outstanding loan after each year of military service.

Student loans are a part of a young person's life long after he or she has graduated from college. So it is important to give careful thought to how much debt to incur and then to develop a realistic plan for loan repayment in the future.

▲ Many campus jobs are part of the Federal Work Study Program that helps college students earn money for school expenses. *What other options exist for college students in need of financial assistance?*

UNIT 6
Individual Rights and Liberties

netw⊙rks

Many of the topics in Unit 6 are controversial ones. Reasonable people often disagree about these issues; and over time, courts and legislatures sometimes change the law in these areas. The debates continue over speech and religious rights, abortion, sexual harassment, and discrimination. These issues can be divisive. But at the same time, the Bill of Rights and our civil rights laws are the hallmarks of the extraordinary freedom Americans have in the area of political and social rights.

◀ Dr. Martin Luther King, Jr., championed the cause of individual rights and liberties for everyone.

CHAPTERS IN BRIEF

CHAPTER 34
Introduction to Constitutional Law

Chapter 34 introduces the study of constitutional law. It describes how the Constitution establishes the basic framework of government and how the Bill of Rights protects basic individual rights.

CHAPTERS 35–37
Freedom of Speech, Freedom of the Press, Expression in Special Places

These chapters focus on freedom of expression and its importance in maintaining a democracy. The chapters investigate the scope of the government's ability to regulate expression and, in some instances, to prevent and punish it.

CHAPTER 38
Freedom of Religion

Chapter 38 explains how the establishment clause and the free exercise clause work together to ensure that religious freedom is protected. The chapter provides examples in which the right of individuals to practice their religion sometimes clashes with the government's obligation not to establish or favor any religion.

CHAPTER 39
Due Process

Chapter 39 explores the concept of due process, which concerns both fair procedures and protection from government interference with certain rights.

CHAPTER 40
The Right to Privacy

Chapter 40 focuses on the contested right to privacy.

CHAPTER 41
Discrimination

Chapter 41 deals with discrimination law and the controversial issue of affirmative action.

▶ The U.S. Constitution was signed in Independence Hall in Philadelphia, Pennsylvania.

The U.S. Constitution is the framework of our government that establishes the executive, legislative, and judicial branches. It is also the supreme law of the land, which all public officials are bound by oath to enforce. Moreover, the Constitution guarantees each American certain basic rights.

One remarkable feature of the U.S. Constitution is its endurance. It is the oldest written national constitution in the world that is still in use. Another remarkable feature of the Constitution is its ability to adapt itself to changing conditions.

Photographs in the Carol M. Highsmith Archive, Library of Congress, Prints and Photographs Division [LC-DIG-highsm-12311]

Amendments to the Constitution

The Founders of the United States anticipated that the Constitution might have to be changed. Therefore, they provided two methods of proposing **amendments,** or changes, to the Constitution. The first method is by a two-thirds vote of both houses of Congress; the second is by a national convention called by Congress at the request of the legislatures in two-thirds of the states. After it is proposed, an amendment does not take effect unless it is ratified either by the legislatures in three-fourths of the states or by special ratifying conventions in three-fourths of the states.

The original Constitution, adopted in 1787, contained only a few provisions guaranteeing individual rights. However, citizens pressured their leaders to add a Bill of Rights. In response, the first ten amendments were adopted by Congress in 1791 and quickly ratified by the states.

These first ten amendments contain many of our basic rights. The First Amendment protects the freedoms of religion, speech, press, assembly, and petition. The Second Amendment protects the right of the people to bear arms. The Third Amendment protects against the quartering of soldiers in private homes, and the Fourth Amendment protects against unreasonable searches and seizures.

The Fifth Amendment provides a right to **due process** of law—fair procedures that are required when government action affects your rights—and gives certain rights to accused people, including protection against self-incrimination. The Sixth Amendment provides the rights to a lawyer, an impartial jury, and a speedy trial in criminal cases.

The Seventh Amendment provides for jury trials in civil cases. The Eighth Amendment prohibits cruel and unusual punishment as well as excessive bail or fines. The Ninth Amendment declares that the rights spelled out in the Constitution are not the only rights that people have. Finally, the Tenth Amendment reserves any powers not belonging to the federal government to the states and the people.

The Bill of Rights was designed to protect Americans against the overuse of power by the *federal* government. Nothing in the unamended Constitution specifically requires *state* governments to abide by the Bill of Rights. But in interpreting the Fourteenth Amendment, which was ratified after the Civil War, the U.S. Supreme Court has applied most protections in the Bill of Rights to the state and local levels of government.

In addition to the Bill of Rights, later amendments provide other important rights. The Thirteenth Amendment forbids slavery and outlaws involuntary servitude, except as punishment for a crime. The Fourteenth Amendment requires **equal protection** of the laws for all citizens. It also provides that no *state* can deprive any citizen of "life, liberty, or property without due process of law."

▲ As this painting *His First Vote* (1868) by Thomas Waterman Wood shows, African American men won the right to vote when the Fifteenth Amendment became law. *How did the Fourteenth and Fifteenth Amendments expand civil rights in the nation?*

amendment (1) one of the provisions of the U.S. Constitution enacted after the original Constitution became law; (2) an addition or change to an existing document or plan

due process the idea stated in the Fifth and Fourteenth Amendments that every person involved in a legal dispute is entitled to a fair hearing or trial. The requirements of due process vary with the situation, but they basically require notice and an opportunity to be heard.

equal protection a constitutional requirement of the Fourteenth Amendment that protects individuals against unlawful discrimination by government

Several amendments protect and broaden the right to vote in federal and state elections. The Fifteenth Amendment forbids denying the right to vote based on race or color. The Nineteenth Amendment gives women the right to vote. The Twenty-third Amendment gives citizens of Washington, D.C., the right to vote in presidential elections. The Twenty-fourth Amendment prohibits poll taxes. The Twenty-sixth Amendment gives all people 18 years of age or older the right to vote.

PROBLEM 34.1

a. The following are some of our most basic and important rights. Based on your opinion, rank these rights in order from the most important to the least important. Explain your rankings.

- Right to counsel
- Right to a jury trial
- Right to freedom of religion
- Right to freedom of speech
- Right to be free from self-incrimination
- Right to bear arms
- Right to freedom of the press
- Right to be free from cruel and unusual punishment
- Right to assemble peacefully
- Right to vote

b. In recent years, constitutional amendments have been proposed in the following areas. Which of these, if any, are needed? Explain.

- To provide for direct election of the president and vice president, abolishing the Electoral College
- To ensure that children who are citizens have a right to a free and adequate education
- To ensure the right of women to obtain an abortion
- To force Congress and the president to agree to a balanced budget, with overspending allowed only in the case of a three-fifths vote of Congress

Basic Constitutional Law Principles

To understand constitutional law, there are three basic ideas to keep in mind. First, the rights guaranteed in the Constitution are not, and cannot be, absolute. The unrestricted exercise of certain rights would, in some instances, restrict the rights of others.

For example, freedom of speech does not mean that anyone can speak about any topic at any time and place. Freedom of the press does not allow a person to intentionally publish false or harmful information about another person. And the freedom of religion does not protect every religious practice.

The courts have designed several "tests" to determine how cases should be decided when conflicts arise over the meaning of the Constitution. These tests are needed because the language of the Constitution is typically brief and often written in general terms. The words are not usually self-explanatory.

In this unit you will study many of the tests developed by the justices of the U.S. Supreme Court. These tests are rules that the Supreme Court requires courts to use in analyzing issues that arise in constitutional law cases. For example, suppose someone yells "Fire!" in a crowded theater as a joke. The exact words protecting freedom of speech are: "Congress shall make no law . . . abridging the freedom of speech . . ." Do these words adequately explain whether the police can arrest the person for shouting "Fire!" falsely?

To analyze this case, courts might use the **compelling interest test**. This means a judge would determine whether the government has a compelling (very important) interest in preventing people from panicking and possibly being hurt in response to someone falsely shouting "Fire!" in a crowded theater. The judge would probably conclude that a compelling interest does exist in this precise situation and that the speaker could be arrested without violating the speaker's First Amendment rights. Many other "tests" the SupremeCourt has developed for analyzing constitutional law cases will be presented throughout this unit.

The second basic idea in understanding constitutional law is that the Constitution protects citizens from certain actions by the *government*. Its protection usually does not extend to situations that are purely private; actions by private citizens, businesses, or organizations are generally not limited by the Constitution. For example, the Fourth Amendment protects against unreasonable searches and seizures by the government. It does not protect against searches and seizures by private individuals. Therefore, if a neighbor comes into your house and seizes your television, this act does *not* violate the Constitution. It may, however, constitute a tort, a crime, or both. As you will learn later, certain private actions, though not unconstitutional, have been made unlawful by congressional or state legislative action.

▲ The rights guaranteed in the Constitution cannot be absolute. *What other ideas basic to understanding constitutional law must you keep in mind?*

compelling interest test The compelling state interest test is satisfied when the government can show a that it has a very important interest that is promoted by the law or action in question and no way to satisfy that interest that interferes less with the rights of others.

The third idea basic to understanding constitutional law is that enforcing one's rights can be time-consuming and expensive. Before trying to enforce a right, you should be aware of the time and money involved. In addition, as noted, rights are not absolute. You might think you have a right in a certain situation and be willing to take the time and spend the money to enforce it. But a court might decide you do not have the right. However, you will study many cases in this unit in which the courts have recognized important individual rights.

Because of the importance of the U.S. Constitution, we sometimes assume that it contains all our rights. But many basic rights are also protected by state constitutions, as well as by laws passed by the U.S. Congress and by state and local legislatures.

The U.S. Constitution provides a so-called constitutional floor, or a minimum level of rights. This means that no government—federal, state, or local—can establish a lower level of legal rights than the level found in the U.S. Constitution. However, governments can be *more* protective of rights than what the Constitution requires. For example, the Supreme Court might find that the Constitution does not require the police to obtain a warrant before conducting a certain type of search. But a state government could pass a law that requires use of a warrant in that state for that same search. In such a case the state is protecting more rights than what the federal Constitution requires.

The individual rights discussed in this chapter can also be called human rights. The world community has adopted a Universal Declaration of Human Rights, as well as a number of other international documents whereby participating countries promise to work to protect these human rights. Most of the human rights included in the U.S. Bill of Rights can be classified as political or civil rights. However, other rights, classified as social and economic rights, are not included in the U.S. Constitution. These include the right to an adequate standard of living, housing, health care, and education.

Some people criticize the United States for acting as a leader in political and civil rights while ignoring the need for social and economic rights. Others say that such rights are not enforceable and that the government should consider them goals rather than enforceable rights.

PROBLEM 34.2

a. What is meant by the statement, "Rights are not absolute"? Give an example of a right that is not absolute, and explain why this is so.

b. How does the U.S. Supreme Court use tests? What test does the Court use when determining whether a state can use a confession obtained by police interrogation of a person in custody?

c. Give an example of an important economic right. Is it provided for in the Constitution? Should it be? Give your reasons.

► Our democracy requires vigilant protection of freedom of speech.

The freedom of speech clause of the First Amendment guarantees the right to express information and ideas. It protects all forms of communication: speeches, books, art, newspapers, telecommunications, and other media. The First Amendment exists to protect ideas that may be unpopular or different from those of the majority. The U.S. Constitution protects not only the person *making* the communication, but also the person *receiving* it. Therefore, the First Amendment includes the right to hear, to see, to read, and in general to be exposed to different messages and points of view. While courts are very protective of this right, freedom of speech, like other constitutional rights, is not absolute.

The Importance of Freedom of Speech

The First Amendment's protection of speech and expression is central to U.S. democracy. The essential, core political purpose of the First Amendment is self-governance: enabling people to obtain information from a diversity of sources, make decisions, and communicate these decisions to the government. In this sense, the First Amendment's protection of speech lies at the heart of an open, democratic society.

Beyond the political purpose of free speech, the First Amendment provides us with a "marketplace of ideas." Rather than having the government establish truth, freedom of speech enables truth to emerge from diverse opinions. People determine the truth by seeing which ideas have the power to be accepted in the marketplace of ideas. This underscores the United States' commitment to trusting the will of the people. The concept of a dynamic marketplace of ideas also encourages a variety of artistic and other creative expression that enriches our lives.

▲ The need for peace and public order must be balanced against the right to express individual opinion. *Why are conflicts involving freedom of expression so difficult to resolve?*

Related to self-government and the marketplace of ideas is the notion that a free, unfettered exchange of ideas and information gives society a "safety valve" that helps the people deal with change in a more orderly, stable way. Through discussion, society can adapt to changing circumstances without resorting to force. Those who disagree with a decision—and such disagreements are inevitable—may be more likely to go along with the majority if they have had a chance to voice their disagreement. The basic theory is that the best response to "bad" speech is "good" speech—as opposed to suppressing the "bad" speech.

The language of the First Amendment seems absolute: "Congress shall make no law . . . abridging the freedom of speech." Yet as the example of shouting "Fire!" falsely in a public place showed, freedom of speech is not absolute and was not intended to be. Nonetheless, the expression of an opinion or a point of view is usually protected under the First Amendment, even if most people disagree with the speaker's message. Remember, the First Amendment was designed to ensure a free marketplace of ideas— even unpopular ideas. Freedom of speech protects everyone, including people who criticize the government or express unconventional views. In some instances, the First Amendment provides people with a right *not* to speak and *not* to associate with others who propose a different message.

In 1943 the Supreme Court considered a case from West Virginia in which children who were Jehovah's Witnesses refused to participate in the pledge of allegiance to the flag at school and were expelled based on a state board of education rule that allowed this punishment. The students asked the Court to protect their right *not* to speak in this case. They argued that the First Amendment prohibited the state from compelling them to declare a specific political belief by saying the pledge of allegiance. While recognizing that the government could encourage national unity and good citizenship, the Court ruled in favor of the students, reversing a precedent from only three years earlier that had upheld the state's authority to require students to pledge allegiance to the flag in school.

In delivering the opinion of the Court, Justice Robert Jackson wrote these often quoted words: "If there is any fixed star in our constitutional constellation, it is that no official, high or petty, can prescribe what shall be orthodox in politics, nationalism, religion, or other matters of opinion, or force citizens to confess by word or act their faith therein."

a. A Supreme Court justice once wrote that the most important value of free expression is "not free thought for those who agree with us, but freedom for the thought we hate." What did the justice mean by this? Do you agree or disagree?

b. Can you think of any public statements or expressions of public opinion that made you angry? How did you feel about protecting the speaker's right to freedom of expression? What is the value of hearing opinions you dislike? What is the danger of suppressing unpopular thought?

c. Assume that the United States is fighting a war and you disagree with the decision to be involved in this war. If you decide to join protests against the war, some people will call you unpatriotic. Is there some way that protest—even during a time of war—can be considered patriotic? Explain.

Conflicts involving freedom of expression are among the most difficult ones that courts are asked to resolve. Free speech cases frequently involve a clash of fundamental values. For example, how should the law respond to a speaker who makes an unpopular statement to which the listeners react violently? Should police arrest the speaker or try to control the crowd? Courts must balance the need for peace and public order against the fundamental right to express one's point of view.

As already noted, freedom of speech may at times be limited by government action. Sometimes government can limit or punish speech because the content of the speech is not fully protected. For example, the First Amendment provides only limited protection to commercial speech and no protection to obscenity, defamation, fighting words, and incitement. Government can also regulate speech even when the content is protected. The section below on time, place, and manner restrictions deals with regulation of protected speech.

Sometimes expressive conduct that communicates through actions rather than words is protected. You will learn about this in the section on symbolic speech. Finally, you will study laws passed to restrict speech that are unenforceable, either because they are unclear and vague or because they are overinclusive, that is, they prohibit expression that should be protected.

Commercial Speech

Commercial speech receives limited protection by the Constitution. Most advertising is considered commercial speech, as is speech proposing a commercial transaction. At one time commercial speech received no protection by the courts. It was assumed that government could regulate commercial speech in much the same way that it could regulate business itself. Today, commercial speech does not receive the same

commercial speech speech that is directed at buying or selling of goods and services. The law treats commercial speech differently from political speech and other forms of expression.

high level of protection accorded to political speech, but most commercial speech receives at least some First Amendment protection.

A case in point involves a state that passed a law making it unprofessional conduct for pharmacists to advertise prescription drug prices. The state's concern was that such advertising might lead to aggressive price competition and ultimately to unprofessional, shoddy services by pharmacists. While the information in these ads was purely commercial, the Supreme Court struck down the law based on the argument that society's interest in information about products was more important than the state's interest in regulating advertising of prescription drugs. In addition, when states tried to ban all advertising by lawyers as being inherently misleading, the Court said that such a concern could not support a total ban on advertising by lawyers.

In general, courts allow government to ban commercial speech that is false or misleading or that provides information about illegal products. If information is not false or misleading and the product or service being advertised is legal, then the government is limited in the ways it can regulate commercial speech. The courts tend to look carefully at such government regulation to see if there is a good reason for it and whether the regulation itself is consistent with that good reason.

In one case the government wanted to keep manufacturers of alcoholic beverages from competing with each other in "strength wars," so it banned statements about alcoholic content on beer cans. A beer company sued,

▼ Commercial speech includes advertising. *In what ways can states regulate commercial speech?*

©TongRo Image Stock/Alamy

arguing that this violated the company's freedom of speech. The Supreme Court agreed with the beer company. While the government had a good reason for its concern about "strength wars," it did not make sense to ban alcohol content from beer labels but not, for example, from wine labels. In other words, the restriction did not sufficiently advance the government's interest.

Obscenity

The portrayal of sex in art, literature, and films and on the Internet is a troublesome topic in American society. Although the First Amendment guarantees freedom of expression, the government has the power to prohibit the distribution of obscene materials. In general terms, **obscenity** is anything that treats sex or nudity in an offensive or lewd manner, violates recognized standards of decency, and lacks serious literary, artistic, political, or scientific value.

As you might expect, courts have had difficulty developing a precise legal definition of *obscenity*. For example, in speaking about pornography, Justice Potter Stewart once said that he could not define it, "but I know it when I see it." In 1957, the U.S. Supreme Court ruled that obscenity is not protected by the Constitution. Later, in the 1973 case of *Miller* v. *California*,

obscenity a general term applying to anything that is immoral, indecent, or lewd

▼ Some people argue that laws meant to protect children from adult content on the Internet also block lawful and meaningful speech for adults. *Why has the Supreme Court found some efforts to protect children from adult content on the Internet unconstitutional?*

the Court set out the following three-part test as a guideline for determining whether expression is obscene:

1. Would the average person applying contemporary community standards find that the material, taken as a whole, appeals to prurient interest (an immoderate, unwholesome, or unusual interest in sex)?

2. Does the work depict or describe, in a patently offensive way, sexual conduct specifically outlawed by applicable state law?

3. Does the work, taken as a whole, lack serious literary, artistic, political, or scientific value?

Applying these standards, an anatomy textbook with pictures of nudity is not obscene, because it has scientific value. But a magazine appealing to prurient interests and filled with photos of nude people committing sexual acts prohibited by state law might be obscene.

Some state and local governments have developed new strategies through lawmaking to deal with pornography. Some communities have tried to ban all pornographic works that degrade or depict sexual violence against women. Such works, they argue, are a form of sex discrimination that may lead to actual violence or abuse against women. Other communities regulate adult bookstores and movie theaters through their zoning laws. Such laws restrict these stores and theaters to special zones or ban them from certain neighborhoods. Finally, most communities have passed laws outlawing child pornography (depictions of children involved in sexual activity) and greatly restricting minors' access to sexually oriented material. The Supreme Court has held that laws against child pornography are constitutional, even when the laws ban material that would not be obscene if it depicts adults.

In 2011 the Supreme Court decided a case in which the State of California tried to help parents guide their children's media choices by banning the sale or rental of violent video games. In a 7–to-2 decision, the Court found that video games are considered speech—in the same way that plays and movies are speech—and therefore entitled to First Amendment protection, even if some think they are offensive. Also, the tradition of allowing the state the power to limit obscenity does not give the state the power to restrict violent speech.

PROBLEM 35.2

a. Should the government be allowed to censor books, movies, the Internet, or magazines? If so, under what circumstances, and why?

b. Who should decide if a book or movie is obscene? What definition should be used?

c. Do you think books and movies that encourage violence against women or encourage racist views should be banned? Explain your answer.

d. Is there a problem with indecent material on the Internet? If so, what should be done about it?

THE **CASE** OF...

The Public Official's Lawsuit for Libel

On March 29, 1960, the *New York Times* printed an advertisement paid for by four African American clergymen. The ad was entitled "Heed Their Rising Voices." It called attention to the civil rights struggle in the South and appealed for funds to be used for various causes, including a legal defense fund for Dr. Martin Luther King, Jr., who had been indicted for perjury in Montgomery, Alabama.

The ad focused on the violence with which the civil rights movement had been met in Montgomery. A portion of the advertisement contained factual errors. For example, the ad said that truckloads of armed police ringed the Alabama State College campus when, in fact, the police were deployed near the campus but did not surround it. The ad also said that Dr. King had been arrested seven times, but he had actually been arrested only four times.

L. B. Sullivan was an elected commissioner of the city of Montgomery, Alabama, and he was responsible for the police department there. While the advertisement did not mention him by name, he contended that references to police included him. Sullivan sued the clergymen and the newspaper for libel in the Alabama courts and was awarded damages of $500,000.

On appeal, the U.S. Supreme Court reversed the decision. The Court viewed the advertisement as communicating information about a public issue of great concern. The Court said that debate on public issues must be "uninhibited, robust, and wide open" and that it may include "vehement, caustic, and sometimes unpleasantly sharp attacks on government and public officials." If critics had to guarantee the complete accuracy of every assertion, it would lead to self-censorship, not free debate.

In the case of *New York Times* v. *Sullivan*, the Court established a rule that a public official cannot recover damages for a defamatory falsehood relating to official conduct unless the official can prove the speaker either knew the statement was false or offered the statement with reckless disregard for its truth. In this case,

▲ Dr. Martin Luther King, Jr., under arrest

the U.S. Supreme Court said that the clergymen and the newspaper did not know the information in the advertisement was false and they did not offer it with reckless disregard for its truth.

In a later case, the Court extended this rule to cover lawsuits brought by all public figures—not just public officials.

PROBLEM 35.3

a. Do you agree or disagree with the U.S. Supreme Court's decision in this case? Explain the reasons for your answer.

b. Does the rule about public officials and public figures reduce the privacy rights of these people? Explain the reasons for your answer.

c. What rights and interests were balanced by the Supreme Court in deciding this case?

Defamation

The First Amendment does not protect defamatory expression. **Defamation** is a false expression about a person that damages that person's reputation. When defamation is spoken, it is called **slander.** Defamation published in a more lasting form—for example, a writing, film, compact disc, or blog—is called **libel.** For example, assume a patient said that her doctor was careless and had caused the death of patients. If others heard this remark, the doctor could sue the patient for slander if the statement had been false. If the patient had written the same thing in a letter, the suit would be for libel. However, if a statement—written or spoken, no matter how damaging or embarrassing—is proven to be true, the plaintiff cannot win a defamation suit in court.

The value placed on freedom of speech in the United States makes it difficult for public officials or public figures to win defamation suits. There is a concern that holding speakers, which include the press, legally responsible for comments about matters of public importance will "chill" or discourage expression.

THE **CASE** OF...

The Offensive Speaker

In 1948, Father Terminiello, a Roman Catholic priest, arrived to make a speech at a Chicago auditorium. Outside the auditorium about 300 people were picketing his speech. Inside, Terminiello criticized Jews and African Americans, as well as the crowd outside. By the time his speech was finished, 1,500 people had gathered outside. A police line prevented the protesters from entering the building. However, the "howling mob" outside was throwing stones and bricks at the building, and the police were unable to maintain control. The crowd was also yelling at and harassing people who came to hear Terminiello speak.

Terminiello was arrested and charged with disorderly conduct under an ordinance forbidding any breach of the peace. He was convicted, and his conviction was upheld in the Illinois courts. However, in a 5-to-4 decision, the U.S. Supreme Court reversed his conviction, ruling that the breach of the peace ordinance was vague and punished some speech that should have been protected.

PROBLEM 35.4

a. What happened in the Terminiello case? Why was he arrested?

b. Should the police have controlled the crowd instead of arresting Terminiello? Did the police violate his First Amendment rights? Why or why not?

c. What did the U.S. Supreme Court decide in this case? Why?

d. Under what circumstances, if any, should people be prohibited from voicing unpopular views? Explain your answer.

Fighting Words, Offensive Speakers, and Hostile Audiences

In addition to obscenity and defamation, there are a few additional situations in which the U.S. Constitution does not protect the content of a person's speech. When a person speaks publicly, two elements are interacting: the speaker and the audience. Protection of a person's speech by the First Amendment depends on how these elements interact in different situations. There are times when certain words may be protected and other times when the same words may not be protected because the surrounding situation is different.

The First Amendment does not protect you if you use words that are so abusive or threatening that they amount to what the U.S. Supreme Court calls **fighting words.** These are words spoken face-to-face that are likely to cause an imminent breach of the peace between the speaker and the listener. Fighting words are like a verbal slap in the face. They do not convey ideas or contribute to the marketplace of ideas. Their value is outweighed by society's interest in maintaining order. Still, courts very rarely use the "fighting words" doctrine today. Even offensive, provocative speech that makes its listeners very angry is generally protected and not considered to be fighting words.

In addition to analyzing face-to-face speech, the police must also decide how to handle the responses of a large audience to speech. Police action may depend on whether the audience is friendly or hostile toward the speaker and whether there is evidence that a serious danger exists if the speech continues.

In The Case of the Offensive Speaker, the police had to deal with an audience that disagreed with the speaker's message. The police must also deal with problems caused when the audience agrees with the message. For example, the government must decide how to deal with speakers who advocate illegal activities. Prior to the 1950s, the courts used the **clear and present danger test.** This test examined the circumstances under which a speech was made and determined whether a clear and present danger of unlawful action existed. The courts generally held that the unlawful action did not have to occur immediately after the speech, for example, when a speaker encourages the audience to overthrow the U.S. government. When there was a clear and present danger of unlawful activity, the government could punish the speaker.

In the early 1950s, the Supreme Court reflected the nation's concern with the Cold War and national security. In *Dennis* v. *United States* (1951), the defendants were convicted for attempting to organize the U.S. Communist Party, whose goal was to overthrow the government. In *Dennis,* the Court used a balancing test that downplayed the likelihood that the harm would occur. Instead, the Court balanced the right of the speaker against the harm the speaker proposed. When the speech advocated very dangerous acts, such as overthrowing the government, the Court required less proof of clear and present danger.

fighting words a legal term applying to words spoken face-to-face that are so abusive that they are likely to cause an imminent fight between the speaker and the person spoken to. Such words are not usually entitled to First Amendment protection.

clear and present danger test a test formerly used by courts to restrict speech when the government thought the speech would create an immediate danger of serious harm

In the 1969 case of *Brandenburg* v. *Ohio*, however, the Supreme Court began using the **incitement test** for cases in which the speaker urged the audience to take unlawful action. This test allowed the government to punish advocacy only when it was directed toward inciting, or producing immediate lawless action from, the audience and when the advocacy was likely to produce such behavior. Unlike the clear and present danger test, the incitement test required that the unlawful action be likely to occur within a short period of time. Therefore, the incitement test gives speakers greater protection.

For example, if a speech causes members of an audience to talk to one another in disagreement, the speaker might not be arrested. However, if the speech urges the audience to throw objects at others and the audience begins to do this, the speaker could be arrested. In practice, the police can face a difficult dilemma in deciding whether to arrest an unpopular speaker or try to control a hostile audience.

Hate Speech

In recent years there has been an effort to punish those who express views, called **hate speech,** motivated by bigotry and racism. This effort has sometimes run afoul of the First Amendment.

Those who support punishment for hate speech argue that strong measures should be taken because of the emotional and psychological impact hate speech has on its victims and its victims' communities. Furthermore, supporters of punishment argue that hate speech amounts to fighting words and thus does not qualify for First Amendment protection. Others argue that so-called speech codes designed to promote tolerance for minorities, women, and gays, while well-intentioned, are vague and difficult to enforce fairly. They claim that such speech codes put the government into the censorship business—favoring certain content or viewpoints and disfavoring others—in violation of the First Amendment. Legal battles over speech codes, primarily on public college and university campuses, have usually resulted in courts striking them down as First Amendment violations. Supporters of the First Amendment argue that the preferred approach to hateful speech is more speech—speech that rebuts bigotry and racism.

▼ White supremacists express views motivated by bigotry and racism. *What are the arguments in support of punishing hate speech? Against it?*

The Supreme Court confronted the issue of whether hateful speech receives First Amendment protection in the 2011 case of *Snyder* v. *Phelps*. In that case members of the Westboro Baptist Church—a group that believes that God hates and punishes America because of its tolerance of homosexuality, especially in the military—picketed near the funeral of Matthew Snyder, a Marine killed in Iraq. The picketers held up signs reading: "Thank God for Dead Soldiers" and "America is Doomed." Matthew Snyder's father saw the tops of the picketers' signs as he was leaving the funeral.

After finding out from news coverage what the signs said, he claimed to suffer extreme emotional distress and sued the Church members and leaders for damages. The Court held that even though the speech was offensive and hurtful to the family of the military officer, it was speech pertaining to public issues and thus entitled to the highest degree of First Amendment protection.

The legal result has been different, however, for state laws that increase criminal punishments for bias-motivated violence and intimidation. In 1993 the U.S. Supreme Court unanimously upheld a Wisconsin law that provides enhanced sentencing when the defendant "intentionally selects the person against whom the crime (is committed) because of . . . race, religion, color, disability, sexual orientation, national origin or ancestry. . . ." Most states now have similar laws providing enhanced penalties for bias-motivated crimes.

PROBLEM 35.5

A school district adopts the following policy: "A student or faculty member may be suspended or expelled for any behavior, verbal or physical, that stigmatizes an individual on the basis of race, ethnicity, religion, national origin, sex, sexual orientation, creed, ancestry, age, marital status, handicap, or veteran status."

a. Decide whether the following actions violate the above policy. If they do, should the student or faculty member be punished?

- After writing a limerick for an assignment, a student reads it aloud in an English class. It makes fun of the reported homosexual acts of a politician.

- A white student writes an article on race relations for the school newspaper. It states that African Americans are more likely than whites to become criminals in the United States, and this point is one reason whites do not mix more with African Americans.

- The athletic director schedules the varsity club's awards dinner on a major Muslim holiday. Several Muslim athletes are unable to attend.

- An African American student hears that a group of Chinese students will not socialize with African Americans. She calls them "typical Chinese racists."

- Wearing white robes and hoods, a white supremacist student group stages a silent march on campus.

b. What are the arguments for and against the above policy? Do you support or oppose it? Can it be improved? If so, how? Are there ways for students to take a stand against hate speech even if there is no code? Explain.

c. Should television and radio stations have their own rules similar to the above policy? Should other private businesses have similar rules? Give your reasons.

d. Think about how racial and ethnic slurs compare with fighting words. In what ways are they the same? How do they differ?

DELIBERATION

Should hate speech be banned in our democracy?

Free speech is essential in democracies. Self-government requires that citizens have accurate and timely information about issues facing their society. Free speech also allows people to advocate for issues important to them, encounter perspectives that are different from their own, and express their complaints with government. In the United States, free speech and other forms of free expression are protected by the First Amendment.

Even democracies, however, limit or prohibit certain kinds of speech. Governments place limits on speech when it conflicts with other democratic values. An example is hate speech. Hate speech is public speech that expresses hate or encourages violence towards a person or group based on something such as race, religion, gender, sexual orientation, or gender identity. Hate speech violates the democratic values of security, tolerance, and equal protection. But different democracies have different ways of dealing with hate speech based, in part, on a country's history.

The United States was born in a war for independence from Great Britain. Americans understood the war, in part, as a rebellion against British restrictions on their rights. As one result, the First Amendment to the Constitution protects freedom of expression. At the same time, however, the United States has a history of slavery, genocide, prejudice, and discrimination that has influenced how some Americans feel about hate speech today.

In the United States, Hispanics, Asian Americans, Jews, Muslims, people with disabilities, immigrants, women, LGBTQ people, and many more groups have also been the targets of hate speech and hate crimes—both in the past and in present day. Many people who have been the targets of hate speech argue that not only does hateful speech prompt real and immediate violence, but that hate speech itself is harmful to their health and well-being. Further, many argue that continuous dehumanization of targeted groups can lead to future violence and denial of rights.

The Supreme Court has weighed in on this debate many times. One type of speech that the Court has said can be limited is speech that is addressed to a specific person or group and calls on them to commit an illegal act. However, the Court has also ruled many times that hate speech is protected if it does not promote imminent violence. In the *Matal* v. *Tam* (2017) case, Justice Alito wrote, "Speech that demeans on the basis of race, ethnicity, gender, religion, age, disability, or any other similar ground is hateful; but the proudest boast of our free speech jurisprudence is that we protect the freedom to express 'the thought that we hate.'"

Clearly, the question of how to handle hate speech is still under debate. Is the answer banning all hate speech? Continuing to protect it? Or somewhere in the middle?

Should hate speech be banned in our democracy? Consider the options.

Hate speech should be banned.

History has shown that demeaning and hateful speech is frequently the first act of persecution against specific persons and groups. The next step may be to criminalize or terrorize the group. Punishing hate speech establishes necessary and appropriate limits on what can be said in a democratic society.

Research shows that being subjected to racist hate speech on a regular basis can cause health problems. These include high blood pressure, anxiety, and depression. Students who experience racist hate speech do not do as well at school. Even when hate speech does not incite violence it causes harm to its victims.

Freedom of speech is not absolute. Society must decide—through its laws—the limits of free speech. By prohibiting hate speech, the government balances freedom of expression with other democratic values like respect and tolerance. If government gets the balance wrong, the people can always change it.

Our government should take a clear stand for what is right. Hatred and intolerance are wrong. By enacting a ban on hate speech, our democracy will set an example of writing our values—tolerance, security, and equal protection—into our laws.

Hate should not be banned.

People will be less likely to say what they really mean if we enact laws punishing hate speech. Once the government has the power to punish expression, the types of prohibited speech will grow. Governments should be permitted to control only what people can and cannot do, not what they say or believe.

People do not agree on what speech is hateful, offensive, or just an opinion with which they disagree. If we cannot agree on what hate speech is, how can we ban it?

Laws prohibiting hate speech do not work. Such laws are often too vague and require the government to determine the intent of the speaker. This is difficult, if not impossible. A word or symbol can mean something to one person, and something very different to another person.

Dealing with hate speech is the price to pay for our freedom. Everything that is legal is not necessarily socially acceptable. It is better to err on the side of allowing some harmful speech than on the side of banning some beneficial speech. A better way to deal with hateful expression is to condemn it.

GUIDING QUESTIONS

1. What are the two most compelling reasons to support the deliberation question?

2. What are the two most compelling reasons to disagree with the deliberation question?

3. What is one area of this deliberation where the two sides might find common ground?

Time, Place, and Manner Restrictions

Some laws regulate expression based on its content. These laws deal with *what* a speaker is allowed to say or not to say. But there is a second type of regulation: other laws that regulate the time, place, and manner of expression. These laws set forth *when, where,* and *how* speech is allowed.

As a general rule, government cannot regulate the content of expression, except in special situations, as noted in the preceding sections. However, government may make reasonable regulations governing the time, place, and manner of speech. For example, towns and cities may require citizens to obtain permits to hold a march, to use sound trucks, or to stage protests in parks, on streets, or on other public property. Towns and cities may also regulate the time during which loudspeakers may be used, the places where political posters may be displayed, and the manner in which political demonstrations may be conducted. Such laws control when, where, and how expression is allowed.

THE **CASE** OF...

The Nazis in Skokie

The American Nazi Party planned a demonstration in the town of Skokie, Illinois. A large number of Skokie's residents were Jewish, and many were survivors of Nazi concentration camps during World War II. Many had lost relatives in the gas chambers. Because of these reasons, many residents strongly opposed the Nazi demonstration in their town.

To prevent violence and property damage, the town passed a law that it hoped would keep the Nazis from demonstrating there. The law required anyone seeking a demonstration permit to obtain $300,000 in liability insurance. However, this requirement could be waived by the town. The law also banned distribution of material promoting racial or religious hatred and prohibited public demonstrations by people in military-style uniforms. The Nazis challenged the law as a violation of their First Amendment rights.

PROBLEM 35.6

a. Why did Skokie's Jewish population feel so strongly about this demonstration?

b. Some people claimed that the purpose of the demonstration was to incite Skokie's Jews and to inflict emotional harm rather than to communicate ideas. Do you agree or disagree? Should the motive of the speaker influence whether a speech is protected by the Constitution?

c. Does the government have an obligation to protect the rights of Nazis and other unpopular groups, even if their philosophy would not permit free speech for others? Should Ku Klux Klan or Communist Party rallies have the same protection as traditional political rallies?

d. Was the law in this case neutral in its viewpoint? Explain.

e. How should this case be decided? In what ways, if any, should the town be able to regulate speech and assembly?

Courts analyze such regulations by first determining whether the site affected is a **public forum,** such as a street or park that is traditionally open to expression—or designated for this purpose—or whether the site is a nonpublic forum, such as a bus terminal or a school. If the site is a public forum, then the regulation will be overturned unless it serves an important government interest. For example, the government may prohibit loudspeakers from blaring in quiet hospital zones or keep marchers off busy main streets when commuters are driving to or from work. In these cases, the government is regulating speech but the regulation serves an important interest. However, regulations for nonpublic forums can be more restrictive and need only be reasonable. For instance, a school district could choose to limit the use of school buildings—a nonpublic forum—to educational purposes.

Regulations for public and nonpublic forums must also be viewpoint-neutral; that is, they cannot promote or censor a particular point of view. The courts will also be more likely to uphold time, place, and manner restrictions if they leave open alternative ways for communicating the information in question.

▲ Public forums, such as streets or parks, are places in which First Amendment rights of expression are traditionally exercised. *How do the courts analyze time, place, and manner restrictions?*

PROBLEM 35.7

Which of the following laws regulate the content of expression, and which regulate the time, place, and manner of expression? Which, if any, violate the First Amendment?

a. A city ordinance prohibits posting signs on public property such as utility poles, traffic signs, and streetlights.

b. A regulation prohibits people from sleeping in federal parks, even though the sleeping is part of a demonstration against homelessness.

c. A federal regulation prohibits public radio stations from airing editorials.

d. An ordinance prohibits commercial billboards within the town limits.

e. A District of Columbia ordinance prohibits the display within 500 feet of a foreign embassy of any sign that tends to bring a foreign government into "public disrepute."

f. A town ordinance prohibits picketing outside abortion clinics.

g. A city ordinance prohibits political or religious organizations from passing out leaflets or asking for donations inside the airport terminal.

public forum any place, such as a park or street, where First Amendment expression rights are traditionally exercised

©Erica Simone Leeds

THE CASE OF...

The Flag Burning

While the Republican National Convention was taking place in Dallas in 1984, Gregory Lee Johnson participated in a political demonstration. Demonstrators marched through Dallas streets, stopping at several locations to stage "die-ins" intended to dramatize their opposition to nuclear weapons. One demonstrator took an American flag from a flagpole and gave it to Johnson.

The demonstration ended in front of the Dallas City Hall, where Johnson unfurled the American flag, doused it with kerosene, and set it on fire. While the flag burned, protesters chanted, "America, the red, white, and blue, we spit on you." There were no injuries or threats of injury during the demonstration.

Of the hundred or so demonstrators, only Johnson was arrested. He was charged under a Texas criminal statute that prohibited desecration of a venerated object (including monuments, places of worship or burial, or a state or national flag) "in a way that the actor knows will seriously offend one or more persons likely to observe or discover his action."

At Johnson's trial, several witnesses testified that they had been seriously offended by the flag burning. He was convicted, sentenced to one year in jail, and fined $2,000. The case was appealed to the U.S. Supreme Court.

PROBLEM 35.8

Assume that you are a justice on the U.S. Supreme Court. Study the two opinions that follow, decide which you would vote for, and in a letter to the editor of a national newspaper, give the reasons for your decision.

Opinion A

Johnson argues that his burning of the flag should be protected as symbolic speech under the First Amendment. The First Amendment literally protects speech itself. However, this Court has long recognized that First Amendment protection does not end with the spoken or written word. While we have rejected the idea that virtually all conduct can be labeled speech and so is protected by the First Amendment, we have recognized conduct as symbolic speech when the actor intended to convey a particular message and there was a great likelihood that those viewing the conduct would understand the message.

In this case, Johnson's conduct is similar to conduct protected as symbolic speech in our earlier cases. However, the First Amendment does not provide an absolute protection for speech. This Court will analyze the Texas law, along with the facts of the case, to determine whether the state's interest is sufficient to justify punishing Johnson's action.

In earlier cases, we upheld the conviction of a protester who burned his draft card. We reached that decision because the government had an important interest in requiring that everyone age 18 and older carry a draft card. In that case we did not punish the protester's speech but rather his illegal act (burning his draft card). However, we have held that freedom of speech was violated when individuals were arrested for displaying a flag decorated with a peace symbol constructed of masking tape and for wearing pants with a small flag sewn into the seat.

In the *Johnson* case, the state argues that it has two important interests: preventing a breach of the peace and preserving the flag as a symbol of nationhood and national unity. The first interest is not involved in this case because there was no breach of the peace or even a threat of such a breach.

The state's other argument—the preservation of the flag as a symbol of nationhood and national unity—misses the major point of this Court's earlier First Amendment decisions: the government may not prohibit expression simply because society finds the ideas presented to be offensive or disagreeable. Johnson was prosecuted for burning the flag to express an idea—his dissatisfaction with the country's policies. His conviction must be reversed because his act deserves First Amendment protection as symbolic speech. The government has not provided sufficient justification for punishing his speech.

Opinion B

For more than 200 years, the American flag has occupied a unique position as the symbol of the nation. Regardless of their own political beliefs, millions of Americans have an almost mystical reverence for the flag. Both Congress and the states have enacted many laws prohibiting the misuse and mutilation of the American flag. With the exception of Alaska and Wyoming, all the states have specific laws prohibiting the burning of the flag. We do not believe that the federal law and the laws in the 48 states that prohibit burning of the flag are in conflict with the First Amendment. Although earlier cases have protected speech and even some symbolic speech related to the flag, none of our decisions has ever protected the burning of a flag.

The First Amendment is designed to protect the expression of ideas. Indeed, Johnson could have denounced the flag in public or even burned it in private without violating the Texas law. In fact, other methods of protest were used and permitted at the demonstration. The Texas statute did not punish him for the ideas that he conveyed but rather for the conduct he used to convey his message. Requiring that Johnson use some method other than flag burning to convey his message places a very small burden on free expression.

We have never held that speech rights are absolute. If Johnson had chosen to spray-paint graffiti on the Washington Monument, there is no question that the government would have the power to punish him for doing so. The flag symbolizes more than national unity. It symbolizes to war veterans, for example, what they fought for and what many died for. It also symbolizes our

▲ The American flag

shared values such as freedom, equal opportunity, and religious tolerance. If the great ideas behind our country are worth fighting for—and history demonstrates that they are—then the flag that uniquely symbolizes the power of those ideas is worth protecting from burning. The conviction should be affirmed.

Landmark Supreme Court Cases

Visit the Landmark Supreme Court Cases Website at **landmark-cases.org** for information and activities about *Texas* v. *Johnson*.

Symbolic Speech

symbolic speech conduct that expresses an idea (for example, wearing a black armband to protest a war)

Expression may be symbolic as well as verbal. **Symbolic speech**, also called expressive conduct, is conduct that expresses an idea. Although speech is commonly thought of as verbal expression, we are all aware of nonverbal communication. Sit-ins, flag-waving, demonstrations, and wearing armbands or protest buttons are examples of symbolic speech. While most forms of conduct could be said to express ideas in some way, only some conduct is protected as symbolic speech. In analyzing such cases, the courts ask whether the speaker intended to convey a particular message and whether it is likely that the message was understood by those who viewed it.

To convince a court that expressive conduct should be punished and not protected as speech, the government must show that it has an important reason. However, the reason cannot be merely that the government disapproves of the message conveyed by the symbolic conduct.

Vagueness and Overinclusive Laws

vagueness indefiniteness, uncertainty, imprecision; not clear or specific

Courts have ruled that laws governing free speech must be clear and specific. This requirement ensures that a reasonable person can understand what expression is allowed and what is prohibited. Laws also need to be clear so they can be enforced in a uniform and nondiscriminatory way. Laws governing free speech that are not clear and specific can be struck down by courts on grounds of **vagueness.**

overinclusive too broad or general. As a legal term this usually refers to a law that punishes speech that should be protected (e.g., by the First Amendment).

In addition, laws that regulate free speech must be narrowly drafted to prohibit only as much as is necessary to achieve the government's goals. Laws that prohibit both protected and unprotected expression are termed **overinclusive.** In specific cases, courts may strike down statutes that are vague or overinclusive, even if the expression in question could have been prohibited or punished under a clearer, more narrowly drafted law.

▶ People have used sit-ins to protest. *How do the courts determine whether conduct is protected as symbolic speech?*

THE **CASE** OF...

The Cross-Burning Law

In the late 1980s, many states and localities passed laws against hate crimes. These laws defined the types of acts that constituted hate crimes and provided criminal penalties for them. St. Paul, Minnesota, was one of many cities to pass such a law. This city's ordinance read as follows:

Whoever places on public or private property a symbol . . . or graffiti, including but not limited to a burning cross or Nazi swastika, which one knows or has reasonable grounds to know arouses anger, alarm, or resentment in others on the basis of race, color, creed, religion, or gender, commits disorderly conduct and shall be guilty of a misdemeanor.

Russell and Laura Jones and their five children were an African American family who had just moved into a mostly white St. Paul neighborhood. Late one night they were awakened by noise outside their bedroom window. When they parted the curtains, they saw a cross burning on their front lawn. St. Paul police arrested an 18-year-old white male. He was prosecuted and convicted under the local ordinance described above.

PROBLEM 35.9

a. What happened in this case? Why was the 18-year-old prosecuted?

b. Could the state have prosecuted the defendant using some other law or ordinance? If so, which ones? Why do you think it used the hate crimes ordinance?

c. Can you identify words or phrases in the ordinance above that are not clear and specific? What are they? Exactly what expression is prohibited?

d. On appeal, what legal arguments can the defendant raise? What legal arguments can the state make?

e. When interviewed by a national newspaper, the lawyer for the defendant stated that, "Everybody's gotten real thin-skinned lately, and I'm defending the right to express yourself in that kind of climate. . . . With an ordinance like this, you open up a doctrine that swallows the First Amendment." What did the defendant's lawyer mean by these comments? Do you agree or disagree with these comments? Give the reasons for your answers.

f. How should this case be decided? Give the reasons for your answer.

g. Assume that a group of students hang a rope ending in a noose from a tree limb near the black cultural studies club at a local high school. Assume the St. Paul ordinance is in effect there. Can this act be prosecuted as a crime? What should school administrators do if this happens?

TAKING ACTION: Law and Democracy

Advising Your City Council

Citizens have come to their representative on the city council and asked for her help in solving the following problem. They are concerned about people on their downtown streets who are approaching local citizens and tourists and asking for money. These people hold out a cup and say "Help the homeless" to passersby. Some people report that they have had their path blocked and have felt harassed.

The city council member is sympathetic to the concerns voiced by her constituents, but she also realizes that this issue might involve the First Amendment and the right to freedom of speech.

A homeless man

PROBLEM 35.10

Assume that you work for this council member. Draft a paper advising her about possible approaches the city council might take. Consider these points:

a. Should a new criminal law be drafted to address this problem? Can an existing criminal law be used to address this problem? Remember that a criminal law that violates the First Amendment would be unconstitutional.

b. Is the phrase "Help the homeless" protected speech under the First Amendment? If so, would the phrase be considered political speech? Commercial speech? Some other type of speech? If the words "Help the homeless" would not be protected, why not? Explain your answers.

c. Even if the words "Help the homeless" are protected, is there some way to regulate this activity according to time, place, and manner that will improve the situation in the community?

d. Draft a proposed law to regulate asking for money on downtown streets. Analyze the law to be sure that it is not vague or overinclusive and that it is not designed to prohibit one particular point of view.

e. Would citizens support passing such a law? Would police support enforcement? Might the law be challenged in court? Explain your answers.

CHAPTER 36
Freedom of the Press

▶ The right of the press to gather and publish information sometimes conflict with other important rights.

censorship (1) the denial of freedom of speech or freedom of the press; (2) the process of examining publications or films for material that the government considers harmful or objectionable

The First Amendment to the U.S. Constitution guarantees freedom of the press. It protects us from government **censorship** of newspapers, magazines, books, radio, television, and film. Censorship occurs when governments examine publications and productions and prohibit the use of material they find offensive. Traditionally, courts have protected the press from government censorship. A free press plays a vital role in our democracy by informing people about public affairs and monitoring government at all levels. A free press exposes scandals, corruption, and abuses of power by the powerful. In the case of *New York Times* v. *Sullivan*, as discussed in Chapter 35, the Supreme Court explained that freedom of the press allows for a "profound national commitment to the principle that debate on public issues should be uninhibited, robust, and wide-open."

While courts typically protect press freedom, politicians, objecting to media scrutiny, sometimes demonize the press. Media bashing by politicians goes back at least to George Washington who referred to the "infamous scribblers" who reported on his administration. But maintaining a free press protects democracy from dictatorship.

Javier Larrea/Pixtal/age fotostock

435

The Framers of the Constitution provided the press with broad freedom. This freedom was considered necessary to the establishment of a strong, independent press in this country, sometimes called "the fourth branch" of government. An independent press can provide citizens with a variety of information and opinions on matters of public importance. However, freedom of the press sometimes clashes with other rights, such as a defendant's right to a fair trial or a citizen's right to privacy. For example, there has been increasing concern about extremely aggressive journalism, including published stories about people's sex lives, their financial dealings, and their families, as well as photographs taken of people when they believed they were in a private setting.

Among the questions that government and the press have confronted are these: When can the government prevent the press from publishing information; keep the press from obtaining information; and force the press to disclose information? Is freedom of the press limited in schools

THE **CASE** OF...

The Candidates' Televised Debate

The Arkansas Educational Television Commission, a state-owned public broadcaster, sponsored debates between the major political party candidates for the 1992 congressional election in Arkansas's Third Congressional District. Ralph Forbes, a ballot-qualified independent, sought permission to participate in the debate. The television station's staff determined that the Forbes campaign had not generated enough enthusiasm from voters and did not include him in the debate. Forbes sued, contending that his exclusion violated his First Amendment rights.

The television station argued that its decision was a viewpoint-neutral exercise of journalistic discretion. The station staff did not invite Forbes because he lacked enough voter support, not because of his views.

Forbes argued that since the station is owned by the state, the government would actually be deciding who is and who is not a viable candidate. This, Forbes contends, is a decision that must be left to the voters. In addition, in an earlier campaign in which he ran as a Republican Party candidate for lieutenant governor, Forbes won a majority of the counties in the Third Congressional District.

PROBLEM 36.1

a. What arguments can the television station make for keeping Ralph Forbes out of the televised debate?

b. What arguments can Forbes make that would enable him to participate in the debate?

c. How should this case be decided? Give the reasons for your answer.

d. How important are televised debates between candidates?

e. Could a third-party candidate with only a modest level of support make a difference in the outcome of an election? Explain.

f. Should our political system do more to encourage participation from candidates who are not members of one of the two major parties? Why or why not?

g. Should a government-owned television station provide an automatic right of access to debates for all candidates who qualify to appear on the ballot? Give your reasons.

or prisons? Are special limits on the press needed during wartime? What special challenges exist when many Americans do not trust the news media to report the news free from political bias?

Not all news today is generated by newspapers and radio and television stations. Social media and Internet sites can turn everyone into real-time publishers of news and opinion. Should traditional First Amendment press protections apply to new media? Look for the law to develop in this area.

Prohibiting Publication

In The Case of the Gag Order below, the judge was concerned about the defendant's Sixth Amendment right to a fair trial. The reporters were concerned about their First Amendment right to freedom of the press. This case presented a conflict between two important constitutional rights: a free press and a fair trial.

In 1976, the U.S. Supreme Court decided that the **gag order** was an unconstitutional limit on the freedom of the press in this case. The Court held that the trial judge should have taken less drastic steps to lessen the effects of the pretrial publicity. It suggested postponing the trial, moving it to another county, questioning potential jurors to screen out those with fixed opinions, and instructing the jury to decide the case based only on the evidence introduced at the trial.

If the gag order in this case had been upheld, it would have amounted to a **prior restraint**—prohibition against any publication—on the press. Attempts to censor publications before they go to press are presumed unconstitutional by the courts. Prior restraint is allowed only

gag order a court order prohibiting public reporting on a case currently before the court

prior restraint any effort to censor a publication before it goes to press

THE **CASE** OF...

The Gag Order

Six people were brutally murdered in their home in a small Nebraska town. The murders and the later arrest of a suspect received widespread news coverage. At a pretrial hearing that was open to the public, the prosecutor introduced a confession and other evidence against the accused. Both the trial judge and the lawyers involved in the case believed that publication of the information presented at the pretrial hearing would make it impossible for the suspect to have a fair trial before an unbiased jury. As a result, the trial judge issued a gag order, which prohibited the news media from reporting the confession or any other evidence against the accused. Members of the news media sued to have the gag order declared unconstitutional and removed.

PROBLEM 36.2

a. What happened in this case? Why did the judge issue a gag order?

b. Should judges be able to close criminal trials to the press? If so, when and why?

c. Which is more important: the right to a fair trial or the right to freedom of the press? Explain your answer.

d. As a practical matter, how could the court protect the rights of the accused in this case without infringing on the rights of the press?

▶ The U.S. government attempted to block publication of documents relating to the Vietnam War.

if (1) publication would cause a certain, serious, and irreparable harm; (2) no lesser means would prevent the harm; and (3) the prior restraint would be effective in avoiding the harm.

A few years after the gag order case, the Court ruled that the public and the press usually have a right to attend criminal (and probably civil) trials. Only if vital government interests are at stake and no less restrictive way exists to protect those interests can trials be closed to the public and the press.

Another example of a government attempt to impose censorship before publication took place in 1971, when a government employee gave top-secret documents about origins of the Vietnam War to several newspapers. The documents outlined the past conduct of the United States regarding the Vietnam conflict. The government sued to block publication of the so-called Pentagon Papers. In the 1971 case of *New York Times* v. *United States*, the Court refused to block publication. It reasoned that the government had not provided enough evidence that the newspaper's actions could cause a "grave and irreparable" danger. However, if the documents had, for example, contained a secret plan of attack during a time of war or endangerd troops currently in a battle zone, the Court might have blocked publication.

PROBLEM 36.3

A whistle-blowing website that aims to reveal secret government and corporate information publishes thousands of confidential messages about American wars and diplomacy. The messages identify specific people—American government employees, foreign diplomats and leaders, and human rights workers. The website is privately financed and hosted on computer servers around the world. The website portrays itself as a journalistic entity. The U.S. government says the website is not journalistic, but political.

a. What are the U.S. government's interests in preventing or prosecuting the publication of the secret documents?

b. What are the website's interests in publishing the secret documents?

c. Should the First Amendment protect the website's publication of state secrets? Why or why not?

Denying the Press Access to Information

Another way in which the government sometimes tries to control the press is by denying the public access to certain information. Some people argue that denying access to information does not violate the rights of the press. Others contend that freedom of the press implies a right to obtain information.

To protect the public's access to government information, Congress passed the *Freedom of Information Act (FOIA)* in 1966. This law requires federal agencies to release certain information in their files to the public. The law allows citizens to obtain government information and records unless the material falls into the category of a special exception, such as information affecting national defense or foreign policy, personnel and medical files, trade secrets, investigatory records, and other confidential information. The *FOIA* applies only to federal agencies and does not create a right of access to records held by Congress, the courts, or local or state government agencies.

The purpose of the *FOIA* is to allow citizens to learn about the business of government. Federal agencies must respond to requests for information within 20 business days. Agencies that refuse to release unprivileged information can be sued in federal court. If you want to request information under the *Freedom of Information Act,* send a letter to the head of the agency or to the agency's *FOIA* officer. You can find the contact information you need online at **www.foia.gov**.

PROBLEM 36.4

The Defense Department has a policy restricting access to a U.S. Air Force base that serves as the main military mortuary for soldiers killed abroad. A group of veterans and photographers argued that this policy restricted needed public access to information. The federal trial court, as well as the court of appeals, however, agreed with the military's argument that the privacy of grieving families was of greater importance and should be protected. The court determined that the policy did not interfere with protected First Amendment rights of the public or the press.

a. Why do you think the veterans and photographers wanted public access to a military base serving as a mortuary?

b. Do you agree with the decision of the court of appeals in this case? Give your reasons.

When you write to request information, it will help if you identify the records you want as accurately as possible. Although you are not required to specify a document by its official name, your request must reasonably describe the information sought. The more specific and limited the request, the greater the likelihood that it will be processed without delay.

You are not required to demonstrate a need or even state your reason for wanting to see the information. If you explain why you want them, however, you are more likely to receive the documents. Many states have laws similar to the *FOIA*. These laws provide citizens with access to state agency files.

During times of war, there may be special issues related to press access to information. For example, the Pentagon allowed hundreds of embedded reporters to accompany troops during the Iraq war in 2003. This strategy provided the public with a great deal of information, virtually in real time, about the war and its aftermath. However, the courts have not been particularly protective of the rights of the press in terms of access to information. In a leading case, the Supreme Court said: "It is one thing to say that the government cannot restrain the publication of news emanating from certain sources. It is quite another to suggest that the Constitution imposes upon the government the affirmative duty to make available to journalists sources of information not available to members of the public generally."

▲ Embedded reporters can sometimes be exposed to danger when reporting from war zones. *What are the advantages of allowing reporters to travel with military troops?*

PROBLEM 36.5

Rumors about a federal prison had circulated for years. Former prisoners claimed that rape, suicide, murder, and mistreatment were all common occurrences. The warden denied the allegations but refused to provide any information about prison conditions.

A newspaper asked permission to inspect the prison and interview the prisoners, but the warden denied the request. The newspaper then asked the federal government for information about the prison. The newspaper asked for a list of inmates and for information about anyone who had died or been injured while in custody. The government refused to provide any information.

The newspaper then did two things. It filed a suit seeking admission to the prison, and it filed a *Freedom of Information* Act request for information about the prison.

a. How would you decide this lawsuit? Explain.

b. What are the newspaper's rights under the *Freedom of Information Act?*

c. What rights or interests does the prison administration have in this case?

d. How would you decide the newspaper's request for information?

e. Give two examples of information held by the federal government that you could access using the *Freedom of Information Act*.

Requiring the Press to Disclose Information

Government and the press also sometimes disagree over the extent to which the First Amendment protects a reporter's sources of information. These conflicts arise because people may give reporters confidential information that is important to a news story. If the people thought they would be identified, they might be less likely to give journalists this information. In one case, a reporter was summoned before a grand jury and asked questions about a crime. The journalist knew this information based on a confidential conversation. The journalist requested a qualified privilege that would have allowed him not to reveal the identity of the source of the confidential information. The U.S. Supreme Court refused to extend any special First Amendment right to the journalist in this situation. The Court did say that states could pass "shield" laws that would give journalists such a privilege. More than half the states have done this, but even the shield laws can come into direct conflict with other very important constitutional rights.

THE **CASE** OF...

The Case of the Satirical Magazine

In 2015, radical Islamist terrorists attacked the offices of Charlie Hebdo, a French satirical magazine that had enraged the attackers by publishing drawings of the prophet Mohammed. In many Muslim communities, creating an image of any of the prophets for any reason is considered to be extremely offensive.

In reporting news of the attack, some news outlets chose to show the drawings as an essential element of the news story, while other outlets chose not to show the drawings in order not to offend. There is no law against mocking religion in the United States, although there are such laws in several European countries and in some other parts of the world.

PROBLEM 36.6

a. If you were the editorial director of a news outlet, what factors would you consider in deciding whether or not to show the drawings? What would you decide? Explain your reasons.

b. Imagine that Congress passed a law that prohibited mocking religion. If this law were challenged in the federal courts, what legal arguments would each side make? Who would win?

▶ Public schools provide only a limited forum for the exercise of First Amendment rights.

public forum any place, such as a park or street, where First Amendment expression rights are traditionally exercised

Schools, military bases, and prisons present special First Amendment problems. The rights of students, military personnel, or inmates may at times conflict with the rights of others or interfere with the need to preserve order. When this conflict occurs, courts must balance the competing interests in each case.

As a general rule, courts allow greater freedom of speech and assembly in parks and on street corners than in public K–12 schools, military bases, and prisons. Courts sometimes speak of places such as public parks and street corners, where First Amendment rights are traditionally exercised, as **public forums.** For the most part, however, courts have found that public schools, military bases, and prisons (and their publications) provide only a limited forum for the exercise of First Amendment freedoms. In these places, you may be able to exercise your rights, but only as long as the expression does not interfere with the purpose of the facility.

©Paul Bradbury/age fotostock

THE **CASE** OF...

The Student Armbands

Mary Beth Tinker and her brother John were opposed to the Vietnam War. They decided to wear black armbands to school as symbols of their objection. When school administrators learned of this, they adopted a policy of asking anyone wearing armbands to remove them. Students who refused would be suspended until they returned to school without the armbands.

The Tinkers and three other students wore black armbands to school. Although some students debated the Vietnam issue in the halls, no violence occurred. The five protesting students were suspended from school until they came back without their armbands. The students sued the school in federal court arguing that their First Amendment rights had been violated.

PROBLEM 37.1

a. What arguments can the students make?

b. What arguments can the principal make?

c. Should wearing armbands at school be considered a form of free expression protected by the Constitution? Give your reasons.

d. How should the court decide this case?

Landmark Supreme Court Cases

Visit the Landmark Supreme Court Cases Website at **landmark-cases.org** for information and activities about *Tinker* v. *Des Moines*.

The First Amendment in Public Schools

In *Tinker* v. *Des Moines School District* (1969), the Supreme Court decided that the right to freedom of expression "does not end at the schoolhouse gate." The Court held that wearing armbands was a form of "symbolic speech" protected by the First Amendment. Before the decision in *Tinker*, the Supreme Court had never recognized a student's First Amendment right to freedom of expression in a public high school. However, the Court also held that the students' right to free speech could be restricted when the school could show that the students' conduct would "materially and substantially disrupt" the educational process or interfere with the rights of other students. Such a disruption did not occur in reaction to the Tinkers' armbands, nor could it reasonably have been predicted, so their suspensions were declared unconstitutional.

The *Tinker* case provides a standard that the courts use to determine whether punishment of student speech by public school officials violates the First Amendment. Although the *Tinker* case clearly involved expression not endorsed or sponsored by the school, in other cases the courts have been asked to determine the extent to which student speech can be controlled as part of school-sponsored activities. In these cases, the courts have balanced students' First Amendment rights against the schools' duty to determine the educational program.

Landmark Supreme Court Cases

Visit the Landmark Supreme Court Cases Website at **landmark-cases.org** for information and activities about *Hazelwood* v. *Kuhlmeier*.

In *Hazelwood* v. *Kuhlmeier* (1988) a high school principal deleted two pages from the year's final issue of the school newspaper because these pages contained one story on student experiences with pregnancy and another about the impact of divorce on students. The principal believed that the stories had been written in such a way that the privacy rights of some students might be violated. He also believed the topics might offend or be inappropriate for some of the younger students at the school. The newspaper was written as part of the school's advanced journalism class. The U.S. Supreme Court ruled in *Hazelwood* that school officials could have editorial control over a school-sponsored newspaper produced in a journalism class. The justices found that this school-sponsored publication should not be treated as a public forum for young journalists. The reasons given for allowing this control were that (1) schools should not have to permit student speech that is inconsistent with their basic educational mission (for example, schools could refuse to sponsor student expression advocating drug or alcohol use), and (2) schools should be allowed to control expression that students, parents, and others in the community might reasonably believe the school has endorsed (for example, students could be stopped from printing vulgar or lewd material in the school newspaper).

This decision gives educators editorial control over the style and substance of school-sponsored student speech if they can show their actions are reasonably related to legitimate educational concerns. However, even with the greater editorial control allowed by the *Hazelwood* decision, a principal who personally opposes (or supports) a contested issue such as gun control, for example, cannot censor a student publication that fairly presents all points of view on that subject.

In addition to cases dealing directly with student speech and press rights, courts have had to consider whether student appearance—in particular the messages on student clothing—is protected expression. For example, students have worn shirts with messages promoting violence, gang membership, drug use, drinking, and sexism. Some educators argue that these clothes transmit a message inconsistent with school and community values and that these messages can lead to school disruption and interfere with the rights of other students. Parents also worry that their children may become targets for violence when wearing such clothing. Some principals have refused to allow students inside their schools when wearing these clothes. Some students argue that the messages on their clothing, even if unpopular, are a form of expression that should be protected by the First Amendment.

▼ The Supreme Court ruling in the *Hazelwood* v. *Kuhlmeier* case stated that school officials have editorial control over a school-sponsored newspaper produced in a journalism class.

High School Student Expression and the First Amendment

Based on the Supreme Court decisions in *Tinker* and *Hazelwood,* analyze each of the following cases. Give arguments both for permitting the expression and for supporting the school's need to prohibit the expression. How should each case be decided?

a. At an assembly before student council elections, a student makes a campaign speech for a friend. While not legally obscene, the speech has many sexual references and makes some students uncomfortable. Others applaud, jeer, and shout additional sexual references. The principal meets with the speaker after the assembly and then suspends him for several days. The student sued the school for violating his right to free speech.

b. Using a computer at his grandmother's house, a student posted a false profile of his high school principal on a social networking site. The profile mocked the principal and contained inappropriate language. The school discovered the profile and suspended the student for ten days. The student sued the school for violation of his First Amendment rights.

c. The major project of a high school drama class is the production of a spring musical. Tickets are sold at the school and at several locations around the community. The students and their drama teacher select the musical Hair, which has several scenes with partially clothed actors and actresses. The drama class begins rehearsals, prints tickets, and starts to publicize the upcoming performances. When the school board learns which musical has been selected, it cancels the production. The drama students sue, alleging violation of their freedom of expression.

▲ Rehearsing for the musical

d. A few parents complain to the high school librarian that several of the school's library books contain negative stereotypes about women as well as certain racial and ethnic groups. The parents ask that the books be removed from the library. The principal agrees and removes the books, even though they are available in the community library. Other students and their parents sue the school for violating the rights of students who want access to those books.

e. With the Olympic Torch Parade scheduled to pass in front of a Juneau, Alaska, high school, students were released from class to watch the festivities. Frederick, an 18-year-old senior at the school, held up a banner that read: "Bong Hits 4 Jesus." He claimed that the message did not have any meaning and was simply an attempt to get on television. The principal, concerned that the banner could be read as encouraging drug use, asked Frederick to take the banner down. When he refused, he was suspended. The student sued, arguing that his First Amendment rights had been violated.

The First Amendment in Prisons and the Military

Schools prepare students for life in our constitutional democracy, with its emphasis on individual freedom. By contrast, both prisons and the military closely regulate almost all aspects of life. Prisons, in particular, physically separate their members from society.

In a 2006 case, the U.S. Supreme Court affirmed its existing rule that a prison regulation that interferes with an inmate's constitutional rights will be upheld as long as it is reasonably related to legitimate **penological** (corrections) objectives. In that case, an inmate in a separate unit for those with consistent disciplinary problems claimed a First Amendment right to receive his daily newspaper. The Court ruled against the inmate, emphasizing that the decision of the correctional officer was related to inmate safety and rehabilitation and that there was an important need to defer to the judgment of prison authorities.

However, inmates do not lose every individual rights case. In 2015, a Muslim inmate in an Arkansas prison sued because prison policy severely limiting growth of facial hair interfered with his religious practice. The prison was concerned that a long beard could be used to hide identity or smuggle contraband. The inmate offered to a compromise—maintaining a one half inch length beard. The prison refused the compromise. In a unanimous opinion, the Supreme Court found in favor of the inmate based on a federal statute (but not the First Amendment) protecting religious exercise in accordance with sincerely held belief.

In 1976, the Court upheld a regulation on a large military base that prohibited all political speeches and the distribution of campaign literature. These cases show that individual rights are often very limited when balanced against the special need for order and discipline in the military.

While the need for military discipline typically trumps free speech rights, the global reach of the web and the explosion of social media tools are raising new challenges to military rules developed in an earlier age. For example, do off-duty military personnel have freedom of speech on social media sites? Can they attend a political rally if not in uniform? Some free speech advocates have noted the obvious irony: "The very people who risk their lives in defense of the First Amendment live under regulations banning their full use of it." (The First Amendment Center)

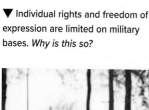

penological of or relating to the criminal corrections process

▼ Individual rights and freedom of expression are limited on military bases. *Why is this so?*

Kefover/Opatrany/McGraw-Hill Education

▶ People practice their religion in many different ways.

The first 16 words of the First Amendment to the U.S. Constitution deal with freedom of religion. These words reflect the deep concern that the Founders of the United States had about the relationship between religion and government and about the right of individuals to practice their religion freely. In addition, Article VI of the Constitution prohibits the government from requiring any religious test for public office.

Religious freedom is protected from government interference by two clauses in the First Amendment: the establishment clause and the free exercise clause. The **establishment clause** prohibits the government from setting up a state religion or building a church. It also prohibits the government from endorsing or supporting religion and from preferring one religion over another. The **free exercise clause** protects the right of individuals to worship or believe, or not, as they choose. Government cannot target religion for unfavorable treatment

establishment clause part of the First Amendment to the U.S. Constitution that prohibits government from establishing a church or preferring one religion over another

free exercise clause part of the First Amendment to the U.S. Constitution that protects individuals' right to worship as they choose

Taken together, the establishment and free exercise clauses generally prohibit the government from either endorsing or punishing religious belief or practice. Some people believe that the two clauses require the government to be neutral toward religion. In other words, the government should not favor one religion over another or favor religion over non religion in its actions or its laws. Others believe that the First Amendment requires the government to accommodate religious belief and practice, as long as it does not establish or promote a state or national religion.

Between 1791 and 1940, the U.S. Supreme Court heard only five cases dealing with church-state relations. Since then, the Court has heard more than a hundred such cases.

Based on data about membership in a religious denomination, the United States is a religious country, and many Americans are religious people. It is also true that the number of people who are non-believers and indicate no religious affiliation is the fastest-growing group in the United States. Many national traditions have religious overtones. For example, U.S. money includes the words "In God We Trust." Since 1954, the Pledge of Allegiance has contained reference to God. Congress and many state legislatures begin their sessions with a brief prayer, and the Supreme Court opens with the words, "God save the United States and this Honorable Court." Although these traditions have been criticized by some people as violating the First Amendment, they have been allowed by the courts.

The Establishment Clause

The establishment clause in the First Amendment prohibits state and federal governments from setting up churches, from passing laws aiding one or all religions, or from favoring one religion over another or over non religion. In addition, the establishment clause prohibits the government from passing laws requiring attendance at any church or belief in any religious idea.

Thomas Jefferson once referred to the establishment clause as a "wall of separation between church and state." In the United States, the wall of separation is not complete. Churches are indirectly aided by government in many ways. For example, churches do not have to pay real estate taxes, even though they receive government services such as police and fire protection.

▲ A Christmas tree and a Hanukkah menorah are displayed on government property. *Do either or both of these displays violate the First Amendment?*

Cases involving the establishment clause have been among the most controversial to reach the U.S. Supreme Court. In these cases, the justices tend to look closely at a wide range of facts before rendering their decision, rather than being driven by one or two facts or rigid standards. In recent years they have relied on several tests. One of these, the *endorsement test,* asks whether the challenged law or government action has either the purpose or the effect of endorsing religion in the eyes of a reasonable, objective person. When using this test, the Court analyzes whether the government has sent a message to nonbelievers that they are outsiders and not full members of the political community.

In addition to the endorsement test, the Supreme Court also uses the following three-part test from the 1971 case of *Lemon* v. *Kurtzman.* Known as "the *Lemon* test," it determines whether a government law or action meets the requirements of the establishment clause:

- The primary *purpose* of the challenged law or government action must be secular, or nonreligious.

- The primary *effect* of the law or action must be neither to advance nor to inhibit, or hold back, religion.

- The operation of the law or action must not foster excessive *entanglement* of government with religion. This means that government does not excessively interfere in the workings of churches or let churches exercise governmental authority.

Establishment clause cases are particularly controversial when they involve aid to **parochial schools** or prayer in public schools. Over the years, the Court has approved some forms of aid to parochial school students and their parents. For example, it has allowed states to provide bus transportation, computers, and loans of certain textbooks to parochial school students. In 2002, the Court approved a program from Ohio that provided vouchers to low-income parents to help pay tuition at a variety of nonpublic schools, including religiously affiliated schools. However, state or federal laws that provide financial aid directly to a religious institution or its instructors are unlikely to be approved.

parochial school a private school supported by or affiliated with a religious organization

Although the topic continues to be very controversial, the Court has held that public school-sponsored prayer violates the establishment clause. Even voluntary school-sponsored prayer has been found to be unconstitutional.

Government displays of the Ten Commandments have led to establishment clause challenges. One side argues that such displays simply send a message about the shared Judeo-Christian cultural heritage of the United States. The other side contends that the message is religious and violates the First Amendment by endorsing certain religions. In these cases, context has mattered, and the Court's decisions have depended on the particular facts of the case. For example, where governments have ordered public schools or courthouses to display the Ten Commandments, the Supreme Court has found a violation of the First Amendment. When a private organization donated a monument that included the Ten Commandments for placement along with other monuments on the grounds between the state capitol and the state supreme court, there was no constitutional violation.

THE CASE OF...

The Rabbi's Invocation

For many years the Providence, Rhode Island, school committee and superintendent have permitted, but not directed, school principals to include religious invocations and benedictions in the graduation ceremonies of the city's public middle schools. As a result, some public middle schools in Providence have included invocations and benedictions in their graduation ceremonies.

The invocations and benedictions are not written or delivered by public school employees but by members of the clergy invited to participate in these ceremonies for that purpose. The schools provide the clergy with guidelines prepared by the National Conference of Christians and Jews. These guidelines stress inclusiveness and sensitivity in preparing nonreligious prayer for public, civic ceremonies. The clergy who have delivered these prayers at graduations in recent years have included ministers of various Christian denominations, as well as Jewish rabbis.

Attendance at graduation ceremonies is voluntary, and parents and friends of the students are invited to attend. Middle school ceremonies are held at the schools.

Daniel Weisman's daughter, Deborah, graduated from Nathan Bishop Middle School, a public school in Providence. Rabbi Leslie Gutterman, from a local synagogue in Providence, delivered the invocation and benediction at the ceremony. Both prayers were consistent with the guidelines that had been sent to him by the school principal.

The Weismans, who are Jewish, filed a case in federal court contending that inviting religious leaders to provide the invocation and benediction at public school graduations violated the separation of church and state required by the First Amendment.

PROBLEM 38.1

a. What happened in this case? Why did the Weismans object to the rabbi's invocation and benediction?

b. What arguments can the Weismans make?

c. What arguments can the school make?

d. Compare this case to the decisions of the U.S. Supreme Court that have found public school-sponsored prayer to be unconstitutional. How is this case like the school prayer cases? How is it different?

e. How should this case be decided?

f. Assume that after the Weismans' complaint the school abandoned its policy of selecting different religious leaders each year and instead sponsored an election for students to elect a peer to write and deliver a prayer at graduation exercises. Would such a policy violate the First Amendment? Explain.

g. Could the school post information on its bulletin board about a community-based baccalaureate service sponsored by local churches for graduating seniors? Would it make a difference if the sign said, "This is not a school-sponsored or school-endorsed activity"?

▲ A graduation ceremony

The Free Exercise Clause

The free exercise clause in the First Amendment protects the right of individuals to worship as they choose. However, when an individual's right to free exercise of religion conflicts with other important interests, the First Amendment claim does not always win. As a general rule, religious *belief* is protected, yet *actions* based on those beliefs may be restricted if they violate an important government interest. As long ago as 1878, the U.S. Supreme Court upheld the conviction of a Mormon man who had violated the criminal law against polygamy—having multiple spouses—even though his religion encouraged this practice at that time.

THE **CASE** OF...

The Amish Children

Wisconsin had a law requiring all children to attend school until age 16. However, the Amish believe that children ages 14–16 should devote that time to Bible study and to training at home in farmwork. The Amish believe that high school is "too worldly for their children." State officials prosecuted several Amish parents for not sending their children to school. The parents defended their actions as an exercise of their religion.

Wisconsin v. *Yoder* reached the U.S. Supreme Court in 1972. The Court weighed the rights of the Amish to practice their religion against the state's interest in requiring school attendance. The Court held that the Amish people's right to free exercise of religion was more important than the two additional years of required schooling. Among the factors the Court considered was the fact that the Amish children were not harmed and became employed, law-abiding citizens after completing their religious education.

▲ An Amish farm

PROBLEM 38.2

a. Do you agree with this decision? Explain.

b. What arguments might the dissenters have put forward in their opinion?

c. This case began in Wisconsin as a prosecution of the parents for not sending their children to school. Their defense at trial, and their arguments in the appeals courts, focused primarily on the rights of the parents. Did the students have rights that might have been considered? What rights and interests might have been asserted on behalf of the students?

Religion and K-12 Public Education

The following situations involve religion and K-12 public education. For each, determine whether the establishment clause, the free exercise clause, or both are involved. Then decide whether the government's action violates the First Amendment to the Constitution. Be sure to give reasons for your answers.

a. A high school student who has been deaf since birth asks his school district to pay for a sign language interpreter to accompany him to classes at a local religious school. A federal law requires school districts to provide for the education of all children with disabilities. The school district (which had provided the student with an interpreter while he attended the public school) refuses to pay.

b. A state law authorizes a one-minute period of silence in all public schools "for meditation or voluntary prayer."

c. A group of high school students requests permission from the school principal to form a prayer club. The group agrees to follow the rules required of all student clubs at the school, which include meeting twice a week at the beginning of the school day during an activity period. A faculty member volunteers to supervise the group. The principal refuses the group's request.

d. A public high school coach gathers his players together before a game and leads them in a brief prayer. One of the players tells the coach he is uncomfortable with the prayer. The coach tells him that it is acceptable for him either to say nothing or to leave the room while the prayer is being said.

e. Eid al-Fitr is an important religious holiday that Muslims celebrate in the days following Ramadan. Muslim students stay home from school during the holiday. Unaware of the holiday, a public school system schedules standardized testing during that time.

▲ A Muslim holiday celebration

f. In a science class, the instructor teaches about the scientific theory of evolution. A student is concerned that evolution contradicts the Biblical story she has learned in church and from her family. Her mother asks that the science teacher also provide a lesson on creationism in order to provide balance.

g. In December, a group of students set up a Christmas tree in the hallway outside the main office of their school. The tree and ornaments are purchased using donations from students and their families. No money from the school's budget was used. Most students who attend the school celebrate Christmas.

h. A school district has a "no hats in school" rule as part of its dress code. A Jewish student wants to wear a yarmulke (skullcap) and a Muslim student wants to wear a hijab (headscarf) as part of their religious practices.

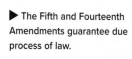

▶ The Fifth and Fourteenth Amendments guarantee due process of law.

procedural due process Generally, a right to fair treatment when government action affects a person's interests.

substantive due process used by courts to protect basic freedoms by making sure that government does not violate a fundamental right without good reason

The idea of due process of law means government has an obligation to treat people fairly. But determining what is fair is seldom easy. The language of the due process clause—no person shall be deprived of life, liberty, or property without due process of law—seems to say that a person cannot lose life, liberty (freedom), or property unless fair *procedures* are first followed by the government. This idea is part of what the due process clause means, and why it is often called **procedural due process.**

Courts have also interpreted the due process clause of the U.S. Constitution, however, as a limit on the substantive powers of the government, meaning that the laws themselves have to be fair. This is known as **substantive due process.** When determining whether there is a violation of substantive due process, courts look at whether a government-passed law or action unreasonably interferes with a fundamental or basic right. Identifying what is a fundamental right has also been a challenge for the courts.

The Fifth Amendment's due process clause protects people against actions by the federal government. The Fourteenth Amendment has almost the same due process language and protects against actions by state and local governments. The Supreme Court has interpreted the two due process clauses as having the same meaning. Some state constitutions also have a due process clause that may provide more protection against state and local government action than what is provided for in federal law.

Procedural Due Process

Many modern due process cases deal with what is called procedural due process, sometimes called fair administration of the law. Due process procedures do not guarantee that the *result* of government action will always be to a person's liking. However, fair procedures do help prevent arbitrary, unreasonable decisions. Due process requirements vary depending on the situation. At a minimum, due process means that people who will be affected by a government decision must be given notice of what the government plans to do and have a chance to comment on the action before it occurs.

Government takes many actions that may deprive people of life, liberty, or property. In each case, some form of due process is required. For example, a state might fire someone from a government job, revoke a prisoner's parole, or cut off someone's Social Security payments. Due process does not prohibit these actions, but it does require that certain procedures be followed before such action is taken.

If a person has a right to due process, the next question is: what process is due? Due process is a flexible concept. The procedures required in specific situations depend on several factors: (1) the seriousness of the harm that might be done to the person; (2) the risk of making an error without following the procedures; and (3) the cost to the government, in time and money, of carrying out the procedures.

According to past decisions of the U.S. Supreme Court, the primary reason for establishing procedural safeguards—when a life, liberty, or property interest is affected by government action—is to prevent inaccurate or unjustified decisions. In a case decided by the Supreme Court in 2003, a sex offender released from prison complained that personal information about him was made available through a state-sponsored Internet site. The site provided information to residents about convicted sex offenders as part of their state's Megan's Law—a law passed in every state and the District of Columbia in memory of a New Jersey girl raped and killed in 1994 by a neighbor who, unbeknownst to the girl's parents, was a convicted sex offender. The former inmate in the 2003 case contended that listing his name and personal information without first having a court hearing to determine whether or not he was *currently* dangerous harmed his reputation—his interest in liberty—and therefore violated his procedural due process rights. The Court found that the operation of Megan's Law was valid because it simply provided residents with truthful information about convicted sex offenders without maintaining that they were currently dangerous. There was no need for individual hearings because there was no substantial risk of error.

In another case, however, the Supreme Court did require that the government provide a hearing before cutting off public assistance to a person. In that case, the Court said that the individual had a property interest that deserved some protection under the due process clause.

THE Constitution

"... nor shall any State deprive any person of life, liberty, or property, without due process of law, ..."

—Fourteenth Amendment

THE CASE OF...

Goss v. Lopez

Ohio law provides for a free education for all children between the ages of 6 and 21. In 1971, widespread student unrest took place in the public schools of Columbus, Ohio. Students who either participated in, or were present at, demonstrations held on school grounds were suspended. Many suspensions were for a period of ten days. Students were not given a hearing before suspension, although at a later date some students and their parents were given informal conferences with the school principal. A number of students, through their parents, sued the board of education, claiming that their right to due process had been violated when they were suspended without a hearing.

In *Goss* v. *Lopez*, the U.S. Supreme Court decided that public school students who are suspended for ten days or less are entitled to certain rights before their suspension. These rights include (1) oral or written notice of the charges, (2) an explanation of the evidence against them (if students deny the charges), and (3) an opportunity for students to present their side of the story.

The Court stated that in an emergency, students could be sent home immediately, and a hearing could be held at a later date. The Court did not give students a right to a lawyer, a right to call or cross-examine witnesses, or a right to a hearing before an impartial person.

In *Goss,* the Court considered the due process interests of harm, cost, and risk. The Court ruled that reputations were harmed and educational opportunities were lost during the suspension; that an informal hearing would not be overly costly for the schools; and that while most disciplinary decisions were probably correct, an informal hearing would help reduce the risk of error.

PROBLEM 39.1

a. What happened in the Goss case? What rights did the Supreme Court say the students should be given prior to a brief suspension?

b. What rights might the students want that they did not receive in this case? What are the arguments for and against providing these additional rights?

c. Do you think this case was decided correctly? Give your reasons.

▲ Meeting with the principal

In addition to providing notice and a chance to be heard, due process may also include factors such as a hearing before an impartial person, representation by an attorney, calling witnesses on one's behalf, cross-examination of witnesses, a written decision with reasons based on the evidence introduced, a transcript of the proceeding, and an opportunity to appeal the decision. Generally, the greater the interests affected by the government's action, the more due process elements are required.

Remember that when the U.S. Supreme Court decides a constitutionality issue, it sets out the minimum protection required by the Constitution. No government can offer less. For example, a state could not decide to do away with the notice requirement in the *Goss* decision. However, government agencies can, and sometimes do, offer greater due process protection than the Constitution requires.

THE **CASE** OF...

The Deportation of Permanent Residents

Hyung Joon Kim came to the United States with his parents in 1984 when he was six. Two years later he got a "green card," which identifies immigrants who are here legally as permanent residents. He was convicted of burglary in 1996 and of petty theft the next year. After serving two years, he was paroled. But soon he was arrested by immigration authorities and jailed as the federal government began deportation proceedings against him. Under the 1996 *Immigration and Naturalization Act*, immigrants—including legal permanent residents—who have already been convicted of certain crimes can be detained without a hearing while the government decides whether to deport them.

From jail, Kim asked a federal judge to release him and to provide him with a due process hearing before further detaining him. Kim wanted the government to justify his detention by showing that he was unlikely to appear for his deportation hearing. Both the trial judge and the federal court of appeals sided with Kim. The government appealed the decision to the U.S. Supreme Court, which found the federal law to be constitutional and not a violation of Kim's right to due process.

Writing for the majority in this 5-to-4 decision, then Chief Justice William Rehnquist said: "This Court has firmly and repeatedly endorsed the proposition that Congress may make rules as to aliens that would be unacceptable if applied to citizens." In dissent, Justice David Souter wrote that the Court was forgetting more than one hundred years of case precedents that protected the basic liberty interests of permanent residents.

Congress had passed the 1996 law out of a concern that many immigrants, once released from jail, would continue to commit crimes and would be hard for authorities to locate. This decision affirms the wide-ranging power the federal government has over immigrants.

PROBLEM 39.2

a. Do you agree with the Court's decision? Explain your answer.

b. Should lawful permanent residents (green-card holders) have the same rights as citizens? Should undocumented immigrants have fewer rights than permanent residents?

Substantive Due Process

If a person challenges a law or government action in court, judges usually require the law or action only to be reasonable in order to be constitutional under the due process clause. Only a law with no rational connection to a legitimate societal purpose will be declared unconstitutional. However, when a law or other government action comes into conflict with a fundamental right, the courts take a closer look. But before the court questions a law's constitutionality, it must be convinced that there is a fundamental right involved.

Some fundamental rights, including freedom of speech, freedom of the press, the right to a fair trial, and protection against cruel and unusual punishment, are stated in the plain text of the Constitution. Other rights, including the right to marry and the right to educate one's children, cannot be found in the text of the Constitution but have been recognized for decades and are deeply rooted in American society. These rights, even though not stated in the Constitution, are sometimes referred to as **unenumerated rights** and are protected by the concept of substantive due process. The right to privacy is sometimes thought of as an unenumerated right.

unenumerated rights rights that are not listed specifically in the Constitution

▼ Parents and children are guaranteed a choice between public and private schools because of substantive due process. *How is substantive due process different from procedural due process?*

The notion of unenumerated rights makes substantive due process controversial. Some believe that substantive due process is critical to achieving the goal of justice because it builds needed flexibility regarding what is fundamental and fair into constitutional interpretation. Others criticize the open-ended nature of this right and believe that it invites judges to substitute their policy choices for those that should be made by elected officials in a democracy.

A law will not necessarily be struck down as unconstitutional because it affects a fundamental right. In some circumstances, the government may be able to show that it has a very strong, or compelling, interest when taking action that affects a fundamental right. For example, as noted above, parents have a fundamental right to raise their children. However, the government has a compelling interest in protecting children and therefore may be able to remove children from the homes of abusive parents and place them in foster care.

The Right to Die

In 1983, Nancy Cruzan was severely injured in an automobile accident. As a result of the accident, she suffered permanent brain damage. She remained unconscious in a state hospital and almost totally unresponsive to the world around her for seven years. She was kept alive by a feeding tube that provided water and nutrition. Her parents asked the hospital to remove the tube, but the hospital refused to do so without a court order. All parties agreed that Nancy would soon die without the feeding tube.

State law required "clear and convincing" proof that Nancy would not want to continue her life in this persistent vegetative state. Both the trial court and the state supreme court found her parents unable to produce this evidence based on some conversations Nancy had held with friends before her accident. In a 5-to-4 decision in 1990, the U.S. Supreme Court affirmed the decision of the state supreme court. However, in holding that a state has a strong interest in preserving life, the Court also said that a competent adult has a liberty interest in not being forced to undergo unwanted medical procedures, such as artificial life-sustaining measures. In this case, Nancy Cruzan was found not competent to make this decision. Comments she had made to others before her accident were not considered by any of the reviewing courts as meeting the state's clear and convincing standard of proof.

Seven years later, a related case came to the U.S. Supreme Court. The State of Washington had passed a law that made assisting a suicide attempt a felony. The law provided: "A person is guilty of the crime when he knowingly causes or aids another person to attempt suicide." This law could be applied to a doctor who assisted a patient with a suicide attempt.

In January 1994, several doctors practicing in Washington, along with three gravely ill patients and a nonprofit organization called Compassion in Dying, filed suit in federal court asking that their

state's assisted suicide law be declared unconstitutional. They argued that the ban on physician-assisted suicide violates a liberty interest protected by the Fourteenth Amendment's due process clause, "which extends to a personal choice by a mentally competent, terminally ill adult to commit physician-assisted suicide." The state argued that the Constitution does not protect a right to physician-assisted suicide and that it has a legitimate interest in prohibiting physician-assisted suicide.

PROBLEM 39.3

a. How are the Cruzan and assisted suicide cases similar? How are they different?

b. What other arguments can you make in favor of allowing physician-assisted suicide?

c. What other arguments can you make against physician-assisted suicide?

d. How should the Court decide the physician-assisted suicide case?

e. Do you believe there should be a right to physician-assisted suicide? Give your reasons.

▶ People expect privacy with their personal belongings.

Although the words *right to privacy* or *right to be let alone* do not appear anywhere in the U.S. Constitution, many people contend that privacy is a basic right that should be protected against unreasonable interference by government.

Since the mid-1960s, the U.S. Supreme Court has recognized a constitutional right to privacy. This right is protected in a variety of situations, including when people want to make certain kinds of important decisions, such as marriage and family planning, free of undue government interference.

In some opinions, the Supreme Court has said that the Constitution creates "zones of privacy." The zones are derived from the freedoms of speech and association (First Amendment), the freedom from unreasonable search and seizure (Fourth Amendment), the right to remain silent (Fifth Amendment), the right to have one's home free of soldiers during peacetime (Third Amendment), and the unspecified rights kept by the people (Ninth Amendment). In addition, because privacy has been found to be a fundamental right, the Court justifies privacy protection in terms of substantive due process. The right generally protects citizens from unreasonable interference with their privacy by the government.

The right to privacy of individual people sometimes conflicts with important government interests. For example, the government may need information about individuals to solve a crime or to determine eligibility for government programs. In such cases, the government can regulate certain acts or activities, even though an individual's interest in privacy is affected. Deciding whether a constitutional right to privacy exists involves a careful weighing of competing private and government interests.

Several cases show how the courts weigh and balance these interests in privacy cases. In one 2011 case, the U.S. Supreme Court upheld a government agency's practice of requiring its contractors to undergo a background check, which included answering questions about illegal drug use. The Court said that this did not violate any right to privacy the contractors might have. The Court also found that these questions were reasonable and furthered the government's interest in managing its operations without unduly intruding into the contractors' privacy.

In another decision, the Supreme Court upheld a state law requiring that notice be given to local youth groups, day care centers, and neighbors that a convicted sex offender lived in the area. The Court determined that the public's right to know and to protect children overrode an offender's right to keep a criminal history private. Giving such notice did not violate the privacy rights of a sex offender.

In recent years, as part of the war on terror, the president has asked Congress and the federal courts for expanded power to obtain information on individuals that some contend should be protected under privacy rights. For the most part, the executive branch has been granted these broad powers.

Surveys regularly show strong popular support among the U.S. population for protecting privacy. In fact, some states have passed privacy laws or added a right to privacy to their state constitutions. There has also been a movement to limit privacy protections that are based on the Constitution. Those who favor such limitations believe that the "zones of privacy" discussed above are the creation of some justices who have gone too far in reading privacy rights into the Constitution. They contend that privacy protections are better left to the people and their elected representatives. Others argue that privacy rights are settled law on which people have come to rely and that these precedents should not be overruled.

▲ Courts have determined that protection of the public, as well as the public's right to know, often overrides a criminal's right to keep his or her criminal record private. *Do you agree with these court decisions?*

© Ekaterina Minaeva/Getty Images

In this chapter you will learn about privacy in a number of contexts: at home, at school, in gathering information, and in the areas of birth control and abortion.

PROBLEM 40.1

For each of the following situations, decide what privacy rights or interests are in conflict and what arguments can be made for each side. Indicate whether you agree or disagree with the law or policy.

a. The government requires taxpayers to reveal the source of their income, even if it is from illegal activities.

b. A law forbids nude sunbathing anywhere at a community's beaches.

c. In a prison that has had several stabbings, inmates are strip-searched every day.

d. A state law requires motorcyclists to wear helmets.

e. The police place a small device in a phone that enables them to record all numbers dialed on that phone.

f. A hospital requires an emergency room patient to list all medications she is taking before treating her.

Privacy in the Home and in Educational Settings

▼ Privacy at home is protected by law. *What do police need in order to search a person's home?*

There is a saying that a person's home is his or her castle. Historically, the law has recognized that people may reasonably expect considerable privacy in their homes. For example, under the Fourth Amendment police usually need a valid search warrant in order to search a person's home.

In a 1986 case, the U.S. Supreme Court considered whether a state had the authority to prosecute consenting adult males for engaging in a sexual act in a bedroom of their own home. In a 5-to-4 decision, the Court held that there was no constitutionally protected right to engage in homosexual conduct—even in the privacy of one's home. The Court found that outlawing homosexual conduct was deeply rooted in the nation's history and traditions. The dissenters, whose reasoning was followed in a Georgia case decided 17 years later, believed that the sexual activities of consenting adults in their own bedrooms should be fully protected under previous privacy decisions and the fundamental "right to be let alone" by the government. In 2003, the Court changed course, overruling the 1986 decision. In the case of *Lawrence* v. *Texas* the Court decided that the gay men could not be prosecuted for consensual sexual practices. This decision is an example of how the reasoning in the dissent in an earlier case (the 1986 case) can sometimes become the reasoning for the majority decision in a later case.

©Tetra Images/Getty Images

THE **CASE** OF...

Possessing Obscene Materials at Home

Georgia had a law prohibiting the possession of obscene or pornographic films. A man was arrested in his own home for violating this law. He said—and the state prosecutor did not challenge him—that he had the films for his own use and did not offer them for sale.

In this case, the U.S. Supreme Court recognized the right to possess obscene materials in one's own home for private use. It indicated that individuals generally have the right to think, observe, and read whatever they please, especially in their own homes. However, the Court has held that states may prohibit the possession and viewing of child pornography, since that kind of law protects the physical and psychological well-being of minors.

Government generally limits students' right to privacy in elementary and secondary schools. For example, most courts have upheld searches of students' desks and lockers. The courts reason that lockers belong to the school and that students cannot reasonably expect privacy on school property. Likewise, the Supreme Court has upheld searches of students' belongings without a warrant and without probable cause, as long as school officials have some reasonable suspicion of wrongdoing.

There is a federal law that protects students' right to some privacy concerning their education records. It is known as the *Family Educational Rights and Privacy Act of 1974 (FERPA).* This law protects privacy by generally prohibiting the release of school records to other parties without a parent's permission. Students who reach age 18 or attend college have a right to see their own records, and at 18 they can also control access to their records. This law gives parents the right to inspect their children's school records. Students age 18 or older also have access to their records. If parents or adult students find any inaccurate, misleading, or inappropriate information, they may insert a written correction to their record. Schools have a duty to inform parents and students of their rights under this law.

THE **CASE** OF...

Peer Grading

The Owasso School District in Oklahoma does not have a formal policy telling teachers how student work is to be graded. Some teachers grade all assignments themselves, while others have students grade some of their own papers after the answers are provided. Still others use peer grading from time to time. This means that students exchange papers and grade each other's work from answers provided.

Mrs. Falvo has four children in the school system. She believes that peer grading humiliates her children and is a violation of their right to privacy under the federal *Family Educational Rights and Privacy Act of 1974 (FERPA)*. The school system believes that peer grading provides immediate feedback to students and avoids the problem of students cheating when they grade their own papers. The school system also contends that peer grading is done for the individual teacher and not for the school system, which does not maintain these educational records (i.e., grades for specific assignments during a semester). Mrs. Falvo wins her case in the lower courts, and the U.S. Supreme Court agrees to review the case in order to decide how *FERPA* applies to peer grading.

PROBLEM 40.3

a. Must the Court decide that a grade on an assignment is part of a student's school record in order for Mrs. Falvo's case to prevail?

b. How should this case be decided? Explain.

Information Gathering and Privacy

Telecommunications has changed the way we live, work, and play. Computers allow businesses and organizations to collect, store, and examine detailed information about individuals. Some organizations sell the data they have collected to businesses or other organizations, often without the knowledge or consent of the individuals.

Computers can be used to store enormous amounts of information. For example, the federal government requires financial institutions to keep copies of all checks written or deposited by their customers. This information can be useful when authorities investigate criminal activity, but it may be unfairly damaging if it falls into the hands of others.

Although laws such as the *Freedom of Information Act* encourage the government to release information to the public, another law restricts access to federal records. The *Privacy Act of 1974* prevents the government from releasing most information about an individual without that person's written consent. It protects an individual's medical, financial, criminal, and employment records from unauthorized disclosure. The law also entitles individuals (with some exceptions) to see information about themselves and to correct any mistakes. If your rights are violated under the federal *Privacy Act of 1974*, you may sue for damages in federal court.

In many ways, the fact that increasing amounts of information held by the government are now available on the Internet is good for democracy. People are better able to monitor and communicate with their government as a result of information available online. But some government records contain information that might be considered private or confidential. Examples include the records of divorce proceedings, bankruptcies, and criminal convictions.

In a digital age, there are evolving challenges related to information gathering and privacy. For example, Internet service providers have the capability to monitor the e-mail of their subscribers. Also, those who download content from the Internet and those who order customized TV programming might be providing data that could be used by others for secondary purposes such as marketing and even government surveillance. Employees, educators, and students should also know that information stored on office or school computers, including e-mail, is not generally protected by privacy laws and can be viewed by employers and school administrators.

▲ Financial institutions are required to keep records of your personal financial information.

THE **CASE** OF...

The Police Officers' Texts

In 2001 a police department distributed pagers to its SWAT officers. The officers were told that they were for official use and that only light personal use would be tolerated. After an officer exceeded the monthly texting limit of the pagers, the department requested a log of the texts to see if they needed to increase their text limit. In reviewing the log, they found many sexually explicit texts and very few work-related texts and disciplined the officer. The officer then sued the city for violating his Fourth Amendment rights.

PROBLEM 40.4

a. The Fourth Amendment protects people from unreasonable searches and seizures by the government. What was the alleged search or seizure in this case?

b. Did the officer have a reasonable expectation of privacy in the texts that he sent on his work pager? Explain.

c. Does it matter, for the purposes of determining whether the search was reasonable, that the police department reviewed the texts in order to determine whether they needed to upgrade their texting limits? Explain.

▼ People on both sides of the abortion issue show their support. *Why is abortion such a controversial issue?*

Reproductive Rights and Privacy

In 1965, the Supreme Court struck down a state law that prohibited the possession of contraceptives by married couples. In 1972, the Court declared that a law prohibiting the sale of birth control devices to unmarried people was also unconstitutional. In both cases, the Court found that these laws had interfered with the fundamental right to bear or not bear children and had violated the right to privacy.

Abortion laws have changed over time. In the early 1800s, abortion was legal in the United States prior to "quickening," when the mother can first feel the fetus moving, usually about 16 weeks. However, by the late 1870s, attitudes changed, and almost every state had laws restricting abortions. As a result, abortion activity went "underground." In the mid-1960s, some people became vocal about the need for legalized and safe abortion. People proposed many arguments on both sides, giving medical, moral, religious, financial, political, and constitutional reasons.

Some people argue that abortion is wrong in all situations. These individuals

Andrew Resek/McGraw-Hill Education

believe that an individual human life begins at conception and must be protected from that moment on. This belief is often referred to as the "right to life," and supporters are said to be pro-life. Others argue that abortion is a constitutional right and a private matter to be decided by a woman. These individuals believe that a woman must be allowed to control her own body and not have it regulated by laws that work against her personal choices. This belief is often referred to as the "right to choose," and supporters are said to be pro-choice.

The U.S. Supreme Court and many state courts have struggled with these issues. In 1973, a landmark Supreme Court decision in *Roe* v. *Wade* made abortion legal in certain circumstances. Based on a woman's constitutional right to privacy, *Roe* held that a woman had a fundamental, though not absolute, right to an abortion. This right was defined on a trimester basis. During the first trimester of pregnancy (the first three months), a woman could have an abortion without interference from the state. During the second trimester (four through six months), the state could regulate abortions for safety but could not prohibit them entirely. During the third trimester (seven through nine months, or late-term), the state could regulate or forbid all abortions except to save the life of the mother.

Landmark Supreme Court Cases

Visit the Landmark Supreme Court Case website at **landmarkcases.org** for information and activities about *Roe* v. *Wade*.

PROBLEM 40.5

a. Why do you think abortion is so controversial?

b. Should abortion be allowed without restriction? Totally banned? Regulated in some way? Would you allow late-term abortions under any circumstances? Explain.

c. What are the advantages and disadvantages of state laws that require minors to obtain consent from a parent before receiving an abortion?

The *Roe* decision did not end the debate over abortion. In some ways, it intensified the debate. Since 1973, the Supreme Court has held that states could not give a husband veto power over his wife's decision to have an abortion. Parents of minor-age, unwed girls also could not have absolute veto power over abortion decisions. However, the Court has said that states may require that pregnant unmarried minors obtain parental consent as long as the minor also has the option to avoid this by going before a judge to obtain permission. While never actually overturning *Roe* v. *Wade,* the Supreme Court has allowed government additional authority to limit the right to an abortion. In 2007, for example, the Court found that a federal law that criminalized the performance of late-term abortions (also called partial-birth abortions) was not a violation of the Constitution.

Abortion has also been an important issue in elections and in judicial nominations. Depending on who is president as well as which party controls Congress, abortion counseling at federally funded clinics has sometimes been permitted and sometimes prohibited. In congressional district and U.S. Senate elections where the public is sharply divided on

THE **CASE** OF...

Abortion Law Challenges

In 1992, the U.S. Supreme Court decided the case of *Planned Parenthood of Southeastern Pennsylvania* v. *Casey*. As a result of that case, a woman continues to have a right to an abortion before the fetus is viable (before the fetus could live independently outside the mother's womb). After fetal viability, however, states have increased power to restrict the availability of abortions. The state maintains the power to restrict some abortions because of its legitimate interests in protecting the health of the woman and the potential life of the fetus.

States can pass some laws that regulate abortion, but these laws cannot place a "substantial obstacle in the path of a woman seeking an abortion," the Court said in the Casey decision. However, the Court declined to define specifically what constitutes a substantial obstacle. The justices ruled that regulations were constitutional if they did not place an "undue burden" on obtaining an abortion. For example, the decision allowed a regulation that requires a woman to give "informed consent" at least 24 hours before the planned abortion takes place.

PROBLEM 40.6

Which of the following laws, if any, would place an undue burden on the right to obtain an abortion? Give reasons for each answer.

a. A state law requires that the father of the baby provide written consent before a woman is able to obtain an abortion.

b. A poor woman is unable to obtain an abortion because her state does not provide public funds to cover such a medical procedure.

c. A state law requires a 24-hour waiting period between the time of the woman's decision to have the abortion and the actual procedure.

d. A state law requires a pregnant minor (someone under the age of 18) to obtain written consent from both of her parents in order to obtain an abortion.

e. A state law requires a pregnant minor to obtain written consent from one parent or from a judge in order to obtain an abortion.

f. A state law requires that doctors have admitting privileges at a hospital that is located no further than 30 miles from where the abortion is performed.

---

this issue, candidates are often reluctant to take a strong stand either for or against abortion rights for fear of alienating an important segment of voters. As long as the public believes that the U.S. Supreme Court is narrowly divided over abortion issues, advocacy groups on both sides of this issue will closely monitor presidential nominations to the Supreme Court and other federal courts.

Abortion policies vary around the world. Some countries, including Canada, allow abortions without restrictions. Others ban abortion completely. Still others allow abortions only to preserve the health of the mother or in cases of rape or incest.

▶ Lyndon B. Johnson meeting with civil rights leaders in the White House April 5, 1968.

The promise of equality is set out in the Declaration of Independence: "We hold these Truths to be self-evident, that all Men are created equal, that they are endowed by their Creator with certain inalienable rights..." This language represents one of our country's most ambitious ideals. But what does equality mean? Does it mean that every American receives the same *treatment*? That everyone has equal *opportunities*? Or does it mean something else? Has equality been achieved only when *results*—in educational, financial, and occupational achievement, for example—are comparable among all groups in a society? Society must decide what the promise of equality means and determine how to respond to the challenge of existing discrimination in a way that is effective and fair to all.

Laws, regulations, constitutional amendments, and court decisions are some ways in which government responds to discrimination. The Thirteenth, Fourteenth, Fifteenth, Nineteenth, and Twenty-fourth Amendments were ratified in attempts to make greater equality a reality.

▲ Changes in societal values forced the Supreme Court to declare that separate educational facilities were unequal and that schools should be integrated "with all deliberate speed." *What were Thurgood Marshall's arguments in the* Brown *case?*

segregation the now unconstitutional practice of separating persons in housing, education, public facilities, and other ways based on their race, color, nationality, or other arbitrary categorization

separate-but-equal the doctrine, now unconstitutional, that allowed facilities to be racially segregated as long as they were basically equal

Jim Crow law a statute or law created to enforce segregation in such places as schools, buses, and hotels

Numerous decisions of the U.S. Supreme Court are regarded as landmarks because of the dramatic changes they called for in the struggle to halt discrimination. In addition, legislatures at local, state, and national levels have passed a number of laws prohibiting discrimination. However, U.S. history is marked by long periods in which these laws were not enforced, unconstitutional practices were permitted, or court rulings had the effect of spreading rather than ending discrimination. Today the country still faces the consequences of some of these bitter chapters in its history.

In 1896, for example, the Supreme Court ruled in *Plessy* v. *Ferguson* that **segregation** was permissible in facilities such as schools, restaurants, railroad cars, and restrooms, as long as those facilities were equal. This doctrine, known as **"separate but equal,"** was in place for nearly 60 years. The *Plessy* case is one example of the Court's power to interpret the Constitution in a manner that resulted in unequal opportunity, at least as this term is understood today.

The power of the Supreme Court to promote equal opportunity is illustrated by its 1954 reversal of the *Plessy* decision in its *Brown* v. *Board of Education* decision. Thurgood Marshall, who later became the first African American Supreme Court justice, presented compelling arguments against separating schoolchildren by race. Asserting that segregation is inherently unequal, Marshall argued that passing and enforcing **Jim Crow laws** had officially maintained segregation. In the *Brown* case, the Court ordered that schools be integrated "with all deliberate speed."

The *Brown* decision launched the civil rights movement, which resulted in significant national legislation. The *Civil Rights Act of 1964* and the *Civil Rights Act of 1968* prohibited discrimination based on race, religion, sex, and national origin in employment and housing. Over the past half century, Americans have also confronted issues of discrimination based on gender, age, disability, citizenship status, and sexual orientation.

In studying discrimination, you will encounter some specific instances in which various civil rights laws collide with one another. For example, do some affirmative action laws protecting people of color actually discriminate against whites? Can the state require a private club to accept members of other races, religions, or the opposite sex without interfering with the existing members' freedom of association or their privacy?

Society suffers when discrimination takes place. If some citizens are prevented from developing their talents, they cannot apply their skills to solving the country's many complex problems. This wasted talent ultimately harms everyone. Hence, all Americans—not just those who are its targets—have an interest in halting discrimination.

What Is Discrimination?

Discrimination occurs when some people are treated differently than others because of their membership in a group, based on, for example, race, age, gender, or religion. However, not all types of discrimination are unfair or illegal. Many laws purposely discriminate. In fact, discrimination is an unavoidable result of lawmaking, and as long as the classifications are reasonable, they usually do not violate the Constitution.

Everyone is familiar with laws that require a person to be a certain age to obtain a driver's license. These laws discriminate but are neither unreasonable nor unconstitutional. However, what if the law required a person to be left-handed to get a driver's license? Or what if whites but not African Americans, or Polish Americans but not Mexican Americans, could get a license? Would these laws be constitutional? Why are they unreasonable when an age requirement is not?

The Fourteenth Amendment provides that no state shall deny to any person the equal protection of the law. To determine whether a law or government practice meets the equal protection requirement, courts use one of three different tests, depending upon the type of discrimination involved.

Landmark Supreme Court Cases

Visit the Landmark Supreme Court Case website at **landmarkcases.org** for information and activities about *Plessy* v. *Ferguson* and *Brown* v. *Board of Education.*

discrimination the decision to treat or categorize persons based on race, color, creed, gender, or other characteristics rather than on individual merit

The Rational Basis Test

In most discrimination cases that go to court, judges use the rational basis test. Using this test, judges will uphold a law or practice that treats some people differently than others if there is a rational basis for the different treatment or classification. A rational basis exists when there is a logical relationship between the treatment or classification of some group of people and the purpose of the law.

For example, states require their citizens to be a certain age before they can drive a car. These laws discriminate against people below a certain age, but they are constitutional. Such a law is based on the idea that, in general, people become more responsible as they get older, and driving a car requires a person to be quite responsible. So there is a rational relationship between the classification and the purpose of the law. For the most part, courts uphold government laws and practices that are judged according to the rational basis test.

▲ Age requirements for driving are upheld according to the rational basis test. *How do the courts apply the rational basis test?*

The Strict Scrutiny Test

Certain laws and practices either discriminate based on race, national origin, or citizenship status or affect some fundamental right set out in the Constitution, such as freedom of religion. In these cases, the courts use a test called strict scrutiny. Judges applying strict scrutiny will find the law or practice constitutional if the state can show that the discriminating law or practice serves a compelling (very important) interest and is "narrowly tailored" to achieve that interest. "Narrowly tailored" is a complicated legal concept, but it means that the law or action must be extremely well-designed to achieve a specific goal and interfere as little as possible with the rights of others.

For example, a state law prohibited marriage between persons of different races. When this case came to the U.S. Supreme Court for review, it presented a clear situation where a state law created a classification based on race. The Court was unanimous in overturning this law because the racial classification did not serve a compelling state interest (*Loving* v. *Virginia*, 1967).

The Substantial Relationship Test

In sex discrimination cases, the Supreme Court uses the less demanding substantial relationship test. By this standard, there must be a close connection—something more than a rational relationship—between the law or practice and its purpose. In addition, laws that classify based on sex must serve an important (but not necessarily compelling) governmental purpose.

For example, a state law prohibited beer sales to males ages 18 to 20 but not to females, because more males had been arrested for drunk driving. Although this law served an important government purpose (reducing drunk driving), it was ruled unconstitutional. The Court held that there was not a close connection between the classification and the purpose, because females were legally free to buy beer and give it to males ages 18 to 20.

Potential Limits of Equal Protection

Equal protection cases are complicated and controversial. Some people have argued, for example, that when the Fourteenth Amendment was ratified in 1868, Congress intended it to protect only against racial discrimination. Others argue that it was intended to protect only African Americans—not women, other racial minorities, or white people—against discrimination. Still others contend that the amendment embodies the national commitment to the fundamental value of equality, and therefore all unfair forms of government discrimination are prohibited by the equal protection clause.

▼ Equal protection generally means that governments cannot draw unreasonable distinctions between different groups of people. *Why are equal protection cases controversial?*

Christopher Robbins/Image Source

The following situations involve some form of discrimination. For each, decide whether the discrimination is reasonable and should be permitted or is unreasonable and should be prohibited. Explain your reasons.

a. An airline requires its pilots to retire at age 60.

b. A business refuses to hire a man with good typing skills for a secretarial position.

c. People who have the HIV virus cannot be hired as prison guards.

d. People under age 18 are not allowed into theaters showing X-rated movies.

e. A child with a disability is not permitted to play at a public playground.

f. In selecting applicants for government jobs, preference is given to veterans.

g. Girls are not allowed to try out for positions on an all-boy baseball team at a public high school.

h. Auto insurance rates are higher for young, unmarried drivers.

i. In order to project a classy image, an expensive seafood restaurant requires that its servers wear tuxedos. The restaurant hires only male wait staff.

Discrimination Based on Race

Most Americans believe that racial discrimination is both morally and legally wrong. Today, almost no one defends segregated public facilities or the operation of separate public school systems for children of different races or ethnic groups. Nevertheless, segregated schools and discrimination are still problems.

Americans are still coming to grips with their history of racial discrimination in light of the Constitution's guarantee of equal protection. In addition to enforcement of antidiscrimination laws, government faces the perplexing dilemma of helping those exposed to racial injustice while avoiding discrimination against others. The troubling issue of how to use just means to rid society of injustice raises complex questions. Does providing greater opportunities for some who have historically been denied equal protection result in fewer opportunities for others? Do antidiscrimination laws that were originally passed to protect minorities serve to protect the majority as well? Must the disadvantaged be treated differently in order to be treated equally?

Today, discrimination is usually more subtle than it was in the past. Moreover, reasonable people sometimes disagree as to what constitutes unlawful discrimination. For example, a town denied a request to rezone land to build townhouses for low- and middle-income tenants. The existing housing in the town was mostly single-family houses, and almost all the residents were white. Critics of rezoning may have objected because the townhouses would have attracted a more diverse population. The Supreme Court upheld the zoning law because the Court found no *intent* to discriminate.

Reasonable people also sometimes disagree as to what constitutes a fair and effective **remedy** for past discrimination. Controversy has often surrounded efforts to **desegregate** public schools, to eliminate unlawful discrimination in the workplace, and to ensure fair representation with respect to voting rights.

Discrimination in Education

Public school segregation was declared unconstitutional in the *Brown* case. In theory, the schools were then opened to students of all races. In many instances, however, segregation continued. Many methods were used to desegregate the schools: allowing students to attend any school they desired in their local school district, redrawing neighborhood school boundary lines, transferring teachers, busing students, and developing magnet schools and charter schools with special programs to attract a racially mixed student population.

Perhaps the most controversial method of school desegregation was busing. Busing as a means of transporting children to school has a long history. For many years, busing was used to segregate schools. However, controversy arose in 1971 when the Supreme Court first allowed busing as a means of achieving school integration.

Supporters of busing claimed that requiring racially balanced schools would help provide equal educational opportunities and quality education for both African American and white children. They believed that racially balanced schools weaken prejudices that are reinforced when children are separated. They also argued that busing, once used to segregate, was an appropriate way to integrate.

▼ Following the *Brown* decision, the federal courts required school districts to desegregate.

Opponents of busing contended that neighborhood schools are better because children are in school with their friends and are closer to home in case of an emergency. Critics also maintained that court-ordered busing caused white families to flee city schools, resulting in even more segregation. Other critics said that it is patronizing to think that a student of color must sit next to a white student in order to learn.

By 2001, after nearly 30 years of what some called a "noble but failed experiment with busing," most court-ordered busing to achieve racial balance had ended. In many communities, a consensus developed in support of neighborhood schools. The parents in these communities preferred that funds that had been spent to bus students instead be used to improve the schools themselves.

However, people in some communities preferred greater diversity in public education. The majority of parents and school officials in these communities believed that students needed preparation to appreciate and participate in their multiracial society.

In 2007, controversial cases came to the U.S. Supreme Court from Seattle, Washington, and Louisville, Kentucky, where parents and school officials had voluntarily adopted race-sensitive high school admission procedures so that students could attend schools more racially diverse than the neighborhoods in which most of them lived. Some parents in those communities objected to the use of race to determine which school their children would attend. The Court was closely divided on whether this race-sensitive approach was constitutional.

In each case, five justices said that the voluntary plans were not narrowly tailored to meet a compelling government interest, and that they therefore violated the Fourteenth Amendment. Four of those five majority justices characterized these plans as "racial balancing" and said that government has no interest in using race to make decisions about where public school students attend school. The four justices who dissented believed that this voluntary plan did not violate the Constitution and was consistent with the promise of the Court in *Brown* v. *Board of Education*. The dissenters found that diversity in K–12 education is an important government interest and that, given segregated housing patterns, failure to use race in school admissions will lead to greater racial isolation.

PROBLEM 41.2

a. Should the government take steps to bring about greater integration of public schools? If so, what should the government do? If not, why not?

b. Some argue that the emphasis should not be on court-ordered integration, but instead on improving schools, regardless of their racial composition. Some also argue that students of color might benefit more by being educated separately from white students. Do you agree with these statements? Give your reasons.

Landmark Supreme Court Cases

Visit the Landmark Supreme Court Cases website at landmarkcases. org for information and activities about *Regents of the University of California* v. *Bakke.*

Affirmative action is another remedy for dealing with the effects of discrimination. Affirmative action involves taking steps to remedy past and current discrimination in employment and education. It goes beyond merely stopping or avoiding discrimination. For example, a university might take affirmative action by starting a program to attract more applications from students who are members of underrepresented groups. Affirmative action plans can be either voluntary or mandatory. Voluntary plans are freely adopted. Mandatory plans are imposed by the government as a condition of government funding or as a court-imposed remedy in discrimination cases.

Affirmative action is controversial, and people in several states have voted to ban or limit these programs. Opponents of affirmative action say that it is a form of "reverse discrimination." They argue that race should not be used as a basis for classification, because special treatment for some means discrimination against others. Supporters of affirmative action say that preferential admission to educational programs is needed because a diverse student body is educationally beneficial to all.

The affirmative action issue was presented to the U.S. Supreme Court in the case of *Regents of the University of California* v. *Bakke* (1978). In this case, the medical school of the University of California at Davis had decided that the best way to increase enrollment from underrepresented groups was to give certain advantages to those applicants. For each

affirmative action steps taken to promote diversity in hiring, promotion, education, etc. by attempting to remedy past discrimination; for example, by actively recruiting minorities and women

▼ In the *Bakke case*, the U.S. Supreme Court found that the special admission policy of the medical school at the University of California at Davis was unconstitutional. The Court stated that racial quotas were illegal but that race could be considered as a factor in the admissions process.

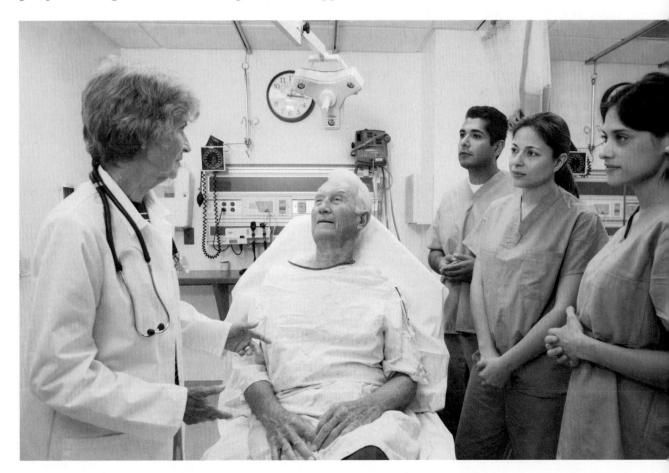

Blend Images/SuperStock

THE **CASE** OF...

Affirmative Action in Higher Education

The Law School Admissions Case

Barbara Grutter was a 49-year-old white mother of two and resident of Michigan who ran her own consulting firm when she applied to the University of Michigan Law School in 1996. She had a 3.8 grade point average and scored in the 85th percentile on the law school admissions test but was not accepted. She sued the law school in federal court, arguing that the law school had discriminated against her because of her race and had denied her equal protection of the law. Grutter objected to the admissions policy, which gave applicants belonging to certain underrepresented racial groups a better chance of being admitted than white students with the same credentials.

The University of Michigan Law School is highly competitive, admitting only 10 percent of its applicants. Its admissions policy focuses on academic ability and a flexible assessment of the applicant's individual talents, experiences, and potential to contribute to law school life and diversity. Diversity is not defined solely in terms of race, but the policy does reaffirm the law school's commitment to achieving a critical mass of African American, Hispanic, and Native American students.

Barbara Grutter won her case before the federal court of appeals, and the university appealed to the U.S. Supreme Court.

The Undergraduate Admissions Case

Jennifer Gratz, a white suburban resident of Michigan, applied for undergraduate admission to the University of Michigan in 1995. Although she met the entrance standards of the university, she was denied admission. The admissions process used a scoring system due to the large number of applications, assigning points to applicants based on high school courses and grades, standardized test scores, a personal essay, geographic diversity, special talents (athletic, musical, etc.), whether the applicant was the child of an alumnus, leadership, and race. This system automatically awarded 20 points toward the total of 150 (a score of 100 was generally required for admission) to students from underrepresented racial groups such as African Americans, Hispanics, and Native Americans. Virtually every qualified applicant from these groups had been admitted under this scoring system. Gratz also sued the university in federal court, but lost. She appealed to the U.S. Supreme Court.

The Supreme Court Decides the Two Cases

Because the issues of diversity and affirmative action in higher education are so important and because federal courts of appeals had issued conflicting decisions, the Supreme Court granted certiorari and agreed to hear both Michigan cases in 2003. In analyzing both cases the justices agreed that racial discrimination was involved and that the Court had to apply strict judicial scrutiny. The state had to show a compelling governmental interest in the use of race and that race could be used to further that interest only if it did not unduly burden the disfavored groups. For example, a race-conscious admissions program cannot use a quota system that sets aside a certain number of places in the entering class for members from selected underrepresented racial groups, although race or ethnicity could be considered a "plus" in a particular applicant's file.

A majority of the justices agreed that student body diversity is a compelling state interest that can justify using race in university admissions.

In a 5-to-4 opinion, the Court found that Michigan's law school admissions policy did not violate Barbara Grutter's rights. Having a critical mass (essential number) of students from underrepresented groups can enrich classroom discussion, produce cross-racial understanding, and break down racial stereotypes.

Rather than emphasizing diversity as justified by past or present discrimination, the Court's opinion in the law school case looked to the future challenges the nation faces: ". . . because universities, and in particular, law schools, represent the training ground for a large number of the Nation's leaders, the path to leadership must be visibly open to talented and qualified individuals of every race and ethnicity." The Court also noted that "the Law School engaged in a highly individualized, holistic view of each applicant's file, giving serious consideration to all the ways an applicant might contribute to a diverse educational environment."

Four justices dissented in the law school case, believing that the "critical mass" notion was simply a disguise for an illegal quota. To the dissenters, the Constitution's prohibition against racial discrimination applies equally to protect all people. They also believed there were nondiscriminatory ways to achieve diversity.

In contrast, Michigan's undergraduate admissions policy was found unconstitutional by a vote of 6 to 3. The majority objected to the program's failure to consider applicants on an individual basis as required by the Court's 1978 *Bakke* decision. While the undergraduate admissions program could use race-conscious affirmative action, it had to be individualized and not mechanical.

The dissenters would have allowed the use of automatic points to achieve diversity because it was an honest, open approach to the role race plays in the admissions process.

PROBLEM 41.3

a. What are the key facts in each of the cases? How are the cases similar? Different?

b. What are the strongest arguments in favor of affirmative action based on race in higher education? Against it?

c. How were the cases decided? Do you agree with the two decisions? Give your reasons.

d. The majority opinion in the law school case includes the following sentence: "We expect that 25 years from now, the use of racial preferences will no longer be necessary to further the interest approved today." Why might this time frame be significant? Will affirmative action be needed in 2028? Explain.

e. Assume that African Americans, Hispanics, and Native Americans make up 30 percent of the high school students in your state but only 12 percent of the undergraduates enrolled at your state's top public university. How would you advise the university's president to address this situation? Explain.

entering class, 16 of 100 places were reserved for applicants from under-represented racial groups. Allan Bakke, a 33-year-old white engineer, was twice denied admission to the medical school. He claimed that without the special admissions program, he would have been admitted because his grades and test scores were higher than those of the students of color. Bakke sued the university, saying that its affirmative action program denied him equal protection of the laws.

The Supreme Court found the medical school's special admissions program unconstitutional and ordered that Bakke be admitted to the university. The Court said that racial quotas were illegal but that race could be considered as one of the factors in the admissions process as part of an effort to obtain a diverse student body.

In the years following *Bakke,* it has been difficult to find an acceptable balance between ensuring diversity by using race as a factor in admissions policies, on one hand, and avoiding the use of unconstitutional racial quotas on the other. As some courts struck down the way state universities used race to ensure diversity, new strategies have been developed to attract a diverse student body. One such approach required state universities in Texas to admit any student graduating in the top 10 percent of his or her high school class.

Discrimination in Employment

In 1964, Congress passed the *Civil Rights Act of 1964. Title VII* of this act prohibits discrimination in employment based on race, color, sex, religion, or national origin by businesses with more than 15 employees or by labor unions. While the Fourteenth Amendment prohibited discrimination by government, *Title VII* extended protection to include discrimination by *private* employers. This law, enforced by the U.S. Equal Employment Opportunity Commission, does permit employment discrimination based on religion, sex, or national origin if it is a necessary qualification for the job. For example, a theatrical company may require that only women apply for female parts in a play.

Affirmative action has been just as controversial in employment as it has been in education. In 1979, the Supreme Court was called on to interpret the *Civil Rights Act of 1964* in a case involving a white employee at an aluminum plant in Louisiana. In that case, the employee's union and the plant voluntarily agreed to an affirmative action plan that

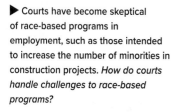

▶ Courts have become skeptical of race-based programs in employment, such as those intended to increase the number of minorities in construction projects. *How do courts handle challenges to race-based programs?*

reserved 50 percent of the training slots for higher-paying, more skilled positions for African Americans. The plan would operate until the level of African Americans in these higher-paying jobs reached the approximate level of African Americans in the local workforce. Before this agreement, African Americans had been dramatically underrepresented in the higher-paying jobs at the plant, compared to their percentage in the local workforce. Brian Weber, a white employee who was not admitted into the training program, brought a lawsuit against the plant because African American employees with less seniority than he had been admitted to the program.

Brian Weber lost his case against the plant. The Supreme Court found that *Title VII* had been passed to improve employment opportunities for members of underrepresented racial groups and that it did not prohibit employers in the private sector from establishing a *voluntary temporary* affirmative action plan designed to end racial imbalance.

The Court reasoned that the purpose of *Title VII* was to end discrimination and to remedy the segregation and underrepresentation that discrimination had caused in the nation's workforce. Because the voluntary affirmative action plan examined in this case mirrored the purposes of *Title VII*, the Court allowed it to stand. The Court believed that it was also important that no one lost a job as a result of the plan and that the plan was designed to operate only temporarily—until underrepresentation was ended.

In recent years, courts have grown increasingly skeptical of race-based programs in employment, just as they have in the area of education. Typical of the kind of program that has come under attack is a requirement that a fixed percentage of a publicly funded project—for example, the building of a road or a school—be set aside for firms owned by people from underrepresented groups. The purpose of these set-asides has generally been to increase the presence of minority contractors in the construction business. When this type of program is challenged as an illegal use of affirmative action, courts require proof that the program is necessary to achieve a compelling governmental interest. Most often, this has resulted in the program being struck down by the court. In other words, the same strict judicial scrutiny that was used to analyze actions that harmed people of color is now also used to analyze race-based federal, state, and local government programs designed to assist them. However, some race-conscious programs can still exist if, for example, they were designed to eradicate the results of past discrimination engaged in by government or a private party.

Some people welcome what they consider to be this new era of race-neutral programs. They argue that the United States can never become a race-neutral society if we continue to rely on race-conscious programs. Others believe that there is no meaningful way to make up for past discrimination without effective affirmative action programs and that justice requires remedies for past injustice.

In a U.S. Supreme Court opinion, a justice once wrote that classifications based on race carry a danger of "stigmatic harm," meaning that the group benefited by the affirmative action program might be harmed in the long run because society might believe that this group cannot succeed without special protection. Do you agree or disagree with this notion? Give your reasons.

Discrimination in Voting Rights

The states have the power to control their elections, and in doing so, certain forms of discrimination are permitted. For example, states can set a minimum voting age and require citizenship and at least a minimal period of residency. However, voting has been found by the Supreme Court to be a fundamental right—in fact, it is one right that helps protect all other rights in a democracy. For this reason, the Court closely scrutinizes any election rule that limits voting.

In 1966, the Court found a state poll tax of $1.50 to be an unconstitutional infringement on the right to vote. The most important legal protections to the right to vote for persons of color are found in the Fifteenth Amendment and in the *Voting Rights Act of 1965* and its later amendments.

Ratified in 1870, the Fifteenth Amendment to the U.S. Constitution provided the right to vote to male citizens of color. It states that, "the right of citizens of the United States to vote [shall not be] denied or abridged... by any State on account of race, color, or previous condition of servitude." However, obstacles to full voting rights continued well into the twentieth century through poll taxes, literacy tests, and intimidation of African Americans who wanted to exercise their voting rights. In addition, women did not win full voting rights until the ratification of the Nineteenth Amendment in 1920.

▼ The *Voting Rights Act of 1965* resulted in a dramatic increase in African American voter registration. *What obstacles to full voting rights existed before the passage of the* Voting Rights Act?

Congress passed the *Voting Rights Act of 1965* at the peak of the civil rights movement. The *Voting Rights Act,* promising equality in the area of political rights, was designed to make good the unfulfilled promise of the Civil War amendments. Congress amended the *Voting Rights Act* several times during the 1970s and 1980s to address persistent obstacles to equal opportunity in voting.

One feature of the *Voting Rights Act* was a requirement that locations with a history of racial discrimination in voting had to get approval from the U.S. Department of Justice before making any changes in its voting rules. This "preclearance" requirement, which applied to nine entire states, mostly in the South, and also to scores of cities and counties across the country, was challenged in a case called *Shelby County v. Holder.*

In a 5-to-4 opinion in 2013, the majority found that the preclearance requirement was based on out of date data and therefore unconstitutional. The majority determined that pre-clearance was a federal intrusion

THE **CASE** OF...

The Redistricting Commission and the State Legislature

Based on census figures that are compiled every 10 years, voting districts are redrawn in each state. Typically they are drawn so that the party in power in the state legislature has favorable boundaries in the coming election cycles. For example, in a state where one national party controls the state legislature, congressional voting districts will be drawn to give that party its best chance of winning as many of the state's congressional seats as possible. Sometimes the districts are compact, meaning, for example, that they are drawn along natural boundaries such as river or county lines. Other times districts can take on unusual shapes best designed to ensure partisan outcomes.

Some states have created bipartisan or nonpartisan commissions to conduct the redistricting process. In some states the commission then sends its recommendations to the state legislature for final approval.

Arizona voters passed a ballot initiative in 2000 creating a bipartisan commission consisting of two Democrats and two Republicans, selected by the legislature, and a fifth person selected by the other

four. The purpose behind the creation of the commission was to draw fairer district lines, mostly free of partisan gerrymandering.

In 2012 the redistricting commission approved a new congressional district map for the state. Once this happened, the state legislature sued, arguing that the commission was created in violation of the U.S. Constitution (First Amendment, section 4: "the Times, Places and Manner of holding Elections for Senators and Representatives shall be prescribed in each state by the Legislature thereof..."). The Arizona legislature argued that the commission was unconstitutional because the Constitution gives the legislature the exclusive power to draw congressional districts.

PROBLEM 41.5

a. What are the best arguments for the state legislature?

b. What are the best arguments for the commission?

c. More than 20 other states have some form of bipartisan or nonpartisan commission in place for redistricting, so the outcome of this case will have a large impact. How should the Court decide this case?

on state sovereignty and a badge of shame on affected jurisdictions that was no longer justified. The dissenters in the case said that the majority was substituting its judgment for that exercised by Congress when the *Voting Rights Act*, with its pre-clearance requirement, was reauthorized in 2006 and extended for another 25 years.

One traditional way to strengthen voting power is to redraw voting district lines to ensure that a particular group of people is included in the same district. This is called **gerrymandering.** These gerrymandered districts are often awkward in shape. Some states have redrawn voting districts to create districts in which underrepresented racial groups constitute the majority of voters. These are sometimes called majority-minority districts. Part of the rationale for the majority-minority districts is the fact that gerrymandering had once been widely used to divide these communities in order to dilute their ability to elect representatives who would work for their interests.

Gerrymandering is a political process and both major political parties—Republicans and Democrats—have at times used this process to protect incumbents (representatives already elected) and even to create additional seats (i.e., greater partisan advantage) for the party in control of the state legislature. This is called *partisan gerrymandering*. Several cases have been brought to the Supreme Court challenging gerrymandering as excessively partisan. But the Court has refused to pass judgment on redistricting plans, considering them part of the political process and largely beyond judicial review.

gerrymandering redrawing voting district lines to ensure that a particular group of people is included in the same districts

Discrimination Based on National Origin and Citizenship Status

Many people think of the civil rights struggle in terms of lawsuits brought by African Americans to end discriminatory practices. During the middle of the twentieth century, the National Association for the Advancement of Colored People (NAACP) and other organizations developed careful strategies for bringing important cases through the federal courts to the U.S. Supreme Court. The lead lawyers in many of those cases was future Supreme Court justice Thurgood Marshall. At the same time, groups representing Latino and Asian plaintiffs also brought significant cases in federal courts. While some of these cases dealt with racial discrimination, others challenged discrimination based on national origin or citizenship status.

Many of the challenged laws and policies treated people as members of a group rather than considering their individual characteristics. For example, courts struck down laws prohibiting noncitizens from becoming lawyers or engineers. State laws excluding noncitizens from all government jobs have also been held unconstitutional, although citizenship may be required for some positions. However, Congress's power to exclude some noncitizens from receiving Medicare benefits has been upheld.

THE **CASE** OF...

Educating the Children of Undocumented People

According to a state law, local school districts receive no money for educating undocumented children not legally admitted into the United States. The same law authorizes local school districts to deny enrollment to such children. A child of parents not legally admitted into the United States is excluded from his local school. That child's parents bring suit against the state, claiming that the law has denied their child equal protection.

▲ Learning fractions

PROBLEM 41.6

Read the two opinions below, and decide which one should be the decision of the U.S. Supreme Court. Give your reasons.

Opinion A

The Fourteenth Amendment says that "No state shall...deny to any person within its jurisdiction the equal protection of the laws." This principle should be applied to all persons, even the children of undocumented people. While our past decisions have allowed states to treat undocumented people differently from those legally admitted, the idea of punishing innocent children for the misconduct of their parents does not fit with our basic idea of fairness. Although there is no federal constitutional right to an education, we recognize that economic opportunity is severely limited for those who are unable to obtain one. This law unconstitutionally places a lifetime of hardship on the children of undocumented parents. It can place social and economic costs on other citizens if these children grow up to be unproductive members of society.

Opinion B

Undocumented people, as opposed to legal residents, are not a group receiving special judicial protection according to our past decisions, and this Court has never held that education is a fundamental right. Therefore, when we look at this new law, we should not be tempted to substitute our wisdom for that of the representatives elected by the state's citizens. Our precedents require only that state laws not violate the Constitution. In this case, the law must have a rational basis. It is certainly not irrational for the state to decline to use its limited financial resources to provide benefits for persons whose presence in this country is illegal. The state law in question does not violate the federal constitution. If the people of the state disagree with this policy, they should address their problem to their elected representatives.

▲ The diverse U.S. population makes protection against discrimination necessary. *What does* Title VII *of the* Civil Rights Act of 1964 *protect against?*

Investigating the Law Where You Live

Find out what state agency handles employment discrimination complaints where you live.

In private (nongovernment) employment, *Title VII* of the *Civil Rights Act of 1964* protects against employment discrimination based on national origin. Employers cannot treat people less favorably on the job because they come from a particular place or because of their ethnicity or their accent. It may be a violation of *Title VII* to require employees to speak English at all times on the job, unless this is necessary for doing the job correctly. However, an employer may not legally hire a person who is in the country without permission.

In the context of criminal law cases and violations of immigration law, persons who are in the country without permission are not given the same due process protections as either citizens or noncitizens who are lawfully in the United States. See Chapter 42 for additional information about immigration law.

Discrimination Based on Sex

The movement to secure equal rights for women has a long history. From the nation's earliest days, women protested against unequal treatment. The first women's rights convention was held in 1848 in Seneca Falls, New York. It set out a list of demands for political, social, and economic equality. The most controversial issue to come out of the Seneca Falls Convention was women's demand for the right to vote. Over 70 years later, women finally won full voting rights with the ratification of the Nineteenth Amendment in 1920.

◀ Congress approved the Equal Rights Amendment (ERA) in 1972, but the amendment ran into opposition when it was sent to the states for ratification. *What did the ERA propose?*

Although women have made many gains, the U.S. Supreme Court was slow to recognize sex discrimination as a problem. Even after passage of the Nineteenth Amendment, it took another 50 years for the Court to find a government policy based on sex to be unconstitutional.

For many years, advocates fought to get the Equal Rights Amendment (ERA) passed. The ERA would have prohibited federal, state, and local governments from passing discriminatory laws or unequally enforcing laws based on sex. The ERA was passed by Congress and sent to the states for ratification in 1972. In 1982, the ERA failed to become part of the Constitution when the ratification deadline passed with the vote still three states short of the 38 needed.

In 1963 Congress passed the *Equal Pay Act,* which made it illegal to pay women less money than men for doing the same job. Under the *Equal Pay Act,* men and women must be given equal pay for equal work performed in the same establishment. If the job requires substantially equal skill, effort, and responsibility under the same working conditions, then equal pay is required, even if job titles are different. In 2018, women were paid $0.78 for every $1.00 men were paid, according to the U.S. Census Bureau. The pay gap was generally even larger for women of color.

THE **CASE** OF...

The Single-Sex School

Virginia Military Institute (VMI) is a taxpayer-supported state military college in Lexington, Virginia. VMI's distinctive mission is to produce citizen-soldiers, men prepared for leadership in civilian life and in military service. In recent years, the military role of VMI has diminished somewhat, with only about 15 percent of VMI's graduates pursuing military careers.

Since its establishment in 1839, VMI has consistently produced an impressive corps of graduates who constitute a loyal, powerful alumni group, many of whom have become leaders in politics, business, and the military. The alumni have developed the largest per-student endowment of any undergraduate college in the United States.

VMI uses a unique approach to instill physical and mental discipline in its cadets while imparting a strong moral code. Similar to a Marine boot camp, this "adversative method" breaks down the individual and then slowly builds him back up again by making him proud of himself and his capacity to survive. This approach includes physical rigor, mental stress, an absence of privacy, extreme regulation of behavior, and indoctrination in desirable values. One aspect of this method is the "rat line," where new cadets must run quickly through a line of more senior cadets while they receive physical punishment.

Between 1988 and 1990, 347 women wrote to VMI for admissions information. They received no response. In 1990, the U.S. Department of Justice brought suit to force VMI to admit women. The Justice Department argued that VMI was denying women the equal protection of the law. VMI argued that women would fundamentally change the character of their school.

Through a series of court decisions and negotiations, VMI agreed to establish a separate Virginia Women's Institute for Leadership (VWIL) rather than admit women to VMI. VWIL did not use the adversative method, but instead used a cooperative methodology based on educational theories that show it is more appropriate for women. The Justice Department did not believe that this adjustment constituted equal protection of the law and sued a second time.

▲ A female cadet

PROBLEM 41.7

a. Why would the state of Virginia want to keep VMI all male? What arguments can Virginia make that it is not denying women the equal protection of the law?

b. What arguments can the Justice Department make that Virginia's operation of VMI violates the Fourteenth Amendment?

c. How should this case be decided? Explain.

d. Assume VMI must be opened to members of both sexes. Does this mean that the exact same program should be offered to men and women? For example, should women have to run through the rat line and shave their heads the way men do? Explain.

e. Do you think that all single-sex schools operated by the government violate the U.S. Constitution? Give your reasons.

One year after the *Equal Pay Act,* Congress passed the *Civil Rights Act of 1964. Title VII* of this act prohibits discrimination by private companies with more than 15 employees against women and people of color in all forms of employment: hiring, firing, working conditions, and promotion. In addition, employees who face discrimination by government because of their sex may sue under the Fourteenth Amendment to the U.S. Constitution, which guarantees "equal protection under the laws." Women or men who think they have been discriminated against because of their sex can contact the U.S. Equal Employment Opportunity Commission (EEOC) or state or local antidiscrimination agencies. The EEOC is responsible for investigating charges of discrimination alleging a violation of *Title VII.*

Alongside legal changes have been increases in women serving in elected office at all levels of government and on the bench. The first woman elected to Congress was Jeannette Rankin, elected to the House from Montana in 1917. The number of women in Congress grew slowly through much of the 20th century with the number almost doubling in the election of 1992. As of 2018, three of the nine Supreme Court justices were women. Approximately 33 percent of judges and a similar percentage of federal judges were women

PROBLEM 41.8

Based on your knowledge of sex discrimination law, analyze each of the following situations and decide whether illegal sex discrimination is occurring. Give reasons for your decisions.

a. A state-supported nursing school does not accept applications from men.

b. A man applies for a job as a used-car salesperson, but the woman who owns the business does not hire him. The reason she gives is that "he is not good-looking enough to entice the young women who come here looking for a car to buy one."

c. A state government provides three months of paid leave to women who become mothers. Paid disability leave for state-employed men who become fathers is limited to four weeks.

d. Women in the military are not allowed to fight in the infantry alongside men in the front line of battle.

Sexual Harassment

An important type of sex discrimination is **sexual harassment.** The federal Equal Employment Opportunity Commission (EEOC) has defined this as "unwelcome sexual advances, requests for favors, and other verbal or physical conduct of a sexual nature" which take place in the workplace. In one type of sexual harassment, a supervisor leads an employee to believe he or she will lose the job if he or she does not submit to the supervisor's sexual advances, or a promotion is offered in exchange for sexual favors. This is called **quid pro quo** (literally, "this for

sexual harassment unwelcome sexual advances, requests for sexual favors, and other verbal or physical conduct of a sexual nature that occurs in the workplace

quid pro quo Latin for "this for that"; an exchange of things or favors

THE **CASE** OF...

The Obnoxious Remarks

Theresa Harris worked as a manager at Forklift Systems. The president of the company, Charles Hardy, made comments to Theresa Harris on the job such as, "You're a stupid woman" and "Let's go to the Highway Hotel to negotiate your raise." He made these comments to Harris in the presence of other employees. In addition, Hardy made sexual comments about Harris's clothes.

In a private meeting, Harris complained to Hardy about his behavior. He apologized, said he had been only joking, and promised to stop the behavior. But the obnoxious comments continued. She filed a lawsuit under *Title VII* of the *Civil Rights Act of 1964,* claiming sexual harassment. At the trial, other female employees testified that they were not offended by Hardy's comments and considered them to be jokes. Harris testified that the comments upset her so much that she began drinking and had to quit her job.

The trial judge concluded that, while Hardy's behavior was annoying and insensitive, it did not create a hostile, abusive environment, nor did it interfere with Harris's work performance. The court believed that the conduct did offend Harris and that it would offend a reasonable woman in the same position as Harris. The court found, however, that the conduct was not so severe as to seriously affect her psychological well-being. Therefore, the court decided that Harris could not win her lawsuit. The court of appeals upheld the trial court's decision, and Harris appealed to the U.S. Supreme Court.

In a unanimous decision, the Court established a new standard for deciding sexual harassment cases. It stated that *Title VII* is violated when a hostile or abusive work environment has been created. The victim must show only that he or she was offended by the conduct in question and that a reasonable person would find the conduct abusive as well. Thus, Harris did not have to show psychological harm in order to win her sexual harassment suit.

The Court found it difficult to say exactly what conduct would be considered abusive or hostile. Instead, courts must look at all the circumstances surrounding the offensive conduct: How often did it occur? How severe was it? Did it unreasonably interfere with the victim's work performance? Was the victim physically threatened or humiliated? No single factor is required to make a case for a hostile or abusive environment. While the mere utterance of an offensive remark certainly does not violate the law, according to Justice Sandra Day O'Connor's opinion, "*Title VII* comes into play before the harassing conduct leads to a nervous breakdown."

PROBLEM 41.9

a. Why is sexual harassment considered a form of sex discrimination? How is it related to *Title VII*'s goal of equal opportunity?

b. What was the standard decided by the U.S. Supreme Court in the *Harris* case? How does this differ from the standard used by the trial court when it first heard the case?

c. Assume the *Harris* case is tried again, this time using the standard announced by the U.S. Supreme Court. As Harris's attorney, what arguments would you make on her behalf? As Hardy's attorney, what arguments would you make on his behalf? If you were the trial judge, would you find sexual harassment in this case? Explain your reasons.

d. What steps should companies take to deal with the issue of sexual harassment in the workplace?

e. What steps do you think an employee should take if he or she has been a victim of sexual harassment?

that") sexual harassment. Employees of either sex are protected from harassment by supervisors of the opposite sex or of the same sex.

The courts have also held that constant vulgar comments, unwelcome physical touching, or other sexual conduct affecting an employee's working conditions constitute sexual harassment. This is called **hostile environment** sexual harassment. The U.S. Supreme Court has defined a hostile work environment as unwelcome conduct of a sexual nature that is so severe or pervasive as to change the conditions of employment. When a hostile or offensive work environment exists, there is no need to show that the employee was in danger of losing his or her job or of being denied a promotion.

▲ Sexual harassment has been a continuing challenge. *Should the law protect women working in traditionally male job settings from sexual harassment?*

hostile environment an uncomfortable working environment in the context of sexual harassment

Surveys show that a high incidence of sexual harassment occurs in the workplace. A majority of women surveyed indicated that they had been the victims of sexual harassment at work. Men are victims less frequently. However, in 1998 the U.S. Supreme Court ruled that a male who is sexually harassed by other males while on the job can make a claim of sexual harassment. The Court's decision stated that just because the plaintiff and the defendant are of the same sex does not mean that there cannot be a valid claim.

Sexual harassment does not occur only in the workplace. Many types of sexual harassment occur in schools as well. There may be harassment from a teacher toward a student, from a student toward a teacher, or from one student toward another. Studies indicate that a significant percentage of both girls and boys are subjected to sexual harassment in school settings. The U.S. Supreme Court has ruled that a public school system can be sued for money damages for failing to respond to known acts of student-to-student harassment that were severe and pervasive.

Many instances of sexual harassment go unreported because of embarrassment or fear of retaliation. However, it is illegal for an employer to take punitive action against an employee because he or she complains in good faith of sexual harassment. An employee can file a complaint with the EEOC or a similar state or local agency or file a sex discrimination case in state or federal court.

In two important 1998 decisions, the Supreme Court ruled that an employer can be held liable for employees' sexual harassment, unless it can prove that it took reasonable steps to prevent harassment and the alleged victim failed to take advantage of the available preventive measures. These decisions encourage employers to establish policies making clear that harassment will not be tolerated, to communicate these policies to all employees, and to provide a meaningful process for handling complaints. Some criticize the development of this area of the law as an attempt to excessively control the workplace and to try to regulate all aspects of interpersonal relationships.

There may be more than one way to handle a sexual harassment situation. It may be possible, for example, to use mediation to manage the conflict. In mediation, an impartial third party assists individuals in discussing and resolving their differences.

PROBLEM 41.10

Which of the following situations, taken alone, constitutes sexual harassment? Why or why not? How should each situation be handled?

a. Fernando and Sylvia are police officers who share the same patrol car. Fernando is the senior officer in charge of the patrol. One night he tells Sylvia he is attracted to her and would like to start dating her.

b. Lois is one of a few female welders. Her male coworkers repeatedly display graphic photographs and drawings of nude women and also make derogatory sexual comments to her.

c. Bart likes to make sexual comments to Ella, who works with him on a construction crew. Ella says she hates his remarks and responds with similar comments only to get back at him for embarrassing her.

d. Stephanie supervises five computer programmers—Victor and four women. She often puts her arm on his shoulder at work and calls him "honey." She also invites Victor, but never the women, to lunch.

e. A male supervisor tells a new male employee, "We only hired you because you are nice to look at."

f. A male high school teacher hugs a female student after she receives high college entrance exam scores. He tells her she has everything going for her, "including smarts and an attractive physique."

g. A female professor testifies before a government committee that her former male boss frequently made sexual remarks to her and asked her out on dates.

h. As part of a "boys against the girls" game at recess, a first-grade boy pulls down a female classmate's pants.

Title IX

In 1972, Congress acted to end sex discrimination in education. *Title IX of the Education Act of 1972* prohibits gender discrimination in all elementary and secondary schools, colleges, and universities that receive federal funds. The affected school activities include curriculum, faculty hiring, and student athletic programs.

Before the enactment of the law, fewer than 30,000 women participated in NCAA intercollegiate sports. In the 2017-2018 academic year, more than 216,000 female athletes were competing, comprising 44 percent of college athletes. At the high school level, there were 3.4 million female athletes representing 43 percent of high school athletes.

Title IX requires equal opportunity for men and women in athletic programs by requiring schools to meet one of the following criteria:

1. that the percentages of male and female athletes are proportionate to the percentages of male and female students enrolled; or

2. that it has a history and continuing practice of expanding opportunities for the underrepresented sex; or

3. that its athletics program fully accommodates the interests and abilities of students of that sex.

Some colleges choose to satisfy the first prong by eliminating some men's teams in order to increase the proportion of female athletes, giving rise to the controversial accusation that they are actually discriminating against male athletes. *Title IX* regulations do not require schools to cut any sports, and the Department of Education encourages schools to fulfill this

▲ Title IX has increased the participation of females in high school and collegiate sports. *Why has* Title IX's *impact on student athletes been controversial?*

Investigating the Law Where You Live

Does your school receive federal funds? (If it is a public school, the answer is yes.) Does your school provide equal opportunities for its female athletes? If you think it doesn't, what change(s) would you suggest?

requirement by increasing opportunities for women. For example, assume a school has a men's basketball team and that it also has a number of women who are interested in playing basketball. The law requires the school either to establish a women's basketball team or to allow women to try out for the men's team. Moreover, if a separate women's team is established, the school cannot discriminate against the women by providing inferior facilities or equipment.

If a few women (not enough to establish a team) are interested in a noncontact sport for which a men's team exists, the school must allow them to try out for the men's team. In contact sports, however, such as football or wrestling, schools can limit teams to members of one sex. Although athletic opportunities must be equal, the law does not require that total expenditures for men's and women's sports be equal.

If a school violates *Title IX*, the government or the person discriminated against can go to court. *Title IX* also allows the federal government to cut off financial aid to schools that discriminate on the basis of sex.

PROBLEM 41.11

Title IX states: "No person in the United States shall, on the basis of sex, be excluded from participation in, be denied the benefits of, or be subjected to discrimination under any education program or activity receiving federal financial assistance."

Which, if any, of the following situations do you believe are in violation of *Title IX?* Assume each school receives federal funds.

a. The music department at the state college has two glee clubs, one for men and the other for women.

b. A school establishes a women's baseball team, which receives used equipment from the men's team.

c. A U.S. history curriculum does not include important contributions made by American women.

d. A small high school competes in volleyball and has a team of only female students. A male student wants to play interscholastic volleyball.

e. A large state university has established separate teams for women in all noncontact sports and has provided them with equivalent equipment. Twice as many males as females participate in the school's interscholastic programs, and 85 percent of the school's athletic scholarship funds go to males.

f. A high school baseball team's parent booster club raises money to build covered dugouts for the baseball field. The softball field used by the girls' team does not have covered dugouts.

◀ Many members of the LGBT community continue to fight for laws that would give them equal rights. *How do state and local laws reflect the changing attitudes toward LGBT people in the United States?*

Discrimination Based on Sexual Orientation and Gender Identity

Throughout much of U.S. history, homosexuality has been a taboo subject. Often, it has been treated as a crime. Today, millions of gay, lesbian, bisexual and transgender (LGBT) people are open about their sexuality and are campaigning for laws that would give them equal rights. These rights include the right to be free from discrimination in employment, housing, and public accommodation.

In the past two decades, American attitudes toward LGBT people have generally become more tolerant. However, some people oppose specific laws that protect members of the LGBT community. These people believe that such laws would give LGBT individuals special rights rather than providing equal rights.

Sexual orientation and gender identity should not be confused. Sexual orientation describes romantic or sexual attraction to other people, whereas gender identity reflects how individuals perceive themselves and what they call themselves—male, female, a blend of both, or neither. One's gender identify can be the same as or different from their sex assigned at birth.

A number of states, cities, and towns have passed laws that provide some protection from discrimination for people who are, or are perceived to be LGBT. These laws vary from place to place and may protect individuals in the areas of employment, housing, education, family matters, and public accommodation. Laws in New York City, for example, allow individuals to inherit the rent-controlled status of apartments from their same-sex partners, prohibit discrimination based on sexual orientation in the workplace, and protect students from harassment and discrimination based on sexual orientation, real or perceived.

At the federal level, Congress has not passed laws to protect people from discrimination based on their sexual orientation. As of 2019, bills to prohibit discrimination against gay, lesbian, and bisexual individuals in the workplace have been proposed by various members of Congress but have not been passed. An executive order signed in 1998 prohibits discrimination in the hiring and firing of executive branch employees based on sexual orientation.

Discrimination in the U.S. military has been particularly controversial. In 1993, President Bill Clinton created a compromise order known as "don't ask, don't tell." This policy prevented the military from investigating the sexual orientation of members of the armed forced but also excluded openly gay, lesbian and bisexual people from service. In 2010, President Barack Obama signed into law a bill repealing this policy. While the U.S. military now allows LGB individuals to serve openly, President Trump introduced a ban on transgender individuals that went into effect in 2019.

Several cases dealing with discrimination based on sexual orientation have come before the U.S. Supreme Court in recent years. In 1996, the Court heard a case from Colorado that dealt with a state constitutional amendment, adopted through a statewide referendum, that prohibited any level of government in the state from passing laws to protect people against discrimination based on sexual orientation. The Supreme Court said that disqualifying a class of persons from the right to obtain specific protection from the law is a denial of equal protection in its most basic sense as described in the Fourteenth Amendment to the Constitution. The Court also found that the amendment was "born of animosity toward the class that it affects." The Court used the rational basis test to strike down the law as having no legitimate legislative purpose.

In 2013, the Court struck down the *Defense of Marriage Act (DOMA)*, a federal law that denied legally married same-sex couples the same federal recognition, rights, and benefits that heterosexual married couples receive under federal law. In 2015 the Supreme Court ruled in *Obergefell* v. *Hodges* that the fundamental right to marry is guaranteed to same-sex couples by the due process clause and the equal protection clause of the Fourteenth Amendment. The ruling requires all 50 states and the District of Columbia to perform and recognize the marriages of same-sex couples.

As of 2018, 27 countries either perform or recognize same-sex marriage. Many other countries have national domestic-partner laws that provide same-sex couples with many of the legal rights enjoyed by married couples. These rights include the right to medical decisions for an incapacitated partner, the right to share health insurance benefits, and the right to inherit property under a will. In the United States some people continue to oppose legal recognition of same-sex couples, arguing that it is inconsistent with the country's mainstream religious teachings, core traditions, and the morality of some people.

Investigating the Law Where You Live

Find out whether there are laws that protect people based on sexual orientation in your town or state. If so, do you think these laws are necessary? If not, should there be such laws?

THE **CASE** OF...

Lawrence v. Texas

On September 17, 1998, Houston police were called to the apartment of John Lawrence based on a report from a neighbor that an armed intruder was "going crazy" in Lawrence's apartment. When police arrived, they found Lawrence and Tyrone Garner engaged in a private consensual sex act. The neighbor later admitted that his allegations were false and was convicted of filing a false report.

Lawrence and Garner were arrested for violating a Texas law prohibiting two persons of the same sex from engaging in certain intimate sexual contact. They were convicted of this misdemeanor and fined $200 each. They appealed their convictions through the state court system, arguing that the Texas law violated their Fourteenth Amendment rights. Specifically, they believed that the law denied them equal protection of the law because it prohibited sexual acts among gay and lesbian people that were permitted among heterosexual couples. They also believed that the due process clause of the Fourteenth Amendment protected the liberty and privacy interests of same-sex and opposite-sex couples and prohibited a state from criminalizing private, consensual sex acts among adults. Relying on the U.S. Supreme Court precedent in *Bowers* v. *Hardwick* (1986), which upheld the constitutionality of a similar law in Georgia, the Texas Court of Criminal Appeals—the highest state court for criminal cases—affirmed the convictions.

The U.S. Supreme Court agreed to hear the case and in June 2003 issued a 6-to-3 decision overturning the Texas law as well as its earlier precedent of *Bowers* v. *Hardwick*. The Court found support for Lawrence's due process argument in earlier privacy rights cases dealing with contraception and abortion.

Writing for the majority, Justice Anthony Kennedy said, "It is a promise of the Constitution that there is a realm of personal liberty which the government may not enter. ... [This case does not involve minors or people paying for sex but rather] two adults who with full and mutual consent ... engaged in sexual practices common to a homosexual lifestyle. [They] are entitled to respect for their private lives. The state cannot demean their existence ... by making their private sexual conduct a crime." Four other justices signed Justice Kennedy's opinion. Justice Sandra Day O'Connor also agreed with the outcome but wrote in her own concurrence that it was their equal protection rather than due process rights that had been violated.

The dissenting justices and other critics of the decision argued that this decision takes away a state's traditional authority to pass laws that set moral standards and reflect the values and views of its citizens. From this perspective, outlawing such behavior was a logical outcome of democracy, not discrimination. Critics also argued that the decision undermines family values.

PROBLEM 41.12

a. What arguments could Lawrence and Garner make for finding the Texas law unconstitutional? What arguments could Texas make for upholding its law?

b. Do you agree with the Supreme Court's decision in this case? Give your reasons.

c. One thing that both supporters and critics of the Court's decision agreed about was its importance. Why was the decision considered to be so important?

d. Explain Justice O'Connor's position on the case.

e. Should states have authority over moral issues? Give reasons to support your answer.

The organization Public Agenda—www.publicagenda.org—helps stimulate discussion about controversial public issues. The following are adaptations of three perspectives for framing the debate that have been developed by Public Agenda.

Perspective 1: *Protect and extend equal rights of all citizens.* The federal government has struggled to provide equal rights to citizens regardless of race, sex, or disability. As part of our overall effort to ensure that all citizens enjoy human rights, there is no legitimate reason to exclude LGBT people who face discrimination in housing, employment, and family matters.

Perspective 2: *Let states and communities choose solutions that work for them.* In a country as large and diverse as ours, where diversity is part of our strength, it is best to let communities make their own decisions on issues as controversial as LGBT rights and fashion workable solutions at the grassroots level. In this area, the federal government should follow, not lead.

Perspective 3: *Support and protect traditional institutions and values.* Tolerating private behavior between consenting adults and granting legal protection for LGBT people are very different. Many people are offended by the notion of same-sex relationships and believe that opposite-sex marriage is a pillar of our civil society.

a. With which perspective described above do you most agree? Give the reasons for your answer.

b. What additional information would be helpful to you in determining your perspective? Where could you find this information?

c. Based on the perspective you have selected, what steps, if any, should be taken to prevent discrimination based on sexual orientation?

Discrimination Based on Age

Mario Campisi, age 55, worked for the same company for 20 years. His boss said that Mario was an excellent worker, but he wanted to bring in someone younger. Mario was given two choices: take a new, lower-paying position or quit. Mario might not have known it, but he had the law on his side.

The *Age Discrimination in Employment Act* protects workers age 40 or older. It forbids discrimination in hiring, firing, paying, promoting, and other aspects of employment. The law applies to private employers of 20 or more people, labor unions, government agencies, and employment agencies.

The law has several important exceptions. It does not apply if age is a bona fide job qualification. There must be a real and valid reason to consider age. For example, an older person could be refused a role playing

◀ Workers age 40 or older are protected by the *Age Discrimination in Employment Act*. Can you identify jobs in which an employer might be justified in refusing to hire an applicant over 40 years of age?

a teenager in a movie. The law also does not apply if an employment decision is made for a good reason other than age. For example, an older employee could be fired for misconduct. Any person who feels he or she has been discriminated against because of age can file a complaint with the Equal Employment Opportunity Commission or a state or local Fair Employment Practice Agency.

THE **CASE** OF...

The Forced Retirement

Massachusetts required state police officers to retire at age 50. The law was designed to ensure that police officers were physically fit. The state police department required complete physical examinations every two years until an officer reached age 40. Then it required exams every year until the officer reached age 50, the mandatory retirement age. Officer Murgia passed all examinations and was in excellent health when the state police retired him on his 50th birthday. Murgia sued the state police, arguing that the mandatory retirement age denied him equal protection. Should the Fourteenth Amendment protect Officer Murgia in this case? Explain the reasons for your answer.

In deciding Officer Murgia's case, the U.S. Supreme Court said, "Drawing lines that create distinctions is... a legislative task and an unavoidable one. Perfection in making the classification is neither possible nor necessary. Such action by a legislature is presumed to be valid." Although Officer Murgia was in good health, the Court accepted the fact that physical fitness generally declines with age. Therefore, it was rational for the state to draw a line at some age, and the Court upheld this law.

PROBLEM 41.14

Do you agree or disagree with the Court's decision? Explain the reasons for your answer.

Age discrimination is not limited to older people. Many laws and practices also discriminate against youth. However, restrictions based on age as it relates to voting, running for public office, making a will, driving, and drinking are generally upheld by the courts as being reasonable.

Although the courts have not used the equal protection clause to protect the rights of youth, some state and local legislatures have passed laws or regulations forbidding age discrimination. In addition, the Twenty-sixth Amendment gives people 18 years of age or older the right to vote in federal and state elections.

Discrimination Based on Disability

According to the U.S. Census Bureau, about one in five Americans (56.7 million people in 2010) has some kind of disability. Just over one in ten has a severe disability. A person who has difficulty performing certain basic functions such as seeing, hearing, talking, or walking or has regular difficulty performing basic activities of daily living is considered to have a disability. A person who is unable to perform one or more daily activities or who needs assistance from another person to perform basic activities is considered to have a severe disability.

Many people with disabilities regularly suffer discrimination in certain areas of daily life. Discrimination often occurs because of prejudice, ignorance, or fear. For example, society may ignore or separate people who are different, believing it may not be appropriate or possible for people with disabilities to participate in certain activities. In addition, other people may not be comfortable seeing people with disabilities participating in everyday activities in society.

Since the 1970s, a number of laws have been passed to prohibit discrimination against people with disabilities. These laws requiring consideration of a person's special needs involve such issues as education, employment, building design, and transportation.

▼ Laws that prohibit discrimination against people with disabilities require consideration of a person's special needs.

Early Legislation

The *Rehabilitation Act of 1973* prohibits discrimination based on disability by the federal government, federal contractors, and recipients of federal financial assistance. This act bans discrimination in employment and requires employers who receive federal benefits to set up programs to assist people with disabilities. Discrimination against people with disabilities is also prohibited in services, programs, or activities provided by all state and local governments.

Education is another area in which the law provides protection. Historically, many children were excluded from attending public schools because of mental or physical disabilities. However, in 1975, Congress passed the *Education for All Handicapped Children Act.* This law, now known as the *Individuals with Disabilities Education Act (IDEA)*, requires states to provide a free and appropriate education to children with special needs in the least restrictive setting possible.

The Student with a Disability

Amy Rowley, who is deaf, was placed in kindergarten and first-grade classes with children who hear without assistance. She attended speech therapy and tutoring sessions in addition to her regular classes and also wore a special hearing aid provided by the school. Amy received passing grades in all her classes. Her parents believed that she would gain much more from her education if she had an interpreter, so they asked the school district to provide one. The school district denied the Rowleys' request, calling it unnecessary and an undue financial burden.

The Rowleys sued the school district under the federal *Education for All Handicapped Children Act.* This law entitles children with disabilities to "a free and appropriate education." The trial judge found that Amy understood only about 60 percent of what was said in class. The case was eventually appealed to the U.S. Supreme Court.

The Court held that under this law schools were required to provide "specialized instruction and related services which are individually designed to provide an educational benefit to the handicapped

▲ A hearing-impaired student

child." A school is not required, however, to provide a program that will maximize the child's potential. With this language, the Court approved the program the school district was already providing to Amy.

PROBLEM 41.15

Do you agree with this decision? Explain.

The Americans with Disabilities Act

In 1990, the *Americans with Disabilities Act (ADA)* was passed to provide much broader protection against discrimination. Many people consider this the most important federal civil rights legislation since the *Civil Rights Act of 1964.* Now many more organizations and businesses are prohibited from discriminating against people with disabilities. This law affects businesses, public accommodations, services provided by state and local governments, transportation, and telecommunications.

The *ADA* defines a person with a disability as someone with "a mental or physical impairment that substantially limits one or more of the major life activities of a person; a record of such an impairment; or being regarded as having such an impairment." It is important to note that, with certain exceptions, the *ADA* does not list specific diseases and impairments under the definition of *disability.* This was done because a specific disease or impairment may not be disabling for one person but may be severely disabling for another.

People with HIV (the virus that causes AIDS) and AIDS, however, are protected under the *ADA*. Alcoholics who are in treatment or rehabilitated are also protected under the *ADA,* as are rehabilitated drug users and those in treatment for drug use.

The primary purpose of the *ADA* is to assist in bringing people with disabilities into the economic and social mainstream of society. For most Americans, a fundamental aspect of life is employment. However, many people with disabilities have been denied the opportunity to participate fully in an employment situation, thus denying them access to economic involvement in society. For this reason, a major portion of the *ADA* deals with employment.

A "qualified individual with a disability" is entitled to "reasonable accommodations" to overcome existing barriers. Some examples of reasonable accommodations include making facilities accessible for workers with mobility difficulties; modifying exams and training materials, such as providing these items in large print; providing qualified readers or interpreters; and providing reserved parking. What constitutes a reasonable accommodation may be different for each person.

THE **CASE** OF...

The Dentist and His HIV-Positive Patient

Sidney Abbott became infected with HIV in 1986. In 1994, Ms. Abbott scheduled a dental appointment with Dr. Bragdon of Maine. She disclosed her HIV-positive status on a patient registration form. At the time of her visit, she had none of the virus's most serious symptoms. Dr. Bragdon informed Ms. Abbott that she had a cavity that needed a filling but that he maintained a policy against filling cavities of HIV-positive patients in his office. Dr. Bragdon did offer to perform the procedure in a hospital at no extra charge. Ms. Abbott would, however, have to pay for the cost of using the hospital facilities.

Ms. Abbott filed suit under the *Americans with Disabilities Act*, alleging that she was discriminated against on the basis of her disability as an individual living with HIV. She argued that the following section of the *ADA* protects her:

"No individual shall be discriminated against on the basis of disability in the full and equal enjoyment of the goods, services, facilities, privileges, advantages or accommodations of any place of public accommodation by any person who... operates a place of public accommodation."

PROBLEM 41.16

a. Should a person who has HIV but who has not yet developed AIDS be considered a person with a disability under the *ADA?* Give your reasons.

b. Could the dentist successfully argue that treatment in his office of a person covered by the *ADA* is not required in this instance, because Ms. Abbott presents a threat to the health of the dentist or his staff?

c. How should this case be decided? Explain.

THE **CASE** OF...

The Golfer and His Golf Cart

Casey Martin is a professional golfer who suffers from a physical condition that makes it impossible for him to walk long distances. Due to the nature of his profession, Martin compensates for this inability by using a golf cart to maneuver around the course. Martin plays well enough to participate in the Professional Golfers' Association (PGA) Tour. However, PGA rules prohibit the use of a golf cart on the tour. The PGA's position is that walking is a basic part of the game of golf and that if Martin cannot walk the golf course, he must be excluded from the PGA Tour.

Martin, who could not play golf professionally without the use of a golf cart, brought a lawsuit against the PGA, claiming that the rule against carts violated his rights under the *Americans with Disabilities Act (ADA)*. The PGA argued that it was a private club and could therefore make its own rules. In addition, famous golfers testified that walking was a critical part of the game of golf.

PROBLEM 41.17

a. What arguments can Casey Martin make that the PGA is violating his rights under the *ADA*?

b. What arguments can the PGA make supporting its decision that Martin not be allowed on the tour if he must use a cart to play golf?

c. How should this case be decided? Give the reasons for your answer.

An employer is not required to make an accommodation if doing so would cause the employer significant difficulty or expense. Such a hardship must be "unduly costly," not just inconvenient, and one that would "fundamentally alter" the business. An employer is not required to make changes ahead of time for any or all possible disabilities. A person with a disability must request an accommodation. In addition, an employer may not ask questions about a particular disability until after a job offer has been made. An employer, however, may ask whether the person will be able to handle tasks that are essential to the job. Note that the *ADA* does allow employers a narrow exception to hire or refuse to hire an individual whose disability would pose a direct threat to the health or safety of the employee or others.

Other federal, state, and local laws also assist people with disabilities. The *Architectural Barriers Act of 1968* requires that all public buildings be made accessible. Restrooms, elevators, drinking fountains, meeting rooms, and public telephones must be designed to accommodate people with disabilities. Similarly, many local laws require wheelchair ramps, Braille signs for the blind, designated parking spaces, and other accommodations for people with disabilities.

People with physical and mental disabilities now have more rights, yet some problems and conflicts remain. For example, people who use wheelchairs need curb ramps, but people who are blind and use canes need curb markers to warn them where sidewalks end.

Discrimination and Disabilities

Evaluate each situation. Does the person have a disability? If so, describe the disability. Is there discrimination based on disability? Should an accommodation be provided? Explain.

a. A high school student who uses a wheelchair needs a ramp installed to reach the stage during graduation. The principal says the diploma can be awarded in front of the stage.

b. Doug applied for a job as a firefighter. He passed the written and physical tests, and the city sent him a letter of appointment. Before he began work, the city learned he was HIV positive and told him not to report for work.

c. A Little League baseball coach who uses a wheelchair is told that, for safety reasons, he can no longer coach his team from the playing field. He may now coach the team only from the dugout.

d. A 59-year-old executive director is fired from her job after her superiors learn that she has brain cancer.

e. A woman who is qualified to be a school lunchroom aide is overweight. When a position for a lunchroom aide becomes available, she applies for it. She is denied the position because of her weight.

Housing Discrimination

Choice of housing is sometimes unfairly limited by unlawful discrimination. For various reasons, some property owners, real estate agents, and mortgage lenders prefer to sell or rent to certain types of people rather than to others.

The federal *Fair Housing Act of 1968* forbids discrimination in the selling, leasing, or financing of housing based on the race, color, religion, sex, or national origin of the applicant. The statute applies to the rental, sale, or financing of a privately owned house or a multifamily dwelling with four or more units. A presidential order prohibits similar forms of discrimination in federally owned, operated, or assisted housing, including public housing. Many states and cities also have antidiscrimination laws that may protect groups of people not mentioned in the federal act.

The act was amended in 1988 to include protections for persons with disabilities and families with children. Accordingly, a landlord cannot discriminate against potential tenants because of a disability. A landlord must permit tenants with disabilities to reasonably modify a dwelling to accommodate their needs, at the tenants' expense. All new multifamily dwellings must be accessible to persons with disabilities.

A landlord also may not refuse to rent to a family because it has children under age 18. This rule is meant to end discrimination against families with children. In certain instances, landlords may still be able to exclude large families from homes that are clearly not large enough to provide them with adequate living space.

The 1988 amendments to the *Fair Housing Act* allow restriction of retirement housing to ssenior citizens if certain criteria are met. Examples of such criteria include the existence of buildings in which all residents are over 62 years of age or the existence of new housing in which over 80 percent of the units will be occupied by someone age 55 or older and in which specific facilities and services for the elderly will be provided. The act prohibits "adults only" housing except for senior citizens.

Discrimination in housing can take many forms. For instance, a real estate agent can be guilty of **steering.** This means directing prospective buyers or renters to particular areas because of their age, race, or some other factor. Some community groups and local governments employ "testers" to uncover steering practices. For example, prospective renters or buyers of different races but similar qualifications may approach an agent. Those agents who show housing to one person, but tell the other that the same housing is unavailable, are guilty of steering. Recent testing reveals that housing discrimination still exists in the United States.

steering a discriminatory practice in which real estate agents direct buyers or renters to particular areas because of their race or for other unlawful reasons

Another type of housing discrimination is called **redlining.** This is the refusal by a bank or other lender to make loans for the purchase of homes in certain neighborhoods. Congress passed the *Community Reinvestment Act of 1977* to stop lenders from routinely rejecting loan applications from people attempting to buy homes in low income and minority neighborhoods. Under this act, a bank cannot purchase another bank or otherwise expand its business unless it can prove that it makes a sufficient number of loans to fund low-income housing.

redlining a discriminatory practice in which certain geographical areas in a community are designated by a bank or other lender as ineligible for mortgage loans

THE **CASE** OF...

The Unwanted Tenant

Since the death of her husband, Amy Weaver has operated a small, five-unit apartment house. She lives in one unit and makes a meager income by renting out the other four. She does not really dislike members of different racial groups but knows that several of her regular tenants have threatened to move out if she rents to people in these groups. She believes she has the right to do whatever she wants in her own building.

Van Tran, an Asian immigrant, is looking for an apartment to rent. When a friend at work tells him about a vacancy at Mrs. Weaver's building, he calls and makes an appointment to see the apartment. When he arrives for the appointment, Mrs. Weaver takes one look at him and tells him the apartment has been rented. "After all," she thinks, "it's my property, and no one has the right to tell me whom I must allow to live here."

PROBLEM 41.18

a. What happened in this case? Why did Mrs. Weaver refuse to rent the apartment to Van Tran?

b. Do you think what Mrs. Weaver did was legal or illegal? Why?

c. Should the law allow landlords to rent to whomever they want?

d. Which do you think is more important: the right to control one's own property or the right to live where one chooses?

e. Is there anything Van Tran can do? Explain.

▲ The *Fair Housing Act* does not allow "adults only" housing except for the elderly. *Why do some older people choose to live in retirement residences?*

Investigating the Law Where You Live

Research to find out what laws prohibit housing discrimination in your state or community. What state or local agencies enforce these laws and investigate complaints?

Not all housing discrimination is illegal. For example, landlords and sellers can refuse to rent or sell to people who have poor credit ratings or whose income is not sufficient to meet the rent or mortgage payments. Other legitimate reasons for discriminating can include poor rental references or unwillingness to follow reasonable rules.

Usually, a major consideration for those who sell or rent is whether the money owed them will be paid in full and on time. To help ensure that this will occur, they usually want to know whether a potential tenant or buyer has a steady income that is likely to continue into the future, whether the income is high enough to enable the person to pay for the housing and meet other fixed expenses, whether the person has a record of paying bills on time and of paying off previous bills or loans, and whether the person will take good care of the property.

If you think you have been illegally discriminated against, you may file a complaint with a state or local agency that deals with housing discrimination or with the U.S. Department of Housing and Urban Development's (HUD's) Fair Housing Office. The state or local agency or HUD has the authority to investigate your complaint and either resolve the problem or bring a lawsuit on your behalf. You also may be able to file a lawsuit in court.

Tetra Images/Getty Images

YOU BE the JUDGE

The Federal Fair Housing Act

Consider each of the following situations, and decide whether you think the action of the landlord, homeowner, lender, or sales agent is legal or illegal under the federal *Fair Housing Act.* If the action is legal, do you think the law should be changed to prohibit the action?

a. A real estate company runs a series of advertisements in a major newspaper featuring photographs that portray all potential tenants as whites. The few people of color who appear are portrayed as janitors or door attendants.

b. A woman seeking a two-bedroom apartment is turned down by the landlord, who thinks the apartment is too small for her and her three children.

c. A landlord refuses to rent an apartment to two men who disclose they are gay and want to share a one-bedroom unit.

d. A homeowner refuses to sell to a Latino couple because he thinks the neighbors will not approve.

e. A woman is rejected for a mortgage by a bank officer who believes her divorce makes her a financial risk.

f. A zoning change to allow a group home for persons with disabilities is blocked by a neighborhood homeowners association.

g. A landlord turns down a rental application from a man who is participating in a drug rehabilitation program, although the man says he no longer uses drugs.

h. A young musician is rejected as a tenant by a landlord who thinks the musician looks like a drug user and might make too much noise.

i. A credit union official discourages an elderly man from buying a house because the official thinks the man will not live long enough to pay off the mortgage.

▲ The wheelchair ramp

j. After receiving permission from the landlord, a tenant who uses a wheelchair has a ramp built near the front door at the tenant's expense. She does this so that she can get to her car without assistance. Other tenants complain to the landlord that the ramp is an eyesore and a nuisance. Tired of the complaints, the owner of the building removes the ramp and suggests that the disabled tenant might be happier living elsewhere.

State and Local Laws Against Discrimination

When the U.S. Supreme Court makes a decision regarding the Constitution, it determines the *minimum* protection that governments must extend to their citizens. However, federal, state, and local governments may offer greater protection than what the Court says the Constitution requires.

For example, the various federal civil rights acts you have studied throughout this chapter prohibit discrimination based on race, national origin, citizenship, sex, age, and disability. Housing discrimination is also prohibited by federal law. In addition, some state and local governments have passed their own antidiscrimination laws. These laws, which can extend beyond the protections offered by federal law, may cover discrimination based on one or more of the following characteristics:

- Age (young or old)
- Marital status
- Personal appearance (e.g., weight and height)
- Source of income
- Sexual orientation
- Gender identity
- Family responsibility (having children)
- Use of service animals
- Matriculation (status of being a student)
- Political affiliation

Some states and municipalities have created commissions that receive, investigate, and resolve complaints based on violations of these antidiscrimination laws. In recent years, there has been an increase in civil rights activity in some state courts. This activity has made state and local laws and state supreme court decisions particularly important for individuals who claim to have been victims of unlawful discrimination.

Other controversial questions that often arise under state and local laws against discrimination involve private clubs that limit their membership based on race, sex, religion, or ethnic background. Small, selective, distinctly private clubs have generally been able to decide who their members will be without violating antidiscrimination laws. For example, prohibiting a church's youth group from requiring that its members be of the same religion might interfere with the basic purpose of the club. However, larger private clubs that regularly serve meals and rent out their facilities to nonmembers for business purposes have usually been deemed by the courts to have lost their "distinctly private" nature. This for-profit activity involving the general public blurs the line between private clubs and public entities that are subject to antidiscrimination laws.

Steps to Take

Actions to Take If Your Rights Are Violated

No single procedure can be followed for all situations in which your rights have been violated. You should know that civil rights are protected by laws at the local, state, and federal levels. Federal law sometimes requires that you first try to solve your problem on a state or local level. Also, some civil rights laws have specific time limits for filing a case. Do not delay if you believe that some action should be taken. If you decide to act, you may wish to consider the following options:

- **Protest in some way.** You can protest verbally, by writing letters, or by demonstrating. Social media can be a helpful tool in spreading information about a violation of rights, and in finding others willing to protest with you.

- **Contact an attorney.** Find an attorney who may be able to negotiate a settlement or file a lawsuit for you.

- **Contact a private organization with an interest in your type of problem.** For example, you may contact the American Civil Liberties Union (ACLU) for First Amendment problems or the Institute for Justice (IJ) if you believe the government is interfering with your property rights.

- **Contact a state or local agency with the legal authority to help.** For example, a state fair-employment commission or a local human rights agency may be able to help you.

- **Contact a federal agency with the legal authority to help.** Most federal agencies have regional offices as well as field offices in larger cities throughout the country. Visit www.usa.gov to find a federal agency that can help you.

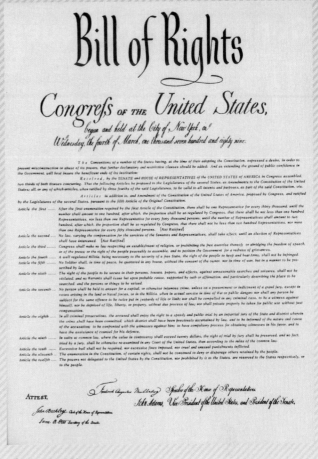

▲ The Bill of Rights

- **Contact the U.S. Commission on Civil Rights.** The commission can provide general information on where to look for help, or it can suggest how to proceed if your complaint goes unanswered.

UNIT 7
Contemporary Issues in Law

networks

The chapters in *Street Law* have traditionally been organized around unit topics that correspond with courses taken in the first or second year of law school. Naturally the presentation of the content has been adapted for high school students with a much greater focus on practicality, skill development, and civic engagement. However, some topics that are now very practical for high school students do not fall neatly within the traditional law school course offerings. These five topics—immigration law, intellectual property, law and terrorism, rights and responsibilities in the workplace, and environmental law—are presented in this final unit.

◄ Contemporary issues in law can be quick to change and sometimes require the Supreme Court to weigh in.

▶ The Statue of Liberty is often seen as a symbol of freedom.

The United States has been a "nation of immigrants" for more than 500 years— many more if you count the earlier migrations of Native Americans across the Bering Strait. Since the nation's founding, the country's immigration laws and policies have changed many times. These changes reflect a persistent tension between the view that immigration should be restricted and the view that immigrants should be welcomed and celebrated.

In 2017, approximately 44.5 million foreign-born people were living in the United States. Approximately three-fourths were legal immigrants, while the remaining one-fourth had entered the country illegally or remained longer than permitted. Between 2000 and 2012, the United States admitted over one million people per year, and from 2008 to 2018 the government removed or deported an average of 358,000 people per year.

The Constitution establishes who is a citizen of the United States. It also gives Congress the power to establish the rules for becoming a citizen (i.e., naturalization) and for passing immigration laws.

Over the years, a variety of immigration laws and policies have set **quotas**, established requirements for immigration, or limited immigration to temporary workers and family immigrants from specific areas of the world. The federal *Immigration and Nationality Act of 1952*, the *Immigration Reform Act of 1965*, and the *1986 Immigration and Reform Control Act* establish the basic immigration law of the United States.

quota a limited or fixed number or amount of people

©TongRo Image Stock/Alamy

◀ People from around the world gain U.S. citizenship through the naturalization process. *How does a person acquire citizenship by birth?*

The Department of Homeland Security (DHS) has a very broad set of responsibilities related to keeping America safe and secure. Some of its agencies carry out immigration law and policy. The U.S. Citizenship and Immigration Services (USCIS) oversees lawful immigration, the Customs and Border Protection (CBP) oversees border security, and Immigration and Customs Enforcement (ICE) enforces violations of immigration laws.

Citizenship

There are two ways to become a U.S. citizen: by birth or by **naturalization**. People born in the United States (other than to diplomats) are citizens. A child born outside the country to a parent who is a U.S. citizen may be a citizen, depending on a number of factors, including whether one or both parents are U.S. citizens.

People born in other countries can apply to become U.S. citizens through a legal process called naturalization. The requirements for naturalization include:

- legal residency in the United States for at least five years (with some exceptions),
- physical presence in the United States during at least half of the past five years,
- being at least 18 years of age,
- having good moral character,
- the ability to speak, read, and write English,
- passing an oral citizenship test on U.S. history and government, and
- swearing allegiance to the U.S. Constitution and loyalty to the United States.

A naturalized citizen can lose citizenship if it was obtained illegally or by fraud.

naturalization a legal process by which persons born in other countries can apply for U.S. citizenship

THE Constitution

To establish an uniform Rule of Naturalization . . . throughout the United States.

—Article 1, Section 8, Part 4

All persons born or naturalized in the United States, and subject to the jurisdiction thereof, are citizens of the United States and of the State wherein they reside.

—Fourteenth Amendment

People who want to become naturalized citizens must pass an oral test about U.S. history and government. Work with three classmates to develop three history questions and three government questions that you think all citizens should be able to answer. Swap your questions with students in two other groups. Can you answer your own questions and theirs?

Then visit the website (www.uscis.gov/) of the U.S. Citizenship and Immigration Services, the government agency that administers the naturalization test. Look at the study guides and sample test questions. How do your questions compare to the actual test questions? Who may be exempt from the tests? What resources does the website offer to help applicants? What is your assessment of the test and the support applicants are given to pass the test?

The spouse of a citizen may apply for citizenship after having permanent residence in the United States for three years and satisfying other naturalization requirements. A child who is a permanent resident and residing in the United States may acquire U.S. citizenship automatically if a parent naturalizes before the child turns 18 as long as the child is in the legal custody of the naturalizing parent.

PROBLEM 42.2

a. Wilfred was born in Germany. His mother is in the military and both of his parents are United States citizens. Is Wilfred a U.S. citizen?

b. Jose attends middle school in Austin, Texas. He was born in the United States. His parents are both graduate students and not U.S. citizens. Is Jose a U.S. citizen?

c. Margot is from Ireland. She has lived in the United States legally for five years, is 21 years of age, and has never been in trouble with the law. She passes the citizenship test and swears allegiance to the U.S. Constitution and loyalty to the United States. Can she successfully apply to be a naturalized citizen?

d. Ying is a naturalized citizen. His eight-year-old son is living with him in the United States. Is Ying's son eligible for U.S. citizenship?

Visitors and Lawful Permanent Residents

visa document that permits a person to visit a country for a specified period of time for a specified purpose, such as to work or study

nonimmigrant visa a visa that allows a person to visit the United States for a specific purpose and stay for a set period of time

The United States welcomes many people each year. Some of them intend to visit while others intend to stay. To enter the country legally, people need to request permission by obtaining a **visa** at a U.S. consulate. There are two main categories of visas: nonimmigrant and immigrant.

Nonimmigrant visas allow people to visit the United States for a specific purpose and to stay in the country for a set period of time. Several types of temporary visas are available. Visitor visas allow people to visit the country for pleasure or on a business trip. Student visas allow people to study at American schools. Temporary work visas allow people in specific occupations or with specialized knowledge to work in the United States for a period of time. These occupations include computer programmers, computer analysts, architects, engineers, lawyers, nurses, doctors, and agricultural workers. Temporary visas are also available for athletes, musicians, government employees, ship or airline crew members, foreign media representatives, and participants in cultural or educational exchanges.

People who wish to stay in the United States permanently need an immigrant visa. In general, foreigners who want **immigrant visas** must be sponsored by either a family member or a potential employer, although sometimes they can petition for themselves. The family member, employer, or self-petitioner must file a visa petition with the U.S. Citizenship and Immigration Services (USCIS) on behalf of the immigrant.

If the petition is approved by the USCIS, the immigrant may be placed on a waiting list at the U.S. Department of State. At some future time, and depending on the type of petition, the immigrant is then invited to apply for status known as a **Lawful Permanent Resident**, or LPR. If granted LPR status, he or she will be issued a **green card**.

LPRs are noncitizens who are allowed to work in the United States. They can remain in the country indefinitely and can travel abroad and freely return with a valid passport from their home country. LPRs are considered "taxable residents" and are required to report their income and, if appropriate, to pay taxes just as citizens do. However, they do not enjoy the full range of benefits associated with citizenship. For example, LPRs cannot vote and can lose LPR status if they engage in criminal activities.

Each year, Congress determines the number of immigrant visas that can be issued in various categories. In 2016, approximately 800,000 family-sponsored immigrants were admitted. Preference is given to spouses, children and parents of adult U.S. citizens who are already lawfully in the United States. An unlimited number of green cards are available for these immediate relatives of U.S. citizens. Other family members

▲ Nonimmigrant visas allow foreign students to attend school in the United States for a set period of time. *What other groups of people may need a nonimmigrant visa?*

immigrant visa a visa that allows a person to stay in the United States permanently

lawful permanent resident a person who has received a green card and is allowed to work in the United States

green card a legal document proving the legitimacy of an immigrant's residency

42.1 Green Cards Issued by Type of Admission

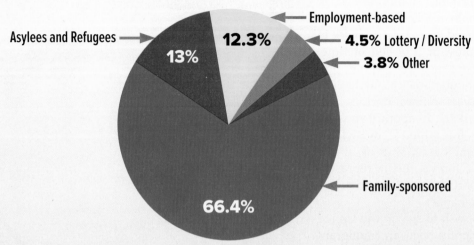

Asylees and Refugees — **13%**

Employment-based — **12.3%**

4.5% Lottery / Diversity

3.8% Other

Family-sponsored — **66.4%**

Year books of Immigration Statistics, 2017, Department of Homeland Security

Lawful Permanent Resident status must be granted before a person can be issued a green card. **ANALYZE THE DATA**
According to this data, what group of people receives the most green cards? Do you agree that group should receive the most? Why or why not?

Investigating the Law Where You Live

Find out if there are any free or reduced-fee legal services available to immigrants in your community. If so, what services are provided? Where is the immigration court nearest to where you live?

asylum a place of refuge or safety from imminent danger

who are not immediate relatives of U.S. citizens may also be able to come to the United States, but for them the wait is usually quite long—often from three to twenty years.

Congress establishes the number and type of employment-based immigrant visas available each year. The number of applicants far exceeds the number of available visas. In 2017, the overall limit for employment-based green cards was 140,000. As they do with temporary work visas, Congress shows a strong preference for highly skilled workers for employment-based immigrant visas.

People Seeking Humanitarian Protection

Every year thousands of people come to the United States who are fleeing persecution or who are unable to return to their homeland due to life-threatening or extraordinary circumstances. The United States provides refuge or humanitarian protection through two programs. The **asylum** program is for people who are already in the United States and their immediate relatives. The asylum program is for people outside the United States and their immediate relatives.

Currently, there are no limits to the number of people who may be granted humanitarian protection, though it is still very difficult to attain. Applicants must be able to prove that they have been persecuted—or have a well-founded fear of persecution—in their home country because of their race, religion, nationality, political opinions, or membership in a particular social or ethnic group. They must also prove they cannot find protection in their home country. A person fleeing poverty, general social unrest, or random violence does not qualify for humanitarian protection.

Some asylum applicants apply when they arrive at a border or port of entry such as an airport or seaport. Others apply after settling in the United States. Under most circumstances, asylum seekers must apply within one year of their arrival or they lose the ability to do so. An asylum officer from USCIS interviews the applicant. The asylum seeker may bring an attorney and any family members they are asking be admitted as part of their application. The applicant must bring an interpreter if he or she is not fluent in English. If the officer rejects the request for asylum, the applicant will be placed in detention. After some period of time, the person will see an immigration judge and will be in removal proceedings, which is the process in which people are removed or deported from the country.

A person can request asylum beyond the one-year time frame if he or she is accused of violating a law and is in removal hearings. Some federal courts have held that immigrants must be advised of their rights to have legal representation and to apply for asylum before being removed.

An asylum claim that is heard in court is similar to the interview described above, but the court case is more formal. An interpreter, if needed, will be provided. Since September 11, 2001, the U.S. government has increased its efforts to block applications for asylum from people who might be members of a terrorist organization or who previously aided such organizations.

◀ Some recent immigrants from the African countries of Ethiopia, Sudan, and Somalia come to the United States seeking asylum. *What must this woman prove in order to receive asylum?*

Each person below has asked for humanitarian protection. Make a ruling as if you were a judge hearing this person's claim. Be sure to give your reasons.

a. Grace is from an African country where female circumcision is practiced. She says that she fears returning to her country because she will be forced to undergo this painful procedure.

b. Wong is a member of a religious sect in China that the Chinese government has declared to be illegal. Some of its members have been arrested and imprisoned in China. Wong has never been arrested.

c. Mohammed has fled his homeland, where he was a member of the political opposition to the dictator who ruled his country. A government official in that country once told him that if he takes action in organizing resistance against the government, he will be arrested.

d. Eva has been the victim of physical abuse by her husband in the country from which she comes. She is applying for asylum because she fears that returning to her home country will result in more abuse.

e. Rashid is an Iraqi who once fought against United States. However, Rashid has since changed sides and now works for the United States in Iraq.

Undocumented Immigrants

undocumented immigrant a foreign-born person who does not have the legal right to be in the United States

People who are in the country without permission are known as undocumented immigrants. Some **undocumented immigrants** came to the United States with a temporary visa, but overstayed the amount of time granted on the visa. Others entered the country without legal permission or with false documents. The goal of many undocumented immigrants is to obtain better-paying work than is available in their home countries. Others come to escape civil war, natural disasters, or other serious problems. Many undocumented immigrants send money back to family members in their home countries.

It is very difficult for undocumented people to find jobs in this country because it is illegal for employers to hire them. Consequently, they often work in low-wage jobs, most commonly working in factories or restaurants, or providing cleaning or landscaping services.

human trafficking the act of controlling a person through force, fraud, or coercion to exploit him or her; a modern form of slavery

Undocumented workers may be paid less than the minimum wage and receive no benefits. In addition, people without documentation can become victims of **human trafficking**.

Detention and Removal of Noncitizens

A person who is in the country illegally who has committed a crime or violated immigration law may be arrested and then removed (or deported) from the country. He or she may be arrested by Immigration and Customs Enforcement (ICE), by a member of the border patrol, or by a police officer who can turn an undocumented immigrant over to the Department of Homeland Security.

Before people are removed, they are typically held in a detention center, which is a facility much like a jail. They wait there until their removal proceeding concludes. They typically do not have the right to bail.

According to the federal government, there were an average of about 42,000 people in detention each day in 2018. Approximately 11 percent of those held are considered violent criminals. The government also estimates that the average length of detention is 31 days, though other groups say that thousands of immigrants wait in detention for months or years. One of the reasons people are detained for so long is that the backlog of cases is extraordinary—more than 800,000 at the end of 2018.

An immigrant in removal proceedings will appear before an immigration judge. Immigration judges differ from state or federal court judges because they are not part of the judicial branch. Instead, they are part of the executive branch and act under the authority of the Department of Justice. Immigration judges vary greatly in leniency or toughness.

Unlike defendants at criminal trials, immigrants do not have a right to a free (government-appointed) lawyer at their removal hearings. They are represented by counsel only if they can pay for a lawyer. Sometimes legal aid programs, volunteer lawyers, or law students provide free or reduced-cost legal assistance. Those who have lawyers are much more successful at this hearing than the people who represent themselves. If the immigrant needs an interpreter at the hearing, the court will provide one.

▼ In some cases, an order of removal against a noncitizen is cancelled if the removal would result in hardship for family members. *Under what other conditions may an order of removal be cancelled?*

Immigrants who lose their removal cases have a right to appeal, though successful appeals are very rare. To appeal, they would have to prove they have resided in the country for at least ten years, have no criminal convictions, demonstrate good moral character, and that their family would suffer extreme hardship if they are forced to leave. If their appeals are successful, their removal orders are canceled, allowing them to stay as Lawful Permanent Residents.

The number of people removed from the United States has increased steadily since the 1970s, when there were fewer than 18,000 removals per year. In 2018 more than 250,000 people were removed.

Immigration Law and Policy

United States policy toward immigrants is controversial, with various people holding a wide range of competing views, particularly regarding those who are in the country illegally. With so many undocumented people in the country, immigration law and policy present a difficult challenge for lawmakers.

One central element of the debate is about how to reduce illegal immigration. Some people think that the United States should spend more money at the border on barriers, patrol agents, and technology. Others think the government's priority should be to provide more economic aid to people in other countries so they will have a better life there. Another approach is to make it more difficult for undocumented people to get and keep jobs in the United States. There are already laws that make it illegal for U.S. employers to hire undocumented workers and to fine employers who do. A continuing pattern of deliberate violations can result in jail time for an offending employer. Critics say these laws are not vigorously enforced.

Advocates for immigrants argue that efforts to reduce illegal immigration should focus on clearing the backlog of people who are trying to get proper documentation. They note that some people who meet the qualifications for a visa or green card can wait any years to get approval. They also say that efforts to reduce illegal immigration must be humane and that it is a fundamental right to migrate in search of a better life.

Another element of the debate is whether some undocumented people should be given a path to citizenship. Supporters of this idea say undocumented people play an important role in the economy and in American society. They point out that the United States is a nation primarily of immigrants and that Americans should welcome new immigrants. In addition, there are enormous practical problems involved in removing the more than 12 million persons here without proper documentation.

amnesty an official pardon for a person who has been convicted of a political offense

Opponents voice concern that the United States is unable to control its borders and that too many people are in the country illegally. Providing **amnesty** for those who have broken the law, it is argued, is contrary to public policy and will encourage others to come here illegally in the future. Some people believe that undocumented immigrants are using social services such as schools, libraries, and parks but are not paying income taxes to support them. They also believe that undocumented workers are taking jobs that should go to people who are here legally. They may believe that immigrants' housing, especially multifamily, is too crowded and that immigrants cause an increase in crime. Some fear that undocumented immigrants who come to the United States are not committed to learning English. Finally, people are concerned that poor control of the country's borders allows drug smuggling and human trafficking, and could also allow terrorists to enter the country.

Traditionally, immigration law has been considered a federal issue. In some communities, however, there is frustration with what some believe is the federal government's inability to deal effectively with immigration law and policy.

The Constitution gives Congress the authority to pass laws and it gives the president the authority to issue **executive orders**, which are presidential directives that have the force of law without the approval of Congress. At times, these powers come into conflict. For example, in 2012, frustrated by a Republican-controlled Congress that would not debate or pass immigration reform, President Barack Obama issued an executive order that put off or "deferred" deportation for some undocumented people who came to the U.S. as children. The order is called *Deferred Action for Childhood Arrivals (DACA)* and it allows them to apply for temporary permission to stay in the U.S. To be eligible for *DACA*, individuals must meet numerous and strict qualifications, including having arrived before the age of 16 and residing in the U.S continuously, passing a criminal background check, and being in school.

DACA was supported by some people and opposed by others. A legal challenge was brought in federal court claiming that President Obama had exceeded his legal authority in issuing these executive orders. The challengers claimed that such action could only be taken based on legislation passed by Congress. The trial judge agreed with the challengers, and the Obama Administration appealed the decision. As of 2019, this issue was still being litigated in federal court.

> **executive order** an order that comes from the president or a government agency and must be obeyed like a law

---

PROBLEM 42.4

What is the appropriate way to deal with undocumented people who come to the United States at a young age? For many, their only language is English.

a. Should they be deported or removed? Give your reasons.

b. If they are allowed to stay in the United States, should they be legal residents or should they have a pathway to citizenship? Give your reasons.

c. How should this policy be determined? By executive order? By Congressional legislation? Is a national decision required or could states act on their own?

In 2017, President Trump issued several executive orders (often referred to as "the travel ban") aimed at limiting admission to the United States of people from several different countries due to security concerns. Initial versions of the travel ban were struck down by various federal courts, but a revised version was deemed lawful by the U.S. Supreme Court in the summer of 2018.

During both the Obama and Trump presidencies, a divided Congress struggled to pass bipartisan legislation related to comprehensive immigration reform and border security.

THE **CASE** OF...

State or Federal Authority Over Immigration Enforcement

In 2010, Arizona passed a law intended to address problems Arizona felt it was having with undocumented immigration in the state. The law did many things, including making it a state crime to fail to register as an immigrant or for undocumented immigrants to work or seek work. It also required local law enforcement to check the immigration status of anyone they stop if they have a reasonable suspicion that the person is an undocumented immigrant.

The federal government sued Arizona to stop the law, saying it has the sole power to regulate immigration. The U.S. Constitution sets up a federalist system of government. This means that some powers are designated specifically to the federal government, while others are left to the states. Some powers are shared by both. When federal and state laws conflict, the federal law takes precedence. However, there is not a conflict every time there is a federal and state law about the same subject.

The case went to the Supreme Court, where the United States argued that Arizona's law was unconstitutional because the federal government is solely responsible for immigration law. Arizona argued that their law complemented, rather than conflicted with, federal immigration law.

PROBLEM 42.5

Read each of the arguments below. Assign each as an argument for the United States, for Arizona, for both, or for neither.

a. The federal government is not effectively dealing with the challenges of illegal immigration, which negatively affect border states like Arizona. The federal government even chose not to enforce completely some of its existing immigration laws.

b. Congress has passed laws that completely regulate immigration, which give the executive branch authority to decide how to enforce these laws. The executive must prioritize limited resources when deciding how to enforce the laws.

c. Immigration policy is something that needs to be done at the federal level, because uniformity is needed across the country. Arizona's law disrupts that necessary uniformity.

d. The Arizona law complements federal law. The state law simply adopts as state crimes some things that are already federal crimes.

e. Immigration enforcement affects the country's relationships with other countries, which are the responsibility of the president.

f. If the Arizona law is allowed, then every state could pass different immigration laws. We can't have a patchwork of uneven immigration laws and enforcement priorities existing among the states.

g. Arizona's law is consistent with the purpose of federal immigration law, which is to discourage employment of undocumented immigrants. Arizona is just using different tools to achieve the same purpose.

TAKING ACTION: Law and Democracy

The U.S. Congress has considered various comprehensive immigration bills. Several reforms have been suggested, including:

- Stronger border protection (wall, fence, greater use of technology, increase in ICE officers)
- Accelerated removal of undocumented immigrants
- A pathway to citizenship for undocumented people
- Increased seasonal and farm worker visas
- Harsher penalties and stricter enforcement of laws that punish employers for hiring people who are not authorized to work in the United States
- Making it harder to obtain asylum in the United Stated and temporarily increasing the number of judges to reduce the backlog of asylum cases
- Making it easier for international students to get student visas for graduate school and providing a quicker way for them to stay in the United States and achieve citizenship if they receive certain graduate degrees

As a member of Congress, you will help search for consensus about the best immigration policies for the country. You will be assigned one of the districts below to represent in the U.S. House of Representatives. Collaborate with other students assigned to represent the same district. Make a preliminary decision about which reforms you might support. Be prepared to explain and defend your position and listen to the other representatives. Attempt to find proposals that can "pass" a vote from the majority of the House of Representatives.

District 1 has many high-tech businesses and universities. Business leaders have said the success of their businesses depends on recruiting more high-tech workers from overseas. Universities want jobs for their students after graduation. They also want to recruit the best professors from around the world. This district has many restaurants, and some may have hired workers not authorized to work here.

District 2 is a rural district whose economy relies heavily on agriculture. The farmers need people to pick their crops. They follow rules that require them to try to hire U.S. workers first, but have trouble recruiting Americans to do the work.

District 3 is an urban district with high rates of unemployment. Some families have lived there for generations, but many others are newcomers, born in other countries. The majority of immigrants are living in the United States legally, though some are unauthorized.

District 4 has a large number of immigrants, including some who call themselves "Dreamers"— young undocumented people who came to the United States as children and want to stay, be able to work legally, and pay in-state tuition to attend college.

District 5 shares a border with Mexico. Many undocumented people cross this border. Some of your constituents are concerned about human trafficking and the possibility that some people crossing the border are smuggling drugs into the country. They are also concerned that increases in crime in their community might be the result of undocumented people who have crossed the border.

District 6 is far from the border and has few immigrants. People there are concerned that giving undocumented people a path to citizenship is a form of amnesty and rewards them for illegal behavior. They believe such a policy will encourage more illegal border crossings. Their focus is on greater border security and removing undocumented people from the country.

PROBLEM 42.6

Work in groups so that each district is represented in each group. Each group should draft a bill that includes its three top priorities. Compare the bills produced by each group. Are there any common priorities? Why do you think Congress has had such difficulty passing comprehensive immigration reform?

▶ The law protects the creations of people's minds as a form of property called intellectual property.

Imagine that you have created a brilliant, action-packed computer game with dazzling 3-D graphics. You are sure that everybody will love it, so you begin to sell copies of your program to people over the Internet. A large software company buys a copy of your game and, without your permission, makes thousands of copies and sells them for a much cheaper price. The company makes millions of dollars by taking credit for and selling the game that you created. Unable to compete with the large company, you have to discontinue your business.

Or perhaps you are a musician and you perform original songs at parties in your neighborhood. What if one day you saw a celebrity musician on television performing a song that you wrote? What if this musician falsely took credit for writing the song, performed it on a hit movie soundtrack, and made a fortune from it without asking your permission or giving you a cent?

Or maybe you are an entrepreneur who has started Exercisers, a shoe company that becomes known for its high-quality athletic footwear. One day you see an ad for Exercizers, a rival shoe company whose name confuses consumers. People start buying Exercizer sneakers thinking they are your Exerciser sneakers. Your sales start falling and stay flat, even during the back-to-school shopping season. When the rival company starts up a website using the word "Exercizer" in its web address, your online sales also drop dramatically. Can you do anything to save your brand name and your business?

Juice Images/Alamy

If people knew that they could not protect their work from being stolen, there would be little incentive to create anything or to show new creations to others. Therefore, the law protects the creations of people's minds as a form of property that can be owned and thus may not be stolen. Since another word for the mind is *intellect*, property in the form of creations of the mind is called **intellectual property**.

Intellectual property law promotes progress in the arts and sciences because it provides an incentive (a reward) for engaging in creative pursuits. Article I, Section 8, of the Constitution gives Congress the power to promote progress in science and the arts by "securing for limited times to authors and inventors the exclusive right to their writings and discoveries." There are three broad categories of intellectual property: patents, copyrights, and trademarks. **Patents** recognize and protect ownership of inventions and discoveries. **Copyrights** recognize and protect forms of creative expression, such as books, movies, computer programs, and songs. And **trademarks** recognize and protect words, phrases, symbols, or designs that are used to identify the source of goods and distinguish them from the goods of other parties. When a person uses a patented, copyrighted, or trademarked work without permission, that person commits a tort called **infringement**.

Patents

Patents protect useful inventions and discoveries such as processes, machines, and new products. However, not everything can be patented. Patents may only be issued to inventors who have thought of something useful that has never been invented before. That is, the idea must truly be new or **novel**. For example, notebooks are usually sold with space for either three or five subjects. You would not be able to get a patent for a four-subject notebook, however, because there is nothing truly novel about the idea. It is an obvious extension of an existing idea. On the other hand, if you invented a notebook with a mechanism that allowed it to be attached to the desk to prevent it from slipping, you would have a better chance of getting a patent for your novel idea.

Patents also do not apply to the laws of nature, physical phenomena, or abstract ideas, because those things are the basic tools for scientific and technological work. Patenting these items could keep others from making future discoveries. For that reason, Sir Isaac Newton would not have been allowed to patent his discovery of the law of gravity. And a person could not patent the discovery of a new mineral, or the equation $e = mc^2$.

Getting a patent can be a lengthy—and often expensive—legal process. You must submit an application to the U.S. Patent and Trademark Office that describes your invention, gives it a name, and explains how to use it in clear and concise terms. You must also explain in detail how your invention is different from other inventions. If drawings are needed to understand your invention, you must include them as well.

An inventor who applies for and gets a patent from the Patent Office has a complete **monopoly** over the invention for 20 years from the date of application. If anyone else tries to sell the invention or profit from the

intellectual property a person's idea or invention that is given special ownership protections

patent federal protection for an invention or design, giving the inventor exclusive ownership rights for a period of time

copyright the protection of a creative fixed expression giving the owner exclusive rights to the expression (For example, Matt Groening has exclusive rights to the *Simpsons* cartoon characters.)

trademark a symbol, word, or words legally registered or established by use as representing a company or product.

infringement the illegal use of someone's intellectual property, such as a copyright, patent, or trademark

novel truly new or unique

monopoly exclusive ownership or possession

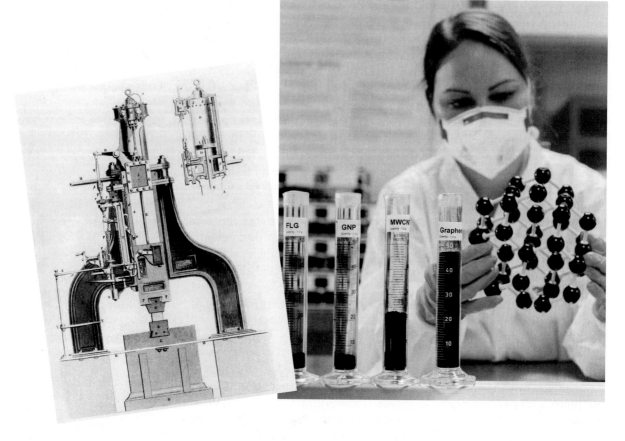

▲ Nasmyth's design (left) for the patent of the steam hammer. A scientist (right) works with a model to test a hypothesis.

idea, the patent holder can sue for infringement. After 20 years the patent expires, and the invention becomes part of the public domain. Anyone may then use or profit from the invention.

(l)Library of Congress Prints and Photographs Division [LC-USZ62-110414], (r)Monty Rakusen/Getty Images

PROBLEM 43.1

Many products that we take for granted today began long ago as patented inventions. Here are just a few of those patents. What would have been novel and useful about each invention at the time the patent for each was issued?

a. U.S. Patent No. 223,898: Electric-Lamp, by T.A. Edison (1880)

b. U.S. Patent No. 775,134: Razor, by K.C. Gillette (1904)

c. U.S. Patent No. 1,800,156: Method and Means for the Atomizing or Distribution of Liquid or Semiliquid Materials (aerosol spray can), by E. Rotheim (1931)

d. U.S. Patent No. 2,495,429: Method of Treating Foodstuffs (microwave), by P.L. Spencer (1950)

e. U.S. Patent No. 4,464,652: Cursor Control Device for Use with Display Systems (computer mouse), by William F. Lapson and William D. Atkinson (1984)

Copyrights

Copyrights protect original works of expression that are somehow fixed (written down, recorded on tape, stored on a computer disk, painted on a canvas, etc.). Unlike a patent, you do not have to go through any legal process to obtain a copyright. Copyright protections exist from the moment a work is created and fixed in a tangible form. As soon as you make your expression fixed or permanent, you automatically have a legal copyright without doing anything else. If you keep a diary, take photos, or write music, then you hold copyrights.

Although copyrights exist as soon as expression is fixed, there are legal benefits to registering the copyright and putting a copyright notice on your work. Many register their works because they want their copyright on the public record and want to have a certificate of registration for their work. You also must have a copyright registration if you want to bring a lawsuit against another party for infringement of your work. Placing the copyright notice on your work serves to warn others that a work is copyrighted. Notice consists of the © symbol, the year the work was created, and the author's name (for example, "© 2015 John Doe"). Registering your original work is not difficult. You only need to send a completed application form to the U.S. Copyright Office.

Copyrights give the owner the exclusive right to reproduce the work, to make **derivative works** (works based on a copyrighted work), to sell or distribute copies of the work, to display copies of the work in public, and to perform the work. Copyright protections exist from the moment the work is created and generally last for the length of the author's life plus an additional 70 years after the author's death.

Exceptions to the exclusive rights of a copyright holder include first sale and fair use. **First sale** means that when the copyright owner sells a copy of the work, the lawful owner of the particular copy may resell that particular copy. First sale does not mean the owner of a copy can make additional copies and sell them. If you purchase a copy of a popular movie on DVD, you are free to sell that DVD to your friend without infringing on the copyright (under first sale). You may not, however, make fifty copies of it and open up your own movie store.

The **fair use** clause of the copyright statute allows limited legal reproduction of copyrighted works for certain noncommercial purposes, such as for criticism, news reporting, scholarship, or research. For example, if you use a video clip during a presentation for your social studies or English class, this would be fair use and not a copyright infringement. The reason is that the material is being used to help educate your classmates. You are not showing

derivative work a work that is very similar to but slightly different from a copyrighted work

first sale the first purchaser of a piece of copyrighted material may legally resell that particular copy of the protected work

fair use a clause of the copyright statute that allows limited reproduction of a copyrighted work for noncommercial purposes

▼ Downloading music files from the Internet raises ethical and legal issues. *How might downloading files or copying songs from a CD be a copyright infringement?*

the entire movie, and you are not charging your classmates to watch the clip. These are all relevant factors in determining whether your use of the copied video is fair to the creator of the movie.

As technology advances, "fair use" questions become more difficult. The most reliable guide may be to imagine that you are the owner of a copyrighted work. Then ask yourself whether it would be fair for people to copy your work without paying you or getting your permission.

FYI For Your Information

Protecting Your Creations

The federal government makes information available online to help you protect your intellectual property and creations. Visit the U.S. Copyright Office online at www.copyright.gov and learn how to search copyright records, register a work, and record a document. Then follow the links to visit the U.S. Patent and Trademark Office— www.uspto.gov—to check the status of patents and trademarks. You can also learn how to search and apply for patents. The Patent and Trademark Office also sponsors the online National Inventors' Hall of Fame at www.invent.org.

PROBLEM 43.2

Gloria has a computer that she uses for schoolwork and entertainment. She must decide what to do with certain content. Consider the law and ethics involved and advise her on what to do in each of the following situations:

a. Gloria buys a DVD of her favorite movie from an online retailer. After watching it repeatedly, she gets tired of it and decides to sell it at her neighborhood yard sale.

b. Gloria's friend Alex wants her to help him start a business in which the two would buy music CDs, copy them, and sell the copies for $5.

c. Gloria wants to download a photograph from a television network's website to use in a report that she is preparing for class.

Trademarks

A trademark is any word, name, slogan, or symbol (or any combination) used to identify and distinguish the source of goods of one party from those of others. In some cases, even a sound, color, or scent can function as a trademark. A trademark is used to identify the source of goods, while a service mark is used to identify the source of services. However, the term *trademark* is generally used in a broad manner to refer to both.

Trademarks fall into four different categories: fanciful, arbitrary, suggestive, and merely descriptive. Fanciful trademarks are unique or coined terms that have no meaning in relation to the goods or services – for example, "VERIZON" or "KODAK". Fanciful marks are the strongest type of trademarks and are given the broadest protection under trademark law. Arbitrary marks are dictionary words but have no meaning in relation to the goods or services. An example would be "APPLE" for electronic goods or services. Suggestive marks are created from words which suggest some meaning related to the good or service but do not literally describe them. The suggestive mark "MICROSOFT" is suggestive of both software and micro-computers. Lastly, merely descriptive marks describe a product's attributes and can function as trademarks if they become distinctive through use. "WEIGHT WATCHERS" is a merely descriptive mark for certain food products.

Under trademark law, a trademark owner can stop others from using a trademark, or one that is confusingly similar, if the trademark is being used in connection with similar or related goods or services. A trademark is confusingly similar if it is "likely to cause confusion" in the minds of the public in how the trademark sounds, how it looks, or what it means.

As with copyrights, you do not need to register a word, name, slogan, or symbol in order to secure trademark protections. You can establish your trademark rights based solely on use of the mark in commerce.

◀ Once you have registered your trademark, you have the right to use the registration symbol "®".

However, owning a trademark registration has several benefits. With a trademark registration, you have the right to use the federal registration symbol "®" and the ability to file a lawsuit against an infringer in federal court. Defenses to a trademark infringement suit include fair use—that the claimed infringement is not confusingly similar—and parody, particularly when the trademark use includes speech protected by the First Amendment. The idea behind parody as a defense is that an artistic or editorial parody of a trademark serves a critical public information role.

Registering a trademark is a lengthy and complex legal process which requires you to comply with trademark statutes and rules. Most people hire an attorney who specializes in trademark matters to assist in the application process. Once registered, it is possible for a trademark registration to remain valid forever if it is periodically renewed. However, trademarks that are not used after a certain period of time may be considered abandoned and could be picked up by a third party. Similarly, third parties can seek to cancel a trademark registration if the mark is not used in the country where it's registered for a certain amount of time.

PROBLEM 43.3

This problem uses the trademark mascot from the U.S. Patent and Trademark Office as an example. Read the scenario and answer the questions that follow.

After seeing his friends buy jackets and vests from designer T. Markey, a high-end fashion and apparel company, a Missouri student started his own clothing and accessories company called Tee Marque. Tee Marque's founder said his company was intended to be a parody of T. Markey. Not amused, T. Markey sued Tee Marque for trademark infringement, arguing that consumers were confused by the competing Tee Marque products. How would you decide if you were the judge in the case? Analyze the photos on this page and also consider:

a. The strength of T. Markey's mark

b. The relatedness of the goods

c. The similarity of the marks

d. Evidence of actual consumer confusion

e. The sophistication of the purchasers

f. Tee Marque's intent

The "T.Markey" and "Tee Marque" images are courtesy of the United States Patent and Trademark Office (USPTO): www.uspto.gov.

TAKING ACTION: **Law and Democracy**

Counterfeit Goods

Counterfeit goods are products manufactured or distributed under someone else's name without their permission. If you have ever purchased a name-brand product for a ridiculously low price, only to discover the product was a fake, then you have been a victim of counterfeiting. Counterfeiting is big business. It is also illegal. Experts estimated the expected value of counterfeit and pirated goods sold worldwide at more than half a trillion dollars in 2016. According to a 2010 report from the Government Accounting Office, "Consumers are particularly likely to experience negative effects when they purchase counterfeit products they believe are genuine, such as pharmaceuticals. Negative effects on U.S. industry may include lost sales, lost brand value, and reduced incentives to innovate; however, industry effects vary widely among sectors and companies. The U.S. government

▲ Discussing a drug prescription

may lose tax revenue . . . and U.S. workers might lose jobs." Counterfeit goods can be poor quality, dangerous, or even deadly to consumers. Counterfeiting is not a victimless crime.

PROBLEM 43.4

Rose has a rare but serious medical condition that requires her to take a patented prescription medicine daily. Rose went to her regular pharmacy last week to refill her prescription, only to find the price of this drug had tripled. Desperate to stay healthy, she searched for a better price online, and purchased what appeared to be the same drug for half the price on a website called CheapieMeds.com.

Rose took her medication as usual. Within a few days, she experienced blurry vision. By the end of the week she could barely see at all. Rose went to her doctor and told him what happened. The doctor, suspecting that the drug Rose had purchased might be counterfeit, contacted the Food and Drug Administration (FDA).

Lab tests confirmed that the product was counterfeit. Although the two drugs looked identical and were similarly packaged, the cheaply-made counterfeit version contained trace amounts of a toxin known to cause blindness. By the time the FDA investigated, CheapieMeds.com's website had mysteriously disappeared.

a. What could Rose's doctor tell patients to pay attention to when buying prescription drugs to avoid the dangers of counterfeit medicines?

b. Did the counterfeit product interfere with the intellectual property rights of the company that manufactured the patented drug? If so, how?

c. What should you do if you suspect you have taken or received a counterfeit medicine, or come across a website that might be associated with counterfeit prescription drugs?

▶ The Pentagon was one target of the terrorist attacks of September 11, 2001.

The battlefield may seem like one of the last places where law would matter. But there have always been rules, both written and unwritten, that governed the actions of combatants. The most well-known set of laws governing war were written at the Geneva Conventions. Nearly 200 countries, including the United States, have agreed to the 1949 version of these rules, which require the humane treatment of civilians, the wounded, and prisoners of war. The rules were developed based on the assumption that conflicts would involve the armed forces of warring countries. However, country against country conflicts have declined and conflicts featuring non-state actors have increased.

For example, during World War II, the United States was at war with the Axis powers—an alliance of Germany, Italy and Japan. However, in 2015 the United States was at "war" with several terrorist organizations whose members are living and fighting in many different countries. This has created new problems when considering law and national security. Which laws of war must be followed when facing a group that does not abide by the rules of war? How should we treat captured terrorists and other non-state actors? Can U.S. laws be enacted to counter a threat on our own soil?

U.S. Navy Photo by Bob Houlihan

After the terrorist attacks of September 11, 2001, law makers considering these issues instituted many new laws and policies. Civil liberties groups and others have challenged some of these laws, arguing they unnecessarily restrict individual rights and harm our national reputation abroad. Those who support antiterrorism measures state that failing to enact such laws would subject the United States to increased risks of terrorist attacks and demonstrate diplomatic weakness to the world.

In past times of crisis, the U.S. government has taken away some of the rights of citizens, and courts have upheld some of these measures. During the Civil War, for example, President Lincoln suspended the right of prisoners to seek the protection of **habeas corpus**, a legal means by which prisoners can challenge the legality in court of their imprisonment. During World War I, the federal government restricted citizens' rights to criticize U.S. involvement in the war, either verbally or in writing. During World War II, the government removed more than 100,000 people of Japanese heritage, most of whom were U.S. citizens, from their homes and detained them in camps. Much of their personal property, including homes and businesses, was never returned to them. In 1944 the removal and detention of Japanese Americans was upheld by the Supreme Court in *Korematsu* v. *United States*. This decision has been widely criticized. In 1988 the U.S. government formally apologized for the detention of Japanese Americans, and Congress approved a reparations payment for surviving detainees.

habeas corpus Latin for "may you have the body"; a writ (court order) which directs the law enforcement officials who have custody of a prisoner to appear in court so the judge determine whether the prisoner is being held lawfully

PROBLEM 44.1

a. Is today's war on terrorism similar to other wars when people's rights have been restricted? How is it the same? How is it different?

b. Assume you were the U.S. president after the September 11, 2001, attacks. What special powers would you want? Give your reasons.

c. Assume you were the leader of a civil liberties organization. What freedoms would you fight hardest to protect? Give your reasons.

d. William Rehnquist, former chief justice of the United States, once wrote: "The laws will thus not be silent in time of war, but they will speak with a somewhat different voice." He also wrote that in times of crisis, "presidents may act in ways that push their legal authority to its outer limits, if not beyond." What do these statements mean?

Surveillance and Searches

Since September 11, 2001, the U.S. government has had more power to conduct surveillance against people both inside and outside the country. These powers were created in the *USA PATRIOT Act (Uniting and Strengthening America by Providing Appropriate Tools Required to Intercept and Obstruct Terrorism)*, which was passed by Congress shortly after 9/11, as well as the updated *Foreign Intelligence Surveillance Act of 2008 (FISA)*. These laws greatly expanded the authority of law enforcement agencies in order to combat terrorism. One aspect of the *PATRIOT Act* allows the government greater authority in tracking and intercepting communications.

▶ Since the September 11, 2001, terrorist attacks, the National Security Agency (NSA) has worked to identify suspected terrorists by tracking international phone calls. *What is the USA PATRIOT Act?*

The *PATRIOT Act* enables law enforcement officials to use a special court known as the FISA Court, whose records and rulings are kept completely secret, to authorize wiretaps to identify terrorists. This court was originally established in 1978 to authorize surveillance to gather foreign intelligence. For that reason, this court is not required to follow the rules that ordinary courts must observe to protect the rights of individuals. For example, the FISA Court can approve wiretaps to monitor an individual's telephone and Internet communications, even if the government has not demonstrated probable cause to believe the individual is involved in criminal activity.

In 2013, a National Security Agency contractor and former CIA agent named Edward Snowden exposed the existence of PRISM, a FISA-authorized intelligence-gathering program built to collect e-mails, chat logs, videos, and other data generated by foreign persons of interest. Though not specifically intended to gather information from U.S. citizens, Snowden disclosed that a great deal of data on U.S. citizens had been collected. After his disclosure, Snowden fled to Hong Kong and then to Russia. He was charged with a violation of the 1917 Espionage Act for providing classified information to unauthorized persons. Some believe that Snowden is a whistle-blower who exposed governmental overreach. Others contend that Snowden's disclosures cost American lives and alerted terrorists to U.S. investigative strategies that will make terrorists more difficult to find and stop in the future.

In defending the PRISM program, President Barack Obama said, "You can't have 100 percent security and then also have 100 percent privacy and zero inconvenience." PRISM and similar programs led to a number of lawsuits by civil rights organizations who believed that such programs violated Fourth Amendment rights. These organizations were successful in having some portions of the *PATRIOT Act* declared unconstitutional; other portions have been upheld.

In addition to their effects at home, the Snowden disclosures also impacted the international community. Upon learning that their citizens were being monitored by the United States, some countries demanded apologies and the termination of the program. Other countries began building or improving their own versions of PRISM.

PROBLEM 44.2

a. On a scale from one to five, with one meaning that you strongly agree and five meaning that you strongly disagree, indicate where you stand on the following statement: "*In a time of heightened concern about domestic terrorism and national security, the government should be allowed to do whatever it believes is reasonably necessary to uncover and arrest terrorists.*"

b. Using the same scale, take a stand on each of the following statements. In each case, assume that Congress has proposed laws giving the federal government the power to take the following actions:

- Look at everyone's e-mail at work.
- Look at everyone's e-mail at home.
- Install surveillance cameras on all public streets.
- Plant small cameras in the homes of suspected terrorists.
- Monitor everyone's library records.
- Check the travel records of people coming into the country.

PROBLEM 44.3

Ed stays in touch by making calls and sending e-mails and faxes on a regular basis to his friend Abdul in Syria. The two met years earlier at a seminar in Europe about international relations. They talk about U.S. foreign policy, and both criticize the U.S. war in Iraq. At one point Ed wires Abdul some money because his family is going through a difficult time financially.

The U.S. government listens in to the calls, reads the e-mails and faxes, and obtains a copy of a financial statement Ed's bank sends him. They also contact Ed's phone company and obtain his phone records showing many calls to Abdul's number in Syria. In addition, the government has evidence that Abdul's brother has been involved in plotting a bombing in Iraq. The government then arrests Ed for "aiding and abetting a terrorist."

a. Can the government take these actions without obtaining a search warrant from either a regular U.S. court or the FISA Court? What are the arguments for and against allowing the government to do this?

b. Does the government have enough evidence to arrest Ed?

c. Would your answer to (a) and (b) change if, before arresting Ed, the government had received information from its intelligence officers that Abdul had been attending meetings of terrorist groups in Syria? Explain your answer.

Law and International Terrorism

The "War on Terror" is not technically a war, as war can only be declared by Congress. The last officially declared war was World War II. The War on Terror, as it is known today, began on September 14, 2001, when Congress passed the *Authorization for Use of Military Force (AUMF)*. Such authorization is required whenever the president wishes to deploy combat troops for an overseas military operation lasting longer than 60 days. This bill gave the president the authority to use "appropriate force" on those who "planned, authorized, committed or aided" the September 11, 2001, attacks. This authorization was used for many years after 2001 when the president determined that a military target was affiliated with al-Qaeda, the radical group that took responsibility for 9/11.

The United States follows a widely accepted body of international laws and customs regarding armed conflict. These laws were developed over time in response to a universal revulsion to certain practices in war. The laws ban chemical and biological weapons, provide guidance on the treatment of prisoners of war, and address the legitimate and illegitimate reasons for starting wars. When a country is believed to have violated these laws—such as when Syria was found to be stockpiling chemical weapons in 2013—the international community is expected to come together to denounce and stop such behavior.

In addition to laws, there are also general principles, which the United States has adopted as official policy, that guide military decisions. These principles require the military to distinguish between combatants and civilians, and to use only the amount of force necessary to further a military objective.

Over the past two decades, the United States has dramatically changed its approach to military action. Two of the biggest changes have been an increase in reliance on special operations forces and an increase in the utilization of drones for both surveillance and strikes. The primary reason for these changes is that the War on Terror represents a new type of conflict in which the enemy consists of non-state groups scattered across many different countries.

Special operations forces are primarily used for targeted strikes, complicated missions, and covert operations. Covert operations are actions that the U.S. wants to conduct in secret. This type of operation would be used if the target of the U.S. action is living in a country that does not allow U.S. forces to enter. For example, the mission that resulted in the death of Osama bin Laden was a covert operation run by special operations forces.

Drones, also known as unmanned aerial vehicles, have become a primary weapon in finding and eliminating suspected terrorists. Those in favor of drones argue that they allow the military to minimize the force and collateral damage necessary to take out a

drone an unmanned aircraft guided by remote control or onboard computers

▼ Some Iraqis who have been detained for interrogation by U.S. troops in Iraq have experienced hostile treatment. *Why did the U.S. government claim that the Geneva Conventions of War did not apply to prisoners captured in Afghanistan and Iraq?*

terrorist because they can fly directly to a target and circle for hours before firing with a smart missile. Opponents argue that the United States is less cautious when using drones and that their use results in many civilians being killed alongside the targets.

As of 2015, the United States continued to rely on the legal authority of the 2001 *AUMF* in order to fight terrorist groups overseas. Although groups such as the Islamic State (also called ISIL or ISIS) did not exist at the time of the 2001 attacks, the United States views them as ideological successors to al-Qaeda with members who "aided" the September 11, 2001, attacks.

FYI For Your Information

Drones

Killing civilians is not against the laws of war provided the civilians were not specifically targeted and the attack used the minimum force necessary to further a valid military objective. Many people have argued that drone strikes lead to excessive civilian casualties. Accurately estimating civilian deaths from drone strikes is difficult. Sources vary greatly, suggesting that 8-30 percent of the people killed in drone strikes in Pakistan, Yemen, and Somalia between 2004 and 2015 were civilians.

In 2013, President Obama announced a new policy for certain drone strikes. Called the "Near Certainty Standard," this policy dictates that no drone strikes occur unless there is "a near certainty" that civilians will not be harmed. This standard has proven difficult to meet in practice, and officials have clarified that the Near Certainty Standard will only apply when the United States takes action outside areas of active conflict.

Originally used by the U.S. military, drones are being developed by many countries for multiple uses. While drones have been used for constructive purposes, they have also been used to deliver drugs, to smuggle illegal products, and for invasion of privacy. In 2018, the Federal Aviation Administration (FAA) ruled that drones weighing less than 55 pounds had to be registered with the FAA. Some states have additional rules.

▲ A U.S. drone over Afghanistan

Law, Torture, and Detainees

One of the difficulties in the War on Terror has been the classification of the participants. Generally, people involved in a conflict are classified as combatants, non-combatants, or civilians. Combatants carry weapons openly and follow the laws of war. It is beneficial to be a combatant because combatants are afforded immunity from punishment based on their actions during an armed conflict, provided they abide by the rules of war. Non-combatants are members of the military who are not taking an active role in the hostilities, like combat medics and military chaplains. Civilians are not members of the armed forces. Non-combatants or civilians who choose to take up arms in a conflict, or those combatants who violate the laws of war, may be tried and punished for such violations. Historically combatants were easy to identity because they represented a nation and wore that country's military uniform. The dramatic increase in conflicts involving non-state actors makes identifying combatants more difficult since the non-state actors are not affiliated with any one country and may not be uniformed.

Following September 11, 2001, the U.S. government held and interrogated many prisoners captured in Afghanistan and later in Iraq. These detainees, most of whom were turned over to U.S. forces in exchange for a bounty, were held awaiting trial by military commissions that did not afford many rights. The government argued that the Geneva Convention dealing with prisoners of war did not apply to these prisoners – also called detainees. Because the detainees were captured during a war against non-state actors like the Taliban and al-Qaeda who do not follow the laws of war, the government stated the Geneva Convention rules were not applicable. Many of the detainees were held at the U.S. military prison at Guantanamo Bay, Cuba. Holding these detainees, in many cases for years without a trial, has been controversial.

In general, the government has maintained that Guantanamo Bay detention is the equivalent of holding prisoners of war on or near a battlefield, and therefore such detainees may be held until the end of the war. Critics of this policy argued that the government was trying to create a "legal black hole"—a place where law did not apply and where courts could not review the legal claims of the detainees.

In 2006, Congress enacted the *Military Commissions Act (MCA)*, which provided a process whereby a detainee's confinement could be reviewed by a military tribunal but not by federal court judges. Lawyers for the detainees filed suit in federal court asking that federal judges be permitted to review the confinement as well. Article I, Section 9 of the U.S. Constitution establishes that the writ of habeas corpus (which allows a judge to determine whether a person is being unlawfully detained by the government) "shall not be suspended, unless when in cases of rebellion or invasion the public safety may require it." Therefore, some critics maintained that the *MCA* violated the Constitution by failing to provide sufficient legal protections for detainees. Others argued that the *MCA* was fair to the detainees, particularly because they were being held outside the United States. In 2008, the Supreme Court ruled that the established military procedures did not provide the detainees a meaningful

◀ The Guantanamo Bay detention camp is a United States military prison located within the Guantanamo Bay Naval Base in Cuba.

opportunity to challenge their detention in federal court and that the detainees did retain the right to habeas corpus.

Approximately 780 prisoners have been sent to Guantanamo since 2002. As of 2019 only 40 remain there. Nearly 20 died in detention, and the others have been transferred to countries all over the world. Virtually none have been transferred to the United States. Of the detainees transferred, some estimate that between 20 percent and 35 percent have returned to the battlefield.

Torture has long been banned in the United States, and confessions obtained by torture have not been allowed as evidence at trials in this country. Torture is also outlawed by the Geneva Conventions, which have been signed and ratified by the United States. The United States is also a signatory to the United Nations Convention against Torture and Other Cruel, Inhuman or Degrading Treatment or Punishment. The *Detainee Treatment Act*, passed by Congress in 2005, imposes severe penalties for torture.

Exactly what constitutes torture, as opposed to "aggressive questioning" or "enhanced interrogation," has been extremely controversial since 2001. A procedure known as "water boarding" has been debated at length. During water boarding a suspect being interrogated can be made to feel as though he is drowning. The technique was employed hundreds of times on at least three high-profile terror suspects before the practice was discontinued in 2006.

Many prisoners were also allegedly subjected to other types of "aggressive questioning" at the U.S. military prison in Guantanamo Bay. While some enhanced interrogation techniques were banned, the issue of torture came up again in 2014 as many of the detainees were conducting hunger strikes. The military instituted a policy of force-feeding detainees on hunger strikes, which they maintain is the only way to keep these detainees alive. Opponents of force-feeding argue that it is an overly aggressive and extremely painful method of delivering food.

Torture is defined under the United Nations Convention against Torture and Other Cruel, Inhuman or Degrading Treatment or Punishment as any act that inflicts severe pain or suffering, physical or mental, and is intentionally inflicted on a person for such purposes as obtaining information. In recent years some government lawyers have proposed an alternative definition of *torture* as "any act that gives rise to pain that would ordinarily be associated with a sufficiently serious physical condition or injury such as death, organ failure or serious impediment of bodily functions."

a. Apply the two definitions of *torture* outlined above to the following situations and decide if the act constitutes torture.

- loud music played continuously for four hours
- hooding the person and then questioning
- using water to simulate drowning (also called "water boarding")
- yelling at the person for one hour
- hanging the person from the ceiling upside down
- keeping the person in total darkness for 24 hours
- keeping the person naked in a small cage

b. Is there a significant difference between these two definitions of *torture*?

c. Yee, a suspected terrorist, is arrested by the FBI. The government has information that he knows where a car bomb is scheduled to go off in two hours in a crowded area of a large city. The FBI interrogates Yee to find out the location of the car bomb and to prevent possible deaths. Are there any limits on the techniques the government can use to obtain this information? If so, what are those limits?

d. The late Senator John McCain, who was tortured as a POW in Vietnam, said the following in a speech opposing the torture of terror suspects: "I agree they are the most evil people in the world—it is not about them, it is about us." What did Senator McCain mean? Do you agree? Explain your answer.

► Everyone has certain rights and responsibilities in the workplace.

©Jetta Productions/Blend Images, LLC

Federal, state, and local laws govern the workplace. In this chapter you will learn the rights and responsibilities of job applicants, employers, and employees during a job search, on the job, and in the event of job loss.

Looking for a Job

When looking for a job, you should keep a number of legal and practical considerations in mind. Issues may arise during job interviews or when job applicants are tested. For example, employers may ask questions about your race, gender, or age. In some instances, such questions are legitimate and necessary. In other instances, such questions may be illegal and could constitute discrimination.

The Job Interview

When you have obtained an appointment for an interview, it is important to be prepared for it. How you dress, act, respond to questions, and otherwise present yourself at an interview may determine whether you get the job. The interview is also a chance for you to learn as much as you can about the position and the organization, so you can decide whether you really want to work there.

Employers ask many questions during job interviews to help them decide whether to hire a particular applicant. Based on employment discrimination laws, as well as generally accepted employment practices, employers should not raise issues in job interviews that may infringe on an applicant's privacy or that could be viewed as evidence of illegal discrimination. Examples include inappropriate references to a person's

541

gender, race, national origin, religion, age, disability, marital status, or personal practices outside the workplace. It *is* appropriate, however, for employers to ask applicants to identify their race, gender, or national origin for statistical purposes.

In preemployment discussions, an employer cannot ask about a person's disability. An employer is allowed, however, to ask questions related to a person's ability to perform a particular task or assignment. The *Americans with Disabilities Act (ADA)* does not require employers to hire a person with a disability who is not qualified for the position. Under the *ADA*, it is illegal to discriminate against a "qualified individual with a disability."

An inappropriate question does not necessarily constitute discrimination. To charge an employer with discrimination, a person must prove that he or she was actually denied the job for unlawful reasons. For example, it may be inappropriate to ask whether an applicant for an administrative position is married, because such a question may be evidence of discrimination. However, the question would not constitute discrimination if the applicant was denied the job because he or she lacked the skills needed for the position.

Employers may legally raise issues such as religion, gender, and national origin in some work-related contexts. For example, a church could require

▲ The *Americans with Disabilities Act* protects individuals with disabilities from discrimination in the workplace. *What does the act require of employers?*

bona fide occupational qualification (BFOQ) an employment requirement that is considered reasonable because it is necessary to perform the job. For example, good vision is a BFOQ for a bus driver; the race or national origin of a bus driver is not a BFOQ.

that a minister hired to lead the church be of a certain religion. In situations where religion, gender, and national origin are job requirements that are reasonably necessary to the normal operation of the business or enterprise, then the law recognizes what is known as a **bona fide occupational qualification (BFOQ)** and considers the discrimination to be legal. Turning down a male actor for a female role in a play would be another example of a reasonably necessary discrimination based on a BFOQ.

All employers must verify whether job applicants are U.S. citizens or have employment authorization. The *Immigration Reform and Control Act of 1986* made it unlawful for employers to knowingly hire, recruit, or continue to employ persons who are in the country without permission. Employers who violate this law are subject to fines and/or criminal penalties.

Whether employers have the right to ask applicants questions about prior arrests and convictions is not as clear. Federal regulations provide, and some federal courts have found, that without proof of business necessity, an employer's use of arrest records to disqualify job applicants is unlawful discrimination. A number of states prohibit employers from asking about arrest records. Making personnel decisions on the basis of records of arrests that did not result in criminal convictions has been found to have a disproportionate effect on employment opportunities for members of some minority groups. As of 2019 more than 30 states had "ban the box" laws. These laws remove the conviction history question from job applications and delay criminal background checks until later in the hiring process.

Employers can inquire about the age of young applicants to determine whether they are old enough to work, to find out how long they have been working, or to help estimate their probable level of maturity. Some states require permits, or "working papers," before young people can be hired. Those between the ages of 12 and 14 may obtain permits in certain states to work during holidays and vacations.

▲ Employers are responsible for verifying that job applicants are U.S. citizens or have authorization to work. *What other information may an employer ask for from a job applicant?*

PROBLEM 45.1

Jill Johnson, age 21, is applying for a job as an assistant hotel manager for a company that operates a chain of hotels throughout the country. She has scheduled a job interview with William Marconi, the regional manager of the company.

a. During the interview, Mr. Marconi asks Ms. Johnson the following questions. Which questions may be illegal? Which questions are legal but inappropriate? Which are legal and appropriate? Give your reasons for each answer.

- How old are you?
- Why do you want this job?
- Are you a U.S. citizen?
- Do you plan to get married and have children in the near future?
- Are you willing to move to another area of the country?
- Have you ever been arrested?
- How tall are you? How much do you weigh?
- Do you speak Spanish?
- Do you have a good credit rating?
- Will you have dinner with me tonight?
- Have you ever been treated for any mental problems?
- Have you ever had, or been treated for, any of the following medical conditions? (Ms. Johnson is given a checklist of diseases and conditions.)

b. Role-play the interview and have Ms. Johnson decide whether and how to answer each question Mr. Marconi asks. How did she answer or respond to any improper or illegal questions? How should she have answered each question? Should any of her answers be different for a better chance at getting the job? If so, which answers? How should she have answered differently? Which answers were particularly good? Give the reasons for your answers.

c. Evaluate how well Ms. Johnson did in the interview.

d. If someone is asked an improper or illegal question in an interview and later is denied the job, can he or she file a lawsuit claiming discrimination? Where can this person go for assistance?

Background Checks and Testing of Applicants

Many employers now conduct background checks before hiring a new employee. In some instances, the person hired might not have the highest grades in school or even the best skills for the job but instead might have had the cleanest background check among all the job applicants. Employers conduct background checks for many reasons, but one of them is to avoid liability for negligently hiring an employee. For example, a day care center could be sued if it hired a staff assistant who later causes harm to a young child on the job, based on a failure to carefully check the employee's background. Background checks often include searches of the following:

- state and national databases of criminal records
- credit history
- employment history
- worker's compensation claim history
- educational history
- sex offender registry
- driver's license history
- Homeland Security database

Employers commonly check an applicant's social networking sites. A photo of a student holding a beer can—even if it's empty and the photo was intended as a joke—can serve as a negative character reference. While some claim that these intensive background checks are overly intrusive or unrelated to the ability to perform on the job, many employers take them seriously. Negative information that shows up in these checks will limit future employment opportunities.

The law allows aptitude, personality, or psychological tests that can be shown to relate to an applicant's ability to do the job. However, such tests have been successfully challenged when they have been shown to be inaccurate or unnecessary for measuring a person's ability to succeed in the job. These tests have also been successfully challenged when they were actually used to discriminate based on such factors as race, gender, age, or national origin.

In addition, a test cannot be used if it screens out people with disabilities unless the tested activity is specifically job-related. For example, in a job that requires fast keyboarding skills, an employer can test for this skill and reject an applicant whose disability affects this skill. In addition, some states have laws prohibiting the use of AIDS testing for hiring purposes. People with HIV and AIDS are protected under the *ADA* as individuals with disabilities.

polygraph test a lie-detector instrument

Some employers contend that lie detector tests, called **polygraph tests,** help prevent the hiring of dishonest employees. However, many question the accuracy of these tests. In 1988, Congress passed the *Employee Polygraph Protection Act,* which makes it illegal for most employers to use such tests to select job applicants. This law does not cover security guards and federal, state, and local government employees.

To reduce the hiring of workers who use drugs and alcohol, many employers conduct drug tests on some or all job applicants. Generally, private corporations have been allowed to require drug testing. However, some states have passed laws limiting such testing, particularly as some states move toward the legalization or decriminalization of marijuana. For many years, the federal government has required drug testing for applicants for military, law enforcement, and certain other positions.

A growing number of states and cities have passed laws limiting the use of credit checks in hiring, firing, or promotion of employees. Those who support these limits argue that credit checks disproportionately affect minority and low-income applicants. They also contend that credit checks are not related to the ability to do most jobs. However, these laws typically have exceptions for jobs in law enforcement or for positions involving access to sensitive or financial information. Also many believe that asking about a credit history is reasonable and should be allowed.

▲ Requiring job applicants to take aptitude, psychological, or lie detector tests is a controversial legal issue. *Should employers use these tests to screen potential employees?*

PROBLEM 45.2

You are the manager of a fast-food restaurant that is opening in your town. You need to hire staff, and you plan to hire some high school students on a part-time basis. They will prepare and serve food and also work as cashiers. You hire a company to conduct background checks and job testing of applicants. What checks and tests do you want the company to conduct on the students you plan to hire? Explain the reasons for your decision.

Conditions on the Job

When on the job, you will find that various local, state, and federal laws apply in the workplace. These laws deal with wages and hours, taxes and benefits, Social Security, unions, health and safety, and privacy issues. Many of these laws exist to regulate the workplace and to protect employees and employers.

Wages and Hours

The vast majority of workers in the United States are covered by the *Fair Labor Standards Act,* which requires that a minimum hourly wage be paid to all employees. The federal minimum wage was $7.25 an hour in 2019. However, more than half of the states have laws that set a minimum wage higher than the federal minimum. When an employee is subject to both state and federal minimum-wage laws, the employee is entitled to the higher of the two minimum wages.

Certain jobs are not covered by the *Fair Labor Standards Act,* and some jobs are designated under federal or state law as having lower minimum wages. These include newspaper delivery and certain part-time retail, service, or agricultural jobs. Some jobs can pay less than the standard minimum wage if employees regularly receive tips to make up the difference.

Federal law also requires employers to pay overtime wages when employees work more than 40 hours per week. In most instances the overtime pay is one and a half times the regular hourly pay. For example, an employee who receives $8.00 per hour but works 50 hours in a week must receive $12.00 per hour for the 10 extra hours of work. Overtime pay rules do not apply to certain types of employees, including administrative and executive employees, professionals who receive fixed salaries and exercise discretion and control in their work, and those who work for commissions (for example, some salespeople).

The federal government has enacted child labor laws to ensure that the workplace is safe for young people and does not jeopardize their health, well-being, or educational opportunities. In addition, each state has its own laws concerning the employment of minors. These laws regulate how many hours a minor may work per day and per week, the minimum age (usually 15 or 16), which hours of the day they cannot work (for example, school hours), whether work permits are required, and what types of jobs minors are prohibited from holding (for example, dangerous activities or selling alcohol). When federal and state standards are different, the rules that provide the most protection for young people will apply.

Employees sometimes have their wages reduced for reasons such as showing up late, leaving early, or not being productive while on the job. If workers believe they have been treated unfairly in such cases, they may be able to file a complaint or even to sue their employer. A problem may occur, for example, when an employee who operates a cash register has less money in the register at the end of the shift than receipts indicate should be there. Whether the employer can reduce the employee's wages may depend on the employment contract, as well as federal and state laws concerning payment of wages.

Investigating the Law Where You Live

Research the minimum wage in your state. What is it? What laws in your state regulate the employment of minors?

Steps to Take

How to Complain About Wage and Hour Problems

- **Contact a government agency.** Employees who think their employer may not be paying them a fair wage should contact the Wage and Hour Division of the U.S. Department of Labor or their state or local government employment agency.

- **Contact the union.** If there is a union, it will have an established grievance procedure for members to follow.

- **File a complaint.** A complaint can be made to the union or to the appropriate government agency if an employer lays off or fires an employee who has complained about a wage and hour problem.

- **Take your case to court.** Employees can also file a case directly in court to enforce wage and hour laws or formal agreements with their employers.

Some states and cities have enacted laws that prohibit employers from requesting salary history information from job applicants. These laws are intended to address the gender wage gaps well as wage discrimination. Women and minorities have historically been paid less than their male or nonminority counterparts, and basing a person's pay on what they have previously been paid perpetuates that trend.

PROBLEM 45.3

a. Should all workers be covered by a minimum wage? Why? Some people favor a lower minimum wage for youths than for adults. What are the advantages and disadvantages of this idea? Do you support it? Explain.

b. As a fast-food cook who is paid $7.50 an hour, you hear that another cook at your restaurant, who is a good friend of the manager, is making $8.50 an hour. Also, last week you worked 42 hours and were paid your regular hourly wage ($7.50 × 42 = $315). What actions, if any, can you take to handle these problems?

c. Vana works as a waitress in a restaurant and is given her own cash bank from which to make change for her customers. At the end of her shift, she is $10 short, based on her receipts. Should she have to pay this money to the restaurant owner?

Investigating the Law Where You Live

Find out the contact information for the fair employment practices agency in your state.

Taxes and Benefits

Employers must withhold federal and state taxes from the paychecks of most employees. These taxes are used to provide government services, such as education, law enforcement, national defense, trash collection, and road building and maintenance. The law requires employers to provide most workers with a W-2 form showing their earnings and the amounts withheld each year by January 31 of the following year. By April 15 of each year, most workers must file state, federal, and sometimes local tax returns based on the information reported on the W-2 form. Depending on the total income for the year, amounts withheld by the employer, and other factors, a worker may either receive a refund from the government or have to pay an additional amount.

In addition to paying wages, employers may decide to provide employees with certain **fringe benefits** free of charge or at reduced cost. These benefits may include life, health, and disability insurance; pension plans; education and training; sick leave, vacations, and holidays; parking; meals; and severance pay in case of job loss. Some cities and states now require that certain employers provide employees with paid sick leave.

In 1993, Congress passed the *Family and Medical Leave Act (FMLA)*. This federal act requires certain employers to grant up to 12 weeks of unpaid leave within a 12-month period to people who want to care for newborn babies, newly adopted children, or ailing relatives. Amendments to the *FMLA* provide additional reasons for protected leave, including to care for a sick or disabled service member. Individual state laws may provide additional benefits. Employees may also bargain individually or collectively to include specific fringe benefits as part of an employment contract.

Social Security is the federal program that pays retirement, disability, or death benefits to eligible workers, their families, or both. Payroll deductions help fund this program. The amount deducted is a percentage of an employee's salary. As of 2019, employers and employees must pay a Social Security tax of 6.2 percent of each employee's salary up to $132,900 each year. The employer and employee each paid a Medicare tax of 1.45 percent of each employee's salary, regardless of the amount.

fringe benefit an item provided by an employer to employees free of charge or at reduced cost

▼ Workers must file tax returns based on the withholding information provided by their employers. *What are taxes withheld from workers' pay used for?*

JGI/Blend Images LLC

a. Bethany, age 22, has just graduated from college and is going to work for a computer company. Bethany is single and would like to return to school someday to earn a master's degree in business. What company fringe benefits will interest Bethany most? Why?

b. The JKR Corporation has 40 employees—25 men and 15 women. The company gives women 10 days of paid maternity leave when they give birth but does not offer a similar benefit to men who become fathers. Chandler, whose wife just had a baby, asks Korey, the president of JKR, for paid paternity leave. What reasons can Chandler present to support his request? What might Korey consider in making his decision? How should this situation be resolved?

c. Russell, age 18 and single, just graduated from high school and plans to work for several years to save money for college. He applies for a job delivering pizzas that requires him to wear a uniform. What fringe benefits might he want the company to provide? Why?

Labor Relations

A newly hired employee will learn whether employees at the company are represented by a union. A union is an organization that represents workers in dealing with the employer. Unions seek to improve wages, benefits and working conditions and to represent workers and resolve grievances with employers. Although union membership has declined since 1983, it was estimated in 2018 that 14.7 million U.S. workers belonged to unions, comprising 10.5 percent of the workforce.

Since 1935, workers in private companies have had the right to join a union under the federal *National Labor Relations Act (NLRA)*. This law is administered by the National Labor Relations Board (NLRB), a federal agency. Workers can choose to be represented by a union through an election in which more than 50 percent of the workers in the bargaining unit vote for it.

The primary purpose of a union is to represent workers in dealing with their employers. Unions engage in collective bargaining with employers to negotiate on behalf of employees.

Union supporters cite higher wages, greater fringe benefits, and better working conditions as results of union activity. Those who favor unions believe that unions accomplish much more for workers, through collective bargaining, than employees can achieve individually. Those who oppose unions say they are costly, unnecessary, disruptive, and interfere with employees' ability to deal directly with their employers. Critics believe that unions push up labor costs, which reduces profits and results in fewer jobs being available.

A **Collective Bargaining Agreement** (CBA) is a contract negotiated between the management of a company and the workers' union. The wages and benefits that workers represented by a union receive are set forth in the CBA. Many CBAs require all workers covered by the CBA to

collective bargaining a required procedure in the National Labor Relations Act providing that under certain circumstances, employers must bargain with official union representatives regarding wages, hours, and other work conditions

be union members and pay union dues or fees for representation. This is based on the argument that the union is the sole bargaining agent for the workers, and all must pay equally for work done on their behalf. Some states have passed "right to work laws," however, which make it illegal to require workers to join unions or to pay dues as a condition of employment. In addition to giving employees the right to join and be represented by unions, the *NLRA* also gives workers the right to engage in other activities together concerning their working conditions. Under the *NLRA,* employees have the right to join and/or support a union, as well as the right not to engage in union activities. Unions have the right to take certain actions, such as organizing strikes (work stoppages) and picketing (public demonstrations) to publicize disputes with employers, including about hazardous and unsafe working conditions. The *NLRA* also prohibits employers and unions from engaging in acts that are defined as unfair labor practices (ULPs). It is a ULP for a union to threaten workers to get them to join the union or to take part in a strike, or for a union not to fairly represent employees. Mass picketing, violence, or other actions that interfere with non-striking workers entering the workplace during a strike are also considered a ULP.

▼ Workers on a picket line

Examples of ULPs by employers include firing workers for joining or trying to organize unions, questioning workers about their union activities, and spying on union meetings. Refusing to bargain with a recognized union or to reinstate workers who take part in a legal strike are other examples of ULPs.

Even if there is no union in a workplace, employees still have the right to engage in "protected concerted activity," and to file ULP charges with the NLRB. Examples of protected activities include circulating petitions for higher wages or better benefits, calling for improved safety at a company meeting, and joining with other employees to protest to management improper payments.

The NLRB investigates ULP charges filed by unions, employers, and workers. After investigating a charge, the NLRB decides whether the case should be prosecuted or dismissed. A charge that is prosecuted will receive a formal hearing before an administrative law judge (ALJ). The ALJ can recommend corrective action if he or she believes a ULP was committed.

Federal employees and some state and local government employees also have the right to join unions, but they generally are not allowed to strike. The rights of federal employees are governed by the *Federal Labor Relations Act*. The rights of state and local public employees are governed by state laws.

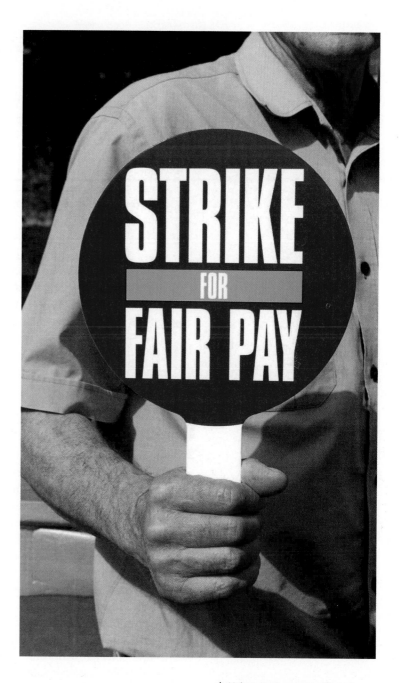

▲ Union members may strike or picket in response to labor disputes. *Would you be willing to demonstrate for or against labor policies?*

a. Why might some workers want to have a labor union in an auto manufacturing plant? Why might other workers in the plant prefer not to have a labor union? What information can you acquire to help you decide whether to support the formation of a labor union in an auto plant? If you worked in the plant, would you support a union? Explain.

b. What is a right-to-work state? What are the arguments in support of a right-to-work law? What are the arguments against a right-to-work law? Do you support or oppose such laws? Explain the reasons for your answer.

c. If city sanitation workers have had the same low salaries for five years and city leaders refuse to increase them, should the workers have the right to strike? Give the reasons for your decision. If a public strike is illegal in their state, what else can the workers do to try to get the city to increase their wages?

d. Should any public employees be allowed to strike? Is your answer different depending on the jobs they do—for example, police officers, firefighters, schoolteachers, government clerks, or maintenance workers at city hall? Explain the reasons for your answer.

Health and Safety in the Workplace

A government study estimated that there were more than 14,000 work-related deaths and 2.2 million injuries on the job in the United States in 1970. As a result of this study, many people became alarmed at the number of deaths and illnesses caused by the effects of lead and mercury poisoning, asbestos-containing materials, cotton dust, pesticides, new toxic substances, and new technologies. In response to these concerns, Congress passed the *Occupational Safety and Health Act.* This law requires that employers provide safe and healthy working conditions for all workers. However, self-employed people and farm families are not covered by this law. The law also does not cover most state and local government employees, who usually receive protection under other laws. Many states have additional laws and standards to further protect the health and safety of workers.

The 1970 *Occupational Safety and Health Act* established a federal agency, the Occupational Safety and Health Administration (OSHA), to issue safety regulations and standards that industries in the United States must follow. The act requires employers to keep records of all job-related illnesses and injuries among their workers. Workers may file safety-related complaints against their employers without making the workers' names known to employers. An employer who discovers the name of a complainant cannot take any disciplinary action against the employee because the employee filed a complaint. If agency inspections show that health or safety hazards exist, OSHA can issue citations requiring employers to take corrective action.

THE **CASE** OF...

The Collapsed Building

In 1987, a building under construction in Bridgeport, Connecticut, collapsed and killed 28 construction workers. A federal investigation showed that unsafe working conditions and practices caused the disaster. The construction site had been inspected once by OSHA six months before the accident because there had been a complaint. After the accident, OSHA issued fines totaling $5.1 million against three construction companies.

▲ A collapsed building

PROBLEM 45.6

What could be done to prevent this type of accident?

The case of the Collapsed Building illustrates a number of problems with the government's attempts to reduce health and safety problems in the workplace. Some people say that OSHA does not administer the regulations properly. Others say that some people in business do not follow the standards. Many think that OSHA has too few inspectors and that it would take millions of additional dollars to do the job right.

To enforce the regulations, OSHA conducts on-site inspections, orders changes, and sometimes fines employers. For example, a large defense contractor was fined $1.5 million for willfully failing to record 251 employee illnesses and injuries and failing to tell workers in 88 instances that they were working with hazardous materials.

OSHA also issues safety and health standards that industries must follow. Standards have been issued for the use of such items as hand tools, power presses, electrical wiring, ladders, hazardous gases, and chemicals. OSHA does not assist workers in filing lawsuits and collecting money damages from employers. Generally, individuals can receive compensation from their employers for injuries only under the workers' compensation system. However, an injured worker may be able to sue a negligent coworker for tort damages. Also, workers are sometimes fired for making safety- and health-related complaints to OSHA, to similar state or local agencies, or to their employer. Under the law, such employees are entitled to file a complaint with OSHA without negative consequences.

Some people criticize OSHA for overregulating businesses and industries and for requiring companies to spend large sums of money to comply with standards they feel are unnecessary. OSHA has also been criticized for expending too much effort on concerns about accidents while

USGS

neglecting the health issues that lead to many work-related illnesses and deaths. Examples of such illnesses include lung cancer resulting from asbestos exposure, black lung disease among coal miners, and brown lung disease in textile workers exposed to cotton dust.

In 2017, 5,147 workers suffered job-related deaths. The most common cause of death on the job was accidents in cars and trucks, followed by falls and homicides. The number of total occupational injuries has been falling steadily for the past decade.

The U.S. Department of Labor reported that there were 2.8 million nonfatal workplace injuries and illnesses in private industry in 2017. Both injuries and illnesses are significantly higher in manufacturing than in service industries. Partly as a result of the *Occupational Safety and Health Act* and similar state laws, workplace injuries and illnesses have been declining in recent years, even as the population of workers has increased.

In response to workers' concerns, the federal government and many state governments have enacted community "right-to-know" laws. These laws require employers using certain hazardous materials to inform their employees about the accident and health hazards of chemicals in the workplace. They must also train employees to properly handle such materials in order to minimize problems. Information about the materials and emergency response plans must be made available to employees and local officials. In addition, many employers offer training programs to inform employees of possible health hazards from assembly-line work or exposure to computer monitors.

Some view cigarette smoke in the workplace as a health hazard. As a result, many states and cities have prohibited smoking inside office buildings. Others have restricted smoking to certain areas of the workplace or required employees to smoke outside.

Violence in the workplace has emerged as an important safety and health issue. Workplace violence ranges from threats and verbal abuse to physical assaults and homicide. It can involve employees, clients, customers, and visitors. While no organization is immune from workplace violence, the heath care and social services industries are particularly susceptible. In response, *OSHA* has developed guidelines and recommendations to reduce worker exposure to this hazard. In addition, some states have enacted legislation aimed at avoiding and combatting workplace violence.

▼ The *Occupational Safety and Health Act* requires that employers provide safe and healthy working conditions for workers. However, *OSHA* has been criticized for neglecting health issues, such as black lung disease, that lead to illnesses and death. *How does* OSHA *help to promote a safe and healthy working environment?*

▲ Many workers have become concerned with the effects on their health of conditions in the workplace, such as noisy equipment and toxic substances. *How has the government responded to such concerns?*

PROBLEM 45.7

a. What is the purpose of *OSHA*? How does it work? Some say that people are safer at work than in their cars. Do you think this is true? If so, is OSHA needed, or is it an example of overregulation by the government?

b. Jack works in a factory where there are strong fumes in the air. He and other workers cough a lot on the job. Jack complains to *OSHA*. He is laid off by the factory manager, who says the company has lost money due to the cost of controlling the fumes as ordered by *OSHA*. What actions can Jack take?

c. Are state laws and local ordinances that prohibit smoking in office buildings a reasonable way to protect nonsmokers or an unreasonable interference with the rights of smokers? Give your reasons.

Privacy at Work

The right to privacy is often referred to as "the right to be let alone." Individuals should be able to determine how much of their personal lives they wish to share with others. Some people say privacy is not possible at work, because an employer has an interest in monitoring, supervising, and evaluating employees' work to ensure that employees do their jobs properly. However, many employees believe that they should not have to give up all rights to privacy.

Those who work for the federal and some state governments generally have greater privacy rights than those who work for private employers. For example, the federal *Privacy Act of 1974* gives federal government employees the right to be told what is in their personnel files, to correct an error in those files, and to limit others' access to the files. Some states provide similar protections for state government employees. Only a few states do so for private employees, however this number is growing. Union contracts may provide some privacy rights.

Employee privacy rights have also become an issue in relation to certain actions that employers have taken to reduce workplace crime. In an effort to cut down on theft by employees, many employers hire private security guards to watch workers, and some use video monitoring as well. The courts have generally allowed employers to take these actions. They have also approved searches of employees' desks and of employees as they arrive at and depart from the workplace, based on the rationale that employers have the right to search their premises for business purposes. If an employer or a security guard goes too far and detains employees against their will without good reason, the workers may have a tort claim for false imprisonment. Evidence of illegal activity found as a result of such searches can usually be used in court, because the Fourth Amendment's exclusionary rule prohibits only the use in court of the results of unreasonable searches by the government.

Wiretapping without a warrant is usually prohibited by federal law, but the courts have allowed telephone monitoring of employees by employers on extension phones. Employers also have other methods of monitoring how much work an employee performs. Employers are also allowed to

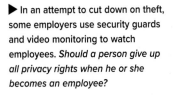

▶ In an attempt to cut down on theft, some employers use security guards and video monitoring to watch employees. *Should a person give up all privacy rights when he or she becomes an employee?*

Aaron Roeth Photography

read employee e-mail and to monitor employee use of the Internet. Employers argue that such monitoring is necessary to make sure employees are doing their jobs properly. Others claim that monitoring creates a negative work atmosphere and should be prohibited.

Employers can generally regulate how employees dress on the job, unless such regulation is a cover-up for some form of illegal discrimination based on race, gender, national origin, or religion. Uniforms, if appropriate to the job, and a neat appearance can be required. This may even include rules regarding length of hair, wearing a beard or mustache, tattoos and piercings, and modes of dress. In recent years, as styles and fashion have changed, some employers have relaxed rules regarding dress and appearance while on the job.

One of the most controversial issues involving privacy in the workplace is that of testing employees for drug use. Many employers test their workers for drugs. These private testing programs are generally legal, unless they are conducted in a state with a strong privacy law or privacy protection in the state constitution. Some labor unions have been able to curtail drug testing through collective bargaining with the employers. Rulings under the *National Labor Relations Act* have held that companies must comply with union requests to negotiate about drug-testing policies. In states the allow medical or recreational use of marijuana, employers may have to adjust their drug-testing practice.

In 1989, the U.S. Supreme Court addressed the drug-testing issue when it decided that blood and urine testing of railroad employees by the federal government after an accident was not a violation of the Fourth Amendment. This case made many references to public safety concerns regarding train accidents. Decisions in future cases will have to determine whether random drug testing of government employees will be allowed or whether reasonable suspicion of individual employees or a special public safety interest relating to the jobs involved will be required.

THE **CASE** OF...

Testing Customs Agents for Drugs

U.S. customs agents work along the country's borders and at airports. One of their duties is to reduce the amount of drugs being smuggled into the United States. The customs commissioner establishes a drug-testing program for all employees who apply for promotion to "sensitive positions." In these positions, employees (1) stop shipments of drugs, (2) carry firearms, or (3) handle classified information. Employees who fail the required urinalysis test are fired, but the results are not turned over to law enforcement officials. Under this program, five customs employees out of 3,600 tested positive for drugs. The customs agents' union files a lawsuit challenging the legality of the drug-testing program.

PROBLEM 45.8

a. What are the arguments in favor of the drug-testing program?

b. What are the arguments against it?

c. If you were the judge in the case, how would you rule, and why?

Employees' Right to Privacy

Decide whether the law should protect the employee's right to privacy in each of the following situations. Then explain the reasons for your answers.

a. Judy, who currently works for a cement company, has applied for a new job with a construction firm. As part of his decision-making process to fill the position, the manager of the construction firm calls the cement company's president. During the phone call the president reads the contents of Judy's personnel file over the phone, including many negative comments about her work and personality.

b. Lionel, an African American salesperson in a store frequented mostly by white people, begins to wear his hair in dreadlocks. His supervisor says Lionel will hurt business if he wears his hair that way while at work and sends him home.

c. Jasper is missing some expensive jewelry from his store. He asks the police to come to the store and search the handbags of the three saleswomen who work for him.

d. Barnes, who owns a painting company, suspects Jenny, one of his painters, of not working very hard when he is not around. Without informing Jenny, he offers $20 to Sally, another one of his painters, to spy on Jenny when he is not present and to tell him how hard she works.

e. To reduce theft in his factory, Jay installs one-way mirrors that enable supervisors to watch employees.

f. Tami owns a business and begins monitoring the e-mail between her employees. She fires Hugo after discovering he has sent messages to other employees criticizing Tami and mentioning that he suspects her of stealing money.

Losing a Job

Few things disturb people more than the thought of losing their jobs. Job loss can occur through firing for cause (for a specific reason) or, in some cases, for no reason at all. Workers also lose their jobs through layoffs, which may be the result of economic problems beyond the employer's control. The fear of unemployment and the resulting loss of income needed to support workers and their families is a serious matter. The law provides some protection from job loss. It also provides some assistance for workers who have lost their jobs.

Employment Contracts

Some jobs are based on oral or written contracts between employees and employers. Employees promise to perform certain duties, and employers promise to pay them and provide other benefits. Many employment agreements between employees and private employers are referred to as **employment-at-will contracts.** Under this doctrine, the employees can quit any time they wish, and the employer can discharge them any time it wishes for any reason or for no reason at all, as long as discharging them does not violate some other law, such as an antidiscrimination law.

employment-at-will contract a work agreement in which the employee can quit at any time, and the employer can fire the employee for any reason or no reason at all as long as the firing does not violate some other law, such as an anti-discrimination law

However government employers must usually follow specific procedures in order to discharge an employee. In some instances a private employer who has negotiated a contract with a union or with nonunion employees may also have to provide certain procedural rights before job termination.

Some written employment contracts specify that the employee must give the employer notice before resigning. If the failure to do so causes the employer to lose money, the employee may be liable.

Opinions differ on whether it is better to have the at-will approach to employment, in which the employer has great freedom to discharge employees, or whether the law should provide greater protection for workers, as it does in a number of other countries. Those in favor of the at-will system argue that it gives businesses the freedom they need to achieve economic success and that restricting them would be inefficient and less profitable. Ultimately workers at inefficient companies wind up losing their jobs. Employers insist that they must be able to get rid of workers who do not show up, are routinely late, do not follow the rules, or cannot perform their jobs. Supporters of at-will employment say the government is not as efficient as private business, at least partly because of restrictions on discharging low-performing employees.

Others call at-will employment unfair. They claim that workers are often discharged without a good business reason or as a cover-up for illegal discrimination. Opponents argue that workers should be discharged only for a good reason, such as inability to do the job.

Courts and state legislatures have made some exceptions to the at-will doctrine by placing more restrictions on the employer's ability to discharge employees. For example, courts have said that there is an implied duty to treat the other party to a contract fairly and in good faith. Specifically, one state court would not allow an employer to end the employment contract of a salesperson in order to avoid paying him commissions he had already earned. The court held that the employer was not treating the worker fairly under his employment contract.

When a Firing May Be Illegal

As noted earlier, federal law provides that employees may not be discharged from their jobs based on race, gender, color, national origin, religion, age (if 40 or older), physical or mental disability, or genetic information. Federal law also prohibits discharge because of membership in a union or union activity. Some state and local laws go further and prohibit discrimination because of factors such as marital status, AIDS, and sexual orientation.

▼ Employees who work for privately owned businesses such as salons and restaurants usually have employment-at-will contracts. Should employers be able to discharge at-will employees for any reason, or for no reason at all?

Assume that the following situations occur at companies with employee handbooks stating that "any employee may be fired at any time for just cause." The following events occur in a state that has recognized such handbooks as implied terms-of-employment contracts. If employees are fired for the following reasons, which firings should the court allow, and which do you think should be declared illegal?

a. Warren is more than 30 minutes late for work two or three times a week and has been warned three times about it.

b. Michael, the owner of the restaurant at which Leona works, has instructed her not to ring up every check on the cash register so he can avoid paying the full sales tax. Leona refuses to follow Michael's instructions.

c. Pierre has an alcohol problem that makes it difficult for him to work most days after lunch.

d. While working on a computer, Naomi accidentally destroys an important company file. She has been warned about the importance of this file and has destroyed files before.

e. Winston and John's inability to get along is harming company operations. After starting a fistfight with Winston, John is fired. Winston does not lose his job.

f. The ice cream company that Chloe works for produces one flavor that is a big seller. She gives the recipe to her friend, who works at another ice cream company.

g. D'Angelo, a government scientist, gives a newspaper reporter classified information showing that a recently issued report to Congress contains false statements.

h. Marnie has been on the job for three months. One morning her son has a bad asthma attack, and she has to take him to the hospital. Marnie calls the boss from the hospital but misses her shift. The boss immediately fires her.

Courts have also held that discharges were unlawful when they determined that the employer's action violated a public policy. In one example, an employee was threatened with losing his job when he refused to lie before a grand jury as ordered by his supervisor. In another case, a discharged employee had been called for jury duty and was told by his supervisor not to serve.

whistle-blowing when an employee tells authorities about his or her employer's illegal acts

Several federal laws protect **whistle-blowing,** which occurs when an employee "blows the whistle" on, or reports, an employer to the authorities for illegal acts. The *Fair Labor Standards Act, Title VII* of the *Civil Rights Act of 1964,* and the *Occupational Safety and Health Act* each protects employees from being fired for making complaints about unfair pay practices, discrimination, and unsafe or hazardous conditions. Some states also have laws that forbid the firing of whistle-blowers. The *Whistleblower*

Protection Act of 1989 protects whistleblowers who work for the federal government and report possible violations of law.

Whistle-blowing might also take the form of telling someone other than the government about a problem. For example, a court ordered the reinstatement of a bank employee who was fired for telling bank vice presidents that the institution was illegally overcharging customers. The employee had done nothing wrong by reporting illegal business practices.

Whistle-blowing raises the conflict between employees' duty of loyalty to their employer and their obligation to act ethically and legally. In situations that do not involve whistle-blowing, loyalty is expected of employees. They can be legally fired for disloyal actions such as selling or giving a company's trade secrets to a competing firm.

Employees must be careful when they complain to someone outside their workplace. For example, employees who call a newspaper to complain that their employer is breaking the law can be fired if they are acting unreasonably—that is, if no effort has been made to confirm the accuracy of the complaint. Workers who complain are required to act reasonably and in good faith. If they do not, the courts are likely to let the firing stand.

▼ Whistle blowers are protected by federal law.

©Chris Ryan/age fotostock

THE **CASE** OF...

The Shoe Store Firing

Mr. Brady works as a salesperson at a shoe store in a mall. He has no written employment contract or employee handbook, and there is no union for store employees. Recently, Mr. Brady was fired by the owner, Mrs. Hinoshita, without a stated reason. Mr. Brady and his coworkers believe that he was fired because he often argued with Mrs. Hinoshita over the way the shoes were arranged in the storeroom, which shifts he worked, breaks, and other issues. The other salespeople in the store believe that Mrs. Hinoshita is a difficult supervisor and that Mr. Brady was a little outspoken, but they do not think he should have been fired.

Mrs. Hinoshita thinks Mr. Brady was more trouble than he was worth and was not a very good salesperson. She also thinks that because it is her store, she should not have to give reasons for firing him.

PROBLEM 45.10

a. Does Mr. Brady have an at-will employment contract? If so, how does this affect his being fired by Mrs. Hinoshita without a stated reason?

b. Should the law allow at-will employment contracts? What are the arguments for and against them?

c. Role-play a meeting between Mrs. Hinoshita and the other shoe salespeople who believe Mr. Brady should be reinstated in his job. If you were Mrs. Hinoshita, what would you do when confronted by the complaints of salespeople? Why? What was the outcome of the meeting?

d. Assume that Mrs. Hinoshita agrees to issue an employee handbook listing the reasons for which an employee can be fired. Draft such a list. Are the reasons listed fair to both Mrs. Hinoshita and the employees? How could you make them fairer?

e. If the employees and Mrs. Hinoshita disagreed on the acceptable reasons for firing people, what other process might be used to come to an agreement that both sides can live with? Should Mrs. Hinoshita care whether the other employees support her firing decisions or think her rules are unfair? Explain your reasons.

▼ At work in a shoe store

Javier Larrea/Pixtal/age fotostock

Procedures Before Job Loss

If a government employee is about to lose his or her job, the U.S. Constitution, the state constitution, or state law will usually require that the employer follow certain procedures. This is not usually required in private employment. In general, most employees do not have to receive notice, and most employers do not have to follow any set procedures.

Sometimes employees are not fired but are laid off. This action often occurs when a company is in trouble financially or experiences a temporary lag in business. After a period of time, laid-off workers may or may not get their jobs back. Depending on the company's policies or its employment contracts, the workers may have rights to continued health insurance or other benefits during the layoff.

In order to give notice of job layoffs to some workers, Congress passed a law requiring most employers with more than 100 employees to warn their workers at least 60 days in advance of an impending plant closing or large-scale layoff. Some states have similar laws. If employers fail to provide such warnings, they may be liable for fines, back pay, and benefits. Notice of job layoffs to employees is not required under some emergency and other special circumstances.

Employees who have been fired or laid off from their job may be eligible for **severance pay.** This is pay to compensate for the loss of their jobs and for time they are not going to work. The amount is determined by the employer, by an employment contract, or by provisions in an employee handbook. Although these employees may be eligible for unemployment compensation, it may not begin for a period of time and may not provide sufficient financial support while they look for other jobs.

Under the *Consolidated Omnibus Budget Reconciliation Act (COBRA),* employers with 20 or more employees are required to let terminated, covered employees and eligible dependents elect to continue their health insurance under the employer's group health plan. However, the former employees and dependents must pay the full cost for such coverage, including a reasonable administrative fee. The ability to purchase health insurance coverage at the employer's group cost can be important for terminated employees, because employers often get a better price than individuals for good health insurance. Coverage is usually available for up to 18 months, unless the employee gets another job that provides for health coverage.

severance pay money paid to employees who have been dismissed (generally through no fault of their own) to compensate for the time they are not going to work because of the job loss

a. Assume that you work for a computer software company. One morning the boss says, "I am sorry, but we have information that you use drugs and even bought some at work one day. We are going to have to let you go. The company has a clearly stated rule against drugs in the workplace." What procedures would you insist on before you were fired? If the employer refused to follow these procedures, what would you do? Explain your answers.

b. If your employer is in financial trouble and going out of business, what are the arguments for and against requiring the owner to give you notice and severance pay? With which point of view do you agree? Explain the reasons for your answers.

c. Can you think of any jobs in which the employee should be required to give the employer notice of intent to leave the job? If so, which ones, and why should notice be required? Should there be a penalty if the worker fails to do this? Explain the reasons for your answers.

unemployment compensation the government system that protects employees who lose their jobs through no fault of their own, by providing them with payments while they look for other jobs

▼ Unemployment compensation is handled by state agencies. *What steps should be taken to help reduce unemployment?*

If You Lose Your Job

All states have a system of **unemployment compensation**—also called unemployment insurance—that protects you if you lose your job through no fault of your own. This system allows you to collect payments from the government while you look for another job. The pay will not be as much as you were earning while you were working, and it is only temporary. However, the money may keep you from using up your savings or going into debt during the period of unemployment. Typically, payments are for up to 26 weeks, although they can continue for longer periods in some states. Congress also has the power to extend unemployment benefits for additional weeks. The unemployment payments come from payroll taxes collected from employers by the federal and state governments.

Some people do not qualify for unemployment compensation. For example, someone who cannot work due to an on-the-job injury is eligible for workers' compensation but is probably not eligible for unemployment benefits.

Someone who was fired for misconduct is not eligible for unemployment compensation. For example, theft would clearly constitute misconduct, whereas an error in filling out a form would not. Generally, a single incident would probably not be considered misconduct, but repeated incidents after being warned might make an employee ineligible for unemployment compensation. An employee fired for poor performance, such as slow typing, may still be able to obtain unemployment compensation. However, a typist who keeps showing up late for work after being warned would probably be ruled ineligible because of misconduct.

Ingram Publishing

People who quit voluntarily are usually not eligible for unemployment benefits unless they can show that the situation at work was unbearable. For example, a person who opposed war as part of his religion and who quit after being transferred to a job producing tanks was allowed to collect unemployment compensation. Someone who becomes physically unable to do a job can also quit and retain eligibility for benefits.

To apply for unemployment compensation, a person must file an application with the state agency that handles these claims. Generally, this can be done by phone or online. It is important to do this as soon as possible after becoming unemployed because it can take several weeks to process the application. Agency staff must investigate all applications, and hearings are sometimes held if employers protest the claims. Employers may sometimes protest the payment of unemployment benefits to a former employee because it can result in higher payroll taxes for the employer in the future.

Investigating the Law Where You Live

Find out the location of the office at which people can apply for unemployment compensation in your area.

PROBLEM 45.12

Assume that the following employees lose their jobs for the stated reasons. Should they be eligible to receive unemployment compensation? Explain the reasons for your answers.

a. Maggie dislikes her boss and says she will no longer do any work he assigns. She is fired.

b. A fellow employee offers Philip some marijuana. Philip is caught smoking it in the men's room and is fired.

c. Sybil stays home from work several times to care for her sick children. Her boss fires her, saying he needs someone who is dependable and that he can count on.

d. When business declines, the company closes the plant where Alonzo works. The company offers him a job at its other plant, which is one and a half hours away by car. Alonzo turns down the new job because he does not want to commute that far to work each day.

▶ The federal Environmental Protection Agency is located in Washington, D.C.

Environmental law in the United States has a long and complicated history that is still evolving. Even though many challenging environmental problems have been addressed, new problems continue to arise as a result of population growth and technological development. Americans continue to learn more about the impacts of human activities on the natural systems that provide life-sustaining necessities like clean air and water, adequate food and shelter, and new medicines.

None of the major environmental laws discussed in this chapter existed until the middle of the twentieth century. In fact, the Environmental Protection Agency (EPA), the principal federal agency charged with combatting pollution, was not established until 1970. Before then, national environmental laws primarily focused on land conservation. In 1872, for example, the U.S. Congress and President Ulysses S. Grant together established Yellowstone National Park. The *Antiquities Act*, which allows the president to designate national monuments, was passed in 1906. And the National Park Service was established a decade later, in 1916.

However, land conservation did not go far enough to protect Americans from the effects of rapid industrialization. By the 1960s, the environment was in crisis. Decades of largely unregulated human activity—burning coal, wood, and even garbage, spraying new pesticides and other hazardous chemicals, and dumping sewage and other wastewater—had taken their toll. Smoke from coal-fired power plants and chemical manufacturing facilities contributed to deadly "killer fog" events in some Midwestern cities. Acid rain, also an unfortunate result of industrialization, caused widespread damage to lakes, forests, and wildlife in New England. The

Cuyahoga River in Cleveland, Ohio, was so full of industrial waste oils that it repeatedly caught fire. California was struggling to crack down on vehicle emissions, a significant cause of that state's asthma-inducing smog.

As a result of these crises, the 1960s and early 1970s saw a wave of national environmental lawmaking that established the foundation for modern environmental regulations. The new laws, most of which remain unchanged nearly 50 years later, have been highly effective in protecting the environment. Across most of the United States, air and water are much cleaner than they were in the 1950s. Some animals have been brought back from the brink of extinction, and many unique natural or historic areas have been protected for future generations.

While the United States has made important progress over the last half-century, the entire world now faces a novel environmental threat that many consider to be the most pressing policy issue of our time: human-induced climate change. As you read about the laws passed in the 1960s and 1970s, and the environmental challenges they helped solve, think about what has worked, what has not, and how you could tackle today's threats.

FYI For Your Information

What is the Environment?

The environment includes many of the things people usually associate with nature: land, air, water, animals, and plants. But the concept also encompasses the public health impacts of pollution. In addition, courts interpret the word *environment* to include social, cultural, and aesthetic aspects of our world—noise levels, historical landmarks, and sites sacred to Native American groups.

PROBLEM 46.1

John Muir, also known as "John of the Mountains" and the "Father of the National Parks," was an influential 19th century conservationist and environmental philosopher. He once wrote, "In walks with Nature, one receives far more than he seeks." What do you think he meant?

The National Environmental Policy Act

The first major environmental law enacted during the law-making wave of the 1960s and 1970s was the *National Environmental Policy Act,* or *NEPA.* Passed in 1969 and signed into law in 1970 by President Nixon, *NEPA* established a national policy of considering the environmental impacts of governmental actions. Under *NEPA,* if a federal government agency plans to undertake an activity that may significantly "affect the quality of the human environment," the agency must first assess the effects of that activity on the human and natural environment. If the effects are significant, the agency must then evaluate and describe them in an extensive **environmental impact statement (EIS).**

NEPA's requirements apply to a wide range of activities in which the federal government is involved, from the construction of a new federal building (*e.g.,* a post office or navy base), to the adoption of a new federal policy. In fact, *NEPA* even applies to the adoption of policies that are not principally about the environment. For example, the Department of Housing and Urban Development (HUD) would have to assess the environmental impacts of a new plan to give funds to low income persons to subsidize their housing costs. *NEPA* applies even if a city or state government is the principal actor, as long as the federal government is playing a substantial role in funding or approving the project.

For *NEPA* to apply, the activity must not only involve the federal government but also "significantly affect" the environment. A state's plan to build a highway using federal funds, for example, would be a federal activity significantly affecting the environment, because it could involve digging up land, filling wetlands, tearing down existing buildings, and possibly even displacing people who live along the project route. Also, the highway would probably increase the amount of traffic in the area, so levels of noise and vehicle emissions would increase. By contrast, a city plan to add a new traffic light at a busy intersection on an existing road might not require federal government involvement, and might not have significant environmental side effects.

The EIS process is important not only because the relevant government agency must gather data and seriously consider how its proposed projects might impact the environment, but also because this process facilitates public involvement in the government project. By requiring the agency to prepare an EIS, and also to share its draft EIS with the public and invite public input, *NEPA* gives the public a chance to weigh in. The public can provide feedback through written comments or they can attend a public hearing on the potential impacts of the project before construction or implementation even begins.

environmental impact statement (EIS) a document prepared to describe the effects of a proposed project on the surrounding environment

PROBLEM 46.2

You are the youth member of the planning commission in your city or town. The high school you attend is severely overcrowded and the school board wants to build a new school. The board is able to use federal funding for part of the construction costs.

a. What issues should the school board address in considering the impacts of this project and determining whether an EIS is required? State the issues in the form of questions. For example, where will the school be built? Is the building site already developed?

b. What are the benefits and costs of seeking public input before making decisions that significantly affect the environment?

NEPA also created the Council on Environmental Quality (CEQ), which is now part of the president's office in the executive branch of the government. CEQ's job is to advise other federal agencies about how to comply with *NEPA*'s requirements. In addition, CEQ keeps the president informed about environmental problems and gives advice to other agencies about the environmental impacts of their activities.

The Clean Air Act

Air pollution poses a serious threat to public health. According to the World Health Organization, air pollution is linked to lung cancer, respiratory infections, strokes, and heart disease. Each year it contributes to millions of premature deaths worldwide.

▼ Smokestacks at energy plants powered by fossil fuels contribute to pollution.

Factories, power plants, chemical manufacturing facilities, trucks, and automobiles are major contributors to air pollution. As a result, although everyone suffers when air is polluted, the communities that suffer most are those located near busy roads and highways, factories, and power plants. These are often low income communities.

Congress passed the *Clean Air Act* (*CAA*) in 1969, the same year as *NEPA*. The *CAA* gives the EPA several difficult tasks: setting national air quality standards based on the best available science; providing guidance about which technologies should be used to reduce pollution; and regulating emissions of certain hazardous air pollutants (like mercury). States are then required to adopt and enforce plans that will meet the EPA's air quality standards.

Congress amended the *CAA* in 1990 to improve enforcement and compliance mechanisms. Since then, the EPA estimates that programs implemented under the *CAA* have prevented up to 160,000 premature deaths per year. Meanwhile, national concentrations of air pollutants targeted by the *CAA* continue to fall.

PROBLEM 46.3

Visit the AirNow website (www. airnow.gov) and enter your zipcode. Use the information you find to answer the following questions.

a. What is the quality of the air where you live today?

b. What is predicted for tomorrow?

c. Is there any information about specific air pollutants where you live?

d. Compare the air quality in your zip code to the air quality in a neighboring zip code. Is there a difference? Can you identify any factors that might lead to these differences air quality?

Tatiana Grozetskaya/Shutterstock

▲ Agricultural runoff—a form of point source pollution—carries topsoil as well as fertilizers and other potential pollutants from unprotected farm fields when heavy rains occur. *Are there areas with harmful agricultural runoff where you live?*

point source pollution any single identifiable source of water pollution from which pollutants are discharged, such as a pipe, ditch, ship, or smokestack

nonpoint source pollution water pollution that is caused by widely dispersed sources of pollutants such as runoff from rain and snow melt, acid rain, and modifications in the form of irrigation, dams, and the like

The Clean Water Act

Have you ever heard the statement, "The solution to pollution is dilution"? This idea embodies the traditional view of water bodies as waste dumps. In fact, until the mid-twentieth century, it was a common practice to pump industrial waste—like chemicals used in manufacturing—directly into nearby rivers or lakes. Sewage and waste from homes and office buildings also ran straight to rain gutters and then to waterways. In addition, electric power plants would often use river water to cool their operating systems and then return the heated water directly back to the river, where it would raise river temperatures.

Such practices harmed aquatic plants and animals. By the latter half of the twentieth century, many streams, rivers, and lakes were unsafe for recreational activities like fishing and swimming. In addition, drinking the polluted water caused significant health problems, including waterborne infections like hepatitis and gastroenteritis, as well as skin, respiratory, and ear infections.

Several federal laws now regulate water pollution. The two most important statutes are the *Clean Water Act* (*CWA*) and the *Safe Drinking Water Act* (*SDWA*). These two laws direct the EPA to establish, implement, and enforce regulations that limit the pollutants entering U.S. waterways and that protect water quality in the groundwater reservoirs, rivers, and lakes that supply drinking water. One significant limitation of these laws, however, is that although they are very effective at reducing **point source pollution,** the statutes do not provide the EPA and state governments with adequate tools to address **nonpoint source pollution.** As a result, this nonpoint source pollution now poses a significant threat to America's waterways.

PROBLEM 46.4

Visit the EPA website (www.epa.gov) and look for the "Your Community" heading on the homepage. From there, select your state in the drop-down menu below "Go to EPA's page about your state." Use the information you find to answer the following questions.

a. What environmental challenges does your state face?

b. What initiatives are underway in your state to meet these challenges?

The Endangered Species Act

Since the early 1900s, U.S. environmental laws have not only taken on the problem of pollution but have also attempted to protect plants and wildlife from over-exploitation and habitat destruction. The most significant of these laws is the *Endangered Species Act* (*ESA*), which was passed in 1973. The *ESA* directs two federal agencies, the U.S. Fish and Wildlife Service (FWS) and the National Marine Fisheries Service (NMFS), to identify and list plant or animal species that are on the brink of extinction. With limited exceptions, individuals are then prohibited from killing or harming those species, and from importing or exporting them to or from the United States. In addition, federal agencies must consult with FWS or NMFS to ensure the agencies' actions do not jeopardize listed species or destroy or harm the species' habitat.

Land Pollution

Land can be polluted in many ways. Examples of land pollution include depositing solid waste such as trash and garbage, old appliances, abandoned cars, etc. on the ground (which also results in visual pollution); piping chemicals and other waste materials into or under the ground; and burying and abandoning tanks of chemicals underground.

Since water pollution laws now prohibit the discharge of most chemicals and wastes into streams, rivers, and lakes, some industries have resorted to storing waste materials and then transporting them to dumping sites known as **landfills**. In addition, to avoid the air pollution caused by burning garbage, many localities dispose of collected trash and garbage by burying it in the ground at municipal landfills. The governing law, the *Resource Conservation and Recovery Act* (*RCRA*), sets the conditions under which such disposal is permitted. It monitors hazardous waste from generation to disposal. However, landfills can still cause significant public health issues for nearby communities, due to groundwater contamination, and airborne particulates.

Stricter regulations apply to landfills that accept hazardous waste. For example, these dumping sites must have impermeable liners and caps to stop the toxins from seeping into groundwater or flooding nearby streams.

Some sites of historic mining, industrial, or waste dumping activity are now so contaminated by hazardous pollutants that they have their own name: **Superfund sites.** These toxic areas are regulated under the *Comprehensive Environmental Response, Compensation, and Liability Act of 1980* (*CERCLA*), which is funded by taxes placed on those that create hazardous waster. *CERCLA*

landfill a place to dispose of refuse and other waste material by burying it and covering it over with soil

Superfund site any land in the United States that has been contaminated by hazardous waste and identified by the EPA as a candidate for cleanup due to health and/or environmental risks

▼ The Iron Mountain Mine near Redding, California, was mined for iron, silver, gold, copper, zinc, and pyrite from the 1890s to 1963. Nearly a century of active mining took an environmental toll. The mine was made a Superfund site in 1983.

requires the EPA, states, tribes, and current and past owners of the sites to work together to clean up and rehabilitate heavily contaminated sites. This can be an extremely expensive undertaking as it often involves digging up contaminated soil (and sometimes even dredging river bottoms), treating the contaminants, or taking them away to carefully regulated hazardous waste landfills. Like many other types of pollution and environmental hazards, Superfund sites disproportionately impact communities with large numbers of people living below the poverty line.

PROBLEM 46.5

Search the EPA website (www.epa.gov) for the Superfund page. Then use the "Sites where you live" link to find the Superfund sites in your state.

a. Is there a site near where you live or go to school?

b. Can you describe any pattern to the Superfund site locations?

Other federal environmental protection laws

A number of federal environmental laws include protections for sites of historical and cultural importance. Passed in 1966, for example, the *National Historic Preservation Act* (NHPA) protects historical landmarks at risk due to construction and other development. States can receive federal grants for the protection, rehabilitation, and reconstruction of sites, buildings, structures, and objects based on a state-wide historic preservation plan. The *NHPA* also protects sites of religious or cultural importance to federally recognized tribes.

▼ Ellis Island, an immigration station that opened in 1892, has been listed on the National Register of Historic Places since 1966. *Are there any sites on this register where you live?*

Noise is a form of pollution. If uncontrolled, it can cause annoyance and even physical harm to humans and other animals. Long exposure to noise above a certain level may eventually cause a loss in hearing. Under the *Federal Noise Control Act of 1972*, the EPA is required to identify major sources of noise, such as airports, and to set standards for the amount of noise that can be made by these sources. The Act provides for criminal penalties—fines or imprisonment—for violators of these standards.

Many states and cities have state- or city-specific pollution laws or regulations, including noise pollution provisions. These various state and city environmental protections complement rather than take the place of the federal laws. Visit www.nonoise.org to find out whether there are local noise control regulations where you live.

a. If you find a law, how does it control noise? If you don't find a local regulation, find a city in your state that has such a law. How does this law work?

b. Is there a noise control problem where you live? How would you get a regulation passed to deal with a local noise problem?

Environmental Regulation at Various Levels of Government

As noted earlier, the EPA was created in 1970 to help oversee and enforce the wave of new federal environmental laws and regulations being passed. The EPA works by itself, with other agencies, with industry and environmental groups, and with state, tribal, and local governments to conduct research, monitor environmental conditions, and enforce regulations.

State and tribal agencies also play a critical role in enforcing environmental regulations. While federal regulations establish minimum standards with which states must comply, states and tribes generally can, and often do, adopt environmental regulations that are stricter than federal standards. In many states there are multiple agencies that deal with environmental issues. These agencies are sometimes called the department of environmental protection, department of water resources, department of conservation, department of waste management, or department of natural resources.

Investigating the Law Where You Live

Research to find the names and primary roles of the agencies in your state responsible for environmental protection.

Since air, water, and other resources are not confined within state boundaries and their quality effects the entire country, the federal government and state governments share in making and enforcing environmental regulations, a concept known as **cooperative federalism.** Historically, this has meant that the federal government passes laws or issues regulations and states have the authority to make their own laws providing they are at least as strict.

a. What are the advantages of the federal government making environmental legislation and regulations? What are the disadvantages?

b. What are the advantages of state governments making environmental legislation and regulations? What are the disadvantages?

c. What are the advantages of cooperative federalism in making environmental legislation and regulations? What are the disadvantages?

cooperative federalism a concept of federalism in which federal, state, and local governments work together collectively to solve problems

DELIBERATION

Should the federal government ban hydraulic fracturing (or fracking)?

Heating your home. Cooking your favorite meal. Turning on the lights and the television. Some consumers in the United States use natural gas for all of these things. But what if the process of taking natural gas from the Earth harms the environment? Do the benefits of natural gas outweigh the problems associated with it?

When plants and animals die, their remains decay into the Earth. Heat and pressure over time lead to those materials changing into coal, oil, and natural gas deep below the Earth's surface. Natural gas collects between layers of rock or in tiny spaces of certain types of rock.

Geologists have learned to detect the places deep below Earth where natural gas is most likely to be found. Once a likely spot is located, a hydraulic fracturing company can use heavy machines to extract it. The companies drill straight down for one to two miles, creating a well. Then they encase their drilled hole in steel or cement to try to stop any leaks in the well. When the drill has reached the deep layer of rock where the natural gas exists, drills can then curve at a 90-degree angle and move horizontally, underground, for up to a mile. Once the drilling is complete, a fluid called slickwater—a mixture of water, chemicals, and sand—is pumped into the wells at high pressure. This fractures the rocks below and make it easier to extract natural gas. The natural gas filters up the well where it is collected to be processed and eventually used by consumers.

This process often involves dangerous materials and it is not foolproof. Slickwater contains chemicals and the water that flows back out of the wells can contain radioactive materials. Companies generally either store this flowback water on-site in pits, inject it into deep wells in the ground, or send it off-site to wastewater treatment facilities.

The federal government and state governments frequently consider regulations to the fracking industry. Since 2005, the federal government has placed few limits on hydraulic fracturing. Unlike other companies that inject substances into the ground, fracking companies do not need to obtain federal permits or report to the federal government the chemicals that they use in their operations.

State governments have varied in their regulations on fracking, from doing very little to passing outright bans. Colorado, for example, requires that well operators report the chemicals they use in drilling. Georgia allows local governments to adopt zoning rules that limit the location and timing of fracking.

Some advocates suggest that a uniform set of federal regulations would better help both the industry and the environment, while others believe that rules about fracking should be firmly in the hands of state governments. Some believe that the federal government should outright ban fracking.

What do you think? Should the federal government ban hydraulic fracturing? Are the rewards of fracking worth the possible risks?

Should the federal government ban hydraulic fracturing (or fracking)? Consider the options.

YES

The federal government should ban hydraulic fracturing.

Fracking can release pollutants into groundwater and the air. Some companies have paid families after contaminating their drinking water wells. In some instances, the company did not properly seal its drilling well and gas traveled into the drinking water. Other instances were the result of poor storage of flowback water.

There are environmental and economic costs in the fracking industry. In extreme cases, fracking can use up to 7 million gallons of water for one well. At least 30 percent of that water cannot be reused. The water often must be transported away from the drilling site, which means that trucks will use gas, producing pollution.

Fracking increases the likelihood of earthquakes. Scientists believe that some earthquakes are a result of waste water disposal that's been pumped deep underground. The pressure from that buildup can create earthquakes. While most of the tremors are mild to moderate, some have caused cracks in houses and bridges.

Critics say methane leaks from fracked wells and pipelines offset any benefits natural gas might have as a bridge fuel. Methane is a much more potent climate-altering gas than carbon dioxide.

NO

The federal government should not ban hydraulic fracturing.

Fracking has lowered natural gas prices by nearly 25 percent. This means that the average American household does not have to spend as much money heating their home or using electricity.

Natural gas is a "bridge" fuel between burning coal for energy and using renewable energy sources. While U.S. consumers still depend on coal as a major source of energy, reliance is decreasing. One reason is that coal causes a lot of pollution, which can harm people's health and contribute to climate change. Increased use of natural gas has reduced air pollution.

Although there are pollution risks with fracking and natural gas, it is usually much cleaner than coal. In fact, natural gas produces less than half as much carbon dioxide as coal. It is not possible right now to shift to 100 percent renewable energy sources, so we need a bridge fuel.

The fracking industry can support millions of new jobs and add billions of dollars to the economy. In 2013, the industry supported 1.7 million jobs in the United States, with estimates of reaching 3 million jobs by 2020. Additionally, it provided $62 billion in government tax revenues.

GUIDING QUESTIONS

1. What are the two most compelling reasons to support the deliberation question?
2. What are the two most compelling reasons to disagree with the deliberation question?
3. What is one area of this deliberation where the two sides might find common ground?

Climate Change

One of the most pressing challenges facing the world today is climate change, also known as global warming. If unchecked, this climate change could have catastrophic consequences worldwide. Indeed, coastal cities and Pacific island nations are already facing threats from warming-fueled sea level rise. In addition, studies are beginning to link natural disasters like severe storms, prolonged drought conditions, and devastating forest fires to climate change.

There is now scientific consensus that the climate is changing, and most people agree that a primary cause is human activity, particularly the reliance on fossil fuels and heavily meat-based diets in many parts of the world. Both fossil fuel use and large-scale animal farming emit significant quantities of greenhouse gases. Greenhouse gases trap heat energy in the upper atmosphere, warming the Earth's land, water, and air. In excess, these gases contribute to global warming.

PROBLEM 46.8

Assume for purposes of this problem that climate change poses a very real threat to human communities, and that a significant cause is human reliance on fossil fuels for transportation, heat, and electricity generation. What steps could be taken to deal with the associated carbon dioxide emissions? Be sure to consider that the problem is global. Who can regulate emissions on a global basis? How can such regulations be enforced?

FYI For Your Information

Global Issues

As of 2019, China was the world's largest source of carbon dioxide and other greenhouse gas emissions. The United States was second, though the U.S. per capita emissions rate—the annual emissions rate of each person in the United States—greatly exceeds that of China. Both countries increased their carbon emissions in 2018. The countries in the European Union, including those that are quite industrialized, have generally been more serious about and had more success in using new technologies to curb their emissions.

The Montreal Protocol is an international treaty that phases out production of substances that deplete the ozone layer. This protocol was agreed to in 1987. As of 2016 there had been nine revisions to the agreement. It has been ratified by all members of the United Nations. However, for various reasons, the United States has refused to ratify (or has withdrawn from) some international agreements designed to protect the environment.

APPENDIX

Contents

The Constitution
of the United States

The Constitution of the United States is a truly remarkable document. It was one of the first written constitutions in modern history. The entire text of the Constitution and its amendments follow. For easier study, those passages that have been set aside or changed by the adoption of amendments are printed in blue. Also included are explanatory notes that will help clarify the meaning of important ideas presented in the Constitution.

Preamble

We the People of the United States, in Order to form a more perfect Union, establish Justice, insure domestic Tranquility, provide for the common defence, promote the general Welfare, and secure the Blessings of Liberty to ourselves and our Posterity, do ordain and establish this **Constitution** for the United States of America.

Article I

Section 1

All legislative Powers herein granted shall be vested in a Congress of the United States, which shall consist of a Senate and House of Representatives.

Section 2

[1.] The House of Representatives shall be composed of Members chosen every second Year by the People of the several States, and the Electors in each State shall have the Qualifications requisite for Electors of the most numerous Branch of the State Legislature.

[2.] No person shall be a Representative who shall not have attained the Age of twenty five Years, and been seven Years a Citizen of the United States, and who shall not, when elected, be an Inhabitant of that State in which he shall be chosen.

[3.] Representatives and direct Taxes shall be apportioned among the several States which may be included within this Union, according to their respective Numbers, which shall be determined by adding to the whole Number of free Persons, including those bound to Service for a Term of Years, and excluding Indians not taxed, three fifths of all other Persons. The actual **Enumeration** shall be made within three Years after the first Meeting of the Congress of the United States, and within every subsequent Term of ten Years, in such Manner as they shall by Law direct. The Number of Representatives shall not exceed one for every thirty Thousand, but each State shall have at Least one Representative; and until such enumeration shall be made, the State of New Hampshire shall be entitled to chuse three; Massachusetts eight, Rhode-Island and Providence Plantations one, Connecticut five, New-York six, New Jersey four, Pennsylvania eight, Delaware one, Maryland six, Virginia ten, North Carolina five, South Carolina five, and Georgia three.

[4.] When vacancies happen in the Representation from any State, the Executive Authority thereof shall issue Writs of Election to fill such Vacancies.

[5.] The House of Representatives shall chuse their Speaker and other Officers; and shall have the sole Power of **Impeachment**.

The Preamble introduces the Constitution and sets forth the general purposes for which the government was established. The Preamble also declares that the power of the government comes from the people. The printed text of the document shows the spelling and punctuation of the parchment original.

Article I.
The Legislative Branch

The Constitution contains seven divisions called articles. Each article covers a general topic. For example, Articles I, II, and III create the three branches of the national government—the legislative, executive, and judicial branches. Most of the articles are divided into sections.

Section 1. Congress

Lawmaking The power to make law is given to a Congress made up of two chambers to represent different interests: the Senate to represent the states and the House to be more responsive to the people's will.

Section 2.
House of Representatives

Division of Representatives Among the States The number of representatives from each state is based on the size of the state's population. Each state is entitled to at least one representative. The Constitution states that each state may specify who can vote, but the Fifteenth, Nineteenth, Twenty-fourth, and Twenty-sixth Amendments have established guidelines that all states must follow regarding the right to vote. *What are the qualifications for members of the House of Representatives?*

Vocabulary

preamble: *introduction*

constitution: *a body of basic principles according to which a state is to be governed*

enumeration: *census or population count*

impeachment: *bringing charges against an official*

The Constitution of the United States **579**

Section 3. The Senate

Voting Procedure Originally, senators were chosen by the legislators of their own states. The Seventeenth Amendment changed this, so that senators are now elected by their state's people. There are 100 senators, 2 from each state.

Section 3. The Senate

Trial of Impeachments One of Congress's powers is the power to impeach—to accuse government officials of wrongdoing, put them on trial, and, if necessary, remove them from office. The House decides if the offense is impeachable. The Senate acts as a jury, and when the president is impeached, the Chief Justice of the United States serves as the judge. A two-thirds vote of the members present is needed to convict impeached officials. *What punishment can the Senate give if an impeached official is convicted?*

Vocabulary

president pro tempore: *presiding officer of the Senate who serves when the vice president is absent*

Section 3

[1.] The Senate of the United States shall be composed of two Senators from each State, chosen by the Legislature thereof, for six Years; and each Senator shall have one Vote.

[2.] Immediately after they shall be assembled in Consequence of the first Election, they shall be divided as equally as may be into three Classes. The Seats of the Senators of the first Class shall be vacated at the Expiration of the second Year, of the second Class at the Expiration of the fourth Year, and of the third Class at the Expiration of the sixth Year, so that one third may be chosen every second Year; and if Vacancies happen by Resignation, or otherwise, during the Recess of the Legislature of any State, the Executive thereof may make temporary Appointments until the next Meeting of the Legislature, which shall then fill such Vacancies.

[3.] No Person shall be a Senator who shall not have attained to the Age of thirty Years, and been nine Years a Citizen of the United States, and who shall not, when elected, be an Inhabitant of that State for which he shall be chosen.

[4.] The Vice President of the United States shall be President of the Senate, but shall have no Vote, unless they be equally divided.

[5.] The Senate shall chuse their other Officers, and also a **President pro tempore**, in the Absence of the Vice President, or when he shall exercise the Office of the President of the United States.

[6.] The Senate shall have the sole Power to try all Impeachments. When sitting for that Purpose, they shall be on Oath or Affirmation. When the President of the United States is tried, the Chief Justice shall preside: And no Person shall be convicted without the Concurrence of two thirds of the Members present.

[7.] Judgment in Cases of Impeachment shall not extend further than to removal from Office, and disqualification to hold and enjoy any Office of honor, Trust or Profit under the United States: but the Party convicted shall nevertheless be liable and subject to Indictment, Trial, Judgment and Punishment, according to Law.

Section 4

[1.] The Times, Places and Manner of holding Elections for Senators and Representatives, shall be prescribed in each State by the Legislature thereof; but the Congress may at any time by Law make or alter such Regulations, except as to the Places of chusing Senators.

[2.] The Congress shall assemble at least once in every Year, and such Meeting shall be on the first Monday in December, unless they shall by Law appoint a different Day.

Section 5

[1.] Each House shall be the Judge of the Elections, Returns and Qualifications of its own Members, and a Majority of each shall constitute a **Quorum** to do Business; but a smaller Number may **adjourn** from day to day, and may be authorized to compel the Attendance of absent Members, in such Manner, and under such Penalties as each House may provide.

[2.] Each House may determine the Rules of its Proceedings, punish its Members for disorderly Behaviour, and, with the **Concurrence** of two thirds, expel a Member.

[3.] Each House shall keep a Journal of its Proceedings, and from time to time publish the same, excepting such Parts as may in their Judgment require Secrecy; and the Yeas and Nays of the Members of either House on any question shall, at the Desire of one fifth of those Present, be entered on the Journal.

[4.] Neither House, during the Session of Congress, shall, without the Consent of the other, adjourn for more than three days, nor to any other Place than that in which the two Houses shall be sitting.

Section 6

[1.] The Senators and Representatives shall receive a Compensation for their Services, to be ascertained by Law, and paid out of the Treasury of the United States. They shall in all Cases, except Treason, Felony and Breach of the Peace, be privileged from Arrest during their Attendance at the Session of their respective Houses, and in going to and returning from the same; and for any Speech or Debate in either House, they shall not be questioned in any other Place.

[2.] No Senator or Representative shall, during the Time for which he was elected, be appointed to any civil Office under the Authority of the United States, which shall have been created, or the **Emoluments** whereof shall have been encreased during such time; and no Person holding any Office under the United States, shall be a Member of either House during his Continuance in Office.

Section 7

[1.] All Bills for raising **Revenue** shall originate in the House of Representatives; but the Senate may propose or concur with Amendments as on other **Bills**.

[2.] Every Bill which shall have passed the House of Representatives and the Senate, shall, before it become a Law, be presented to the President of the United States; If he approve he shall sign it, but if not he shall return it, with his Objections to that House in which it shall have originated, who shall enter the Objections at large on their Journal, and proceed to reconsider it. If after such Reconsideration two thirds of that House shall agree to pass the Bill, it shall be sent,

Vocabulary

quorum: *minimum number of members that must be present to conduct sessions*
adjourn: *to suspend a session*
concurrence: *agreement*
emoluments: *salaries*
revenue: *income raised by government*
bill: *draft of a proposed law*

Section 6. Privileges and Restrictions

Pay and Privileges To strengthen the federal government, the Founders set congressional salaries to be paid by the United States Treasury rather than by members' respective states. Originally, members were paid $6 per day. In 2011, all members of Congress received a base salary of $174,000.

Section 7. Passing Laws

Revenue Bill All tax laws must originate in the House of Representatives. This ensures that the branch of Congress that is elected by the people every two years has the major role in determining taxes.

together with the Objections, to the other House, by which it shall likewise be reconsidered, and if approved by two thirds of that House, it shall become a Law. But in all such Cases the Votes of both Houses shall be determined by yeas and Nays, and the Names of the Persons voting for and against the Bill shall be entered on the Journal of each House respectively. If any Bill shall not be returned by the President within ten Days (Sundays excepted) after it shall have been presented to him, the Same shall be a Law, in like Manner as if he had signed it, unless the Congress by their Adjournment prevent its Return, in which Case it shall not be a Law.

[3.] Every Order, **Resolution**, or Vote to which the Concurrence of the Senate and House of Representatives may be necessary (except on a question of Adjournment) shall be presented to the President of the United States; and before the Same shall take Effect, shall be approved by him, or being disapproved by him, shall be repassed by two thirds of the Senate and House of Representatives, according to the Rules and Limitations prescribed in the Case of a Bill.

Section 8

[1.] The Congress shall have the Power to lay and collect Taxes, Duties, Imposts and Excises, to pay the Debts and provide for the common Defence and general Welfare of the United States; but all Duties, Imposts and Excises shall be uniform throughout the United States;

[2.] To borrow Money on the credit of the United States;

[3.] To regulate Commerce with foreign Nations, and among the several States, and with the Indian Tribes;

[4.] To establish an uniform Rule of **Naturalization**, and uniform Laws on the subject of Bankruptcies throughout the United States;

[5.] To coin Money, regulate the Value thereof, and of foreign Coin, and fix the Standard of Weights and Measures;

[6.] To provide for the Punishment of counterfeiting the Securities and current Coin of the United States;

[7.] To establish Post Offices and post Roads;

[8.] To promote the Progress of Science and useful Arts, by securing for limited Times to Authors and Inventors the exclusive Right to their respective Writings and Discoveries;

[9.] To constitute Tribunals inferior to the supreme Court;

[10.] To define and punish Piracies and Felonies committed on the high Seas, and Offences against the Law of Nations;

[11.] To declare War, grant Letters of Marque and Reprisal, and make Rules concerning Captures on Land and Water;

[12.] To raise and support Armies, but no Appropriation of Money to that Use shall be for a longer Term than two Years;

[13.] To provide and maintain a Navy;

[14.] To make Rules for the Government and Regulation of the land and naval Forces;

Section 7. Passing Laws

How Bills Become Laws A bill may become a law only by passing both houses of Congress and being signed by the president. The president can check Congress by rejecting— vetoing—its legislation. *How can Congress override the president's veto?*

Section 8. Powers Granted to Congress

Powers of Congress Expressed powers are those powers directly stated in the Constitution. Most of the expressed powers of Congress are listed in Article I, Section 8. These powers are also called enumerated powers because they are numbered 1–18. *Which clause gives Congress the power to declare war?*

Vocabulary

resolution: *legislature's formal expression of opinion*

naturalization: *procedure by which a citizen of a foreign nation becomes a citizen of the United States*

[15.] To provide for calling forth the Militia to execute the Laws of the Union, suppress Insurrections and repel Invasions;

[16.] To provide for organizing, arming, and disciplining, the Militia, and for governing such Part of them as may be employed in the Service of the United States, reserving to the States respectively, the Appointment of the Officers, and the Authority of training the Militia according to the discipline prescribed by Congress;

[17.] To exercise exclusive Legislation in all Cases whatsoever, over such District (not exceeding ten Miles square) as may, by Cession of particular States, and the Acceptance of Congress, become the Seat of Government of the United States, and to exercise like Authority over all Places purchased by the Consent of the Legislature of the State in which the Same shall be, for the Erection of Forts, Magazines, Arsenals, dock-Yards, and other needful Buildings; And

[18.] To make all Laws which shall be necessary and proper for carrying into Execution the foregoing Powers, and all other Powers vested by this Constitution in the Government of the United States, or in any Department or Officer thereof.

Section 9

[1.] The Migration or Importation of such Persons as any of the States now existing shall think proper to admit, shall not be prohibited by the Congress prior to the Year one thousand eight hundred and eight, but a Tax or duty may be imposed on such Importation, not exceeding ten dollars for each Person.

[2.] The Privilege of the Writ of Habeas Corpus shall not be suspended, unless when in Cases of Rebellion or Invasion the public Safety may require it.

[3.] No Bill of Attainder or ex post facto Law shall be passed.

[4.] No Capitation, or other direct, Tax shall be laid, unless in Proportion to the Census or Enumeration herein before directed to be taken.

[5.] No Tax or Duty shall be laid on Articles exported from any State.

[6.] No Preference shall be given by any Regulation of Commerce or Revenue to the Ports of one State over those of another: nor shall Vessels bound to, or from, one State, be obliged to enter, clear, or pay Duties in another.

[7.] No Money shall be drawn from the Treasury, but in Consequence of Appropriations made by Law; and a regular Statement and Account of the Receipts and Expenditures of all public Money shall be published from time to time.

[8.] No Title of Nobility shall be granted by the United States: And no Person holding any Office of Profit or Trust under them, shall, without the Consent of the Congress, accept of any present, Emolument, Office, or Title, of any kind whatever, from any King, Prince, or foreign State.

Section 10.
Powers Denied to the States

Limitations on Powers Section 10 lists limits on the states. These restrictions were designed, in part, to prevent an overlapping in functions and authority with the federal government.

Article II.
The Executive Branch

Article II creates an executive branch to carry out laws passed by Congress. Article II lists the powers and duties of the president, describes qualifications for office and procedures for electing the president, and provides for a vice president.

Section 1.
President and Vice President

Former Method of Election In the election of 1800, the top two candidates received the same number of electoral votes, making it necessary for the House of Representatives to decide the election. To eliminate this problem, the Twelfth Amendment, added in 1804, changed the method of electing the president stated in Article II, Section 3. The Twelfth Amendment requires that the electors cast separate ballots for president and vice president.

Section 10

[1.] No State shall enter into any Treaty, Alliance, or Confederation; grant Letters of Marque and Reprisal; coin Money; emit Bills of Credit; make any Thing but gold and silver Coin a Tender in Payment of Debts; pass any Bill of Attainder, ex post facto Law, or Law impairing the Obligation of Contracts, or grant any Title of Nobility.

[2.] No State shall, without the Consent of the Congress, lay any Imposts or Duties on Imports or Exports, except what may be absolutely necessary for executing its inspection Laws: and the net Produce of all Duties and Imposts, laid by any State on Imports and Exports, shall be for the Use of the Treasury of the United States; and all such Laws shall be subject to the Revision and Controul of the Congress.

[3.] No State shall, without the Consent of Congress, lay any Duty of Tonnage, keep Troops, or Ships of War in time of Peace, enter into any Agreement or Compact with another State, or with a foreign Power, or engage in War, unless actually invaded, or in such imminent Danger as will not admit of delay.

Article II

Section 1

[1.] The executive Power shall be vested in a President of the United States of America. He shall hold his Office during the Term of four Years, and, together with the Vice President, chosen for the same Term, be elected, as follows.

[2.] Each State shall appoint, in such Manner as the Legislature thereof may direct, a Number of Electors, equal to the whole Number of Senators and Representatives to which the State may be entitled in the Congress: but no Senator or Representative, or Person holding an Office of Trust or Profit under the United States, shall be appointed an Elector.

[3.] The Electors shall meet in their respective States, and vote by Ballot for two Persons, of whom one at least shall not be an Inhabitant of the same State with themselves. And they shall make a List of all the Persons voted for, and of the Number of Votes for each; which List they shall sign and certify, and transmit sealed to the Seat of the Government of the United States, directed to the President of the Senate. The President of the Senate shall, in the Presence of the Senate and House of Representatives, open all the Certificates, and the Votes shall then be counted. The Person having the greatest Number of Votes shall be the President, if such Number be a Majority of the whole Number of Electors appointed; and if there be more than one who have such Majority, and have an equal Number of Votes, then the House of Representatives shall immediately chuse by Ballot one of them for President; and if no person have a Majority, then from the five highest on the List the said House shall in like Manner chuse the President. But in chusing the President, the Votes shall be taken by States, the Representation from each State having one Vote; A quorum for this Purpose shall consist of a Member or Members from two thirds of the States, and a Majority of all the States shall be necessary to a Choice. In every Case, after the Choice of the President, the Person having the greatest Number of Votes of the Electors shall be the Vice President. But if there should remain two or more who have equal Votes, the Senate shall chuse from them by Ballot the Vice President.

[4.] The Congress may determine the Time of chusing the Electors, and the Day on which they shall give their Votes; which Day shall be the same throughout the United States.

[5.] No Person except a natural born Citizen, or a Citizen of the United States, at the time of the Adoption of this Constitution, shall be eligible to the Office of President; neither shall any Person be eligible to that Office who shall not have attained to the Age of thirty five Years, and been fourteen Years a Resident within the United States.

[6.] In Case of the Removal of the President from Office, or of his Death, Resignation, or Inability to discharge the Powers and Duties of the said Office, the Same shall devolve on the Vice President, and the Congress may by Law provide for the Case of Removal, Death, Resignation or Inability, both of the President and Vice President, declaring what Officer shall then act as President, and such Officer shall act accordingly, until the Disability be removed, or a President shall be elected.

[7.] The President shall, at stated Times, receive for his Services, a Compensation, which shall neither be encreased nor diminished during the Period for which he shall have been elected, and he shall not receive within that Period any other Emolument from the United States, or any of them.

[8.] Before he enter on the Execution of his Office, he shall take the following Oath or Affirmation:—"I do solemnly swear (or affirm) that I will faithfully execute the Office of President of the United States, and will to the best of my Ability, preserve, protect and defend the Constitution of the United States."

Section 2

[1.] The President shall be Commander in Chief of the Army and Navy of the United States, and of the Militia of the several States, when called into the actual Service of the United States; he may require the Opinion, in writing, of the principal Officer in each of the executive Departments, upon any Subject relating to the Duties of their respective Offices, and he shall have Power to grant Reprieves and Pardons for Offences against the United States, except in Cases of Impeachment.

Section 1.
President and Vice President

Qualifications The president must be a citizen of the United States by birth, at least 35 years of age, and a resident of the United States for 14 years.

Section 1.
President and Vice President

Vacancies If the president dies, resigns, is removed from office by impeachment, or is unable to carry out the duties of the office, the vice president becomes president. (see Amendment XXV)

Section 1.
President and Vice President

Salary Originally, the president's salary was $25,000 per year. The president's current salary is $400,000 plus a $50,000 nontaxable expense account per year. The president also receives living accommodations in two residences—the White House and Camp David.

Section 2.
Powers of the President

Cabinet Mention of "the principal officer in each of the executive departments" is the only suggestion of the president's cabinet to be found in the Constitution. The cabinet is an advisory body, and its power depends on the president. Section 2, Clause 1 also makes the president the head of the armed forces. This established the principle of civilian control of the military.

Section 2.
Powers of the President

Treaties The president is responsible for the conduct of relations with foreign countries. *What role does the Senate have in approving treaties?*

Section 3.
Powers of the President

Executive Orders An important presidential power is the ability to issue executive orders. An executive order is a rule or command the president issues that has the force of law. Only Congress can make laws under the Constitution, but executive orders are considered part of the president's duty to "take care that the laws be faithfully executed." This power is often used during emergencies. Over time, the scope of executive orders has expanded. Decisions by federal agencies and departments are also considered to be executive orders.

Section 4. Impeachment

Reasons for Removal From Office This section states the reasons for which the president and vice president may be impeached and removed from office. Only Andrew Johnson and Bill Clinton have been impeached by the House. Richard Nixon resigned before the House could vote on possible impeachment.

Article III.
The Judicial Branch

The term *judicial* refers to courts. The Constitution set up only the Supreme Court but provided for the establishment of other federal courts. The judiciary of the United States has two different systems of courts. One system consists of the federal courts, whose powers derive from the Constitution and federal laws. The other includes the courts of each of the 50 states, whose powers derive from state constitutions and laws.

[2.] He shall have Power, by and with the Advice and Consent of the Senate, to make Treaties, provided two thirds of the Senators present concur; and he shall nominate, and by and with the Advice and Consent of the Senate, shall appoint Ambassadors, other public Ministers and Consuls, Judges of the supreme Court, and all other Officers of the United States, whose Appointments are not herein otherwise provided for, and which shall be established by Law: but the Congress may by Law vest the Appointment of such inferior Officers, as they think proper, in the President alone, in the Courts of Law, or in the Heads of Departments.

[3.] The President shall have Power to fill up all Vacancies that may happen during the Recess of the Senate, by granting Commissions which shall expire at the End of their next Session.

Section 3

He shall from time to time give to the Congress Information of the State of the Union, and recommend to their Consideration such Measures as he shall judge necessary and expedient; he may, on extraordinary Occasions, convene both Houses, or either of them, and in Case of Disagreement between them, with Respect to the Time of Adjournment, he may adjourn them to such Time as he shall think proper; he shall receive Ambassadors and other public Ministers; he shall take Care that the Laws be faithfully executed, and shall Commission all the Officers of the United States.

Section 4

The President, Vice President and all civil Officers of the United States, shall be removed from Office on Impeachment for, and Conviction of, Treason, Bribery, or other high Crimes and Misdemeanors.

Article III

Section 1

The judicial Power of the United States, shall be vested in one supreme Court, and in such inferior Courts as the Congress may from time to time ordain and establish. The Judges, both of the supreme and inferior Courts, shall hold their Offices during good Behaviour, and shall, at stated Times, receive for their Services, a Compensation, which shall not be diminished during their Continuance in Office.

Section 2

[1.] The judicial Power shall extend to all Cases, in Law and Equity, arising under this Constitution, the Laws of the United States, and Treaties made, or which shall be made, under their Authority;—to all Cases affecting Ambassadors, other public Ministers and Consuls;—to all Cases of admiralty and maritime Jurisdiction;—to Controversies to which the United States shall be a Party;—to Controversies between two or more States;—between a State and Citizens of another State;—between Citizens of different States,—between Citizens of the same State claiming Lands under Grants of different States, and between a State, or the Citizens thereof, and foreign States, Citizens or Subjects.

[2.] In all Cases affecting Ambassadors, other public Ministers and Consuls, and those in which a State shall be Party, the supreme Court shall have **original Jurisdiction**. In all the other Cases before mentioned, the supreme Court shall have **appellate Jurisdiction**, both as to Law and Fact, with such Exceptions, and under such Regulations as the Congress shall make.

[3.] The Trial of all Crimes, except in Cases of Impeachment, shall be by Jury; and such Trial shall be held in the State where the said Crimes shall have been committed; but when not committed within any State, the Trial shall be at such Place or Places as the Congress may by Law have directed.

Section 3

[1.] Treason against the United States, shall consist only in levying War against them, or in adhering to their Enemies, giving them Aid and Comfort. No Person shall be convicted of Treason unless on the Testimony of two Witnesses to the same overt Act, or on Confession in open Court.

[2.] The Congress shall have Power to declare the Punishment of Treason, but no Attainder of Treason shall work Corruption of Blood, or Forfeiture except during the Life of the Person attainted.

Article IV

Section 1

Full Faith and Credit shall be given in each State to the public Acts, Records, and judicial Proceedings of every other State. And the Congress may by general Laws prescribe the Manner in which such Acts, Records and Proceedings shall be proved, and the Effect thereof.

Section 2

[1.] The Citizens of each State shall be entitled to all Privileges and Immunities of Citizens in the several States.

[2.] A Person charged in any State with **Treason**, Felony, or other Crime, who shall flee from Justice, and be found in another State, shall on Demand of the executive Authority of the State from which he fled, be delivered up, to be removed to the State having Jurisdiction of the Crime.

[3.] No Person held to Service of Labour in one State, under the Laws thereof, escaping into another, shall, in Consequence of any Law or Regulation therein, be discharged from such Service or Labour, but shall be delivered up on Claim of the Party to whom such Service or Labour may be due.

Section 2. Jurisdiction

General Jurisdiction Federal courts deal mostly with laws passed by Congress, treaties, and cases involving the Constitution itself.

Section 2. Jurisdiction

The Supreme Court A court with "original jurisdiction" has the authority to be the first court to hear a case. The Supreme Court generally has "appellate jurisdiction" in that it mostly hears cases appealed from lower courts.

Section 2. Jurisdiction

Jury Trial Except in cases of impeachment, anyone accused of a crime has the right to a trial by jury. The trial must be held in the state where the crime was committed. Jury trial guarantees were strengthened in the Sixth, Seventh, Eighth, and Ninth Amendments.

Vocabulary

original jurisdiction: *authority to be the first court to hear a case*

appellate jurisdiction: *authority to hear cases appealed from lower courts*

treason: *violation of the allegiance owed by a person to his or her own country, for example, by aiding an enemy*

Article IV. Relations Among the States

Article IV explains the relationship of the states to one another and to the national government. This article requires each state to give citizens of other states the same rights as its own citizens, addresses the admission of new states, and guarantees that the national government will protect the states.

Section 1. Official Acts

Recognition by States This provision ensures that each state recognizes the laws, court decisions, and records of all other states. For example, a marriage license issued by one state must be accepted by all states.

New States Congress has the power to admit new states. It also determines the basic guidelines for applying for statehood. Two states, Maine and West Virginia, were created within the boundaries of another state. In the case of West Virginia, President Lincoln recognized the West Virginia government as the legal government of Virginia during the Civil War. This allowed West Virginia to secede from Virginia without obtaining approval from the Virginia legislature.

Article V. The Amendment Process

Article V explains how the Constitution can be amended, or changed. All of the 27 amendments were proposed by a two-thirds vote of both houses of Congress. Only the Twenty-first Amendment was ratified by constitutional conventions of the states. All other amendments have been ratified by state legislatures. *What is an amendment?*

Vocabulary

amendment: *a change to the Constitution*

ratification: *process by which an amendment is approved*

Article VI. Constitutional Supremacy

Article VI contains the "supremacy clause." This clause establishes that the Constitution, laws passed by Congress, and treaties of the United States "shall be the supreme Law of the Land." The "supremacy clause" recognizes the Constitution and federal laws as supreme when in conflict with those of the states.

Section 3

[1.] New States may be admitted by the Congress into this Union; but no new State shall be formed or erected within the Jurisdiction of any other State; nor any State be formed by the Junction of two or more States, or Parts of States, without the Consent of the Legislatures of the States concerned as well as of the Congress.

[2.] The Congress shall have Power to dispose of and make all needful Rules and Regulations respecting the Territory or other Property belonging to the United States; and nothing in this Constitution shall be so construed as to Prejudice any Claims of the United States, or of any particular State.

Section 4

The United States shall guarantee to every State in this Union a Republican Form of Government, and shall protect each of them against Invasion; and on Application of the Legislature, or of the Executive (when the Legislature cannot be convened) against domestic Violence.

Article V

The Congress, whenever two thirds of both Houses shall deem it necessary, shall propose **Amendments** to this Constitution, or, on the Application of the Legislatures of two thirds of the several States, shall call a Convention for proposing Amendments, which, in either Case, shall be valid to all Intents and Purposes, as Part of this Constitution, when ratified by the Legislatures of three fourths of the several States, or by Conventions in three fourths thereof, as the one or the other Mode of **Ratification** may be proposed by the Congress; Provided that no Amendment which may be made prior to the Year One thousand eight hundred and eight shall in any Manner affect the first and fourth Clauses in the Ninth Section of the first Article; and that no State, without its Consent, shall be deprived of its equal Suffrage in the Senate.

Article VI

[1.] All Debts contracted and Engagements entered into, before the Adoption of this Constitution, shall be as valid against the United States under this Constitution, as under the Confederation.

[2.] This Constitution, and the Laws of the United States which shall be made in Pursuance thereof; and all Treaties made, or which shall be made, under the Authority of the United States, shall be the supreme Law of the Land; and the Judges in every State shall be bound thereby, any Thing in the Constitution or Laws of any State to the Contrary notwithstanding.

[3.] The Senators and Representatives before mentioned, and the Members of the several State Legislatures, and all executive and judicial Officers, both of the United States and of the several States, shall be bound by Oath or Affirmation, to support this Constitution; but no religious Test shall ever be required as a Qualification to any Office or public Trust under the United States.

Article VII

The Ratification of the Conventions of nine States, shall be sufficient for the Establishment of this Constitution between the States so ratifying the Same.

Done in Convention by the Unanimous Consent of the States present the Seventeenth Day of September in the Year of our Lord one thousand seven hundred and Eighty seven and of the Independence of the United States of America the Twelfth. In witness whereof We have hereunto subscribed our Names,

Article VII. Ratification

Article VII addresses ratification and states that, unlike the Articles of Confederation, which required approval of all thirteen states for adoption, the Constitution would take effect after it was ratified by nine states.

Signers

George Washington,
President and Deputy from Virginia

New Hampshire
John Langdon
Nicholas Gilman

Massachusetts
Nathaniel Gorham
Rufus King

Connecticut
William Samuel Johnson
Roger Sherman

New York
Alexander Hamilton

New Jersey
William Livingston
David Brearley
William Paterson
Jonathan Dayton

Pennsylvania
Benjamin Franklin
Thomas Mifflin
Robert Morris
George Clymer
Thomas FitzSimons
Jared Ingersoll
James Wilson
Gouverneur Morris

Delaware
George Read
Gunning Bedford, Jr.
John Dickinson
Richard Bassett
Jacob Broom

Maryland
James McHenry
Daniel of St. Thomas Jenifer
Daniel Carroll

Virginia
John Blair
James Madison, Jr.

North Carolina
William Blount
Richard Dobbs Spaight
Hugh Williamson

South Carolina
John Rutledge
Charles Cotesworth Pinckney
Charles Pinckney
Pierce Butler

Georgia
William Few
Abraham Baldwin

Attest: William Jackson, Secretary

Amendment I

Congress shall make no law respecting an establishment of religion, or prohibiting the free exercise thereof; or abridging the freedom of speech, or of the press; or the right of the people peaceably to assemble, and to petition the Government for a redress of grievances.

Amendment II

A well regulated Militia, being necessary to the security of a free State, the right of the people to keep and bear Arms, shall not be infringed.

The Amendments

This part of the Constitution consists of changes and additions. The Constitution has been amended 27 times throughout the nation's history.

The Bill of Rights

The first 10 amendments are known as the Bill of Rights (1791). These amendments limit the powers of the federal government. The First Amendment protects the civil liberties of individuals in the United States. The amendment freedoms are not absolute, however. They are limited by the rights of other individuals. *What freedoms does the First Amendment protect?*

Vocabulary

quarter: *to provide living accommodations*

warrant: *document that gives police particular rights or powers*

common law: *law established by previous court decisions*

Amendment 5

Rights of the Accused This amendment contains protections for people accused of crimes. One of the protections is that government may not deprive any person of life, liberty, or property without due process of law. This means that the government must follow proper constitutional procedures in trials and in other actions it takes against individuals. *According to Amendment V, what is the function of a grand jury?*

Amendment 6

Right to Speedy and Fair Trial A basic protection is the right to a speedy, public trial. The jury must hear witnesses and evidence on both sides before deciding the guilt or innocence of a person charged with a crime. This amendment also provides that legal counsel must be provided to a defendant. In 1963, in *Gideon* v. *Wainwright*, the Supreme Court ruled that if a defendant cannot afford a lawyer, the government must provide one to defend him or her. *Why is the right to a "speedy" trial important?*

Amendment 9

Powers Reserved to the People This amendment prevents government from claiming that the only rights people have are those listed in the Bill of Rights.

Amendment III

No Soldier shall, in time of peace be **quartered** in any house, without the consent of the Owner, nor in time of war, but in a manner to be prescribed by law.

Amendment IV

The right of the people to be secure in their persons, houses, papers, and effects, against unreasonable searches and seizures, shall not be violated, and no **Warrants** shall issue, but upon probable cause, supported by Oath or affirmation, and particularly describing the place, to be searched, and the persons or things to be seized.

Amendment V

No person shall be held to answer for a capital, or otherwise infamous crime, unless on a presentment or indictment of a Grand Jury, except in cases arising in the land or naval forces, or in the Militia, when in actual service in time of War or public danger; nor shall any person be subject for the same offence to be twice put in jeopardy of life or limb; nor shall be compelled in any criminal case to be a witness against himself, nor be deprived of life, liberty, or property, without due process of law; nor shall private property be taken for public use without just compensation.

Amendment VI

In all criminal prosecutions, the accused shall enjoy the right to a speedy and public trial, by an impartial jury of the State and district wherein the crime shall have been committed, which district shall have been previously ascertained by law, and to be informed of the nature and cause of the accusation; to be confronted with the witnesses against him; to have compulsory process for obtaining Witnesses in his favor, and to have the assistance of counsel for his defence.

Amendment VII

In Suits at common law, where the value in controversy shall exceed twenty dollars, the right of trial by jury shall be preserved, and no fact tried by a jury, shall be otherwise reexamined in any Court of the United States, than according to the rules of **common law**.

Amendment VIII

Excessive **bail** shall not be required, nor excessive fines imposed, nor cruel and unusual punishments inflicted.

Amendment IX

The enumeration in the Constitution, of certain rights, shall not be construed to deny or disparage others retained by the people.

Amendment X

The powers not delegated to the United States by the Constitution, nor prohibited by it to the States, are reserved to the States respectively, or to the people.

Amendment XI

The Judicial power of the United States shall not be construed to extend to any suit in law or equity, commenced or prosecuted against one of the United States by Citizens of another State, or by Citizens or Subjects of any Foreign State.

Amendment XII

The electors shall meet in their respective states and vote by ballot for President and Vice-President, one of whom, at least, shall not be an inhabitant of the same state with themselves; they shall name in their ballots the person voted for as President, and in distinct ballots the person voted for as Vice-President, and they shall make distinct lists of all persons voted for as President, and of all persons voted for as Vice-President, and of the number of votes for each, which lists they shall sign and certify, and transmit sealed to the seat of the government of the United States, directed to the President of the Senate;—The President of the Senate shall, in the presence of the Senate and House of Representatives, open all the certificates and the votes shall then be counted;—The person having the greatest number of votes for President, shall be the President, if such number be a **majority** of the whole number of Electors appointed; and if no person have such majority, then from the persons having the highest numbers not exceeding three on the list of those voted for as President, the House of Representatives shall choose immediately, by ballot, the President. But in choosing the President, the votes shall be taken by states, the representation from each state having one vote; a quorum for this purpose shall consist of a member or members from two-thirds of the states, and a majority of all the states shall be necessary to a choice. And if the House of Representatives shall not choose a President whenever the right of choice shall devolve upon them, before the fourth day of March next following, then the Vice-President shall act as President, as in the case of the death or other constitutional disability of the President. The person having the greatest number of votes as Vice-President, shall be the Vice-President, if such number be a majority of the whole number of Electors appointed, and if no person have a majority, then from the two highest numbers on the list, the Senate shall choose the Vice-President; a quorum for the purpose shall consist of two-thirds of the whole number of Senators, and a majority of the whole number shall be necessary to a choice. But no person constitutionally ineligible to the office of President shall be eligible to that of Vice-President of the United States.

Amendment 10

Powers Reserved to the States
This amendment protects the states and the people from the federal government. It establishes that powers not given to the national government and not denied to the states by the Constitution belong to the states or to the people. These are checks on the "necessary and proper" power of the federal government, which is provided for in Article I, Section 8, Clause 18.

Amendment 11

Suits Against the States The Eleventh Amendment (1795) provides that a lawsuit brought by a citizen of the United States or a foreign nation against a state must be tried in a state court, not in a federal court. The Supreme Court had ruled in *Chisholm* v. *Georgia* (1793) that a federal court could try a lawsuit brought by citizens of South Carolina against a citizen of Georgia.

Vocabulary

bail: *money that an accused person provides to the court as a guarantee that he or she will be present for a trial*
majority: *more than half*

Amendment 12

Election of President and Vice President The Twelfth Amendment (1804) corrects a problem that had arisen in the method of electing the president and vice president, which is described in Article II, Section 1, Clause 3. This amendment provides for the Electoral College to use separate ballots in voting for president and vice president. *If no candidate receives a majority of the electoral votes, who elects the president?*

Amendment XIII

Section 1

Neither slavery nor involuntary servitude, except as a punishment for crime whereof the party shall have been duly convicted, shall exist within the United States, or any place subject to their jurisdiction.

Section 2

Congress shall have power to enforce this article by appropriate legislation.

Amendment XIV

Section 1

All persons born or naturalized in the United States, and subject to the jurisdiction thereof, are citizens of the United States and of the State wherein they reside. No State shall make or enforce any law which shall **abridge** the privileges or immunities of citizens of the United States; nor shall any State deprive any person of life, liberty, or property, without due process of law; nor deny to any person within its jurisdiction the equal protection of the laws.

Section 2

Representatives shall be apportioned among the several States according to their respective numbers, counting the whole number of persons in each State, excluding Indians not taxed. But when the right to vote at any election for the choice of electors for President and Vice President of the United States, Representatives in Congress, the Executive and Judicial officers of a State, or the members of the Legislature thereof, is denied to any of the male inhabitants of such State, being twenty-one years of age, and citizens of the United States, or in any way abridged, except for participation in rebellion, or other crime, the basis of representation therein shall be reduced in the proportion which the number of such male citizens shall bear to the whole number of male citizens twenty-one years of age in such State.

Section 3

No person shall be a Senator or Representative in Congress, or elector of President and Vice President, or hold any office, civil or military, under the United States, or under any State, who, having previously taken an oath, as a member of Congress, or as an officer of the United States, or as a member of any State legislature, or as an executive or judicial officer of any State, to support the Constitution of the United States, shall have engaged in insurrection or rebellion against the same, or given aid or comfort to the enemies thereof. But Congress may by a vote of two-thirds of each House, remove such disability.

Section 4

The validity of the public debt of the United States, authorized by law, including debts incurred for payment of pensions and bounties for service in suppressing **insurrection** or rebellion, shall not be questioned. But neither the United States nor any State shall assume or pay any debt or obligation incurred in aid of insurrection or rebellion against the United States, or any claim for the loss or emancipation of any slave; but all such debts, obligations and claims shall be held illegal and void.

Section 5

The Congress shall have power to enforce, by appropriate legislation, the provisions of this article.

Amendment XV

Section 1

The right of citizens of the United States to vote shall not be denied or abridged by the United States or by any State on account of race, color, or previous condition of servitude.

Section 2

The Congress shall have power to enforce this article by appropriate legislation.

Amendment XVI

The Congress shall have power to lay and collect taxes on incomes, from whatever source derived, without **apportionment** among the several States and without regard to any census or enumeration.

Amendment XVII

Section 1

The Senate of the United States shall be composed of two Senators from each State, elected by the people thereof, for six years; and each Senator shall have one vote. The electors in each State shall have the qualifications requisite for electors of the most numerous branch of the State legislatures.

Section 2

When **vacancies** happen in the representation of any State in the Senate, the executive authority of such State shall issue writs of election to fill such vacancies: *Provided,* That the legislature of any State may empower the executive thereof to make temporary appointments until the people fill the vacancies by election as the legislature may direct.

Section 3

This amendment shall not be so construed as to affect the election or term of any Senator chosen before it becomes valid as part of the Constitution.

Amendment XVIII

Section 1

After one year from ratification of this article, the manufacture, sale, or transportation of intoxicating liquors within, the importation thereof into, or the exportation thereof from the

Amendment 14. Section 4

Public Debt The public debt acquired by the federal government during the Civil War was valid and could not be questioned by the South. However, the debts of the Confederacy were declared to be illegal. *Could former slaveholders collect payment for the loss of their slaves?*

Amendment 15

Voting Rights The Fifteenth Amendment (1870) prohibits the government from denying a person's right to vote on the basis of race. Despite the law, many states denied African Americans the right to vote by such means as poll taxes, literacy tests, and white primaries.

Amendment 16

Income Tax The origins of the Sixteenth Amendment (1913) date back to 1895, when the Supreme Court declared a federal income tax unconstitutional. To overturn this decision, this amendment authorizes an income tax that is levied on a direct basis.

Amendment 17

Direct Election of Senators The Seventeenth Amendment (1913) states that the people, instead of state legislatures, elect United States senators. *How many years are in a Senate term?*

Vocabulary

insurrection: *rebellion against the government*

apportionment: *distribution of seats in House based on population*

vacancy: *an office or position that is unfilled or unoccupied*

Amendment 18

Prohibition The Eighteenth Amendment (1919) prohibited the production, sale, or transportation of alcoholic beverages in the United States. Prohibition proved to be difficult to enforce. This amendment was later repealed by the Twenty-first Amendment.

Amendment 19

Woman Suffrage The Nineteenth Amendment (1920) guaranteed women the right to vote. By then women had already won the right to vote in many state elections, but the amendment made their right to vote in all state and national elections constitutional.

Amendment 20

"Lame-Duck" The Twentieth Amendment (1933) sets new dates for Congress to begin its term and for the inauguration of the president and vice president. Under the original Constitution, elected officials who retired or who had been defeated remained in office for several months. For the outgoing president, this period ran from November until March. Such outgoing officials, referred to as "lame ducks," could accomplish little. *What date was chosen as Inauguration Day?*

Amendment 20. Section 3

Succession of President and Vice President This section provides that if the president elect dies before taking office, the vice president elect becomes president.

Vocabulary

president elect: *individual who is elected president but has not yet begun serving his or her term*

United States and all territory subject to the jurisdiction thereof for beverage purposes is hereby prohibited.

Section 2

The Congress and the several States shall have concurrent power to enforce this article by appropriate legislation.

Section 3

This article shall be inoperative unless it shall have been ratified as an amendment to the Constitution by the legislatures of the several States, as provided in the Constitution, within seven years from the date of the submission hereof to the States by the Congress.

Amendment XIX

Section 1

The right of citizens of the United States to vote shall not be denied or abridged by the United States or by any State on account of sex.

Section 2

Congress shall have power by appropriate legislation to enforce the provisions of this article.

Amendment XX

Section 1

The terms of the President and Vice President shall end at noon on the 20th day of January, and the terms of the Senators and Representatives at noon on the 3d day of January, of the years in which such terms would have ended if this article had not been ratified; and the terms of their successors shall then begin.

Section 2

The Congress shall assemble at least once in every year, and such meeting shall begin at noon on the 3rd day of January, unless they shall by law appoint a different day.

Section 3

If, at the time fixed for the beginning of the term of the President, the **President elect** shall have died, the Vice President elect shall become President. If a President shall not have been chosen before the time fixed for the beginning of his term, or if the President elect shall have failed to qualify, then the Vice President elect shall act as President until a President shall have qualified; and the Congress may by law provide for the case wherein neither a President elect nor a Vice President elect shall have qualified, declaring who shall then act as President, or the manner in which one who is to act shall be selected, and such person shall act accordingly until a President or Vice President shall have qualified.

Section 4

The Congress may by law provide for the case of the death of any of the persons from whom the House of Representatives may choose a President whenever the right of choice shall have devolved upon them, and for the case of the death of any of the persons from whom the Senate may choose a Vice President whenever the right of choice shall have devolved upon them.

Section 5

Section 1 and 2 shall take effect on the 15th day of October following the ratification of this article.

Section 6

This article shall be inoperative unless it shall have been ratified as an amendment to the Constitution by the legislatures of three-fourths of the several States within seven years from the date of its submission.

Amendment XXI

Section 1

The eighteenth article of amendment to the Constitution of the United States is hereby repealed.

Section 2

The transportation or importation into any State, Territory, or possession of the United States for delivery or use therein of intoxicating liquors, in violation of the laws thereof, is hereby prohibited.

Section 3

This article shall be inoperative unless it shall have been ratified as an amendment to the Constitution by conventions in the several States, as provided in the Constitution, within seven years from the date of the submission hereof to the States by the Congress.

Amendment XXII

Section 1

No person shall be elected to the office of the President more than twice, and no person who had held the office of President, or acted as President, for more than two years of a term to which some other person was elected President shall be elected to the office of the President more than once. But this Article shall not apply to any person holding the office of President when this Article was proposed by the Congress, and shall not prevent any person who may be holding the office of President, or acting as President, during the term within which this Article becomes operative from holding the office of President or acting as President during the remainder of such term.

Section 2

This article shall be inoperative unless it shall have been ratified as an amendment to the Constitution by the

Amendment 21

Repeal of Prohibition The Twenty-first Amendment (1933) repeals the Eighteenth Amendment. It is the only amendment ever passed to overturn an earlier amendment. It is also the only amendment ratified by special state conventions instead of state legislatures.

Amendment 22

Presidential Term Limit The Twenty-second Amendment (1951) limits presidents to a maximum of two elected terms. The amendment wrote into the Constitution a custom started by George Washington. It was passed largely as a reaction to Franklin D. Roosevelt's election to four terms between 1933 and 1945. It also provides that anyone who succeeds to the presidency and serves for more than two years of the term may not be elected more than one more time.

legislatures of three-fourths of the several States within seven years from the date of its submission to the States by the Congress.

Amendment XXIII

Section 1

The District constituting the seat of Government of the United States shall appoint in such manner as the Congress may direct:

A number of electors of President and Vice President equal to the whole number of Senators and Representatives in Congress to which the District would be entitled if it were a State, but in no event more than the least populous State; they shall be in addition to those appointed by the States, but they shall be considered, for the purposes of the election of President and Vice President, to be electors appointed by a State; and they shall meet in the District and perform such duties as provided by the twelfth article of amendment.

Section 2

The Congress shall have power to enforce this article by appropriate legislation.

Amendment XXIV

Section 1

The right of citizens of the United States to vote in any primary or other election for President or Vice President, for electors for President or Vice President, or for Senator or Representative in Congress, shall not be denied or abridged by the United States or any State by reason of failure to pay any poll tax or other tax.

Section 2

The Congress shall have power to enforce this article by appropriate legislation.

Amendment XXV

Section 1

In case of the removal of the President from office or his death or resignation, the Vice President shall become President.

Section 2

Whenever there is a vacancy in the office of the Vice President, the President shall nominate a Vice President who shall take the office upon confirmation by a majority vote of both Houses of Congress.

Section 3

Whenever the President transmits to the President pro tempore of the Senate and the Speaker of the House of Representatives his written declaration that he is unable to discharge the powers and duties of his office, and until he

Amendment 23

D.C. Electors The Twenty-third Amendment (1961) allows citizens living in Washington, D.C., to vote for president and vice president, a right previously denied residents of the nation's capital. The District of Columbia now has three presidential electors, the number to which it would be entitled if it were a state.

Amendment 24

Abolition of the Poll Tax
The Twenty-fourth Amendment (1964) prohibits poll taxes in federal elections. Prior to the passage of this amendment, some states had used such taxes to keep low-income African Americans from voting. In 1966 the Supreme Court banned poll taxes in state elections as well.

transmits to them a written declaration to the contrary, such powers and duties shall be discharged by the Vice President as Acting President.

Section 4

Whenever the Vice President and a majority of either the principal officers of the executive departments or of such other body as Congress may by law provide, transmit to the President pro tempore of the Senate and the Speaker of the House of Representatives their written declaration that the President is unable to discharge the powers and duties of his office, the Vice President shall immediately assume the power and duties of the office of Acting President.

Thereafter, when the President transmits to the President pro tempore of the Senate and the Speaker of the House of Representatives his written declaration that no inability exists, he shall resume the powers and duties of his office unless the Vice President and a majority of either the principal officers of the executive department or of such other body as Congress may by law provide, transmit within four days to the President pro tempore of the Senate and the Speaker of the House of Representatives their written declaration that the President is unable to discharge the powers and duties of his office. Thereupon Congress shall decide the issue, assembling within forty-eight hours for that purpose if not in session. If the Congress, within twenty-one days after receipt of the latter written declaration, or, if Congress is not in session, within twenty-one days after Congress is required to assemble, determines by two-thirds vote of both Houses that the President is unable to discharge the powers and duties of his office, the Vice President shall continue to discharge the same as Acting President; otherwise, the President shall resume the power and duties of his office.

Amendment XXVI

Section 1

The right of citizens of the United States, who are eighteen years of age or older, to vote shall not be denied or abridged by the United States or by any State on account of age.

Section 2

The Congress shall have power to enforce this article by appropriate legislation.

Amendment XXVII

No law, varying the compensation for the services of Senators and Representatives, shall take effect, until an election of representatives shall have intervened.

Amendment 25

Presidential Disability and Succession The Twenty-fifth Amendment (1967) established a process for the vice president to take over leadership of the nation when a president is disabled. It also set procedures for filling a vacancy in the office of vice president.

This amendment was used in 1973, when Vice President Spiro Agnew resigned from office after being charged with accepting bribes. President Richard Nixon then appointed Gerald R. Ford as vice president in accordance with the provisions of the Twenty-fifth Amendment. A year later, President Nixon resigned during the Watergate scandal, and Ford became president. President Ford then had to fill the vice presidency, which he had left vacant upon assuming the presidency. He named Nelson A. Rockefeller as vice president. Thus, individuals who had not been elected held both the presidency and the vice presidency. *Whom does the president inform if he or she cannot carry out the duties of the office?*

Amendment 26

Voting Age of 18 The Twenty-sixth Amendment (1971) lowered the voting age in both federal and state elections to 18.

Amendment 27

Congressional Salary Restraints The Twenty-seventh Amendment (1992) makes congressional pay raises effective during the term following their passage. James Madison offered the amendment in 1789, but it was never adopted. In 1982 Gregory Watson, then a student at the University of Texas, discovered the forgotten amendment while doing research for a school paper. Watson made the amendment's passage his crusade.

The Universal Declaration of Human Rights

The Universal Declaration of Human Rights was written and adopted by the United Nations in 1948. It is a statement of basic human rights and standards for government that has been agreed upon by the international community. The declaration proclaims that all people have the right to liberty, education, political and religious freedom, and economic well-being. It also bans torture and says that all people have the right to participate in their country's governmental process.

Original Text	Plain Language Version*
Article 1 All human beings are born free and equal in dignity and rights. They are endowed with reason and conscience and should act towards one another in a spirit of brotherhood.	**Article 1** When children are born, they are free and each should be treated in the same way. They have reason and conscience and should act towards one another in a friendly manner.
Article 2 Everyone is entitled to all the rights and freedoms set forth in this Declaration, without distinction of any kind, such as race, colour, sex, language, religion, political or other opinion, national or social origin, property, birth or other status. Furthermore, no distinction shall be made on the basis of the political, jurisdictional or international status of the country or territory to which a person belongs, whether it be independent, trust, non-self-governing or under any other limitation of sovereignty.	**Article 2** Everyone can claim the following rights, despite • a different sex • a different skin colour • speaking a different language • thinking different things • believing in another religion • owning more or less • being born in another social group • coming from another country. It also makes no difference whether the country you live in is independent or not.
Article 3 Everyone has the right to life, liberty and security of person.	**Article 3** You have the right to live, and to live in freedom and safety.
Article 4 No one shall be held in slavery or servitude; slavery and the slave trade shall be prohibited in all their forms.	**Article 4** Nobody has the right to treat you as his or her slave and you should not make anyone your slave.
Article 5 No one shall be subjected to torture or to cruel, inhuman or degrading treatment or punishment.	**Article 5** Nobody has the right to torture you.
Article 6 Everyone has the right to recognition everywhere as a person before the law.	**Article 6** You should be legally protected in the same way everywhere, and like everyone else.

* The plain language version is given only as a guide. This version is based in part on the translation of a text, prepared in 1978 for the World Association for the School as an Instrument of Peace, by a Research Group of the University of Geneva, under the responsibility of Prof. I Massarenu. In preparing the translation, the Group used a basic vocabulary of 2,500 words in use in the French-speaking part of Switzerland.

Original Text	Plain Language Version*
Article 7 All are equal before the law and are entitled without any discrimination to equal protection of the law. All are entitled to equal protection against any discrimination in violation of this Declaration and against any incitement to such discrimination.	**Article 7** The law is the same for everyone; it should be applied in the same way to all.
Article 8 Everyone has the right to an effective remedy by the competent national tribunals for acts violating the fundamental rights granted him by the constitution or by law.	**Article 8** You should be able to ask for legal help when the rights your country grants you are not respected.
Article 9 No one shall be subjected to arbitrary arrest, detention or exile.	**Article 9** Nobody has the right to put you in prison, to keep you there, or to send you away from your country unjustly, or without a good cause.
Article 10 Everyone is entitled in full equality to a fair and public hearing by an independent and impartial tribunal, in the determination of his rights and obligations and of any criminal charge against him.	**Article 10** If you must go on trial this should be done in public. The people who try you should not let themselves be influenced by others.
Article 11 1. Everyone charged with a penal offence has the right to be presumed innocent until proved guilty according to law in a public trial at which he has had all the guarantees necessary for his defence. 2. No one shall be held guilty of any penal offence on account of any act or omission which did not constitute a penal offence, under national or international law, at the time when it was committed. Nor shall a heavier penalty be imposed than the one that was applicable at the time the penal offence was committed.	**Article 11** You should be considered innocent until it can be proved that you are guilty. If you are accused of a crime, you should always have the right to defend yourself. Nobody has the right to condemn you and punish you for something you have not done.
Article 12 No one shall be subjected to arbitrary interference with his privacy, family, home or correspondence, nor to attacks upon his honour and reputation. Everyone has the right to the protection of the law against such interference or attacks.	**Article 12** You have the right to ask to be protected if someone tries to harm your good name, enter your house, open your letters, or bother you or your family without a good reason.
Article 13 1. Everyone has the right to freedom of movement and residence within the borders of each State. 2. Everyone has the right to leave any country including his own, and to return to his country.	**Article 13** You have the right to come and go as you wish within your country. You have the right to leave your country to go to another one; and you should be able to return to your country if you want.

Original Text	Plain Language Version*
### Article 14	### Article 14
1. Everyone has the right to seek and enjoy in other countries asylum from persecution. 2. This right may not be invoked in the case of prosecutions genuinely arising from non--political crimes or from acts contrary to the purposes and principles of the United Nations.	If you are frightened or being badly treated in your own country, you have the right to run away to another country to be safe. You lose this right if you have killed someone and if you, yourself, do not respect what is written here.
### Article 15	### Article 15
1. Everyone has the right to a nationality. 2. No one shall be arbitrarily deprived of his nationality nor denied the right to change his nationality.	You have the right to belong to a country and nobody can prevent you, without a good reason, from belonging to another country if you wish.
### Article 16	### Article 16
1. Men and women of full age, without any limitation due to race, nationality or religion, have the right to marry and to found a family. They are entitled to equal rights as to marriage, during marriage and at its dissolution. 2. Marriage shall be entered into only with the free and full consent of the intending spouses. 3. The family is the natural and fundamental group unit of society and is entitled to protection by society and the State.	As soon as a person is legally entitled, he or she has the right to marry and have a family. In doing this, neither the colour of your skin, the country you come from nor your religion should be impediments. Men and women have the same rights when they are married and also when they are separated. Nobody should force a person to marry. The government of your country should protect your family and its members.
### Article 17	### Article 17
1. Everyone has the right to own property alone as well as in association with others. 2. No one shall be arbitrarily deprived of his property.	You have the right to own things and nobody has the right to take these from you without a good reason.
### Article 18	### Article 18
Everyone has the right to freedom of thought, conscience and religion; this right includes freedom to change his religion or belief, and freedom, either alone or in community with others and in public or private, to manifest his religion or belief in teaching, practice, worship and observance.	You have the right to profess your religion freely, to change it, and to practice it either on your own or with other people.
### Article 19	### Article 19
Everyone has the right to freedom of opinion and expression; this right includes freedom to hold opinions without interference and to seek, receive and impart information and ideas through any media and regardless of frontiers.	You have the right to think what you want, to say what you like, and nobody should forbid you from doing so. You should be able to share your ideas also—with people from any other country.

Original Text	Plain Language Version*
### Article 20 1. Everyone has the right to freedom of peaceful assembly and association. 2. No one may be compelled to belong to an association.	### Article 20 You have the right to organize peaceful meetings or to take part in meetings in a peaceful way. It is wrong to force someone to belong to a group.
### Article 21 1. Everyone has the right to take part in the government of his country, directly or through freely chosen representatives. 2. Everyone has the right of equal access to public service in his country. 3. The will of the people shall be the basis of the authority of government; this will shall be expressed in periodic and genuine elections which shall be by universal and equal suffrage and shall be held by secret vote or by equivalent free voting procedures.	### Article 21 You have the right to take part in your country's political affairs either by belonging to the government yourself or by choosing politicians who have the same ideas as you. Governments should be voted for regularly and voting should be secret. You should get a vote and all votes should be equal. You also have the same right to join the public service as anyone else.
### Article 22 Everyone, as a member of society, has the right to social security and is entitled to realization, through national effort and international cooperation and in accordance with the organization and resources of each State, of the economic, social and cultural rights indispensable for his dignity and the free development of his personality.	### Article 22 The society in which you live should help you to develop and to make the most of all the advantages (culture, work, social and welfare) which are offered to you and to all the men and women in your country.
### Article 23 1. Everyone has the right to work, to free choice of employment, to just and favourable conditions of work and to protection against unemployment. 2. Everyone, without any discrimination, has the right to equal pay for equal work. 3. Everyone who works has the right to just and favourable remuneration ensuring for himself and his family an existence worthy of human dignity, and supplemented, if necessary, by other means of social protection. 4. Everyone has the right to form and to join trade unions for the protection of his interests.	### Article 23 You have the right to work, to be free to choose your work, and to get a salary which allows you to live and support your family. If a man and a woman do the same work, they should get the same pay. All people who work have the right to join together to defend their interests.
### Article 24 Everyone has the right to rest and leisure, including reasonable limitation of working hours and periodic holidays with pay.	### Article 24 Each work day should not be too long, since everyone has the right to rest and should be able to take regular paid holidays.

Original Text	Plain Language Version*
Article 25	**Article 25**
1. Everyone has the right to a standard of living adequate for the health and well-being of himself and of his family, including food, clothing, housing and medical care and necessary social services, and the right to security in the event of unemployment, sickness, disability, widowhood, old age or other lack of livelihood in circumstances beyond his control. 2. Motherhood and childhood are entitled to special care and assistance. All children, whether born in or out of wedlock, shall enjoy the same social protection.	You have the right to have whatever you need so that you and your family do not fall ill; do not go hungry; have clothes and a house; and are helped if you are out of work, if you are ill, if you are old, if your wife or husband is dead, or if you do not earn a living for any other reason you cannot help. The mother who is going to have a baby, and her baby, should get special help. All children have the same rights, whether or not the mother is married.
Article 26	**Article 26**
1. Everyone has the right to education. Education shall be free, at least in the elementary and fundamental stages. Elementary education shall be compulsory. Technical and professional education shall be made generally available and higher education shall be equally accessible to all on the basis of merit. 2. Education shall be directed to the full development of the human personality and to the strengthening of respect for human rights and fundamental freedoms. It shall promote understanding, tolerance and friendship among all nations, racial or religious groups, and shall further the activities of the United Nations for the maintenance of peace. 3. Parents have a prior right to choose the kind of education that shall be given to their children.	You have the right to go to school and everyone should go to school. Primary schooling should be free. You should be able to learn a profession or continue your studies as far as you wish. At school, you should be able to develop all your talents and you should be taught to get on with others, whatever their race, religion or the country they come from. Your parents have the right to choose how and what you will be taught at school.
Article 27	**Article 27**
1. Everyone has the right freely to participate in the cultural life of the community, to enjoy the arts and to share in scientific advancement and its benefits. 2. Everyone has the right to the protection of the moral and material interests resulting from any scientific, literary or artistic production of which he is the author.	You have the right to share in your community's arts and sciences, and any good they do. Your works as an artist, a writer, or a scientist should be protected, and you should be able to benefit from them.
Article 28	**Article 28**
Everyone is entitled to a social and international order in which the rights and freedoms set forth in this Declaration can be fully realized.	So that your rights will be respected, there must be an "order" which can protect them. This "order" should be local and worldwide.

Original Text	Plain Language Version*
### Article 29	### Article 29
1. Everyone has duties to the community in which alone the free and full development of his personality is possible. 2. In the exercise of his rights and freedoms, everyone shall be subject only to such limitation as are determined by law solely for the purpose of securing due recognition and respect for the rights and freedoms of others and of meeting the just requirements of morality, public order and the general welfare in a democratic society. 3. These rights and freedoms may in no case be exercised contrary to the purposes and principles of the United Nations.	You have duties towards the community within which your personality can only fully develop. The law should guarantee human rights. It should allow everyone to respect others and to be respected.
### Article 30	### Article 30
Nothing in this Declaration may be interpreted as implying for any State, group or person any right to engage in any activity or to perform any act aimed at the destruction of any of the rights and freedoms set forth herein.	In all parts of the world, no society, no human being, should take it upon her or himself to act in such a way as to destroy the rights which you have just been reading about.

Major Federal Civil Rights Laws

In the 1950s, a tide of protest began to rise in the United States against deeply rooted attitudes of racism and discrimination. The campaign for equality grew and gained momentum in the 1960s. For example, women and minority groups began to challenge predominant ethnic, racial, and gender stereotypes and worked to overturn laws that restricted their rights and freedoms. At the end of the twentieth century, an important civil rights law—the Americans with Disabilities Act (ADA)—was passed to protect persons with disabilities. The civil rights movement continues into the twenty-first century, meeting both old and new challenges.

Equal Pay Act of 1963 (Amended in 1972)
- Requires equal pay for equal work, regardless of sex.
- Requires that equal work be determined by equal skill, effort, and responsibility under similar working conditions at the same place of employment.
- Requires equal pay when equal work is involved even if different job titles are assigned.

(Enforced by the Equal Employment Opportunity Commission and private lawsuit.)

Civil Rights Act of 1964 (Amended in 1972, 1978, and 1991)
- Prohibits discrimination based on race, color, religion, or national origin in public accommodations (for example, hotels, restaurants, movie theaters, sports arenas). It does not apply to private clubs closed to the public.
- Prohibits discrimination in employment based on race, color, sex, religion, or national origin by businesses with more than 15 employees or by labor unions. (This section is commonly referred to as Title VII.)
- Prohibits discrimination based on race, color, religion, sex, or national origin by state and local governments and public educational institutions.
- Prohibits discrimination based on race, color, national origin, or sex in any program or activity receiving federal financial assistance. It authorizes ending federal funding when this ban is violated.
- Permits employment discrimination based on religion, sex, or national origin if it is a necessary qualification for the job.

(Enforced by the U.S. Equal Employment Opportunity Commission and private lawsuit.)

Voting Rights Act of 1965 (Amended in 1970, 1975, 1982, and 2006)
- Bans literacy and "good character" tests as requirements for voting.
- Requires bilingual election materials for most voters who don't speak English.
- Reduces residency requirements for voting in federal elections.
- Establishes criminal penalties for harassing voters or interfering with voting rights.

(Enforced by the U.S. Department of Justice and private lawsuit.)

Age Discrimination in Employment Act of 1967 (Amended in 1974, 1978, 1986, and 1990)
- Prohibits arbitrary age discrimination in employment by employers of 20 or more persons, employment agencies, labor organizations with 25 or more members, and federal, state, and local governments.
- Protects people aged 40 and older.
- Permits discrimination where age is a necessary qualification for the job.

(Enforced by the U.S. Equal Employment Opportunity Commission, a similar state agency, and private lawsuit.)

Civil Rights Act of 1968 (Amended in 1988 and 1992)
- Prohibits discrimination based on race, color, religion or national origin in the sale, rental, or financing of most housing.

(Enforced by the U.S. Department of Justice, the U.S. Department of Housing and Urban Development, and private lawsuit.)

Title IX of the Education Act Amendments of 1972
- Prohibits discrimination against students and others on the basis of sex by educational institutions receiving federal funding.

- Prohibits sex discrimination in a number of areas, including student and faculty recruitment, admissions, financial aid, facilities, and employment.
- Requires that school athletic programs effectively accommodate the interest and abilities of members of both sexes; equal total expenditure on men's and women's sports is not required.
- Does not cover sex stereotyping in textbooks and other curricular materials.

(Enforced by the U.S. Department of Education's Office of Civil Rights.)

Rehabilitation Act of 1973 (Amended in 1998)
- Prohibits government employers and private employers receiving government assistance from discriminating on the basis of physical handicap.
- Requires companies that do business with the government to undertake affirmative action to provide jobs for the handicapped.
- Prohibits activities and programs receiving federal funds from excluding otherwise qualified handicapped people from participation or benefits.

(Enforced by lawsuit in federal court and, in some cases, state or local human rights or fair employment practices commissions.)

Americans with Disabilities Act of 1990 (ADA)
- Prohibits discrimination against individuals with disabilities.
- Prohibits discrimination in employment. This covers such things as the application process, testing, hiring, evaluation, assignments, training, promotion, termination, compensation, leave, and benefits. *(Title I)*
- Prohibits discrimination in public services. This title covers state and local -government services and all services, programs, and activities provided or made available by these gov-ernments. This includes entities such as state metro rail systems and AMTRAK. (Title II)
- Prohibits discrimination in public accommo-dations and services operated by private entities. This includes entities such as private taxi companies, schools, restaurants, hotels, and grocery stores. *(Title III)*
- Prohibits discrimination in telecommunications. This covers relay services for hearing -impaired and speech-impaired -individuals, and closed-captioning of public service announcements. *(Title IV)*
- Prohibits discrimination in such activities as construction, prohibits retaliation and coercion, and regulates the Architectural and Transportation Barriers Compliance Board. (Title V)

(Enforced by various methods including administrative complaint to a specific federal agency or private lawsuit.)

Civil Rights Act of 1991
- Addresses discrimination in the workplace.
- Addresses discrimination at any point in the employment relationship, including private and governmental discrimination.
- Allows individuals who prove intentional employment discrimination on the basis of sex, disability, or religion to collect compensatory and punitive damages.
- Creates a limit on damages.

(Enforced by private lawsuit.)

Individuals with Disabilities Education Act of 1991 (IDEA) (Amended in 1997)
- Guarantees a "free appropriate public education" for all children with disabilities.
- Entitles each child with a disability to free special services, including medical services necessary to secure an appropriate education.
- Requires schools to develop an "individualized education program" (IEP) for each child with a disability.
- Requires parental approval of "individualized education programs" (IEP) and all changes in plan or placement.
- Includes learning disabilities, behavioral disorders, and mental and physical impairments within the definition of "disability."

(Enforced by private lawsuit and state and federal departments of education.)

—————————— **A** ——————————

abduction involves taking away a person against that person's will

abortion a premature end to a pregnancy. Abortion can result from a medical procedure performed in the early stages of pregnancy or as in a miscarriage, when the fetus leaves the womb before it can survive on its own.

abused children minors who have been sexually, physically, or emotionally mistreated

acceleration clause a provision in a contract that makes the entire debt due immediately if a payment is not made on time or if some other condition is not met

acceptance the act of agreeing to an offer and becoming bound to the terms of a contract

accessory a person who helps commit a crime but usually is not present at the crime. An accessory before the fact is one who encourages or helps plan a crime. An accessory after the fact is someone who, knowing a crime has been committed, helps conceal the crime or the criminal.

accomplice a person who voluntarily helps another person commit a crime; an accomplice is usually present or directly aids in the crime.

acquaintance rape sexual assault by someone known to the victim, such as a date or neighbor (also called date rape)

adjudicatory hearing the procedure used to determine the facts in a juvenile case; similar to an adult trial, but generally closed to the public

adjustable-rate mortgage a home loan in which the interest rate can change over time

adoption the legal process of taking a child of other biological parents and accepting that child as your own, with all the legal rights and

responsibilities there would be if the child were yours by birth

adultery voluntary sexual intercourse between a married person and someone other than his or her spouse

adversarial system the judicial system used in the United States. It allows opposing parties to present their legal conflicts before an impartial judge and jury.

advocacy active support or argument for a cause

advocate a person who speaks for the cause of another or on behalf of someone or something

affidavit a written statement of facts sworn to or made under oath before someone authorized to administer an oath

affirmative action steps taken to promote diversity in hiring, promotion, education, etc. by attempting to remedy past discrimination; for example, by actively recruiting minorities and women

aftercare the equivalent of parole in the juvenile justice system. A juvenile is supervised and assisted by a parole officer or social worker.

agency an administrative division of a government set up to make and carry out certain laws

aggravating circumstances factors that tend to increase the seriousness of an offense. The presence of such circumstances must be considered in the sentence.

alibi a Latin word meaning "elsewhere;" an excuse or plea that a person was somewhere else at the time a crime was committed

alimony a court-ordered allowance a husband or wife (or an ex-husband/ex-wife) pays to his or her spouse after a legal separation, after a divorce, or while the case is being decided

allegation a criminal accusation that has not been proven

amendment (1) one of the provisions of the U.S. Constitution enacted after the original Constitution became law; (2) an addition or change to an existing document or plan

annual percentage rate (APR) the interest rate paid per year on borrowed money

annulment a court or religious order that declares a marriage never legally existed

appeal to take a case to a higher court for a rehearing

appeals court a court in which appeals from trial-court decisions are heard

appellant one who signs or files an appeal of a trial decision

appellate court *see* appeals court

arbitration a way of settling a dispute without going to trial. The parties who disagree select one or more impartial persons to settle the argument. If the arbitration is binding, then all parties must accept the decision.

arraignment a court session at which a defendant is charged and enters a plea. For a misdemeanor this is also the defendant's initial appearance, at which the judge informs him or her of the charges and sets the bail.

arrest to take a person suspected of a crime into custody

arrest warrant a court-ordered document authorizing the police to arrest an individual on a specific charge

arson the deliberate and malicious burning of another person's property

assault an intentional threat, show of force, or movement that causes a reasonable fear of, or an actual physical contact with, another person. Can be a crime or a tort.

assumption of risk a legal defense to a negligence tort, whereby the plaintiff is considered to have voluntarily accepted a known risk of danger

asylum a place of refuge or safety from imminent danger

attachment the act of taking a debtor's property or money to satisfy a debt, by court approval

attempt an effort to commit a crime that goes beyond mere preparation but does not result in the commission of the crime

attractive nuisance doctrine that says if a person keeps something on his or her premises that is likely to attract children, that person must take reasonable steps to protect children against dangers the condition might cause

B

bait and switch a deceptive sales technique in which customers are "baited" into a store by an ad promising an item at a low price and then "switched" to a more expensive item

balloon payment a financing agreement in which the last payment of a loan is much higher than the regular monthly payments

bankruptcy the procedure under the *Federal Bankruptcy Act* by which a person is relieved of all debts once he or she has placed all property and money in a court's care

bar association an organization that licenses lawyers in some states. In other states lawyers are licensed by their state supreme court.

battery any intentional, unlawful physical contact inflicted on one person by another without consent. In some states, this is combined with assault. A battery can also be a crime. *See also* assault.

bench trial trial that takes place before a judge without a jury

best interest of the child a doctrine used to determine custody by examining factors that will best benefit a child

Glossary

beyond a reasonable doubt the level of proof required to convict a person of a crime. It does not mean "convinced 100 percent," but does mean there are no reasonable doubts as to guilt.

bigamy the crime of being married to more than one person at a time

bill (1) a proposed law being considered by a legislature; (2) a written statement of money owed

bill consolidation a form of credit in which the lender combines all of a person's debts into a single monthly payment. In effect, this is a refinancing of a person's existing debts, often with an additional, higher interest charge

Bill of Rights the first ten amendments to the Constitution, which guarantee basic individual rights to all persons in the United States

black-market adoption a form of adoption, illegal in many states, that bypasses licensed adoption agencies by using a go-between to negotiate between the expectant mother and the adopting parent(s)

bona fide a Latin term, meaning "in good faith"; (1) characterized by good faith and lack of fraud or deceit; (2) valid under or in compliance with the law

bona fide occupational qualification (BFOQ) an employment requirement that is considered reasonable because it is necessary to perform the job. For example, good vision is a BFOQ for a bus driver; the race or national origin of a bus driver is not a BFOQ.

bond a mandatory insurance agreement or obligation. A bail bond is the money a defendant pays to secure release from jail before the trial.

booking the formal process of making a police record of an arrest

breach the violation of a law, duty, or other form of obligation, including obligations formed through contracts or warranties

bullying a version of assault and battery in which peers or acquaintances intimidate, or put others in fear

burden of proof the requirement that to win a point or have an issue decided in one party's favor, the party must show that a certain amount of the weight of the evidence is on his or her side. In a civil case, the burden of proof is on the plaintiff, who must usually prevail by a preponderance (majority) of the evidence. In a criminal case, the state must prove its case beyond a reasonable doubt. The weight of the evidence is more than the amount of evidence. It is also concerned with the believability of the evidence.

burglary breaking and entering a building with the intention of committing a crime

business necessity the legally acceptable reason for employee selection requirements. A business must show it can operate well only if these selection requirements are met by potential employees.

———————— **C** ————————

capital punishment the death penalty; putting a convicted person to death as punishment for a crime

carjacking a crime in which the perpetrator uses force or intimidation to steal a car from a driver

causation the reason an event occurs; that which produces an effect. It is one of the four elements that must be proven in a negligence case. Causation is subdivided into cause in fact and proximate cause.

cause in fact one of the elements a plaintiff must prove in order to establish causation in a negligence suit. It means that if the harm would not have occurred without the wrongful act, the act is the cause in fact of the harm.

caveat emptor Latin phrase meaning "let the buyer beware"

cease and desist order an order given by an administrative agency or a judge to stop some illegal or deceptive activity

censorship (1) the denial of freedom of speech or freedom of the press; (2) the process of examining publications or films for material that the government considers harmful or objectionable

certiorari *see* petition for certiorari

charge the formal accusation of a crime

checks and balances the power of each of the three branches of government (legislative, judicial, executive) to limit the other branches' power, so as to prevent an abuse

child abuse neglect or mistreatment of a child

child neglect the failure of a parent to properly feed, clothe, provide shelter for, educate, supervise, or provide for the medical needs of a child

child support a court-determined payment that the parent not living with the child must pay to help provide for the child's needs

citizenship legal residency in a country by either birth or oath and the rights and privileges therein

civil action a noncriminal lawsuit, brought to enforce a right or redress a wrong

civil law all law that does not involve criminal matters, such as tort and contract law. Civil law usually deals with private rights of individuals, groups, or businesses.

civil union a legal status that allows two persons to establish a relationship that protects many of the same spousal benefits that would apply to partners in a traditional marriage

class action a lawsuit brought by one or more persons on behalf of a larger group

clause a paragraph, sentence, or phrase in a legal document, such as a contract, lease, or will

clear and present danger test a test formerly used by courts to restrict speech when the government thought the speech would create an immediate danger of serious harm

closing statement at the end of a trial, the comments a lawyer makes to summarize the evidence presented

cohabitation agreement a written or oral contract outlining how unmarried couples want to deal with their money, property, or responsibilities during and after their q21relationship

collaborative divorce a form of divorce that involves informal discussions and conferences attended by both parties and their lawyers to settle all issues

collateral money or property given as security in case a person is unable to repay a debt

collective bargaining a required procedure in the *National Labor Relations Act* providing that under certain circumstances, employers must bargain with official union representatives regarding wages, hours, and other work conditions

collective rights rights that apply more to people acting together in a group than to individuals acting on their own; examples include the right to bear arms, freedom of assembly and of petition, and even freedom of the press

collision coverage insurance that pays for damage to the insured's own car caused by an automobile collision

commercial speech speech that is directed at buying or selling of goods and services. The law treats commercial speech differently from political speech and other forms of expression.

common law a system in which court decisions establish legal principles and rules of law

common-law marriage a marriage created without legal ceremony by a couple living together and publicly presenting themselves as married. Such a marriage can be formed only in certain states.

community policing a strategy whereby the community works actively with the local police to lower the crime rate in its area

community property property acquired during a marriage that is owned by both husband and wife, regardless of who earned it or paid for it

commute to change a sentence to another less severe sentence

comparative negligence in a tort suit, a finding that the plaintiff was partly at fault and, therefore, does not deserve full compensation for his or her injuries. For example, if an accident was 40 percent the plaintiff's fault, the plaintiff's damages are reduced by 40 percent.

comparison shopping looking at several products and comparing quality and price before deciding which item best meets one's needs

compelling interest test The compelling state interest test is satisfied when the government can show a that it has a very important interest that is promoted by the law or action in question and no way to satisfy that interest that interferes less with the rights of others.

compensatory damages in a civil case, money the court requires a defendant to pay a winning plaintiff to make up for harm caused. This harm can be financial (for example, lost wages, medical expenses, etc.), physical (for example, past, present, and future pain and suffering), and, in some jurisdictions, emotional (fright and shock, anxiety, etc.).

competent a person's having the capacity and function to make legal decisions on their own behalf

complaint (1) the first legal document filed in a civil lawsuit. It includes a statement of the wrong or harm done to the plaintiff by the defendant and a request for a specific remedy from the court. (2) A complaint in a criminal case is a sworn statement regarding the defendant's actions that constitute the crime charged.

comprehensive coverage the portion of an insurance policy that protects an individual against automobile damage or loss from events other than collisions. It includes damages and losses due to fire, vandalism, or theft.

compulsory voting mandatory voting; voting that is required by all citizens

computer crime the unauthorized access to, and tampering with, someone else's computer system

concealment the crime of attempted shoplifting that is recognized by some states

concurring opinion an additional written court opinion in which a judge or judges agrees with the outcome reached by the court, but for reasons different from those used to support the majority opinion

confession an accused person's voluntary admission of wrongdoing

consent written, spoken, or assumed agreement to something

consent decree a voluntary agreement to stop a practice that is claimed to be illegal

consideration something of value offered or received that must be present in every valid contract

conspiracy an agreement between two or more persons to commit a crime along with a substantial act toward committing the crime

consumer anyone who buys or uses a product or service

consumer protection laws statutes that protect consumers by prohibiting unfair or misleading trade practices; setting standards for quality, safety, and reliability of many goods and services; and establishing agencies to enforce consumer laws and help consumers

contempt of court any act to embarrass, hinder, or obstruct the court in the administration of justice

continuance the postponement of the court proceedings in a case to a future time

contraband any items that are illegal to possess

contraceptive a precautionary item such as a condom or birth control pills designed to prevent or reduce the chance of pregnancy

contract a legally enforceable agreement between two or more people to exchange something of value

contributory negligence a legal defense in which it is determined that the plaintiff and defendant share the fault for a negligence tort. If proven, the plaintiff cannot recover damages.

conversion in tort law, the taking or controlling of another's property without consent. If the property is not returned to the rightful owner, the court can force the defendant to give the plaintiff the monetary value of the property.

conviction the finding that a person is guilty of a crime or wrongdoing

cooperative federalism a concept of federalism in which federal, state, and local governments work together collectively to solve problems

copayment an amount of money that a person with health insurance is required to pay at the time of each visit to a doctor or when purchasing medicine

copyright the protection of a creative fixed expression giving the owner exclusive rights to the expression (For example, Matt Groening has exclusive rights to the *Simpsons* cartoon characters.)

corporal punishment physical punishment, such as spanking or paddling

corrective advertising a remedy imposed by the Federal Trade Commission requiring that any false claim in an advertisement be admitted and corrected in all future ads for a specified period of time

corroborate to confirm information

cosign to sign a legal document, guaranteeing to pay off the debt or contract if the original signer defaults or if the contract is unenforceable against the original signer

counterclaim a claim made by a defendant against the plaintiff in a civil lawsuit

covenant a solemn promise to do or not do something. Similar to a contract except that consideration is not required.

covenant marriage a special type of marriage in which the couple surrenders, in advance, their right to a no-fault divorce

credit (1) a deduction from what is owed; (2) purchasing goods with delayed payment, as with a credit card; (3) money that is loaned

creditor a person who provides credit, loans, money, or delivers goods or services before payment is made

credit property insurance insurance against theft or damage of items purchased with loans

credit life/disability insurance insurance that guarantees payment of owed balances should the buyer die or become disabled

crime an act or failure to act that violates a law and for which a government has set a penalty (usually a fine, jail, or probation)

crime of omission failing to perform an act required by criminal law

criminal fraud knowingly misstating or misrepresenting an important fact, with the intent to harm another person

criminal homicide the killing of another person intentionally and with malice

criminal justice process the system by which government enforces criminal law. It includes everything from the arrest of an individual to the individual's release from control by the state.

Glossary

criminal law the branch of law dealing with crimes and their punishment

criminal sexual assault a category of crimes that includes rape, attempted rape, and statutory rape.

cross examination the questioning of the opposing side's witnesses during a hearing or trial

custodial interrogation questioning by law enforcement officers after a person has been taken into custody or otherwise deprived of his or her freedom of movement

custody the care and keeping of something or someone, such as a child

cybercrime describes a wide range of actions that involves computers and computer networks in criminal activities

cyberstalking stalking or harassment using electronic communications

— **D** —

damages (1) money asked for or paid by court order to a plaintiff for injuries or losses suffered; (2) the injuries or losses suffered by one person due to the fault of another

date rape *see* acquaintance rape

death penalty a sentence to death for commission of a serious crime, such as murder; *see also* capital punishment

debit card also called a *check card;* a card used to make purchases in which the purchase price is deducted from your bank account

debtor a person who owes money or buys on credit

decree an official decision of a court, setting out the facts found in a case and the legal results. It orders that the court's decision (for example, a divorce decree) be carried out.

deductible the amount an insured person agrees to pay toward repairs before the insurance company pays anything.

deep pockets a description of the person or organization, among many possible defendants, best able to pay damages and therefore most likely to be sued in a tort case

defamation written or spoken expression about a person communicated to a third person that is false and damages that person's reputation

default failure to fulfill a legal obligation, such as making a loan payment or appearing in court on a specified date and time

default judgment a ruling against a party to a lawsuit who fails to take a required action (for example, failing to file a paper on time)

defendant the person against whom a claim is made. In a civil suit, the defendant is the person being sued; in a criminal case, the defendant is the person charged with committing a crime.

defense a denial, answer, or plea by a defendant, disputing the correctness of charges against the defendant

defense of property the use of reasonable force, which would otherwise be illegal, to defend your home or other property

deinstitutionalization a policy of releasing a mentally ill patient from a mental hospital into the community

deliberate intentional

delinquent offender a minor who has committed an act that, if committed by an adult, would be a crime under federal, state, or local law. Such offenders are usually processed through the juvenile justice system.

derivative work a work that is very similar to but slightly different from a copyrighted work

desegregate to end the policy of imposing legal and social separation of races, as in housing, schools, and jobs

desertion the act of abandoning one's spouse with no intention of returning or of reassuming the duties of marriage. Desertion is usually grounds for divorce.

deterrence measures taken to discourage illegal actions; usually some form of punishment. It is the belief that punishment will discourage the offender from committing future crimes and will serve as an example to keep others from committing crimes.

direct action an action that consumers take to make an impact on a business's or other organization's operations or profits

direct examination the questioning of a witness by the side calling the witness to the stand

direct file gives prosecutors discretion to file charges against juveniles in adult criminal court

disability a condition that makes performing certain basic functions or activities difficult

disclaimer a clause or statement in a contract or agreement that limits responsibility for anything not expressly promised

discovery the pretrial process of exchanging information between the opposing sides

discrimination generally, choosing or selecting. In law, it may be the decision to treat or categorize persons based on race, color, creed, gender, or other characteristics rather than on individual merit. Also, the denial of equal protection of the law.

disposition the final sentence or result of a case

dispositional hearing the procedure in which a judge decides what type of punishment or sentence a juvenile offender should receive

dissenting opinion in a trial or appeal, the written opinion of the minority of judges who disagree with the decision of the majority

divorce the ending of a marriage by court order

DNA evidence biological evidence, derived from testing samples of human tissues and fluids, that genetically links an offender to a crime

domestic partnership allows an employee's heterosexual or homosexual live-in partner to receive the same employment and health benefits a spouse would receive

double jeopardy a defendant cannot be prosecuted a second time for the same crime. This limit on government power is based on the Fifth Amendment.

down payment cash that must be paid up front when something is bought by paying in installments over time

driving under the influence/driving while intoxicated DUI/DWI refers to a person's blood alcohol concentration (BAC). Although the legal levels of BAC vary from state to state, an individual generally is considered *impaired* when the BAC is between 0.05g/dl and 0.08g/dl, and *intoxicated* when the BAC is 0.08g/dl or greater

drug courier profile using commonly held notions of what typical drug couriers look and act like in order to be able to question a person without establishing individualized suspicion

drunk driving the operation of a motor vehicle while intoxicated (overcome by alcohol to the point of losing control over one's conscious faculties). A drunk person's blood-alcohol concentration is above a predefined level set by state law.

due process the idea stated in the Fifth and Fourteenth Amendments that every person is entitled to fair treatment by the government. The requirements of due process vary with the situation, but they require at a minimum notice and an opportunity to be heard.

Glossary

duress unlawful pressure on a person to do something that he or she would not otherwise do. Duress may be a defense to a criminal charge.

duty a legal obligation

duty to mitigate (damages) the legal responsibility to make damages from a harm such as breaching a contract less severe if possible

— **E** —

emancipated the condition of having reached legal adulthood; usually at age 16, 18, or 21

emancipation the freeing of a child from the control of parents and allowing the child to live on his or her own or under the control of others. It usually applies to adolescents who leave the parents' household by agreement or demand. Emancipation may also end the responsibility of a divorced parent to pay child support.

embezzlement the taking of money or property by a person to whom it has been entrusted; for example, a bank teller or a company accountant

employment-at-will contract a work agreement in which the employee can quit at any time, and the employer can fire the employee for any reason or no reason at all, as long as the firing does not violate some other law, such as an anti-discrimination law

entrapment an act by law enforcement officials to persuade a person to commit a crime that the person would not otherwise have committed. If proven, entrapment is a valid defense to a criminal charge.

equal protection a constitutional requirement of the Fourteenth Amendment that protects individuals against unlawful discrimination by government

environmental impact statement (EIS) a document prepared to describe the effects of a proposed project on the surrounding environment

Equal Rights Amendment a proposed amendment to the U.S. Constitution preventing gender discrimination. It was not ratified by enough states, so it was not added.

equitable distribution a system for dividing property at the end of a marriage in which each spouse is entitled to his or her separate property brought into or acquired during the marriage. Marital property is divided according to factors such as need and length of the marriage.

error of law a mistake made by a judge in legal procedures or rulings during a trial that may allow the case to be appealed

escrow money or property that a neutral party, such as a bank, holds for someone until that person fulfills some obligation or requirement

establishment clause part of the First Amendment to the U.S. Constitution that prohibits government from establishing a church or preferring one religion over another

estate an individual's personal property, including money, stocks, and all belongings

eviction the action by a landlord of removing a tenant from a rental unit

exclusionary rule a legal rule that prohibits the use of illegally obtained evidence against the defendant at trial; generally applies to violations of Fourth, Fifth, or Sixth Amendment rights

exclusive remedy the only solution, or compensation, available to a plaintiff in a particular legal situation

executive branch the administrative branch of a government; responsible for carrying out (enforcing) laws. This branch includes a chief executive, executive offices, and agencies.

executive order an order that comes from the president or a government agency and must be obeyed like a law

expectation damages money the breaching party in a contract dispute must pay to make

Glossary

the other party as well off as if the contract had not been breached

express warranty a statement of fact or a demonstration concerning the quality or performance of goods offered for sale

expunge to seal or destroy a criminal record. Some states allow the expungement of a juvenile record when the juvenile reaches a certain age.

extortion taking property illegally through threats of harm (often called blackmail)

extradition the legal process in which one country or state asks another to surrender a suspected or convicted criminal

———————— **F** ————————

fair use a clause of the copyright statute that allows limited reproduction of a copyrighted work for noncommercial purposes

false imprisonment the intentional or wrongful confinement of another person against his or her will

family car doctrine a legal rule stating that the owner of a car will be liable for damage done by any family member driving the car

family foster care a system of licensed families in each state who act as temporary parents for children who cannot live with their families

family mediator a professional who works directly with a divorcing couple, helping them preserve their relationship for the future. To save time and money, this person helps the couple reach some agreements out of court.

family responsibility laws laws that require adult children to care for their elderly parents

family reunification the process a family goes through to make the necessary changes to provide a safe home for a foster child to return to

federalism the division of powers between the states and the federal government

felony a serious criminal offense punishable by a prison sentence of more than one year

felony murder the killing of someone during the commission of certain felonies, regardless of intent to kill (which is usually required for a murder charge)

fighting words a legal term applying to words spoken face-to-face that are so abusive that they are likely to cause an imminent fight between the speaker and the person spoken to. Such words are not usually entitled to First Amendment protection.

finance charge additional money owed to a creditor in exchange for the privilege of borrowing money

fine a monetary penalty imposed upon someone

first-degree murder *see* murder

first sale the first purchaser of a piece of copyrighted material may legally resell that particular copy of the protected work

fixed-rate mortgage a home loan in which the interest rate remains the same throughout the term of the loan

fixture (1) anything attached to land or a building; (2) those things that, once attached, may not be removed by a tenant

food stamps coupons given to people with incomes below a certain level. The coupons can be exchanged like money for food at authorized stores.

for-cause challenge a lawyer's request that a potential juror be eliminated for some specific reason, for example, if a juror knew the defendant or the victim in the case

foreclosure a bank's taking possession of a property to resell it, due to the owner's failure to make mortgage payments

forgery the act of making a fake document or altering a real one with the intent to commit fraud

Glossary

formulary an official list giving details of medicines that may be prescribed

foster parents a couple or family who take in and care for a child who is without parents or who has been removed from the custody of his or her parents

fraud an intentional deception, lie, or dishonest statement made to cheat someone resulting in harm

free exercise clause part of the First Amendment to the U.S. Constitution that protects individuals' right to worship as they choose

fringe benefit an item provided by an employer to employees free of charge or at reduced cost

frivolous lawsuits cases without merit, sometimes filed in an effort to force the defendant to offer a cash settlement rather than going to the expense of defending the lawsuit

G

gag order a court order prohibiting public reporting on a case currently before the court

garnishment the legally authorized process of taking a person's money, generally by taking part of the person's wages in order to pay creditors

gerrymandering redrawing voting district lines to ensure that a particular group of people is included in the same districts

grand jury a group of 16 to 23 people who hear preliminary evidence to decide whether there is sufficient reason to formally charge a person with a crime

grassroots lobbyist a person, or group of people, who works to convince a lawmaker to vote for or against a particular issue by participating in rallies, meeting with representatives, or letter writing campaigns

green card a legal document proving the legitimacy of an immigrant's residency

group home a residence in which several children in foster care live together under the supervision and care of licensed individuals

guilty but mentally ill a verdict that allows convicted criminal defendants to be sent to a hospital and later transferred to a prison after recovery from mental illness

H

habeas corpus Latin for "may you have the body"; a writ (court order) which directs the law enforcement officials who have custody of a prisoner to appear in court so the judge determine whether the prisoner is being held lawfully

hate speech bigoted speech attacking or disparaging a social or ethnic group or a member of such a group

hearing the process by which a judge or other court officer hears evidence to determine the factual or legal issues in a case

home confinement the type of sentence in which the defendant must serve the term at home and usually can leave only for essential purposes, such as work or school

homicide the killing of another person. Homicide can be criminal, noncriminal, or negligent. *See also* manslaughter *and* murder.

hostile environment an uncomfortable working environment in the context of sexual harassment

housing codes the municipal ordinances that regulate standards of safety and upkeep for buildings

human rights basic privileges a person has as a human being

hung jury the situation in which a jury cannot reach a unanimous decision

I

immune exempt from penalties, payments, or legal requirements; free from prosecution

immunity freedom from; protection from some action, such as being sued or prosecuted

implied consent an unwritten agreement to submit to forms of interrogation or searches in exchange for certain privileges, such as driving or flying

implied warranty the unwritten minimum standard of quality the law requires of products offered for sale

imprisonment confinement, usually in jail or prison. *See also* false imprisonment.

incapacitation a reason for criminal punishment that stresses keeping a convicted person confined to protect society

incarceration imprisonment by the government

incest sexual relations between people who are closely related to each other

inchoate crimes crimes that are committed before or in preparation for committing another crime

incitement test a method used by courts to determine whether to restrict or punish expression based on its potential to cause immediate unlawful behavior

indictment a grand jury's formal charge or accusation of criminal action

indigent term used to describe a defendant who does not have the financial means to hire an attorney

individual mandate a requirement by law that most Americans purchase or otherwise obtain health care or pay a tax penalty

infancy the legal defense of a person considered not yet legally responsible for his or her actions; the time before which a person

becomes entitled to the legal rights and responsibilities normally held by citizens

information a prosecuting attorney's formal accusation of the defendant, detailing the nature and circumstances of the charge

infringement the illegal use of someone's intellectual property, such as a copyright, patent, or trademark

inheritance property received from a deceased person either by intestacy laws or from a will

initial hearing a preliminary examination of the validity of a youth's arrest, during which the state must prove that an offense was committed and that there is reasonable cause to believe the accused youth committed it. Decisions are made about further detention and legal representation, and a date is set for a hearing on the facts.

initiative a procedure by which voters can propose a law and submit it to the electorate or the legislature for approval

injunction a court order requiring a person to do, or refrain from doing, a particular act

in loco parentis Latin for "in place of a parent"; person or institution (such as a school) that is entrusted with a minor's care and has intentionally assumed some or all of the rights of a parent over the minor

inquisitional system a European method for handling disputes in which the judge plays an active role in gathering and presenting evidence and questioning witnesses

insanity a defense used in criminal law cases. The insanity defense varies from state to state and is based on the idea that the defendant could not tell right from wrong.

insanity defense defense raised by a criminal defendant stating that because of mental disease or defect, the defendant should not be held responsible for the crime committed

insurance a contract in which one party pays money and the other party promises to reimburse the first party for specified types of losses if they occur

intake the informal process in which court officials or social workers decide if a complaint against a juvenile should be referred to juvenile court

intellectual property a person's idea or invention that is given special ownership protections

intentionally with purpose

intentional infliction of emotional distress a tort in which a defendant purposely engages in an action that causes extreme emotional harm to the plaintiff

intentional tort an action taken deliberately to harm another person and/or his or her property; intentional wrong

intentional wrong *see* intentional tort

interest money paid for the use of someone else's money; the cost of borrowing money. Money put in a savings account earns interest, while borrowing money incurs an interest charge.

interrogate to question a witness or suspected criminal

intoxication a state of drunkenness or similar condition created by the use of drugs or alcohol

involuntary manslaughter *see* manslaughter

irreconcilable differences disagreement between a couple that is grounds for a no-fault divorce

----------------- **J** -----------------

jail a place of short-term confinement for persons convicted of misdemeanors or awaiting trial

Jim Crow law a statute or law created to enforce segregation in such places as schools, buses, and hotels

joint custody a custody arrangement in which divorced or separated parents have equal rights

in making important decisions concerning their children

judgment a court's decision in a civil case

judicial branch the branch of government that interprets laws and resolves legal questions

judicial integrity as used in discussing search and seizure, this is an argument for the use of the exclusionary rule, which emphasizes that courts should not permit lawbreaking by the police

judicial review the process by which courts decide whether the laws passed by Congress or state legislatures are constitutional

jury in a legal proceeding, a body of men and women selected to hear and examine certain facts and determine the truth

juvenile a person not yet considered an adult for the purposes of determining either criminal or civil liability; a minor

juvenile waiver allows juvenile court judges to send juveniles to adult court for prosecution

----------------- **K** -----------------

kidnapping taking away a person against that person's will

kinship care placement of a vulnerable youth in the continuous care and supervision of relatives who are not his or her parents as directed by a social services or other child welfare agency. Such an arrangement also often occurs informally.

----------------- **L** -----------------

labor relations law the branch of law that determines how unions and employers may operate

landfill a place to dispose of refuse and other waste material by burying it and covering it over with soil

landlord the property owner who leases or rents space

Glossary

larceny the unlawful taking of another's property with the intent to steal it. Grand larceny, a felony, is the theft of anything above a certain value (often $100 or more). Petty larceny, a misdemeanor, is the theft of any thing below a certain value (often $100).

lawful permanent resident a person who has received a green card and is allowed to work in the United States

lease a rental contract between a landlord and a tenant for the use of property for a specified length of time at a specified cost

lease application a form the landlord uses to determine whether someone qualifies for a rental property

legal authority (1) legal rights granted to officials, giving them certain powers; (2) the body of statutes, case law, and other sources that serve as legal guidance

legal defense a legally recognized excuse for a defendant's actions, such as implied consent, privilege, and self defense, which may remove liability for certain offenses

legal separation a situation in which the two spouses are separated but still maintain some marital obligations

legislative branch the branch of government that passes laws. The U.S. Senate and House of Representatives comprise the legislative branch of the federal government.

legislative intent what the lawmakers who passed a law wanted the law to mean. If the language of a statute is unclear, judges will often look at the legislative intent to help them interpret the law.

liability legal responsibility; the obligation to do or not do something. The defendant in a tort case incurs liability for failing to use reasonable care, resulting in harm to the plaintiff.

liability insurance the type of coverage or insurance that pays for injuries to other people or damage to property if the individual insured is responsible for an accident during the term of the contract

liable legally responsible

libel a written expression about a person that is false and damages that person's reputation

lien the right to take possession of or hold a debtor's property until the debt for the property is paid in full

limited government a basic principle of our constitutional system. It limits government to powers provided to it by the people

litigator a trial attorney; a barrister

loan sharking lending money at high, often illegal, interest rates

lobbying influencing or persuading legislators to take action to introduce a bill or vote a certain way on a proposed law

loss leader something (as merchandise) sold at a loss (or for very little profit) in order to draw customers into a store

---

M

malice ill will; deliberate intent to harm someone

malpractice failure to meet acceptable standards of practice in any professional or official position; often the basis for lawsuits by clients or patients against their attorney or physician

mandatory sentencing laws that require courts to sentence convicted criminals to prison terms of a certain specified length

manslaughter the killing of a person without malice or premeditation, but during the commission of an illegal act. Manslaughter can be either voluntary, when intentional but not premeditated, resulting from the heat of passion or the diminished mental capacity of the killer; or involuntary, when unintentional but done during an unlawful act of a lesser nature. *See also* homicide *and* murder

marital property property acquired during a marriage, including joint bank accounts, real estate, automobiles, etc. Such property is considered to be owned equally by both spouses.

marriage counselor a person who is trained to help couples settle their marital problems

mediation the act or process of resolving a dispute between two or more parties

Medicaid a government program that provides medical care to people with low incomes

medical coverage insurance which covers an individual's own medical expenses resulting from accidents

Medicare the federal health insurance program available to people who are eligible for Social Security or Social Security Disability Insurance

mens rea the Latin term used by lawyers when they discuss the requirement for a guilty state of mind

mental cruelty acts of emotional or psychological abuse against one's spouse

minor a child; a person under the legal age of adulthood, usually 18 or 21

Miranda warnings rights that a person taken into custody must be informed of by police or other officials before questioning begins. These include the right to remain silent, to contact a lawyer, and to have a free lawyer provided if the person arrested cannot afford one.

misdemeanor a criminal offense, less serious than a felony, punishable by a jail sentence of one year or less

mistrial the termination of a trial before its normal conclusion because of procedural error; statements by a witness, judge, or attorney which prejudice a jury; a deadlock by a jury without reaching a verdict after lengthy deliberation (a "hung jury"); or the failure to complete

a trial within the time set by the court. A new trial must be ordered and the case starts over from the beginning.

mitigating circumstances factors that tend to lessen the seriousness of an offense. The presence of these factors must be considered in the sentence.

monopoly exclusive ownership or possession

month-to-month lease a lease enabling the tenant to leave with 30 days' notice and the landlord to raise the rent or evict the tenant with 30 days' notice

mortgage a loan in which land or buildings are put up as security

motion a request made by one party to a lawsuit that a judge take specific action or make a decision

motion for change of venue a request to change the location of a trial to avoid community hostility, for the convenience of a witness, or for other reasons

motion for a continuance a request to postpone a lawsuit to gain more time to prepare the case

motion for discovery of evidence a request by the defendant to examine, before trial, certain evidence possessed by the prosecution

motion to suppress evidence a motion filed by a criminal defense attorney, asking the court to exclude any evidence that was illegally obtained from the attorney's client

motive the reason a person commits a crime

murder the unlawful killing of a person with malice aforethought. Murder in the first degree is planned in advance and done with malice or during the commission of a dangerous felony. Murder in the second degree does not require malice or premeditation but is the result of a desire to inflict bodily harm. It is done without excuse, and is therefore more serious than manslaughter. *See also* manslaughter, homicide, *and* malice.

N

national origin country where one was born or from which one's ancestors came

naturalization a legal process by which persons born in other countries can apply for U.S. citizenship

necessities those things that parents have a legal obligation to provide to their children and that one spouse has the responsibility to provide to the other. These usually include food, clothing, housing, and medical care.

necessity a defense to a criminal charge that shows a just or lawful reason for the defendant's conduct

neglect the failure of a parent or guardian to properly feed, clothe, shelter, educate, or tend to the medical needs of a child

negligence the failure to exercise a reasonable amount of care in either doing or not doing something, resulting in harm or injury to another person

negligent homicide causing death through criminally negligent behavior

negotiation the process of discussing an issue to reach a settlement or agreement

no-fault divorce a divorce in which neither party is charged with any wrongdoing. The marriage is ended on the grounds that there are irreconcilable differences (i.e., basic disagreements) that caused the marriage to break down.

no-fault insurance a form of automobile or accident insurance (available in only a few states) in which each person's insurance company pays up to a certain share of damages, regardless of fault

nolo contendere Latin phrase meaning "no contest"; a defendant's plea to criminal charges that does not admit guilt but also does not contest the charges. It is equivalent to a guilty plea, but cannot be used as evidence in a later civil trial for damages based on the same facts.

nominal damages a token amount of money awarded by a court to a plaintiff to show that the claim was justified, even if the plaintiff is unable to prove economic harm

nonbinding arbitration a method in which disputants agree to have a third party listen to arguments from both sides and make a decision that is not final (i.e., either party may still take other steps to settle the dispute)

nonpoint source pollution water pollution that is caused by widely dispersed sources of pollutants such as runoff from rain and snow melt, acid rain, and modifications in the form of irrigation, dams, and the like

notice a written statement intended to inform a person of some proceeding in which his or her interests are involved

novel truly new or unique

nuisance an unreasonable interference with the use and enjoyment of one's property, usually repeated or continued for prolonged periods of time

O

obscenity a general term applying to anything that is immoral, indecent, or lewd

offer a specific proposal by one person to another to make a deal or contract

ombudsperson a person who has the power to investigate reported complaints and help achieve fair settlements

opening statement at the start of a trial, one side's explanation of what it expects to prove and how it intends to prove it

ordinance a county or city law

overinclusive too broad or general. As a legal term this usually refers to a law that punishes speech that should be protected (e.g., by the First Amendment).

overt open; clear (For example, an overt act in criminal law is more than mere preparation to do something; it is at least the first step of actually attempting the crime.)

──────── **P** ────────

palimony the support payment that one partner may make or be ordered by a court to make to the other when an unmarried couple, romantically involved and living together, breaks up and no longer cohabitates

pardon release from guilt or remission of punishment; an order that releases a person from legal punishment

parens patriae Latin for "parent of the country"; the doctrine that allows the government to take care of minors and others who cannot legally take care of themselves

parochial school a private school supported by or affiliated with a religious organization

parole release from prison before the full sentence has been served, granted at the discretion of a parole board

parties the people directly concerned with or taking part in any legal matter

patent federal protection for an invention or design, giving the inventor exclusive ownership rights for a period of time

paternity fatherhood

paternity leave a temporary absence from work for men to care for their infants

paternity suit a lawsuit brought by a woman against a man she claims is the father of her child. If paternity is proven, the man is legally responsible for contributing to the support of the child.

pedophile a person who engages in the sexual abuse of a minor

penological of or relating to the criminal corrections process

peremptory challenge part of the pretrial jury selection. Attorneys on opposing sides may dismiss a certain number of possible jurors without giving any reason. There is one exception: peremptory challenges cannot be used to discriminate based on race.

personal property property or belongings that can be moved, such as cars, clothing, furniture, and appliances

personal recognizance a release from legal custody based on a defendant's promise to show up for trial. An alternative to cash bail, this practice is used if the judge decides that the defendant is likely to return.

petition (1) to file charges in a juvenile court proceeding; (2) a request to a court or public official

petitioner one who signs and/or files a petition. The party initiating or appealing a case to the Supreme Court is referred to as the petitioner.

petition for certiorari *Certiorari* is a Latin word meaning "to be informed of." It is a formal application by a party to have a lower-court decision reviewed by the U.S. Supreme Court, which has discretion to approve or deny any such application.

physical cruelty acts of violence or physical abuse against one's spouse

picketing a gathering of individuals in a public place to express their opposition to certain views or practices

plaintiff in a civil case, the injured party who brings legal action against the alleged wrongdoer

plea bargaining in a criminal case, the negotiations between the prosecutor, defendant, and defendant's attorney. In exchange for the defendant agreeing to plead guilty, the prosecutor agrees to charge the defendant with a less serious crime, which usually results in a reduced punishment.

point source pollution any single identifiable source of water pollution from which pollutants are discharged, such as a pipe, ditch, ship, or smokestack

polygamy the practice of having more than one spouse at the same time. Polygamy is illegal in the United States.

polygraph test a lie-detector instrument

precedent appellate court decision on a legal question that guides decisions in future cases representing similar questions

preliminary hearing pretrial proceeding at which the prosecutor must prove that a crime was committed and establish the probable guilt of the defendant. If the evidence presented does not show probable guilt, the judge may dismiss the case.

premeditated deliberate, or having thought about doing something before actually doing it

premiums payments made for insurance coverage

prenuptial agreement a contractual agreement between a couple prior to marriage. It often includes provisions for the disposal of property in the event of separation, divorce, or death.

preponderance of the evidence usually the standard of proof used in a civil suit; the burden of proof that a party must meet in order to win the lawsuit. To win, a party must provide evidence that is more convincing than the other side's evidence.

presentence report a probation officer's written report that gives the sentencing judge information about the defendant's background and prospects for rehabilitation

pretrial motion a document by which a party asks the judge to make a decision or take some action before the trial begins

preventive detention detaining a person if the individual is a danger to himself/herself or the community

principal the person who commits a crime

prior restraint any effort to censor a publication before it goes to press

prison a place of confinement for criminals who are serving long-term sentences

privacy the state of being left alone

privilege (1) an advantage, right to preferential treatment, or excuse from a duty others must perform; (2) a right that cannot be taken away; (3) the right to speak or write personally damaging words because the law specifically allows it; (4) the right and the duty to withhold information from others because of some special status or relationship of confidentiality. These privileges include spousal, doctor-patient, and attorney-client.

privilege against self-incrimination the rule, derived from the Fifth Amendment, that says suspects have a right to remain silent and cannot be forced to testify against themselves.

probable cause a reasonable belief, known personally or through reliable sources, that a specific person has committed a crime

probate the process of proving to a court that a will is genuine; distributing property according to the terms of a will

probation a system of supervised freedom, usually by a probation officer, for persons convicted of a criminal offense. Typically, the probationer must agree to certain conditions such as getting a job, avoiding drugs, and not traveling outside a limited area.

procedural due process a citizen's right to fair access to the courts and to fair treatment in those courts. Generally, a right to fair treatment when government action affects a person's interests.

Glossary

product liability the legal responsibility of manufacturers and sellers for injuries caused by defective products they produce or sell

pro se Latin term meaning "for oneself" or "on one's own behalf"; typically used to describe a person who represents himself or herself in court

prosecution the side bringing a criminal case against another party

prosecutor the state or federal government's attorney in a criminal case

protective order in family law, a court order directing one spouse not to abuse the other spouse or the children. The penalty for violating a protective order is jail.

proximate cause in negligence law, this concept limits damages the defendant must pay to only those harms that are reasonably predictable consequences of the defendant's wrongful acts. *See also* foreseeable harm.

public domain property that belongs to the public; the point at which an unprotected idea or invention reaches the public and no longer belongs to the creator

public forum any place, such as a park or street, where First Amendment expression rights are traditionally exercised

public hearings proceedings that are open to the public. During these proceedings, evidence is considered and then a decision is reached based on this evidence.

puffing an exaggerated statement or advertisement as to the desirability or reliability of a product or service

punitive damages awards in excess of the proven economic loss. In a tort action, they are awarded to the plaintiff to punish the defendant and to warn others not to engage in such conduct.

Q

quid pro quo Latin for "this for that"; an exchange of things or favors

R

racial profiling the use of race as a factor in identifying people who may break or who may have broken the law

rape unlawful sexual intercourse. It is committed when one party forces another party to have sexual intercourse. It implies lack of consent.

ratify to confirm a previous act even though it was not approved beforehand.

real property land and all items attached to it, such as houses, crops, and fences

reasonable-person standard the idealized standard of how a community expects its members to act. It is based on how much care a person of ordinary prudence would exercise in a particular situation.

reasonable suspicion evidence that justifies an officer in stopping and questioning an individual believed to be involved in criminal activity; based on less evidence than probable cause but more than a mere hunch

rebuttal argument the presentation of facts to a court, demonstrating that the testimony of a witness or evidence presented by the opposing party is not true

recall the removal of an elected official from office by a vote of the people

receiving stolen property receiving or buying property that is known or reasonably believed to be stolen

redlining a discriminatory practice in which certain geographical areas in a community are designated by a bank or other lender as ineligible for mortgage loans

reentry a program designed to reduce crime committed by ex-offenders

referendum a procedure in which issues are voted on directly by the citizens rather than by their representatives in government

regulation a rule made by a government agency

rehabilitation the process through which a convicted person is changed or reformed, in order to lead a productive life rather than commit another crime

rehabilitative alimony after a divorce, money awarded to a spouse for the purpose of regaining or developing job skills

release (1) the giving up of a claim or right by a person; (2) a landlord's act of excusing a tenant from all duties related to the apartment or house and the lease

remedy what is done to compensate for an injury or to enforce some right

removal for cause part of the jury selection process. After voir dire, opposing attorneys may request removal of any juror who does not appear capable of rendering a fair and impartial verdict.

rent control a law that limits how much existing rents can be raised. Large cities often have such laws.

repossess to take back a debtor's property because the debtor failed to repay a debt

rescission the act of canceling a contract and treating it as if it never existed

reservation a legal way of making a provision less enforceable than it might otherwise be

respondent the party that wins the case and has to respond to the appeal to the higher court by the petitioner

restitution the act of restoring something to its owner; the act of making good for loss or damage; repaying or refunding illegally obtained money or property

restorative justice a concept in criminal justice that emphasizes reparation to the victim or the affected members of the community by the offender, as by cash

retribution punishment given as a kind of revenge for wrongdoing

revoke to take back or cancel

right of entry or access the provision of a lease that allows a landlord and his or her agents to enter a tenant's premises to make repairs, collect rent, or enforce other provisions of the lease

right to die the right of terminally ill (or comatose) patients not to be kept alive by artificial or extraordinary means

right to quiet enjoyment a tenant's basic right to use and enjoy a rented or leased property without unnecessary disturbance by the landlord or other tenants

right-to-work state a state in which it is illegal to require workers to pay union dues as a condition of employment

robbery the unlawful taking of property from a person's immediate possession by force or intimidation

S

search warrant a court order issued by a judge or magistrate, giving police the power to search a person or to enter a building to search for and seize items related to a crime

second-degree murder *see* murder

secular not of a religious nature

secured credit credit for which the consumer must put up some kind of property as protection in the event a debt is not repaid

security deposit refundable money that a landlord requires a tenant to pay before moving in; used to cover any damages, cleaning costs, or unpaid rent, if such fees arise

segregation the now unconstitutional practice of separating persons in housing, education, public facilities, and other ways based on their race, color, nationality, or other arbitrary categorization

self-defense the right to defend oneself with whatever force is reasonably necessary against an actual or reasonably perceived threat of personal harm

self-incrimination giving evidence and answering questions that would tend to subject one to criminal prosecution

separate-but-equal doctrine the rule, now unconstitutional, that allowed facilities to be racially segregated as long as they were basically equal

separate property a system under which property owned by either spouse before the marriage remains that person's property throughout the marriage, and any property acquired during the marriage belongs to the person who acquired it

separation agreement a written document that lists the continuing legal rights and duties of each spouse when a couple separates, including alimony, child custody, support, and division of property

separation of powers the division of power among the branches of government (executive, legislative, and judicial)

service charge a fee for service, such as using a bank's ATM

set-asides certain amounts of government money and work reserved for companies owned by members of minority groups

settlement a mutual agreement between two sides in a civil lawsuit, made either before the case goes to trial or before a final judgment is entered, that settles or ends the dispute

severance pay money paid to employees who have been dismissed (generally through no fault of their own) to compensate for the time they are not going to work because of the job loss

sexual assault unwelcome sexual contact against another individual committed through the use of force, threat, or intimidation, or enabled because the victim is incapacitated due to drugs, alcohol, or mental disability

sexual harassment unwelcome sexual advances, requests for sexual favors, and other verbal or physical conduct of a sexual nature that occurs in the workplace

shoplifting a form of larceny in which a person takes items from a store without paying or intending to pay

slander spoken expression about a person that is false and damages that person's reputation

small claims court a court that handles civil claims for small amounts of money. People usually represent themselves in this type of court rather than hire an attorney.

solicitation the act of requesting or strongly urging someone to do something. If the request is to do something illegal, solicitation is considered a crime.

specific performance a remedy available in civil court in which the breaching party must do exactly what he or she promised under the contract

spouse abuse the physical, sexual, psychological, or emotional harm by one spouse against the other

stalking the act of following or harassing another person, causing the fear of death or injury

standard of proof the level of certainty and the degree of evidence necessary to establish proof in a criminal or civil proceeding. The standard of proof in a criminal trial is generally beyond a reasonable doubt, whereas a civil case generally requires the lesser standard of preponderance of the evidence. *See* preponderance of the evidence.

Glossary

stare decisis the rule stating that precedent must be followed, providing the legal system with predictability and stability

state of mind what you are thinking; most crimes require that the actor have a guilty state of mind, meaning that he or she purposefully commits the prohibited act

status offender a minor who has committed an act that would not be a crime if committed by an adult, such as truancy from school, running away from home, or being habitually disobedient. They are considered beyond the control of their legal guardians.

status offense an illegal act that can only be committed by a juvenile (for example, truancy or running away from home)

statute of limitations a deadline for filing a lawsuit that requires a tort claim to be filed within a certain period after the injury was suffered. In most states, the statute of limitations for filing a tort lawsuit is either two or three years.

statutes written laws enacted by legislatures

statutory exclusion requires certain offenses committed by juveniles to be prosecuted in adult court

statutory rape the act of unlawful sexual intercourse by an adult with someone under the age of consent, even if the minor is a willing and voluntary participant in the sexual act

steering a discriminatory practice in which real estate agents direct buyers or renters to particular areas because of their race or for other unlawful reasons

stop and frisk to "pat down" or search the outer clothing of someone whom the police believe is acting suspiciously

stop payment a depositor's order to a bank to refuse to honor a specified check drawn by him or her

strict liability the legal responsibility for damage or injury even if you are not negligent

strike the act in which employees stop, slow down, or disrupt work to win demands from an employer

sublease clause the provision of most standard leases that requires the tenant to obtain the landlord's permission before allowing someone else to live on the premises and pay all or part of the rent

subpoena a court order to appear in court or turn over documents on a specified date and time

subsidy money that is paid usually by a government to keep the price of a product or service low or to help a business or organization to continue to function

substance a chemical, often mind-altering, that people abuse, such as alcohol, drugs, and tobacco

substance abuse the harmful overuse of chemicals, such as drugs or alcohol

substantiated provided with a reasonable basis for objective claims that are made by a seller or advertiser in its ads

substantive due process used by courts to protect basic freedoms by making sure that government does not violate a fundamental right without good reason

suicide the deliberate taking of one's own life

Superfund site any land in the United States that has been contaminated by hazardous waste and identified by the EPA as a candidate for cleanup due to health and/or environmental risks

supremacy clause the provision in Article VI of the Constitution stating that U.S. laws and treaties must be followed even if state and local laws disagree with the Constitution and these treaties

Glossary

surrogate mother a woman, other than the wife, who agrees to be artificially inseminated to carry the resulting child to term, and to release legal custody to the individual or couple immediately following birth

suspended sentence a sentence issued by the court but not actually served. The individual is usually released by the court with no conditions attached.

symbolic speech conduct that expresses an idea (for example, wearing a black armband to protest a war)

---------------- **T** ----------------

telemarketing the practice of selling or marketing goods and services by phone

temporary legal guardian the state's role in making most decisions for children whose parents are temporarily unable to care for them. The parents usually retain limited rights.

tenancy at will an arrangement in which a tenant remains on rented property beyond the end of the lease with the understanding that the tenant may leave, or be asked to leave, at any time.

tenancy for years any lease for a fixed period of time. This type of lease specifies that the tenant may live on the property for a single definite period of time, during which the landlord may not raise the rent or evict the tenant.

tenant a person who rents property

tender years doctrine the presumption (now rejected by most states) that a young child is always better off living with his or her mother

term (1) a word; (2) a condition of an agreement; (3) a length or duration of time

terminate parental rights a court decision ending the rights of an unfit parent, leaving the child available for adoption by the foster family, relatives, or others

testify to provide evidence under oath

throwaways children, usually older teenagers, whose parents have refused to continue to care for them

tort a breach of some obligation, causing harm or injury to someone; a civil wrong, such as negligence or libel

tort action a civil lawsuit for damages

tort reform the movement that focuses on changing the process of settling tort claims. It emphasizes methods other than going to court or establishes limitations on how much money the winning party may receive.

toxic torts a lawsuit against a manufacturer of a toxic substance for harm caused by the manufacture or disposal of that substance

treaty a pact between nations; if entered into by the United States through its executive branch, the pact must be approved by "two-thirds of the senators present," under Article II, Section 2 of the Constitution, to become effective.

trespass the unauthorized intrusion on, or improper use of, property belonging to another person. This can be the basis of an intentional tort case or a criminal prosecution.

trial a court proceeding

trial courts courts that listen to testimony, consider evidence, and decide the facts in a disputed situation

truant a child who stays away from school without permission

---------------- **U** ----------------

unauthorized use of a vehicle unlawful taking of a car by someone who intends only to use it temporarily

unconscionable (1) unfair, harsh, oppressive; (2) a sales practice or term in a contract that is so unfair that a judge will not permit enforcement of it

unconstitutional conflicting with some provision of the Constitution

unemployment compensation the government system that protects employees who lose their jobs through no fault of their own, by providing them with payments while they look for other jobs

unenumerated rights rights that are not listed specifically in the Constitution

unfair labor practices the failure by an employer or a union to abide by the regulations of the *National Labor Relations Act*

uninsured motorist coverage insurance that protects drivers from those with no insurance or inadequate insurance. It compensates the insured for the personal injuries or damage the uninsured driver caused.

union an association of workers that seeks to secure favorable wages, improve working conditions and hours, and resolve grievances with employers

unlawful imprisonment confining a person against that person's will and in violation of the law

unsecured credit credit based only on a promise to repay in the future

U.S. Constitution the written document that contains the fundamental laws of the nation and the principles of a free, representative democracy

usury the unlawful act of charging interest for various types of credit at rates higher than the state's legal limit

uttering offering to someone as genuine a document known to be a fake

— V —

vagueness indefiniteness, uncertainty, imprecision; not clear or specific

vandalism the deliberate destruction or defacement of another person's property; also known as malicious mischief

variable interest rate interest charged for credit at a rate that changes slightly from time to time, going up or down within certain limits, depending on changes in the economy

verdict a jury's decision on a trial case

veto prohibit; in government, the veto is the power of a chief executive to prevent enactment of a bill (i.e., to prevent the bill from becoming a law)

visa document that permits a person to visit a country for a specified period of time for a specified purpose, such as to work or study

visitation rights following a divorce or separation, the right of the parent without custody of the children to visit and spend time with those children

voir dire from the French phrase meaning "to speak the truth." It is the screening process in which opposing lawyers question prospective jurors to ensure as favorable or as fair a jury as possible

voluntary manslaughter *see* manslaughter

— W —

waive to give up some right, privilege, or benefit voluntarily

waiver of tort liability a lease clause in which the tenant agrees to give up the usual right to hold the landlord responsible for personal injuries

warrant a paper signed by a judge authorizing some action, such as an arrest or search and seizure

warranty a guarantee or promise made by a seller or manufacturer concerning the quality or performance of goods offered for sale

warranty of fitness for a particular purpose a seller's promise, implied by law, that the item sold will meet the buyer's stated purpose

Glossary

warranty of habitability the implied, or unwritten, obligation of a landlord to provide a unit fit for human habitation

warranty of merchantability an implied promise that the item sold is of at least average quality for that type of item

warranty of title the seller's promise that he or she owns and may transmit title to the item being offered for sale

waste damages caused by a tenant's misuse or neglect of property. The landlord can force the tenant to make repairs or can sue for damages.

welfare financial or other aid provided, especially by the government, to people in need

whistle-blowing when an employee tells authorities about his or her employer's illegal acts

will a legal document that states what a person wants done with his or her belongings after death

workers' compensation system a system of compensating employees who are injured on the job. These benefits are paid no matter who caused the accident, but limit a worker's ability to collect damages through the tort system.

work release the type of sentence in which a defendant is allowed to work in the community but is required to return to prison at night or on weekends

writ a judge's order, or authorization, for something to be done

wrongful conduct unreasonable behavior that violates an individual's duty to others

————— **Y** —————

youth court a proceeding for sentencing minors who have taken responsibility for their actions. The system aims to involve the community directly and to teach the young offenders the impact of their acts. *See also* restorative justice.

Glossary

Index

Index

Index

Index

F

Index

N

Index

O

P

Index

Index

Q

R

S

Index

U

V

Index

Index